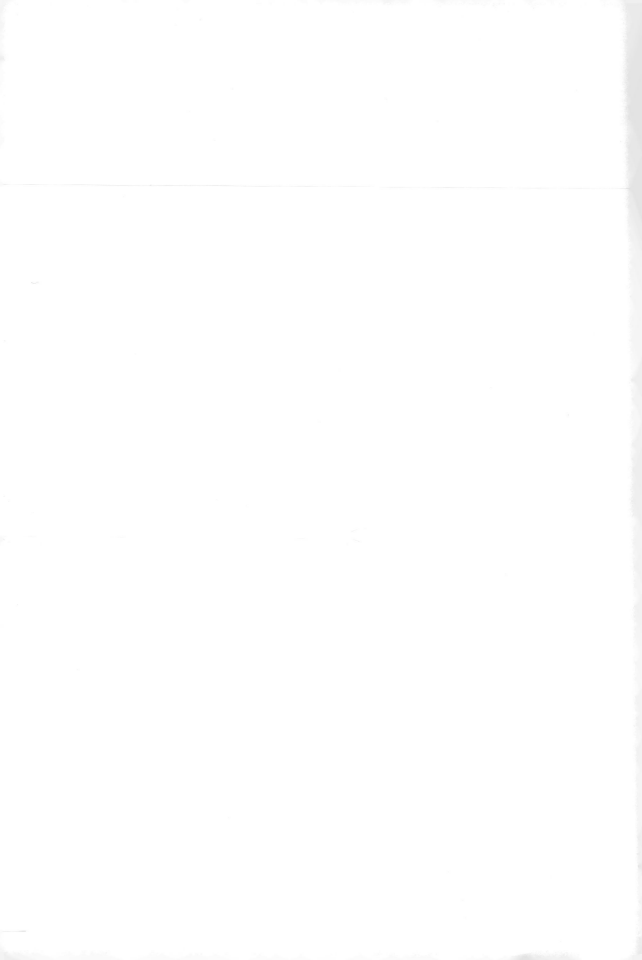

WOMEN AND MUSIC IN AMERICA SINCE 1900

WOMEN AND MUSIC
IN AMERICA
SINCE 1900

An Encyclopedia
Volume 1, A–K

Edited by Kristine H. Burns

An Oryx Book

GREENWOOD PRESS
Westport, Connecticut • London

Library of Congress Cataloging-in-Publication Data

Women and music in America since 1900 : an encyclopedia / edited by Kristine H. Burns
    p.   cm.
   Includes bibliographical references and index.
   ISBN 1–57356–267–X (alk. paper)—ISBN 1–57356–308–0 (vol. 1)—ISBN
1–57356–309–9 (vol. 2)
   1. Women musicians—United States—History—20th century—Encyclopedias. 2.
Music—United States—20th century—Encyclopedias. I. Burns, Kristine Helen.
ML82 .W625 2002
780'.82'0973—dc21   2001054570

British Library Cataloguing in Publication Data is available.

Library of Congress Catalog Card Number: 2001054570
ISBN: 1–57356–267–X (set)
     1–57356–308–0 (vol. 1)
     1–57356–309–9 (vol. 2)

First published in 2002

Greenwood Press, 88 Post Road West, Westport, CT 06881
An imprint of Greenwood Publishing Group, Inc.
www.greenwood.com

Printed in the United States of America

The paper used in this book complies with the
Permanent Paper Standard issued by the National
Information Standards Organization (Z39.48–1984).

10 9 8 7 6 5 4 3 2 1

Contents

Preface

The major role that women have played and continue to play in the musical culture of the United States is indisputable. Although this role has been described in many books and articles, no single reference book to date has been published that thoroughly covers the subject. Herein lies the major difference between this encyclopedia and other reference books on music or on women and music. Some works, for example, limit coverage of women to only classical musicians. Other publications may be strictly biographical or may cover one type of musician, such as composers or songwriters. *Women and Music in America since 1900* represents the first major effort to describe the role of women in all forms of music in the twentieth century in the United States; it includes entries on gender issues, education, genres, honors and awards, organizations, individuals, and professions.

The field of music is quite vast, and women have been very active in it for a long time. This encyclopedia encompasses a wide range of women and issues. Although this two-volume project represents many people and genres, it simply cannot cover every individual and every issue involved in the field. An exhaustive encyclopedia of women and music would occupy many more pages.

DEFINING TERMS

For the purposes of this encyclopedia, the term "American" is applied to someone who meets the following criteria. First, the person must have been born in the United States, resided in the United States, or made most of her contributions in the United States. Although there are many women involved in music who were born outside of the United States, those who have had a significant career while living in the U.S. are included here. For example, although Lotte Lehmann was born in Germany, she performed extensively and influenced generations of opera performers throughout the United States.

The second criterion for inclusion in this project is that the individual must have been born in or lived primarily during the twentieth century. For example, although the field of hymnody dominated American Protestantism in the nineteenth century, the women composers associated with this music (Fanny J. Crosby, Clara H. Scott, Phoebe Palmer

Knapp, and others) lived into the twentieth century. Theirs are still some of the most widely heard songs and hymns in the world.

Third, an individual must have made major contributions as a musician, composer, scholar, activist, or the like that have advanced the role of women in music. For example, her compositions have won many awards, she was the first woman editor of an important periodical, she was the first woman conductor of a major orchestra, or her band was the most successful rock group, female or otherwise, of the 1980s.

THE ADVISORY AND EDITORIAL BOARD

The Advisory and Editorial Board members who oversaw the development of this book represent a highly knowledgeable group of individuals, all of whom have blazed new paths in the field of women in music. The Advisory Board was composed of three individuals—Harriet Hair, Pauline Oliveros, and Judith Tick. Harriet Hair is an internationally known music educator whose primary area of research is children's musical responses; her service in professional music organizations is widely known. In addition to serving as a role model for an entire generation of musicians—both men and women—Pauline Oliveros iconizes the quintessential spirit of an American composer. An internationally renowned musicologist, Judith Tick is one of the foremost scholars of women in music.

The associate editors included Judith A. Coe, Stephen M. Fry, Suzanne L. Gertig, Deborah Hayes, Cristina Magaldi, Patricia O'Toole, and Sally Reid. Among her many activities, Judith A. Coe serves as co-chair of the College Music Society Committee on Women,

Music, and Gender, and she also serves on the Board of Directors of the International Alliance for Women in Music. Stephen M. Fry is a noted researcher of women in jazz and for many years organized the Pauline Alderman Award for excellence in women in music research. In addition to performing as a professional harpist and working as a music librarian, Suzanne L. Gertig is one of the leading Sophia Corri Dussek scholars. Highly respected musicologist Deborah Hayes has not only published many essays and articles on various topics on women in music, but she has also authored the book *Peggy Glanville-Hicks: A Bio-Bibliography* (Greenwood). Additionally, Hayes serves on the Board of Directors of the International Alliance for Women in Music. Cristina Magaldi is an important scholar specializing in Latin American music and music of the Americas. She has contributed entries to *The New Grove Music Dictionary of Women Composers* and *The New Grove Dictionary of Music and Musicians*, and she served as editor of the music section for the publication *Handbook of Latin American Studies*. Patricia O'Toole is a scholar whose work involving issues in qualitative methodologies and gender inequities produced through standard choral practices is well known. Her groundbreaking research is found in numerous books and articles. Composer Sally Reid is the past president of the International Alliance for Women in Music, one of the most important women in music organizations in the world. Her extraordinary leadership has led this organization to increased membership and higher visibility.

TOPICS

Members of the Advisory and Editorial Board suggested topics for inclusion in this publication. The Advisory Board was ultimately responsible for final analysis of the encyclopedia: who would be included and why, what topics were relevant, and how the material should be organized. The wisdom of the board's advice has ultimately provided a comprehensive approach to the topic of twentieth-century American women in music.

The *headword* list of topics includes individuals from all areas of music (rock, pop, classical, jazz, etc.) as well as all types of musicians (performers, composers, researchers, etc.). Associate editors were responsible for writing a *foundation entry* in their area of expertise. The foundation entries include topics such as gender issues, women in music technology, women in rock and popular music, and many more. These foundation entries present a broad historical overview of a particular area and provide the reader with background on a wide range of women musicians. The vast majority of text is devoted to these longer entries.

As each music-related area was shaped by the insight of the specific associate editor, the headword list was further refined, and experts from all areas of music were asked to serve as contributing authors for the project. These contributing authors wrote the entries, drawing from both primary and secondary sources, including books, articles, correspondence, and interviews.

The nearly 200 contributing authors, associate editors, and advisors come from a wide variety of musical backgrounds and experiences. These women and men include academics, professional musicians, and independent authors, musicians, and critics.

ORGANIZATION

This encyclopedia is organized alphabetically. However, several broad topic areas serve as the foundation for all other entries. These topics include associations, blues, classical music, country and folk music, education, experimental music, gender issues, gospel, honors and awards, jazz, multicultural musics, music technology, and rock and popular music.

Although many musicians defy strict categorization, every attempt has been made to include women active in both mainstream and non-mainstream areas of music. Significance of contributions, rather than popularity, has determined who or what appears in individual entries and longer histories. For example, although computer and electronic music have always had a small audience, exponents such as Laurie Spiegel and Pauline Oliveros have served as very important role models for many young women in the field. And although relatively few women to date perform as rap and hip hop artists, Queen Latifah continues to influence the next generation of women artists by performing alongside men in concert and on television. In short, women who are universally regarded as the best, most important in their field, whether it is rap or systematic musicology, have been included in these volumes.

Although there are certainly a large number of individual entries, this project does not provide "Top 10" lists of the most popular women in each category. Rather, the vast majority of prose is dedicated to longer histories to categorize a particular genre of music or trend in history. These comprehensive entries are better able to cut across disciplines, including performance, academia, sociology, and education. Occasionally an issue is so broad that it requires coverage in several places. Discrimination is such an issue because of its relevance in nearly every arena.

Entries for various honors and awards have been included for the most important women-only and mixed-gender awards and honors in various fields. Each such entry describes the award or honor and lists the women winners. Organizations, associations, publishers, and institutions include those groups primarily dedicated to women and music. Additionally, important women's subcommittees within other organizations are covered, as are associations in which women have been historically underrepresented. Entries discuss the history, development, nature, purpose, success, and influence of the particular group, in addition to size of membership, important individuals, and other issues. Topics in education and gender studies include not only specific women educators and researchers but also methods of addressing women's issues both in and out of the classroom.

Finally, each entry concludes with "For Further Reading," a short list of reference materials that will enhance and supplement the information presented. The second volume concludes with a comprehensive bibliography for the entire encyclopedia.

Kristine H. Burns
Editor-in-Chief
May 2000

Acknowledgments

Hundreds of contributors from across the world have come together to assist with the research for this project, thus providing valuable information that has never before been published. The countless hours spent with personal interviews, telephone calls, and correspondence have provided the most detailed account of women musicians in the United States to date. Of special note are the contributions from the International Alliance for Women in Music. Without the personal assistance and support of its nearly 800 members, this project would not have been completed.

Additionally, the encyclopedia certainly could not have been accomplished without the assistance of many spouses, siblings, parents, and children of the musicians listed herein. I would especially like to thank Colby Leider, my husband. Without his many hours of extra housework and child care, this project most certainly would not have been completed.

My greatest debt of gratitude is owed to Henry Rasof, senior acquisitions editor at Oryx Press, and to my Advisory Board. Henry assisted with every step in the process of developing this encyclopedia. Without his input and advice, the project would never have been completed. His knowledge and insight into musical issues were refreshing and very much appreciated. The Advisory Board—Harriet Hair, Pauline Oliveros, and Judith Tick—provided invaluable input as to whom and what should be included in the scope of this encyclopedia. They also assisted with identifying individual authors and researchers. The associate editors—Judith A. Coe, Stephen M. Fry, Suzanne L. Gertig, Deborah Hayes, Cristina Magaldi, Patricia O'Toole, and Sally Reid—worked countless hours adjusting the list of entries, procuring authors, editing, polishing the individual entries, and, as experts in their individual areas, writing entries of their own. Their effort has now been rewarded as this publication reaches fruition.

Introduction: Historical Overview

Much legislation has affected, for better or worse, the ability of women to achieve absolute equality. Women as a group have been affected by key twentieth-century legislation, including the Nineteenth Amendment and the Equal Pay Act. In 1920, the Nineteenth Amendment was ratified. This law guarantees women the right to vote by stating that "The right of citizens of the U.S. to vote shall not be denied or abridged by the U.S. or by any State on account of sex." In 1963, President Kennedy signed the Equal Pay Act, which states that men and women should receive equal pay for equal work.

Although women have had many legal successes, many indiscretions still exist in the enforcement of these laws. For instance, Congress established the Age Discrimination Act over 30 years ago, yet there are still a number of women who are reticent to divulge their actual ages for fear of age discrimination by employers. Therefore, when requested, birth year information has been omitted for certain individuals listed within these pages. All other birth and death information has been provided whenever possible.

Although women have achieved many professional successes in music, they have fought fiercely for equality. In 1907, Frances Elliott Clark became the first woman president of the Music Supervisors National Conference (later called the Music Educators National Conference). Other education groups were formed in the twentieth century to help facilitate women music educators. For example, in 1903, Eva Vescelius created the first journal of music therapy. In 1946, the service sorority Tau Beta Sigma was chartered to serve the needs of the growing number of women band musicians throughout the United States, and the Women Band Directors National Association was formed in Chicago, IL, in 1969. Finally, in 1984, the National Association of Jazz Educators Women's Caucus held its first meeting in Columbus, OH.

To reach the growing number of women composers in the United States, the Society of American Women Composers was founded in 1924 with Amy Marcy Cheney Beach as president. In 1930, Ruth Crawford Seeger became the first woman to win the prestigious Guggenheim Fellowship in music composition. During her time in Europe she composed her String Quartet (1931), one of the most significant string quartets written in the twentieth century. In 1975, Nancy Van de Vate established the International League of Women Composers, an organization that helped unite women composers through performances, recording projects, and mentorship. Other groups such as the American Women Composers and the International Congress for Women in Music soon followed. However, it was not until 1995 that these three important groups united to form a single coalition: the International Alliance for Women in Music.

Women composers and educators made great strides during the twentieth century, and so did performers and conductors. In 1936, Marian Anderson became the first African American singer to perform at the White House. Although the Daughters of the American Revolution refused to allow her to perform at a 1939 Constitution Hall concert because of her race, Anderson demonstrated her amazing range and vitality when Eleanor Roosevelt invited her, instead, to perform on the steps of the Lincoln Memorial on Easter Sunday. In 1938, Antonia Brico became the first woman to conduct the New York Philharmonic Symphony Orchestra.

Contemporary popular musicians have often found favor with the American public; however, respect and equality have been hard won. In 1959, Berry Gordy Jr. established Motown and immediately signed Mable John, Claudette Robinson, and Mary Wells among the first acts. One year after the Rock and Roll Hall of Fame was established, Aretha Franklin became the first woman inducted in 1987. Lilith Fair was founded in 1996 to assist women performers and singer-songwriters by providing performance venues all over the United States. Although it lasted only three years, Lilith Fair had a huge impact on numerous musicians and audiences.

In 1940, Carl Seashore wrote in "Why No Great Women Composers?" (*Music Educators Journal* 25/5, March 1940) that "Married women have not produced great compositions, but they have produced great composers." In 1999, Donald R. Vroon, editor of the *American Record Guide* (May–June 1999), stated that "no outstanding composer was a woman. . . . All the great composers were white males, and no amount of research will change that. . . . Nothing we have uncovered in the rush to find 'women composers' has affected that in the least." The views are clearly uninformed: not only have there been numerous outstanding women composers, but there have also been remarkable women performers, educators, and researchers. The present encyclopedia is testament to this fact. Over the years, countless articles and books have been written to dispute both statements, and more will certainly be written.

These two volumes present over 400 entries that address significant women composers, performers, researchers, singer-songwriters, computer programmers, radio DJs, electronica artists, and many, many others. There should be no question that women have contributed, and will continue to contribute, significantly to the field of music. The only question remaining is to what extent women will become even more involved in the music roles of the more traditionally male-dominated areas such as higher education and administration, audio production, music management, and computer music.

Twentieth-century American women

have possessed the indomitable pioneering spirit that defined the development of the country. Indeed, women have flourished and prospered in the face of adversity and discrimination. This publication is dedicated to those women musicians who came before us and those who will follow.

Chronology

1902　Gertrude "Ma" Rainey begins stage career and sets the pace for all blues women.

1903　Eva Vescelius creates the first journal of music therapy.

1904　The Musicians Union ends its exclusion of women when it joins with the American Federation of Labor.

1907　Barbara Duncan, perhaps the first woman music librarian, begins her career at the Boston Public Library.

Frances Elliott Clark becomes the founding chairperson of the Music Supervisors National Conference (later the Music Educators National Conference).

1915　Federation of Music Clubs establishes Young Artist Auditions.

1919　Margaret Anderton institutes the first college course work in music therapy (Columbia University).

1920　The Nineteenth Amendment is ratified. It guarantees women the right to vote by stating that "The right of citizens of the U.S. to vote shall not be denied or abridged by the U.S. or by any State on account of sex."

1924　The Society of American Women Composers is founded, with Amy Marcy Cheney Beach as its president.

1926　New York's first major choral concert is conducted by a woman, Margarete Dessoff.

1930　Ruth Crawford Seeger becomes the first woman to win the prestigious Guggenheim Fellowship.

1938　Antonia Brico becomes the first woman to conduct the New York Philharmonic Symphony Orchestra.

1939　Marian Anderson performs on the steps of the Lincoln Memorial on Easter Sunday. The concert is arranged by Eleanor Roosevelt to protest the refusal of the Daughters of the American Revolution to allow Anderson to perform in Constitution Hall because of her race.

American Music Center is established to build "a national community for new American music."

1940　In his essay "Why No Great Women Composers?" psychologist Carl Seashore states that "Married women have not produced great compositions, but they have produced great composers."

1943　Federation of Music Clubs establishes the Young Composers Contest.

1946　Tau Beta Sigma is chartered to serve the needs of the growing number of women band musicians throughout the United States.

1955　The first woman cantor in the United States, Betty Robbins, officiates at a worship service.

1956   Bebe Barron and her husband, Louis, create the score for *Forbidden Planet*, the first film score comprised entirely of electronic sounds.

1957   The Grammy Award is established to recognize excellence in the recording industry.

The Chicago Symphony Chorus is founded by Margaret Hillis.

1959   Berry Gordy Jr. establishes Motown and signs Mable John, Claudette Robinson, and Mary Wells.

1963   President John F. Kennedy signs the Equal Pay Act, which states that men and women should receive equal pay for equal work.

The Foundation for Contemporary Performance Arts, Inc., is founded.

1964   Title VII of the Civil Rights Act of 1964, as amended, prohibits discrimination in employment on the basis of sex, race, color, national origin, or religion.

1965   The Voting Rights Act is established to ensure that anyone over the age of 21 can legally register to vote, no matter what their ethnicity.

1966   The National Endowment for the Arts Composers Assistance Program is established to aid composers by providing funds for copying and completing scores and parts for orchestral presentation, as well as commissioning and preparing works for performances. The organization is later renamed the Composer/Librettist Fellowship, and still later the Composers Program.

1967   The Age Discrimination in Employment Act is established "To prohibit age discrimination in employment."

1969   The Women Band Directors National Association is formed in Chicago.

Barbara Kolb becomes the first woman recipient of the American Rome Prize for Musical Composition.

1970   Mother Maybelle Addington Carter and Sara Dougherty Carter Bayes, members of the Carter Family, become the first women elected to the Country Music Hall of Fame.

1972   The Equal Employment Opportunity Act of 1972 expands the Civil Rights Act of 1964 to include academic employment.

1973   Olivia Records, the first women's record label, is founded in Washington, DC, by Linda Tillery and Mary Watkins.

Patsy Cline becomes the first woman solo artist to be elected to the Country Music Hall of Fame.

1975   Ellen Taaffe Zwilich becomes the first woman to receive a doctorate in composition from the Juilliard School.

Nancy Van de Vate establishes the International League of Women Composers.

1976   Tommie Ewert Carl founds the American Women Composers, Inc. (AWC), "for the express purpose of alleviating the gross inequities that women composers have experienced in all areas of the music world."

1977   The U.S. Army commissions the first two women to serve as bandmasters: Nancy Bodenhammer and Ginny Allen.

1978   The Kennedy Center Honors is established to recognize excellence and life achievement in the performing arts. Marian Anderson is the first woman musician to be honored in its inaugural year.

Jeannie Pool establishes the National Congress on Women in Music.

1980   The Equal Employment Opportunity Commission recognizes sexual harassment as a form of sex discrimination and thus a violation of Title VII of the Civil Rights Act of 1964.

1982   American Women Composers, Midwest, Inc., is formed.

1983   Ellen Taaffe Zwilich becomes the first woman to win the Pulitzer Prize in music.

The Rock and Roll Hall of Fame is established in Cleveland, OH.

The Massachusetts Chapter of American Women Composers is formed.

1984   The National Association of Jazz Educators Women's Caucus holds its first meeting in Columbus, OH.

Gladys Stone Wright becomes the first woman to be elected to membership in the prestigious American Bandmasters Association.

New York Women Composers, Inc., is founded.

1986   First inductions into the Rock and Roll Hall of Fame are made; however, no women are honored until 1987.

The Pauline Alderman Prize is established to honor the authors of published and unpublished books and articles about women in music. Nancy B. Reich becomes the first woman to be honored for her book *Clara Schumann: The Artist and the Woman*.

Los Angeles Women in Music is founded to increase awareness of women's contributions to the business and art of music.

The Maud Powell Foundation is established to educate the public about the life and art of violinist Maud Powell.

1987   Aretha Franklin becomes the first woman to be inducted into the Rock and Roll Hall of Fame.

1990   Susan Slaughter founds the International Women's Brass Conference.

Joan Tower becomes the first woman to win the Grawemeyer Award for Music Composition for her orchestral composition *Silver Ladders*.

1991   The U.S. Navy appoints its first woman bandmaster, Lorelei Conrad.

Seeking to be placed in the same pay group as her male colleagues in the Munich Philharmonic, Abbie Conant goes to trial and wins. Although the decision is appealed, Conant wins again in 1993.

1993   Catherine Masters and Marcia Shein establish the Women in Music Business Association.

The Center for Women in Music is formed at New York University.

1995   The Audio Engineering Society Women in Audio: Project 2000 is created to increase the opportunities for women in the audio industry over the next five years.

The International Alliance for Women in Music is established.

1996   Lilith Fair is founded.

1997   Women Musicians' Alliance is established to serve the central Florida region by promoting independent women creators and performers of contemporary music.

1998   The National Women Conductors Initiative is established.

1999   Mary Simoni becomes the first woman to be elected president of the International Computer Music Association.

Cosette René Collier becomes chair of the Audio Engineering Society, Women in Audio Committee.

2000   Eunice Boardman is honored with the Illinois Music Educators Association's President's Award.

Barbra Streisand is awarded the Cecil B. DeMille Award, the highest honor for contribution to the field of entertainment bestowed by the Hollywood Foreign Press Association.

After nearly 40 years of performing, Cher receives her first Grammy Award, winning for her dance hit "Believe."

Guide to Related Topics

BROAD TOPIC CATEGORIES

Education

Children's Choirs
Choral Education
Dalcroze Eurhythmics
Early Childhood Music Educators
Gender and Feminist Research in Music Education
General Music
Instrumental Education
Jazz Education
Kodály Method
Music Education
Music Educators National Conference
Music Learning Theory
Orff Approach
Piano Pedagogy
Researchers in Music Education
String Education

Gender Issues

Aptitude
Bifocal History
Canon
Chilly Climate
Compensatory History
Constructivism
Cultural Appropriation
Discrimination
Equality
Essentialism
Exceptional Woman
Female Inferiority, Theories of
Feminist Music Criticism
Feminist Music History
Feminist Music Theory
Feminist Musicology
Gender and Curricula
Gender and Repertoire
Gender Coding
Gender in Music Analysis
Gender Issues
Gendered Aspects of Music Theory
Historiography
Internet Resources
Journals
Lesbian Music
Male Gaze
Multifocal History
Patronage
Professionalism
Pseudonyms
Separate Spheres—Sexual Aesthetics
Social Darwinism
Women-Identified Music

Women's Sphere

Women's Voice

Womyn's Music

Genres and Movements

African American Musicians

Asian American Music

Bands, Pop Rock

Barbershop Quartet

Bluegrass

Blues

Church Music

Classical Music

Country Music

Disco

Electronic Dance Music

Experimental Music

Film Composers

Folk Music

Garage Rock and Heavy Metal Bands

Gospel Music

Hymnody

Improvisation

Indie-Rock

Industry, Rock Music

Jazz

Jewish Musicians

Latin American Musicians

Motown

Multicultural Musics

Multimedia

Music Technology

Musical Theater

Native American Musicians

New Age Music

Performance Art

Rap

Rock and Popular Music Genres

Ska

Sound Design

Underground

Honors and Awards

Academy Awards

American Rome Prize in Musical Composition

Country Music Hall of Fame

Foundation for Contemporary Performance Arts, Inc.

Fulbright Fellowship Program

Grammy Award

Grawemeyer Award for Music Composition

Guggenheim Award

MacArthur Fellows Program

National Endowment for the Arts Composers Program

Prizes, Composer and Performer

Publication Awards

Pulitzer Prize

Rock and Roll Hall of Fame

Tony Awards

Musicians

Allyson, June

Amacher, Maryanne

Amos, Tori

Anderson, Laurie

Anderson, Marian

Andrews Sisters

Anonymous 4

Baez, Joan

Bailey, Pearl

The Bangles

Barkin, Elaine R.

Barron, Bebe

Battle, Kathleen

Bauer, Marion

Beach, Amy Marcy Cheney

Beardslee, Bethany

Bentley, Alys E.

Berberian, Cathy

Bianchi, Louise Wadley

Bish, Diane Joyce

Black, Shirley Temple

Bley, Carla

Boardman, Eunice

Boswell Sisters

Boyer-Alexander, René

Brown, Ruth

Bryant, Clora

Bryn-Julson, Phyllis

Caldwell, Sarah

Carabo-Cone, Madeleine

Carlos, Wendy

Carpenter, Karen

Carpenter, Mary-Chapin

Carr, Vikki

Carter, Betty

Carter, Mother Maybelle Addington

Cash, June Carter

Casterton, Elizabeth

Channing, Carol

Chapman, Tracy

Chen Yi

Cher

Clark, Frances Elliott

Clark, Frances Oman

Clarke, Rebecca

Cline, Patsy

Clooney, Rosemary

Cole, Natalie

Collins, Judy

Comden, Betty

Conant, Abbie

Cooper, Adrienne

Covell, Rebekah Crouch

Crane, Julia Ettie

Crawford Seeger, Ruth

Crider, Paula Ann

Crow, Sheryl

Cruz, Celia

D'Cückoo

Day, Doris

Dearie, Blossom

DeGaetani, Jan

Deutsch, Diana

Diemer, Emma Lou

DiFranco, Ani

Dudziak, Urszula

Durbin, Deanna

Eder, Linda

Estefan, Gloria

Etheridge, Melissa

Falletta, JoAnn

Fine, Vivian

Fitzgerald, Ella

Fluxus

Franklin, Aretha

Fullman, Ellen

Galás, Diamanda

Ganz, Isabelle

García, Adelina

Garland, Judy

Gideon, Miriam

Glanville-Hicks, Peggy

Glenn, Mabelle

The Go-Go's

Goetze, Mary

González, Celina

Gore, Lesley

Grant, Amy

Grigsby, Beverly Pinsky

Guillot, Olga

Haasmann, Frauke Petersen

Hackley, Emma Azalia Smith

Hair, Harriet Inez

Handy, D. Antoinette

Harry, Deborah (Debbie)

Hayes, Pamela Tellejohn

Hill, Emily

Hill, Lauryn

Hillis, Margaret

Hoffman, Mary E.

Holiday, Billie

Hood, Marguerite Vivian

Hoover, Katherine

Horne, Lena

Horne, Marilyn

Purim, Flora

Queen Latifah

Rainey, Gertrude "Ma"

Raitt, Bonnie

Ran, Shulamit

Rao, Doreen

Reynolds, Debbie

Richter, Marga

Rimes, LeAnn

Ritchie, Jean

Rockmore, Clara

Rodríguez, Albita

Ronstadt, Linda Maria

Ross, Diana

Rowe, Ellen H.

Sager, Carole Bayer

Sainte-Marie, Buffy

Salt-N-Pepa

Scaletti, Carla

Schonthal, Ruth

Selena

Sembrich-Kochanska, Marcella

Semegen, Daria

Shenandoah, Joanne

Shields, Alice Ferree

The Shirelles

Shocked, Michelle

Sills, Beverly

Simone, Nina

Slick, Grace

Smith, Bessie

Smith, Kate

Smith, Patti

Sobrino, Laura Garciacano

Spiegel, Laurie

Staple Singers

Streisand, Barbra

The Supremes

Suzuki, Pat

Svigals, Alicia

Swift, Katharine (Kay)

Talma, Louise Juliette

Tharpe, Sister Rosetta

Thome, Diane

Thorton, Willie Mae "Big Mama"

Tick, Judith

Tillis, Pam

Tower, Joan

Tripp, Ruth

Tucker, Sophie

Tucker, Tanya

Turner, Tina

Ulali

Vaughan, Sarah

Vega, Suzanne

Vincent, Rhonda

Walker, Shirley

Warwick, Dionne

Washington, Dinah

Waters, Ethel

Wells, Kitty

Williams, Mary Lou

Wilson, Anne and Nancy

Wilson, Nancy

Wynette, Tammy

Young, Phyllis

Zaimont, Judith Lang

Zwilich, Ellen Taaffe

Organizations, Associations, and Agencies

American Composers Forum

American Music Center

American Women Composers, Inc.

American Women Composers, Massachusetts Chapter

American Women Composers, Midwest, Inc

Center for Women in Music

Committees

Conferences and Festivals

Country Music Association

Ensembles, Jazz

Fraternities and Sororities, Professional

Grand Ole Opry

Indiana Home Economics Club Choruses
International Alliance for Women in Music
International Congress on Women in Music
International League of Women Composers
International Women's Brass Conference
Libraries and Archives
Lilith Fair
Los Angeles Women in Music
Maud Powell Society for Music and Education
Meet the Composer
National Federation of Music Clubs
New York Women Composers, Inc.
Organizations, Music Education
Organizations, Performer
Organizations, Professional Audio
Organizations, Regional Arts
Organizations, Research
Performance Ensembles, Classical
Performing and Mechanical Rights Organizations
Publishers, Women's Music
Sweet Adelines
Tau Beta Sigma
Women Band Directors International
Women in Music Business Association
Women Musicians' Alliance
Women's Philharmonic

Professions

Arranger
Audio Production
Composer
Conductor, Choral
Conductor, Instrumental and Opera
Copyist
DJ, Club
Ethnomusicology
Librettist
Military Music
Music Critic
Music Librarian
Music Management
Music Programmer/Host

Music Psychology
Music Theorist
Music Therapy
Musicologist
Performer, Brass
Performer, Choral and Vocal Ensemble
Performer, Keyboard
Performer, Live Electronics
Performer, Percussion
Performer, String
Performer, Vocal
Performer, Woodwind
Production Manager
Singer-Songwriter
Software Designer/Programmer
Songwriter
Sound Installation Artist

INDIVIDUALS ACCORDING TO GENRE AND PROFESSION

Alternative

Chapman, Tracy
Crow, Sheryl
D'Cückoo
DiFranco, Ani
Indigo Girls
Merchant, Natalie

Classical

Anderson, Marian
Anonymous 4
Barkin, Elaine R.
Battle, Kathleen
Bauer, Marion
Beach, Amy Marcy Cheney
Beardslee, Bethany
Berberian, Cathy
Bish, Diane Joyce
Bryn-Julson, Phyllis
Caldwell, Sarah
Chen Yi

Clarke, Rebecca
Conant, Abbie
Crawford Seeger, Ruth
DeGaetani, Jan
Diemer, Emma Lou
Falletta, JoAnn
Fine, Vivian
Ganz, Isabelle
Gideon, Miriam
Glanville-Hicks, Peggy
Grigsby, Beverly Pinsky
Hillis, Margaret
Hoover, Katherine
Horne, Marilyn
Kolb, Barbara
Lam, Bun Ching
Larsen, Libby
LeBaron, Anne
Lehmann, Lotte
León, Tania
Moore, Undine Smith
Musgrave, Thea
Norman, Jessye
Parker, Alice
Perry, Julia
Price, Leontyne
Ptaszynska, Marta
Ran, Shulamit
Richter, Marga
Rockmore, Clara
Schonthal, Ruth
Sills, Beverly
Talma, Louise Juliette
Thome, Diane
Tower, Joan
Zaimont, Judith Lang
Zwilich, Ellen Taaffe

Conductors

Caldwell, Sarah
Crider, Paula Ann
Falletta, JoAnn

Hillis, Margaret
León, Tania
Parker, Alice

Country

Carpenter, Mary-Chapin
Carter, Mother Maybelle Addington
Cash, June Carter
Cline, Patsy
The Judds
Lee, Brenda
Lynn, Loretta
Maddox, Rose
Mandrell, Barbara
McEntire, Reba
Parton, Dolly
Rimes, LeAnn
Tillis, Pam
Tucker, Tanya
Wells, Kitty
Wynette, Tammy

Educators, Patrons

Bentley, Alys E.
Bianchi, Louise Wadley
Boardman, Eunice
Boyer-Alexander, René
Carabo-Cone, Madeleine
Casterton, Elizabeth
Clark, Frances Elliott
Clark, Frances Oman
Covell, Rebekah Crouch
Crane, Julia Ettie
Crider, Paula Ann
Glenn, Mabelle
Goetze, Mary
Haasmann, Frauke Petersen
Hackley, Emma Azalia Smith
Hair, Harriet Inez
Hayes, Pamela Tellejohn
Hoffman, Mary E.

Hood, Marguerite Vivian
Inskeep, Alice C.
Jarjisian, Catherine
Jorgensen, Estelle Ruth
Kemp, Helen Hubbert
Lamb, Roberta
Larimer, Frances Hiatt
Lawler, Vanett
Liston, Melba Doretta
Low, Henrietta G. Baker
McElwee (Gonzales), Ileane
Monsour, Sally A.
Pitts, Lilla Belle
Rao, Doreen
Rowe, Ellen H.
Tripp, Ruth
Williams, Mary Lou
Young, Phyllis

Music Technology

Barron, Bebe
Carlos, Wendy
Grigsby, Beverly Pinsky
Hutchinson, Brenda
Klein, Judith (Judy) Ann
Knowles, Alison
McLean, Priscilla
Payne, Maggi
Rockmore, Clara
Scaletti, Carla
Semegen, Daria
Shields, Alice Ferree
Spiegel, Laurie

Experimental Music

Amacher, Maryanne
Anderson, Laurie
Berberian, Cathy
Fluxus
Fullman, Ellen
Galás, Diamanda

La Barbara, Joan
Lam, Bun Ching
Lockwood, Annea
Monk, Meredith
Moorman, Charlotte
Oliveros, Pauline
Ono, Yoko
Phillips, Liz

Folk, Bluegrass

Baez, Joan
Collins, Judy
Krauss, Alison
Lewis, Laurie
Mitchell, Joni
Ritchie, Jean
Sainte-Marie, Buffy
Vincent, Rhonda

Jazz, Blues, Motown, and Soul

Bailey, Pearl
Bley, Carla
Boswell Sisters
Brown, Ruth
Carr, Vikki
Carter, Betty
Clooney, Rosemary
Cole, Natalie
Fitzgerald, Ella
Franklin, Aretha
Holiday, Billie
Horne, Lena
Jackson, Janet
Joplin, Janis Lyn
Kaye, Carol
Kitt, Eartha
Knight, Gladys
LaBelle, Patti
Lee, Peggy
Liston, Melba Doretta
McPartland, Marian

McRae, Carmen
Rainey, Gertrude "Ma"
Raitt, Bonnie
Ross, Diana
The Shirelles
Simone, Nina
Smith, Bessie
The Supremes
Thornton, Willie Mae "Big Mama"
Vaughan, Sarah
Washington, Dinah
Waters, Ethel
Williams, Mary Lou
Wilson, Nancy

Multicultural Musics

Chen Yi
Cooper, Adrienne
Cruz, Celia
Dudziak, Urszula
Estefan, Gloria
Ganz, Isabelle
Gideon, Miriam
González, Celina
Guillot, Olga
La Lupe
Lam, Bun Ching
Little Coyote, Bertha
Masoaka, Miya
Mendoza, Lydia
Miranda, Carmen
Miyamoto, Nobuko Joanne
Montaner, Rita
Ptaszynska, Marta
Purim, Flora
Ran, Shulamit
Rodríguez, Albita
Ronstadt, Linda Maria
Sainte-Marie, Buffy
Selena
Sembrich-Kochanska, Marcella
Shenandoah, Joanne

Sobrino, Laura Garciacano
Suzuki, Pat
Svigals, Alicia
Tucker, Sophie
Ulali

Musical Theater and Film

Allyson, June
Barron, Bebe
Black, Shirley Temple
Carlos, Wendy
Channing, Carol
Comden, Betty
Durbin, Deanna
Eder, Linda
Garland, Judy
Jones, Shirley
LuPone, Patti
MacDonald, Jeanette
Martin, Mary Virginia
Merman, Ethel
Miranda, Carmen
Peters, Bernadette
Powell, Jane
Reynolds, Debbie
Suzuki, Pat
Swift, Katherine (Kay)
Tucker, Sophie
Walker, Shirley

Rap

Hill, Lauryn
Queen Latifah
Salt-N-Pepa

Researchers

Barkin, Elaine R.
Deutsch, Diana
Handy, D. Antoinette
Krumhansl, Carol L.
Lamb, Roberta

Tick, Judith
Zaimont, Judith Lang

Rock, Pop, and Punk

Amos, Tori
Andews Sisters
The Bangles
Carpenter, Karen
Cher
Day, Doris
Estefan, Gloria
Etheridge, Melissa
The Go-Go's
Gore, Lesley
Harry, Deborah (Debbie)
King, Carole
Lauper, Cyndi
Madonna
Midler, Bette
Minnelli, Liza
Nicks, Stephanie "Stevie"
Nyro, Laura

Phranc
Ronstadt, Linda Maria
Sager, Carol Bayer
Shocked, Michelle
Slick, Grace
Smith, Kate
Smith, Patti
Streisand, Barbra
Turner, Tina
Vega, Suzanne
Warwick, Dionne
Wilson, Anne and Nancy

Sacred, Hymnists, Religious, and Gospel

Dearie, Blossom
Grant, Amy
Jackson, Mahalia
Patty, Sandi
Staple Singers
Tharpe, Sister Rosetta

WOMEN AND MUSIC
IN AMERICA
SINCE 1900

A

Academy Awards

The Academy Awards (also known as the "Oscars") have been presented annually in Los Angeles, CA, since 1929 by the Academy of Motion Picture Arts and Sciences. The categories and nature of these awards have changed over time, reflecting the film industry's own evolution. The Academy of Motion Picture Arts and Sciences was founded in 1927 by a group of film executives and artists, and actor Douglas Fairbanks Sr. served as its first president.

The Oscar in the category of Best Score was first given in 1934. Initially, this award went to the head of a movie studio's music department, rather than to the composer who had written the score. In 1938 the Academy changed its rules, giving the Oscar directly to the composer. Women were rarely nominated in the first decades of the award, and then often only as collaborators with male composers. Since its inception, there have been over 400 films with Academy Award nominations for music scoring. Although many of the nominees worked on the scoring alone and there were numerous collaborations over the years,

only five women have been nominated for an Academy Award in music scoring, and only two have won.

In 1945, during the eighteenth season of the award presentations, Ann Ronell (b. 1908) became the first woman ever nominated for an Academy Award in film scoring; she shared this honor with Louis Applebaum for the film *The Story of G.I. Joe*. The next nomination for a woman was not until 1970 with Tylwyth Kymry and Fred Karlin for the film *The Baby Maker* for Original Song Score. Angela Morley (b. 1945) was nominated for Scoring: Original Song Score and Adaptation or Scoring: Adaptation along with Alan Jay Lerner, Frederick Loewe, and Douglas Gamley for *The Little Prince* in 1974. Then, at the fiftieth anniversary of the Academy Awards, Morley was nominated again, this time with Richard M. Sherman and Robert B. Sherman, for Original Song Score and Its Adaptation or Adaptation Score for *The Slipper and the Rose—The Story of Cinderella*. Finally, the first woman to win an Oscar in a music category was Marilyn Bergman, who, along with Michel Legrand and Alan Bergman, won the award for Original Song Score or Adaptation Score for the movie *Yentl* in 1983. However, not until 1996 was the Oscar for Best Score given to a single woman without collaborator: Rachel Portman.

Rachel Portman (b. 1960), an English composer, was awarded the Best Original Score Oscar for her music for the film *Emma* (1996). (When she received the Oscar, the category was no longer known as Best Score; rather, it had been split into smaller, more specific categories.) Another of these newer subdivisions (Best Original Musical or Comedy Score) proved to be fruitful for a second English composer, Anne Dudley (b. 1956), who won the Oscar in this category for her score to *The Full Monty* (1997). No American woman composer has ever won an Academy Award in any of these categories.

A category in music where women have more recognition is that of Best Song (later called Best Original Song). Usually this presence has been, again, as a collaborator, and often as the lyricist of a songwriting team. The first such award-winning lyricist was Dorothy Fields (1905–1974), who, along with Jerome Kern, won in 1936 for the song "The Way You Look Tonight," from the film *Swing Time*. A later, even more successful lyricist was Marilyn Bergman, who, in collaboration with her husband, Alan Bergman, and others, won in 1968 for "The Windmills of Your Mind" (from *The Thomas Crown Affair*, in collaboration with Michel Legrand) and in 1973 for "The Way We Were" (from the film of the same name, in collaboration with Marvin Hamlisch).

Composer-lyricists without collaborators have also been nominated in this category. Sylvia Fine (wife of the actor Danny Kaye) had been successfully writing songs for Kaye's films for years. Her first Oscar nomination was in 1953 for "The Moon Is Blue" (in collaboration with Herschel Burke Gilbert), and she was later nominated in 1959 for the title song to the film *The Five Pennies*.

Ann Ronell was an early exception in the male-dominated field of songwriting for film. She began her songwriting career in 1934 with the movie *Down to Their Last Yacht*, followed by a number of hits during that decade. Because of these hits she was hired by Walt Disney Studios (where she wrote the famous lyrics to "Who's Afraid of the Big Bad Wolf?"). Ronell was the first woman to score for films and to conduct her own scores. She wrote the music for *Champagne Waltz* (1937), *Algiers* (1939), and (with Louis Applebaum) *The Story of G.I. Joe* (1945). The song "Linda" from this film (which she had written without collaboration) was nominated for an Academy Award that year.

More recently, such composer-lyricist nominees have included Dolly Parton (b. 1946) for "9 to 5" in 1980 (from the film of the same name) and Diane Warren for "How Do I Live" in 1997 (from *Con Air*) and "I Don't Want to Miss a Thing" in 1998 (from *Armageddon*), but the only composer-lyricist to ever actually win this award without sharing it was Carly Simon (b. 1945) for "Let the River Run" from the film *Working Girl* (1988).

See also Film Composers; Walker, Shirley

For Further Reading

Sackett, Susan. *Hollywood Sings! An Inside Look At Sixty Years of Academy Award-Nominated Songs.* New York: Billboard Books, 1995.

Shale, Richard. *Academy Awards—An Ungar Reference Index.* New York: Ungar, 1978.

Welcome to the Academy of Motion Picture Arts and Sciences. Available: http://www.oscars.org

Jeremy Beck

Women Who Have Received an Academy Award in Music: Best Original Song

Composer or Lyricist	Year	Composition	Category
Anne Dudley	1997	Score for *The Full Monty*	Best Original Musical or Comedy Score
Rachel Portman	1996	Score for *Emma*	Best Original Score
Carly Simon	1988	"Let the River Run" from *Working Girl*	Best Original Song
Irene Cara with Giorgio Moroder, Keith Forsey	1983	"Flashdance . . . What a Feeling" from *Flashdance*	Best Original Song
Buffy Sainte-Marie with Will Jennings, Jack Nitzsche	1982	"Up Where We Belong" from *An Officer and a Gentleman*	Best Original Song
Carole Bayer Sager with Peter Allen, Burt Bacharach, Christopher Cross	1981	"Arthur's Theme (Best That You Can Do)" from *Arthur*	Best Original Song
Angela Morley with Richard M. Sherman and Robert B. Sherman	1977	*The Slipper and the Rose—The Story of Cinderella*	Original Song Score and Its Adaptation or Adaptation Score
Barbra Streisand with Paul Williams	1976	"Evergreen" from *A Star Is Born*	Best Original Song
Tylwyth Kymry with Fred Karlin	1970	Song score for *The Baby Maker*	Best Original Song Score
Marilyn Bergman with Alan Bergman, Marvin Hamlisch	1973	"The Way We Were" from *The Way We Were*	Best Song
Marilyn Bergman with Alan Bergman, Michel Legrand	1968	"The Windmills of Your Mind" from *The Thomas Crown Affair*	Best Song
Dorothy Fields with Jerome Kern	1936	"The Way You Look Tonight" from *Swing Time*	Best Song

African American Musicians

Female African American musicians have played substantial roles in the history of music in the United States. As instrumental and vocal performers, composers, and publishers, their contributions span many styles from blues to classical to rap music. African American women musicians have also been pioneers in the struggle for racial equality and recognition in the United States, and this is often reflected in their music. For example, in 1963 gospel singer Mahalia Jackson (1911–1972) was on the forefront of the civil rights movement. She was a featured singer at the march on Washington, DC, the event where Martin Luther King gave his famous "I Have a Dream" speech. But the prominence and notoriety of African American women in music actually began long before that.

Blues. In the early 1920s and 1930s, African American women were associated with what was known as Classic Blues, a style that transformed cities such as Chicago and New York into blues recording industries. With their rich voices and elaborate costumes, Classic Blues singers were in essence "divas," similar to female opera singers. Because many of the African American female blues singers of this time had been performers in vaudevilles and theatrical shows, they brought to the blues tradition a high sense of drama in their musical expressions by linking music and lyrics with the everyday experiences of black women in the United States. Classic Blues singers sang about the hardships of broken homes, love relationships, and poverty.

In the 1920s record producers realized that African American women blues singers could bring in a profit and began marketing records to be sold exclusively in the black community. Mamie Smith (1883–1946) became the first African American to record the blues. With her rendition of "Crazy Blues" she dominated what was known as the "race market." Other women to make a great impact in this period include Gertrude "Ma" Rainey (1886–1939) (often called the "Mother of the Blues"), and Bessie Smith (1894–1937).

Jazz. Just as in blues, women have been major innovators in jazz as singers, bandleaders, and composers. Lillian Armstrong (also known as Lil Harding [1898–1971]) served as a pianist with Joe King Oliver's Band, one of the earliest African American jazz ensembles. As one of the composers of this ensemble, her rendition of "Struttin' with Some Barbecue" contributed to making her husband, Louis "Satchmo" Armstrong, a major jazz sensation. Mary Lou Williams (1910–1981) was another pianist and composer who impacted the world of jazz by working with such legends as Andy Kirk, Duke Ellington, and Dizzy Gillespie. Williams has been revered as a distinguished forerunner of a whole generation of female musicians. In 1996 she was honored at the first of an annual series of Mary Lou Williams Women in Jazz Festivals at the Kennedy Center in Washington, DC.

Another noted jazz performer was Ella Fitzgerald (1917–1996). Deemed America's leading female interpreter of popular songs for approximately 45 years, Fitzgerald also popularized "scatting," a style of jazz singing that involves nonsense syllables instead of words. In the 1940s and 1950s Sarah Vaughan (1924–1990) became the most prominent female singer of bebop. Referenced alongside bebop instrumentalists Charlie Parker and Dizzy Gillespie, Vaughn's vocal range was comparable to that of a trumpet or a saxophone.

Gospel. Throughout the twentieth century gospel music has served as a source of inspiration for African American existence in the United States. The contribution of Mahalia Jackson (1911–1972), known today as the "Queen of Gospel Music," made gospel singing a great legacy. Her 1947 recording of "Move On Up a Little Higher" transformed gospel music into a commercial enterprise, selling over two million copies. Other noted female gospel musicians include Sallie Martin (1896–1988), who established her own gospel music training school, and Roberta Martin (1907–1969) and Clara Ward (1924–1973), both of whom organized choral groups and gospel music workshops throughout the United States.

Classical. Classical music has been one of the most difficult fields of acceptance for African American women. Because of the lack of racial tolerance and acceptance, many African American classical musicians had to first establish themselves as artists in Europe before they were readily accepted as concert artists in the United States. One of the most important trailblazers in classical music was Marian Anderson (1897–1993), whose perseverance in becoming an operatic singer made it possible for later musicians to succeed in the classical music genre. Anderson made her debut in New York City in 1922, but her success did not occur until 1930, when she acquired European management. Even after several performances in many European opera houses, Anderson continued to be denied performances in the United States. Because of her race, in 1939 Anderson was prohibited from singing in Constitution Hall in Washington, DC. Instead, she sang on the steps of the Lincoln Memorial to an audience of more than 75,000 people, a performance that increased the awareness of prejudice in the United States.

In 1955 Marian Anderson became the first African American operatic singer to appear in a lead role at the Metropolitan Opera House in New York. Following Anderson's legacy, Leontyne Price (b. 1927) made her debut in 1957 in San Francisco and also became the first African American artist to sing in an opera telecast with the Metropolitan Opera House in New York. Today there are many other African American female opera singers who continue to strive toward greatness in the operatic field; they include Grace Bumbry (b. 1937), Jessye Norman (b. 1945), and Kathleen Battle (b. 1948). Prominent African American women composers of classic music include Julia Perry (1924–1979), Undine Smith Moore (1904–1989), Florence Price (1887–1953), Margaret Bonds (1913–1972), and Dorothy Rudd Moore (b. 1940).

Popular Genres. African American women continue to bring major innovations to popular musical genres such as rhythm and blues, funk, soul, and rap. Aretha Franklin's (b. 1942) "soulful type" of singing earned her the title of "High Priestess of Soul Music." Other popular music divas include Whitney Houston (b. 1963) and Patti LaBelle (b. 1944). As rap has become one of the most popular contemporary styles, women have also started to play a significant role. Although the style began in the late 1970s with male disc jockeys in the Bronx, NY, in the late 1980s African American women began to emerge in rap with the music of Queen Latifah (b. 1970). Her success in rap music has opened the door for other African American women to become rappers.

See also Blues; Classical Music; Jazz; Multicultural Musics; Rock and Popular Music Genres

For Further Reading

Green, Mildred Denby. *Black Women Composers: A Genesis.* Boston, MA: Twayne, 1983.

Stewart-Baxter, Derrick. *Ma Rainey and the Classic Blues Singers.* New York: Stein and Day, 1972.

Walker-Hall, Helen. *Black Women Composers: A Century of Piano Music.* Bryn Mawr, PA: Hildegard Publishing, 1992.

Clarence Bernard Henry

Allyson, June (1917–)

June Allyson is an American film musical legend. She had one of the most successful careers in Hollywood as a singer, dancer, and actress. Her "girl next door" personality was characterized by the similarity of her sung and spoken voice, and it was enhanced by her remarkable dancing and genuine "star quality."

Because many of the female film musical stars were sopranos, the husky alto quality of Allyson's voice is instantly recognizable. Her straightforward presentation of lyrics and clear pronounciation endowed her performances with an engaging narrative quality. She starred opposite many Hollywood legends such as Lucille Ball, Mickey Rooney, Judy Garland (1922–1969), and Gene Kelley. Her vocal performances are included on recent compilation compact discs such as *That's Entertainment! The Best of the M-G-M Musicals* (Rhino 72463) and *That's Entertainment! Part 3* (Angel 55215).

Born Eleanor Geisman on 17 October 1917 in the Bronx, NY, Allyson experienced a difficult childhood. It was complicated by a traumatic injury that ocurred when she fell at age eight. After many years in leg braces, Allyson started swimming as part of a physical therapy program. She regained her strength and took up dancing lessons despite her physician's reservations.

Allyson began her career as a Broadway singer and dancer when she was cast in the Metro-Goldwyn-Mayer (MGM) film *Best Foot Forward* (1943), thus securing a contract with MGM beginning in 1942. In 1952 Allyson won a Golden Globe award for her role as Cynthia Potter in *Too Young to Kiss* (1951). Her "sweet girl" movie role lasted through most of the 1940s and 1950s, until she was cast as Helen Berger Miller in *The Glenn Miller Story* (1954) starring opposite Jimmy Stewart. Though Allyson has appeared in more recent film roles in *Blackout* (1978) and *That's Entertainment! Part 3* (1994), her film movie career ended when she turned to the new medium of television in 1959, where she starred in *The Dupont Show with June Allyson*, which ran until 1961. Throughout her career, Allyson returned to her roots

as a nightclub singer when her work as an actress was sparse.

Beyond her long and significant career as a multifaceted entertainer—appearing in over 60 feature and musical films as well as numerous television appearances—Allyson is also known today for her extensive work with the American Urogynecologic Society. In 1987 she was appointed by President Ronald Reagan to the Federal Council on Aging. Allyson has continued to be an outspoken advocate on programs for senior citizens.

June Allyson has been married three times. In 1945 she married actor Dick Powell, with whom she had two children. When Powell died in 1963, she married and later divorced Glenn Maxwell, and since 1976 she has been married to Dr. David Ashrow.

For Further Reading

Allyson, June. *June Allyson*. New York: Berkley Publishing Group, 1983.

Parish, June, and Ronald L. Bowers. *The MGM Stock Company: The Golden Era*. New Rochelle, NY: Arlington House, 1973.

Daniel DiCenso

Amacher, Maryanne (1946–   )

Installation artist Maryanne Amacher has been creating experimental sound environments for over 30 years, using the physical properties of the individual room to create a wide range of sonic environments. Amacher has won many prestigious awards, including a John Simon Guggenheim Memorial Foundation Fellowship (1997) and the Prix Ars Electronica Golden Nica Distinction in Computer Music (1997).

Born in 1946, Amacher began musical training with piano study at the Philadelphia Conservatory of Music. She completed undergraduate and graduate degrees in music and computer science at the University of Pennsylvania. She has served as a Bunting Institute Fellow at the Mary Ingraham Bunting Institute of Radcliffe College, Harvard University (1978–79); a guest artist at the Deutscher Akademischer Austauschdienst (DAAD) in Berlin; and the first Rosekrans Artist-in-Residence at Mills College (1993). She has also collaborated with such artists as choreographer Merce Cunningham and visual artists including Scott Fisher, Luis Frangella, and architect Juan Navarro Baldeweg.

Amacher's installations may be divided into three categories: *City Links #1–22* (1967–), *Music for Sound-Joined Rooms* (1980–), and *Mini-Sound Series* (1985–). *City Links #1–22* uses sound from multiple sites within a single city or multiple cities; ambient sounds (e.g., water, traffic, and factories) are transmitted to the exhibition space. These displaced sounds are then presented within the installation, and the space is transformed into an "adventure." Installations of *City Links #1–22* have been presented at the Music of Contemporary Art (Chicago), Walker Arts Center (Minneapolis), and The Kitchen (New York).

The *Music for Sound-Joined Rooms* installation series uses the sonic, visual, and spatial features of a group of rooms, or as much as the entire building, to develop the "stage" for each performance. *Music for Sound-Joined Rooms* reexamines how the audience perceives the sound, including its origin and movement. The audience walks through the space, immersed in sound throughout the experience.

Mini-Sound Series is a modified version of *Music for Sound-Joined Rooms* in which the time span of the installation is expanded to utilize sounds found over a four- or five-week period of continuous evolution. Amacher uses the idea of a "television mini-series" in order to create

an evolving narrative in which the composition unfolds in episodes, rather than as a continuous installation.

Her compact disc *Sound Characters (making the third ear)* (TZ 7043) is available on Tzadik.

See also Sound Installation Artist

For Further Reading

Gann, Kyle. *American Music in the Twentieth Century*. New York: Schirmer Books; London: Prentice-Hall International, 1997.
Licht, Alan. "Expressway to Your Skull." *Omni* 181 (1999): 42–45.

Kristine H. Burns

American Composers Forum

One of the most active and effective proponents of new music in the last part of the twentieth century has been the American Composers Forum. New music always has needed champions. In the past, wealthy patrons occasionally arranged for concerts of music by their favorite composers. Famous virtuosi showcased works written especially for them. Prominent orchestras held competitions that pledged performance of the winning piece. Although all of this remains common, specialized institutions have emerged in recent years to help bring artists and audiences together.

Founded in 1973 by Libby Larsen (b. 1950) and Stephen Paulus, then graduate students at the University of Minnesota, the organization was first known as the Minnesota Composers Forum. Its primary mission was to support the creation and performance of recently composed music by local artists. Dedicated to composer service, the Forum sponsored public readings and panel discussion sessions, presented concerts, produced a monthly radio series, published a newsletter and a membership directory, and provided practical assistance in recording and photocopying. From the very beginning, women were well represented within the Forum's membership, staff, and governing board, and a genuine spirit of inclusiveness characterized its programs. As the group's activities grew, its reputation spread outside the Minneapolis and Saint Paul metropolitan area, and in 1982 it began accepting members from outside Minnesota. Its mission also gradually expanded to that of a more comprehensive new-music advocacy organization. In addition to providing services and resources not readily available to individual artists working in isolation, the Forum became more and more concerned with educating listeners, developing enthusiastic audiences, establishing new sources of financial support, and forging closer ties between living composers and their communities. In 1995 the organization's name was changed to the American Composers Forum (ACF), to better reflect its national stature and broader mandate.

At the start of the twenty-first century, the American Composers Forum has nine regional chapters, including affiliates in New York, Chicago, and the San Francisco Bay area. It sponsors several concert series, including the traveling Sonic Circuits ElectroAcoustic Music Festival. In addition, there is a commissioning program, which supports the work of emerging composers; a fellowship program for Minnesota-based artists; and a visiting composer program, which underwrites residencies for non-Minnesotans. An innovative church and synagogue program funds year-long residencies in congregations of different faiths, and a new nationwide commissioning program called Continental Harmony is designed to elicit new music for rural and underserved communities. Educational programs co-sponsored by the ACF and various orchestras enable emerging composers to hear expert readings of their works and receive valuable feedback from performers and an experienced composer-consultant. Finally, a recording assistance program enables ACF members to produce and distribute a compact disc of their music on the *innova* recording label. Significant women participants in American Composers Forum programs have included Mary Ellen Childs, Jennifer Higdon, Libby Larsen, Janika Vandervelde, and Judith Lang Zaimont (b. 1945), among others.

See also Larsen, Libby

For Further Reading

American Composers Forum. Available: http://www. composersforum.org

James William Sobaskie

American Music Center

The American Music Center (AMC) seeks to build "a national community for new American music," and since its founding in 1939 it has become one of the largest organizations for the promotion of American music. Its six founders, Marion Bauer (1897–1955), Aaron Copland, Howard Hanson, Otto Luening, Harrison Kerr, and Quincy Porter, envisioned two mechanisms to meet their charge: a library of scores and recordings to serve as a core representation and a central repository, and an information-gathering and distribution service to disseminate otherwise difficult to obtain information for the promotion of contemporary music. Currently the library houses over 60,000 scores and recordings (many unavailable elsewhere), and its Information Services Program responded to almost 35,000 requests for information in 1998 alone. With projects such as the Copy Assistance Program and Meet the Composer, as well as commissions and support for programming and recording these works, the Center is actively involved with all aspects of the music creation process.

Founder Marion Bauer, ever a proponent of new music, leads the list of some very impressive women composers associated with the AMC. Around 30 percent of the AMC's over 2,500 members are women, including Laurie Anderson (b. 1947), Joan La Barbara (b. 1947), Libby Larsen (b. 1950), Thea Musgrave (b. 1928), Pauline Oliveros (b. 1932), Ursula Oppens, Joan Tower (b. 1938), and Ellen Taaffe Zwilich (b. 1939). Additionally, all these women have served on the board of directors.

The last 20 years have witnessed much broader attempts to promote American music. In 1985 the AMC conceived the national music festival American Music Week, funded by a network of corporations, foundations, and the National Endowment for the Arts. The AMC sponsored one of the first music sites on the World Wide Web in the early 1990s, and with its interface to the Center's database, the site is an important organ for information distribution. A recent development on their World Wide Web site is the monthly column "American Music: In the First Person," where distinguished members are provided a forum to communicate anything they choose on or about American music.

Members are eligible to apply for copy and recording assistance grants and receive a monthly Opportunity Update with a comprehensive list of calls for scores, competitions, grants, and performance and study programs. Members are also allowed borrowing privileges to the score and recording library and are given the opportunity to include biographical and professional information on the AMC World Wide Web site.

The AMC responded to the practical needs of its members by launching a series of workshops tailored to career-related issues. Begun in New York, the workshops will eventually be held in cities throughout the United States and will include topics such as music publishing and self-publishing, crossing over into film composition, marketing strategies, receiving permission to use a text for a composition, and ways for high school students to embark on a career as a composer. Another career-outreach program brings together composers and performers along with producers, managers, lyricists, and librettists in Networking Groups to foster professional business networking. In each of these endeavors, the AMC strengthens its commitment both to new American music and to the community that creates and performs it.

See also Meet the Composer; National Endowment for the Arts Composers Program

For Further Reading

The American Music Center. Available: http://www.amc.net

Richardson, Susan. "Defining a Place for Composers: The Early History of the American Composers Alliance and the American Music Center, 1937–1950." Ph.D. diss., University of Indiana, 1997.

Gregory Straughn

American Rome Prize in Musical Composition

Sponsored by the American Academy in Rome, the American Rome Prize in Musical Composition is one of the most prestigious prizes in classical music composition. Prizes are awarded annually by the Academy to individuals working in the fields of archaeology, architecture, classical studies, design arts, historic preservation and conservation, history of art, landscape architecture, literature, modern Italian studies, musical composition, post-classical humanistic studies, and visual arts. In 1894 the first American Rome Prizes were awarded to architects, and in 1923 the American Academy in Rome awarded its first two prizes in Musical Composition to Howard H. Hanson and Leo Sowerby.

The process begins when music composition applicants submit compositions to jurors who may award as many as two prizes each year. During their 11-month residency, fellows compose, study, and prepare for performances of their works at Academy-sponsored concerts. In its long history, only eight of the 103 prize recipients have been women.

In 1969 Barbara Kolb (b. 1939) became the first woman recipient of the American Rome Prize in Musical Composition. Kolb attended Hartt College of Music of the University of Hartford (B.M. 1961 with honors, M.M. 1964). After her Rome Prize fellowship (1969–1971), she was named a trustee of the Academy in Rome from 1972 to 1975, and she returned as composer in residence in 1975. Kolb has an exclusive contract with Boosey and Hawkes. Many of her works are available on the following labels: Bridge, CRI, Desto, Galaxia, Leonarda, New World, Opus One, Turnabout. Her lengthy catalogue of composition includes *Voyants* (solo piano and chamber orchestra), *All in Good Time* (orchestra), and *Millefoglie* (chamber ensemble and computer tape). In 1999 she prepared a marimba concerto for Evelyn Glennie. Kolb presently teaches at the Eugene Lang College of the New School (NY).

Sheila Silver (b. 1946) studied composition with Edwin Dugger at the University of California, Berkeley (B.A. 1968); with Erhard Karkoscka and György Ligeti in Stuttgart; and with Arthur Berger, Harold Shapero, and Seymour Shifrin at Brandeis University, where she received her Ph.D. (1976). At Tanglewood she studied with Jacob Druckman. Silver's music is published by MMB Music, Studio 4, and Argenta Music and is recorded by CRI, Mode, and Leonarda. Her most important compositions include *To the Spirit Unconquered* (piano trio) and a piano concerto. Silver has also worked on commissions for harpist Heidi Lehwalder, cellist Yehuda Hanani, and violist Rivka Golani. She continues artistic collaboration with her husband, the filmmaker John Feldman, and is professor of music at the State University of New York, Stony Brook.

Tamar Diesendruck (b. 1946) attended Brandeis University (B.A. Fine Arts 1969, *magna cum laude*) and the University of California in Berkeley (M.A. 1979, Ph.D. 1983). Her teachers include Seymour Shifrin and Andrew Imbrie. Visiting artist at the American Academy in Rome in 1989, Diesendruck has received many other fellowships including those awarded by the Guggenheim, Goddard Lieberson, and Bunting Institute. She co-founded several new music groups including Earplay. Important experimental chamber works include *Theater of the Ear* (a cycle of five works) and *the grief that does not speak*. Recordings are available from Centaur. Other projects in 1999 include commissions for the Pro Arte Quartet and for Wu Man (pipa), and premieres of *Every Which Wave* (orchestra) and *Strange Lines and Distances* (violin and cello).

Kathryn Alexander (b. 1955) studied flute at Baylor University (B.M. 1978) and at the Cleveland Institute of Music

(M.M. 1981, A.D. 1983). While at the Cleveland Institute, she also studied composition (B.M., M.M. 1983). At the Eastman School of Music (D.M.A. 1997) she studied with Samuel Adler, Barbara Kolb, Allan Schindler, and Joseph Schwantner. Recordings of Alexander's work are available from EDIPAN, Edizioni Musical, and New World Records.

Her compositions, published by Edizioni Musicali in Europe, include *And the Whole Air Is Tremulous* (flute and electronic tape), *Enraptured with Flame* (string quartet), and *New Work* (clarinet, bassoon, and piano). At Yale University, where she teaches, Alexander directs the Group for New Music, in which she plays an Akai Electronic Wind Instrument.

Women Who Have Won the American Rome Prize in Musical Composition

Recipient	Fellowship Years	Compositions Prepared for American Academy in Rome Concerts
Barbara Kolb	1969–1971	*Trobar Clus* (chamber ensemble) *Solitaire* (piano and prerecorded tape) *Soundings* (chamber ensemble and prerecorded tape or orchestra)
Sheila Silver	1978–1979	*Canto* (baritone and a chamber ensemble of nine players) *Dynamis* (solo horn) *Chariessa: A Cycle of Six Songs on Fragments from Sappho* (soprano and orchestra)
Tamar Diesendruck	1983–1984	*Quartet* (clarinet/bass clarinet, violin, cello, and piano) *Mana* (solo clarinet)
Kathryn Alexander	1988–1989	*Dance the Orange!* (solo trombone) *Rainbows Stretched Like Endless Reins* (solo violin) *One Haze, One Incandescence* (dancer and electronic tape)
Michelle Ekizian	1988–1989	*Octoéchos* (double string quartet and soprano) *Swan Song* (high voice alone)
Bun Ching Lam	1991–1992	*Bittersweet Music II* (solo piccolo) *After Spring* (two pianos) *Another Spring* (alto flute, cello, and piano) *L'Air du Temps* (string quartet) *Last Spring* (piano quintet)
Shih-Hui Chen	1999–2000	(submitted for the 1999–2000 competition) *String Quartet number 3* *Moments* (full orchestra) *66 Times* (soprano and chamber ensemble)
Carolyn Yarnell	1999–2000	(submitted for the 1999–2000 competition) *Love God* (electronic piece) *Paintings for Jacob* (symphony), in memory of Jacob Druckman *The Same Sky* (mega piano and computer)

Michelle Ekizian (b. 1956) studied composition at the Manhattan School of Music (B.M. 1977, M.M. 1978) and at Columbia University (D.M.A. 1988). Her teachers included Chou Wen-chung, Mario Davidovsky, Nicolas Flagello, and Vladimir Ussachevsky. New World Records offers a compact disc of Ekizian's *Octoéchos* (double string quartet and soprano). Her music is published by G. Schirmer and includes *Red Harvest* (concerto for violin and orchestra) and *Symphony No. 1: When Light Divided*, featuring folk-singer Richie Havens. Ekizian serves as composer-in-residence for the Interfaith Committee of Remembrance at New York City's Cathedral of St. John the Divine. In 1999 she received an Artslink Award from CEC International Partners for a residency with the Armenian Philharmonic.

Bun Ching Lam (b. 1954) studied piano at the Chinese University of Hong Kong (B.A. 1976) and composition at the University of California at San Diego (Ph.D. 1981). Her mentors include Bernard Rands, Robert Erickson, and Pauline Oliveros (b. 1932). Labels carrying Lam's work are Tzadik, CRI, Nimbus, Koch International Classics, Sound Aspect, and Tellus. Her publisher is Notevole Music Publishing, Inc. Lam's important works include *Sudden Thunder* (pipa and orchestra) and *The Child God* (opera for shadow theater). Other projects include *Wenji* (chamber opera), commissions from Chamber Music America and the New Jersey Symphony, and an orchestral piece marking Macao's handover to China. Lam has taught at Cornish College of the Arts and at Yale.

Shih Hui Chen (b. 1962) studied composition at the Taiwan National Academy of the Arts (Diploma 1982), Northern Illinois University (M.M. 1985 and 1986), and Boston University (D.M.A. 1993). Chen helped to organize the 4th International Conference on Chinese Music for April 2000 at the Longy School of Music, where she taught during the previous year. Performances of her works in 2000 included East and West Coast premieres of *Silent Spring* by Duo Asiatica and Earplay, respectively; *Fu II* by the Pittsburgh New Music Ensemble; and *66 Times* (soprano and chamber orchestra) by the Cleveland Chamber Symphony Orchestra.

Carolyn Yarnell (b. 1961) studied composition at the San Francisco Conservatory of Music (B.M. 1986) and at Yale University (M.M. 1989). In 1999 she was composer in residence at the Seal Bay Festival in Maine, and she received commissions from the Seattle Symphony, Tanglewood, the American Composers Orchestra, and Dogs of Desire. Yarnell's orchestral works include *Symphony*, *Paintings for Jacob*, and *Living Mountains*. Sonic Vision publishes her compositions. Common Sense Composers' Collective on the CRI Emergency Music label offers a recording of Yarnell's *Sage* (chamber ensemble).

See also Kolb, Barbara; Prizes, Composer and Performer

For Further Reading

American Academy in Rome. Available: http://www.aarome.org

American Academy in Rome Report: 1968–1973. New York: American Academy in Rome, 1973.

La Farge, C. Grant. *History of the American Academy in Rome*. New York: American Academy in Rome, 1915.

Valentine, Lucia, and Alan Valentine. *The American Academy in Rome: 1894–1969.* Charlottesville: University Press of Virginia, 1973.

Ruth Robertson

American Society for Composers, Authors, and Publishers

See Performing and Mechanical Rights Organizations

American Women Composers, Inc.

In April 1976, Tommie Ewert Carl founded American Women Composers, Inc. (AWC), "for the express purpose of alleviating the gross inequities that women composers have experienced in all areas of the music world" (*AWC News/Forum* 5, 1984). The organization was to "disseminate the work of American women composers, past and present; to create a network for the exchange of information; and to encourage the active participation of American women composers in American musical life." The AWC was certainly one of the most significant women-in-music organizations in the United States during the latter half of the twentieth century, and eventually the AWC would merge with several other organizations to form the International Alliance for Women in Music.

Among the charter members in AWC were Emma Lou Diemer (b. 1927), Ursula Mamlock, Marga Richter (b. 1926), Ruth Schonthal (b. 1924), Jeanne Singer, Joan Tower (b. 1938), and Vice Presidents Alexandra Pierce, Margaret Meier, and Judith Lang Zaimont (b. 1945). Zaimont initiated several advocacy projects and, working with the planning committee of Richter and Singer, put together a four-concert PANORAMA of Women Composers presented at La Guardia Community College, City University of New York (May 1979), and broadcast on radio (*The Listening Room*, WQXR; WFUV, WNYC, and a series of programs with WGMS). Four programs with Radio France Culture were arranged by Liaison Officer Julia Stilman. Concerts in such venues as the Kennedy Center, Wolftrap, the Library of Congress, Piccolo Spoleto Festival, and the National Gallery contributed to the goal of the AWC mission statement "AMER-ICAN WOMEN COMPOSERS, INC. brings music by women, past and present, into the mainstream of contemporary culture by presenting works to a broad concert audience."

Under Carl's leadership, concerts were organized at the Wolf Trap Barns, the Corcoran Gallery, the Library of Congress, and the British Embassy in Washington, DC, the Bruno Walter Library in New York City, and the Piccolo Spoleto in Charleston, SC, during several successive seasons. Anne LeBaron (b. 1953), vice president for program development, and Tommie Carl initiated the tenth anniversary celebrations of AWC with 15 programs of works by women in various Washington, DC, venues, including the Frances and Armand Hammer Auditorium, Corcoran Gallery of Art, Dumbarton United Church, and the Coolidge Auditorium, Library of Congress.

The *AWC News/Forum* publication was an important asset of the organization as a networking tool, publishing profiles and interviews with composers, conductors, and performers, notices of score calls, conferences and festivals, listings of recent acquisitions of the AWC library, and scholarly articles. Its editorial board included Catherine Pickar, Suzanne Cusick, and Fred Everett Maus. Three recordings of "New American Music" were released on AWC's Bravura label.

Regional chapters of AWC were formed in Massachusetts, the Midwest (Chicago), Virginia, and Washington. In 1984 AWC Massachusetts and Tufts University co-sponsored a three-day conference called "Women in Music." In the following year AWC Massachusetts and Boston University co-sponsored the "Women's Music Festival."

Tommie Carl served as AWC president from 1976 to 1988 and was succeeded by transitional leadership including Patricia Morehead, Carolyn Duignan, and Ruth Lomon during 1988–1989. Judith Shatin (b. 1949) became the second president of the AWC (1989–1993). During her tenure the acclaimed concert program at the National Women's Museum in Washington, DC, was inaugurated. In this venue the winning scores from the annual AWC Call for Scores were performed. The work of Vice Presidents Priscilla Little (Programming), Mary Kathleen Ernst (Development), and *News/Forum* editor Catherine Pickar contributed to a renaissance of the AWC. Other important leaders within the organization have included Janet Crossen, Carolyn Duignan, Gary Martin, Pam Settlage, and the late Colonel Haskell Small, as well as composers and performers Mary Kathleen Ernst, Priscilla Little, Mary Meyers, Janet Peachey, Suzanne Summerville, and Linda Dusman (b. 1956).

Shatin's *Letter from the President*, published in the 1993 issue of the *AWC News/Forum*, urged working "in a cooperative manner with other organizations with similar aims, such as International League of Women Composers (ILWC)" (*AWC News/Forum* 11, 1993). In 1993 Stefania de Kenessey, as the third AWC president, served as co-chair of the AWC/ILWC merger committee, making possible the merger of the two groups and the formation of the International Alliance for Women in Music (IAWM) in January 1995. DeKenessey served as president of the newly formed IAWM for its first year.

The AWC score library was housed at the Levine School of Music in Washington, DC, from 1986 to 1993, when it was also home to the national office of the AWC. After the national office was transferred to George Washington University and the AWC merged to form the IAWM, Catherine Pickar secured a permanent home for the AWC Score Collection in the Gelman Library of George Washington University. The, 1673 scores represent the work of 245 composers. These works may still be accessed through the World Wide Web. The collection may be viewed in person by setting up an appointment with Elizabeth Harter, librarian for the humanities.

See also American Women Composers, Massachusetts Chapter; American Women Composers, Midwest, Inc.; International Alliance for Women in Music

For Further Reading

Ammer, Christine. *Unsung.* Revised and expanded second edition. Portland, OR: Amadeus Press, 2001.

Halstead, Jill. *The Woman Composer: Creativity and the Gendered Politics of Musical Composition.* Aldershot, Hampshire, UK: Ashgate Publishing, 1997.

Shatin, Judith. "American Women Composers, Inc." *IAWM [International Alliance for Women in Music] Journal* 1/1 (June 1995): 3–4.

Ruth Lomon

American Women Composers, Massachusetts Chapter

As one of the largest regional organizations of the American Women Composers, Inc. (AWC), the Massachusetts Chapter of American Women Composers had a very strong and vital membership. The Massachusetts Chapter of AWC was formed in 1983, seven years after the founding of the national American Women Composers, Inc., organization in Washington, DC. Its members, women musicians from the Boston area, united to perform and promote music by women, both past and present. Although the purpose of the group was clearly defined, activities varied considerably.

Besides a concert series at the Longy School of Music, there was a collaborative concert series with Chamber Music in Watertown, an annual marathon concert, several festivals, a newsletter, a Directory and Information Guide listing women musicians in the Boston area, and a few out-of-state concerts.

By June 1984, the organization had grown sufficiently to sponsor a weekend conference at Tufts University directed by Vivian Taylor and Ruth Lomon celebrating women's music in concerts and lectures. In addition to local musicians, there were speakers and performers from Canada, Washington, and New York and a performance by Rosemary Platt of the nine *Preludes* by Ruth Crawford Seeger (1901–1953), followed by a lecture by Judith Tick (b. 1943). There was also a concert of music by black women composers and a lecture on Native American women's music.

In October of the following year, Boston University co-sponsored the Women's Music Festival/85 directed by Marjorie Merryman and Elizabeth Vercoe. This four-day event included an opening concert by Alea III directed by Theodore Antoniou, a concert by the Pro Arte Chamber Orchestra conducted by Gunther Schuller, programs by the university orchestra and other ensembles, a dance concert by the Beth Soll Dance Company, poetry readings, student performances, and several premiere performances. Publicity was good: the *Christian Science Monitor* featured the festival in a front-page story, the *Boston Globe* reviewed all the major concerts, and *MS Magazine* carried a preview.

Highlights of the 1986–1988 seasons included a program of experimental music for voice performed by Joan La Barbara (b. 1947) on the Longy concert series, a performance in Washington, DC, by Marimolin (a marimba and violin duo), and a concert of chamber music at the Nouveau Théâtre Mouffetard in Paris, France.

In 1993 a lecture series entitled Women of Note was inaugurated at Lesley College in Cambridge. Members talked about and performed their music, and guests were invited to speak about music publishing and recording. The annual marathon concerts continued, adding some features of the large-scale festivals with multiple concerts and panel discussions. The last of these was held in 1995 while Lynn Steele was president. The event was chaired by Leslie Holmes and held at Northeastern University.

Various Massachusetts arts organizations supported the group. There were grants for technical support and commissions from the Massachusetts Arts Council, as well as assistance for concerts from the Polaroid Foundation, the New England Foundation for the Arts, and the Boston Arts Lottery. But there were divisions in the group, a waning of participation, and a feeling among some members that expanding opportunities for women meant that separate concerts for women composers were no longer necessary. The group decided to disband at the end of the 1995–1996 concert season.

See also American Women Composers, Inc.; American Women Composers, Midwest, Inc.

For Further Reading

Shatin, Judith. "American Women Composers, Inc." *IAWM [International Alliance for Women in Music] Journal* (June 1995): 3–4.

Elizabeth Vercoe

American Women Composers, Midwest, Inc.

American Women Composers, Midwest, Inc. (AWC), is a regional group of composers, performers, and non-musicians, both men and women, who work to bring performance opportunities, recognition, and support to women composers living in the United States and to acquaint the public with the centuries-long tradition of women composers worldwide. The organization was founded in 1982 in Chicago as a chapter of the American Women Composers, Inc., organization that had been established in Washington, DC, in 1976 by composer Tommie Carl. The founding composers of AWC Midwest, Darleen Cowles Mitchell (the first president), Charmian Tashjian, Jan Remer, and Janice Misurell-Mitchell, joined with Chicago performers, flutist Mary Stolper and soprano Marybeth Evensen, to present concerts of both contemporary and historic women composers. During the 1980s the group expanded in membership and visibility, establishing itself as a concert presenter in the Chicago area with occasional performances in Washington, DC, for the national AWC, the National Women's Studies Association Conventions, and the annual Boston Women's Music Festival.

By the mid-1980s AWC Midwest began to build its programs around a theme, combining jazz and new music, folk music and classical music, and to promote music by African American women composers (particularly those who lived and worked in Chicago) in programs at local colleges and on radio. The first major concert of this type was the Ruth Crawford Seeger Retrospective in 1985. This was followed in subsequent years by concerts of music of African American women, including orchestral and choral works as well as newly commissioned works, collaborations with choreographers, and early music groups. One such project united several groups in a series of theatrical concerts about music by women performed at the Women's Building at the 1893 Columbian Exposition in Chicago.

In the early 1990s the group expanded its venues. Major concerts from this period included music by Soviet women, performances at the Art Institute of Chicago, music from the eighteenth to twentieth centuries hosted by guest composer Tania León (b. 1943) at the Ravinia Festival, and music featuring Chicago composers performed in the Ballroom of Orchestra Hall by members of the Chicago Symphony. Each of these venues became incorporated into the concert season on a fairly regular basis, and this visibility brought new supporters to the organization. It was during this period that AWC Midwest rented its own office space and hired staff to assist in running the organization and in fundraising. The group also began to make a greater effort to attract student members and to provide services for them.

AWC Midwest developed an outreach program in 1991. Originally designed for high school students, the program was expanded to include grade school students and has proved highly successful. Performances focus on the work of women composers whose race or ethnic background reflects the Chicago student population: Latino, African American, Eastern European, and Asian.

In 1997 the group celebrated its 15th anniversary and continues to receive both public attention and substantial funding. Future plans include a newsletter, further collaborations with local organizations and performing ensembles, and the development of a concert series that will present a multifaceted view of music by women.

See also American Women Composers, Inc.; American Women Composers, Massachusetts Chapter

For Further Reading

American Women Composers, Midwest, Inc. Available: http://music.acu.edu/www/iawm/wimusic/awcmid.html

Shatin, Judith. "American Women Composers, Inc." *IAWM [International Alliance for Women in Music] Journal* (June 1995): 3–4.
Janice Misurell-Mitchell

Amos, Tori (1963–)

Tori Amos is one of the most successful pop singer-songwriters of the 1990s. Drawing from artists of the 1970s such as Joni Mitchell (b. 1943), she has revitalized the singer-songwriter tradition. Additionally, Amos has helped to revive the piano as a rock and roll instrument.

Born Myra Ellen Amos on 22 August 1963 in Newton, NC, she began playing the piano at a very early age. Amos entered the Peabody Institute (Baltimore) by the age of five. Though clearly a talented performer, she struggled with the strictly classical focus of the program and was eventually dismissed from Peabody several years later. As a teenager, she performed her own pop songs at bars and clubs throughout Washington, DC, before changing her name to "Tori" and moving to Los Angeles.

Her first break came when Atlantic Records signed her band Y Kant Tori Read, though she abandoned the act shortly thereafter to begin working on her own more intimate material. Amos released her first solo album, *Little Earthquakes* (Atlantic 82358–2), in 1992, featuring the much sparser sound of only piano and vocals. The single "Me and a Gun," a recounting of her own experience with acquaintance-rape, displayed the confessional lyrical style that has won her the devotion of a multitude of predominantly female fans. That same year she released the extended play album

Tori Amos in performance in New York City in July 1998. *Photo © Mitchell Gerber/ CORBIS.*

Crucify (Atlantic 82399), which featured mainly cover songs, including her own version of Nirvana's "Smells Like Teen Spirit."

Her next full-length album, *Under the Pink* (Atlantic 82567), solidified her pop-star status with the sale of millions of copies. She followed in 1996 with *Boys for Pele* (Atlantic 82862), which debuted at number two on the *Billboard* Top-20 Chart, before adding a backup band for the 1998 release of *From the Choirgirl Hotel* (Atlantic 83095). Released in 1999 *To Venus and Back* (Atlantic 83230), garnered substantial critical acclaim and continued her string of best-selling albums in the 1990s.

A very personal and outspoken public

persona, Amos has been a strong advocate for women musicians and women's rights. She also contributed to the formation of the Rape, Abuse, and Incest National Network (RAINN), a hotline for survivors of sexual assault.

See also Singer-Songwriter

For Further Reading

RAINN (Rape, Abuse, and Incest National Network). Available: http://www.rainn.com

Roger, Kalen. *Tori Amos: The Authorized Bibliography: All These Years*. London: Omnibus Press, 1994.

Jeff Herriott

Anderson, Laurie (1947–)

Performance artist Laurie Anderson has successfully extended the boundaries of both the popular and avant-garde musical genres, including innovations in electronic performance media and new uses of technology in music. Best known for her large-scale multimedia shows, Anderson has used technology and gender as important themes in her performances. Her place in music is unique in that she has maintained followings in both popular music and avant-garde electronic and multimedia music.

Anderson was born on 5 June 1947 in Chicago, IL, and studied violin at an early age. She moved to New York, where she studied visual arts, earning a B.A. in art history from Barnard College (1969) and an M.F.A. in sculpture from Columbia University (1972). Her career as a performance artist started during her graduate work, when she began including music and stories with her films and sculptures, creating intermedia installations that she presented in local venues.

In 1982 her self-produced single *O Superman (for Massenet)*, released privately the year before, unexpectedly reached number two on the British pop charts.

Laurie Anderson performing at the Wiltern Theatre in Los Angeles in February 1990. *Photo © Neal Preston/CORBIS.*

Shortly thereafter Anderson signed a contract with Warner Brothers Records and co-produced (with Roma Baran) her first album, *Big Science* (Warner Brothers 2–36741982). Included on *Big Science* were excerpts from what would become her first major multimedia touring production, *United States*. *United States* was a vast production, taking two nights to perform. In the show, Anderson used several instruments that she invented or helped to invent. The most notable of these was the tape-bow violin—a violin that uses a bow made of magnetic tape, and that has a tape head in place of the strings. The bow was drawn at varying speeds across the tapehead in order to play the prerecorded sounds on the tape at different speeds, and forward or backward. Other distinctive sounds used in her shows include the vocoder, a device used to alter her voice; extended vocal techniques; and contact microphones used to amplify the sounds of the body.

Several more albums followed with Warner Brothers, including *Home of the Brave* (Warner Brothers Records 25400–1), *Strange Angels* (Warner Brothers Records 9 25900–2), and *Bright Red* (Warner Brothers Records 9 45534–2); most of these albums contain music from her live productions. In 1986 the concert video for her *Home of the Brave* show was released. There are numerous other more recent projects. *Puppet Motel* (Voyager DCRM 1296500) is an interactive CD-ROM produced with designer Hsin-Chien Huang that allows the user to explore the rooms of the virtual hotel experiencing both previously released music and new audio and visual material derived from her stage productions. In 1994 Anderson's book *Stories from the Nerve Bible* was published, detailing the 20-year development of her career as an artist.

In 1999 Anderson signed with Nonesuch Records and began touring with her new production, *Songs and Stories from Moby Dick*. Her latest album, *Life on a String* (Atlantic 75939), includes three pieces from the tour, in addition to new material.

See also Experimental Music; Music Technology; Performance Art

For Further Reading

Anderson, Laurie. *Stories from the Nerve Bible: A Retrospective, 1972–1992*. New York: Harper Collins, 1994.

Gaar, Gillian G. *She's a Rebel: The History of Women in Rock and Roll*. Seattle: Seal Press, 1992.

Leslie Stone

Anderson, Marian (1897–1993)

Considered one of the finest singers of the twentieth century, Marian Anderson would be noteworthy for that accomplishment alone. In addition, she is significant for the way she effectively advanced black civil rights and combated racism in the United States. She broke the racial barriers and paved the way for African American artists to succeed in the field of music.

Although Anderson was considered a contralto, voice descriptions and recorded evidence reveal an amazing range of nearly three octaves; her voice possessed a warmth and richness that always served the words and music of whatever she sang. Her voice was particularly compelling in the Negro spirituals with which she often ended her concerts. Many recordings have been made of her remarkable voice, including *Great Voices of the Century* (Memoir Classics 432) and *Spirituals* (RCA 63306).

Anderson was born on 17 February 1897 in Philadelphia. She displayed an early love of music and sang in the choirs of her family's church from the age of six. She had no formal music lessons until she was 15 years old, despite the fact that her voice was remarkable and she often substituted for absent soloists. Giuseppe Boghetti became her teacher shortly before she left high school. In 1925 Boghetti entered Anderson in a competition to appear in concert with the New York Philharmonic. She placed first out of 300 contestants and subsequently performed in concert with the Philharmonic. However, true success did not come until she went to Europe.

In October 1930 Anderson made her debut in Berlin, followed by a successful concert tour of Scandinavia. Between 1930 and 1935 she achieved much ac-

Marian Anderson in performance ca. 1945. *Photo courtesy of Hulton/Archive Photos.*

claim from concert tours throughout Europe. She appeared at the Salzburg Festival (1935), where she sang for Arturo Toscanini; it was there that he made the famous remark, "a voice like hers comes only once in a century." When Anderson returned to the United States later that year she was an established, world-class artist. Following rave reviews of her New York recitals at Town Hall and Carnegie Hall, she embarked on a coast-to-coast performance tour of the United States. In 1936 she became the first African American singer to perform at the White House. The event that secured Anderson's place in history books, however, was the outdoor concert she gave at the Lincoln Memorial on Easter

Sunday 1939 before an audience of 75,000. Called America's first civil rights rally, this concert was arranged to protest the Daughters of the American Revolution refusal to let her perform in its Constitution Hall because of her race.

Another of Anderson's many triumphs was her Metropolitan Opera debut as Ulrica in Giuseppe Verdi's *Un Ballo in Maschera* (1955). Although it occurred late in her career, this performance marked the first performance of an African American soloist at the Metropolitan Opera.

During the decade before her retirement, Anderson served as a delegate to the United Nations Committee on Human Rights and received the Presidential Medal of Freedom. Following a farewell recital at Carnegie Hall on Easter Sunday 1965, she retired. On 8 April 1993 she died at age 96 in Portland, OR.

See also Performer, Vocal

For Further Reading

Anderson, Marian. *My Lord What a Morning*. New York: Viking Press, 1956.
Sims, Janet. *Marian Anderson: An Annotated Bibliography and Discography*. Westport, CT: Greenwood Press, 1981.

Jenny Williams

Anderson, Roberta Joan

See Joni Mitchell

Andrews Sisters

An American institution that symbolized the swing era and the World War II years, the Andrews Sisters entertained and uplifted civilian and military audiences with their cheerful, escapist novelty songs and sincere ballads. Their act, with its distinctive close three-part harmony and an optimistic, enthusiastic delivery, made them the most popular of all women's vocal groups; they had hits from 1937 to 1953 and sold over 80 million records. Though they brought fun, hope, and relief to their audience, the sisters had a turbulent relationship, at times squabbling or refusing to talk to each other.

All three sisters were born in Mound, MN. Patty (b. 1918), the lead vocalist, was playful and personable with a flair for comedy; she acted as the group's leader and spokesperson. Maxene (1916–1995) sang the high harmony part. LaVerne (1911–1967) sang the low harmony and played piano; she was the only sister who could read music. As children they took dancing lessons and frequented a vaudeville theatre near their parents' restaurant. LaVerne taught her younger siblings songs she had heard on the radio. In 1937, after years of touring in vaudeville, they were on radio themselves. Booking agent Lou Levy heard them and brought them to Decca Records, where they remained for 16 years. Levy became their manager, and in 1941 he married Maxene.

The Andrews Sisters' first hit was a huge one: "Bei Mir Bist Du Schoen (Means That You're Grand)" made them stars in 1938. With its Yiddish title, it set the pattern of translations and adaptations of songs from other countries, among them "Beer Barrel Polka" (1939) from Czechoslovakia, "Ferryboat Serenade" (1940) from Italy, and "Rum and Coca Cola" (1944) from Trinidad—all top hits. Accompanied by Vic Schoen and his orchestra, the sisters popularized many kinds of songs: polka, calypso, novelty, boogie-woogie, rhythm and blues, country and western, nostalgic, patriotic, and Christmas. Their numerous recordings include *All-Time Greatest Hits* (MCA 1121) and *20th Century Masters—The Millennium Collection: The Best of the Andrews Sisters* (MCA 112230).

Regular guests on radio shows, they worked with other top artists such as Glenn Miller. Stars they recorded with include Carmen Miranda (1909–1955), Guy Lombardo, Ernest Tubb, Burl Ives, Les Paul, Danny Kaye, and, longest and most successfully, Bing Crosby. Big hits with Crosby include "Don't Fence Me In" and "Ac-cent-tchu-ate the Positive." In the 1940s the Andrews Sisters appeared in 15 movies and added voices to two Walt Disney cartoons—*Make Mine Music* (1946) and *Melody Time* (1948). Whether playing socialites, amateur singers, elevator operators, club hostesses, or factory workers, they injected

The Andrews Sisters (from left, LaVerne, Patty, and Maxene) during a 1940s performance. *Photo courtesy of Archive Photos.*

vitality and hit songs into these unso-phisticated films. In the 1950s the trio separated for a period to try solo careers but soon reunited, performing until shortly before LaVerne's death in 1967.

In 1973 a new version of their 1941 hit "Boogie Woogie Bugle Boy" by Bette Midler (b. 1945) led to renewed interest in the Andrews Sisters. Patty and Maxene appeared on Broadway in 1974 and continued to perform, much loved, into the 1990s. Maxene's memoirs were published in 1993.

See also Grammy Award

For Further Reading

Andrews, Maxene, and Bill Gilbert. *Over Here, Over There: The Andrews Sisters and the USO Stars in World War II*. New York: Kensington Publishing, 1993.

Garvin, James. *The Andrews Sisters: Their Greatest Hits and Finest Performances*. Program notes to a 3-CD box set: Reader's Digest 3349, 1996.

Parish, James Robert, and Michael R. Pitts. *Hollywood Songsters*. New York: Garland Publishing, 1991.

Craig Morrison

Anonymous 4

Anonymous 4 is a unique vocal ensemble founded in 1986 by four women to perform medieval chant and polyphony. In the 1980s, medieval vocal music was largely considered the purview of male voices, but this group of female singers, in emulating nuns singing in a convent, has found a natural place in the performance of the repertoire. Anonymous 4 has received superlative reviews for their exquisite blend of sound and precise unisons, the result of a meticulous rehearsal style described by a member of the group as "obsessive-compulsive." Their concerts are often a combination of song (including chant, monophonic song, and polyphony) and spoken poetry or narrative.

From 1986 to 1998 the four performers were Ruth Cunningham, Marsha Genensky, Susan Hellauer, and Johanna Maria Rose. Ruth Cunningham left the group in 1998 and was replaced by Jacqueline Horner. The name Anonymous 4 is a tongue-in-cheek reference to the scholarly practice of naming unsigned medieval music treatises—Anonymous IV being a treatise on musical practice written at the cathedral of Notre Dame in Paris around 1200.

Although the group has a devoted following among medieval music aficionados, it has also caught the imagination of New Age music devoteés. The group's debut album produced in 1992 by Harmonia Mundi, *An English Ladymass: 13th and 14th-century Chant and Polyphony in Honor of the Virgin Mary* (Harmonia Mundi 907080), rose to *Billboard* magazine's classical Top 10 list and remained there for two years. Since then, the group has produced ten more recordings for Harmonia Mundi, including *On Yoolis Night: Medieval Carols and Motets* (HMU 907099), *Love's Illusion: Music from the Montpellier Codex, 13th Century* (HMU 907109), *The Lily and the Lamb: Chant and Polyphony from Medieval England* (HMU 907125), *Miracles of Sant'iago: Music from the Codex Calixtinus* (HMU 907156), *A Star in the East: Medieval Hungarian Christmas Music* (HMU 907139), *11,000 Virgins: Chants for the Feast of St. Ursula* (HMU 907200), *A Lammas Ladymass* (HMU 907222), *1000: A Mass for the End of Time* (HMU 907224), *Legends of St. Nicholas* (HMU 907232), and *The Second Circle: Love Songs of Francisco Landini* (HMU 907269). Anonymous 4 has recently branched out into contemporary music, premiering works by John Taverner and Steve Reich and recording Richard Einhorn's *Voices of Light* (Sony 62006).

Anonymous 4 currently performs about 70 concerts per year, spending four months on the road. For many years an ensemble-in-residence at St. Michael's Church in New York City, in 1998 they moved their base of operation to that city's Corpus Christi Church. They have a repertoire of about a dozen programs and have performed in concert, on broadcasts, and in festivals in the United States, England, France, Germany, Holland, and Spain. In 1998 they appeared in a festival in Bingen, Germany, celebrating the 900th birthday of Hildegard of Bingen. They have also appeared on the television show *CBS Sunday Morning*, on National Public Radio's *Performance Today* and *Weekend Edition*, and on Garrison Keillor's *A Prairie Home Companion*.

See also Performer, Choral and Vocal Ensemble

For Further Reading

Anonymous 4 Website: Available: http://www.anonymous4.com/

Ellison, Cori. "Help Wanted: Fourth Singer, Able to Make a Singular Sound." *New York Times*, 20 September 1998.

Anita Breckbill

Aptitude

Musical aptitude, talent, imagination, creativity, and related attributes in women as compared to men have been discussed in terms of biological (essentialist) and sociological (constructivist) factors. Music has historically been considered a *feminine* pursuit, and women have been considered to have an advantage in aptitude for some musical activities, such as singing. Girls do not resist singing activities in school, and their voices do not change register during puberty, a problematic event for boys. Attempts to explain women's apparent inferiority in other areas of music, as represented by the seeming lack of women composers of large orchestral scores, have often hypothesized an innate or *essential* lack of aptitude. According to social Darwinism, a pervasive and widespread doctrine in the United States in the early twentieth century, women are less highly evolved than men are and thus are unable to understand music theory or compose in the so-called higher forms.

In 1940 Carl Seashore, a psychologist specializing in musical aptitude testing, maintained that in the matter of innate musical attributes—native talent, intelligence, musical temperament, creative imagination, musical precocity, education, and endurance—girls and boys are equally endowed. There is "no clear support in genetics" for the theory that women's creative imagination is "less sustained" than men's, he writes, and any difference is probably owing to "environmental influences." Because "the outcropping of genius is above social considerations," the reason the great composers have all been men is that "woman's fundamental urge is to be beautiful, loved, and adored as a person," whereas "man's urge is to provide and achieve in a career" (367).

Other research has addressed gender as a factor in children's and adults' aptitude for instrumental performance, improvisation, composition, and various components of musical creativity. Mar-

ianne Hassler in the journal *Psychoneuroendocrinology* (1992) reports a study of creative musical behavior, musical intelligence, and spatial ability in relation to the presence of the hormone testosterone in subjects' saliva. Researchers compared a cross-sectional study with 117 adults and an eight-year longitudinal study with 120 adolescents, composers, instrumentalists, and non-musicians of both sexes (63 men, 54 women). The study revealed that an optimal salivary testosterone (ST) range may exist for the expression of creative musical behavior, and this range may be at the bottom of normal male ST range and at the top of normal female ST range. In addition, musicians attained significantly higher spatial test scores than did non-musicians in an eight-year period of adolescent development and in adulthood.

Lucy Green (1997) addresses the development of musical aptitude in girls or boys in elementary school, citing research in England and North America; she observes that gender research became a significant component of music education only in the 1990s. Malcolm Gladwell in the *New Yorker* (1997) discusses gender and racial differences in aptitude and training in athletics and mathematics that may be applied to music performance, music theory, and composing complicated music. He compares girls and boys according to psychological "attribution theory," specifically "effort attribution" (girls) versus "ability attribution" (male). Boys doing well in mathematics, for example, attribute their achievement to their own ability; however, if a boy is doing poorly, he blames the teacher or his own lack of motivation, rather than a lack of general ability. Girls say they are doing well because they work hard; if a girl does not do well, she says she is not smart enough, and this low self-image may eventually thwart her progress.

Malcolm Gladwell concludes that success depends on three factors: genes; a belief in one's own ability; and a desire and passion to succeed. Along this line, studies of "chilly climate" and other forms of discrimination on college campuses maintain that if women do not believe in their own ability, it is because teachers tend to attribute women's successes not to their ability but to luck or an apparent lack of difficulty for the specified task. The message seems to be that a woman's success is owing to external factors over which she has little control.

Green and others decry the all-male repertoire of classical music in general music classes. Many say it discourages girls from thinking of themselves as potential composers. A few say that it deprives both girls and boys of experience with the "feminine aesthetic," although others, including some women who compose, question whether there is such a thing as a feminine aesthetic. It appears that aptitude for music needs the support of adequate training and appropriate self-esteem. When girls and young women with significant musical aptitude are made aware that women have succeeded in every area of musical activity, then they can be encouraged in the direction best suited to their abilities and interests.

See also Chilly Climate; Discrimination, Female Inferiority, Theories of; Social Darwinism

For Further Reading

Gladwell, Malcolm. "The Sports Taboo: Why Blacks Are Like Boys and Whites Are Like Girls." *New Yorker* (19 May 1997): 50–55.

Green, Lucy. "The Music Curriculum and the Possibilities for Intervention." Chapter 9 in *Music, Gender, Education*. Cambridge: Cambridge University Press, 1997.

Hassler, Marianne. "Creative Musical Behavior and Sex Hormones: Musical Talent and Spatial Ability in the Two Sexes." *Psychoneuroendocrinology* 17/1 (March 1992): 55–70.

Seashore, Carl E. "Why No Great Women Composers?" *Music Educators Journal* 25/5 (March 1940): 21, 88. Reprinted: in Carl E. Seashore, *In Search of the Beautiful in Music* (New York: Ronald Press, 1948); as "A 1940 Perspective" in *Music Educators Journal* 65/5 (Jan. 1979): 42ff; and as section 47 in *Women in Music: An Anthology of Source Readings from the Middle Ages to the Present*, ed. by Carol Neuls-Bates (New York: Harper and Row, 1982; rept, Boston: Northeastern University Press, 1996).

Carolyn Bremer
Deborah Hayes

Arrangers

Arrangers create new versions of music that may involve elaboration, simplification, transcription, or orchestration. The most successful arrangers demonstrate a special skill for writing idiomatically by capturing the best qualities of the instruments or voices for which they are arranging. Arrangements may be for publication, performance, or recording. In the twentieth century, women arrangers found success in both instrumental and choral settings, and in all major genres of music—jazz, classical, country, and rock and popular music.

One of the most prolific choral arrangers of the twentieth century is Alice Parker (b. 1925), with well over 400 published choral arrangements. Many of these were written for the Robert Shaw Chorale during her long association with that organization. Sally Terri (1922–1996) worked with the Roger Wagner Chorale in a role comparable to Parker's with the Robert Shaw Chorale. Her published arrangements include the major works *Shaker Worship Service* and *Moravian Love Feast*, as well as the Sally Terri Choral Series. Both Parker's and Terri's choral arrangements have been widely recorded by professional and university groups.

Significant instrumental arrangers include Cynthia Dobrinski (b. 1950), Anne McGinty (b. 1945), Julie Giroux (b. 1961), and Linda Perkins. Dobrinski has over 150 publications, including a large number of arrangements for handbells. Anne McGinty has a reputation for excellent idiomatic writing; she has over 160 instrumental arrangements and original compositions for all levels of performance ability. Julie Giroux has a number of works published for band. Additionally, she is an Emmy Award–winning arranger for broadcasts and has arranged music for recordings by Celine Dion, Michael Jackson, and Reba McEntire (b. 1954). She was a member of the team of arrangers that wrote the music for eight Academy Awards broadcasts. Linda Perkins made her living solely by arranging during the early 1980s in Houston, TX. Her work was for local big bands, charity events and shows, and various schools and churches, among others. Although much of the demand for big bands and large charity shows declined after Houston's economic downturn of the mid-1980s, Perkins continues to work as an arranger and member of the local musicians union.

See also Copyist; Librettist

For Further Reading

Alice Parker Home. Available: http://www.alice parker.com/

Gresham, Mark. *Choral Conversations: Selected Interviews from Chorus! Magazine by Mark Gresham.* San Carlos, CA: Thomas House Publications, 1997.

Allyson Brown Applebaum

Arts Midwest

See Organizations, Regional Arts

Asian American Music

Asian American music primarily gained public awareness in the United States after World War II. Cutting across racial barriers and essentially becoming cultural ambassadors to their ethnic groups, these musicians paved the passage for the continuation of Asian American music today.

Among the first to be ordained into the elite group of Asian American women in music was Pat Suzuki (b. 1930). Often compared to female vocal giants such as Sarah Vaughan (1924–1990), Ella Fitzgerald (1917–1996), and Judy Garland (1922–1969), singer-actress Suzuki performed in a wide range of venues from night clubs to Broadway. One of the first Asian American women to earn the starring role in the original 1958 Broadway production of *Flower Drum Song*, Suzuki transcended negative attitudes fostered by post–World War II America toward Japanese Americans and soared to popularity. Suzuki's success enabled others to follow.

Racial stigma toward Asian Americans, particularly toward Japanese Americans owing to their internment, continued to exist in post–World War II America, giving rise to the emergence of the Asian American movement in the 1960s and 1970s. This movement was aimed at counteracting racial discrimination and creating Asian American solidarity. Addressing politically charged issues in their creative endeavors, the first generation of Asian American women such as Sumi Tonooka, Nobuko Miyamoto (b. 1939), June Kuramoto, and Miya Masaoka (b. 1958) arrived on the music scene.

Sumi Tonooka's composition *Out from the Silence*, which documents the experiences of Japanese Americans interned in camps during World War II, best represents the politically oriented artistic wealth of this generation. A *sansei* (third-generation) Japanese American dancer and composer, Nobuko Miyamoto has been closely involved in the Asian American movement since the 1970s. Recognizing the importance of the performing arts as a platform to address cultural and political issues, Miyamoto continues to be politically active, choosing to represent the achievements and struggles of Asian Americans through performance.

Popular among Asian American musicians is the use of jazz and jazz improvisation as the basic creative idiom to which traditional Asian music is incorporated to construct unique Asian American musical expressions. Sumi Tonooka, Keiko Matsui, and Miya Masaoka largely fit this aesthetic model. Tonooka's use of traditional Japanese instruments and compositional techniques pays homage to her Asian heritage while successfully fusing Japanese and American jazz music. Similar to Tonooka, Matsui is an acclaimed Japanese keyboardist who performs in the jazz idiom. Trained in Japanese court music, and a performer on the Japanese koto (a 13-string board zither), sansei Japanese American Miya Masaoka has applied her musicianship toward creating new music. Combining jazz, computer music, and traditional Japanese musical instruments, Masaoka primarily explores experimental music.

June Kuramoto, a koto innovator, was a founder of Southern California's popular Asian American band Hiroshima. Nominated for a Grammy Award, Hiroshima was formed during the 1970s to address issues pertinent to the Asian American movement. Although Kuramoto utilizes improvisation, she prefers to preserve the authenticity of Japanese koto music. Less politically oriented than her contemporaries, Ikoko Yuge is a performer of *gagaku* (traditional Japanese court music) on the koto and shamisen (a traditional Japanese three-string instrument). Like Kuramoto, Yuge has dedicated her life to the preservation of authentic Japanese musical traditions. Since 1957, Yuge has been an instructor at the University of California, Los Angeles, where she directs the gagaku ensemble (1957–2000). Her dedication to education is matched only by her commitment to the dissemination of traditional Japanese music in Southern California.

Trained in both Western Classical music and traditional Chinese music, composer Chen Yi (b. 1953) integrates Chinese music into the Western Classical idiom. Her main contribution lies in her efforts to expose American audiences to Chinese music and to use her music to create a Chinese American identity. Chen has been composer in residence with many ensembles, including Chanticleer and the Women's Philharmonic (San Francisco).

The San Francisco–based "Asian Improv" company has played an important role in promoting Asian American musicians since the 1970s—providing them with a record label that was dedicated to preserving Asian American music. Today the Asian Improv label has afforded recognition for Asian American women artists such as the members of Pinay and the artist Jocelyne Enrique. Formerly a member of Pinay Divas (a Filipina *a cappella* group who sing in English and Tagalog), Filipina Jocelyne Enrique has now launched a solo career and is no longer considered to represent Asian American music, as she has crossed over into mainstream popular music. Also from Northern California, Linda Low is currently climbing to success with her dance and electronic music.

In this second generation we encounter Asian American women such as Lea Salonga, who has continued to perform on Broadway in addition to lending her voice to animated characters in films such as *Aladdin* (1992) and *Mulan* (1998). Increasingly, the pressures to accommodate to the music industry's specifications have led Asian Americans to abandon their role as cultural activists and to cross over to the mainstream popular music industry. Thus we find cross-over artists such as gospel singer Junko; and Hawaiian-Filipino rhythm and blues singer Faith; and rhythm and blues, and pop singer Tatyana Ali; and Filipina and African American rapper Foxy Brown (b. 1979). Magdalen Hsu-Li (b. 1970), who expresses Chinese American societal concerns, as well as rhythm and blues, and rock singer Anggun, who is influenced by her traditional Indonesian music, continue to make political statements in their music—providing critical discourse through art, as did their predecessors. Yoko Ono (b. 1933) is another Asian American woman who has enjoyed notoriety in the American entertainment industry.

Contemporary Asian American women musicians continue to expand their artistic reach by participating in globalization as they affiliate themselves with educational and commercial institutions worldwide. International presence has afforded them popularity and facilitated the dissemination of their art. Is it ironic, however, that documentation of Asian American women in music can best be described as scanty when compared with the academic and commercial publication of their male counterparts. The discussion of Asian American women in music, however, should not be restricted to those in the performing arts. There are also many Asian American women musicologists and ethnomusicologists who have cultivated an awareness about Asian American musical culture in the United States. It is largely owing to the scholarship of Asian American women such as Susan Asai, Cynthia Wong, Deborah Wong, and Adelaida Reyes Schramm that we are beginning to find discussion of Asian American music and see mention of Asian American women in music.

See also Multicultural Musics

For Further Reading

Asai, S. "Sansei Voices in the Community: Japanese American Musicians in California." In *Musics of Multicultural America: A Study of Twelve Musical Communities*, eds. Kip Lornell and Anne Rasmussen. New York: Schirmer Books, 1997.
———. "Transformations of Tradition: Three Generations of Japanese American Music Making." *Musical Quarterly* 79/3 (1995): 429–453.
Barkin, Elaine. "The New Music of Chen Yi." *Journal of Music in China* 1 (1999): 147–149.
Jong, Richard Kenneth. "An Urgency in Our Insurgency: Perspectives on the Formation and Maintenance of an Asian American Music Collective." Master's thesis, University of California, Los Angeles, 1996.
Komai, Chris. "Miss Ponytail Returns." *Rafu Shimpo*, 11 May 1994.
Noriyuki, Duane. "Nobuko Miyamoto, Civil Rights Activist." *Los Angeles Times*, 19 July 1995.
Wong, Deborah. "Just Being There: Making Asian American Space in the Recording Industry." In *Musics of Multicultural America: A Study of Twelve Musical Communities*," eds. Kip Lornell and Anne Rasmussen. New York: Schirmer Books, 1997.

Vasana De Mel

Audio Engineering Society

See Organizations, Professional Audio

Audio Production

The field of audio production, which includes people working as producers and engineers, has historically been more dominated by men than other areas of the recording industry, such as executive or performance careers. The producer or engineer often works behind the scenes in the recording studio with mixing boards, microphones, audio recorders, and computer audio software.

Three industry organizations that provide support for, and recognition of, audio production personnel—the Audio Engineering Society (AES), the Society of Professional Audio Recording Services (SPARS), and the National Academy of Recording Arts and Sciences (NARAS)—recognize that women are underrepresented, and they provide networking opportunities for women interested in audio production careers. However, the AES is the only organization that has formed a standing committee to address women's issues related to audio careers.

In 1991 only 15 percent of applicants for admission to audio engineering programs at trade schools, colleges, and universities were women (Nunziata, 1991). Part of the problem is the lack of role models who might encourage young women to major in audio production degrees. As a result, a paradox exists: very few women are prepared to enter audio careers, therefore very few role models and mentors exist to encourage potential students of audio.

There are several reasons why women tend to avoid careers as audio engineers or producers. Shirley Kaye, executive director of the Society of Professional Audio Recording Services (SPARS), cites the unorthodox hours of recording environments as a key factor for women. In order to complete an album in a fairly short period of time, recording sessions typically consume many hours per day. It is not uncommon for engineers and producers to work through the night in order to use the studios—booked by the day—as cost effectively as possible.

Because American society has historically placed the burden of childcare on wives rather than husbands, the women in heterosexual marriages typically must select from two options: have children, or have a career in audio.

Shirley Kaye owned and operated a recording studio prior to becoming the executive director of SPARS. She is credited with hiring the first woman engineer and first woman assistant engineer while a studio owner. After several years of serving as the only woman member of the SPARS board of directors, Kaye became executive director. She has served as a panelist for the Audio Engineering Society—Women in Audio project and is considered one of the most influential role models for women interested in audio recording careers.

Dyana Williams, president of the International Association of African American Music (IAAAM), believes quite strongly that women are discouraged from entering certain careers within the music industry. Cosette Collier, chair of the AES Women in Audio committee and audio recording professor, agrees with Williams. Collier draws upon personal experiences from when she was an engineer. A recording studio manager did not want her to work at night because he felt she "would not be safe" after normal business hours. Another deterrent for women is the myth that women are not as proficient as their male counterparts at technical tasks.

In 1991 an AES Education Committee identified several issues that were in need of further investigation. One of those issues, the challenges women face in audio technology–related jobs, was assigned to a subcommittee for review. In 1995 the AES Women in Audio: Project 2000 was created to increase the opportunities for women in the audio industry over the subsequent five-year period. Project 2000 presented panels of successful women producers and engineers to discuss current problems and present suggestions for other women hoping to enter or progress in the industry. When the successful five-year pilot program ended, AES created a standing committee called AES Women in Audio.

Cosette Collier, who became chair of AES Women in Audio in 1999, plans to continue presenting annual panels featuring successful women audio engineers and producers at national conventions and other public forums. Collier hopes to establish a mentoring program, using successful professionals who agree to donate some of their time, to inform women of the options available for entry-level careers and advancement in the industry. AES Women in Audio also hopes to present a program called Audio Careers directed at young women who may not be aware of potential educational programs and careers in audio. The AES Women in Audio World Wide Web site contains current information about issues pertaining to women in audio engineering and producing careers.

In addition to Kaye, Williams, and Collier, there have been several other important women in the field of audio production. These include Sylvia Massy, Jennifer Monnar, Susan Rogers, Zoe Thrall, and Flory Ramirez Turner. Sylvia Massy has engineered or produced artists representing an extremely diverse array of genres. Massy began her career working at her college's student radio station. Her experience recording commercials left her with a yearning to learn more about the recording process. She "started sweeping floors at a music studio" in an effort to work her way into an audio engineering position (Ricker, 1997).

Massy's credits include: Tool, Smash-ing Pumpkins, Tom Petty, Johnny Cash, the Red Hot Chile Peppers, R.E.M., GetoBoys, Love and Rockets, Melissa Etheridge, Oingo Boingo, Luscious Jackson, Aerosmith, Paula Abdul, Prince, Mojo Nixon, and Greta.

Jennifer Monnar is one of only a few women who has entered the male-dominated genre of urban music as a producer and engineer. Her projects include the controversial and critically acclaimed album by Me'shell Ndegéocello. Her entry into the rap and hip hop world lead to producer and engineer credits for successful albums by R. Kelly and Dr. Dre. Monnar's discography also includes works by Luther Vandross, Ras Kass, the Gregory Hines Show, King T, Anthrax, and Mickey Hart.

Susan Rogers is one of four women producers recognized by *Billboard* magazine and who began gaining international attention in 1991 (Nunziata, 1991). Rogers has produced, co-produced or engineered albums for: Rusted Root, Jill Sobule, Barenaked Ladies, the Artist formerly known as Prince, David Byrne, Queen, Geggy Tah, David Poe, Tricky, Nil Lara, Paul Westerberg, Michael Penn, and Violent Femmes. Recording artist David Poe complimented Rogers's style and said, "She let the music cradle the songs instead of take away from them" (Bessman, 1998).

Zoe Thrall is president of Avatar Recording Studios in New York City and is the first woman to become president of a major recording facility in the nation. Thrall's career in audio began as an intern at the Power Station Recording Studios in 1981. She was subsequently hired full-time by the studios and worked as an assistant engineer on projects for numerous artists including Bruce Springsteen and Aerosmith.

Thrall met producer Steven Van

Zandt and worked with him on his solo album as both an assistant engineer and performer. This collaboration sparked a 12-year relationship in which she toured and recorded with Little Steven. In 1994 Thrall returned to the Power Station Recording Studios as vice-president of studio operations. When the studios were sold to Voikunthanath Kanamori and brought into the Avatar Entertainment Corporation organization, Thrall was appointed president. In addition to her executive duties, she serves on the board of directors for SPARS.

Flory Ramirez Turner is one of a very few women concert production crew members touring the world today. She and other crew members for the Rolling Stones' "Voodoo Lounge" tour were recognized as the top touring production crew in the world by *Performance Maga-zine*. Turner has been on production crews for Bruce Springsteen, Michael Bolton, Mariah Carey, the Rolling Stones, Luther Vandross, Enrique Englesias, and Tina Turner (no relation).

See also Organizations, Professional Audio

For Further Reading

Bessman, Jim. "Black's 'Road' Ready—Anticipation High for Arista/Austin Set." *Billboard* (18 July 1998).

Nunziata, Susan. "Few Producers, Engineers Are Women, But Chances Improve." *Billboard, the Billboard Report* (12 October 1991): 1.

Ricker, Di Mari. "Tough Money: Entertainment . . ." *Los Angeles Times*, 24 March 1997, D2, p. 19, Financial Desk.

Richard Barnet

Avant Garde Music

See Experimental Music

B

Baez, Joan (1941–)

Singer-songwriter Joan Baez brought solo performance of folk music to prominence during the 1960s as rock bands were beginning to dominate the American music scene. Her performance of Bob Dylan's songs broadened both his audience and her own and helped forge the alliance between folk and rock music. Featuring her clear, crystalline soprano voice, five of the albums she released between 1960 and 1971 sold over 1,000,000 copies and, therefore, were certified Gold, including her 1968 Grammy Award–nominated double album of Dylan songs *Any Day Now* (Vanguard VCD-79306/7). From the start, Baez appealed to an unusually diverse audience and was a featured performer at both the Newport Folk Festival and at Woodstock. Known first as a fine interpreter of the songs of others, Baez later began composing original songs. She is also known for her political activism. Jailed in the 1960s for antiwar activities, she has since been honored as much for her public service as for her music.

Born on 9 January 1941 in Staten Island, NY, Baez is of Mexican-English heritage. She began performing songs with guitar during her high school years in California. When her father accepted a teaching position at the Massachusetts Institute of Technology in 1958, Baez suddenly found herself in the midst of Boston's thriving urban folk movement. After only a few months of coffeehouse appearances, Baez was invited to sing with Bob Gibson at the first Newport Folk Festival. The success of that event opened the way to new opportunities as she signed with Vanguard Records. Her first album, released in 1960, was an immediate success. Her second and third albums followed in 1961 and 1962. In 1962, when she appeared on the cover of *Time* magazine, all three of her albums were on the charts.

Throughout the 1960s, Baez continued releasing at least one album each year. She became increasingly involved with civil rights and antiwar activities and with Bob Dylan and his politically charged music. Dylan and Baez undertook a joint U.S. concert tour in 1965. In 1964 she published *The Joan Baez Songbook*, which has since reprinted 20 times.

In 1969 Baez released *David's Album*

Joan Baez performing at the Bread and Roses Festival of Music in Berkeley, CA, in October 1979. *Photo © Roger Ressmeyer/ CORBIS.*

(Vanguard VCD-79308) as her husband, David Harris, began serving a prison term for draft resistance. Her singing of "Joe Hill" is featured in the *Woodstock* movie, filmed later that same year. In 1971 her cover of "The Night They Drove Old Dixie Down" was a Top 10 single. Her politics became increasingly international, with visits to Southeast Asia, Ireland, Moscow, and Central and South America; and on Christmas day 1972, Baez was in Hanoi as U.S. bombs fell on the city. In 1975 A&M Records released her album *Diamonds and Rust* (A&M Records CD-3233), including her original compositions. Her pace slowed through the 1980s, though she continued to receive awards and recognition for both her musical and political activities.

After four decades, Baez remains an artistic influence in popular music. She has recently appeared with singer-

songwriters such as Mary-Chapin Carpenter (b. 1958) and the Indigo Girls. In 1992 her compact disc *Play Me Backwards* (Virgin Records 86458–2) was nominated for a Grammy Award. The success of her album *Gone from Danger* (Guardian 7 2438–59357–2) prompted a new world tour in 1997 and 1998.

See also Rock and Popular Music Genres; Singer-Songwriter

For Further Reading

Baez, Joan. *Daybreak*. New York: Dial Press, 1968.
Baggelaar, Kristin, and Donald Milton. *Folk Music: More Than a Song*. New York: Crowell, 1976.
The Joan Baez Web Pages. Available: http://baez. woz.org

Kathleen Pierson

Bailey, Pearl (1918–1990)

Pearl Bailey was a popular singer and actress and even a United Nations delegate. Her performances were sultry and earthy. A personable jazz and show singer, Bailey's exuberant performances left a memorable mark both on stage and in concert.

Bailey was born on 29 March 1918 in Newport News, VA. Her parents supported her early musical interests. Her family moved to Washington, DC, and after her parents divorced, she and her three siblings moved to Philadelphia with their mother. The adolescent Bailey began winning dance and singing contests in Washington, DC, and at the Apollo Theater in New York. At age 15 she left school. She worked in a series of nightclubs in the Philadelphia area, but returned to Washington, DC, after an early failed marriage.

In 1940 she performed as a big-band vocalist and dancer with Noble Sissle; then she sang with the bands of "Cootie" Charles Williams and Count Basie. She

Pearl Bailey on stage at the Strand Theatre in New York City in 1945. *Photo courtesy of Frank Driggs Collection.*

also performed on a United Service Organizations tour (1941–1943). She debuted her solo career in 1944 at New York's Village Vanguard and at the Blue Angel. While performing at the Blue Angel in 1945, she began a long and successful association with bandleader and performer Cab Calloway. Calloway's band at the Strand Theater in New York featured gospel singer Sister Rosetta Tharpe (1915–1973). When Tharpe became ill, Bailey replaced her for three weeks; she did the same for 16 weeks with Calloway at the Zanzibar nightclub in New York.

Bailey made her Broadway debut in *St. Louis Woman* (original score recording available Capitol L-355), for which she earned the Donaldson Award for best Broadway newcomer. From the 1950s through the 1970s she performed in films and on the stage. One of her trademark songs, "Tired," was performed in her first film, *Variety Girl* (1947). In 1968 she received a special Tony Award for her performance in an all-black version of *Hello Dolly*. Bailey also performed and recorded with her new husband, jazz drummer Louis Bellson. In the 1960s she began suffering from ill health. Her albums include *The One and Only Pearl Bailey Sings* (Mercury MG-20187) and *The Intoxicating Pearl Bailey* (Mercury MG-20277).

In 1985 she received her B.A. in theology from Georgetown University.

Pearl Bailey died on 17 August 1990 in Philadelphia.

See also Jazz; Tony Awards

For Further Reading

Bailey, Pearl. *The Raw Pearl*. New York: Harcourt, Brace, and World, 1968.
———. *Talking to Myself*. New York: Harcourt, Brace, Jovanovich, 1971.

Monica J. Burdex

Bands, Pop Rock

All-women pop rock bands—individuals and groups that performed their own instruments as well as sang—were a rarity in the United States until the 1980s, when the Go-Go's and the Bangles achieved commercial success. The few examples prior to this decade encountered formidable chart competition from their male counterparts and sometimes suffered from poor management. Equally unusual were women instrumentalists in otherwise male-dominated bands; with the ascendancy of the new wave movement of the late 1970s, they would be more frequently encountered.

During the 1960s the only all-woman pop rock band was Goldie and the Gingerbreads. Founded in 1963 and originally based in New York, its members were Polish-born lead singer Goldie (b. 1940 as Genya Zelkowitz), guitarist Carol McDonald, organist Margo Crocitto, and drummer Ginger Panebianco. Their rhythm and blues–style vocals and prominent Hammond B-3 organ characterized the group's sound. The group had its first break when the English group the Animals heard them play and recommended the band to their management team. Their suggestion that the Gingerbreads relocate to Britain in 1964 initially proved fortuitous; the band opened for the Kinks, Yardbirds, Hollies, and Rolling Stones; did a Beatles-like

stint at Hamburg's Star Club; and released a successful U.K. single, "Can't You Hear My Heartbeat?" From here, though, the group's luck ran out. Their management team broke apart, with one of its members, Mickie Most, obtaining the rights to the Gingerbreads' British single. Most enlisted his recent hot group, Herman's Hermits, to record the song; theirs beat the Gingerbreads' version to the U.S. airwaves and became a hit. Goldie returned to England in 1965 to embark on a solo career, leaving the remaining trio to soldier on unsuccessfully before breaking up in 1967. McDonald would later found other groups, most notably the all-woman band Isis of the mid-1970s, a jazz-rock act prominently featuring congas and horns. Goldie's career would encounter a number of unusual twists, including solo turns under this name and Genya Ravan, membership in the band Ten Wheel Drive, and production of various albums for other artists, most notably *Young, Loud, and Snotty* (Sire 26981) by the Dead Boys.

All-woman groups of the 1970s had only marginally more success. The most notable was Fanny, a Los Angeles–based pop-rock quartet (showing modest boogie, folk, and soul influences) that bore the distinction of being the first all-woman band signed by a major U.S. label. Initially named the Svelts, then Wild Honey, its members included sisters Jean (b. 1950) and June (b. 1949) Millington on bass and vocals and guitar and vocals, respectively; Nickey Barclay on keyboards; and Alice de Buhr on drums. They recorded four albums, *Fanny* (Reprise 6416), *Charity Ball* (RS-6456), *Fanny Hill* (MS-2058), and *Mothers Pride* (MS-2137), and nudged the bottom of the charts with the single "Charity Ball." They also served as backing band on Barbra Streisand's album *Stoney End*. The act collapsed briefly in 1973 and then re-formed with Patty Quatro replacing June Millington and Brie Brandt-Howard replacing de Buhr; they released one more album, *Rock 'n' Roll Survivors*, before permanently dissolving in 1975. Their biggest commercial success came as the band was breaking up, when the single "Butter Boy" reached the Top 40. During their run the act received much publicity, most notably bumper stickers asking listeners to "get behind Fanny."

If anything, the Fanny slogan campaign saddled onto rival band Birtha proved even more unseemly ("Birtha has balls"). The latter act's personnel consisted of Shele Pinizzotto (guitar and vocals), Rosemary Butler (bass and vocals), Sherry Hagler (keyboards), and Liver Favela (drums). A boogie-oriented hard-rock outfit in the mould of Uriah Heep, they recorded two albums, *Birtha* (Dunhill 50127) and *Can't Stop the Madness* (Dunhill 50136), and experienced no chart success before breaking up.

The Deadly Nightshade was the most eclectic of the women pop bands of the 1970s, sporting music that exhibited pop, rock, country, and bluegrass influences, as well as overtly feminist lyrics; their sole flirtation with the charts was a disco-styled send-up of the theme to the television show *Mary Hartman, Mary Hartman*. The Deadly Nightshade members, Anne Bowen (guitar and vocals), Helen Hooks (guitar and vocals), and Pamela Brandt (bass and vocals), were veterans of two earlier short-lived all-women acts, the Moppets and Ariel. They released two albums, *The Deadly Nightshade* (RCA 10955) and *F & W* (RCA 11370), before folding.

Founded by producer Kim Fowley in 1975, the proto-punk Runaways turned out music showing influences of pop and glam-rock. They recorded four albums during the decade, *The Runaways* (Touchwood 4), *Queens of Noise* (Touchwood 5), *Waitin' for the Night* (SRM-1-3705), and *And Now . . . the Runaways* (Cherry Red 3), and are perhaps best remembered for the bratty number "Cherry Bomb." The group's marginally skilled, adolescent-aged personnel varied considerably, but this classic lineup consisted of Joan Jett (b. 1960) on guitar and vocals, Cherie Currie (b. 1960) on vocals, Lita Ford (b. 1958) on guitar and vocals, Jackie Fox (b. 1960) on bass, and Sandy West (b. 1960) on drums. Both Jett and Ford went on to highly successful careers leading their own otherwise all-male hard-rock bands during the 1980s.

The next decade saw a few such acts experience significant commercial prosperity. The California-based Go-Go's released an output influenced equally by girl-group pop and their punk-based roots. Founded as the Misfits in 1978 by Belinda Carlisle (b. 1958) on vocals and Jane Wiedlin (b. 1958) on guitar and vocals, the final membership during its heyday also included Charlotte Caffey (b. 1953) on guitar, vocals, and keyboards, former Runaway Kathy Valentine (b. 1959) on bass, and Gina Schock (b. 1957) on drums. Their three best-selling albums, *Beauty and the Beat* (IRS 44797-5021-2), *Vacation* (IRS 44797-5031-2), and *Talk Show* (IRS 44797-5041-2), contained the chart singles "We Got the Beat," "Our Lips Are Sealed," "Vacation," and "Head over Heels."

After the band's tumultuous breakup in 1985, Carlisle enjoyed a lucrative solo career, but Caffey and Schock found less illustrious outfits. The Go-Go's reunited briefly in 1990 and 1994 to give a limited number of live concerts. England's pop-metal group Girlschool deserves mention here as a proving ground for Valentine and guitarist Kathy Johnson, who later teamed up to form the U.S. outfit World's Cutest Killers.

The Bangles, a Los Angeles band formed in 1981 and initially named the Colours, the Supersonic Bangs, and the Bangs, first consisted of Susanna Hoffs (b. 1957) on guitar and vocals, Annette Zilinskas on bass and vocals, and sisters Vicki (b. 1960) and Debbi (b. 1961) Peterson on guitar and vocals and drums and vocals, respectively. Zilinskas left just before the group signed a major-label contract and was replaced by another former Runaway, Michael Steele (b. 1954). The band's work showed clear debts to 1960s pop and featured three successful albums, *All Over the Place* (Columbia CK-39220), *Different Light* (Sony International 505474), and *Everything* (Columbia CK-44056), as well as a host of hit singles, most notably "Manic Monday," "Walk Like an Egyptian," "In Your Room," and "Eternal Flame." In 1989 the Bangles collapsed in dissention, with Hoffs moving on to a solo career.

The 1990s act best fitting this category was the New York–based quartet Luscious Jackson. Drawing its name from a 1960s basketball player and consisting of Jill Cunniff (bass and vocals), Gabrielle Glaister (guitar and vocals), Kate Schellenbach (drums)—all friends since their teen years—and Vivian Trimble (keyboards), the group forged a bass and samples–driven style incorporating elements of rap, funk, folk, and indie-rock. Prior to the act's formation in 1991, Cunniff and Glaister had started a short-lived punk outfit, Jaws, and Schellenbach had performed with the Beastie Boys and Hippies with Guns. The band released the extended play album *In Search of Manny* (Grand Royal/Capitol 1), as well as three proper albums, *Natural Ingredients* (Grand Royal/Capitol 28356), *Fever*

In Fever Out (Grand Royal/Capitol 35534), and *Electric Honey* (Grand Royal 72). Generally, the group experienced critical rather than commercial success, though they scored a modest hit with "City Song."

Prior to the late 1970s, accomplished women rock instrumentalists in male-dominated bands were infrequently encountered. Examples in the United States included Bo Diddley guitarist Peggy "Lady Bo" Jones, 1960s session bassist Carol Kaye (b. 1935), Sly and the Family Stone trumpeter Cynthia Robinson (b. 1946) and keyboardist Rosie Stone, and Velvet Underground drummer Maureen "Moe" Tucker. A few vocalists, Heart's Nancy Wilson (b. 1954) on guitar, the Carpenters' Karen Carpenter (1950–1983) on drums, as well as Fleetwood Mac's Christine McVie (b. 1943) and Jefferson Airplane's Grace Slick (b. 1939), both on keyboards, showed notable ability as instrumentalists. The new wave and indie-rock movement in the United States saw an influx of women bass players, starting with Tina Weymouth (b. 1950) of Talking Heads and the Tom Tom Club; other examples were Sonic Youth's Kim Gordon (b. 1953), Black Flag's Kira Roessler (b. 1962), the Feelies' Brenda Sauter, the Pixies' Kim Deal, Smashing Pumpkins' D'Arcy Wretzky, Concrete Blonde's Johnette Napolitano, and the Blake Babies' Juliana Hatfield (b. 1967). Even in this seemingly more enlightened era, able women guitarists, keyboardists, drummers, and saxophonists remained relatively rare. Examples in "no-wave" bands included guitarist Pat Place and keyboardist Adele Bertei of the Contortions, drummer Ikue Mori of DNA, and guitarist China Berg and drummer Nancy Arlen of Mars. The Cramps sported two such performers, longtime guitarist "Poison" Ivy Rorschach and less permanent drummer Miriam Linna. Tara Key played guitar with the Babylon Dance Band and Antietam. Guitarists Joan Jett and Lita Ford, discussed above, also deserve mention here, as do U.S.-born British expatriates bassist Suzi Quatro (b. 1950), guitarist Chrissie Hynde (b. 1951), and saxophonist Lene Lovich (b. 1949).

See also Rock and Popular Music Genres; Rock Music

For Further Reading

Frost, Deborah. "Garageland." In *Trouble Girls: The Rolling Stone Book of Women in Rock*, ed. Barbara O'Dair. New York: Random House, 1997, 415–425.

McDonnell, Evelyn. "She's in the Band: Maureen Tucker, Tina Weymouth, and Tara Key." In *Trouble Girls: The Rolling Stone Book of Women in Rock*, ed. Barbara O'Dair. New York: Random House, 1997.

O'Brien, Lucy. "Can the Can: Whatever Happened to the Rock Chick?" In *She Bop: The Definitive History of Women in Rock, Pop, and Soul*. London: Penguin Books, 1995.

David Cleary

The Bangles

Originally known as the Colours (and later the Bangs), The Bangles were a dominant all-woman rock and roll band of the 1980s. Formed in 1981 by Susanna Hoffs (b. 1957), sisters Debbi (b. 1961) and Vicki (b. 1960) Peterson, and Annette Zilinskas, the California natives shared the musical taste for harmonies reminiscent of 1960s groups such as the Beatles and The Mamas and The Papas. Although the Go-Go's had a similar sound and development, they had a more punkish sound than did The Bangles. With each woman possessing the ability to play an instrument and sing, the group began playing live performances on the Los Angeles club circuit. Because of their affinity for 1960s rock revival, they be-came part of what was labeled the "paisley underground." In 1983 Zilinskas left the group and was replaced by Michael Steele (b. 1954). Shortly thereafter, The Bangles signed with CBS Records and toured as an opening act for Cyndi Lauper (b. 1953).

The Bangles' second album, *Different Light* (CK-40039), pushed the group into true stardom. *Different Light* contained the hit single "Manic Monday" (written by pop star Prince under the name Christopher) as well as "Walk Like an Egyptian," which not only topped the *Billboard* charts but created an entirely new dance that was a craze in and of itself. "Egyptian" captured Single of the Year and Best Music Television (MTV) Video Performance.

Following successful tours, The Bangles released a third album, *Everything* (CK-44056), in 1989; it included "Eternal Flame," a title that became the band's second number one hit. As the lead vocalist on "Eternal Flame," Susanna Hoffs began to be labeled by the media as The Bangles' lead singer. Subsequent tension surrounding the media attention, coupled with ongoing dissatisfaction with management, ultimately lead to the group's dissolution in 1989.

Ten years after the band broke up, The Bangles informally reunited to record a new track, "Get the Girl," which was included on the soundtrack for the film *Austin Powers: The Spy Who Shagged Me* (1999). There are also plans for a concert tour and new studio albums.

See also Bands, Pop Rock

For Further Reading

Baker, Mark A. *Goldmine Price Guide to Rock n Roll Memorabilia*. Iola, WI: Krause Publications, 1997.

Gaar, Gillian G. *She's a Rebel: The History of Women in Rock and Roll*. Seattle, WA: Seal Press, 1992.

O'Dair, Barbara (ed.). *The Rolling Stone Book of Women in Rock: Trouble Girls*. New York: Random House, 1997.

William G. Biddy

Barbershop Quartet

Barbershop quartet singing displays the influence of early four-part American hymnody, which featured the melody in an inner voice with harmony above and below it. Although it can be traced back to the middle of the nineteenth century, barbershop singing, with its unique *a cappella* style, had its heyday from the late 1890s to the years between the two world wars when professional male quartets performed and even recorded the traditional repertoire. At first, women played a peripheral and primarily social role as supporters of the male amateurs in their families who sang in harmony clubs, or as audiences of barbershop quartets performing in minstrel shows and later in vaudeville. However, by the 1940s women had begun to take an active role in barbershop singing. By the end of that decade the Sweet Adelines, the first women's barbershop organization, claimed almost 1,500 members; today, nearly 35,000 women worldwide are active barbershop performers.

Although scholars have yet to document specific women's roles in barbershop history, members of Sweet Adelines International and its offshoot, Harmony, Inc., have compiled unofficial chronicles. Some claim that because she sang alto harmony above the melody, the first woman barbershop singer was Abby Hutchinson, who, along with her three brothers, Judson, John, and Asa, sang abolition and temperance songs as the Hutchinson Family. Two issues work against this theory, however: Abby also performed solos, and more important, the Hutchinsons' arrangements do not feature the characteristic chordal "swipes" or the "lock and ring" technique that produces the overtones associated with the true barbershop sound. Others more reasonably maintain that even though women may have joined together to improvise songs in barbershop style, it is difficult to say exactly when women became active performers. Save for odd cases, such as the emergency substitution of Inez Barbour in the Premiere Quartet's recording of "Carry Me Back to Old Virginny," professional quartets were all male.

The first name that can be connected to the organization of a women's barbershop movement was that of Edna Mae Anderson (1903–1959), whose husband, William, was a member of the Society for the Preservation and Propagation of Barber Shop Quartet Singing in America (SPEBSQSA). Receiving support in 1945 from that group's co-founder, Owen C. Cash, who referred to the women's group as the "Corseteers" and the "Bustle Auxiliary," Anderson put out the call for women ("no prima donnas wanted") who were interested in singing, socializing, and obtaining music education. Named for the popular barbershop song, Anderson's creation, the Sweet Adelines, attracted amateurs, music students, and career singers. One of the benefits of the organization in those early years, claim its current members, was that it brought together working women and homemakers, allowing them to develop as artists and leaders.

Not only have women performing this repertoire maintained the gendered title of "barbershop," but they also employ the traditional male voice-part terms. The tenor line, often assigned to sopranos with light, clear tones and no excessive vibrato, has a range between f' and g" (c' = middle C). Because the tenor sings above the melody, major chords in barbershop style are voiced "do-sol-do-mi" rather than "do-mi-sol-do." The lead, who sings the melody, must possess both a warm tone and an acute sense of pitch; her range is between a and c". The baritone, with a range from g to a', moves above and below the melody line, blending with either the tenor or the bass. Finally, the bass, with the fullest tone of the quartet, insuring the traditional "cone-shaped" or bottom-heavy sound of barbershop music, sings between d and f'. Both the baritone and bass lines are normally notated an octave below the sung pitch. Because these singers are women, there might be a temptation to refer to them as "beautyshop" quartets. This term, however, refers to *a cappella* drag groups who have no connection to barbershop singing style. Instead, wearing outrageous frocks, bouffant wigs, and curlers, they satirize the stereotypical beauty parlor clientele of the 1950s and 1960s.

In addition to Sweet Adelines International, with members in the United States, Canada, Sweden, the Netherlands, Germany, Australia, and New Zealand, other organizations include the above-mentioned Harmony, Inc.; the Ladies Association of Barbershop Singers in the United Kingdom; Barbershop in Germany; and Holland Harmony. Other choruses and quartets, many found on college and university campuses, function outside of these organizations. Aside from furthering the cause of performing barbershop by holding annual conventions that feature competitions as well as workshops in choreography, choral and quartet performance (members first join choruses from which quartets are formed), and artistic presentation, the larger organizations continue to further one of Anderson's original aims—education. Members receive training in choral directing, music arranging, and competition judging as well as in development of leadership skills, enabling them to administer the groups' national, regional, and local hierarchy. Outreach programs also bring music to young women and educators whose institutions may have suffered cutbacks in arts education; in addition, the major organizations award music and academic scholarships. Choruses also frequently perform benefit concerts for charity and community functions.

See also Hymnody, Sweet Adelines

For Further Reading

Harmony, Inc. Home. International Organization of Women Barbershop Singers. Available: http://www.harmonyinc.org

Kaplan, Max (ed.). *Barbershopping: Musical and Social Harmony.* Rutherford, NJ: Fairleigh Dickinsen University Press, 1993.

Sweet Adelines International. Available: http://www.sweetadelineintl.org

Denise Gallo

Barkin, Elaine R. (1932–)

Elaine R. Barkin is one of the most significant music composers and researchers of the twentieth century. Additionally, she has served as associate editor of the distinguished journal *Perspectives of New Music.* Barkin's compositional output includes over 50 works, composed for a wide variety of sources including electronic media, Balinese and Javanese gamelan, and voice, as well as works for traditional western instruments. Her compositions range in conception from theater pieces (*Media Speak*, 1981), compositions with graphic scores (*Quilt Piece*, 1984), symphonic wind ensemble (*Poem*, 1999) and chamber pieces (*Legong Dreams* for solo oboe, 1990) to pieces requiring improvisation (*Demeter and Per-*

sephone, 1986). Barkin has been the recipient of numerous awards, including a Meet the Composer/National Endowment for the Arts Commission for which Barkin, in collaboration with I Nyoman Wenten, composed the work *Touching All Bases/Di Mana-Mana* (1996) for basso bongo (Robert Black, electronic bass, and Amy Knoles, MIDI [Musical Instrument Digital Interface—a communications protocol for synthesizers and computers] percussion) and Balinese gamelan.

Elaine Barkin was born Elaine Radoff on 15 December 1932 in the Bronx, NY. She received a B.A. in music from Queens College (1954), an M.F.A. in composition from Brandeis University (1956), a Certificate in composition and piano from the Hochschule für Musik, Berlin (1957), and a Ph.D. in composition and theory from Brandeis University (1971). Barkin served on the faculty at the University of California, Los Angeles, as an associate professor (1974–1977) and as a full professor (1977–1997), where she taught theory and composition. Prior to her appointment at the University of California, Los Angeles, she taught at Queens College (1964–1970), Sarah Lawrence College (1969–1970), the University of Michigan (1970–1974), Princeton University (Spring 1974), Victoria University, Wellington, New Zealand (Spring 1994) and Semester at Sea, Institute for Shipboard Education (Fall 1996).

Since 1990 she has been co-producer of the publications series OPEN SPACE. Barkin has been in residence at the Rockefeller Foundation Study and Conference Center at Villa Serbelloni, Bellagio, Italy; the MacDowell Colony; Edna St. Vincent Millay Colony; Briarcombe Foundation Colony; and the Djerassi Foundation SMIP Ranch. Cur-

rently is she professor emerita at the University of California, Los Angeles.

See also Meet the Composer; National Endowment for the Arts Composers Program

For Further Reading

Ammer, Christine. *Unsung.* Revised and expanded second edition. Portland, OR: Amadeus Press, 2001.

Barkin, Elaine. *e: an anthology of music texts and graphics (1975–1995).* Red Hook, NY: Open Space, 1997.

Pendle, Karin (ed.). *Women and Music: A History.* Bloomington: Indiana University Press, 1991.

Amy Dunker

Barron, Bebe (1927–)

Electronic music pioneer and composer Bebe Barron, along with her husband and collaborator, Louis Barron, conducted some of the earliest experiments in electronic music. The Barrons maintained a studio for electronic music in New York City, where many other composers came to collaborate on new works. It was in this studio that the Barrons created many of their compositions, including the electronic film scores for which they are best known.

Pioneers in the use of electronic sounds in film music, the Barrons created scores that were not even described as "music." In fact, the credits for the film *Forbidden Planet* (1956) called the score simply "electronic tonalities." The Barrons' film accompaniments ranged from ethereal "bubbling" and "gurgling" sound effects to ambient background passages.

Barron was born Charlotte Wind in Minneapolis, MN, on 16 June 1927. She studied political science at the University of Minnesota while also taking composition lessons with Roque Cordero. After moving to New York she took lessons with both Henry Cowell and Walling-ford Riegger. She married Louis Barron in 1948, and in the following year the Barrons opened their studio for electro-acoustic music in New York. Their studio became the site for many important early projects in electronic music, including John Cage's *Imaginary Landscape No. 5* and *Williams Mix*.

Together the Barrons wrote more than 40 film scores. In 1956 they composed their best known: the score for the Metro-Goldwyn-Mayer science fiction film *Forbidden Planet*. This was one of the first entirely electronic scores for a full-length motion picture. The Barrons created and performed all their own circuitry for their scores. Other scores include those for *Bells of Atlantis* (1952), *The Computer Age* (1968), and *Cannabis* (1975). Although the Barrons divorced in 1970, they continued working together until Louis's death in 1989.

Barron was a founding member of the Society for Electro-Acoustic Music in the United States (SEAMUS) and served as secretary for the organization for two years. She (and Louis, posthumously) received the SEAMUS lifetime achievement award in 1997 for contributions to the field of electro-acoustic music.

See also Film Composers; Music Technology

For Further Reading

Clarke, Frederick, and Steve Rubin. "Making Forbidden Planet." *Cinefantastique* vii/2–3 (1979): 42–54.

Griffiths, Paul. *A Guide to Electronic Music.* New York: Thames and Hudson, 1979.

Rubin, Steve. "Retrospect: Forbidden Planet." *Cinefantastique* iv/1 (1975): 4–13.

Leslie Stone

Battle, Kathleen (1948–)

Kathleen Battle has gained the reputation of being one of the finest, if most tem-pestuous, coloratura lyric sopranos in the history of opera. She did what very few lyric sopranos have ever done: attain diva status performing essentially supporting roles. Her warm, bell-like voice, charming acting, and overt pandering to the audience are characteristic of Battle's performances.

Kathleen Battle was born on 13 August 1948 in Portsmouth, OH. As a young girl she sang in the church choir and played piano. At the urging of her high school music teacher, Battle studied music in college instead of math. She received both bachelor's and master's degrees in music education from the University of Cincinnati College-Conservatory of Music, and upon graduation she obtained a teaching position in the Cincinnati Public Schools.

While teaching elementary school in the early 1970s, Battle performed and took various auditions. She had the opportunity to audition for James Levine, who was directing the Cincinnati May Festival. Immediately taken with her voice, Levine suggested that she return to her voice studies and pursue a performing career more actively. Battle took his advice and went back to school to study vocal performance.

After a few years singing professionally, Battle made her New York City Opera debut in 1976 as Susanna, in Wolfgang Amadeus Mozart's *Le Nozze di Figaro*. One year later she debuted at the Metropolitan Opera as both the shepherd in Richard Wagner's *Tannhäuser* and in the larger role of Sophie in Jules Massenet's *Werther*. After her Met debut, she performed throughout Europe and the United States regularly. Appearing on magazine covers and in television broadcasts, Kathleen Battle saw her name become essentially a household word.

As Battle's fame grew, so did rumors

about her mistreatment of crew members and fellow cast members in opera houses worldwide. After appearances with the San Francisco Opera, members of the cast had T-shirts made that said "I Survived the Battle." During rehearsals for a production of Richard Strauss's *Der Rosenkavalier* at San Francisco in 1993, differences with conductor Christian Thielemann over tempi caused Battle to quit the production. One year later Battle was fired from New York's Metropolitan Opera. The *New York Times* cited "unprofessional actions" as the cause of her dismissal.

Her most notable recordings include *Kathleen Battle Sings Mozart* (DS-38297 Angel), which received three Grammy Awards, and *Kathleen Battle at Carnegie Hall* (435 440-2 Deutsche Grammophon). Battle continues to have a highly successful career as a classical singer. She performs frequently with James Levine and other conductors all over the world.

See also Classical Music; Performer, Vocal

For Further Reading

Gates, David, et al. "Soap Opera at the Met." *Newsweek* 123/8 (1994): 60–61.
Page, Tim. "Interrupted Melody." *Opera News* 58/14 (1994): 16–17.

Amy Evers

Bauer, Marion (1897–1955)

Marion Eugenie Bauer, a composer and champion of new music, was the only woman among the founders of the League of Composers and a co-founder of the American Music Guild. She contributed articles to numerous musical journals, served as editor of the *Musical Leader*, and wrote the book *Twentieth Century Music*, as well as several popular titles.

Bauer's music remained basically impressionistic throughout her career, with its emphasis on coloristic harmony, programmatic titles, and narrative through-composed forms. Bauer often made use of non-Western elements in her music ranging from Native American influences (*Indian Pipes*, for orchestra, 1927) to African themes (*A Lament on African Themes*, for chamber orchestra, 1928).

Marion Bauer was born on 15 August 1897 in Walla Walla, WA. She studied in Portland (OR), Paris, and Berlin. Her teachers included Nadia Boulanger, Henry Holden Hess, Eugene Heffley, Walter Henry Rothwell, Paul Ertel, Andre Gedalge, and violinist Raoul Pugno. From 1926 to 1951 Bauer served on the faculty of New York University, where she taught music history and composition. She also taught at the Juilliard School, Mills College, and the Cincinnati Conservatory of Music. Bauer was frequently in residence at the MacDowell Colony in Peterborough, NH.

In her article "Why Not Teach Music of Today?" (*Associated Music Teachers League Bulletin*, November 1951), Bauer challenged composers and educators alike to invest in education and to cultivate the interest of young people in new music. In addition to writing didactic compositions (*American Youth Concerto*, 1943), Bauer wrote orchestral, chamber, and choral music including Symphony No. 1 (1950), Violin Sonata, Op. 22 (1935), and *China* (1945). In 1947 her composition *Sun Splendor* was first performed by the New York Philharmonic with Leopold Stokowski conducting. This was the only composition by a woman composer performed by that organization in the previous 25 years.

She died on 9 August 1955 in South Hadley, MA, a few days before her 68th birthday.

See also Classical Music; Composer

For Further Reading

Ammer, Christine. *Unsung.* Revised and expanded second edition. Portland, OR: Amadeus Press, 2001.

Pendle, Karin (ed.). *Women and Music: A History.* Bloomington: Indiana University Press, 1991.

Amy Dunker

Beach, Amy Marcy Cheney (1867–1944)

Amy Marcy Cheney Beach was America's leading woman composer in the early part of the twentieth century, the first American woman to have a successful career as a composer of large-scale art works, the first to have a symphony played by a major orchestra, and the first woman to make a career as a pianist with American training. She was a leader, model, and mentor for the following generation of women composers. Beach's early works are in late-Romantic style, with long lyrical lines, a fine sense of prosody, lush and often dissonant harmonies, and modulations to remote keys. Later works show changes from late Romanticism to Expressionism, with dissonances left unresolved, leaner and more contrapuntal textures, while retaining her lyricism and passion. For many years she was the most frequently performed composer of her generation, and she was known as the dean of American women composers.

Born in West Henniker, NH, on 5 September 1867, Beach grew up surrounded by music. Before she was one year old she was singing—according to her mother—40 songs, and by age two,

Amy Marcy Cheney Beach. *Photo courtesy of Milne Special Collections and Archives Department, University of New Hampshire Library, Durham, NH.*

singing alto to her mother's soprano. By age four she was playing by ear, improvising, and composing. The family moved to Chelsea, a suburb of Boston, in 1871, and in 1875 to Boston proper. Her mother denied her early dream of becoming a concert pianist, determined she would grow up, marry, and make music in private as her mother did.

Clara Cheney, however, agreed to teach her daughter piano beginning at age six; by age seven the girl played in a local recital and was reviewed as a prodigy. In the following year Amy changed piano teachers, who prepared her for the concert stage. At age sixteen she made her debut, playing solo and with orchestra to rave reviews. For the next two years she gave local recitals, making debuts in 1885 with the Boston Symphony playing the Frederic Chopin Concerto in F Minor and with the Theodore Thomas Orchestra playing Felix Mendelssohn's D Minor Concerto.

At age 17 she had sought a composition teacher, expecting to both compose and perform. Advised, however, to teach herself—women were not expected to benefit from training—she learned theory, harmony, counterpoint, orchestration, and composition. In December 1885 she married Henry Harris Aubrey Beach and agreed to curtail her performance career in order to concentrate on composition. During the next 25 years she wrote and published 150 works, almost all performed, some many times. Outstanding are the Mass in E-flat, op. 5; the Symphony in E-minor ("Gaelic"), op. 32; the Violin Sonata, op. 34; the Service in A, op. 63; the choral cantata the *Chambered Nautilus*, op. 66; and the Piano Quintet, op. 67. The Mass made her famous, the Symphony won her acceptance by leading composers, and her art songs—she wrote a total of about 120 songs—won devoted audiences numbering in the thousands. Beach was involved in the ongoing controversy over whether women should become composers; indeed, she was named by feminists as the person who proved that women could compose works of value.

Widowed in 1910, Beach went to Germany (1911–1914), changed her name from Mrs. H. H. A. Beach to Amy Beach, revived her career as a performer, and had her major compositions played and reviewed. Returning in triumph to the United States at the start of World War I, she toured during the winters as a composer-pianist (from 1930 on, based in New York) and composed during the summers at the MacDowell Colony in Peterborough, NH (1921–1941). Outstanding among her later works are the *Theme and Variations for Flute and String Quartet*, op. 80; her *Prelude and Fugue* for piano, op. 81, on a theme that spells out A-B-E-A-C-H; the *Quartet for Strings (in One Movement)*, op. 89; two *"Hermit Thrush"* pieces for piano, op. 92, based on bird calls; the song *Rendezvous*, op. 120; the opera *Cabildo*, op. 149; and the *Piano Trio*, op. 150. Outstanding among her late sacred choral works is the *Canticle of the Sun*, op. 123. Her works totaled over 300.

Amy Beach died in New York on 27 December 1944.

See also Classical Music

For Further Reading

Block, Adrienne Fried. *Amy Beach, Passionate Victorian: The Life and Work of an American Composer, 1867–1944*. New York: Oxford University Press, 1998; rev. ed., 2000.

Jenkins, Walter S. *The Remarkable Mrs. Beach, American Composer: A Biographical Account Based on Her Diaries, Letters, Newspaper Clippings, and Personal Reminiscences*, ed. John H. Baron. Warren, MI: Harmonie Park Press, 1994.

Tick, Judith. "Passed Away Is the Piano Girl." In *Women Making Music: The Western Art Tradition, 1150–1950*. Urbana and Chicago: University of Illinois Press, 1986.

Adrienne Fried Block

Beardslee, Bethany (1927–)

Bethany Beardslee is a lyric soprano whose precise intonation, wide range, and flute-like tone have proven very effective in interpreting twentieth-century vocal music. Princeton University awarded her an honorary doctorate in 1977. Beardslee's academic appointments as a voice teacher have come from Westminster Choir College, the University of Texas at Austin, the University of California at Davis, and the City University of New York (Brooklyn College).

Bethany Beardslee was born in Lansing, MI, on 25 December 1927. Following study at Michigan State University, she received a scholarship to the Juilliard School and made her vocal debut in New York City in 1949. Together with her first husband, Jacques-Louis Monod, she gave recitals and presented the U.S. premieres of works by Alban Berg, Arnold Schoenberg, Ernst Krenek, and Igor Stravinsky. Mastering the art of *sprechstimme* ("sung speech") led to brilliant performances of works like Schoenberg's *Pierrot Lunaire* (Columbia Masterworks M2S 679). Beardslee also released the album *A Tribute to Bethany Beardslee, Soprano* in 1969; this album featured her performing compositions by well-known contemporary composers such as George Perle and Godfrey Winham, whom she married in 1956.

Between 1957 and 1960 she partnered with the now-defunct New York Pro Musica in a series of memorable concerts of medieval and renaissance music. In 1962 the American Composers Alliance awarded Beardslee its Laurel Leaf in recognition of her significant contributions to American music. Two years later Beardslee used a Ford Foundation grant to commission and perform Milton Babbitt's *Philomel* (recorded on *Electo Acoustic Music*, 450–74 Neuma), a monodrama scored for soprano and tape.

See also Performer, Vocal

For Further Reading

Higginbotham, Diane. "Performance Problems in Contemporary Vocal Music and Some Suggested Solutions." Ed.D. diss., Columbia University Teachers College, 1994.

Hollander, John. "Notes on the Text of *Philomel*." *Perspectives of New Music* 6/1 (1967): 134–41.

Judith L. Marley

Bentley, Alys E. (1869–1951)

Alys E. Bentley was an early pioneer in music education in the United States. She articulated strong views on the training of children's voices, advocated for musical teachers to teach music in schools, generated exemplary teaching materials, integrated movement with music, and took part in early organizational movements. Bentley's work was part of the liberal child-centered movement of the early twentieth century, which led to the incorporation of music into schools curricula. Music was increasingly regarded as a medium through which the child's character and aesthetic awareness could be formed. Thus music was essential in the curriculum for all children.

Alys E. Bentley was one of 104 music supervisors who attended the Music Supervisors Conference in Keokuk, IA, in 1907, and she became one of the 69 charter members of the new organization emerging from this historical meeting. Originally convened to demonstrate P. C. Hayden's methods of teaching rhythm, the conference inspired attendees to form a national conference, which ultimately became the Music Educators National Conference.

Bentley gave the first presentation at Keokuk; her topic was the child's voice. She illustrated ways to improve vocal quality by having a group of first graders imitate buzz saws, drums, bells, and other sounds. She noted that "It will also be found that this imitative singing is one of the surest cures of the monotone. It is so effective in helping these backward singers that very few monotones are found above the first grade."

Bentley generated influential music books such as *The Song Series*, published by A. S. Barnes in 1907 and 1910. Her books incorporated movement experiences as well as songs she had composed. Bentley believed that song and the love of music were essential as the motivation and basis for instruction. According to

Bentley, technical exercises and sight-reading were part of music making, but they were not the reason for the music making. This approach contradicted previous music pedagogy.

Bentley's work with movement paralleled Emile Jaques Dalcroze's work in Europe. A passage in the proceedings of the Music Supervisors National Conference in Pittsburgh notes: "Beginning with the large muscle masses and guided by carefully selected music the child is led to a series of correlated movements. ... Through this perfected rhythmical body, the student is then led on to express the feeling awakened in him by various musical compositions." (1915, 38–39).

Bentley continued to teach dance and music in Washington, DC, and New York for over 50 years. She served as director of music in Washington, DC, public schools for 20 years and maintained a studio in Carnegie Hall from 1912 to 1938. Alys E. Bentley died in Malone, NY, in 1951.

See also Dalcroze Eurhythmics; Music Education

For Further Reading

Clark, Frances Elliott. "The Fruits of the 'Spirit of Keokuk'." *Music Educators Journal* 33/6 (June 1947): 26–28.

Goodman, A. Harold. *Music Education: Perspectives and Perceptions*. Dubuque, IA: Kendall Hunt, 1982.

Journal of Proceedings of the 8th Annual Meeting of the Music Supervisors National Conference, Pittsburgh, PA, 1915: 38–39.

Kari K. Veblen

Berberian, Cathy (1925–1983)

Catherine (Cathy) Berberian was a celebrated performer of classical music, a mezzo-soprano with a specialty in avant garde works of the 1950s and 1960s. Her vocal range spanned a remarkable three octaves—much wider than most sopranos; and she was able to meld a stunning array of sounds and special effects into her singing, making her one of the most virtuosic and flexible performers of the time.

Berberian's reputation ran beyond that of the contemporary music scene, as is evidenced by the fact that she was profiled in mainstream classical music magazines and received mention in the lyrics to the song "Your Gold Teeth" by the rock group Steely Dan.

Berberian, of Armenian heritage, was born in Attleboro, MA, on 4 July 1925 (not 1928, as listed in some sources) but spent most of her formative years in New York. She pursued an eclectic educational course, taking classes in opera, mime, and script writing at Columbia and New York universities as well as attempting further studies in dance, costuming, and Hindu. She performed solo dance works with a New York Armenian folk group and played summer stock. In 1950 she won a Fulbright Scholarship, allowing her to pursue vocal studies in Milan with Girogina del Vigo. Her professional debut occurred in Naples in 1957 in an Incontri Musicali concert. One year later, a performance of John Cage's *Aria with Fontana Mix* in Rome brought her widespread renown, which was further solidified by her U.S. debut at the Berkshire Music Festival in 1960. She concertized and recorded extensively from this point on, finding time during the 1970s to teach at the Rheinische Musikschule (Cologne) and the University of Vancouver.

Numerous composers wrote compositions for her, including Igor Stravinsky, Hans Werner Henze, Darius Milhaud, and Luciano Berio. Berberian was married to Berio from 1950 to 1966, and he

Cathy Berberian. *Photo courtesy of Olympia Publifoto.*

composed a number of his major vocal pieces for her, including *Circles*; *Epifanie*; *Recital I*; *Sequenza III*; and *Visage*.

Although she is most remembered today as a new-music performer, she successfully sang a wide variety of repertoire, including Baroque period opera, salon pieces, folksongs, and Beatles songs. Berberian was also a composer of music in avant garde style, her best-known works being *Stripsody* (1966) for solo voice and *Moriscat(h)y* (1971) for piano. She appears on numerous recordings, including *MagniCathy* (WER 60054-50) and *Cathy Berberian Sings Claudio Monteverdi* (Telefunken 6.41956 AW).

She died, apparently of a heart attack, on 6 March 1983 in a Rome hotel.

See also Experimental Music; Performer, Vocal

For Further Reading

Moor, Paul. "The First Lady of Far-Out Song." *Musical America* 109/3 (1989): 76–77.

Soames, Nicholas. "Cathy Berberian." *Music and Musicians* 26/6 (1978): 8–12.

David Cleary

Bianchi, Louise Wadley (1912–1998)

Louise Wadley Bianchi distinguished herself in piano pedagogy as a teacher, administrator, and author. She established a model program for training piano teachers at Southern Methodist University (SMU), where she taught for more than 25 years. After earning the M.M. degree in piano performance at SMU, Bianchi joined the music faculty and established a piano preparatory department. The preparatory department served as a laboratory program for intern teaching and as a revenue source for the pedagogy program. It was one of the first preparatory programs in the United States to offer extensive opportunities for supervised practice teaching in piano coordinated with coursework in piano pedagogy. The program served as a model for the many preparatory programs that were established to facilitate teacher training in U.S. colleges and universities. In 1967 Bianchi established a curriculum for an M.M. degree in piano pedagogy. The curriculum for the pedagogy program at Southern Methodist University was featured as a case study in *The Piano Pedagogy Major in the College Curriculum*, co-authored by Frances Larimer (b. 1929) and Marienne Uszler and published by the National Conference on Piano Pedagogy.

During the 1970s Louise Bianchi collaborated with Lynn Freeman Olson and Marvin Blickenstaff to produce *Music Pathways*, a method series for beginning students in piano. The 36-book series, published by Carl Fischer, offered a comprehensive approach to teaching young piano students the essentials of reading, theory, technique, and improvisation. In developing the curriculum for *Music Pathways*, the three co-authors adopted the most successful elements of the educational concepts of Frances Clark (1905–1998) and Robert Pace. The series modified the intervallic approach to teaching music reading by using five C pitches as landmarks across the grand staff. This novel approach to reading offered young students the opportunity to use a wide range of the keyboard from the earliest lessons. The method series was highly successful because of its excellent curriculum and the musical appeal of the original compositions.

Bianchi earned a national reputation not only for her educational publications and pedagogy training but also for the many workshops that she presented for the continuing education of piano teachers. A strong believer in high-quality repertoire as an essential factor in student motivation, Bianchi's lecture entitled "Pupil Savers" was one of her most popular. The lecture offered teachers a graded list of repertoire that would motivate even the most reluctant students to continue lessons and to practice.

See also Music Education; Piano Pedagogy

For Further Reading

Blickenstaff, Marvin. "What is the Pedagogical Legacy of Louise Bianchi?" *Keyboard Companion* 10 (1999): 38–41.
Holland, Samuel. "Louise Wadley Bianchi's Contributions to Piano Pedagogy." Ph.D. diss., University of Oklahoma, 1996.

Kenneth Williams

Bifocal History

Bifocal history, or "contribution history," examines women's contributions to male-dominated society; human experience is conceptualized primarily in dualist categories—female/male, private/public, nature/transcendence, nature/culture—and women's oppression is taken into account. The term was coined in 1975 by Gerda Lerner in her classification of phases in historiography. Specifically in music, a bifocal approach explores the reasons for women musicians' relative invisibility and analyzes social factors that have prevented them from gaining recognition.

A precursor to what is now known as bifocal history, Judith Tick's essay about American music history, "Why Have There Been No Great Women Composers?" (1975), states the basic feminist theory that because history is written by and about the dominant social class (men), women's work is simply not included because women are a "marginal" group. Edith Borroff, in "Women Composers: Reminiscence and History" (1975), cites the "duress" under which women have worked as a significant historical fact. In the United States in the early twentieth century, she reports, Isabella Beaton, Mary Anderson Lucas, and Marion Bauer "inserted a wedge into cultural consciousness" but did not receive the recognition they deserved; for the younger generation, Borroff observes, "barriers are slowly yielding and their history will be different."

Diane Jezic's *Women Composers: The Lost Tradition Found* (1988), although conceived as compensatory history, or a study of notable women, includes observations about the oppression American women have suffered that illustrate the bifocal approach and feminist history as well, as Elizabeth Wood's foreword to the book makes explicit. Wood points out the elitism of traditional male history and compensatory women's history, in her observation that many of the composers Jezic highlights (including eight American women) enjoyed advantages and opportunities similar to the best male composers—birth or marriage to a musical family, a technical and theoretical education, performance experience, publishers, and financial sponsorship. Moving to the bifocal approach, she notes that these successful women still faced a set of attitudes that threatened to silence and defeat them: "A persistent sneer of patronage, tokenism, and trivialization that pronounced women fragile; that domesticated women's work; that kept women out of professions, out of history books, and out of positions, and even genres, of prestige and power." She notes that only in the twentieth century did attitudes begin to change. Finally, she urges academics to "give our students the chance to meet musicians whose lives and works are exemplary models—not merely symbols—of women's contributions both to music's traditions and also

to the ongoing process of cultural change"; her reference to women as participants in cultural change touches on the feminist approach.

Carol Neuls-Bates's *Women in Music: An Anthology of Source Readings from the Middle Ages to the Present* (1982; rev. ed., 1996), an example of all-inclusive feminist history, includes several sections that can be termed bifocal in outlook as they illustrate theories of women's inferiority, the unequal educational opportunities for women, sexual aesthetics, and related issues. Because women internalize patriarchal attitudes about their own inferiority, the history of female patronage in the United States shows that women have often denied other women the support they grant to men. Beth Macleod in " 'Whence Comes the Lady Tympanist?': Gender and Instrumental Musicians in America, 1853–1990" (1993) finds historical precedents for some twentieth-century ideas about women instrumentalists. Catherine Parsons Smith's essay " 'A Distinguishing Virility': Feminism and Modernism in American Art Music" (1994) shows how antiwoman attitudes were essential to musical modernism in America after World War I; male hostility effectively suppressed the work of women as composers and shut them out of the modernist movement. Only a few are known today, such as Ruth Crawford Seeger (1901–1953), who abandoned modernist composition at an early age; Louise Talma (1906–1996); Miriam Gideon (1906–1996); and Elinor Remick Warren (1900–1991). Others, such as Elizabeth Sprague Coolidge (1864–1953), Minna Lederman, and Claire Reis, turned instead to female-identified careers as patrons, impresarios, or literary advocates of the male modernists.

The bifocal approach is an important

component of all research about women and music. Jane Bowers concludes from an exhaustive survey of "Feminist Scholarship and the Field of Musicology" (1989–1990) that women's activities have been made invisible through a continuous historical process, and that "musicologists and critics"—women as well as men—have been "accomplices in this process." Although the bifocal approach may give rise to an unfortunate picture of women as victims, its documentation of women's exclusion and oppression is an effective way of countering ideas of women's inferior status as representing some kind of personal failure of the individual woman in music.

See also Compensatory History; Feminist Music History; Historiography; Separate Spheres—Sexual Aesthetics

For Further Reading

Macleod, Beth Abelson. " 'Whence Comes the Lady Tympanist?': Gender and Instrumental Musicians in America, 1853–1990." *Journal of Social History* 27/2 (Winter 1993): 291–308.

Smith, Catherine Parsons. " 'A Distinguishing Virility': Feminism and Modernism in American Art Music." In *Cecilia Reclaimed: Feminist Perspectives on Gender and Music*. Urbana and Chicago: University of Illinois Press, 1994, 90–106.

Tick, Judith. "Why Have There Been No Great Women Composers? Notes on the Score of Sexual Aesthetics." *International Musician* 74/6 (July 1975): 6, 22.

Deborah Hayes

Bish, Diane Joyce (1941–)

Diane Joyce Bish is a renowned organist, concert and recording artist, composer, conductor, and international television personality. Her major compositions include *Festival Te Deum* (1974) for organ and orchestra; *Passion Symphony* (1976) for organ and narrator; *Symphony of Hymns* or *Morning Has Broken* (1983) for double choir, orchestra, narrator, and organ; and *Symphony of Psalms* (1988) for choir, organ, and orchestra. Appearing weekly on televised broadcasts, Bish has gained national recognition. She is in demand not only as a concert artist but as a recording artist as well. She is the first American woman organist to record on the "Mozart" organ at St. Bavo's Cathedral in the Netherlands and on all four organs of Freiburg Cathedral in Germany.

Bish was born on 25 May 1941 in Wichita, KS. Exhibiting an early interest in music, she began piano lessons at age five. At age 11 she began organ lessons. Bish attended Asbury College in Kentucky and the University of Oklahoma, studying organ with Era Wilder Peniston and Mildred Andrews. During her senior year she won three significant music competitions: the American Guild of Organists Competition; the National Federation of Music Clubs' National Organ Competition; and the Composition Competition of the music fraternity Mu Phi Epsilon. She also completed an M.M. degree at the University of Oklahoma.

Upon graduating she secured a position as organist at East Heights United Methodist Church in Wichita, KS. Because of her dynamic playing, Bish's reputation grew and she was soon in demand as a concert artist. At a concert for the 1968 Dallas convention of Mu Phi Epsilon, she first exhibited what would become her performing trademark—a lavish, colorful concert attire. In 1965–66 Bish was awarded a Fulbright Scholarship to study organ and harpsichord with scholar and musician Gustav Leonhardt at the Conservatory of Amsterdam. In 1969 she was awarded a Fondation des Etats-Unis scholarship to study organ in Paris with Marie Claire Alain. She also studied music theory with Nadia Boulanger.

In 1971 Bish joined the staff of Coral Ridge Presbyterian Church in Fort Lauderdale, FL as senior organist and artist-in-residence, beginning what would be a fruitful 20-year relationship with the church. She co-founded the church's concert series and its workshops for church musicians entitled *Church Music Explosion*. She also wrote, transcribed, and arranged numerous compositions for organ and choir.

Bish realized a personal dream in 1983, when she became the first classical woman organist to produce and host her own television program, *The Joy of Music*. Seen by over 100 million people weekly around the world, the program brings together great organ music, world-renowned guest soloists, ensembles and orchestras, and inspirational narratives against the backdrop of the world's greatest churches, cathedrals, and monasteries. In 1989 for her service to the musical, artistic, and cultural life of the nation, she was awarded the prestigious National Citation by the National Federation of Music Clubs of America. She continues to divide her time between her television programming, concerts, and recording activities. Among her numerous recordings are *Music for Brass and Organ* (Word 701–8908–507) and *The Artistry of Diane Bish* (Suncoast Concert Management).

See also National Federation of Music Clubs; Performer, Keyboard

For Further Reading

Birkby, A. "1st Lady of the Organ." *Clavier* 20/10 (1981): 13–15.

Woodruff, Warren L. *First Lady of the Organ, Diane Bish: A Biography.* Atlanta: SW Concerts, 1994.

Gary W. Mayhood

Black, Shirley Temple (1928–)

Shirley Temple Black was one of the most successful and most famous child stars in the history of American film music. Owing to her cheerful and spirited singing style in such popular tunes as "On the Good Ship Lollipop," she was beloved by all. Following her first film appearance at age four, her popularity was such that in spite of the nation's hard economic times, Temple became the greatest moneymaker of her day and, at that time, the greatest moneymaker in film history.

Born on 23 April 1928 in Santa Monica, CA, Shirley Temple was an unprec-

Shirley Temple Black in a January 1936 promotional photo for the film *Captain January. Photo courtesy of Pictorial Parade/Archive Photos.*

edented sensation and international celebrity during the 1930s. Her first lead role, and perhaps most famous film musical, was *Stand Up and Cheer* (1934). This film and her performance of "Baby, Take a Bow" thrust her into instant stardom. Known for her perfect curls, dimples, and lively personality, Temple won many roles from 1934 to 1938 as a singer and dancer in films such as *Little Miss Marker* (1934), *The Little Colonel* (1935), *Captain January* (1936), *Wee Willie Winkie* (1937), *Heidi* (1937), *Rebecca of Sunnybrook Farm* (1938), and *The Little Princess* (1939). Though Temple starred alongside some of the greatest adult actors and actresses of her day—Lionel Barrymore, Adolph Menjou, Sidney Blackmer, Alice Faye, Robert Young, Cesar Romero, Jimmy Durante, and C. Aubrey Smith, among others—she always managed to steal the spotlight. She won her first and only Academy Award in 1934 for *Bright Eyes* (1934).

Temple's booming success as a child actress was short-lived. Although she continued making films throughout her teen years, including *Miss Annie Rooney* (1942), *I'll Be Seeing You* (1944), *Since You Went Away* (1944), *The Bachelor and the Bobbysoxer* (1947), and *Fort Apache* (1948), her appeal to audiences as a young woman could not compete with her earlier success as a child.

In 1949 she retired from acting at the age of 21. But Temple's retirement from film was hardly the end of her public life. From 1957 to 1959 Temple narrated the television series *Shirley Temple's Story Book*. In 1967, as the wife of Charles A. Black, Shirley Temple Black ran unsuccessfully for the U.S. House of Representatives. Despite this initial disappointment, Temple Black went on to hold several high-ranking political offices. In 1969 she was appointed a dele-gate to the United Nations General Assembly. From 1974 to 1976 she served as U.S. ambassador to Ghana; she was chief of protocol for the White House from 1976 to 1977; and she served as U.S ambassador to Czechoslovakia from 1989 to 1992. In 1998 she was the recipient of Kennedy Center Honors, and today she remains active with the United Nations.

See also Academy Awards; Musical Theater

For Further Reading

Black, Shirley Temple. *Child Star: An Autobiography.* New York: McGraw Hill, 1988.
Edwards, Anne. *Shirley Temple: American Princess.* New York: William Morrow, 1988.
Windeler, Robert. *The Films of Shirley Temple.* Secaucus, NJ: Citadel Press, 1978.

Daniel DiCenso

Bley, Carla (1938–)

Carla Bley is one of the most significant composers of large form, post-bop jazz. Her music incorporates numerous styles and cultures to produce a highly individual type of "hyper-modern" jazz. She is an unorthodox jazz composer with outrageous and extraordinary "far-out" music. She has composed music for ensembles ranging from duets to big bands, but mostly she prefers the 10-piece band for her own music.

Born on 11 May 1938 as Carla Borg in Oakland, CA, she learned to play piano from her father, a piano teacher and church organist, at an early age. Her main musical experiences were singing in church choirs and working as a church organist. At age 17 she moved to New York and worked at the Birdland jazz club as a cigarette girl. She married Paul Bley in 1957 and began composing jazz pieces at this time. Her free-jazz improvisations were sought by the likes of Art

Farmer, Charlie Haden, Jimmy Giuffre, and Gary Burton.

She was a charter member of the Jazz Composers Guild in New York in 1964, which eventually became the Jazz Composers Guild Orchestra. Two years later she helped to found the Jazz Composers Orchestra Association with her second husband, Michael Mantler. Known by her jazz opera *Escalator over the Hill* (ECM 839310-2), Bley has helped lead the movement to give jazz musicians a degree of independence, control, and self-determination within the music industry.

The formation of the Jazz Composers Guild Orchestra provided her the opportunity to produce works of an epic scale for large forces. Her two largest works, *A Genuine Tong Funeral (Dark Opera without Words)* (One Way 34510) and *Escalator over the Hill*, were conceived as a kind of musical theater. *Escalator over the Hill*, which won the Melody Makers Jazz Poll Top Album of the Year Award, took four years for Bley to write. The opera incorporates Eastern chants and wails, jazz, avant garde, western dance, and circus music. Throughout the 1980s Bley played keyboards and led small- to medium-sized bands, but it is her compositional style that led to her tour with the Very Big Carla Bley Band in the early 1990s. She continues to convincingly handle orchestral forces and to champion musicians' rights.

See also Improvisation; Jazz

For Further Reading

AMG: All Music Guide. Available: http://www. allmusic.com

McManus, Jill. "Women Jazz Composers and Arrangers." In *The Musical Woman: An International Perspective I*, ed. Judith Lang Zaimont. Westport, CT: Greenwood Press, 1984.

Brad Eden

Bluegrass

Bluegrass, part of country music, emerged in the 1940s as a stylized version of the traditional mountain music of Kentucky, Tennessee, Virginia, North Carolina, and neighboring states. It celebrates its rural origins with an all-acoustic lineup of instruments and a repertoire of songs of home, intense emotion, and Christian upbringing. A deep nostalgia pervades much of the music, as it chronicles the effects of time and urbanization on people and places.

The characteristic "high lonesome sound" of bluegrass comes from combining a ringing banjo, a swirling fiddle, a river of fast mandolin notes, a strummed or flat-picked guitar, and an upright bass playing an "oom-pah" rhythm. Sometimes a "Dobro"—a guitar with a resonator at the soundhole, played flat using a metal bar to slide along the strings—is added, but purists dislike the use of electric bass or drums. Earnest, hard-driving vocals, solo or in harmony, ride above the band. Though clearly based on the hillbilly stringband, bluegrass has a stronger influence from the blues (indiscernible to those who cannot hear past the style's twang); incorporates sentiment, songs, and vocal style from gospel; and has borrowed from jazz the idea of showing off highly developed instrumental ability. The exciting result is, for fans around the world, a thrilling affirmation of the human spirit and a connection to earthy values and a cherished musical tradition.

The pioneering activities and artistic choices of Bill Monroe, the mandolinist regarded as the father of bluegrass, have affected the course of the style from its inception to the present. Monroe's influence shows in the typical high-pitched singing, the instrumentation, and the categories of repertoire—from tender waltzes to fast instrumental "breakdowns." Several Monroe compositions have become bluegrass standards, and the style's name is derived from the name of his band—Bill Monroe and the Bluegrass Boys (chosen to underline their origins in Kentucky, "the Bluegrass State"). Even the format of calling a band "a man [or two] and the [insert geographical reference] boys" was copied by many other bands, such as Jimmy Martin and the Sunny Mountain Boys, and Jim and Jesse and the Virginia Boys. However masculine sounding the band names were, some women were members: bassist Bessie Lee Mauldin played for a time as one of the Bluegrass Boys. A few later bands with all women members were named in reaction to this tradition, such as the Good Ol' Persons, and the All Girl Boys.

Prior to the 1970s, when women-led bluegrass bands began to multiply, partly in response to the rise of folk festivals, most women in the style belonged to family bands, as siblings, daughters, cousins, or wives of male stars. Because of the social and musical conservativeness of the bluegrass industry, which expected women to remain in the home making soft parlor music if any, women's participation was at first derided and resented by many fans and some musicians. This attitude comes in part from the social and religious values handed down from pioneer stock and may be extrapolated from typical bluegrass lyrics. Some describe an idealized, rural homeland of parents, sweetheart, and familiar hills. Often portrayed is a man, in search of his fortune, who leaves for the big city, the industrial job, or the lure of the road. In a song like the Stanley Brothers' "Rank Stranger," the man returns only to find that death has preceded him and change in the form of urbanization has obliterated the sights

of childhood. Against such forces, the strength of the family can seem to be preserved by womenfolk. If they were to abandon their traditional roles to play the stages, schoolhouses, festivals, and studios of the world, the family would risk fragmentation.

When featured women band members and bandleaders did emerge, they often came from folk revival and collegiate backgrounds, and they brought articulate, emotionally revealing songs and sensibilities to bluegrass from the singer-songwriter movement. Their connection to bluegrass came from exposure to recordings and touring artists as much as from any rural imprinting. When they played for audiences, they had to deal with comments like "she plays pretty good for a woman" (or, more likely, "a girl"). Some women musicians have expressed the feeling that they had to prove themselves even more in the face of such attitudes, not to mention figuring out how to present their visual image: to draw attention to or away from their gender?

Women in bluegrass certainly took inspiration from Monroe, the Stanley Brothers, Flatt and Scruggs, Mac Wiseman, and other men who were architects and stars of the music; but they also sought out their "foremothers" in country music. Cathy Fink in particular has uncovered and broadcast the history of women in music, as a performer and through her efforts in conjunction with the Smithsonian Institute. Among the many predecessors looked to were Sara (1899–1979) and Maybelle (1909–1978) Carter of the Carter Family, country music's first star ensemble; Cousin Emmy, whose song "Ruby" was covered by the Osborne Brothers and became a bluegrass standard; and the Coon Creek Girls from Kentucky, the first all-women hillbilly band, formed in 1937. Another pioneer was Rose Maddox (1925–1998), who as a child came from Alabama to California with her family in the 1930s to escape the great drought and the Depression. Performing with her older brothers as the Maddox Brothers and Rose, they were stars of radio, playing earthy country and proto-bluegrass. After they disbanded, in the 1960s Rose recorded bluegrass albums, including one with Bill Monroe.

Quite influential was the singing of style of Molly O'Day (1923–1987), which was compared to that of Hank Williams by Mac Wiseman who picked up O'Day's influence as he passed through her band early in his career. O'Day's approach also affected Wilma Lee Cooper (b. 1921), who performed with her husband as Wilma Lee and Stoney Cooper and the Clinch Mountain Clan. Cooper was a Grand Ole Opry member whose punchy mountain singing style was popular with country and bluegrass audiences. Like Cooper, Hazel Dickens (b. 1935) came from West Virginia; she has been a source of strength and great songs that are widely covered, such as "Mama's Hands." The albums Hazel Dickens made in the 1970s and 1980s, the first two in duo with Alice Gerrard, have had a major impact.

Delia Bell, whose first album appeared in 1978, was championed by Emmylou Harris (b. 1947), who produced it and sang Bell's "Roses in the Snow" as the title track to her own bluegrass album two years later. Besides Harris, many other country stars, including Dolly Parton (b. 1946), Patty Loveless (b. 1957), and Kathy Mattea (b. 1959), have acknowledged their connection to bluegrass by recording and performing it. The Whites, comprised of Sharon (b. 1953) and Cheryl (b. 1955) White and

their father, Buck, moved from bluegrass into mainstream country, a path also followed by the Dixie Chicks.

From the 1990s, fiddler and vocalist Alison Krauss (b. 1971), with her band Union Station, was one of the most popular stars of bluegrass, bringing new fans to the style through television appearances and radio hits. Krauss named Missouri native Rhonda Vincent (b. 1962) as her main inspiration. Laurie Lewis (b. 1950) is another of the top artists in the field.

Two of the most admired bluegrass bands on the scene in recent decades have as their core a husband and wife team. Claire Lynch (b. 1954), a fine songwriter and award-winning singer, formed the Front Porch String Band in 1974 with her mandolin-playing husband, Larry Lynch. After the band (not the marriage) broke up, she returned to the scene under her own name. Born in Texas, Lynn Morris (b. 1948) played guitar in high school but did not hear a bluegrass band until 1970 when she went to college in Colorado. She soon switched to banjo and in 1974 won a National Banjo Picking Championship in Kansas, she won again in 1981. After many years of experience as a band member, in 1988 with her husband, bassist Marshall Wilborn, she formed the Lynn Morris Band. It soon became one of the most admired in the style.

Helped by the artistry and groundbreaking efforts of the women named above, and many others, bluegrass has changed. From the conservative, virtually all-male, and geographically restricted style of its early days, it has evolved into one that accepts new influences and new participants regardless of gender, and it now has devotees from Europe to Japan and beyond.

See also Carter, Mother Maybelle Addington; Country Music; Krauss, Alison; Lewis, Laurie; Vincent, Rhonda

For Further Reading

Bufwack, Mary A., and Robert K. Oermann. *Finding Her Voice: The Saga of Women in Country Music*. New York: Crown Publishers, 1993.

Seymour, Chris. *Bluegrass*. New York: Friedman/Fairfax Publishers (Life, Times & Music Series), 1996.

Willis, Barry R. *America's Music—Bluegrass: A History of Bluegrass Music in the Words of Its Pioneers*. Franktown, CO: Pine Valley Music, 1998.

Craig Morrison

Blues

Women have sung the blues since it emerged as a popular music form in the early 1900s. African American blueswomen played an important role in the development of the American recording industry and became major figures in the history of American entertainment.

Throughout its history, there has been confusion about what "the blues" is. In its strictest definition as a music form, blues has a straight AAB verse pattern, 12 bars, and a I-IV-I-V-I chord progression; but in reality blues has frequently intermixed with other popular song forms. The blues songs the blueswomen sang often added an introduction, a bridge, or a chorus to the standard blues verse form. To provide variety and to please their audiences, blues musicians sang other popular songs as well. Many blueswomen of the 1920s were accompanied by jazz musicians or small jazz bands. Mixing of genres and styles characterized the songs the blueswomen sang but did not hinder their ability to sing "the blues" as they defined it.

Blues musicians themselves have a simple definition: blues is the truth. This definition refers not only to the situation a song depicts but even more to its emo-

tional impact. Blues originated in African American folk culture and comes from the same tradition as the earlier work songs and spirituals. It shares with them an aspect of complaint and a down-to-earth vocal style that pulls the listener into the song, to identify emotionally with the singer. Paradoxically, even when a blues song is a complaint about mistreatment, the purpose of singing the blues is to lose the blues: to tell the truth about a situation and thus to transcend it. The blueswomen were popular because they were effective truth-tellers, and as such they made blues a vehicle for African American expression.

Little is known about traditional blues in private, domestic settings, in which women must have participated as singers and musicians. Women began singing the blues on stage soon after 1900. Gertrude "Ma" Rainey (1886–1939), one of the earliest and greatest of the blueswomen, began her stage career in 1902. By the 1920s, billed as "The Mother of the Blues," Rainey traveled through the South with her own troupe, performing in tent shows and theaters.

The 1920s have been called the era of Classic Blues, the term used to distinguish the more polished music performed by the blueswomen from "country blues," usually considered to be cruder and closer to its folk roots. The Classic Blues singers were theatrical performers, and they often sang songs written by popular songwriters in addition to songs they wrote themselves. They cultivated stage personas with elaborate scenery, costumes, and jewelry that made them figures of power and glamour to their audiences, who were predominantly working class African Americans. The blueswomen worked hard, however. Life on the theatrical circuit was arduous, involving long hours of travel, constant economic uncertainty, and even physical hardship, especially in the racially segregated South, where much of the audience for blues resided. Nevertheless, the blueswomen symbolized independence and success, especially to the women in their audiences, whose only choices of employment were field labor, domestic service, or prostitution.

Performing live was crucial to the careers of the early blueswomen. Most gained their early experience in traveling shows. As they became successful in the 1920s and 1930s, major performers like Bessie Smith (1894–1937), Clara Smith (1894–1935), and Ida Cox (1896–1967) took to the road with their own troupes. Other blueswomen, including Mamie Smith (1883–1946), Trixie Smith (1895–1943), and Lucille Hegamin (1894–1970), were vaudeville singers who simply followed a trend and added blues songs to their repertoires. Still others, including Ethel Waters (1896–1977), Alberta Hunter (1895–1984), and Victoria Spivey (1906–1976), began their careers in clubs and cabarets and then moved to theater or films.

What gave the blueswomen their national popularity—and their greatest historical importance—was the advent of blues recording. The earliest blues recordings were jazz instrumentals, but in 1920 the songwriter Perry Bradford convinced Okeh Records of New York City to record African American vaudeville singer Mamie Smith. After one modestly successful record with standard popular tunes, she recorded Bradford's "Crazy Blues" in August 1920. Bradford's song was as close to the popular song style of Tin Pan Alley as it was to hard core blues. Record sales were phenomenal, however, especially among African Americans, who flocked to buy a recording of their own music sung by one of

their own. The recording companies, recognizing a profitable market, began to seek out other blueswomen to record. The companies numbered their recordings in special "race" series aimed at black record buyers, inventing a system of targeting audiences by race that is still present today in less overt forms.

During the 1920s record companies such as Okeh, Paramount, Columbia, and Vocalion signed many blue singers, known and unknown, to keep up with popular demand for blues recordings. In 1920, almost immediately after the issue of "Crazy Blues," Lucille Hegamin, another vaudeville artist, began recording blues songs, and Ethel Waters and Alberta Hunter, both popular cabaret artists, recorded in 1921. By 1923 Gertrude "Ma" Rainey and Bessie Smith made their first recordings. Country blues did not catch on with the record companies until 1924, but it ultimately became hugely popular as well, and women artists with a more "country" sound, among them Lucille Bogan (1897–1948), Elvie Thomas, and Louise Johnson, also made recordings. During the 1920s blues, along with jazz, defined African American popular music.

Some blueswomen also performed in Europe. African American musicians had traveled to Europe to perform since the nineteenth century, but the 1920s marked a new craze for jazz, and African American theatrical performers like Florence Mills (1895–1927) and Josephine Baker (1906–1975) created a sensation. Though not blueswomen themselves, they began a trend that some blueswomen followed successfully. Europe was not the place for "down home" performers like Gertrude "Ma" Rainey, whose following was primarily in the American South, or even for Bessie Smith, who occasionally joined theatrical productions in New York, with mixed success. It was the more sophisticated actress/singers who succeeded overseas. Lizzie Miles (1895–1963), who sang in clubs and cabarets, was the first blueswoman to have a record released in England (1923). Edith Wilson (1896–1981) was featured as a singer in Florence Mills's *Dover Street to Dixie* revue in London in 1924. Alberta Hunter appeared in Paul Robeson's London production of *Show Boat* in 1928.

The women who performed overseas shared with cabaret performers Josephine Baker and Ada "Bricktop" Smith (1894–1984) the versatility to perform popular styles other than blues and the ability to sing in languages other than English. Though they often started out in tent shows or black nightclubs, and they recorded blues songs for the race record series of the American recording companies, their broader repertoires were intended to appeal to white theater-goers and to the patrons of segregated nightclubs, and thus they transferred effectively to European audiences.

The 1920s were the heyday of blues recording, but the situation changed after the onset of the Great Depression. Hard times hit the recording industry. Some blues-oriented labels like Paramount, a power in the 1920s, actually failed. Other companies cut back and recorded only their most popular singers. Bessie Smith and Victoria Spivey continued to record during the 1930s, and new artists, like Merline Johnson, known as "The Yas Yas Girl," and the immensely popular Memphis Minnie (born Lizzie Douglas, 1897–1973), actually began their recording careers during the Depression, but many less popular blueswomen sank out of sight. Gertrude "Ma" Rainey, who had been on the road singing the blues for more than 30 years, retired in 1935 and

died in 1939. Victoria Spivey, Ida Cox, and Bessie Smith continued touring. Bessie Smith, on tour in Mississippi, was killed in a tragic automobile accident in 1937. Trixie Smith, Mamie Smith, and Ethel Waters turned to theater and films. Alberta Hunter moved to Europe, where she toured widely and stayed until World War II. On the whole, the blueswomen were not able to benefit from the rise of radio, which was dominated by the big bands and singers popular with white audiences.

Memphis Minnie is unique among the blueswomen. Stylistically she was a country blues singer who wrote her own songs and accompanied herself on the guitar. She was one of the most prolific singer-songwriters of the 1930s, providing an outspoken, woman's point of view about relationships and personal experiences. She performed in blues combos and experimented with electrified instruments, never losing her country sound. Thus, in a period when Classic Blues was in decline, she is a pivotal figure.

Blues experienced a new prominence in the late 1940s, though by then the music had adapted to changes in popular musical taste, instrumentation, technology, and even terminology. After World War II the big bands gave way to smaller combos. It had become standard to amplify the traditional blues instruments, harmonica, and guitar. By the late 1940s the recording industry had recovered from its economic problems. In 1949 *Billboard*, the music industry publication that charted record sales, changed its terminology for black popular music from "race records," (used by the recording industry since the 1920s and now considered anachronistic and demeaning), to "rhythm and blues."

The term "rhythm and blues" (or simply "r&b") denotes a change in popular taste to a faster, more rhythmic and danceable style of blues influenced by the jitterbug style of the big bands. The swing-influenced "jump blues" stressed honking saxophones, electric guitars, and a driving beat. An equally new but more "down home" sound was achieved in the electrified urban blues of the midwestern cities, especially Chicago. Women performed rhythm and blues in all its forms, although the change in terminology has meant that the women rhythm and blues singers have not been recognized as blueswomen at all.

Like the Classic Blues singers of the 1920s, the blueswomen of the 1940s and 1950s were most often singers, not instrumentalists, who sang popular songs in addition to straight-ahead blues. Live performance was still their chief means of support. They performed on their own or traveled with revues, playing theaters and dance halls. However, rhythm and blues artists were much more dependent on the recording industry to maintain their popularity with live audiences. Independent record labels such as Chess in Chicago, King in Cincinnati, Atlantic in New York, Duke and Peacock in Houston, and Aladdin in Los Angeles all featured prominent women vocalists. Some, like Dinah Washington (1924–1963), leaned toward jazz. Marie Adams (b. 1925) and Esther Phillips (1935–1984), both of the Los Angeles–based Johnny Otis Show, were capable of jump blues and straight blues, as well as other pop material. La Vern Baker (1929–1997), Etta James (b. 1938), and Ruth Brown (b. 1928) achieved a solid blues vocal sound despite the stylistic diversity of their songs. The most "down home" of the rhythm and blues women, like Willie Mae "Big Mama" Thornton (1926–1984) and Koko Taylor (b. 1935), never strayed far from traditional blues. All were de-

nied a mainstream audience because any hit songs they achieved were immediately re-recorded, or "covered," by white artists to be sold to white record buyers.

Unlike the 1920s, when women pioneered in recording and fronted their own vaudeville troupes, the blues scene of the 1940s and 1950s was a man's world. The electrified urban blues gave extra prominence to male instrumentalists. Most women did not achieve the independence of the classic blueswomen, despite their popularity, and for the most part the image they portrayed, for all their glamour, was much in keeping with postwar images of feminine domesticity and dependence. There was a certain amount of good-time party music, like "Wang Dang Doodle," a hit in a rollicking rendition by Koko Taylor, but the music performed by the women rhythm and blues artists dealt mainly with relationships between men and women.

The 1960s brought a revived interest in American traditional music among young whites. Older blues musicians who had not performed for years were rediscovered and had second performing careers in folk clubs and festivals. Among the blueswomen able to take advantage of the folk revival were Willie Mae "Big Mama" Thornton, Sippie Wallace (1898–1986), Victoria Spivey, and Alberta Hunter. Victoria Spivey formed her own record company, Spivey Records. Ida Cox recorded a new album of songs, *Blues for Rampart Street* (Riverside RLP-9374) in 1961, and recordings by Gertrude "Ma" Rainey, Bessie Smith, and others were reissued on LP compilations. Both Wallace and Hunter eventually became subjects of documentary films: *Sippie* in 1982, and *Alberta Hunter: My Castle's Rockin'* in 1988.

During the 1960s and 1970s young white women were also attracted to the blues. Bonnie Raitt (b. 1949) learned her guitar style from the bluesmen, but she also befriended and performed with Sippie Wallace. Blues-rock diva Janis Joplin (1943–1970) had one of her biggest hits with Willie Mae "Big Mama" Thornton's "Ball and Chain." The 1980s brought the likes of pianist Marcia Ball, guitarist Rory Block, and a racially mixed group, Saffire, billing themselves as "the uppity blueswomen."

Despite the implications of a "blues revival" among white fans, blues never left the African American community, where it appeals especially to older listeners. Malaco Records in Jackson, MS, has made this audience its own, issuing recordings by blueswomen Denise Lasalle (b. 1939) and Valerie Wellington (b. 1959), whose untimely death in 1993 cut short a promising career. Ichiban Records of Atlanta appeals to a similar audience with recordings by Francine Reed and Millie Jackson (b. 1944).

Blues also appeals to mainstream fans, and there are still opportunities to perform. Until her death in 1999, New Orleans singer/pianist Katie Webster (b. 1939) continued a career that began in the 1950s. Today in Chicago, blueswomen including Bonnie Lee, Zora Young (b. 1948), and Big Time Sarah (Sarah Streeter, b. 1953) regularly appear and record as featured performers with some of Chicago's best blues bands. Koko Taylor, though she tours nationally, is the acknowledged queen of Chicago blues. Shirley King is following in the footsteps of her father, bluesman B. B. King. Ruth Brown's honors include a Tony Award (for *Black and Blue*, 1989) a Grammy Award for Best Jazz Female Vocal Performance (in 1990, for an album entitled *Blues on Broadway*, Fantasy FCD-9662–2), and induction into the Rock and Roll Hall of Fame (1993)—ex-emplifying again the power of blueswomen to transcend genre boundaries in American popular music.

Because of their historical importance and their woman-oriented songs, feminist scholars have studied the blueswomen of the 1920s seriously. Far less study has been devoted to the rhythm and blues singers of the 1940s and 1950s. How do the blueswomen of today fit into the tradition? Though these issues remain to be explored further, the important role that the blueswomen have played in the development of American popular music cannot be overlooked or denied.

See also African American Musicians; Jazz

For Further Reading

Brown, Ruth, and Andrew Yule. *Miss Rhythm: The Autobiography of Ruth Brown, Rhythm and Blues Legend.* New York: Donald I. Fine Books, 1996.

Davis, Angela Y. *Blues Legacies and Black Feminism: Gertrude "Ma" Rainey, Bessie Smith, and Billie Holiday.* New York: Pantheon Books, 1998.

Harrison, Daphne Duvall. *Black Pearls: Blues Queens of the 1920s.* New Brunswick, NJ: Rutgers University Press, 1988.

Suzanne Flandreau

Boardman, Eunice (1927–)

In her role as a teacher educator, as an author and editor, and as the developer of the *Generative Theory of Musical Learning* (Boardman, 1988), Eunice Boardman is characterized by her ability to link major ideas from research and scholarship in education, psychology, and philosophy to the field of music education. Her contributions have been many, and in 2000 Boardman was honored with the Illinois Music Educators Association's President's Award.

Boardman's professional and scholarly contributions are grounded in her early work as a music specialist and choral director. After graduating with a B.M.E. degree from Cornell College (1947), she taught in the elementary and secondary schools of Iowa. Boardman completed her M.M.E at Teachers College, Columbia University (1951). She began her career as a professor of music and education in 1956 and earned an Ed.D. from the University of Illinois (1963). Boardman held various professorships before being appointed in 1975 as a professor of music and education at the University of Wisconsin—Madison. Five years later she was elected as director of its School of Music. In 1989 Boardman moved to the University of Illinois—Champaign as professor and director of graduate studies in music education, a position she held until her retirement in 1998.

Boardman's broad interests are reflected in the courses she taught regularly at the University of Illinois, such as Philosophical Foundations of Music Education, Psychological Foundations of Music Education, and Contemporary Trends in Music Education Research. Her influence is extended through the work of many current professors of music education who were taught, supervised, or advised by her throughout their doctoral studies.

Boardman influenced classroom practice in general music education through co-authoring: the *Individualized Music Program* (1972) for elementary schools; three elementary school music textbook series: *Exploring Music* (1966, 1972, 1975), *The Music Book* (1980, 1984), and *Holt MUSIC* (1988); and a text for preservice music educators, *Musical Growth in the Elementary School* (Bergethon and Boardman, 1963, 1972, 1975, 1979; Bergethon, Boardman, and Montgomery, 1986, 1996).

Boardman's ability to link music education to more general educational issues placed her in great demand as a clinician and speaker. Her writings on, for example, teacher education curriculum, research, teacher education reform, and music education curriculum illuminated connections for music educators. Through chairing two conferences on Qualitative Research in Music Education, Boardman helped establish a context for reconsidering current practice in music education research. Boardman also served as editor of the *Bulletin of the Council for Research in Music Education* (1992–1999).

Her own research and scholarship has focused on the development of the *Generative Theory of Musical Learning*. As a leader in music education, Boardman has argued that "our instructional decisions are, must be founded in the underlying assumptions about music and about the purpose of schooling, as well as in a well-founded understanding of how people learn" (Boardman, 1988, "Generative Theory of Musical Learning: Part I," 5). Through teaching, scholarship, writing, and professional service, she has sought a deeper understanding of these assumptions and foundations and has encouraged others in the same pursuit.

See also Music Education

For Further Reading

Boardman, Eunice. "Generative Theory of Musical Learning: Part I." *General Music Today* 2/1 (1988): 4–5, 26–30.

———. "Generative Theory of Musical Learning: Part II." *General Music Today* 2/2 (1988): 3–6, 28–32.

Mary Hookey

Boswell Sisters

The Boswell Sisters were among the best and most talented jazz vocal groups of the first half of the twentieth-century.

Their New Orleans background assisted the sisters in creating fantastic harmonies and performing vocal gymnastics that have rarely been equaled. Connee (1907–1976), Martha (1908–1958), and Helvetia (1909–1988) Boswell grew up singing blues and southern gospel music together in New Orleans. These sisters were a rarity among blues and gospel performers because they were white. Starting with a vaudeville act, they began singing on local radio stations in 1925. Even though Connee had been crippled and confined to a wheelchair since childhood, she generally led the trio in both singing and instrumental playing. Connee usually played cello, guitar, and saxophone; Helvetia played guitar, banjo, and violin; and Martha accompanied on piano.

Their vocal talents led to appearances in New York and Chicago, and they began recording for Victor in 1930. They reached the Hit Parade in 1931 with "When I Take My Sugar to Tea," sung in the Marx Brothers' film *Monkey Business* and featuring the Dorsey Brothers Orchestra. They also appeared in the 1932 film *The Big Broadcast* with Bing Crosby and Cab Calloway. Their song "The Object of My Affection" made it to the top of the Hit Parade in 1935 and was featured in the movie *Time Square Parade*. Numerous albums were recorded, including *St. Louis Blues* (Silver Swan 1001), *Syncopating Harmonists from New Orleans* (Take Two 406), and *The Three Syncopatin' Boswell Sisters from the Sunny South* (Totem 1042), as well as compilation albums such as *The Boswell Sisters 1932–1934* (Biograph 3). In 1936 the group broke up so that Martha and Helvetia could pursue married life. Connee continued her solo career after the group disbanded. She hit the top of the charts twice in the late 1930s, with "Alexander's Ragtime Band" and "Bob White (Whatcha Gonna Swing Tonight)" in duet versions with Bing Crosby. She continued recording well into the 1960s.

See also Blues; Jazz

For Further Reading

Erlewine, Michael (ed.), et al. *All Music Guide to Jazz*, 2d ed. San Francisco: Miller Freeman Books, 1996.

Hassinger, Jane. "Close Harmony: Early Jazz Styles in the Music of the New Orleans Boswell Sisters." In *Women and Music in Cross-Cultural Perspective*, ed. Ellen Koskoff. New York: Greenwood Press, 1987.

Brad Eden

Boyer-Alexander, René (1950–)

René Boyer-Alexander has played a major role in the movement for multiethnicity in general music curricula and school choral music. A versatile educator, she holds the position of professor of music education at the University of Cincinnati College–Conservatory of Music (CCM) while maintaining a personal partnership with the inner-city schools, presenting clinics at state and national conferences, working with the choir at New Jerusalem Baptist Church, and teaching and conducting abroad.

Boyer-Alexander was born on 2 April 1950 in San Diego, CA, and spent her childhood and youth in East St. Louis, MO. As a child, René and her siblings spent entire days at the home of Marjorie Olive, their piano teacher. At home, the children competed for their turn at the piano. Boyer-Alexander's grandmother, a church musician, nicknamed her "Little Professor." René has always wanted to teach and feels that that desire and ability is a gift from God. Following bachelor's and master's degrees in music at Southern Illinois University, Boyer-Alexander taught high school chorus and elementary music in the Normandy School District in St. Louis. In 1975 Washington University, an institution that has actively sought people of color in order to diversify its student body, offered René a full fellowship and stipend to pursue a doctoral degree. At Washington, she found a mentor in Dr. Lewis B. Hilton and wrote her dissertation on the development of an eclectic curriculum for American elementary schools. Upon completion of her Ed.D. (1978), Boyer-Alexander joined the faculty of CCM.

Boyer-Alexander is co-author of *Music Fundamentals, Methods, and Materials for the Elementary Classroom Teacher*; contributor to *Share the Music*, a school music series published by Macmillan McGraw-Hill; and coordinator and director of the Orff-Schulwerk Certification Program at CCM. Her approach to classroom music emphasizes singing and the creative use of instruments, reflecting her dual certification in Orff and Kodály methods. President of the Black Music Caucus of the Music Educators National Conference, Boyer-Alexander is completing an anthology of children's spirituals that will include parts for Orff instrumentation.

Conference presentations, including "Getting the Middle Schooler's Attention in Music Class: Hook, Line and Sinker," "Shocked Beyond Reality—Inclusion of the Middle School Non-Singer," and "Jazzin' It Up in the Music Classroom" reflect not only Boyer-Alexander's deep concern for middle school students but also her dynamic approach to instruction.

See also Kodály Method; Music Education; Orff Approach

For Further Reading

Rozmajzl, Michon, and René Boyer-White. *Music Fundamentals, Methods, and Materials for the Elementary Classroom Teacher*. White Plains, NY: Longman Publishers USA, 1996.

Carolyn Bryan

Brown, Ruth (1928–)

Ruth Brown, the legendary "Miss Rhythm" of rhythm and blues music, is one of the most popular blues singers of the twentieth century. She helped to create the Rhythm and Blues Foundation in 1988. She also received the Foundation's first Career Achievement Award in 1989. In that same year she also received a Tony Award and a Blues Alive Award for her Broadway show *Black and Blue*. In 1990 she received a Grammy Award for *Blues on Broadway* (Fantasy 9662), and in 1993 she was inducted into the Rock and Roll Hall of Fame.

Ruth Brown was born Ruth Weston on 12 January 1928 in Portsmouth, VA, the oldest of seven children. She grew up singing in a church choir that her father directed. In her teens, Ruth began singing in nightclubs and United Service Organization shows at military bases in the area. Her parents assumed that she was at choir practice and would have been unhappy at the knowledge that she was singing the "devil's music," that is, the blues. She believes, however, that her father secretly boasted about her talent with his friends. It was in these places that she began refining her singing style, which was influenced by many types of music, including blues singers, and stylists like Billie Holiday (1915–1959) and Ella Fitzgerald (1917–1996).

Her strongly rhythmic and spirited outbursts of expression, as well as a preference for the organ instead of the piano, can probably be attributed to her attendance at the Revival Weeks in the local Baptist churches. Her hooting sounds probably may be attributed to the "hill-

Ruth Brown performing at the Atlantic Records 40th anniversary concert at Madison Square Garden in May 1988. *Photo © Neal Preston/CORBIS.*

028) to her most recent *Good Day for the Blues* (Bullseye Blues 619613), recorded when she was 70 years old.

During the early 1960s, with the popularity of rock and roll, her bookings decreased, and from 1964 to 1974 she was not very active as a performer. The late comedian Redd Foxx had a part written for her on his hit television show *Sanford and Son* in 1974. This gave impetus to her career as an actress, and she began appearing on the stage, on television shows, and in motion pictures. In addition, she had two weekly radio shows, *Blues Stages* and *Harlem Hit Parade*, on National Public Radio.

See also Blues; Jazz

For Further Reading

Brown, Ruth, with Andrew Yule. *Miss Rhythm: The Autobiography of Ruth Brown, Rhythm and Blues Legend.* New York: Donald I. Fine, 1996.
Deffaa, Chip. *Blue Rhythms: Six Lives in Rhythm and Blues.* Urbana and Chicago: University of Illinois Press, 1996.
Shaw, Arnold. *Black Popular Music in America: From the Spirituals, Minstrels, and Ragtime to Soul, Disco, and Hip-Hop.* New York: Schirmer Books; Collier MacMillan, 1986.

Monica J. Burdex

billy" or country and western music she heard on the radio. She was also influenced by the top popular singers and groups of the time.

After high school, Brown began her career in earnest. Her career began its ascent when she was introduced to Blanche Calloway (sister of Cab), who became her manager, and she signed a recording contract with Ahmet Ertegun, founder of Atlantic Records. She had many hits for the label from 1949 to 1961; in fact, Atlantic Records became known as the "house that Ruth built." She has numerous albums to her credit, including her very earliest albums *Ruth Brown* (Atlantic 8004 and *Along Comes Ruth* (Phm-200-

Bryant, Clora (1927–)

Clora Bryant is a pioneering Los Angeles bebop jazz trumpeter as well as a vocalist, drummer, arranger, composer, teacher, writer, and mother of four. In June 1957 she recorded her only album, *Gal with a Horn: Clora Bryant* (VSOP 42). The recording features Clora Bryant, vocals and trumpet; Roger Fleming, piano; Ben Tucker, bass; and Bruz Freeman, drums; assisted by Walter Benton, tenor sax, and Normie Faye, trumpet. Bryant's performances typically include driving bebop-style trumpet playing, reminiscent of her mentor, Dizzy Gillespie, and an entertaining, fluid vocal style.

Bryant was born in Denison, TX, on 30 May 1927. She began to sing in church and school choruses and to play piano early in her youth. In the 1940s she learned to play the trumpet that her brother Fred left behind when he was drafted for World War II. Majoring in music at Prairie View Agricultural and Mechanical University near Houston, TX, she started to write her own trumpet solos and joined the Prairie View Coeds, an all-woman swing band.

In 1945 she moved with her father to Los Angeles, where she became one of the few women who jammed at the city's Central Avenue jazz clubs. Initially she played mostly with women's groups, such as the Sweethearts of Rhythm and the Darlings of Rhythm. In 1951 she played with the first women's band on a musical variety television show, the Queens of Swing, but the television station changed the group's name to the Hollywood Sepia Tones. The program lasted only six weeks because the station received complaints about blacks being on the air and because the band could not find sponsors. From 1949 to 1959 Bryant was married to bass player Joe Stone.

Though Los Angeles remained her base, she toured internationally, playing with such notables as Gillespie, Billie Holiday (1915–1959), Clark Terry, Charlie Parker, Dexter Gordon, Harry James, and Louis Armstrong, and with some of her children, including drummer Kevin and vocalist Darrin. She was a member of the big band that backed Sammy Davis Jr. in the 1960 film *Pepe*. In 1961 and 1962 she appeared with the Billy Williams Revue at the Riviera Hotel in Las Vegas, where she developed her famous impersonation of Louis Armstrong. During this time Bryant ap-

peared on the *Tonight Show* and with the Billy Williams Revue on the *Ed Sullivan Show*. For six weeks in Australia, she and her brother Mel performed on a television show twice a week from their hotel.

In the late 1970s she replaced trumpeter Blue Mitchell in Bill Berry's big band but found it increasingly difficult to find jobs. She returned to school at University of California, Los Angeles, to study composition and obtained a bachelor's degree in music. She subsequently completed her five-movement *Suite for Dizzy* with the assistance of three grants from the National Endowment for the Arts. As an additional example of her perseverance, in 1988 she tried to get work abroad by writing to Soviet leader Mikhail Gorbachev, which resulted in five concerts in Moscow and Leningrad.

In 1990 Bryant was diagnosed with chronic bronchitis, and since then she has mainly been teaching jazz history courses, writing, composing, arranging, participating in conferences, and giving some private lessons. The University of Massachusetts at Amherst honored her in 1993 for her work in American music.

For Further Reading

Bryant, Clora (ed.) et al. *Central Avenue Sounds: Jazz in Los Angeles.* Berkeley: University of California Press, 1998.

California Soul: Music of African Americans in the West, eds. Jacqueline Cogdell DjeDje and Eddie S. Meadows. Berkeley: University of California Press, 1998.

Victor Cardell

Bryn-Julson, Phyllis (1945–)

Phyllis Bryn-Julson is one of the most highly regarded interpreters of twentieth-century vocal music. She has served on the voice faculties of Kirkland-Hamilton College, the University of Maryland, and the Peabody Conservatory of Music. She conducts master classes in both the United States and England. She has served as master teacher for the twentieth-century vocal literature course at the renowned Britten-Pears School for Advanced Musical Studies in Aldeburgh (Suffolk, United Kingdom).

Bryn-Julson was born in Bowdon, ND, on 5 February 1945; she studied voice, piano, organ, and violin at Concordia College in Moorehead, MN. Impressed with her facility at sight-reading 12-tone music, an aptitude fueled by perfect pitch, a three-octave range, and clarity of timbre, composer Gunther Schuller encouraged her to study voice at the Berkshire Music Center, where conductor Erich Leinsdorf offered additional guidance.

Bryn-Julson completed her vocal studies at Syracuse University. On 28 October 1966 she made her formal debut as a soloist in Alban Berg's *Lulu Suite* with the Boston Symphony Orchestra. Ten years later she made her operatic debut as Malinche in the American premiere of Roger Session's *Montezuma*. Although Bryn-Julson's repertoire is quite broad,

she has achieved greatest success on stage and in recordings with a wide variety of twentieth-century works, many written especially for her by composers like David Del Tredici and Phillip Rhodes. Bryn-Julson's husband is the organist Donald Sutherland, with whom she often collaborates in recitals and on recordings.

Her many recordings include *Phyllis Bryn-Julson* (CRI SD 498), a solo album of contemporary music; Pierre Boulez's *Pli Selon Pli* (2292-45376-2); and *20th-Century Voices in America* (CDX 5145 VoxBox).

See also Classical Music; Performer, Vocal

For Further Reading

Drucker, Arno. "The Britten-Pears School in Aldeburgh: Summer Courses with Elly Ameling and Phyllis Bryn-Julson." *The Journal of Singing: The Official Journal of the National Association of Teachers of Singing* 54/5 (1998): 27–30.

Judith Marley

Bullock, Annie Mae

See Tina Turner

Burce, Suzanne Lorraine

See Jane Powell

Caldwell, Sarah (1924–)

Sarah Caldwell—impresaria, conductor, stage director—has received numerous honors for her tireless efforts on behalf of American music and culture. She is generally regarded as one of the most influential personalities in twentieth-century American opera. Caldwell highlights the drama in her productions. Her operatic stagings often feature impressive and unusual visual elements, including lasers, black lights, and film. Her staging of Engelbert Humperdinck's opera *Hänsel und Gretel* even required a witch to fly over the heads of the audience.

Caldwell was born in Maryville, MO, on 6 March 1924. A precocious child, she began violin lessons at the age of four. She attended Hendrix College and the University of Arkansas, studying both music and psychology. In the early 1940s she went to the New England Conservatory to continue her violin study, but soon she took up an interest in opera production and stage design. Her principal violin teachers were Richard Burgin of the Boston Symphony Orchestra and, later, George Flourel. In 1946 she attended the Berkshire Music Festival at Tanglewood, studied conducting (the only woman student) with Serge Koussevitsky, and played the viola in the student orchestra. She returned in 1947 and, under the tutelage of Boris Goldovsky, directed her first opera, Ralph Vaughan Williams's *Riders to the Sea*. After completing her studies at the New England Conservatory, she became Goldovsky's assistant with the New England Opera Company. He gave her the opportunity to conduct her first opera, Wolfgang Amadeus Mozart's *La finta giardiniera*.

From 1952 to 1960 she was head of the Boston University Opera Workshop. In 1958 she organized what later became the Opera Company of Boston. Despite financial constraints and the lack of an operatic tradition in Boston, Caldwell developed an enthusiastic following in New England and, later, throughout the country. She developed the reputation for courageous and imaginative programming, skillful conducting, and innovative stage direction. She is credited with the American premieres of numerous twentieth-century works, including Paul Hindemith's *Mathis der Maler*, Sergei

Prokofiev's *War and Peace*, Luigi Nono's *Intolleranza*, Bernd Alois Zimmermann's *Die Soldaten*, Arnold Schoenberg's *Moses und Aron*, Peter Maxwell Davies's *Taverner*, and Rodion Shchedrin's *Dead Souls*. She also premiered many works by American composers, among them Roger Sessions, Gunther Schuller, and Robert di Domenica. Caldwell discovered and promoted the careers of numerous young American singers, but she also helped maintain the careers of Beverly Sills (b. 1929) and Shirley Verrett before they became recognized by the Metropolitan Opera.

The company survived numerous financial problems over the years, but Caldwell was unable to successfully combine the roles of administrator and artistic director. Despite the company's demise in the late 1980s, Caldwell's work became more and more recognized around the world. In 1976 she was the first woman to conduct an opera at the Metropolitan Opera, Guiseppe Verdi's *La Traviata*. She was also a frequent guest conductor with orchestras and opera companies around the world. She continued to develop numerous new projects, such as a collaborative company in the Philippines and exchange programs with the Soviet Union and the People's Republic of China. In 1983 she became the artistic director of the New Opera Company of Israel. In the late 1990s Caldwell returned to the University of Arkansas as distinguished professor of opera.

See also Conductor, Instrumental and Operatic

For Further Reading

Goldovsky, Boris. *My Road to Opera: The Recollections of Boris Goldovsky.* Boston: Houghton Mifflin, 1979.
Sadie, Stanley (ed.). *The New Grove Dictionary of Opera.* London: Macmillan Press; New York: Grove's Dictionaries of Music, 1992.

Robert B. Dundas

Canon

In American music the canon, or standard "classical" repertoire, consists of the works of a succession of important composers, all of them men, in the European-American art music tradition. In its oldest meaning in music, a canon is a compositional procedure of imitative counterpoint. Only since the mid-1980s has the term been widely used to refer to a body of exemplary works of music, analogous to the literary canon. Musicians may not always find the literary analogy appropriate, perhaps because music, unlike literature, derives much of its beauty and appeal from unwritten, undocumented elements. Nevertheless American concert programs, histories, textbooks, and anthologies provide a consensus as to what works are presumed to be most deserving of repeated performance, scholarship, and teaching. Criteria of greatness exemplified in the classical canon include the existence of a written score, construction on the basis of certain Germanic formal and theoretical principles and procedures, virtuosity, originality, public performance, and critical attention. Although these criteria are not gender-specific, they are derived from a one-gender repertoire.

In "A Survey of College Music Textbooks: Benign Neglect of Women Composers?" (1986), Diane Jezic and Daniel Binder show that in spite of all the recovery of women's work, music appreciation and music history textbooks rarely mention any woman musician. The most widely used classroom anthologies today contain music by, at most, one or two prominent American women such as

Ruth Crawford Seeger (1901–1953) or Ellen Taaffe Zwilich (b. 1939).

Marcia Citron's *Gender and the Musical Canon* (1993) is a detailed study of the classical canon and the musical and cultural values it represents. To explain the exclusion of music composed by women, Citron draws on a wealth of writings about music, literature, philosophy, and aesthetics from the last 200 years, juxtaposing traditional views and recent feminist critiques. To bring music by women to the attention of audiences, historians, and students, Citron considers the relative merits of mainstreaming and separatism. Mainstreaming, or the integration of music by women into the canon, has the advantage of representing the two genders as existing in a common society and cultural unit, and it maintains familiar stylistic and historical outlines; it can also result, however, in the women's repertoire being overwhelmed by the imperialistic tendencies of the mainstream. Separatism, or the formulation of a counter-canon of music by women, preserves women's identity and individualism and allows the recognition of a women's tradition; a separate repertoire, however, can be ignored as marginal or unimportant. Citron thus advocates a "contrapuntal" interweaving of mainstreaming and separatism, so that women are represented as part of music's social and economic context, and as part of certain female patterns as well (Citron, 219–221).

Besides the women's movement, other historic changes in American society since the 1960s and 1970s have challenged the importance of the canon. The civil rights movement for African Americans and other racial and ethnic minorities, as well as increasing numbers of non-European immigrants, have resulted in an unprecedented pluralism in American culture that finds expression in a multitude of musical traditions, oral as well as written. The classical canon is only one of many important American repertoires. The musicologist Don Randel, in "The Canons in the Musicological Toolbox" (1992), discusses the contributions of feminist criticism and feminist musicology to an understanding of canons and canon formation.

See also Feminist Music Criticism; Feminist Musicology

For Further Reading

Citron, Marcia. *Gender and the Musical Canon*. Cambridge: Cambridge University Press, 1993.

Jezic, Diane, and Daniel Binder. "A Survey of College Music Textbooks: Benign Neglect of Women Composers?" In *The Musical Woman: An International Perspective II*, ed. Judith Lang Zaimont. Westport, CT: Greenwood Press, 1986, 445–469.

Randel, Don Michael. "The Canons in the Musicological Toolbox." In *Disciplining Music: Musicology and Its Canons*. Chicago: University of Chicago Press, 1992, Chapter 2.

Deborah Hayes

Carabo-Cone, Madeleine (1915–1988)

Madeleine Carabo-Cone became known in the 1960s and 1970s through her workshops and writing and for her new approach to music education. Her influence on the way music is taught to preschool and elementary-age children is acknowledged less often.

Born Madeleine Carabo on 2 June 1915 in Scarsdale, NY, she studied violin at the Juilliard School, where she received the Frederick Stock Award and a Juilliard Graduate Fellowship. Her violin teachers were Georges Enesco, Nathan Milstein, Mischa Mischakoff, Adolfo Betti, and Carl Friedberg. She married pianist Harold Cone. Madeleine Carabo-Cone became the first woman to join the first violin section of the Cleveland Orchestra. In New York City she presented concerts at Carnegie Hall and Town Hall and gave the city's first performances of works by Charles Ives, Henry Cowell, and Roy Harris. She appeared as guest violinist with American orchestras such as the Chicago Symphony.

After several years of teaching music, she developed the Carabo-Cone method. Endeavoring to motivate a student who preferred playing with friends to studying music, she invited the child's friends into the classroom. In her words, "Soon the walls and floors were covered with musical drawings and cutouts. The familiar children's games were being translated into musical terms, and new games were developing as musical needs presented themselves. For the youngsters, the emphasis was on play, but gradually, and without their realizing it, they were learning basic musical concepts and instrumental techniques" (Carabo-Cone and Royt, 1953, ix).

Influenced by the learning theories of Jean Piaget and Jerome Bruner, the Carabo-Cone method allows for different learning styles by involving children in planned visual, tactile, and motor experiences. Reliance on sense perception more than on verbalization gives children from varying backgrounds an equal opportunity to learn. Carabo-Cone made the classroom a structured environment where the musical staff is constantly encountered. By physically entering a gigantic grand staff, children "become" various musical elements and discover concepts of tone and duration, for example, in relation to themselves. Five levels on the child's own body—feet, knees, waist, shoulders, and head—can represent the five lines of the staff. The Carabo-Cone method became widely accepted, even by those who were unaware of its name or origin. Educators soon appropriated these ideas for music learning games and began to decorate their classrooms with icons that could help children become musically literate. Thus Carabo-Cone's sensory-motor approach came to influence music teachers everywhere.

Madeleine Carabo-Cone died on 14 August 1988 in Westchester, NY.

See also Music Education

For Further Reading

Carabo-Cone, Madeleine. *The Playground as Music Teacher*. New York: Harper and Brothers, 1959.

Carabo-Cone, Madeleine, and Beatrice Royt. *How to Help Children Learn Music*. New York: Harper and Brothers, 1953.

Mark, Michael. *Contemporary Music Education*, 2d ed. New York: Schirmer, 1978.

Carolyn Livingston

Cardona, Florencia Bisenta de Casillas Martínez

See Carr, Vikki

Carlos, Wendy (1939–)

Wendy Carlos—composer, film scorer, electronic instrument designer—is perhaps best known for *Switched-On Bach*, her Grammy Award–winning album of electronic music. Her music has been described as "avant garde," "ambient," "classical," and even "New Age," although none of these terms per se accurately or adequately describe her music.

Born in Pawtucket, RI, on 14 November 1939, Carlos showed an early interest in both music and science and began piano lessons at age six. She studied both music and physics at Brown University and subsequently earned an M.A. in composition at Columbia University. While at Columbia she studied with electronic music pioneers Vladimir Ussachevsky and Otto Luening. Upon graduation Carlos worked as a recording engineer and, along with long-time producer Rachel Elkind, released the album *Switched-On Bach* (CBS/Sony MK 7194). *Switched-On Bach*, in addition to winning three Grammy Awards, was the first classical album to command platinum sales, and it is still one of the best-selling classical music releases in history. This album helped bring electronic music—and in particular, the Moog synthesizer—to a wider audience. *The Well-Tempered Synthesizer* (CBS MS 7286) quickly followed *Switched-On Bach*. In 1972 her album *Sonic Seasonings* (ESD 81372) again charted new territory in its cross-over appeal to classical, electronic, and the new ambient and New Age audiences.

Carlos composed music to accompany Stanley Kubrick's film *A Clockwork Orange* (1971), one of the first such works to extensively employ synthesized human voices. Her other film scores include music for Kubrick's *The Shining* (1980) and Disney's *Tron* (1982). With the score for *Tron*, Carlos began exploring the notion of imitative synthesis, exploiting the perceptual boundaries between synthesized and acoustic sounds. This exploration culminated in her *Digital Moonscapes* (Columbia MK-39340), where Carlos's synthesized "LSI Philharmonic Orchestra" attempted to create electronic textures indistinguishable from the sounds produced by an acoustic orchestra.

From an early age, Carlos had been interested in alternate tuning systems. At age 16 she retuned her parents' spinet piano in various ways, and with her study of electronic music she applied her expertise to the composition of electronic music in various tuning systems. Examples include her 1986 classic *Beauty in the Beast* (Audion SYN 200), which employs various non-Western tuning systems (e.g., Balinese and Javanese), and *Switched-On Bach 2000* (Telarc 30323), which juxtaposes historical tunings of Bach's time with modern electronic orchestrations.

Carlos's work with tuning systems led her to espouse a theory on the correspondence between tuning and timbre. It has also led to her discovery of the so-called *alpha*, *beta*, and *gamma* equal-tempered scales. These scales are comprised of asymmetrical, non-integer divisions of the octave in which key intervals (such as the third and the fifth) are almost perfectly in tune—more so than in traditional 12-tone equal temperament. Carlos even invented instruments to aid in her quest to explore other tunings: her little-known invention, the Circon, is a modification of the Theremin (an early electronic instrument that produced "eerie" voicelike sounds), whereby the player indicates the pitch being played on a graphical keyboard scale.

Carlos's more recent work includes *Tales of Heaven and Hell* (East Side Digital 81352), which she describes as "an unusual musical dramatic work which combines themes from *A Clockwork Orange* with a dark and forbidding gothic Mass," and the score to the British film *Woundings* (1998). Wendy Carlos continues to innovate, explore, and chart new musical territory.

See also Film Composers; Music Technology

For Further Reading

Chadabe, Joel. *Electric Sound: The Past and Promise of Electronic Music.* Upper Saddle River, NJ: Prentice Hall, 1997.

Karen Carpenter during a performance of the Carpenters in the 1970s. *Photo courtesy of Frank Driggs/Archive Photos.*

Milano, Dominic. "Wendy Carlos." *Keyboard Magazine* (November 1986): 50–65.

Colby Leider

Carpenter, Karen (1950–1983)

Karen Carpenter was the vocalist and drummer in the popular brother-sister duo the Carpenters of the 1970s. Her mellow alto, natural vocal expression, and crystal clear diction were enhanced with the duo's use of vocal overdubs, full rich harmonies, and polished presentation. Along with her distinctive, warm voice and the steady string of hits, Karen is perhaps best remembered for her death at age 33 of a heart attack brought on by a history of anorexia nervosa.

Karen Carpenter was born on 2 March 1950 in New Haven, CT, four years after her brother Richard. The family moved to Downey, CA, in 1963. She began her musical career playing drums in the high school marching band and in 1965 joined her first group, the Carpenter Trio, which included Richard on keyboards and a friend on bass. After the trio broke up in 1967, Richard and Karen formed a larger group, Spectrum, which played in Los Angeles clubs. When Spectrum broke up, Karen began to study voice with California State, Long Beach, music teacher Frank Pooler. With Pooler's encouragement, Richard and Karen came up with their signature multitrack vocal recording style and decided to try their luck as a duo.

A Carpenters demo eventually attracted the attention of trumpeter Herb Alpert, who signed the duo to A&M Records. Their second single, Burt Bacharach and Hal David's "(They Long to Be) Close to You," complete with understated piano arrangement, shot to the top of the charts in 1970. The song was a massive hit around the world and ushered in an era of chart domination by the duo.

Some of their most popular hits include "For All We Know," "Rainy Days and Mondays" (both available on *Carpenters*, A&M 393502), "Sing," and "Yesterday Once More" (both available on *Now & Then*, Polygram 9055). In 1971 the Carpenters received Grammy Awards for Best New Artist and Best Vocal Performances.

Having abandoned the drums in concert and eager to try her own standing as a singer, Karen attempted to launch a solo career. She recorded a solo album in 1979, working with producer Phil Ramone. But that project was destined to remain unreleased in her lifetime; Richard persuaded her to abandon it to work on a new Carpenters album, *Made in America* (A&M 75021-3723-2), which provided the duo's last hit single, "Touch Me When We're Dancing." Karen's increasingly poor health and her decision to seek professional treatment for her anorexia forced the duo to maintain a low profile in the early 1980s. Karen Carpenter died on 4 February 1983 in Downey, CA, of heart failure. Her solo album was finally released in 1996—13 years after her death—on an album entitled *Karen Carpenter* (A&M 540588).

The pleasant, laid-back tone of their material seemed a refreshing relief in an age of chaos and represented a return to "traditional values" in the aftermath of the counterculture explosion. Although their polished allure made the Carpenters famous in the mid-1970s, it earned them the disapproval of boomer rock critics. Later audiences perceived a tortured Karen who was seen as an object of fascination: a young woman trapped between the big business of pop stardom

and the overwhelming constraints of her family's expectations. Once thought of as being too bland and "nice," the Carpenters' standing in popular music has risen once again.

See also Rock and Popular Music Genres; Rock Music

For Further Reading

Gaar, Gillian G. *She's a Rebel: The History of Women in Rock and Roll*. Seattle: Seal Press, 1992.

O'Dair, Barbara. *Trouble Girls: The Rolling Stone Book of Women in Rock*. New York: Random House, 1992.

Warner, Jay. *Billboard's American Rock 'n' Roll in Review*. New York: Schirmer Books, 1997.

Lisa Dolinger

Carpenter, Mary-Chapin (1958–)

Singer-songwriter Mary-Chapin Carpenter initially aspired to a career in pop music. Although not influenced directly by country music during her childhood, she listened to folk-revival and folk-rock performers such as Judy Collins (b. 1939) and the Weavers, and she developed a love for acoustic genres. As a youngster Mary-Chapin taught herself to play guitar while accompanying phonograph records. She has continually honed her gift as a beautifully descriptive storyteller to become one of the country music industry's most well loved songwriters. Like her contemporary, Pam Tillis (b. 1957), Mary-Chapin suffered isolation and loneliness during her childhood years and countered that loneliness by spending many hours in her room playing the guitar, expressing herself in song.

Unlike other country performers, Carpenter did not spend decades trying to break into the music business. Born in Princeton, NJ, on 21 February 1958, she does not boast rural or agrarian roots,

Mary-Chapin Carpenter. *Photo courtesy of Globe Photos.*

and her family was not poor or uneducated. In fact, her rise to success has been surprisingly direct. Upon graduation from Brown University (1981) with a degree in American civilization, Carpenter worked as a coffeehouse singer in the Washington, DC, folk scene and as an arts organization's grant consultant. Her first recording, designed for sale locally at Washington, DC, shows, was heard by CBS Records executives, resulting in a 1985 recording contract and her 1987 debut album *Hometown Girl* (CK 40758). Although her first album built predominantly a cult following, her second release, *State of the Heart* (CK 44228), found wider favor with country audiences and radio station disc jockeys, and it established her as an artist with great promise for an enduring professional career.

Carpenter has consistently produced beautifully crafted stories set to music. The range of topics and emotions explored and celebrated through her writing and performance encompass a wide spectrum of human experience. Some stories are melancholy and touchingly personal; others explore topics of more global import. She portrays an image simultaneously wholesome and raucous: the girl-next-door juxtaposed with the sassy vixen. In this, she joins the growing list of women country artists who have effectively broken free from cultural constraints on women performers of earlier generations.

Mary-Chapin Carpenter has won numerous awards including the Academy of Country Music's Top New Female Vocalist honor in 1989, the Grammy for Best Female Country Vocal Performance annually from 1991 through 1994, the 1992 and 1993 Country Music Association's Female Vocalist of the Year honors, and 1994 Grammy Awards for Best Country Album and Best Country Song. She has expanded her activities to include writing and performing songs for motion pictures and Broadway shows. She is a published author who has written books for children and has essays included in edited works.

Paramount among the activities that define Mary-Chapin Carpenter as a significant personality within the music industry is her participation in humanitarian activities. She is a vocal supporter of numerous environmental, literacy, and social concerns, and proceeds from her children's books are donated to charities. She strongly supports women's issues, and has participated in United Nations Children's Fund concerts and in United Service Organization concerts for American troops in Bosnia, the Middle East, and the Persian Gulf.

See also Singer-Songwriter

For Further Reading

Bufwack, Mary A., and Robert K. Oermann. *Finding Her Voice: The Saga of Women in Country Music.* New York: Crown, 1993.

Elison, Curtis W. *Country Music Culture: From Hard Times to Heaven.* Jackson: University of Mississippi Press, 1995.

Amy Corin

Carr, Vikki (1941–)

Vikki Carr is one of the most successful Mexican American vocalists to date. She has headlined the world's most prestigious nightclubs in Las Vegas, New York, the Netherlands, Germany, Spain, France, England, Australia, and Japan. She joined Danny Kaye in a three-week tour of military bases in Vietnam, which she described as one of her more rewarding experiences. In 1972 she was honored as Singer of the Year by the American Guild of Variety Artists. She has great vocal control and can move quickly from one style into another. Supple tone and clear phrasing provide her with the tools to easily perform the popular standards of the 1940s and 1950s.

Born Florencia Bisenta de Casillas Martínez Cardona on 19 July 1941 in El Paso, TX, Carr is the eldest of seven children. She was raised in the San Gabriel Valley, the east portion of Los Angeles County. In high school, she began studying music and playing leading roles in the school's musical productions. Fol-

lowing graduation she was offered a job as a soloist with the Pepe Callahan Mexican-Irish Band and opened as "Carlita" at the Chi-Chi Club in Palm Springs. Following this initial public exposure in the early 1960s, she changed her stage name to Vikki Carr and signed a long-term contract with Liberty Records. Following a highly successful tour to Australia, with a hit record, "He's a Rebel," Carr joined the Ray Anthony television series as the featured vocalist.

Carr also has performed musical comedy, including such shows as *South Pacific*, *The Unsinkable Molly Brown*, and *I'm Getting My Act Together and Taking It on the Road*, and she has made numerous dramatic television appearances. In 1967 she performed for Queen Elizabeth II and the next year appeared in her own Vikki Carr Show at the London Palladium. Carr has performed for state dinners and other events at the White House. In 1990 she sang at the inauguration of the Richard M. Nixon Library, where Presidents Bush, Reagan, Ford, and Nixon were in attendance.

Carr has recorded over 50 best-selling albums in both English and Spanish. Her first appearance in her grandparents' native Mexico took place in 1972 at the Hotel Aristos in Mexico City. After subsequently hosting two Mexican television specials, she received the Visiting Entertainer of the Year Award. Since then, Carr's career has focused on singing in Mexico and the rest of Latin America. Since her recording of "Y el amor" in 1980, she has accumulated 14 Gold records for her albums recorded in Spanish, all on the CBS International label. She received a Grammy Award for the Mexican American category in 1986 for her album *Simplemente mujer* (Sony CD-80206). In 1989 the single "Mala suerte" from her album entitled *Esos hombres*

(Sony CD-80057) became a major hit throughout Latin America and the Hispanic areas of the United States. She was awarded another Grammy in 1992 in the Latin Pop category.

In 1971, with funds earned from a television commercial, Carr established the Vikki Carr Scholarship Foundation to award higher education scholarships to young Mexican Americans. In recognition of her many philanthropic endeavors, Carr received the *Los Angeles Times* Woman of the Year Award in 1970 and the Hispanic Women's Council Hispanic Woman of the Year Award in 1984. She has also received honorary doctorates from St. Edwards University and the University of San Diego.

See also Latin American Musicians; Multicultural Musics

For Further Reading

Loza, Steven. *Barrio Rhythm: Mexican American Music in Los Angeles.* Urbana and Chicago: University of Illinois Press, 1993.

Steve Loza

Carter, Betty (1929–1998)

Betty Carter, "Betty Bebop," a brilliant and uncompromising jazz singer, performed with jazz greats such as Lionel Hampton, Dizzy Gillespie, and Charlie Parker. Because she did not like to sing in a conventional, commercial manner, she did not record with many major labels. Rather, she formed her own label, Bet-Car, in 1970.

Carter was born Lillie Mae Jones on 16 May 1930 in Flint, MI. From childhood, music was her interest. At Midwestern High School in Detroit she played in the band and developed a consuming interest in bebop jazz. By the age of 16 she was going to nightclubs to listen to great jazz musicians, and occasionally she would sing with some of the leading bebop performers, including Dizzy Gillespie and Charlie Parker. She studied piano and music theory at the Detroit Conservatory of Music. At age 18, as "Lorraine Carter," she was hired and fired several times by Lionel Hampton. Hampton called her "Betty Bebop," a name she regretted. However, she kept the name "Betty" and began singing as "Betty Carter."

Using her strong musical training, she learned how to arrange music for Hampton's band and toured with that group from 1948 until 1957. In 1951 the band arrived in New York, bringing Carter to the center of bebop style. By 1957, when she left Hampton's band, she began singing in various New York City nightclubs, perfecting her highly original and "pure" approach to vocal jazz. Her style was patterned after horn players, rather than singers. Improvisation and scatting were her norm, and singing a standard tune as written was uncommon.

Two of the five albums she released in 1970, *The Audience with Betty Carter* (Verve 835684-2) and *Whatever Happened to Love* (Verve 835683-2) were nominated for Grammy Awards. In 1981 Bet-Car received an Indy award for the best independent recording label in the United States. She went on to receive another Grammy in 1988 for her album *Look What I've Got* (Verve 835661-2). She continued singing and serving as an advocate for jazz, and in 1997 she received a National Medal of Arts award. Betty Carter died on 26 September 1998 at her home in Brooklyn, NY.

See also Jazz

For Further Reading

Bourne, Michael. "Betty Carter: It's Not about Teaching. It's about Doing." *Down Beat* 16/12 (1994): 16–20.

Gourse, Leslie. "Betty Carter: Guru of 'Out'." In *Louis' Children: American Jazz Singers*, ed. Leslie Gourse. New York: William Morrow, 1984, 324–336.

Jones, James T., IV. "Betty Carter: Look What We've Got!" *Down Beat* 56/8 (1989): 24–27.

Monica J. Burdex

Carter, Mother Maybelle Addington (1909–1978)

Country music legend Maybelle Addington Carter was a driving force in the development of country music in the United States during the late 1920s and 1930s. Her unique style of guitar picking was copied for generations following her 1927 debut. First as a member of The Carter Family, and then as the matriarch of the Carter Sisters and Mother Maybelle, Maybelle Addington Carter remains one of the most highly regarded women in country music.

Carter was born on 10 May 1909 into a family of 10 children in the rural community of Nickelsville, VA. Music was an integral part of her experiences while growing up. Her mother, Margaret Addington, led the Fair Oak Methodist Church Women's Choir, where Maybelle learned gospel songs at a very early age. From her mother she learned traditional sentimental parlor songs and ballads as well. Both her sister and mother played banjo, which Maybelle also mastered, and she acquired skills on the autoharp and guitar while still quite young. During her childhood Maybelle and her sister Madge often amused themselves by playing music with their cousin Sara, and Maybelle, with her brothers, frequently played for local community square dances. With all of her musical abilities, however, it was Maybelle's self-taught guitar-playing style that ultimately became her trademark and influenced

Mother Maybelle Addington Carter. *Photo courtesy of Frank Driggs Collection.*

greatly the future development of country music.

Maybelle's professional career began as a member of The Carter Family, comprised of Maybelle, Alvin Pleasant (A. P.), and Sara Carter (1898–1979). The Carter Family broke new ground in the recording industry in August 1927 when 36-year-old A. P. drove his wife, their baby, and then-pregnant 18-year-old sister-in-law Maybelle to Bristol, TN, to participate in auditions for Victor Records. Ralph Peer, Victor A&R director, was impressed with the trio and immediately contracted the group to record for Victor. In the following seven years the association between The Carter Family and Victor Records produced recordings that defined the future direction of the country music industry.

The hallmark sound of The Carter

Family was realized by the combination of Sara's beautiful soprano voice supported by Maybelle's alto harmonies and A. P.'s occasional bass vocals, as well as Sara's musical accompaniment on autoharp or guitar, and Maybelle's guitar-picking style. Maybelle's guitar style, a technique in which she picked a melody on the guitar bass strings with her thumb while alternately strumming chords on the treble strings with brushing strokes from her fingers, became not only a signature of the Carter sound but the epitome of technique to be mastered by southern country guitarists.

Maybelle and Sara also paved the way for future generations of women in country music with their vocal style. Even though A. P. was the group's leader and did, in fact, find, rearrange, standardize, and copyright the mostly traditional British ballads, parlor tunes, and gospel songs recorded by the family, he often chose not to perform. It fell therefore to the two cousins to record consistently as a vocal duet in an era when women's music was almost exclusively performed at home, in the parlor, rather than in public venues. Their vocal style, carefully intertwined with the instrumental accompaniment, both rhythm and melodic riffs, essentially standardized the country song.

When The Carter Family broke up in 1943, Maybelle formed Mother Maybelle and the Carter Sisters with her daughters June (b. 1929), Helen (b. 1927), and Anita (b. 1933). By 1950 they had become mainstays on the Grand Ole Opry, where they remained for the next 17 years. Chet Atkins became the group's guitar player, and Mother Maybelle, with the second generation of the Carter Family, began performing with Johnny Cash, who eventually married daughter June in 1961. Mother Maybelle Carter died on 23 October 1978.

See also Cash, June Carter; Country Music; Grand Ole Opry

For Further Reading

Bufwack, Mary A., and Robert K. Oermann. *Finding Her Voice: The Saga of Women in Country Music*. New York: Crown, 1993.

Dew, Joan. *Singers and Sweethearts: The Women of Country Music*. Garden City, NY: Doubleday, 1977.

Tichi, Cecelia. *High Lonesome: The American Culture of Country Music*. Chapel Hill: University of North Carolina Press, 1994.

Amy Corin

Cash, June Carter (1929–)

June Carter Cash represents the second generation of successful women performers belonging to commercial country music's founding family, the Carter Family. Married to country music icon and singer-songwriter Johnny Cash, June has performed professionally since the age of 10. She is an accomplished comedienne, actress, instrumentalist, singer, producer, playwright, and published author with two autobiographical works, *Among My Klediments* (1979) and *From the Heart* (1987), to her credit.

The daughter of Carter Family matriarch Mother Maybelle Addington Carter and Maybelle's husband, Ezra, June was born on 23 June 1929 in Maces Springs, VA, two years after the Carter Family's auspicious 1927 recording sessions in Bristol, VA. In 1938 the Carter Family performed a series of broadcasts originating in Del Rio, TX, at radio station XERF. During their first season, Maybelle brought June's sister Anita (b. 1933), and her aunt Sara Carter (1898–1979) brought daughter Janette to work with the family. June and her 12-year-old sister, Helen (b. 1927), joined them the following year for their second season in Del Rio. During this period the sisters also recorded their own radio shows as a trio. One year later they gained further experience with the Carter Family during a series of performances at a radio station in Charlotte, NC.

When the original Carter Family disbanded in 1943 due, in no small part, to tensions created by Sara's divorce from A. P. Carter a decade earlier, Maybelle and her three daughters formed Mother Maybelle and the Carter Sisters. The all-woman band initially featured Maybelle's signature guitar style, June playing the autoharp, Anita the bass, and Helen the accordion. Although the women's fledgling act was undeniably lacking in sophistication at the onset, in time they became more polished performers. Helen became the most proficient instrumentalist, and Anita's beautiful soprano voice led the group vocally, but it was June who developed into the most competent entertainer.

After June's high school graduation in 1946, the women continued their rise to success through a sequence of appearances at ever more significant barn dance shows. In 1949 they moved to the Ozark Jubilee in Springfield, MO, where Mother Maybelle hired then unknown guitarist Chet Atkins to accompany them. In 1950 Mother Maybelle and the Carter Sisters became permanent members of Nashville's famed Grand Ole Opry.

In addition to her work with her family's singing group, June honed her acting skills in New York, studying at the Actors Studio with Elia Kazan. She performed on the *Gary Moore* and the *Jackie Gleason* television shows and, from 1969 to 1971, was seen weekly on ABC Television's *Johnny Cash Show*. Following that series, June has appeared in more than 30 television specials and in a dramatic leading role during an episode of *Dr. Quinn,*

Medicine Woman. Her songwriting credits include tunes now considered classic in the country music repertoire, including "Ring of Fire" co-written with Merle Kilgore. June Carter Cash has been honored with two Grammy Awards, in 1967 and 1970, for duet recordings with husband Johnny Cash. She has numerous recordings available, including songs and performances that appear on *The Carter Family* (Arhoolie 412), At San Quentin (CBS PCT-9827), and *The Man in Black: 1963–1969* (Bear Family 15588).

June Carter has married three times: the first, in 1952, to honky-tonk singer Carl Smith; the second to Rip Nix in 1960; and finally to country superstar Johnny Cash in 1968. Whereas the first two unions were brief, the marriage to Cash endured and established a country music dynasty. In addition to their overwhelming career successes, Carter and Cash have seen a number of their children become performers, claiming their birthright as members of country music's founding family.

See also Country Music; Grand Ole Opry; Songwriter

For Further Reading

Cash, June Carter. *Among My Klediments*. Grand Rapids, MI: Zondervan Pub. House [1979], 1981.

———. *From the Heart*. New York: Prentice-Hall, 1987.

Elison, Curtis W. *Country Music Culture: From Hard Times to Heaven*. Jackson: University of Mississippi Press, 1995.

Amy Corin

Casterton, Elizabeth (1877– 1946)

Elizabeth Casterton was a nationally prominent leader in music education in the early 1900s. While music supervisor for the Bay City, MI, schools, she served three summers on the faculty of the American Institute of Normal Schools in Boston (1906–1908). From 1907–1916 she took the position of music supervisor in Rochester, NY, and from 1909 to 1915 she sat on the Board of Directors of the Music Supervisors National Conference (MSNC)—later known as the Music Educators National Conference (MENC). In 1914 she served as the Conference president.

Casterton was born in 1877 in Parnanssus, PA. Little is known about her life before she took on leadership in music education. Casterton was outspoken in her plea to correlate music with other branches of the school curriculum. She asked, "Does the pupil get all the benefits to be obtained when music is in a separate class period? Wouldn't each course be enhanced by a more intimate association?" (Casterton, 1905). She was one of the scrutinizing corps of teachers at the turn of the century that observed children could read notes but could not make music. In her public addresses she called for the profession to move away from the then-prevalent emphasis on sight-reading and progress toward valuing the artistic possibilities of song.

Casterton also advocated creating musical sociological learning opportunities through teaching children folk musics of various European heritages. But above all else, she strongly supported teaching and cultivating contemporary U.S. works, stating, "Since we are a music loving nation we must have American Music" (Music Supervisors National Conference, 1914).

In 1915 she retired from the music profession, leaving behind her national prominence to marry John MacDonell of Medina, NY. However, while she raised her two children she remained on the advisory council of the MSNC and contin-

ued to take an active part in the musical life of her community. In this era before women's rights, Casterton had braved the hardships of national travel to help shape the direction of music education in the United States. Elizabeth Casterton died on 4 November 1946 at age 69.

See also Music Education

For Further Reading

Casterton, Elizabeth. "Correlation of Music with Other Branches of the Curriculum." *School Music Monthly* 5 (1905): 24–28.
MENC Historical Center. *Elizabeth Casterton File.* College Park: University of Maryland Performing Arts Library.

Kilissa M. Cissoko

Center for Women in Music

Created in 1993 at New York University (NYU), the Center for Women in Music (CWIM) presents concerts featuring women composers, sponsors lectures and panel discussions featuring prominent women musicians, and serves as a clearinghouse for information on women musicians. On 24 April 1993, during discussions at the Women in Music Conference, the participants developed a proposal to promote and support women in music. Featured guests, panelists, and performers at the conference included Claudette Sorel (1932–1999), Deborah Borda, Edith Borroff (b. 1924), Doriot Anthony Dwyer (b. 1922), Nancy Clarke, Virginia Eskin, and Catherine French. Linda Kernohan, composer, pianist, and master's candidate at NYU, served as co-ordinator of CWIM.

In 1994–1995, "The Year of the Conductor," CWIM recognized three outstanding women: Judy Collins (b. 1939), for co-directing a film about Antonia Brico (1902–1989), the first significant woman conductor in the United States; JoAnn Falletta (b. 1954), conductor of the Louisville Philharmonic and Bay Area Women's Philharmonic; and Eve Queler (b. 1936), a conductor known for presenting rarely performed operas.

The CWIM established an Internet database and published the first *Center for Women in Music Newsletter* in 1995. Organization awards and lectures promoting women in music continued throughout the 1990s. In 1996 composer Chen Yi (b. 1953) was awarded $5,000. In 1998 David Dubal, professor at the Juilliard and Manhattan Schools of Music, presented a program entitled "Lionesses of the Keyboard." And New York City mayor Rudolph Giuliani proclaimed 7 April 1998 as "Women in Music Day." A nationwide choral composition competition was organized in 1998; the two winners received cash awards and performances. The compositions were published by Marks Music and distributed by Hal Leonard Company. In 1999 the Board of Directors included Berge Avedisian and Walter Kilmer. Claudette Sorel served as president until her death in 1999.

See also Libraries and Archives

For Further Reading

CWIM [Center for Women in Music] Newsletter, Spring 1995.

"CWIM Press Release, June 1995." *IAWM [International Alliance for Women in Music] Journal* (June 1995).

Speciale, Rosalie. "World Loses Great Artist and Teacher . . . Fraternity Loses Honored Member." *Triangle of Mu Phi Epsilon* 93/4 (Winter 1999–2000): 12–13.

Mary Etta Hobbs

Channing, Carol (1921–)

Carol Channing, the actress-singer whose career has spanned over half a century, made her stage debut in 1941 in *No for an Answer*. Her voice is one of the most

Carol Channing in her role as Dolly Gallagher Levi in *Hello Dolly!* Photo courtesy of *Jay Thompson/Globe Photos*.

distinctive in the American musical theater. This, taken with her immense smile, wide-open eyes, and blonde hair, has made her one of the most easily recognizable and most treasured of all Broadway icons. Her raspy-voice soubrette characters usually reveal a person who is more intelligent and thoughtful than the audience would first believe. After several smaller roles and a nightclub career, she made her Broadway debut in the 1948 revue *Lend an Ear*. This led to her being cast as Lorelei Lee in *Gentlemen Prefer Blondes* (CBS 48013), providing her with the opportunity to introduce such songs as "I'm Just a Little Girl from Little Rock" and the colossally successful "Diamonds Are a Girl's Best Friend." She succeeded Rosalind Russell in the role of Ruth Sherwood in *Wonderful Town* (1953), and her nightclub-act-turned-one-woman show *Show Girl* reached Broadway in 1961.

Born in Seattle, WA, on 31 January 1921, Channing began her career as a soprano but evolved into a true Broadway belter. Channing is best known for the role of Dolly Gallagher Levi in *Hello, Dolly!* (RCA 3814-2-RG). She won both a Tony Award and the *Variety* Drama Critics Award for her performance as the effervescent matchmaker whose songs included "So Long, Dearie," "Before the Parade Passes By," and the show's immortal title song. She received a special Tony Award in 1968. In 1973 she reprised the role of Lorelei Lee on Broadway in *Lorelei* (subtitled "Gentlemen Still Prefer Blondes"), a revised version of the earlier musical. Channing re-created the title role of *Hello, Dolly!* in the show's 1994 Broadway revival, 30 years after its premiere (the 30th anniversary cast recording is available on Varese 5557). To quote a line from the title song, Channing, like Dolly, was "still going strong." She received a second special Tony Award, this one for Lifetime Achievement, in 1995.

Channing's success on stage made her a popular guest on various television game and talk shows, including *Password*, *To Tell the Truth*, the *Merv Griffin Show*, and the *Ed Sullivan Show*. She appeared in several films, the most important of which was *Thoroughly Modern Millie* (1967). Her co-stars in the film included Julie Andrews and Mary Tyler Moore.

See also Musical Theater

For Further Reading

Frommer, Myrna Katz, and Harvey Frommer. *It Happened on Broadway: An Oral History of the Great White Way*. New York: Harcourt, Brace, 1998.

Ramczyk, Suzanne Mary. "A Performance Demands Analysis of Six Major Female Roles of the American Musical Theatre." Ph.D. diss., University of Oregon, 1986.

William A. Everett

Chapman, Tracy (1964–)

Singer-songwriter Tracy Chapman is given almost universal praise for her vocal style, which has been described as husky, sturdy, emotional, and unwavering in performance. Her lyrics have been criticized at times for being excessively preachy, but it is the political content of her songs that has helped her retain a loyal following.

Born on 20 March 1964, Chapman was raised primarily by her mother in Cleveland, OH. By the time she attended high school in Connecticut, she was writing her own songs and accompanying herself on guitar. In the early 1980s she began performing at folk venues in Boston while attending Tufts University. Chapman signed her first record contract after being brought to Elektra's attention by a classmate's father who was involved in the music publishing business.

In 1988 Tracy Chapman's self-titled debut album (Elektra 60774-2) brought her song writing to a mass audience. The single, "Fast Car," which was a commentary on the economics of the times, made it to the Top 10. The success of the album and the single was aided by Chapman's appearance at a concert celebrating Nelson Mandela's 70th birthday. Her involvement in South African politics was also apparent in her second album, *Crossroads* (Elektra 60888-2), which featured "Freedom Now." Chapman's third release, *New Beginning* (Elektra 61850), almost duplicated the commercial success of her debut album. The single from *New Beginning* "Give Me One Reason" is an

Tracy Chapman. *Photo courtesy of Mark Allan/Globe Photos.*

unadorned 12-bar blues. Despite the blues form's immeasurable influence on popular music at the end of the twentieth century, it was startling to hear such a stripped-down blues amid the numerous other trends in contemporary music. Chapman's later album, *Telling Stories* (Elektra/Asylum 62478), continued to mix songs that address personal struggles with songs that express her trademark themes of political and social concern.

See also Singer-Songwriter

For Further Reading

Gaar, Gillian G. *She's a Rebel: The History of Women in Rock and Roll.* Seattle, WA: Seal Press, 1992.

O'Dair, Barbara (ed.). *Trouble Girls: The Rolling Stone Book of Women in Rock.* New York: Random House, 1997.

Garth Alper

Chen Yi (1953–)

Composer Chen Yi is one of the most prolific and highly respected composers living in the United States. In 1986 she became the first woman to receive the M.A. degree in composition in mainland China. She has served as composer-in-residence for many ensembles, including Chanticleer and the Women's Philharmonic. She blends Chinese and Western traditions and techniques in her compositional style.

Born on 4 April 1953 in Guangzhou, China, Chen began violin and piano studies at the age of three. During the height of the Cultural Revolution in 1968, Chen was sent to the countryside for two years to do forced labor. She took her violin in hopes of continuing her studies and often entertained the local peasants and her colleagues with violin transcriptions of revolutionary folk songs. It was during this period that she became interested in Chinese folk and traditional musics. She continued practicing her Western art music repertoire in secret, as Western music was deemed anti-revolutionary during those years and she faced dire consequences if discovered. She returned to Guangzhou at age 17 and served as concertmaster of and composer for the local Beijing Opera troupe.

In 1977 Chen was admitted to the Central Conservatory of Music in Beijing, where she studied composition with Wu Zu-Qiang and British visiting professor Alexander Goehr. She continued studying the violin at the Central Conservatory with Lin Yao-Ji and began a systematic study of Chinese traditional music and music theory. When she received her M.A. (1986), she was honored by the Chinese Musicians Association, the Central Conservatory of Music, Ra-

Chen Yi (left) and percussionist Evelyn Glennie rehearse Chen Yi's Percussion Concerto for its world premiere in Singapore in March 1999. *Photo by Zho Long.*

dio Beijing, and CCTV with an entire program devoted to her orchestral works. In 1986 Chen was awarded a fellowship to study composition with Chou Wen-Chung and Mario Davidovsky at Columbia University in the United States. She received her D.M.A. with distinction (1993). In that year Chen was appointed, through the Meet the Composer program, to a three-year term as composer-in-residence for the Women's Philharmonic orchestra, Chanticleer vocal ensemble, and the Aptos Creative Arts Programs in San Francisco. Upon completion of her term, she joined the composition faculty of Peabody Conservatory. In 1998 Chen joined the faculty of the University of Missouri, Kansas City, as the Cravens/Milsap/Missouri

distinguished professor in composition. In December 2000, Chen Yi received the second Charles Ives Living Prize from the American Academy of Arts and Letters. This award (worth $225,000) is the largest cash prize available to a living composer and will allow Chen to dedicate the next three years to only composing.

Chen's compositions are modernist approaches to the "essence" and spirit of Chinese and Western musics and ideas. Examples of her compositions include *Duo Ye No. 2, Ge Xu* ("Antiphony"), *Piano Concerto*, and *Second Symphony*, which make use of pentatonic scales and musics of Chinese minority cultures in the Western orchestral idiom. Her *Chinese Myth Cantata for Male Choir and Orchestra* is based on three Chinese creation myths: Pan Gu, Nu Wa, and the Weaver Maiden and the Cowherd. Many of these compositions appear on the compact disc recording of *The Music of Chen Yi* (NA090). To date 20 of her compositions have been recorded by major classical music labels in the United States, China, and Europe.

Chen Yi has received fellowships and awards from such organizations as the American Academy of Arts and Letters; the National Endowment for the Arts; the Ford, Rockefeller, Guggenheim, Fromm, Civitella Ranieri, and Koussevitzky Foundations; and Chamber Music America. Her honors include a first prize from the Chinese National Composition Competition, the Lili Boulanger Award, one Sorel Medal, the Albert Award, and the Eddie Medora King Composition Prize.

See also Asian American Music

For Further Reading

Daines, Matthew. "Finding Her Way to the Top of Two Worlds." *New York Times* Late Edition (9 June 1996): 2:32.

Kosman, Joshua. "Classical Convergence: Composer Chen Yi's Music Merges Modern with Traditional, East with West." *San Francisco Chronicle* (9 June 1996), Sunday Edition Notebook: 36.

Cynthia Wong

Cher (1946–)

As a solo singing artist and with her husbands, Cher has embraced not only pop and rock but also dance, folk-pop, gospel, rhythm and blues, adult contemporary, popular standards, and even Latin music. Though her voice itself is not often praised, Cher's singular personality, unique delivery, and her ease with many genres and subgenres of pop and rock

serve as the foundation of her remarkable longevity.

Born Cherilyn Sarkasian LaPier in El Centro, CA, on 20 May 1946, Cher grew up fatherless. She fell in love with musician Salvatore "Sonny" Bono when she was 16 years old, and their relationship was a platonic one at first. Bono was record producer Phil Spector's protégé, and Cher began following him to work at Spector's legendary Gold Star Studios. She ended up working with Spector as a back-up singer for groups like the Ronettes and the Righteous Brothers while still in her teens.

Cher's relationship with Sonny matured into an artistic as well as a romantic partnership, and they became one of the most popular acts of the mid-1960s, with hits such as "The Beat Goes On" and "I Got You, Babe." Cher also hit the pop charts on her own with "You Better Sit Down, Kids" and "Bang, Bang (My Baby Shot Me Down)." After trouble with the Internal Revenue Service and a couple of movie flops (*Good Times* [1967] and *Chastity* [1969]), they lost their money, stopped producing hits, and were forced to play supper clubs and open for other more popular entertainers.

Cher's acid wit and the couple's natural chemistry propelled them toward their CBS television series, of the early 1970s, *The Sonny and Cher Comedy Hour*. Cher began to chart again as a solo performer, as well as with Sonny. This time her Native American heritage and dark intensity were reflected in her material, including the number-one hits "Gypsies, Tramps and Thieves" (*Gypsies, Tramps and Thieves*, Movie Play 74017), "Dark Lady" (*Dark Lady*, MCA 2113), and "Half Breed" (*Half Breed* MCA MCAD 20210).

In 1974 Sonny and Cher's marriage, already in distress, crumbled completely;

and only days after their 1975 divorce, Cher married rock musician Gregg Allman. After the failure of both a reunion show with Sonny and her own television show *Cher*, her music career took a turn for the worse. During this difficult time Cher kept busy as a sold-out performer in Las Vegas and Atlantic City, and in the early 1980s she began pursuing her long-delayed acting career.

She won Best Actress at the Cannes Film Festival for her performance in *Mask* (1985) and an Academy Award as Best Actress for *Moonstruck* (1987). She also had one of her most spectacular solo recording successes to date with her 1989 release *Heart of Stone* (Geffen 2-24239), which included the hits "Just Like Jesse James" and "If I Could Turn Back Time." In February 2000, after nearly 40 years in the music business, she received her first Grammy Award, winning for her omnipresent global dance hit "Believe" (*Believe*, Warner Brothers 47121) in the Best Dance Recording category.

See also Rock and Popular Music Genres; Rock Music

For Further Reading

Cher, and Jeff Coplon. *The First Time*. New York: Pocket Books, 1998.

Rees, Dafydd, and Luke Crampton. *VH1 Rock Stars Encyclopedia*. New York: DK Publishing, 1999.

Romanowski, Patricia, and Holly George-Warren (eds.). *Rolling Stone Encyclopedia of Rock and Roll*. New York: Rolling Stone Press, 1995.

Leslie Stratyner

Children's Choir

The American children's choir movement, defined as children with treble voices ages eight through 16, was developed during the late 1970s by visionary conductors and educators, predominantly women, who advocated quality choral education for young singers. They sought increased educational opportunities for teachers and conductors who worked with children; better choral education programs in the schools; increased singing opportunities for children in community, school, and church choirs; and the development of quality resources in printed and audio format.

The history of children's choirs in the United States is somewhat limited. Few community-based children's choirs existed in the United States until the 1980s. Of those in existence, most were centered in large cities and developed mid-century. The most notable of these choirs included the Chicago Children's Choir founded in 1956, the Texas Girls' Choir (Fort Worth, TX) founded in 1962, Glen Ellyn Children's Chorus (Chicago, IL) founded in 1965, Northwest Girlchoir (Seattle, WA) founded in 1972, and the Young Singers of Callanwolde (Atlanta, GA) founded in 1975. Other notable youth choirs of long-standing tradition in the United States were predominantly boy choirs under the leadership of male conductors who frequently adopted the European model of choral training. Prior to the formation of the significant choirs mentioned, the work of Helen Kemp (b. 1918) inspired people who worked with young singers beginning in the 1950s.

During the 1960s many public school choirs existed in elementary and junior high schools throughout America. Events of the 1970s resulted in numerous music education programs falling prey to budget cuts. Elimination of music in a "back to basics" emphasis of education and a movement toward arts-related programs caused a great decline in choral education programs. In many places school choirs existed only where strong teachers advocated for their continuation. Often chorus rehearsals were relegated to before or after school hours, during lunchtime, or were offered in direct conflict with other activities.

As a result of the decline of singing in the schools, community-based choirs were formed where children could continue to study, learn, and perform choral music. Numerous choirs were formed in the late 1970s and early 1980s, such as the Children's Chorus of Maryland, the Colorado Children's Choir, Red River Boy Choir, Pueri/Puellae Cantores at the University of Nebraska, Indiana University Children's Choir, Duquesne University Festival Children's Chorus, the Syracuse Children's Chorus, Seattle Girls' Choir, and the St. Louis Children's Choir.

The development of American children's choirs was greatly influenced by the formation of the American Choral Directors Association (ACDA) National Committee on Children's Choirs under the encouragement of Colleen Kirk, ACDA national president and music educator. Kirk influenced many emerging leaders of the children's choir movement, including Doreen Rao (b. 1950), Mitzi Groom, and Lynn Gackle. Other organizations that have influenced teachers and conductors include the Organization of Kodály Educators (OAKE), the Music Educators National Conference (MENC), and the Choristers Guild. At the present time Chorus America has provided additional leadership related to the organizational structure, management, and artistic visibility of children's choirs.

In 1981 under the leadership of Doreen Rao, children's choirs became a recognized area in the Repertoire and Standards structure of the ACDA. The first meeting of the National Committee on Children's Choirs officially started what would later become a thriving choral movement in the United States. Rao chaired the ACDA National Committee on Children's Choirs from 1981 to 1988. Subsequent national chairs included Barbara Tagg (1988–1995), Debbie Mello (1995–1998), and Rebecca Rottsolk (1998–).

The rapid growth of the children's choir movement was guided in part by the strong leadership of the ACDA National Committee on Children's Choirs. The committee provided the organization with visionary ideas about children's singing. They advocated for the development of printed resources and established standards of artistic excellence. The structure of Repertoire and Standards in ACDA allowed information to be dispersed through the local, state, division, and national conventions and publications. Fifty state chairs were appointed to assist with the long-term and short-term goals of the committee. The ACDA National Committee on Children's Choirs was responsible for many historic firsts in the organization. In 1983 the committee introduced the honors choir concept to ACDA. In 1989 they introduced the first consortium choir for an Interest Session combining three outstanding children's choirs that were used as a demonstration choir with a record 1,000 people attending. In 1994 the first elementary school choir performed with orchestra at an ACDA national convention. The Chevy Chase Elementary School Chorus (Joan Gregoryk, director) sang in a performance of *Carmina Burana* with the National Symphony Orchestra. At the same convention the first research poster session was held; it was devoted to the topic of children's choirs.

Many professional publications, including the *Kodály Envoy, Orff Echoes*, and the *Music Educators Journal*, were increasing the number of articles devoted to children's choir topics. In 1989 the first issue of the *Choral Journal* devoted to a single Repertoire and Standards committee area appeared; Doreen Rao served as guest editor. In 1993 a second issue was published with Barbara Tagg and Linda Ferreira as guest editors. The Music Educators National Conference and ACDA undertook a joint project in 1990 that resulted in publication of *Choral Music for Children: An Annotated List*. Contributors under the leadership of Doreen Rao included Linda Baupre, Nancy Boone, Mary Goetze (b. 1943), and Joan Gregoryk.

American children's choirs first appeared on the stage of Carnegie Hall in 1990. Nine choirs participated in this international event: Syracuse Children's Chorus, Amadeus Children's Choir, Los Angeles Children's Choir, St. Louis Children's Choir, Red River Boy Choir, Northwest Girlchoir, Winnipeg Mennonite Children's Choir, Vox Aurea, and the Indianapolis Children's Choir. Participating choirs sang under their own director and in a massed choir under the direction of Doreen Rao.

Through increased performances by children's choirs at national conventions, many composers became aware of the artistic capability of children during the 1980s and 1990s. Published women composers writing for children's voices during the 1980s included Betty Bertaux, Carolee Curtright, Lori-Anne Dolloff, Victoria Ebel-Sabo, Mary Goetze (b. 1943), Crystal LaPoint, Libby Larsen (b. 1950), Nancy Telfer, and Ruth Watson Henderson.

Technology was changing during this time as well. During the early 1980s self-produced cassette tapes of children's choirs were available on a very limited basis for national distribution. Compact discs were beginning to become more widely available. By 1993 quality recordings in compact disc format were more readily available in national retail markets from such choirs as the Toronto Children's Chorus, Glen Ellyn Children's Chorus, the San Francisco Girls Chorus, and the Chevy Chase Elementary School Chorus recorded with the National Symphony Orchestra. Since that time, many fine recordings of children's choirs have been nationally produced. With the increased availability of high-quality recordings, broadcasts of outstanding children's choirs have been heard on National Public Radio's *Performance Today* and *The First Art*. Indeed, American children's choirs have been broadcast throughout the world on radio and television.

During the 1980s the music publishing industry took note of the growing children's choir movement. Anne Schelleng of Boosey and Hawkes was one of the first women leaders in the field advocating for quality music for young singers in published format. She states, "We as publishers have contributed to this movement through a rapid increase in the amount of new repertoire available. At the same time, the higher standard in quality literature for treble voices has become the criterion by which conductors and teachers base their curricula" (Tagg, 7). Other outstanding women in publishing who were advocates for the publication of quality repertoire for treble singers included Susan Brailove (Oxford University Press) and Judith Tischler (Transcontinental Music Publishers). Major publishers in addition to Boosey and Hawkes, which provided quality music for reading sessions at ACDA conventions, included Walton Music, Lawson Gould Music Publishers, E. C. Schirmer,

G. Schirmer, earthsongs, and others. Newer publishing houses include Alliance Music Publications and Morning Star Music Publishers.

Few festivals devoted to children's choirs in the United States existed at the beginning of the children's choir movement. By 1993, 10 festivals were listed in the *Choral Journal* specific to children's choirs, several of which were located in the United States. In 1994 the first World Honors Children's Choir was held for the International Society of Music Education (ISME) World Conference in Tampa, FL. The 1993 ACDA National Honors Choir became the core of this first world children's choir made up of singers from England, Canada, Finland, and the United States. Since that time numerous festivals for young singers have continued to develop across America and throughout the world.

See also Choral Education; Music Education

For Further Reading

Rao, Doreen. "Children and Choral Music in ACDA: The Past and the Present, the Challenge and the Future." *Choral Journal* 29/8 (March 1989): 6–14.

Schelleng, Anne L. "A Perspective from a Publisher." *Choral Journal* 33/8 (March 1993): 23.

Tagg, Barbara. "Building the American Children's Choir Tradition." *Choral Journal* 33/8 (March 1993): 7–9.

Tagg, Barbara, and Linda Ferreira (eds.). "Focus: Repertoire—Selected Literature for Children's Choirs." *Choral Journal* 33/8 (March 1993): 41–54.

Barbara Tagg

Chilly Climate

"Chilly climate" is the phrase used by Bernice Sandler and others at the Project on the Status and Education of Women of the Association of American Colleges to describe the discouraging environment for women students, faculty members, and administrators on American college and university campuses. Many people believe that discrimination ended in the 1960s and 1970s with laws and other measures codifying women's rights to equal pay and equal access to education and employment. Women enrolled in higher education in increasing numbers and are now the majority of students in many areas, including music. Many women hold faculty positions, at least at the lower levels, and most campuses have one or two highly placed women administrators. Women are treated pleasantly by men. Yet discriminatory attitudes persist. Moreover, although the campus climate has been researchers' principal concern, women in music find it a chilly climate elsewhere as well.

The Classroom Climate: A Chilly One for Women? (1982) reports several concerns: the continuing low enrollment of women in traditionally male-dominated fields; the fact that women undergraduates feel less confident about their preparation for graduate school than do men attending the same institution; and the surprising decline in academic and career aspirations experienced by many women students during their college years.

Many factors contribute to the chilly climate, including the disproportionate number of male faculty, faculty behavior that discourages women from classroom participation, and faculty members' use of sexist humor and disparaging comments about women as a group. The report describes how both men and women faculty, even those most concerned about sex discrimination, may inadvertently communicate to their students preconceptions about abilities, professional behaviors, career directions, and personal goals that are based on sex rather than on individual interest and ability.

Women students are less likely to be called upon directly than students who are men, they are interrupted more often, and their questions and comments are likely to receive less response. Moreover, many of the problems experienced by women students generally are often exacerbated in the case of minority women and older women. Patterns of speech valued in higher education, such as highly assertive remarks and competitive interchanges, are more often found among men than among women speakers.

The Campus Climate Revisited: Chilly for Women Faculty, Administrators, and Graduate Students (1986) analyzes the subtle ways in which women at all professional levels are made to know that they are not quite first-class citizens. Based on an examination of the extensive literature on the subject and numerous anecdotes reported during investigators' campus visits, the report discusses common behaviors that create a chilly professional climate; the report features sections such as "Collegiality: Can a Woman Be 'One of the Boys'?," "Attractiveness and Sexuality," "Sexual Harassment," "Humor: Why Can't a Woman Take a Joke Like a Man?," "Men's and Women's Communication Styles—Another Double Bind," and "Minority Women on Campus—An Endangered Species." The report includes numerous recommendations for change, an institutional self-evaluation checklist, suggestions for a campus workshop, and a list of resources.

See also Gender Issues

For Further Reading

Hall, Roberta M., and Bernice R. Sandler. *The Classroom Climate: A Chilly One for Women?* Washington, DC: Association of American Colleges, Project on the Status and Education of Women, 1982.

Katz, S. Montana, and Veronica J. Vieland. *Get Smart: What You Should Know (But Won't Learn in Class) about Sexual Harassment and Sex Discrimination*, 2d ed. New York: Feminist Press at the City University of New York, 1993.

Sandler, Bernice R., and Roberta M. Hall. *The Campus Climate Revisited: Chilly for Women Faculty, Administrators, and Graduate Students*. Washington, DC: Association of American Colleges, Project on the Status and Education of Women, 1986.

Deborah Hayes

Choral Education

The tradition of choral education in America has its roots in the singing schools beginning in 1770. These singing schools were made up of approximately 50 students and were in session from one to three months. They met in churches, taverns, or meeting houses. Pupils were taught to sing in parts and to read music. Attention was given to vocal production, style of performance, and deportment. A public performance was given at the end of the school term. Singing schools led to choral societies, which proliferated on the East Coast in particular. Choral societies were important to the development of American choral music because they set high standards for all musicians. They became associated with academic institutions during the second half of the nineteenth century. The Oberlin Musical Union, the University Choral Union of the University of Michigan, and the Madison Choral Union of the University of Wisconsin were considered important choral societies.

In the early twentieth century, the *a cappella* choir came into vogue. The St. Olaf Lutheran Choir, founded in 1912 with F. Melius Christansen as the conductor, set the standards that became the performance practices of the *a cappella* tradition in senior high schools and colleges throughout the United States. After the 1930s, state organizations began to promote excellence in choral singing by sponsoring contests, festivals, and honor choirs at local and state levels.

In the 1940s the mainstream of American choral music began to move away from the *a cappella* ideal toward a new emphasis on the integrity of the musical score, a varied concept of choral tone, and a higher level of formal training for choral music educators. Robert Shaw became an influential leader in the field of choral music. Shaw developed a uniquely personal and intensive approach to the structural and contextual score analysis of choral masterpieces. He believed there was a distinctly different choral concept of sound based on the different style periods and composers. Shaw emphasized performances of extended choral compositions.

The launching of the Sputnik satellite by the Soviet Union in 1957 inaugurated the era of curricular reform in the United States. There grew a new urgency to the considerations of the place of choral music in the school curriculum. Projects and seminars including the Young Composers Project, Yale Seminar, Contemporary Music Project, and Tanglewood Symposium clearly articulated a program of comprehensive musicianship.

The first choral music experience in contemporary American schools occurs in the elementary general music classrooms. The junior high and middle school choral program follows. The secondary ensemble possibilities are continued or expanded at the high school level. The typical choral music program at the high school level has both select (auditioned) and non-select (non-auditioned) choirs. Sometimes these ensembles fit into the model of a beginning choir and an advanced choir. In a beginning choir the students learn how to read music, develop basic musicianship, and master the fundamental principles of proper choral vocal techniques. This beginning choir, usually made up of ninth or tenth graders, contains a variety of voices at different stages of maturity. Proper voice classification is essential to successful singing with students. A variety of repertoire is performed, and public performances are an integral part of the program.

The advanced choir (usually 11th and 12th grades) has more mature voices with extensive training. Students continue to develop proper choral technique and sight-reading skills. The advanced choir usually performs a varied repertoire from traditional Western-style periods to non-Western and contemporary. Within the last two decades multicultural music has become an important part of the repertoire as the world becomes interconnected along with the heightened interest in celebrating the diversity of cultures. The African American spiritual also is a vital part of the standard repertoire as a continuation of the folk tradition being passed from one generation to another.

A chamber ensemble, varying from four to 24 members, is frequently a part of a high school choral program. This ensemble provides an opportunity for the advanced student to be further trained and challenged. Typically the ensemble performs music from all historical periods; however, the ensemble may also specialize in music of the Renaissance and only perform madrigals.

The swing choir, show choir, and vocal jazz ensemble are all relatively new ensembles in the high school choral program, each with a specific type of repertoire. These ensembles are typically chamber ensembles. The swing choir is the oldest of the three. Beginning in the 1940s, groups varying from 12 to 16 students would sing Broadway show tunes and popular numbers. Choreography was added in the 1960s, with professional models being the Johnny Mann Singers and Fred Waring and the Pennsylvanians. An instrumental combo was added in the 1970s, and costumes became a part of the presentation. The term "swing" began to disappear in the 1980s when the "show choir" became more prominent. In the show choir movement, choreography was emphasized, along with staging and lighting. However, the repertoire continued to be the variety of popular tunes, Broadway tunes, and contemporary songs made famous by groups such as the King's Singers and the New Swingle Singers.

The vocal jazz ensemble has educational roots rather than the professional roots of the swing and show choirs. The vocal jazz styles developed from the African American culture and evolved from the instrumental jazz band. The first vocal jazz ensembles appeared in the Northwest in the 1960s. Improvisation, "scat" syllables, and syncopated rhythms characterize this style of singing. Vocal jazz ensembles place the emphasis on the vocal sound rather than on the visual aspects of the other two contemporary ensembles. Ensembles are frequently amplified and use instrumental jazz combo groups. Quite often, these ensembles are larger than the swing and show choir ensembles.

There are numerous gender issues that accompany choral practices and policies. In most choral programs girls outnumber boys 3:1, and because boys are rare commodities they are afforded numerous privileges for which girls have to compete fiercely. When auditioning for choirs, boys are almost always guaranteed positions because of their scarcity. However, because choral directors limit themselves to balanced mixed-voice ensembles, girls' membership may be limited to the number of available boys. For example, 112 sopranos, 65 altos, 23 basses, and 15 tenors audition for an honor choir that will take only 10 of each voice type (O'Toole, 1998). Therefore, 91 percent of the sopranos and 84 percent of the altos will not be accepted into the choir, whereas only 55 percent of the basses and 30 percent of the tenors will be rejected. Administrators, teachers, parents, and students rarely examine these numbers and question these policies; they accept the limitations girls experience because they are the majority.

Girls who do not pass the auditions to be placed in the more select ensembles are frequently placed in women's choirs, which have become professionally known as the "dumping ground." This scenario holds true for school choirs, state honor choirs, and summer choral camp programs. Further problems arise in these competitive mixed-voice choirs in that the girls, because of the competition, are usually more talented and focused than the boys. This means that the girls' education is limited by the abilities of the male singers.

Choral practices are steeped in sexist beliefs that have become professional common sense. For example, boys are encouraged to develop the full extent of their ranges (falsetto to bass) and can perform most choral repertoire without women, as exemplified by the popular all-male groups the King's Singers and Chanticleer. However, girls are limited to appropriately feminine ranges, namely, the higher registers. Although there are professional women singers with low, appealing voices, they often exist only in jazz or popular music. The choral profession in general does not acknowledge this lower range as appropriate for women. Finally, the vast majority of repertoire written for mixed-voice and women's choirs is written by composers who are men, from men's perspective, and about men's experiences. This suggests to women singers that only men compose and only men's experiences are worth singing about.

Several women have played influential roles in the successes in choral education in America. Charlene Archibeque and Sandra Willetts are choral conductors at the collegiate level and are considered to be the top in their field. Janet Funderburk-Galvan is known for her work with children's choirs and women's choirs. Tamara Brooks is respected for her championing of contemporary choral music. Doreen Rao (b. 1950) and Jean Ashworth have contributed extensively to the field of children's choirs. Patti Hennings is known for her work with new music for treble voices. Constantina Tsoulanos is a frequent festival conductor and is an English diction specialist.

See also Music Education

For Further Reading

Hoffer, Charles. *Teaching Music in the Secondary Schools*, 4th ed. Belmont, CA: Wadsworth Publishing, 1991.
O'Toole, Patricia. "A Missing Chapter from Choral Methods Books: How Choirs Neglect Girls." *Choral Journal* 39/5 (1998): 9–32.
Roach, Donald. *Complete Secondary Choral Music Guide*. West Nyack, NY: Parker Publishing, 1989.
Roe, Paul. *Choral Music Education*. Englewood Cliffs, NJ: Prentice-Hall, 1983.

Marla Butke

Church Music

Although women have been active in church music, that is, music used to accompany religious services and functions, since the turn of the twentieth century, early leaders of the field were primarily men. At the beginning of the century, church music consisted mainly of choir and organ music. Much of the music was from the "classical masters" of the past. Congregational singing included mainly hymns based on ancient tunes and newly composed tunes. Almost all of this music developed from the European models adopted and adapted by American composers. By the 1960s there was a strong movement away from many of the more traditional church music forms. Folk and popular styles of music were introduced into the worship service. Ethnically diverse hymns and other musics were included, and many familiar hymns were reworded to correct gender-specific wording.

The 1990s saw the introduction of many new hymnals in most denominations. These new hymnals included songs from the traditions of Native Americans, African Americans, South and Central Americans, Korea, China, Japan, and many other non-European countries. Contemporary praise songs and choruses with styles ranging from rock, jazz, and electronic music, to gospel and blues, were also added. Some denominations developed praise bands, worship teams, gospel choirs, and other new ensembles. However, traditional hymns and gospel music remained important in congregational singing.

The field of church music has provided women with many career opportunities, including composer, accompanist, church music educator in private schools or as part of the church program, and adult, youth, or children's choir director. Other positions include director of handbell choirs, soloist or choir singer (many of these are salaried positions), worship team (a small group of singers that lead the singing in contemporary style services), praise band (instrumental group that accompanies contemporary style services), and cantor.

Women in church music have made their mark in a variety of ways. Composers who have been involved in multicultural church music include Undine Smith Moore (1904–1989) and Melva Costen (b. 1933). Moore, a composer and educator, wrote many African American spirituals and other sacred works. Costen, a music professor, author, and theologian, is an expert on African American worship and was the editor of the most recent Presbyterian hymnal, which included many songs from other cultures and numerous adaptations of hymn texts to correct gender-specific language. Costen also wrote many arrangements of African American hymns.

Outstanding organists include concert and recording artist, composer, conductor, and international television personality Diane Bish (b. 1941); and the director of church music at Northwestern University and past president of the American Guild of Organists, Margaret McEwain Kemper (b. 1938).

Contemporary Christian performing artists like Sandi Patty (b. 1957) and Amy Grant (b. 1960) have led the way in the use of more popular styles in church music. Mahalia Jackson (1911–1971) was a pioneer in popularizing the African American gospel style that has developed into groups such as the Brooklyn Tabernacle Choir and the Atlanta Mass Choir.

Helen Kemp (b. 1938), music educator, has been a leader in developing children's choirs and has had a great influence on church music education.

Conductors like Charlene Archebeque (b. 1935) and Ann Howard Jones have been involved in the training of new conductors through university programs and training workshops. Others, like Elaine

Render, have been involved in developing new ideas in liturgical music.

See also Hymnody; Jewish Musicians

For Further Reading

Claghorn, Charles E. *Women Composers as Hymnists: A Concise Biographical Dictionary*. Metuchen, NJ: Scarecrow Press, 1984.

Dean, Talmage. *A Survey of Twentieth Century Protestant Church Music*. Nashville, TN: Broadman, 1988.

Wilson-Dickson, Andres. *The Story of Christian Music: From Gregorian Chant to Black Gospel— An Authoritative Illustrated Guide to All the Major Traditions of Music for Worship*. Oxford: Lion, 1992.

John Augenblick

Ciccone, Madonna Louise Veronica

See Madonna

Clark, Frances Elliott (1860–1958)

Frances Elliott Clark, known affectionately as "Mother Clark," was one of the most influential American music educators in the twentieth century, pioneering the use of the new recording technology in music education. In 1907 she was the founding chairperson of the Music Supervisors National Conference (MSNC). From 1911, as educational director for RCA Victor, Clark pioneered the use of recorded music in education. She shaped the fundamental nature of American music education through her idealistic mission: to hear more beautiful music, well sung and well played, by and for children; to bring more and better music to all the schoolchildren of America; and to ensure that music would be an integral part of education.

Clark was born in Angola, IN, on 27 May 1860. At age 10 she moved with her family to the woods of northern Michigan, where she attended a rural music school. She married John Clark, a Canadian, but was soon widowed and supported her young son through dressmaking while teaching herself music. She attended Tri-State College at Angola, graduating in 1880, and taught music in Indiana, Illinois, and Iowa before becoming music supervisor in Milwaukee, WI. Clark held leadership positions in several organizations, including the National Education Association. In 1907 she presided at the founding meeting of the MSNC—which became known as the Music Educators National Conference (MENC) after 1934. Characteristically rising to the occasion, Clark became the first chairperson and for the next 50 years remained a driving force in the Conference.

Clark's primary achievement was in promoting the use of the newly developed audio technology in music education. As Milwaukee schools' music supervisor, in 1909 she introduced the use of recordings on a wide scale for the first time in the United States. In 1911 the Victor Talking Machine Company invited Clark to head a newly formed educational department. In this position she built libraries of recordings suitable for educational purposes and produced the first records made especially for school use. By 1916 schools in more than 4,000 towns and cities had adopted the use of phonographs, ushering in the era of "music appreciation." At the peak Clark managed a staff of 33 former educators who demonstrated the use of records in schools nationwide. She advocated the use of masterworks by fine performers as well as folk songs and dances. In 36 years Clark produced over 500 school records before she retired as director emerita.

Frances Clark also authored the widely read *Music Appreciation for Children*. In 1928 Temple University conferred upon her the Doctor of Music degree. A member of the Daughters of the American Revolution, Clark died in Salt Lake City, UT, on 14 June 1958.

See also Music Education; Music Educators National Conference

For Further Reading

Birge, Edward B. "Supervisor Sketches: Frances Elliott Clark." *Musician* 37/6 (1932): 9.

Cooke, James F., L.V. Hollweck, Marie M. Keith, and Hazel G. Kinscella. "Frances Elliott Clark." *Music Educators Journal* 46/5 (1960): 20–24.

Kendel, John C., G. Josephine Airy, Franklin Dunham, Ellsworth E. Dent, and Birdie Alexander. "Clark Centennial Memorial Tributes: A Selection from Letters from Friends." *Music Educators Journal* 46/5 (1960): 78–79.

Kilissa M. Cissoko

Clark, Frances Oman (1905–1998)

Frances Oman Clark has been called the "Inventor of Piano Pedagogy," "America's First Lady of Piano Education," and the "Dean of Pedagogues." These tributes honor a woman who spent a lifetime developing a philosophy and methodology for teaching piano. Clark held the philosophical conviction that "there is music in every child" and that it is the teacher's responsibility to create experiences from which the child will learn to play the piano. Her methodology developed from this philosophy and led to her co-authoring, with long-time colleague Louise Goss (b. 1926), a vast library of piano study materials entitled The Frances Clark Library for Piano Students. These materials include original works written by Clark, works commissioned from contemporary and international composers, and works selected from existing repertoire for their pedagogical value.

Frances Clark was born on 28 March 1905 in Sturgis, MI, and graduated with a B.A. in English from Kalamazoo College (1928). This was followed by graduate study at the University of Michigan, the Juilliard School, the Paris Conservatory, and the Fountainbleau Academy. She received honorary doctorates from Kalamazoo College and Westminster Choir College, and she held the Master Teacher Certificate from the Music Teachers National Association. She was an honorary member of the National Society of Arts and Letters and of Alpha Sigma Iota Honorary Music Fraternity, and she received the Women of Distinction Award from Rutgers University. In 1984 she received the only Lifetime Achievement Award ever offered by the National Conference on Piano Pedagogy.

Because of Clark's success in training piano teachers, she was asked by her alma mater, Kalamazoo College in 1945 to develop the first four-year undergraduate degree program in piano pedagogy in the United States. Ten years later she started a similar program at Westminster Choir College, and in 1960 she and Goss founded the New School for Music Study—a postgraduate center for piano pedagogy and music research, and the nation's only independent research center devoted to keyboard teaching and teacher education. In 1981 Clark created a master's degree curriculum in piano pedagogy as a joint program offered by the New School for Music Study and Westminster Choir College of Rider University. For many years Clark shared her expertise in workshops and study courses on college and university campuses and served as consultant to those institutions creating piano pedagogy de-

gree programs. For 26 years readers of *Clavier Magazine*, published monthly, benefited from a question and answer column that she wrote for piano teachers. These columns were published in book form in 1992.

Clark died on 17 April 1998 in Princeton, NJ, at age 93.

See also Music Education; Piano Pedagogy

For Further Reading

Allen, Doris. "Women's Contributions to Modern Piano Pedagogy." *The Musical Woman: An Interdisciplinary Perspective*, Vol. 2, USA (1984–85): 411–44.

Clark, Frances. *Questions and Answers*. Available through *Clavier Magazine*, 200 Northfield Rd., Northfield, Illinois 60093.

Kern, Robert Fred. "Frances Clark: The Teacher and Her Contributions to Piano Pedagogy." D.A. diss., University of Northern Colorado, 1984.

Florence Aquilina

Clarke, Rebecca (1886–1979)

Violist and composer Rebecca Clarke was the most distinguished British-American woman musician of her generation, but she was also a highly accomplished violist, one of the first six women to be a full member of the Wood's New Queen's Hall Orchestra, and an active and renowned chamber musician. Clarke studied violin at the Royal Academy of Music (1902–1910), but her overbearing father forced her to leave because her harmony teacher, Percy Miles, proposed marriage. Beginning in 1907, Clarke also studied composition with Charles Villiers Stanford, who persuaded her to switch from the violin to the viola. She eventually studied viola privately with Lionel Tertis. Shortly after leaving the Royal Academy, Clarke argued with her father and was banished from the family home. She never returned. She completed her studies with the help of friends and benefactors while supporting herself primarily by playing the viola.

Clarke was born in Harrow, England, on 27 August 1886. She first came to the United States in 1916. In 1919 her Sonata for Viola and Piano placed second in the composition competition sponsored by Elizabeth Sprague Coolidge (1864–1953). Having originally tied for first with composer Ernest Bloch's Suite for Viola and Piano, Coolidge broke the tie by choosing the Bloch work. Interested parties were astonished to learn afterwards that the second-place work had been composed by a woman. From the early 1920s until the early 1940s, Clarke divided her performing and composing time between the United States and England. By the early 1940s arthritis made playing difficult, and Clarke replaced most performance activities with a lecture series on a New York classical radio station and supplemental employment as a nanny. In 1944 she married American pianist and composer James Friskin, a fellow student from the Royal Academy of Music, then living in New York. Following her marriage, Clarke ceased composing and performing entirely.

Clarke's works fall into two large categories: instrumental music (strings with or without piano) and songs. Best known are the Sonata for Viola and Piano and the Piano Trio. Along with the Rhapsody for Viola and Piano, these two works form the nucleus of her musical output. Clarke's compositions appear to have a Brahmsian foundation punctuated strongly with post-Impressionistic idioms. Closer examination, however, reveals three primary influences: Claude Debussy, Ralph Vaughan Williams, and Ernest Bloch. The style of Clarke's music may be described as a combination of post-tonal chromaticism and late Romantic textures and rhythms. In recent years performances of her instrumental works, particularly the Sonata for Viola and Piano have become more common, but her songs have yet to receive the attention they deserve. Recordings of Clarke's music are available on *Music for Viola* (Northeastern, NR 121-CD), *Piano Trios by Rebecca Clarke and Katherine Hoover* (Leonarda LPI 103), and *Songs of America* (Wea/Atlantic/Nonesuch 79178). Rebecca Clarke died in New York City on 13 October 1979.

See also Performer, String

For Further Reading

Curtis, Liane. "Rebecca Clarke and Sonata Form: Questions of Gender and Genre." *Musical Quarterly* 81 (1997): 393–429.

Kohnen, Daniela. *Rebecca Clarke: Kompositin und Bratschistin*. Frankfurt am Main: Verlag Hansel-Hohenhausen, 1999.

MacDonald, Calum. "Rebecca Clarke's Chamber Music I." *Tempo: A Quarterly Review of Modern Music* 160 (1987): 15–26.

Robert Follet

Classical Music

The genre of classical music is often referred to as "art music," "high art," or "concert music." Despite the ongoing discrimination against women composers, performers, and conductors of classical music, the twentieth century saw an explosion in the sheer numbers of women professionally active in classical music. The number of women composers and conductors who have made significant contributions to classical music far exceeds the boundaries of the present entry. In the Western European tradition from which much of classical music in the United States was conceived, it is music composed within the confines of Western European cultural standards of rhythm, melody, and harmony. The major areas associated with classical music do not vary significantly from those of popular or traditional music, save the area of conducting. Composition and performance, along with conducting for those ensembles requiring it, are necessary components in classical music expression.

Major genres of classical music include large instrumental or vocal ensembles, chamber combinations of many kinds, and solo works (including electro-acoustic media). In spite of the large body of works composed by women, few women composers and their works appear within the accepted canon of performed works or works to be studied in music history, literature, and appreciation books. Historic changes in American society in the last 40 years of the twentieth century with regard to the contributions of racial and ethnic minorities, and non-European immigrants, while challenging the traditional classical canon, have not altered it significantly.

Notable as the first American woman to write both a symphony and a mass, Amy Marcy Cheney Beach (1867–1944) had large compositions performed both in America and in Europe quite frequently until the end of World War I. The latter years of the twentieth century, saw a significant rekindling of interest in her music. Born in the same year as Beach, Margaret Lang was a composer whose works saw their greatest interest with the public in the 1890s. Singer and composer Mary Turner Salter (1856–1938) wrote over 200 songs as well as other vocal works in western Massachusetts. George Chadwick's pupil Helen Hood (1863–1949) was most notable for her songs, whereas another of Chadwick's students, Mabel Wheeler Daniels (1879–1971) achieved considerable suc-

cess in both vocal and instrumental composition. A Scottish woman, Helen Hopekirk (1856–1945), moved to Boston permanently in 1897, and although she composed some large-scale works around the turn of the nineteenth century, the vast majority of her compositions were chamber and solo pieces including over 100 songs. A German woman, Adele Lewing (1896–1943), was active in both piano teaching and composition. The English-born Clara Kathleen Barnett Rogers (1844–1931) was both opera singer and composer. She taught at New England Conservatory and published books about singing.

Lily Strickland, Harriet Ware, and Mana-Zucca (Augusta Zuckermann) were active in many genres of classical composition, although their works including voice are the most memorable. Strickland's song *Lindy Lou* became a favorite encore song for recitals. Active in many genres, Ware (1877–1962) composed the symphonic poem *The Artisan*, which was programmed in 1929 by the New York Symphony Orchestra. Zuckermann was said to have published over 1000 works during her lifetime. Although Eva Munson Smith's *Women of Sacred Song* (1885) lists 52 women composers, there were certainly a greater number of composers for the church in the nineteenth and early twentieth centuries. Along with Beach, Mabel Daniel and Mary Howe both composed major sacred works that were performed during their lifetimes.

Trained as a pianist, in the early 1920s Mary Howe (1882–1964), like Amy Marcy Cheney Beach before her, turned toward composition. Along with her composition, which was influenced by European impressionism, Howe was important for organizing festivals, including the first Coolidge Festival in Washington, DC, and the Chamber Music Society, which became Friends of Music of the Library of Congress. She raised the funds to establish the National Symphony Orchestra. George Barrère's Little Symphony in New York programmed a number of Howe's compositions, and her works were programmed regularly by the Society of American Women Composers. In 1954 three of her symphonic poems were programmed by the Vienna Symphony (Austria).

African American composer Florence Smith Price's (1887–1953) music reflected her southern roots. Her Symphony in E Minor, which made effective use of black melodies and rhythms, was performed by the Chicago Symphony as a result of her capturing two Wanamaker Foundation Awards.

Remembered as a champion of contemporary music, like Howe, Marion Bauer (1887–1955) employed impressionistic idioms in her compositions. Bauer is remembered equally as composer and teacher who taught a generation of American composers at various prominent colleges, universities, and conservatories. Active in writing about music, Bauer wrote or co-authored several books on music, contributed articles to music encyclopedias, and was the New York correspondent to Chicago's *Musical Leader* until her death. She was the only woman on the executive board of the American Composers Alliance. California-born Elinor Remick Warren's (1906–1991) neo-Romantic works spanned the major genres of classical composition. Her works were programmed by major orchestras, including the Los Angeles and New York Philharmonics and the Detroit Symphony.

With the beginning of the twentieth century, one of the most innovative of American composers was born. Ruth Crawford Seeger (1901–1953) assimi-lated all the elements of musical style and current contemporary movements and forged her own tightly organized and highly individual style. The first woman to win a Guggenheim Fellowship (1930), Crawford composed her String Quartet, which became her best-known work during that year abroad. Nadia Boulanger's student Louise Talma (1906–1996) was the only American who was allowed by Boulanger to teach at the American Conservatory in Paris. In the 1950s Talma explored 12-tone music, not adopting the style completely but incorporating the technique of row writing as part of her own style. She was the recipient of a number of awards, including a Senior Fulbright Research grant (1955) and a Koussevitsky Music Foundation commission (1959). She was elected to the National Institute of Arts and Letters in 1974. Like Talma, composer, writer, and teacher Dika Newlin (b. 1923) was influenced in her writing style by the 12-tone school. Newlin was the first person to receive a Ph.D. in musicology from Columbia University. Newlin wrote many of her important works for piano, and in the 1970s she used taped and computer-generated sounds in her works.

A pupil of Florence Price while in high school, Margaret Bonds (1913–1972) was educated at Northwestern University. Moving to New York, she studied with composers Roy Harris, Robert Starer, and Emerson Harper. Her over 200 works show the influence of blues, jazz, and spiritual style melodies. Boulanger and Luigi Dallapiccola student Julia Perry's (b. 1924) use of African American musical idioms is subtler than Bonds's and Price's. A Kentucky native, Perry studied at Westminster Choir College and the Juilliard School prior to working with Dallapiccola at Tanglewood and in Europe with Boulanger. Winner of both the Boulanger Grand Prix (1952) and a Guggenheim Fellowship (1954), she concentrated on instrumental works after 1950; this effort resulted in over 12 symphonies for various instrumental ensembles. African Americans Evelyn LaRue Pittman's (b. 1910) and Lena Johnson McLin's (b. 1929) works incorporate black musical idioms. Whereas a considerable percentage of Pittman's compositions were written to fill a need for teaching materials for her students and for the choral ensembles she conducted, a great number of McLin's works fulfilling that same need employ later blues, gospel, jazz, and rock styles along with the older African American spirituals and work songs. Although not African American, Alice Parker (b. 1925) used southern idioms and American subjects in her arrangements and compositions. Like Parker, Gena Branscombe (1881–1997) was active in composing vocal music, choral conducting, and compositions on American subjects. Between 1929 and 1931 she was president of the Society of American Women Composers.

Both Julia Frances Smith (1911–1989) and Radie Britain (1903–1994) incorporated the American musical idiom of the rural West and Southwest into their compositions. In the 1940s Smith taught both theory and counterpoint at The Juilliard School, also taught at New Britain State Teachers College, and founded the music education department at the Hartt School of Music. Britain's *Heroic Poem* for orchestra won both the International Hollywood Bowl Prize in 1930 and the Juilliard Publication Award in 1945 (the first time that award was given to a woman composer).

From the beginning of women's participation in the art of music in America, the acceptance of women as singers, but not as instrumentalists, has led to a historic imbalance in composition for instruments, of women instrumental players (save keyboard and harp), and conductors. Opera as a genre of composition was a middle ground where the woman composer explored her art in both vocal and instrumental areas. Along with solo and ensemble vocal works, the number of professional opera performers exceeds that of instrumentalists.

Early twentieth-century operas were composed by women born much earlier in the preceding century, such as Eleanor Everest Freer (1864–1942). Other opera composers active earlier in the century include Jane Van Etten, Celeste Massey Hecksher, Elsie Maxwell, Gerrish Jones, and Mary Carr Moore.

Scenes from composer and conductor Emma Steiner's (1852–1929) operas *The Man from Paris* and *The "Burra Pundit,"* along with the overture to her opera *Fleurette*, were the first of the operatic genre by a woman to be performed by the Metropolitan Opera. Australian-born Peggy Glanville-Hicks (1912–1990) received a Ford Foundation commission for her opera *Sappho* in 1963. Spending many years in the United States, Scottish-born Thea Musgrave (b. 1928) composed and conducted a number of her own works with major orchestras and opera houses.

After mid-century, the emergence of electronic instruments, electronic and computer-generated sounds, and multimedia works opened new creative vistas for composers. Composer Marga Richter (b. 1926) used electrified guitars and tamboura, and other non-Western instruments, along with standard orchestral forces for her second piano concerto. The consolidation of old and new techniques was the compositional concern of German-born Ursula Mamlok (b. 1928).

The unusual use of traditional instruments and the human voice is found as a hallmark of the works of Joyce Mekeel (b. 1931). Lucia Dlugoszweski (b. 1931 or 1934) has also used traditional instruments in nontraditional ways along with instruments she invented herself. Aleatory composition is associated with the output of Netty Simons (b. ca. 1918), and microtonal works with Tui St. George Tucker (b. 1924).

The Prix de Rome in composition went to an American woman for the first time in 1969. Barbara Kolb (b. 1939) received the honor and went to the American Academy in Rome. Kolb's creative works, both in subject and in the use of prerecorded instruments, and other electronically generated sounds along with live performance, have generated numerous commissions for the composer. Having composed in almost every medium, Jean Eichelberger Ivey (b. 1923) turned to electronic composition in the late 1960s. By 1970 she combined live performance with taped music. Involved during her career with several electronic music centers, German-born Daria Semegen (b. 1946) composes both electronic and non-electronic compositions. Computer-generated sounds are discovered in the works beginning in the late 1960s and early 1970s of both Laurie Spiegel's (b. 1945) computer music and Suzanne Ciani's (b. 1946) analog synthesizers. Pauline Oliveros's (b. 1932) use of real-time tape compositions, sound sculpture, astro-bio-geo-physical recorded activities, and multimedia compositions attest to that composer's early use of unconventional sound. Beth Anderson (b. 1950) is known for her multimedia compositions that create sound environments for the listener. Composer Laurie Anderson (b. 1947) provides a model of an artist who uses multimedia art and performance.

Born well into the twentieth century, Sarah Caldwell (b. 1928) has had a distinguished career as conductor, producer, and stage director. Eve Rabin Queler (b. 1936), founder of the Opera Orchestra of New York, has had appointments and numerous conducting assignments, in both opera and symphonic music. Judith Somogi (1943–1988), the first woman to conduct a Naumberg series concert; Italian-born Alberta Maisello, assistant conductor of the Metropolitan Opera; and Belgian-American Frédérique Petrides (1903–1983) also made significant inroads for women conductors. Margaret Hillis's (1921–1998) founding of the Chicago Symphony Chorus and extensive experience with conducting vocal ensembles led also to a successful career in orchestral conducting. Hillis was the first woman to conduct the Chicago Symphony. Despite their talent, some conductors experienced difficulty in getting management representatives. Beatrice Brown (1918–1997) in the 1950s and 1960s and Antonia Brico (1902–1989) in the 1930s experienced the unspoken prejudice against women on the podium. In the 1970s the Affiliate Artists Conductors Program helped to provide experience for conductors early in their careers. As a result, a number of talented women conductors received the exposure they needed to assume podium positions in opera and symphony orchestras previously not available to them. In the final 20 years of the twentieth century, younger conductors like JoAnn Falletta (b. 1954) and Marin Alsop (b. 1956) forged distinguished careers.

Classical music prizes, fellowships, and awards have encouraged women in the field to achieve success in their creative areas. Earlier in the twentieth century,

Ruth Crawford Seeger became the first woman to win the Guggenheim Fellowship in composition. In 1933 her *Three Songs* were selected to represent the United States at the International Society for Contemporary Music Festival. Kolb's Prix de Rome has already been mentioned. The coveted Pulitzer Prize in music was awarded for the first time to a woman composer in 1983: Ellen Taaffe Zwilich received the Pulitzer for her Symphony No. 1: Three Movements for Orchestra (New World Records 336), commissioned by the American Composers Orchestra. Both the Kennedy Center Freidheim Award and the Grawemeyer Award for Music Composition were awarded Joan Tower for the same composition, her *Silver Ladders* (Nonesuch 79245) for orchestra. Tower is further distinguished by being the first woman to win a Grawemeyer Award given by the Louisville Orchestra for musical composition. In music technology, the prestigious first prize in the program division given in the International Electroacoustic Music Competition, Bourges, was awarded for the first time to an American woman in 1986: Vivian Adelberg Rudow (b. 1936) received this prize for her composition *With Love*. The National Endowment for the Arts National Medals began to be awarded in the early 1970s. Several women opera singers (Marilyn Horne, Roberta Peters, Beverly Sills, Marian Anderson, and Leontyne Price) have received the medal to date. Composers and conductors who have been recipients of the medal are conductor Sarah Caldwell (1996) and composers Margaret Garwood (1973), Pril Smiley (1974), Vivian Fine (1977), and Marga Richter (1977).

See also Conductor, Choral; Conductor, Instrumental and Operatic; Experimental Music

For Further Reading

Ammer, Christine. *Unsung*. Revised and expanded second edition. Portland, OR: Amadeus Press, 2001.

Pendle, Karen (ed.). *Women and Music: A History*. Bloomington: Indiana University Press, 1991.

Sadie, Julie Anne, and Rhian Samuel. *The Norton/Grove Dictionary of Women Composers*. New York: W.W. Norton, 1994.

Suzanne L. Gertig

Cline, Patsy (1932–1963)

In an era when women in the country music industry were expected to project a demure image, often dressed in gingham, singer Patsy Cline garnered a reputation as a hell-raiser. Her feisty, sexually aggressive image matched the outspoken woman who kept a pint of whiskey in her handbag and insisted upon dressing in sexy cowgirl costumes until the final few years of her life. During a time when women country singers occupied roles supportive to performers who were men, Patsy Cline became a headliner. Her peers, including singers Loretta Lynn (b. 1935) and Dottie West (1932–1991), and generations of women singers to follow, credit her with having paved the way for their future successes within the country music industry.

Cline was born on 8 September 1932 to a 16-year-old mother in Winchester, VA; her given name was Virginia Patterson Hensley. She exhibited a love for music and driving ambition to become a country music star from her earliest years. Virginia started playing the piano at the age of seven and discovered Nashville's Grand Ole Opry radio broadcasts at age 10. She began singing in local clubs at age 14 and in the same year became a regular with Joltin' Jim McCoy and his Melody Playboys on McCoy's live Saturday radio show broadcast on local radio station WINC. Abandoned by

Patsy Cline, ca. 1950s. *Photo courtesy of Frank Driggs/Archive Photos.*

her alcoholic father at age 15, she quit school to sing with local bands at night while clerking in a drug store by day.

At age 16 Virginia unsuccessfully auditioned for the Grand Ole Opry but returned undaunted to Winchester, continuing to sing in nightclubs and other local venues while sporting her mother's hand-sewn cowgirl costumes. She took the name Patsy Hensley in 1951 when she joined Bill Peer and his Melody Boys, and in 1953 she married local playboy Gerald Cline.

Her rise to success began in earnest when, in the mid-1950s, she signed a personal management contract with country promoter and radio station owner Connie B. Gay; she also signed with Four Star Records, which leased her recordings to Decca Records for distribution. Patsy subsequently appeared on Arthur Godfrey's *Talent Scouts* television show in New York, winning first place for her hit "Walkin' after Midnight." In 1960 she became a member of the Grand Ole Opry and released the most successful recording of her career, "I Fall to Pieces," which remained on the *Billboard* charts for a remarkable 39 weeks. Although there are numerous reprints and compilation discs available of Cline's recordings, some of the original albums and hit singles are found on *Patsy Cline* (MCA MCAD-25200), *Showcase* (MCA), and *Sentimentally Yours* (MCA MCAD-90).

Although she clearly defined herself as a country performer, many considered Patsy's voice more suited to pop music. Decca Records producer Owen Bradley tried repeatedly to move her career toward more pop-styled songs and instrumental backing, but Cline tenaciously clung to her preference for country-oriented material and vocal techniques. Her career illustrates tensions experienced by country performers in the 1950s and early 1960s. During this period, Nashville's producers transitioned from earlier country and honky-tonk styles, developing what became known as "the Nashville sound," appealing to rock and roll as well as pop and country music audiences. Patsy Cline died while returning from a benefit performance on 5 March 1963, in a plane crash that also took the lives of performers Cowboy Copas and Hawkshaw Hawkins.

See also Country Music

For Further Reading

Dew, Joan. *Singers and Sweethearts: The Women of Country Music*. Garden City, NY: Doubleday, 1977.

Nassour, Ellis. *Honky Tonk Angel: The Intimate*

Story of Patsy Cline. New York: Bantam Books, Mass Market Paperback, 1994.

Amy Corin

Clooney, Rosemary (1928–2002)

Rosemary Clooney, American singer and actress, has made a lasting mark on jazz and popular music with her refined and enduring vocal style in a long and outstanding career. In her autobiography *Girl Singer*, Clooney termed herself "a sweet singer with a big band sensibility." Clooney has recorded with many musical icons, including Bing Crosby, Percy Faith, Mitch Miller, Tony Pastor, Nelson Riddle, and Frank Sinatra. Her acting career spanned several decades, from films such as *The Stars Are Singing* (1953) and *White Christmas* (1954) to the television series *The Rosemary Clooney Show* (1957–1958) and episodes of *ER*, which earned her a 1995 Emmy nomination.

Born on 23 May 1928 in Maysville, KY, Clooney grew up in poverty and helped raise her siblings. She began singing with her sister Betty on a radio show in the mid-1940s, and then the Clooney Sisters worked with Tony Pastor (1945–1949). In 1953 Clooney married the actor José Ferrer. Divorce proceedings ensued in 1961, after which they were reunited, but a final divorce occurred in 1967. Clooney and Ferrer had five children together. In 1997 Clooney married dancer Dante DiPaolo.

Clooney overcame depression and an addiction to prescription drugs during the late 1960s and early 1970s. In 1976 she revived her singing career with Bing Crosby in a celebratory concert, and in 1977 she started recording with the Concord Jazz label, issuing an album annually. Clooney was awarded the James Smithson Bicentennial Medal in 1992, an award "to persons who have made distinguished contributions to the advance-

Rosemary Clooney. *Photo courtesy of Frank Driggs Collection.*

ment of areas of interest to the Smithsonian." In 1999 Clooney's recording "Hey There" was inducted into the Grammy Hall of Fame. She has recorded primarily on the Columbia, Concord Jazz, MGM, and RCA labels. Among her notable recordings are the 1951 single "Come On-a My House" (available Bear Family CD 15895) and the 1954 album *Irving Berlin's White Christmas* (Columbia C-6338). Her performances are characterized by skillful phrasing, keen timing, and careful attention to the dramatic elements of the lyrics.

In 1988 Rosemary Clooney opened the Betty Clooney Center for persons with brain injuries, a facility dedicated to her sister. Rosemary Clooney died on 29 June 2002 of lung cancer.

See also Grammy Award

For Further Reading

Clooney, Rosemary, and Joan Barthel. *Girl Singer*. New York: Doubleday, 1999.

Clooney, Rosemary, and Raymond Strait. *This for Remembrance*. Chicago: Playboy Press, 1977.

Laura Gayle Green

Cole, Natalie (1950–)

Singer Natalie Cole, daughter of Nat "King" Cole, established a voice of her own over the last quarter of the twentieth century. In 1991 Cole's landmark album *Unforgettable—With Love* (Elektra 61243-2/4) earned seven Grammy Awards. On this technological landmark recording, Natalie Cole sang with her late father on 22 of his songs.

Natalie Cole was born on 6 February 1950 in Los Angeles, CA, to legendary entertainer Nat "King" Cole and jazz vocalist Maria Cole. While her parents traveled, Cole and her sisters were raised by an aunt, but her family's affection and a strong attachment to her father were unforgettable influences on Cole's career. Her parents valued education above

Natalie Cole. *Photo courtesy of Jeff Mayer/ Globe Photos.*

all and expected their children to enter non-musical professions. However, upon hearing her teenage rendition of an Ella Fitzgerald (1917–1996) song, Natalie's father encouraged her musical interests. Throughout her early years she enjoyed the celebrity of her attractive and talented family, and she was deeply affected by her father's death in 1965.

After completing a degree in psychology at the University of Massachusetts, Cole began to perform in earnest. Her work with Chuck Jackson and Marvin Yancey, whom she married, led to her first Grammy Awards in 1976, for Best Rhythm and Blues Female and Best New Artist for the album *Inseparable* (Capitol C2-97769). However, the 1980s were difficult years marked by divorce, drug abuse, and physical debilitation that included vocal polyps. Cole sought treatment for her addictions and illnesses and has celebrated her permanent recovery in frequent public declarations of religious faith and gratitude to her family.

Cole's *Take a Look* (Elektra 61496-2/4) celebrated famous black singers and established her as an independent, mature musician with a distinctive personal style. After recording several albums of standards, she returned to her pop and soul beginnings. *Snowfall on the Sahara* (Elektra 62401-2/4), her 21st album, produced in 1999 to observe Cole's 25th anniversary in the music profession, offered a widely varied program. She continues to perform concerts and record music that inspires her many fans.

See also Rock and Popular Music Genres

For Further Reading

Nathan, David. *The Soulful Divas: Personal Portraits of Over a Dozen Divine Divas from Nina Simone, Aretha Franklin, and Diana Ross, to Patti LaBelle, Whitney Houston, and Janet Jackson*. New York: Watson-Guptill, 1999.

Nicholson, Delores. "Natalie Cole." In *Notable Black American Women, Book II*, ed. Jessie Carney Smith. New York: Gale Research, 1996.

Paula Elliot

Collins, Judy (1939–)

Judy Collins is a notable historic figure in folk and popular music. From her earliest recordings of traditional folksongs to her innovative albums of the 1960s and 1970s to her current work, Collins's originality and seriousness of purpose have left their mark. She has been involved in humanitarian activities, authored several books, and produced and co-directed an award-winning documentary film about her teacher, orchestral conductor Antonia Brico (1902–1989). Folk music artist and beat poet Richard Fariña described Collins's voice in this way: "If amethysts could sing, they would sound like Judy Collins." Her performances are marked by a wistful sound and delicate delivery of lyrics.

Collins was born on 1 May 1939 in Seattle, WA. When she was four years old the family moved to Los Angeles, and five years later they moved again, to Denver, where her father arranged for Collins to study classical piano with Brico. Following years of performing classical repertoire, Collins shifted her focus to folk music. She began performing in coffeehouses and soon was singing in Chicago and New York. Following an appearance at the Village Gate in 1961, Collins was signed by Elektra Records and over the next three years released three albums of traditional folk songs. Her fourth and fifth albums, reflecting on her life in New York City, included songs written by urban folk musicians such as Bob Dylan and Gordon Lightfoot. Her 1966 album *In My Life* (Elektra 74027-2), including works by Leonard Cohen, Jacques Brel, and the Beatles, transcended her previous "folk" categorization and characterized her trademark adventurous programming.

In 1967 Collins achieved artistic and commercial success with the release of *Wildflowers* (Elektra 74012), her first album to sell over one million copies. This produced both her first Grammy nomination (1968) and the first of her chart hits (her cover of Joni Mitchell's "Both Sides Now"). Selections ranged from Cohen and Brel to an authentic rendition of a fourteenth-century Landini ballata, in addition to two songs that Collins had written herself, "Sky Fell" and "Albatross." Joshua Rifkin's strikingly original arrangements in *Wildflowers* featured harpsichords and orchestral instruments.

In 1969 she published *The Judy Collins Songbook* and then continued to release one album a year throughout the 1970s, achieving Platinum status in 1975 with her 14th album, *Judith* (Elektra 111-2). Collins also took up acting, playing the role of Solveig in the New York Shakespeare Festival's production of *Peer Gynt*. She produced and co-directed the film *Antonia: Portrait of the Woman*, which won the Christopher Award and the Independent Film Critics Award, was named one of the Top 10 films of 1974 by *Time* magazine, and was nominated for an Academy Award for Best Documentary. Collins was also active in projects such as Women Strike for Peace and helped with voter registration.

Less active artistically and politically through the 1980s, Collins has recently returned to prominence in performing, in publishing, and in public service. As a United Nations Children's Fund (UNICEF) Special Representative for the Arts, she composed "Song for Sara-

Judy Collins. *Photo courtesy of by George Pickow.*

jevo" in an attempt to draw awareness to the UNICEF Landmine Awareness Program. The song appeared on her *Come Rejoice!: A Judy Collins Christmas* (Mesa/Bluemoon 479085). She has also published a novel, *Shameless* (1995), and a best-selling memoir, *Singing Lessons* (1998).

See also Singer-Songwriter; Songwriter

For Further Reading

Baggelaar, Kristin, and Donald Milton. *Folk Music: More Than a Song.* New York: Crowell, 1976.
Collins, Judy. *The Judy Collins Songbook.* New York: Grossett and Dunlap, 1969.

Kathleen Pierson

Comden, Betty (1917?–)

A leading lady of the American musical theater for over half a century, Betty Comden has co-written the book or lyrics for numerous award-winning stage and screen musicals. Comden is remarkable not only for her longevity but for her success in what has been a field dominated by men. Few women lyricists, if any, can boast of her accomplishments.

Betty Comden was born Basya Cohen in Brooklyn, NY, on 3 May, probably in 1917, although various sources cite years from 1915 to 1919. Comden was educated at the Brooklyn Ethical Culture

School, Erasmus Hall High School, and New York University, at which she majored in dramatic arts and English. She married Steve Kyle (born Siegfried Schutzman) in 1942, and they had two children, Susanna and Alan. Kyle died in 1979; her son, in 1990.

Comden's career as a lyricist really began when she met Adolph Green in 1938. They, along with three others, including Judy Tuvim (later Judy Holliday), formed a group called the Revuers, which performed its own songs and sketches. The group garnered some attention, but the other three members left, two for Hollywood and one for defense work. Comden and Green were then approached by Leonard Bernstein, Paul Feigay, and Oliver Smith about the possibility of writing a musical inspired by the Bernstein and Jerome Robbins ballet *Fancy Free*. From this collaboration came their first hit stage show, *On the Town*, which made its debut at the Adelphi Theatre on 28 December 1944. Other shows followed, including *Wonderful Town* (1953), *Hallelujah Baby* (1968), *Applause* ([1970] Polygram 159404), and *Will Rogers Follies* (1991), which all won Tony Awards for Best Musical. *On the Twentieth Century* (1978) won a Tony Award for Best Score. Comden and Green also worked on movie musicals in Hollywood. They were asked to create a show around songs previously written by Arthur Freed and Nacio Herb Brown. The result was *Singin' in the Rain* (1952), widely regarded as the best movie musical ever made. Among Comden and Green's other movies are *On the Town* ([1949] Sony 2038), *The Band Wagon* (1953), and *It's Always Fair Weather* ([1955] Heritage 0058). These, along with *Singin' in the Rain*, won Screenwriter's Guild of America awards.

Although now octogenarians, Comden and Green remain active in their art. In 1998 they created a new libretto for the Richard Strauss operetta *Die Fledermaus* for the Metropolitan Opera. In 1999 they performed an anthology of their songs in *An Intimate Party with Betty and Adolph* at Joe's Pub at the Papp Village Theater. In 1991 Comden and Green were acknowledged for their body of collaborative work, receiving the Lifetime Achievement Award from the Songwriters Hall of Fame, the Kennedy Center Honors, and recognition from the Academy of Motion Picture Arts and Sciences.

See also Librettist; Musical Theater

For Further Reading

Comden, Betty. *Off Stage*. New York: Simon & Schuster, 1995.

Robinson, Alice M. *Betty Comden and Adolph Green: A Bio-Bibliography*. Westport, CT: Greenwood Press, 1983.

Michele Wolff

Committees

Cultural diversity committees and committees of the status of women and minorities have been increasingly found in many organizations. In addition, many organizations provide Special Interest Groups (SIG) or Roundtables where individuals may gather to share information and to find support. To increase awareness of women's issues within various musical disciplines, many professional organizations include committees that focus on women and gender.

The American Musicological Society (AMS) is a nonprofit organization whose purpose is to "advance research in the various fields of music as a branch of learning and scholarship." The AMS belongs to the American Council of Learned Societies. Its membership encompasses 3,000 people and 1,250 institutions from 40 nations. The Committee on the Status of Women (CSW) examines the representations of women in AMS activities, surveys the number of papers by women in its journal and other scholarly journals, surveys the number of women chosen to read papers and chair panels at annual meetings, and holds open meetings with panels at annual gatherings that address such issues as employment, promotion, tenure, researching, and teaching the History of Women in Music, Women's and Gender Studies, and Feminist Musicology. This committee has held meetings every year since 1991. All CSW documents are housed at the University of Pennsylvania in Philadelphia. Online, the CSW maintains a bibliography, syllabi, resources, and related links. Judy Tsou serves as the committee chair.

The College Music Society (CMS) is a consortium of colleges, conservatories, universities, and independent musicians and scholars; CMS is a member of the International Society for Music Education. The organization is dedicated to the science of learning and the art of teaching. CMS generates dialogue about the progress of music teaching, philosophy and practice of music, and participation in music on all levels. One of the most significant CMS forums focuses on women and gender. Additionally, CMS allies with many other professional organizations and provides three special committees—mentoring, student concerns, and advocacy. Workshops and performances explore issues, including teaching about women and gender, and music technology. The 20-year-old committee on music, women, and gender sponsors studies, projects, and conferences. Four "institutes" have been presented to date, including "Women, Music, and Technology." Judith A. Coe currently chairs the CSW.

The Society for American Music (for-merly the Sonneck Society for American Music) was founded in honor of Oscar Sonneck as a nonprofit scholarly and educational organization to "stimulate the appreciation, performance, creation, and study of American music in all its historical and contemporary styles and contexts." Members who have similar interests form groups and have sessions at annual conferences. There are 12 interest groups, including Research on Gender in American Music, Research Resources, and Twentieth-Century Music. The Research on Gender in American Music special interest group has most recently been chaired by Kay Norton.

The Society of Composers, Inc. (for-merly the American Society of University Composers), is a professional society formed to promote new and contemporary music through composition, performance, and understanding. Members include performers and composers in and outside of academia. There is an executive committee, which includes officers, editors of publications, the producer of the compact disc series, the electronic mail coordinator, and others. The Society of Composers, Inc., has a special committee on minorities that has been chaired by Marshall Bialosky. In 1997 at the Tenth International Congress on Women in Music (Valencia, CA), Bialosky was honored for his many years of service to promote the participation of women and minorities within the SCI organization.

The Society for Music Theory (SMT) was established in 1977 in order to promote music theory as a scholarly and pedagogical discipline. The Society's intention is to support the development of various aspects of music theory through workshops and professional development. The Society publishes the *Music Theory Spectrum* semiannually.

The SMT has an executive board with five officers, committees, and interest groups. One of the most important committees—the Committee on the Status of Women (CSW)—now a standing committee, has developed one of the largest "Bibliographies of Sources Related to Women's Studies, Gender Studies, Feminism and Music on the Web." It aims to promote gender equity and feminist scholarship related to music theory and to be a source of information about women and music. The CSW has developed the "Guidelines for Nonsexist Language," which covers terms such as "generic man" and subjects such as masculine pronouns, sex-role stereotypes, and exclusionary language. Additionally, the CSW has a wide-ranging mentoring program with database match-up capabilities. Also available on the World Wide Web is an archive of syllabi of women and music courses. Elizabeth Sayrs chairs the CSW.

See also Organizations, Music Education; Organizations, Professional Audio; Organizations, Research

For Further Reading

American Music Network. Available: http://American-Music.org
AMS [American Musicological Society] Website. Available: http://www.sas.upenn.edu/music/ams/
The Society for Music Theory. Available: http://smt.ucsb.edu/smt-list/smthome.html
Welcome to the College Music Society. Available: http://www.music.org

Alicia RaMusa

Compensatory History

The term "compensatory history," which implies that the research compensates or makes amends to women for past exclusion and neglect, originated in the 1970s and reflects that era's political movements toward improving women's status and achieving greater equality. The historian Gerda Lerner in a 1975 essay described compensatory history as preliminary to other, more informative phases of women's historiography that may be designated bifocal history, feminist history, and multifocal history. Because compensatory history seeks to identify women whose work seems to have met the standards of the accepted canon of great male composers and great works, the terms "exceptional woman" and "woman worthy" are used for women so depicted as exceptions to the general rule that women's work is insignificant. Identifying outstanding black and other nonwhite women and men in white-identified areas of music may also be termed a compensatory activity.

Early studies, such as those by Rupert Hughes, Arthur Elson, and Otto Ebel, highlight women of achievement in a way that later historians might call compensatory. Arthur Elson's *Woman's Work in Music* (1903) includes a chapter on "America" with much information about Amy Marcy Cheney Beach (1867–1944) and briefer coverage of Margaret Rutheven Lang, Clara Rogers, Julia Rivé-King, Emma Steiner, Helen Josephine Andrus, Mildred Hill, and others. Otto Ebel in *Women Composers: A Biographical Handbook of Woman's Work in Music* (1902) presents a long article on Beach and shorter articles on Lang ("her published compositions promise well for the future"), Carrie Jacobs Bond (identified as a composer and writer), Caroline Richings Bernard (composer and celebrated singer), Amy Fay (musician and author), Jean Parkman Brown (author of *Intervals, Chords and Ear Training*), Louisa Cappiani (talented New York vocal teacher), and many composers of songs and hymns, including Helen Hood, Gertrude Griswold, and Mary

Knight Wood. Claire Reis in *Composers in America* (1947) presents information about the lives and works of 17 prominent women: Marion Bauer (1897–1955), Beach, Jeanne Behrend, Evelyn Berckman, Gena Branscombe (1881–1977), Radie Britain, Ulric Cole, Ruth Crawford Seeger (1901–1953), Mabel Daniels, Vivian Fine (1913–2000), Florence G. Galajukian, Miriam Gideon (1906–1996), Mary Howe, Dorothy James, Beatrice Laufer, Eda Rapoport, Louise Talma (1906–1996), and Mabel Wood-Hill.

Compensatory history is especially evident in the last three decades of the twentieth century. Edith Borroff's "Women Composers: Reminiscence and History" (*College Music Symposium*, 1975) identifies significant women in each era of Western classical music. Julia Smith's *Directory of American Women Composers with Selected Music for Senior and Junior Clubs* (1970) and E. Ruth Anderson's *Contemporary American Composers: A Biographical Dictionary* (1976; 2d ed., 1982) include many prominent women. Anya Lawrence's *Women of Notes: 1,000 Women Composers Born before 1900* (1978) includes several Americans, using information largely from Ebel and Elson. Jeannie G. Pool's "America's Women Composers: Up from the Footnotes," in a special women's issue of the *Music Educators Journal* (1979), reviews women's achievements since colonial times, as does Mary Brown Hinely's survey of "The Uphill Climb of Women in American Music," published in the same journal five years later (1984), in two parts: (I) performers and teachers, and (II) composers and conductors. Aaron I. Cohen's *International Encyclopedia of Women Composers* (1981; 2d ed., 1987) and the *New Grove* (also *Norton/Grove) Dictionary of Women Composers* (1995) both include hundreds of Americans. Sally Placksin in

American Women in Jazz, 1900 to the Present: The Words, Lives, and Music (1982) and Linda Dahl in *Stormy Weather: The Music and Lives of a Century of Jazzwomen* (1984) explore more recent history. Mildred Denby Green's *Black Women Composers: A Genesis* (1983) examines the lives and works of five prominent Americans of the twentieth century: Florence Price (1887–1953), Margaret Bonds (1913–1972), Evelyn LaRue Pittman (1827–1903), Julia Perry (1924–1979), and Lena McLin. Diane Jezic's *Women Composers: The Lost Tradition Found* (1988), a survey beginning in medieval Europe, contains sections on Beach, Clarke, and six recent U.S. composers: Katherine Hoover (b. 1937), Ellen Taaffe Zwilich (b. 1939), Ruth Schonthal (b. 1924), Barbara Kolb (b. 1939), Marga Richter (b. 1926), and Judith Lang Zaimont (b. 1945). Although the title suggests a compensatory view, much of the book is also bifocal in approach insofar as Jezic takes into account women's inferior social and cultural status.

Catalogs and studies of concert music composed by women begin to appear in great numbers in the 1980s. These include: Miriam Stewart-Green's *Women Composers: A Checklist of Works for the Solo Voice* (1980); Joan Meggett's *Keyboard Music by Women Composers* (1981); "Music for Clarinet by Women Composers," compiled by Elsa Ludewig-Verdehr and Jean Raines (in *Clarinet*, 1981); *Guitar Music by Women Composers : An Annotated Catalog*, compiled by Janna MacAuslan and Kristan Aspen (1997); Heidi Boenke's *Flute Music by Women Composers* (1988); Rose-Marie Johnson's *Violin Music by Women Composers* (1989); Adel Henrich's *Organ and Harpsichord Music by Women Composers: An Annotated Catalog* (1991); Helen Walker-Hill's *Piano Music by Black Women Composers* (1992); and Colette Ripley's "Concert Organ Music by Women Composers from the United States" (in *American Organist*, 1997). Other studies of women and their work include: Jane Weiner LePage's *Women Composers, Conductors, and Musicians of the Twentieth Century* (3 vols, 1980–1988); D. Antoinette Handy's *Black Women in American Bands and Orchestras* (1981); Charles Claghorn's *Women Composers and Hymnists* (1984) and *Women Composers and Songwriters* (1996); Carolynn Lindeman's *Women Composers of Ragtime* (1985); and Virginia Grattan's *American Women Songwriters: A Biographical Dictionary* (1993).

Intended for classroom use, James Briscoe's *Historical Anthology of Music* (1987), which begins with medieval Europe, includes music by nine American women, with introductory essays about each composer's life and work: Beach, Rebecca Clarke (1886–1979), Crawford Seeger, Gideon, Talma, Perry, Fine, Pauline Oliveros (b. 1932), and Zwilich. Briscoe's *Contemporary Anthology of Music by Women* (1998), reflecting an increasing diversity in the 1990s, includes composers of popular and country music, musical theater, and jazz, 20 of whom are American: Emma Lou Diemer (b. 1927), Kolb, Joan La Barbara (b. 1947), Libby Larsen (b. 1950), Tania León (b. 1943), Babbie Mason, Joni Mitchell (b. 1943), Meredith Monk (b. 1942), Undine Smith Moore (1904–1989), Alice Parker (b. 1925), Dolly Parton (b. 1946), Shulamit Ran (b. 1949), Jean Ritchie (b. 1922), Lucy Simon, Natalie Sleeth, Grace Wiley Smith, Joan Tower (b. 1938), Nancy Van de Vate (b. 1930), Mary Lou Williams (1910–1981), and Zaimont. For student ensembles, Jane Palmquist and Barbara Payne offer "The Inclusive In-strumental Library: Works by Women" (*Music Educators Journal*, 1992).

Recordings are indispensable to historical study, and several new labels, such as Leonarda Productions, Rosetta Records, and Northeastern, which specialize in music by women, date from the 1970s and 1980s. Jane Frasier's *Women Composers: A Discography* (1983), Aaron Cohen's *International Discography of Women Composers* (1984), later updated and published in his *International Encyclopedia of Women Composers*, 2d ed. (1987), and Jan Leder's *Women in Jazz: A Discography of Instrumentalists, 1913–1968* (1985) provide valuable information about recorded performances, including some issued by small, little-known companies.

Bibliographers have published indexes to the coverage of women musicians in standard music reference sources; early examples are Susan Stern's *Women Composers: A Handbook* (1978) and JoAnn Skowronski's *Women in American Music: A Bibliography* (1978). As an indication of the increased recognition of women musicians, Don Hixon and Don Hennessee's *Women in Music: A Biobibliography* (1975), which lists existing references to American and European women in one slim volume, expands to two large volumes in the second edition, retitled *Women in Music: An Encyclopedic Biobibliography* (1993).

The so-called compensatory approach has come under criticism for the scholarly conservatism of its dependence on criteria derived from the elitist male canon. Elizabeth Wood, in a "Review Essay: Women and Music" (*Signs*, 1980), asserts that discussions of women's work "in terms of the dominant musical culture or methodology alone" are lacking in "scholarly substance." Jeannie Pool, in "A Critical Approach to the History of Women in Music" (*Heresies*, 1980), likewise observes that biographies of notable women merely constitute a defensive response to questions of greatness, a canonic concept. Yet, almost 10 years later, Jane Bowers, in an extensive survey of "Feminist Scholarship and the Field of Musicology" (*College Music Symposium*, 1989–1990), maintains the importance of such "fact-finding" research, along with imaginative new interdisciplinary methodologies and organizing ideas.

See also Bifocal History; Exceptional Woman; Feminist Music History; Historiography; Multifocal History

For Further Reading

Bowers, Jane M. "Feminist Scholarship and the Field of Musicology [I, II]." *College Music Symposium* 29 (1989): 81–92; vol. 30, no. 1 (Spring 1990): 1–13.

Wood, Elizabeth. "Review Essay: Women and Music." *Signs: Journal of Women and Culture in Society* 6/2 (1980): 283–297.

Deborah Hayes

Composer

Although historically women composers have met with great difficulty, the late twentieth century saw many women active in all genres of composition. Women have gained more recognition, had more performance and recording opportunities, and have obtained levels of education previously only available to men. Whether working in academia or as independent composers, women achieved more during the twentieth century than ever before.

A primary source of income for composers may be a commission: a contractual agreement to write music for a fee supplied by a commissioning organization. Details about the work are stipulated by the commissioning organization, such as duration, performers, premiere date, and who retains performance rights and copyright. Although most commissions are arranged between parties familiar with each other's work, there are some commissioning programs and competitions available to all composers. These usually require anonymous submissions to ensure that women are considered equally with men. Women currently making their living through commissions include Libby Larsen (b. 1950) and Ellen Taaffe Zwilich (b. 1939).

Women composers who routinely hold residencies include Pauline Oliveros (b. 1932) and Joan Tower (b. 1938). Composers who are "in-residence" are hired by an institution or ensemble to create an unspecified amount of music during a given period, such as a year. Another source of income for composers is grants. Many government organizations and foundations offer grants and fellowships. Unlike the commission, grants and fellowships usually do not stipulate details about the music to be written, beyond those proposed by the composer in the grant application. Grants are designed to give the composer a set amount of time to concentrate on composing. Although grant applications are not usually submitted anonymously, blind judges are often used at some stage of the selection process to help prevent discrimination. Additionally, there are grants available specifically for women artists and women's projects.

In the commercial music industry, there are many opportunities for composers. Film scoring, or composing the music for a movie, television show, or industrial film, is a common field for the trained composer. Additionally, there are fields in advertising, radio, theater, and even books-on-tape that employ composers. Many composers run their own studios and businesses, supplying music for commercial purposes. The World

Wide Web has provided many additional venues for the dissemination of both women's music and their composition-related business ventures. Wendy Carlos (b. 1939) has composed many scores for movies, and Shirley Walker (b. 1945) is a highly acclaimed film and television composer.

Composers often supplement composition income with related activities that draw upon their specialized skills. Many conservatories and colleges employ composers to teach composition and related classes, including orchestration, counterpoint, theory, and arranging. Because they are traditionally underrepresented among faculties, special efforts have been made recently to hire women and minorities at most campuses. Some composers give master classes where they meet with students for brief but intensive workshops. Others work as copyists, preparing scores and parts for composers and publishing companies. Still others work as arrangers, creating arrangements of existing music for specific ensembles, such as setting a popular tune for marching band. Arrangers are also used extensively to orchestrate and prepare parts for performers who will record film and television scores, and by publishers to prepare piano arrangements of popular tunes. Although not composition, these activities require the skill and knowledge of a professional composer.

See also Fulbright Fellowship Program; Guggenheim Award; Performing and Mechanical Rights Organizations; Prizes, Composer and Performer

For Further Reading

IAWM [International Alliance for Women in Music] Journal. A publication of the International Alliance for Women in Music.
Women and Music: A Journal of Gender and Culture. Annual. Lincoln: University of Nebraska Press.
Dorothy E. Hindman

Conant, Abbie (1955–)

Trombonist Abbie Conant is one of the most important brass musicians of the twentieth century. Her landmark gender discrimination case against the Munich Philharmonic culminated in victory after a protracted court battle. It stands today as one of the first and most publicly documented cases in the history of women orchestral musicians. Hired as a solo trombone performer in 1980, Conant successfully completed her probationary year and was granted tenure by a vote of the orchestra. Nonetheless she was demoted to second trombone in 1982 by Music Director Sergiu Celibidache, who stated, "You know the problem: we need a man for solo trombone." Conant filed a sex discrimination suit, and in 1988 the court ruled in her favor. Although Conant was immediately reinstated to her position of solo trombone, the orchestra refused to pay her as a solo trombonist or to deliver her the back pay she was entitled to until they received the three-page written judgment from the judge that arrived two years later. The orchestra then placed Conant in a lower salary group than all 15 of her (male) solo-wind colleagues. In 1991 Conant won the lawsuit; this decision was appealed, but Conant won again in 1993. After 13 years of litigation, Conant finally regained the position she had won in 1980, receiving the same pay and seniority as her male colleagues. Vindicated, Conant left the orchestra and accepted a tenured position at the State Conservatory of Music in Trossingen, Germany. She was replaced in the Munich Philharmonic by a 17-year-old man with no orchestral experience.

Abbie Conant was born on 14 March 1955 in Pryor, OK. She began her trombone studies in the eighth grade and received her high school diploma from Interlochen Arts Academy in 1973. She received a Bachelor of Music degree *cum laude* in 1977 from Temple University as a student of M. Dee Stewart and a Master of Music degree in 1979 from the Juilliard School as a student of Per Brevig. Other teachers include Vinko Globokar at L'Accademia di Chigiana in Siena (Master Course 1979) and Branimir Slokar at the Staatliche Hochschule für Musik Köln (Soloists Diploma 1984). Conant was solo trombonist of the Royal Opera of Turin (1979–1980 season) and solo trombonist of the Munich Philharmonic (1980–1993). She has been professor of trombone at the Staatliche Hochschule für Musik in Trossingen, Germany, since 1992.

In 1992 Conant was elected to the Board of Directors of the International Trombone Association, and in 1998 she was the first woman to serve on the jury of the International Trombone Competition in Geneva, Switzerland. She has been a featured soloist at many professional conferences. She has made the recording *Trombone and Organ* (Audite 97.410) and was featured as the cover story for journal articles published by the International Trombone Association and the British Trombone Society. In addition to having roles in two other feature films, Conant was the subject of the musical documentary film *Abbie Get Your Gun* (1994). She tours extensively with the Wasteland Theatre Company, performing music-theater works by her composer husband, William Osborne.

See also Classical Music; Performer, Brass

For Further Reading

Buzzarté, Monique. "We Need a Man for Solo Trombone: Abbie Conant's Story." *Journal of the International Alliance for Women in Music* (February 1996): 8–11.

Magliocco, Hugo. "A Special Endurance." *International Trombone Association Journal* 20/2 (Spring 1992): 22–28.

Monique Buzzarté

Concert Series

See Conferences and Festivals

Conductor, Choral

A choral conductor is responsible for artistic, and often administrative, direction of either a professional or amateur chorus. From the beginning of the 1900s, women choral conductors were more prevalent than women orchestral conductors. The number of women church and school choir directors grew significantly, and the mainstream public became aware of women's directorial capabilities. Nevertheless it took the first several decades of the twentieth century for women to enter the professional world of choral conducting in substantial numbers.

By the 1920s, women's names first appeared as leaders of recognized ensembles on the East Coast. New York's first major choral concert conducted by a woman took place in 1926: the Schola Cantorum was led by German-born Margarete Dessoff (1874–1944). Soon afterward, she founded both a women's choir and a mixed chorus. These groups merged in 1929 and became the Dessoff Choirs; they continued to perform in New York City well into the late twentieth century.

Canadian American pianist, composer, and conductor Gena Branscombe (1881–1977) began her conducting career in the early 1920s with the MacDowell Colony Chorus. She frequently conducted her own choral compositions in Canada, England, and the United States. In 1934 she formed her own semiprofessional women's chorus, the Branscombe Choral, and led it for the next 20 years.

A group of outstanding women conductors emerged in the late 1940s and 1950s. Lorna Cook de Varon (b. 1922) studied with Robert Shaw at Tanglewood and joined the faculty in 1953 as conductor of the Tanglewood Festival Chorus. In 1947 de Varon accepted a professorship at the New England Conservatory. The large choral group she formed in 1950 made many recordings with the Boston Symphony.

The contributions made to the musical life in Chicago and to choral music in general by Margaret Hillis (1921–1998) cannot be overvalued. She studied at the Juilliard School with Robert Shaw and in 1950 founded the Tanglewood Alumni Chorus. Seven years later Fritz Reiner asked her to organize a permanent professional chorus to give regular performances with the Chicago Symphony. It was the first chorus of its kind in the United States. Hillis led the group more than 600 times and took part in 45 recordings, nine of which won Grammy Awards.

Iva Dee Hiatt (1919–1980), after a brief career as a teacher at the San Francisco Conservatory and the University of California Extension Division Music School, did not have private money to form her own professional chorus, so she joined the Smith College faculty as director of choral activities in 1948. At Tanglewood's Berkshire Music Center in 1948, she was the first woman to conduct a work for chorus and orchestra in the Tanglewood Shed. Hiatt returned to Tanglewood as a staff conductor during the 1960s and prepared choruses for Erich Leinsdorf, Charles Munch, Pierre Monteux, and Leonard Bernstein. She later served on the staff of the Aspen Choral Institute and was director of the Cambridge Society for Early Music from 1965 to 1977. Hiatt was the inspiration and mentor for dozens of women choral conductors who now hold positions all over the country.

Robert Shaw was also important in the career of conductor, composer, and choral arranger. Alice Parker (b. 1925), who is known internationally for her settings of American hymns, folksongs, and spirituals as well as for Melodious Accord, a 16-voice professional chorus she founded in 1985. Parker travels throughout the United States and abroad conducting concerts and workshops for professional and amateur groups of all ages.

One of the most important contributors to choral music in the United States during the latter half of the twentieth century was Margaret Hawkins (1937–1993). She started the Milwaukee Symphony Chorus in 1976 and remained its conductor until her untimely death. Besides conducting multiple Christmas programs with her singers, she led many concerts on the Symphony Orchestra's regular schedule. Hawkins founded an annual program under which 200 Wisconsin high school students are invited to sing major works with the orchestra. During her tenure the Chorus made important recordings of unusual repertoire including Sergei Prokofiev's *Alexander Nevsky* and Berlioz's *Lélio*, as well as Antonin Dvorák's *Stabat Mater* and *Te Deum*.

Elaine Brown (1910–1997) founded Singing City in 1948 and made it into one of Philadelphia's premier music organizations. Brown took her group to the Soviet Union, Israel, and the Middle East. Following the U.S. Supreme Court's 1955 school desegregation decision and during civil rights struggles of the 1960s, Brown and her choir made several tours through the southern United States. Singing City's 50th anniversary season was a celebration of Brown's dream to "create a choir with a difference," an ensemble of artistic excellence that would not only sing but also generate a sense of community with its singers and audiences.

Emily Remington (b. 1916) founded two important vocal organizations. The Augusta Choral Society, begun in 1951, performed under her baton for a total of 25 years. Remington joined the College of Charleston faculty in 1976. When an earlier Charleston Choral Society had transformed itself into an opera company, Remington was asked to begin a new group to perform with the symphony. This group is now known as the Charleston Symphony Singers' Guild. Remington remained its artistic director until her retirement in 1996.

In America's far north, it was women conductors who early in the twentieth century took positions of leadership in choral music performance. The Fairbanks Oratorio Society, under the direction of Dr. Aline Bradley, presented a performance of *The Holy City* during the winter of 1907–1908, a scant five years after the founding of Fairbanks as a gold mining camp. Three years later, Jeanette Drury Clark reorganized the Oratorio Society under the name Fairbanks Choral Club. She felt that "during the quiet winter months, choral work will be a pleasure and a benefit to those taking part, while providing some entertainment for the camp at large."

Lorene Harrison (b. 1905) founded the Anchorage Community Chorus in 1946 and the Anchorage Concert Association in 1950. Mary Hale (b. 1920) took over the Community Chorus in 1950 but left it six years later to organize the Alaska Festival of Music. Hale was responsible for Robert Shaw's initial invitation to take part in the 49th state's musical activities. Following in the pioneering path of Harrison and Hale, Elvera Voth (b. 1923) became the Community Chorus's third director in 1959. She was a major figure in Anchorage's myriad of choral and operatic activities until she returned to her Kansas roots in 1994. Voth now heads the Lyric Opera of Kansas City Chorus and the East Hill Singers, an inmate chorus she started at the State Prison in Lansing.

Virginia Davidson (b. 1928) was the founder and director of the New York Treble Singers, a group of 12 professional singers that celebrated its 15th anniversary 1999. She also conducts the Davidson Singers, a touring ensemble, and the Great Neck Choral Society. Before opening her New York studio, she founded the Winter Haven, FL, Youth Symphony; the Florida Camerata; and the Bach Festival of Central Florida.

In the closing decades of the twentieth century, a third group of women conductors became active throughout the United States. Amy Kaiser (b. 1945) guided the Dessoff Choirs in New York for 12 years and is currently director of the Saint Louis Symphony Chorus. She has prepared choruses for New York Philharmonic, Ravina Festival, Mostly Mozart Festival, and the Opera Orchestra of New York, to mention but a few. In 2000 she returned for a sixth season to the Berkshire Choral Festival. Kaiser has conducted more than 25 operas for the Berkshire Opera, the Opera Ensemble of New York, and the Metropolitan Opera Guild.

Judith Clurman (b. 1953), founding director of the New York Concert Singers and the Judith Clurman Chorale, is on the faculty of the Juilliard School. Her ensembles have been featured in performances with major orchestras, including the New York Philharmonic, the Boston Symphony Orchestra, and Orchestra of St. Luke's, as well as on Great Performances at Lincoln Center. Her outreach to contemporary popular culture includes directing Lincoln Center's annual Christmas Tree Lighting Ceremony and television appearances with David Letterman and the Sesame Street Muppets.

Frances Fowler Slade (b. 1949), is founder and music director of Princeton Pro Musica, a 120-voice chorus of professional and volunteer singers dedicated to the performance of major choral works with orchestra. This chorus has performed concerts at Carnegie and Merkin Halls in New York City, as well as in New Jersey and Pennsylvania. Slade studied with Margaret Hillis and led the choral program at Douglass College of Rutgers University for 12 years.

Upon graduation from the University of Oregon, Kathy Salzman Romey (b. 1956) continued her studies with Helmut Rilling in Frankfort, Germany. There she was a member of his professional choir, the Gächinger Kantorei, assisted at Stuttgart's Memorial Church, and was on the staff of Rilling's International Bach Academy. Romey headed choral activities at Macalester College from 1985 to 1992 and then joined the University of Minnesota faculty. After serving as assistant director of the Minnesota Chorale from 1992 to 1995, she was appointed its artistic director. The Chorale performs with both the Minnesota Orchestra and the St. Paul Chamber Orchestra, and Romey has prepared the group for appearances under the baton of major international conductors. Since 1984,

Romey has returned to her home state as a staff member of the Oregon Bach Festival. She currently prepares the Festival's professional chorus for performances and recordings.

J. Michele Edwards (b. 1945) studied conducting with Margaret Hillis, Daniel Moe, and James Dixon. In 1976 she founded Harmonia Mundi, a professional double wind quintet and piano ensemble. Edwards has been active in commissioning and premiering new works and has a strong commitment to the performance of music by women composers. Edwards began teaching at Macalester College in 1974, where she held a dual appointment in Women's and Gender Studies until her retirement in 2001. Edwards has been director of choral activities for the College Music Society's Institute on Women, Music and Gender (1996) and the Summer Institute on the Study and Teaching of Women in Music (1993). She currently directs the Calliope Women's Chorus.

Anne Howard Jones is the director of choral activities at Boston University where she conducts the symphonic and chamber choruses and heads the master's and doctoral programs in choral conducting. She also conducts the University's Tanglewood Institute Chorus, an auditioned ensemble of high school singers who perform at Tanglewood each summer. From 1984 to 1999, Jones was the assistant conductor for choruses with the Atlanta Symphony under the late Robert Shaw. She also assisted with the Robert Shaw Chamber Singers, was one of the founders of the Robert Shaw Institute, and assisted with the Festival Singers in the United States and France.

Judith Willoughby (b. 1953) is the founding artistic director of both the Choral Society of Montgomery County

(PA) and the Temple University's Children's Choir. The Choral Society has performed neglected works by Monteverdi, Handel, and Telemann. Her Children's Choir has performed at regional and national meetings of American Choral Directors Association and has sung with the Philadelphia Orchestra. During the summer of 2000 the ensemble participated in the Pacific International Children's Choral Festival and sang the *St. Matthew Passion* at the Oregon Bach Festival.

Anne Harrington Heider, director of choral ensembles at Chicago Musical College of Roosevelt University, lists Iva Lee Hiatt, Andrea von Ramm, and Alice Parker among her mentors. As artistic director of His Majestie's Clerkes, a professional *a cappella* chamber choir, she has produced a long list of programs for National Public Radio and several Chicago-area radio stations. Heider has prepared His Majestie's Clerkes for concerts with Simon Preston, Paul Hillier, and Alice Parker and has conducted the group on most of its numerous recordings. Almeda Berkey (b. 1947), singer, conductor, lyrist, and former director of choral activities at the University of Nebraska at Omaha, is the founder and music director of the professional ensemble Soli Deo Gloria Cantorum of Omaha. Norman Luboff and Eric Ericson were her choral mentors. She currently works closely with her husband, composer and arranger Jackson Berkey. Her diverse activities include conducting concerts and making recordings with the Cantorum and touring as keyboardist with Mannheim Steamroller.

In the western United States, numerous conductors have enriched the world of choral music with their teaching abilities and compositions as well as through their leadership in the manifold aspects of choral management. The following are but three examples of the varied talents to be found among today's women directors. Nina Gilbert (b. 1956), associate conductor of choirs, University of California—Irvine, and Monica Hubbard (b. 1943), director of choral activities at the California Institute of Technology for 27 years, are prime representatives of those women who have extended their involvement in the world of choral music beyond a campus setting and into editing and publishing, outreach to music programs in the public schools, consultations for boards of directors, and national committees on choral standards and repertoire. Karen P. Thomas (b. 1957) divides her time between composing and serving as artistic director and conductor of Seattle Pro Musica, a position she has held since 1987.

As the 1900s became the second millennium, women choral conductors had traveled far—from the schoolroom and church choir rehearsals, to the stages of many important concert venues in the United States and abroad. Their talents have been recognized by major critics and, even more important, by the boards of directors of many leading musical institutions; by the thousands of vocalists, both amateur and professional, who find singing in a group one of their life's most important and enriching activities; and by the audiences who attend the thousands of choral concerts presented each year.

See also Choral Education; Conductor, Instrumental and Operatic; Performer, Choral and Vocal Ensemble

For Further Reading

Ammer, Christine. *Unsung*. Revised and expanded second edition. Portland, OR: Amadeus Press, 2001.

Jepson, Barbara. "American Women in Conducting." *Feminist Art Journal* (Winter 1975/76): 13–18.

Suzanne Summerville

Conductor, Instrumental and Operatic

The instrumental and operatic conductor is responsible for orchestra, opera, ballet, and academic ensembles. Although there have been many important women choral conductors throughout the twentieth century, the history of women instrumental and operatic conductors does not enjoy the same history. Instrumental and operatic conducting has traditionally been a male-dominated career; however, beginning in the 1970s more women began to graduate from conservatories, entered the field and gained professional positions. The opportunities for women conductors have gradually become more widespread.

A professional orchestra conductor in a music director position oversees the performance endeavors including programming the season's repertoire, selecting guest artists, and auditioning musicians. The music director is often involved in many aspects of activities, including long-range planning, community outreach, organizational functions and programs, and as spokesperson. The training of a conductor usually begins at an early age. Thorough training includes sight singing, ear training, harmony, counterpoint, instrumentation, orchestration, music history, styles, performance practice, conducting technique, and a wide spectrum of repertoire study. A conductor often attends rehearsals and performances, master classes, recital and chamber music concerts, and the like to gain deeper understanding of all the musical fields and subjects. Very often the valuable training continues after degree programs and in music festivals, workshops and intense professional conducting programs. Some individuals gain opportunities in apprentice positions before entering assistant, associate, resident, and music director positions in the professional field.

During the early part of the twentieth century there were few opportunities for women conductors. Antonia Brico (1902–1989) and Ethel Leginska (1886–1970) were among the first women conductors in the United States. Leginska conducted the Women's Symphony Orchestra (Chicago) from 1927 to 1930, and later the National Women's Symphony Orchestra (New York). Brico became the first woman to conduct the Berlin and New York Philharmonic orchestras. Other important women conductors in the United States include Sarah Caldwell (b. 1924), Fiora Contino, Eve Queler (b. 1936), Catherine Comet, JoAnn Falletta (b. 1945), Tania León (b. 1943), Victoria Bond (b. 1945), Kay George Roberts, Anne Manson (b. 1960), Marin Alsop (b. 1956), Gisele Ben-Dor, Kate Tamarkin, Apo Hsu (b. 1956), Carol Crawford, Diane Wittry, Keri-Lynn Wilson, and Janna Hymes Bianchi.

See also Conductor, Choral

For Further Reading

Collins, Judy, and Jill Godmilow. *Antonia: Portrait of the Woman*. New York: Phoenix Films, 1974.
LePage, Jane Weiner. *Women Composers, Conductors, and Musicians of the Twentieth Century: Selected Biographies*. Metuchen, NJ: Scarecrow Press, 1985.

Apo Hsu

Conferences and Festivals

Women contributed to the sociological phenomenon of American music conferences and festivals throughout the twentieth century. These are organized events in the history of American music where people gathered together for performance, research, celebration, or fellowship. The first half of the century can be said to have the general characteristic of "women for music," whereas the second half of the century was more clearly a period of "music for women."

Two late-nineteenth-century events foreshadowed the participation of women in musical happenings of the twentieth century. In 1876 Fanny Raymond Ritter addressed the Association for the Advancement of Women at the Centennial Congress held in Philadelphia. In her address, "Woman as a Musician: An Art-historical Study," Ritter issued three directives: (1) that music composition should be an elective if not a required subject at women's colleges; (2) that women should be encouraged to study instruments other than the piano; and (3) that women should take on the role of patron in the formation of music libraries, collections of rare musical instruments, and societies for music performance.

In July 1893 at the Art Institute of Chicago during the convention of the American College of Musicians and the Music Teachers National Association, the Woman's Musical Congress presented three sessions at which women read papers by women educators and performed the music of women composers. These attracted the largest audiences because of the participation of leading women in music, the interesting subject matter of the papers, and the fact that the sessions had a unifying theme: the contributions of American women in music. Women would indeed make significant contributions as composers, performers, librarians, patrons, philanthropists, producers, hosts, lecturers, and afficionados

of music happenings during the following century.

The "women for music" paradigm of the first half of the century is reflected in the National Federation of Music Clubs (NFMC). Chartered in 1898, the initial purposes of NFMC were to foster new clubs, organize state federations, and turn private concerts by well-known artists into public fund-raising events. However, the emphasis quickly shifted to managing artists' concerts and promoting music by American composers. At the fourth annual convention in Denver (1905), songs by Mary Turner Salter were performed and the Olive Mead Quartet gave a concert. In 1907 the NFMC established an American Music Department, which directed clubs to give preference to American artists and American music and established a biennial competition for American composers.

Another important organization, the National League of American Pen Women, held conventions at which its composer-members performed, including Mary Howe, Dorothy Raddle Emery, and Marianne Genet. In 1925 the first festival sponsored by the League featured works by Karolyn Wells Bassett, Frances Marion Ralston, Harriet Ware, and Amy Marcy Cheney Beach (1867–1944). In 1932 the League presented 23 recitals and a "national concert" featuring compositions by Ruth Crawford Seeger (1901–1953), Pearl Adams, Mary Carr Moore, and Marjorie Dudley. Many of the composers featured at the American Pen Women conventions were also charter members of the Society of American Women Composers formed in 1924. Amy Marcy Cheney Beach served as the organization's first president.

On the local level, the impact of women's music clubs was significant. Between 1899 and 1930 the Artists Series of the Women's Club of Columbus, OH, produced 10 major symphony orchestras, three opera companies, and six chamber ensembles. Mrs. Charles B. Kelsey and the St. Cecilia Club of Grand Rapids, MI, erected a building for their concerts. In 1911, Claire Raphael Reis (1888–1978), better remembered as the executive director of the International Composers Guild and later of the League of Composers, established the People's Music League, presenting some 200 free concerts each year for arriving immigrants in New York schools. Ella May Smith (1860–1916), president of the Music Club of Columbus from 1903 to 1916, organized convention programs around the music of American composers and African American composers for conventions of the Ohio State Music Teachers Association. One woman was especially known for her managerial skills: Adella Prentiss Hughes (1869–1950) of Cleveland's Fortnightly Music Club. Anna Schoen-René (1864–1942), known as the "Musical Czarina" of Minneapolis, paid for the renovations of the city's exposition hall and formed the first organized branch of the Mozart Society. In 1910 an article appeared in *Musical America* declaring that club women had obtained "an executive ability equal in its results with that of the majority of successful men" and suggesting that "a musical foundation is being built that nothing can topple."

Even as the grass-roots and national efforts of women's clubs across the United States sustained considerable support for music happenings in America, a few individuals contributed directly to the establishment of important festivals. One of the most influential women patrons of the early twentieth century was Ellen Battell Stoeckel (1851–1939). In 1900 she and her husband formed the

Norfolk Music Festival in Connecticut. For 22 years the festival hosted performances by some of the finest performers in America and Europe. Among the women who performed at the Norfolk Festival were Fanny Bloomfield-Zeisler, Maud Allen, Alma Gluck, and Louise Homer. Maud Powell (1867–1920), a premier violinist of the time and a devotee of contemporary music, performed often at the festival and premiered many new works by Max Bruch, Jean Sibelius, and Samuel Coleridge-Taylor. Works were often commissioned by Stoeckel for the festival, including *The Oceanides* by Sibelius in 1914, with the composer conducting the premiere performance. Other commissions went to George Chadwick, Victor Herbert, Horatio Parker, and Percy Grainger.

Another patroness whose contributions had a lasting impact on the festival scene in America was Elizabeth Sprague Coolidge (1846–1953). In 1918, two years after forming the Berkshire Quartet, Coolidge established the Berkshire Festival of Chamber Music in western Massachusetts. Later she became known as the "Patron Saint" and the "Lady Bountiful of Chamber Music" in America. Her philanthropy extended to festivals and concerts in California and Europe and the establishment of the Founder's Day Festivals at the Library of Congress, where Aaron Copland's *Appalachian Spring* and Samuel Barber's *Hermit Songs* were premiered.

Elizabeth Coolidge later served as honorary president for Henry Hadley's Berkshire Symphonic Festival (Tanglewood), in 1934. Similarly, Gertrude Robinson Smith, Mrs. Owen Johnson, and Mrs. William Fulton Barrett were instrumental in the success of this festival. In the same year Mary Aspinwall Tappan and her niece, Mrs. Andrew H. Hepburn, donated the land at Tanglewood for the site of the festival. A similar donation of land and funding for indoor and outdoor theaters was made by Catherine Filene Shouse for the Wolf Trap Festival. Other leaders in the "women for music" movement of the first half of the twentieth century include Ruth Haller Ottaway Sokoloff (1886–1955), president of NFMC from 1929 to 1933, delegate to the Anglo-American Music Conference in Lucern in 1929, and chairwoman of the music committee within the National Council of Women; Lillian Baldwin, administrator of the internationally recognized plan for children's concerts known as the "Cleveland Plan" from 1929 to 1956; Emma Roderick, instrumental in organizing the New England Festival Association; Caroline Beebe, New York pianist and founder of the New York Chamber Music Society; Emma Azalia Hackley (1867–1922), responsible for organizing conventions and concerts in African American communities in the East and South; Blanche Wetherill Walton (1871–1963), whose patronage assisted many budding composers, including Henry Cowell, Ruth Crawford Seeger, and Charles Seeger, and whose apartment offered a location for the first meeting of what became the American Musicological Society; and Marion Bauer (1897–1955), the only woman among the founders of the League of Composers.

The second half of the twentieth century witnessed the birth of a new class of music that has come to be known as "women-identified" music, or "women's music." This "music for women" characteristic reflected the changing roles of women in American society influenced by the women's liberation movement and the changes in self-image and self-realization that came with it; women found new ways to contribute to music

happenings in America. Additionally the evolution of new musical styles and languages (e.g., folk, soul, rock and roll, country, and jazz) offered a new meaning to the definition of "festivals" and "conventions." While women increased their activity in the performance, research, and celebration of classical music, popular music opened up new venues for self-expression, including pop and rock festivals. This moved women from behind-the-scenes "women for music" to the stage and lectern, "music for women."

There was little room in the misogynist world of rock for the evolving American woman. Her growing independence and continued self-awareness could not tolerate the music and lyrics of rock's male-dominated industry. Janis Joplin (1943–1970) arose to perform rock from a woman's perspective. However, her success, launched at the Monterrey International Pop Festival of 1967, came to an untimely end with her death in 1970. Without a pioneer and unable to sway the anti-feminine direction of rock, women of the 1960s and 1970s responded to the alienation and misogyny by forming their own groups. Early women-identified music was written and performed by Maxine Feldman, Alix Dobkin, Kay Garner, the Chicago Women's Liberation Rock Band, and the New Haven Women's Liberation Band. Their music reflected the socio-political paradigm of the times, which included lesbian and feminist themes. The titles alone reveal examples of these themes: "A Woman's Anger," "Whole Woman," "Woman to Woman," and "Talking Gay Bar Blues."

From the mid-1970s to the turn of the century, music festivals celebrating the liberation of women proliferated. The first Women's Music Festival was formed by Kate Miller in 1973 at Sacramento

State University, followed by the first National Women's Music Festival in 1974 at the University of Illinois at Champaign-Urbana. By the turn of the century, some 27 festivals survived to offer annual events including the Michigan Womyn's Music Festival (1976), Boston Women's Music Festival (1975), Wiminfest, New Mexico (1981), and the West Coast Lesbian Festival, California (1992). Performers and producers associated with these festivals include Meg Christian, Holly Near (b. 1945), Cris Williamson, Deadly Nightshade, Margie Adams, the New Miss Alice Stone Ladies' Society Orchestra, Melissa Etheridge (b. 1961), Tracy Chapman (b. 1964), Mary Byrne, Barbara Price, the Indigo Girls, and Tribe 8.

In addition to the popular women's music festivals of the latter half of the century such as Lilith Fair and others, women in professional music organizations held "music happenings" in the form of conferences and festivals. The Music Library Association, the professional organization in the United States devoted to music librarianship and founded in 1931, held annual meetings providing a forum for study and action on issues affecting music libraries and their users. Its members made significant contributions to librarianship, publishing, standards of scholarship, and the development of new information technologies. Women who played important early roles in this organization include Eva Judd O'Meara, Anna Harriet Heyer (b. 1909), Catherine Keyes Miller, and Virginia Cunningham.

Jeannie Pool established the National (later International) Congress on Women in Music in 1978. The first of these congresses was held as a collaborative project with the International League of Women Composers. These congresses bring together professional and amateur musicians—performers, composers, and researchers of women's music—from many cultures and backgrounds.

With support from the International Alliance for Women in Music, the Fourth and Fifth International Festivals of Women Composers were held at the Indiana University of Pennsylvania in 1996 and 1998. These festivals were organized by Susan Wheatley and Sarah Mantle.

American women have affected significant changes in the standards of scholarship through their participation in other professional music organizations. Woman-centered and feminist strategies of music analysis and research did not fully take shape until the last decade of the twentieth century. The annual meeting of the American Musicological Society in 1988 provided a watershed experience for women in the field, presenting landmark works by Ruth Solie, Susan McClary, and Susan C. Cook. Other pioneers include Suzanne G. Cusick, Judith Tick, Carolyn Abbate, Caryl Flinn, Marcia J. Citron, Christine Ammer, Karen Peterson, and Ellen Koskoff. In June 1991 the first major conference devoted to feminist theory and music was held at the University of Minnesota.

See also International Congress on Women in Music; Lilith Fair

For Further Reading

Gaar, Gillian. *She's a Rebel: The History of Women in Rock and Roll.* Seattle: Seal Press, 1992.

Locke, Ralph P., and Cyrilla Barr (eds.). *Cultivating Music in America: Women Patrons and Activities since 1860.* Berkeley: University of California Press, 1977.

Morris, Bonnie J. *Eden Built by Eves: The Culture of Women's Music Festivals.* Los Angeles: Alyson Books, 1999.

Rabin, Carol Price. *Music Festivals in America: Classical, Opera, Jazz, Pops, Country, Old-Time*

Fiddlers, Folk, Bluegrass, Cajun, 4th ed. Great Barrington, MA: Berkshire House, 1990.

Stephen J. Rushing

Constructivism

Constructivism in relation to gender and music is the belief that differences between women and men musicians, and between women's music and men's music, are social and cultural constructs. Constructivism is contrasted with essentialism, the belief that differences between women and men are biologically determined essences. A parallel distinction is between culturally constructed gender (feminine, masculine) and biological sex (female, male). The difference is one between "nurture" (constructivism) and "nature" (essentialism) as determinants of human behavior and destiny. In the feminist revival in the 1960s and 1970s both views gave rise to effective feminist slogans: the personal is political (constructivist), and anatomy is destiny (essentialist).

In music history and aesthetics, the issue has been whether differences between women's and men's creativity and aesthetic response should be attributed to gender differences or to sex differences. Prevailing opinion has shifted since 1900. In the early decades, women's perceived inferiority as creative musicians was usually ascribed to innate female qualities, as explained by social Darwinism and related doctrines. The constructivist view, that social factors—institutionalized exclusion of women, definitions of creativity, and the like—are responsible, became the prevailing view in later decades. The constructivist view is strengthened by observations of how music itself helps to construct culture, including gender; music's constructive power has been revealed in considerations of gender in music analysis and the analytical approaches of feminist music theory.

At the same time, scientists continue to demonstrate that nature and nurture are mutually dependent. Human genome research reveals that even at the level of the chromosome certain genetic codes operate only in response to environmental stimuli. Such observations indicate that both constructivism and essentialism are valid with respect to women, men, and music.

See also Essentialism; Female Inferiority, Theories of; Feminist Music Theory; Gender in Music Analysis; Social Darwinism

For Further Reading

Burkett, Lyn. "Feminist Music Scholarship: An Informal Guide to 'Getting It.' " *Indiana Theory Review* 17/1 (1996): 65–76.

Deborah Hayes

Cooper, Adrienne (1946–)

Adrienne Cooper is a feminist Yiddish vocalist; she believes that singing Yiddish songs provides an opportunity to transmit a vocabulary of Jewish expressive culture through music. Cooper is a member of the faculty of the Academy of Jewish Religion and presents master classes in Yiddish Song throughout the world, including Russia, where she travels each summer to train Jewish musicians. Cooper is currently director of program development for the Workmen's Circle/Arbeter Ring and resides in New York.

Cooper was born on 1 September 1946 in Oakland, CA. Her grandmother made homemade wax discs of Yiddish folk and liturgical music, and her grandfather was a baritone *ba'al tfilah*. Adrienne's mother was an opera and musical theater performer and a prominent concert performer of Yiddish and

Hebrew music. Cooper began studying voice in her late teens with her mother's teacher, Mary Groom Jones. She continued studying classical art song with Mina Lief at the Rubin Academy of Music in Jerusalem. She then attended Hebrew University and received a B.A. in history. Later she continued voice training with Jennie Tourel and Simon Sargon. After returning to the United States she studied at the University of Chicago, where she received an M.A. in history. She first performed Yiddish songs in graduate school.

In 1975 Cooper moved to New York and was coached by Lazar Weiner. She also studied with Yiddish poet and lyricist Wolf Younin. After taking summer courses in Yiddish language, she became assistant director of the YIVO Institute for Jewish Research. In 1985 she cofounded with Henry Sapoznik the multigenerational Yiddish Folk Arts Program, popularly known as "Klezkamp." Klezkamp successfully trains upcoming music professionals and others interested in a folk education.

Cooper has presented concerts in Russia, Poland, Germany, Israel, Canada, and the United States, and she has performed and recorded with top klezmer bands including the Klezmatics, Hasidic New Wave, the Flying Bulgar Klezmer Band, Kapelye, and Frank London's Shekhine Big Band. Her singing can be heard at the U.S. Holocaust Memorial Museum and on compact discs such as *Remember the Children* (1991) and *Hidden Histories: Songs from the Kovno Ghetto* (1997). In 1989 Cooper recorded *Partisans of Vilna* (HC-VAR-10D). In 1995 she produced a solo album, *Dreaming in Yiddish* (AC432), accompanied by Joyce Rosenzweig. She also produced several collaborations with Zalman Mlotek, including her compact discs *On the Wings*

of Song, *Pearls of Yiddish*, and *Ghetto Tango* (Traditional Crossroads 4297; this label released some previously unknown theater and cabaret music created during World War II). In 1998 Cooper debuted with Mikveh, a women's klezmer band, in Eve Ensler's V-Day Benefit; and she produced the recording *Mikveh* (Transitional Crossroads 4305) in 2000.

See also Jewish Musicians; Multicultural Musics

For Further Reading

Rubin, Ruth. *Voices of a People: The Story of Yiddish FolkSong*. Philadelphia: Jewish Publication Society of America, 1979.
Sapoznik, Henry. "Music, Yiddish." In *Jewish-American History and Culture: An Encyclopedia*, eds. Jack Fischel and Sanford Pinsker. New York: Garland, 1992.
Slobin, Mark. *Tenement Songs: The Popular Music of the Jewish Immigrants*. Urbana: University of Illinois Press, 1982.

Judith S. Pinnolis

Copyist

The music copyist transcribes the composer's, arranger's, or orchestrator's notation of musical scores and extracts individual instrumental parts from the scores, transposing as needed. For most of the twentieth century this copying was done by hand with special pens and inks and with the aid of a variety of drafting tools. By the late 1990s most professional copyists had begun to use music notation software. However, the level of musical knowledge and the sense of layout and design required have not lessened since the advent of software usage.

Always in the background of the processes of musical performance, production, and publication, copyists are not credited in concert programs or on album liners and are rarely acknowledged in musical scores. The only woman copyist in the twentieth century who achieved great recognition for such work was Mathilde Pincus (1911–1988). Originally a violist, Pincus began copying instrumental parts for the Broadway production of *Finian's Rainbow* in the early 1950s. By the middle of the decade she and orchestrator Don Walker had established Chelsea Music, a copying service. The business took another partner, Al Miller, but eventually Mathilde Pincus was the sole proprietor.

Over the years Pincus was the principal copyist for Broadway composers Stephen Sondheim and John Kander, among many others. She devised a new method for copying for the musical theater in order to accommodate the many changes that take place during rehearsals. This new approach allowed spacing at the beginning for new introductions that might be added, and it kept multiple blank measures in small groups so that individual lines of music could be replaced, rather than whole pages or parts. In the decades that preceded notation software and photocopying, her time-saving concepts were revolutionary. Mathilde Pincus received a Tony Award in 1976 for outstanding service to the Broadway Musical Theater. After her death in 1988 a special tribute was held for her on Broadway, for which all the composers and orchestrators for whom she had worked over the years contributed music.

See also Arrangers

Allyson Brown Applebaum

Country Music

Women singers, songwriters, and instrumentalists have been crucial to the development of country music since its inception. They have, however, fought a continuously uphill battle for inclusion,

recognition, and equity in the field. During the early twentieth century, social constraints severely limited the public participation of women; musical performance by women was restricted to domestic, parlor, and church-related contexts. When women did perform publicly, they were confined to support roles, appearing with husbands or within family musical groups.

The creation of the country music recording industry can be traced to 1923, when Okeh Records representative Ralph Peer created a label called "Old Time Tunes" aimed at the rural, white market. The Carter Family—Alvin Pleasant Carter, his wife, Sara (1898–1979), and Sara's cousin, Maybelle Addington Carter (1909–1978)—was among the first national stars in the fledgling country music industry to record for Peer. The women of the family became models both for their contemporaries and for generations of future women performers. When The Carter Family disbanded, Mother Maybelle Addington Carter and the Carter Sisters, comprised of Maybelle and her three daughters, June (b. 1929), Helen (b. 1927), and Anita (b. 1933), continued performing, expanding both their popularity and the visibility and versatility of women performers in the field of what had then become known as "hillbilly" music.

Beginning in the 1920s, country music performers began to reach a wide audience via radio barn dance shows. Women found unprecedented acceptance and success in the radio barn dance shows that came to the forefront in the years just prior to the Great Depression. Country music shows originating from many major urban radio stations, including WSB in Atlanta, WBAP in Fort Worth, KDKA in Pittsburgh, and WSM in Nashville, reached well beyond the cities and into the homes of thousands of rural folks. The barn dance format itself was begun in 1924, when Chicago's radio station WLS launched "The National Barn Dance." Here, portrayal of the sweet gingham-clad country girl coexisted with the part tomboy, part cowboy's sweetheart image that was becoming increasingly popular as romantic western movies gained favor in the 1930s. The National Barn Dance established the careers of cowgirl sensation Patsy Montana (1914–1996), whose 1935 hit "I Want to Be a Cowboy's Sweetheart" was the first by a woman country singer to sell over a million records. The National Barn Dance was also the first to produce live road shows featuring its performers, and it provided the model for a number of future barn dance radio shows, including Nashville's Grand Ole Opry.

World War II found many male country performers drafted into the military services. Although many women enlisted as well, the void created in all areas of American life provided an opportunity for the inclusion of women in fields heretofore closed to them. In country music, however, new women stars were rare during this period while existing celebrities tenuously hung on to their careers. Most notable among these war years performers were Patti Page (b. 1927), Dinah Shore (1917–1994), and Jo Stafford (b. 1920), some of the first women performers from country backgrounds to cross over to pop music stardom.

Male performers still dominated the country music field after World War II. In the 1950s, however, women began to make strides in both record sales and their ability to draw audiences for personal appearances. Grand Ole Opry star Kitty Wells (b. 1918), the first "Queen of Country Music," emerged as the predominant woman country singer to attain stardom, blending a traditional, demure, gingham-clad country girl image with a new honky-tonk musical style focused on drinking, infidelity, and divorce. In spite of resistance from record producers who at that time believed that "girl singers" could not be viable solo artists, a number of other important women country performers emerged in Wells's footsteps, including Jean Shepard (b. 1933), Jean Chapel, and Martha Carson (b. 1921).

The mid-1950s also saw the emergence of rock and roll. Although traditional country artists found themselves losing a substantial share of the record-buying public to the new genre, some women artists such as Brenda Lee (b. 1944), Wanda Jackson (b. 1937), and Lorrie Collins (b. 1942) actively embraced the new style. The movement to counter rock and roll and recapture the country record–buying audience led directly to a 1960s era realization of guitarist producer Chet Atkins's vision for the "Nashville sound." This addition of pop music production values, instrumentation, and background vocals to the recordings of country artists clearly established Nashville as the home of country music and saw the rise in popularity of an unprecedented number of women performers. The success of Patsy Cline (1932–1963) was soon followed by Loretta Lynn (b. 1935), Dottie West (1932–1991), Barbara Mandrell (b. 1948), Tammy Wynette (1942–1998), Dolly Parton (b. 1946), Jan Howard (b. 1932), and Skeeter Davis (b. 1931).

The 1970s ushered in an era of crossover between pop and country markets. Building on the influence of the folk-country and folk-rock hybrid genres popular in the previous decade, women performers such as Olivia Newton-John, Anne Murray, Bobby Gentry (b. 1944), and Lynn Anderson (b. 1947) bridged the gap between the polished productions and image of the pop star and the folksy material and presentation of earlier country artists. Women country performers such as Donna Fargo (b. 1949), Dolly Parton, and Barbara Mandrell were also increasingly visible as stars of television shows and weekly series. Another trend during the decade paired women singers with country stars who were men: Tammy Wynette with George Jones; Jeannie Seely (b. 1940) with Jack Greene; Susan Raye (b. 1944) with Buck Owens; Dolly Parton with Porter Wagoner; and Helen Cornelius (b. 1950) with Jim Ed Brown.

The 1970s and 1980s brought new opportunities to the careers and musical choices of country's women performers and became the era of country "glamour queens." During this period country women finally found performing homes in glitzy Las Vegas strip showrooms, sporting sexy, glamorous costumes, some performing intricately choreographed productions supported by elaborate musical arrangements. Barbara Mandrell was fully involved in the new trend, and the era saw the ascent of Loretta Lynn's sister, Crystal Gayle (b. 1951). The 1980s also launched and supported the careers of a number of women "new traditionalists." Led by trailblazer Emmylou Harris (b. 1947), the new movement included singer-songwriters Nanci Griffith (b. 1953), Kathy Mattea (b. 1959), and Mary-Chapin Carpenter (b. 1958), all influenced by 1960s folk-revival performers like Joan Baez (b. 1941), Joni Mitchell (b. 1943), Odetta (b. 1930), and Buffy Sainte-Marie (b. 1941), popular a generation earlier.

As the 1980s gave way to the final decade of the twentieth century, women performers in the field of country music finally saw their inclusion as fully participating members of the country music community. No longer willing to have their images restrained and crafted by others, contemporary country women such as Pam Tillis (b. 1957), Wynonna Judd (b. 1964), the Forester Sisters, the Dixie Chicks, Carlene Carter (b. 1955), Paulette Carlson (b. 1953), Rosanne Cash (b. 1955), K. T. Oslin (b. 1942), and Reba McEntire (b. 1954) have taken center stage, often banding together to ensure that the place of women in country music is secure and that the opportunities now available to them might be protected for generations to come.

See also Country Music Association; Country Music Hall of Fame; Grand Ole Opry

For Further Reading

Elison, Curtis W. *Country Music Culture: From Hard Times to Heaven.* Jackson: University of Mississippi Press, 1995.

Haslam, Gerald W. *Working Man Blues: Country Music in California.* Berkeley: University of California Press, 1999.

Peterson, Richard A. *Creating Country Music: Fabricating Authenticity.* Chicago: University of Chicago Press, 1997.

Tichi, Cecelia. *High Lonesome: The American Culture of Country Music.* Chapel Hill: University of North Carolina Press, 1994.

Amy Corin

Country Music Association

The Country Music Association (CMA) was established in 1958 as the professional trade organization of the country music industry, the first to promote a type of music. Since then, the CMA membership has grown from 233 members to over 6,800 individuals and organizations, all of whom have made significant contributions to the industry.

Headquartered in Nashville, the CMA works to promote and enhance country music throughout the world. A driving force in the establishment of all these activities was Jo Walker-Meador (b. 1925). Hired in 1958 as the first employee of the CMA, Walker-Meador soon became executive director, a post she held from 1961 to 1991. Other women who have played important roles in the CMA are Frances Preston, chair from 1964 to 1965 and president in 1973; Connie Bradley, president in 1989 and chair in 1990; Kitty Moon Emery, who served as chair in 1995 and president the following year; and Donna Hilley, chair of the association from 1997 to 1998.

The CMA created the Country Music Hall of Fame in 1961 to honor inductees' contributions to country music. And in 1967 the CMA helped to open the Country Music Hall of Fame Museum. A subset of the CMA provides the nominations for new Hall of Fame inductees, and members in good standing are responsible first for narrowing the field of nominations and then voting. CMA members also vote for the recipients of the CMA Awards. The awards ceremony is broadcast annually with high ratings and includes presentations to artists in 12 categories. Another popular promotional event, co-hosted by the Country Music Association and the Grand Ole Opry, is the International Country Music Fan Fair, held every June in Nashville since 1972.

See also Country Music; Country Music Hall of Fame; Grand Ole Opry

For Further Reading

CMA World. Available: http://www.cmaworld.com
Country.com. Available: http://www.country.com
Kingsbury, Paul (ed.). *The Encyclopedia of Country Music. The Ultimate Guide to the Music*. New York: Oxford University Press, 1998.

Leslie Stone

Country Music Hall of Fame

Fourteen women have been elected to the Country Music Hall of Fame, an organization established by the Country Music Association (CMA) in 1961 to honor contributions to country music. In all, more than 70 individuals and groups have been elected, including performers, songwriters, comedians, and music industry executives.

On 1 April 1967 the Country Music Hall of Fame and Museum opened in Nashville, with the first inductees announced on 3 November 1961. Jimmie Rodgers, Hank Williams, and Fred Rose were honored with plaques displayed in the Tennessee State Museum. The Hall of Fame is administered by the Country Music Federation, a group formed at that time to preserve the traditions of country music.

Voting occurs annually. The 12 members of the Hall of Fame Nominating Committee (a subset of the over 6,000 members of the Country Music Association) selects 10 to 20 nominations for each category from the nominations of the director of the Country Music Federation and the executive director of the Country Music Association. The Committee then presents the nominations to the Panel of Electors, all CMA members who have been active in country music for at least 10 years and who have not missed voting in two elections in a row. The Panel first narrows the field in each category to five nominations and then votes to determine a winner.

Each year the Nominating Committee chooses nominees in an "Open" category. The CMA has also established that nominations be made in a "non-performer" category, beginning in 1989 and every third year thereafter.

The first women inducted into the

Women in the Country Music Hall of Fame

Year Inducted	Name
1970	Mother Maybelle Addington Carter, Sara Carter (as members of The Carter Family)
1973	Patsy Cline
1975	Minnie Pearl
1976	Kitty Wells
1988	Loretta Lynn
1991	Felice Bryant
1992	Frances Preston
1995	Jo Walker-Meador
1996	Patsy Montana
1997	Brenda Lee
1997	Cindy Walker
1998	Tammy Wynette
1999	Dolly Parton

Country Music Hall of Fame were Sara Dougherty Carter Bayes (1898–1979) and Mother Maybelle Addington Carter (1909–1978). They were elected in 1970 as members of The Carter Family, a trio organized by A. P. Carter in the 1920s. Sara, A. P.'s wife, sang lead vocals and played the autoharp; Maybelle, A. P.'s sister-in-law, sang harmony and played the guitar. As one of the earliest country acts, they had a strong influence on the emerging country genre.

In 1973 Patsy Cline (1932–1963) became the first woman solo artist elected to the Hall of Fame. Cline's career, including three years with the Grand Ole Opry and several hit singles, although brief, significantly influenced country music. Kitty Wells (b. 1918), also an Opry cast member, was elected to the Hall of Fame in 1976, 24 years after distinguishing herself as the first woman solo act to have a number one song on the country music charts.

No other women were added to the Hall of Fame until Loretta Lynn (b. 1935) was inducted in 1988. Like Lynn, Tammy Wynette (1942–1998) and Dolly Parton (b. 1946) were recognized for their extraordinary contributions as performers and songwriters as well as for their strong influences on the changing roles of women in country music and their status as country music personalities. Other solo women performers elected to the Hall of Fame were child pop star Brenda Lee (b. 1944), who achieved great success on the country music charts, and Patsy Montana (1908–1996), best known for her yodeling singing style and her influence as an early role model for women in country music.

Not all honorees have been country music singers. Like many of her associates in the Hall of Fame, Minnie Pearl (nee Sarah Ophelia Colley Cannon, 1912–1996) was a member of the Grand Ole Opry cast. She is, however, the only comedienne elected. Felice Bryant (nee Scaduto, b. 1925) was elected in 1991 with her husband, Boudleaux. The Bryants were a songwriting team whose songs became hits not only for many country artists, including the Everly Brothers. Cindy Walker (b. 1918) also earned recognition because of her prolific (more than 450 songs recorded) contribution as a songwriter.

Frances Preston was inducted in 1992 for her role in establishing rights for performers and songwriters, including her service as president and chief executive officer of Broadcast Music Inc., an important performing rights organization in the United States. Jo Walker-Meador (b. 1925) was also elected to the Hall of Fame for her role as executive director of the Country Music Association from 1962 to 1991, notably during the time when the Hall of Fame and Museum and Country Music Federation were established. Both Walker-Meador and Preston played critical roles in the increase in popularity experienced by country music during the 1960s.

See also Country Music; Country Music Association

For Further Reading

Country Music Federation. *Country: The Music and the Musicians.* New York: Abbeville Press, 1994.

Country.com. Available: http://www.country.com

Kingsbury, Paul (ed.). *The Encyclopedia of Country Music.* New York: Oxford University Press, 1998.

Leslie Stone

Covell, Rebekah Crouch (1939–)

Rebekah Crouch Covell, a leading collegiate conductor and music educator, served 25 years on the faculty of the Crane School, where she conducted the Crane Symphonic Band, one of the first women to hold such a position. Her other conducting positions included music director and conductor for the Crane Opera, and guest appearances with various wind and string ensembles, including the Crane Wind Ensemble. An advocate for new music, she was a featured conductor with Lukas Foss for the Gala Concert of the inaugural Crane New

Music Festival. At the 1980 Winter Olympics in Lake Placid, Covell served as conductor of ceremonial bands, which included an extended appearance on international television at the Gold Medal ceremonies for the U.S. hockey team. In 1988 she participated in a project at California State University, San Bernardino, involving a select number of women conductors in the establishment of a videotape library. Additionally, Covell frequently appeared as guest conductor and clinician for high school bands and wind ensembles throughout the Northeast.

Rebekah Crouch Covell, born on 4 May 1939, is professor emerita of music at the Crane School of Music at the State University of New York at Potsdam, having served until her retirement in 1996. A devoted pedagogue, Covell taught conducting, trumpet, brass techniques, and basic musicianship for many years. Additionally, she developed the Business of Music program for the Crane School and served as coordinator until her retirement. For the final three years of her tenure at Crane, Covell assumed administrative responsibilities, serving as director of advising and scheduling. The recipient of numerous awards from both faculty and students, she received the Crane Student Music Educators National Conference (MENC) Chapter Faculty Appreciation Award in 1992 and was honored at the 1993 Potsdam College commencement with the President's Award for Excellence in Academic Advising.

Covell earned her Ph.D. and M.M.E. degrees from Florida State University and her B.S. degree from East Carolina University. Before joining the faculty of the Crane School in 1971, she taught at Midwestern State University in Wichita Falls, TX, and in public school in Virginia. Covell had an active interest in the history and literature of the wind band throughout her career and published several articles on the subject.

See also Music Education; Music Educators National Conference; Women Band Directors International

For Further Reading

Crouch, Rebekah Ellen. "The Contributions of Adolphe Sax to the Wind Band." Ph.D. diss., Florida State University, 1968.

———. "The Contributions of Adolphe Sax to the Wind Band (Part 1)." *Journal of Band Research* 5/2 (1969): 29–42.

———. "The Contributions of Adolphe Sax to the Wind Band (Part 2)." *Journal of Band Research* 6/1 (1969): 59–65.

Daryl Kinney

Crane, Julia Ettie (1855–1923)

Julia Ettie (Etta) Crane founded the Crane Normal Institute of Music in Potsdam, NY, in 1886, the first music teacher education program affiliated with a normal school, an undergraduate teacher-training institution, in the United States. During the mid-1800s public school music was taught by classroom teachers or conservatory-trained musicians. In the latter part of the century Julia Crane advanced the systematic training of public school music teachers by integrating teaching methods with the development of music skills.

Julia Crane was born on 19 May 1855 in Hewittville, near Potsdam, NY. She entered Potsdam Normal School at age 14 and began a public school teaching career after her graduation five years later. During the next two summers Crane studied vocal music in Boston, then moved to Shippensburg, PA, to teach music, mathematics, and calisthenics in a normal school. In 1880 Crane returned to Potsdam, where she opened a success-

ful voice studio. Crane resumed her voice studio teaching in Potsdam during 1882–1884, after which time she was approached to join the faculty of the Potsdam Normal School. Crane was initially reluctant to accept this position because of her commitment to studio voice teaching and because she did not consider the time and resources within the Normal School curriculum to be sufficient for a good music program. She accepted the faculty position after being assured that she could develop a music teacher education program that would meet her ideals. During the first two years of her appointment Crane developed an innovative program that allowed students to pursue music throughout their normal school training. A Special Music Teachers Curriculum was initiated in 1886 in conjunction with the founding of the Crane Normal Institute of Music in the same year. This joint program between the Institute and the Normal School represented the first specialized music teacher-training program for public school education in the United States. The first class of "special music teachers" graduated in 1888.

Julia Crane's system of K–12 music instruction was explained in her *Music Teacher's Manual*, first published in 1889. This popular method of instruction went through eight editions, the last of which was completed by Marie Schuette in 1923. Crane's philosophy and method focused on rote learning experiences before the introduction of music notation, music literacy, and appreciation of "good" music. She advocated music for the masses and believed that music was important in the development of every child. Her influence became widespread through her writing, workshops, lectures, and professional affiliations. Following Julia Crane's death on 11 June 1923, the

Crane Normal Institute was operated as a private corporation for a short time before it was purchased by the State of New York. It is now known as the Crane School of Music at the Potsdam College of the State University of New York.

See also Music Education

For Further Reading

Crane, Julia E. *Music Teacher's Manual*, 8th ed. Potsdam, NY: Herald Recorder Presses, 1923.

———. "A Standard Course as Outlined by the Educational Council." *Journal of the Proceedings of the 15th Annual Meeting of the Music Supervisors National Conference* (1922): 46–50.

———. "The Training of the Music Supervisor." *Journal of the Proceedings of the 12th Annual Meeting of the Music Supervisors National Conference* (1919): 83–85.

Patricia Flowers

Crawford Seeger, Ruth (1901–1953)

In the predominantly masculine world of musical composition in America during the first half of the twentieth century, Ruth Crawford Seeger made a name both as a composer and as a folksong transcriber and compiler. Along with composers like Henry Cowell, Charles Ives, and Charles Ruggles, Crawford helped define American dissonant modernism. As a folksong transcriber, she tied her interest in modernism to American traditional music.

Crawford was born on 3 July 1901 in East Liverpool, OH. Her family moved several times, settling in 1912 in Jacksonville, FL. Crawford studied piano, and after high school graduation she taught for three years at the School of Musical Art. She moved to Chicago in 1921 to attend the American Conservatory and studied piano with a variety of teachers, including Djane Lavoie Herz. Piano study was an acceptable pursuit for women at the

time, but a significant change of focus came with Crawford's studying composition with Adolf Weidig. During this time she developed a friendship with Carl Sandburg and later wrote *Three Songs* (1932) based on his poetry. Also, Composer Henry Cowell became a good friend and remained a staunch advocate of Crawford throughout her life. In this milieu, Crawford was influenced by theosophy and oriental mysticism, and she developed a dissonant, experimental style of composition. One work in this style, Sonata for Violin and Piano (1926), had several performances in Chicago and New York and was pronounced "virile" by a critic.

Crawford spent the summer of 1929 at the MacDowell Colony in New Hampshire and then moved to New York beginning studies with the composer and musicologist Charles Seeger. In New York, she experimented with serializing all parameters of her compositions, including rhythm. Becoming the first woman to win the Guggenheim fellowship in composition, Crawford spent 1930–1931 in Europe. While there, she wrote perhaps the finest of her 40 or so works, the String Quartet (1931). She returned to New York to marry Charles Seeger.

Ruth Crawford Seeger wanted a family but was concerned with the effect that caring for children would have on her career. This dual-directional pull stayed with her throughout her life and was never completely resolved. She called her work from 1933 to 1943 "composing babies" and managed four such compositions in all: Michael, Peggy, Barbara, and Penny.

The Seegers became involved with the Composer's Collective, a group of musicians with ties to the Communist Party. This association underscored an interest

Ruth Crawford Seeger with children at the Green Acres Nursery School in Washington, DC, in the early 1950s. *Photo by Buckingham Studio Inc., Washington, DC (1952). Courtesy of the Seeger Family.*

in folk music, or music of "the people." From 1936 on, Crawford essentially put composition aside and, along with her husband (who was employed by the Works Progress Administration in Washington, DC), focused on folk music transcription. Crawford participated in the publication of *Our Singing Country* (1941) with Alan and John Lomax. In addition, she published several children's songbooks on her own, including *American Folk Songs for Children* (1948), with folksongs that she had tried out with children at the Silver Springs (MD) Co-operative Nursery. Fueled by folksong collecting trips and her transcribing work, Crawford, along with her stepson, Peter, and her children Michael and Peggy, became involved in the folk music revival—Crawford as a teacher, tran-

scriber, and compiler, and her children as performers. In 1952 Ruth Crawford Seeger returned briefly to composition, completing the *Suite for Wind Quintet.* Her music has been recorded on albums such as *Ruth Crawford Seeger: Chamber Works* (CPO 999670), *Portrait* (Deutsche Grammophon 449925), and *Music of Marion Bauer and Ruth Crawford Seeger* (Albany Records 297). She died from cancer on 18 November 1953.

See also Classical Music; Experimental Music

For Further Reading

Gaume, Matilda. *Ruth Crawford Seeger: Memoirs, Memories, Music.* Metuchen, NJ: Scarecrow Press, 1986.

Straus, Joseph Nathan. *The Music of Ruth Crawford Seeger.* New York: Cambridge University Press, 1995.

Tick, Judith. *Ruth Crawford Seeger: A Composer's Search for American Music*. New York: Oxford University Press, 1997.

Anita Breckbill

Crider, Paula Ann (1944–)

Paula Ann Crider is an outstanding band director who has been recognized for her numerous contributions to the field of music education. She has had a distinguished teaching career spanning over 30 years in which she left an indelible mark on music and musicians in the state of Texas. In the early part of her career she was only one of a few successful women high school directors in the nation. By the end of her career she had paved the way for successive generations of young women conductors who aspired to be high school and college band directors. She has received numerous honors and awards, including two "Eyes of Texas" teaching excellence awards, the National Band Association Citation of Excellence, and the Tau Beta Sigma Outstanding Service to Music Award. She is a member of the prestigious American Bandmaster's Association. In 1997 Crider's name was added to the Historic Roll of Honor of High School Concert Bands, and she was awarded the Sudler Order of Merit by the John Philip Sousa Foundation in recognition of her special contributions in the excellence of bands and band music.

Crider attended the University of Southern Mississippi beginning in 1962. Recognized as a talented musician, she was encouraged to become a conductor by Director of Bands William J. Moody. She studied to be an instrumental music teacher and eventually graduated with honors in music and English literature. After graduation she secured her first instrumental teaching position in Purvis,

MS; however, she soon left her home state to continue her education and career in Austin, TX. Crider followed her mentor, Moody, to the University of Texas in order to pursue a master's degree in music education. Her connection with the university turned out to be the beginning of a long, rich tradition of instrumental teaching and musical excellence for the state of Texas.

She eventually left public school teaching and began a career in university teaching. In 1982 Crider was appointed associate professor and assistant director of the University of Texas Longhorn Bands. In 1995 Professor Crider was appointed to the coveted position of director of the University of Texas Longhorn Band. Regularly performing before crowds of 80,000, the Longhorn Band earned national recognition for musical and marching excellence under her leadership. She is the only woman to ever conduct a university band in the Big 12 Conference.

Crider devoted many hours of service to her profession. She conducted and adjudicated in 29 states, Australia, Ireland, and the United Kingdom. She has written many articles for the *Instrumentalist, the Band Director's Guide*, and the *National Band Association's Journal*. She was the first woman elected to serve as the president of the National Band Association. Throughout her career she inspired generations of students with her dedication, excellence, love, and passion for music teaching. Crider retired from the University of Texas in 1999.

See also Music Education

For Further Reading

Conway, Colleen M. "Gender and Musical Instrument Choice: A Phenomenological Investigation." *Bulletin of the Council for Research in Music Education*, in progress.

Grant, Denise Elizabeth. "The Impact of Mentoring and Gender-Specific Role Models on Women College Band Directors at Four Different Career Stages." Ph.D. diss., University of Minnesota, 2000.

Jill Sullivan

Crow, Sheryl (1962–)

Sheryl Crow is one of the most important recording artists and songwriters of the 1990s. Released in 1993 to tremendous popular and critical acclaim, her first album, *Tuesday Night Music Club* (A&M 314–540126–2), sold more than nine million copies, helped establish her as a significant new voice in popular music, and won her the Grammy Award for Best New Artist. Her raspy voice lends itself perfectly to the moody folk-rock melodies she writes.

Crow was born on 11 February 1962 in Kennett, MO, to a musical family. She attended the University of Missouri before becoming a public school music teacher. In 1986 she moved to Los Angeles, where she became a backup singer for Stevie Wonder, Michael Jackson, George Harrison, and Don Henley. Despite the apparent simplicity of the first single and video from *Tuesday Night Music Club*, "All I Wanna Do," the album showcased a talented singer-songwriter who could not be placed into a singular stylistic category. Her musical influences range from the Beatles, Rolling Stones, and Bob Dylan to Johnny Cash, Hank Williams, and Emmylou Harris (b. 1947), to Bessie Smith (1894–1937) and Billie Holiday (1915–1959). Her influences as a lyricist include Bob Dylan, John Steinbeck, Mark Twain, John Irving, and Walt Whitman (her song "Riverwide" was inspired by Whitman's "Leaves of Grass").

With the release of her second album, *Sheryl Crow* (A&M 540587), and its two

Sheryl Crow performing at Madison Square Garden in November 1994. *Photo © Mitchell Gerber/CORBIS.*

hit songs, "If It Makes You Happy" (written as a diatribe against her former band members) and "Everyday Is a Winding Road" (recorded by The Artist in 1999), Crow staked a place for herself as an independent and powerful voice. The song "Love Is a Good Thing," with the lyric "watch our children while they kill each other with a gun they bought at Walmart discount stores," drew the ire and corporate censorship of the Walmart Corporation. Despite its substantial pressure, Crow refused to change the lyrics and Walmart refused to stock and sell the album.

Her third album, *The Globe Sessions* (A&M 540959), was self-produced in her New York studio and represented her attempt at more proficient and technical music and studio production, as well as songs that were more autobiographical than her previous efforts. Particularly noteworthy at the end of the album is a hidden two-minute track that criticized those politicians who were resolved to impeach President Clinton. Bob Dylan showed his respect for Crow by letting her be the first to record his song "Mississippi" on this album.

Sheryl Crow's live album released in 1999, *Sheryl Crow and Friends Live from Central Park* (Interscope 490574), is essentially a "greatest hits" album. Her songs have appeared in the films *The Faculty* (1998) and *Message in a Bottle* (1999). She has also raised money for the Vietnam Veterans–sponsored "Campaign for a Landmine Free World."

See also Grammy Award; Singer-Songwriter

For Further Reading

Sheryl Crow. Available: http://www.sherylcrow. com/

E. Michael Harrington

Cruz, Celia (1924–)

Celia Cruz has been the most popular vocalist of Afro-Cuban and salsa music since the 1950s in the United States and abroad. Twenty of Cruz's albums have reached Gold status, selling over 1,000,000 copies. She has performed in Spain, Germany, Italy, Greece, Portugal, England, France, Japan, and every Latin American country with the exception of Bolivia and Paraguay. In the 1980s and 1990s Cruz was something of an icon for international Cuban music and salsa: she was generally referred to as the "Queen of Salsa" and was the subject of the book *Reina Rumba* (The Rumba Queen) by Colombian author Umberto Valverde.

Born on 21 October 1924 to a working-class family in Havana, Cuba, Cruz began her career in the 1930s as a teenager by entering amateur contests on radio stations. In the 1940s she sang professionally on Havana radio and in nightclubs accompanied by a variety of musical groups and performing the entire gamut of Cuban music, from *boleros* to *sones*, Afro-themes, and even Argentine tangos. During this period she recorded her first albums and began to travel abroad, first to Mexico and then to Venezuela. Her rise in popularity dates to the early 1950s, when Cruz began to sing catchy danceable tunes accompanied by the group Sonora Matancera, with whom she traveled to several countries including Haiti, Puerto Rico, and Colombia. Cruz and the Sonora Matancera were featured in the Caracas carnival each year from 1955 to 1958.

In the 1950s Cruz performed frequently in Havana's luxury nightclubs, as well as on radio and television. She left Cuba in 1960 and lived in Mexico for a few years before moving to New York City, where in the late 1960s she recorded a series of albums with famed percussionist Tito Puente. In general, the 1960s represented a lull in her career. In the 1970s, however, her fortunes changed when Cruz became identified with the success of the salsa phenomenon in New York, Colombia, and Puerto Rico. She recorded a number of popular record albums, first with Dominican bandleader Johnny Pacheco and later with New York trumpeter Willi Colón. In these recordings Cruz included not only old Cuban dance standards but also tunes from other Latin American countries such as Brazil, Peru, Uruguay, and Panama, which she interpreted in the Afro-Cuban salsa mode. Her many recordings include *La Candela* (Fania 19), *Azucar*

(Charly 630), and *La Reina de Cuba* (International Music 50313). She also performed with several artists from New York's recording label Fania. Her recording with drummer Ray Barreto, *Ritmo en el Corazón* (Fania 651), received a Grammy Award.

Cruz has received dozens of prizes and awards, including honorary doctoral degrees from Yale University and Florida International University, and the keys to many cities including Paris, New York, and Lima. She appeared in several movies in the 1990s such as *Mambo Kings* (1992) and *The Perez Family* (1995). Through her work she continues to popularize the rich, rhythmic, danceable sounds of her native Cuba.

Celia Cruz set the standard by which all women salsa vocalists are measured. She was one of the pillars on which home-grown U.S. salsa was built. The current popularity of Latin jazz and all manner of Spanish Caribbean–flavored music in the United States owes much to the work and artistic talent of Celia Cruz.

See also Latin American Musicians; Multicultural Musics

For Further Reading

Aparicio, Frances. "The Blackness of Sugar: Celia Cruz and the Performance of (Trans) Nationalism." *Cultural Studies* 13/2 (1999): 223–236.

Fernández, Raúl. "Celia Cruz: Artista de América Latina." *Deslinde* (July–Sept. 1997): 102–121.

Valverde, Umberto. *Celia Cruz: Reina Rumba*. Bogotá: Arango Editores, 1995.

Raúl Fernández

Cultural Appropriation

The term "cultural appropriation" is understood to be the use by a person who identifies with one culture or group of some characteristic aspect of another culture or group. It is a late-twentieth-century term often associated with a power imbalance between the user and the group or culture from which the appropriation is made. Most often it results from hierarchical constructions associated with differences in race, national origin, class, and sometimes gender. Cultural appropriation may also involve adapting usages common to one audience to another audience, which may only know the appropriated form. The appropriation may be deliberate or inadvertent. It is seen as an aspect of cultural oppression when the borrower profits substantially or fails to acknowledge the contribution of others.

Although music performance is often seen as an individual art, musical interaction among individual music makers is the norm, and the borrowing of others' material is a common characteristic of artistic production. The line between borrowing, acknowledged or not, and appropriation is not always clear and is likely to be interpreted differently depending on the position of the observer. Two examples will illustrate. A relatively clear example of cultural appropriation is the borrowing by white blues singers such as Janis Joplin (1943–1970) from a blues style initially cultivated by a series of African American singers. The fact that the white singers were more acceptable to white audiences and were therefore able to profit from a style invented by others emphasized the differences associated with race in American society. In an earlier example, Amy Marcy Cheney Beach (1867–1944) incorporated Celtic and Inuit melodies into her concert works (a symphony and a string quartet) but rejected the use of African American melodies. At that point her usages were considered as legitimate borrowings from "folk" music, and no charge of appropriation was made.

Much more speculative is the application of the term "cultural appropriation" to borrowings of musical styles across gender lines. In the nineteenth century, according to the concept of separate spheres, a sharp distinction was made between public performance and private, domestic music making. The former was dominated by men (except for women singers) and the latter associated with women's sphere. When men performed in public, they were often making use of skills initially learned at the hands of women teachers. Composing "in the larger forms" and orchestration were generally considered beyond the reach of women who were composers. The range of emotional and expressive states was divided into the "feminine" and the "masculine," usually by male writers. As a matter of course, composers who were men were expected to portray the entire gamut of emotion in their music, but women composers were expected to limit themselves to the "smaller forms" and "feminine" emotions. It is not at all clear

that women had much to say in the construction of this "masculine—feminine" expressive duality, however, so whether the use of the "feminine" by men amounts to cultural appropriation is not clear. It does appear that in some cases the role of the woman as "muse" and inspiration to the man may conceal more substantial creative contributions. The apparent creative silence of women until the last quarter of the twentieth century and the highly developed critical language that belittles their work may have more to do with outright cultural oppression than with appropriation.

See also Separate Spheres—Sexual Aesthetics

For Further Reading

McClintock, Anne, Aamir Mufti, and Ella Shohat (eds.). *Dangerous Liaisons: Gender, Nation, and Postcolonial Perspectives*. Minneapolis: University of Minnesota Press, 1997.

Ziff, Bruce, and Pratima V. Rao (eds.). *Borrowed Power: Essays on Cultural Appropriation*. New Brunswick, NJ: Rutgers University Press, 1997.

Catherine P. Smith

D

D'Cückoo

D'Cückoo is an all-women music ensemble that combines layered vocals, multicultural rhythmic harmonies, and custom-designed digital samples, forming a genre of music that the group describes as "cybertribal world-funk." Based in the San Francisco Bay area, the ensemble was created in 1987 by Candice Pacheco, Patti Clemens, and Tina Blaine and has featured an ever-changing lineup of musicians over the course of its history, including Jennifer Hruska, Tina Phelps, Janelle Burdell, Terrie Wright, Susan Jette, Shalonda Smith, Ava Maria Square, Janet Koike, and Luanne Warner.

D'Cückoo creates music with various instruments, such as traditional and electronic percussion, electric keyboards, guitars, basses, and synthesizers. Electronic percussion instruments, all of which were invented, designed, and built by members of the band, include MIDI (Musical Instrument Digital Interface—a communications protocol for synthesizers and computers) marimbas, multi-pad MIDI drum controllers (nicknamed "turtles" because of their shape), MIDI bamboo trigger sticks (known as "D'Koostix"), and electronic taiko drums. Many individuals thought the women were crazy to attempt to build their own electronic instruments, hence the choice of the name D'Cückoo for the band.

Along with their music, D'Cückoo's energetic live performances contain video presentations and computer graphics, such as RigBy, an animated, computer-generated puppet displayed on a large screen behind the band who banters with the audience in real-time. A unique feature of any D'Cückoo concert is the Midiball, a giant, helium-filled sphere with MIDI triggers in its surface, which, when touched by members of the audience, produce sampled sounds and computer visuals, thereby allowing the audience to jam with the band. Choreography is also an integral facet of their live performances, as each band member dances and trades instruments throughout the show. D'Cückoo has produced two albums—*D'Cückoo*, which features a cover of Brian Eno's "No One Receiving," and *Umoja* (RGB 501), Swahili for "unity." Candice Pacheco, a founding band member of D'Cückoo, has produced two solo albums: *The Vortex* (RGB 502) and *If Then . . . Else* (RGB 503).

See also Music Technology; Performer, Percussion

For Further Reading

Campbell, Clyde. "D'Cückoo." *Percussive Notes* 33/ 3 (June 1995): 69.

Erin Stapleton-Corcoran

Dalcroze Eurhythmics

Dalcroze eurhythmics is a method of music education that integrates rhythmic movement, aural training, and improvisation. Emile Jaques-Dalcroze (1865–1950) was a Swiss musician and educator who developed a new approach to the study of music through movement. Music is abstract; it moves through time. Movement is concrete; it moves through space. By connecting listening with movement, Dalcroze set out to clarify abstract musical concepts. His work with children and adults helped him to discover that rhythmic movement in response to intelligent and sensitive listening develops both the tonal and rhythmic senses, enhancing the understanding, the joy, and the performance of music. There have been many American women disseminating this important music method.

The study of eurhythmics is valuable at all ages, but benefits are clearly evident when lessons begin in early childhood. Eurhythmics classes for young children are designed to awaken musical instinct and imagination along with sensitizing children to the varied and multileveled cues in music prior to or concurrent with formal instruction. A eurhythmics lesson is based on elements of music that can be demonstrated through movement such as tempo, dynamics, accents, beat, patterns, meter, phrasing, form, and style. These elements are explored in a spiral approach, requiring a more sophisticated response as the students advance in their understanding of tonal and rhythmic nuances in music. Transfer in learning occurs as students manipulate these elements in unfamiliar compositions. Although the basic elements of music are inseparable, the teaching of a concept within a specific composition or improvisation can provide the instructor with immediate feedback on learning.

Rhythmic solfege, the second element in the Dalcroze approach, is aural training that incorporates movement, singing, and games. Sequential exercises in aural development aid in the understanding of music theory, in music literacy, and in the practice of scales, modes, intervals, melody, harmony, modulation, counterpoint, and vocal improvisation. The goal of rhythmic solfege is to develop music literacy, accurate hearing, and refined intonations in the students.

Improvisation is the third aspect of the Dalcroze approach. The goal of improvisation is to develop skillful techniques of using rhythm (through movement) and sound (both vocal and instrumental) in creative, spontaneous, and expressive combinations to create music. Improvisation may arise from movement, stories, poems, sounds, or pictures. The creativity and imagination of the students in the class form the springboard for improvisation. The instructor fosters and guides the germination of ideas through questioning and sequential selection. Both the teacher and the students approach improvisation as a means to develop the ability to express quickly and clearly ideas and feelings about any musical subject or combination of subjects, and to combine this ability with the competence to transform other people's music into a lively, re-creative performance.

As the approach was being developed, Jaques-Dalcroze used rhythmic movement to assist students at the Geneva Conservatory in improving their sight-singing and rhythmic skills. The first rhythmic methods classes were offered at the Conservatory in 1902. Jaques-Dalcroze continued to teach these classes in Geneva until 1910, when he moved to Dresden-Hellerau to teach eurhythmics in a planned community for the arts. In 1915 Dalcroze returned to Geneva and established his own institute. The Institute Jaques-Dalcroze functions today and is the site of a Dalcroze training center for children through adults. Teacher-training centers have also been established in New York, Boston, Pittsburgh, and Seattle. A eurhythmics teacher is required to have an acute sense of pitch and rhythm, movement experience, keyboard skills, and improvisation skills in movement, in voice, and on an instrument. Consequently, teachers of eurhythmics are in strong demand by conservatories and music schools around the world. The following is a summary of American women who have made a strong contribution to music education through Dalcroze eurhythmics.

Elsa Findlay (1892–1975) studied with Jaques-Dalcroze during the Hellerau years. Notables who were in Hellerau from 1910 through 1914 included Serge Diaghilev, Vaslav Nijinsky, Anna Pavlova, George Bernard Shaw, Constantin Stanislavski, Darius Milhaud, Ingacy Paderewski, and Serge Rachmaninoff. From Hellerau, Findlay moved to England to begin her career as a Dalcroze teacher. After several years of teaching in Manchester and Liverpool, she moved to New York and taught in the music department of Teacher's College, Columbia University. Elsa Findlay taught briefly in Los Angeles before arriving at the Cleveland Institute of Music, where she taught for the remainder of her career. Students from her 50 years of teaching described Elsa Findlay as a woman of wit and wisdom, of strong personal loyalties and high artistic standards; quick and impatient, demanding much from her students, but giving in return much more; affection, sympathy and advice, sharp criticism and generous praise, unflagging enthusiasm and ever-present laughter. Elsa Findlay is credited with beginning a degree program in eurhythmics at the Cleveland Institute of Music, a program that continues today. Her book *Rhythm and Movement: Applications of Dalcroze Eurhythmics* (1971 Summy-Birchard Music; reprinted 1999) continues to be a valuable resource for music educators.

Henrietta Rosenstrauch (1887–1982) was both an educator and a tireless promoter of Dalcroze eurhythmics. Born in Cologne, she took her early musical training in Germany. Rosenstrauch became an established pianist, specializing in *lieder* (songs) before discovering eurhythmics. After studying in Hellerau and in Geneva, Rosenstrauch taught eurhythmics in Frankfurt from 1921 until 1933, when Adolf Hitler came to power. She later taught eurhythmics in England and in 1937 moved to Pittsburgh to teach at the Carnegie Institute of Technology (CIT), now Carnegie Mellon University. Her tenure at CIT was from 1937 to 1964, interrupted with a few years of teaching at the Institute Jaques-Dalcroze in Geneva.

Henrietta Rosenstrauch was chiefly known for her use of percussion instruments as teaching aids in her eurhythmics classes. Her significant publications include *Percussion, Rhythm, Music, Movement* (Peripole, no date); *Percussion, Movement and the Child* (Peripole, 1960);

and *Essays on Rhythm, Music, Movement* (Volkwein, 1973). She wrote extensively on the meaning of rhythm studies and the purpose of Music Education for the People, a course that Rosenstrauch taught for many years, which encouraged students toward *understanding* rather than *knowledge.*

Her countless students remember Henrietta Rosenstrauch as open, intelligent, frank, and uncompromisingly honest. Further, her knowledge of music and literature was profound. Rosenstrauch, on occasion a strict disciplinarian, was a role model to her young students, through her dedication to the principles of Dalcroze and to excellence as a way of life.

Hilda Schuster (?–1997) studied with Jaques-Dalcroze in Geneva. She later taught at the Oberlin Conservatory, Duquesne University, and Carnegie Institute of Technology before moving to New York to teach at the Dalcroze School of New York. In 1945 Jaques-Dalcroze appointed Schuster to be director of the New York school, a position she held for 48 years until her retirement in 1993. Schuster was a tireless promoter of Dalcroze eurhythmics. As director of the first Dalcroze eurhythmics school in the United States, she attracted many foreign and American students to the program. Students of Hilda Schuster went on to become respected Dalcroze educators. These include Ruth Alperson, Brunhilde Dorsch (1914–1996), Anne Farber, Annabelle Joseph, and Lisa Parker.

Brunhilde Dorsch received her eurhythmics training from Cecil Kitkat at the Carnegie Institute of Technology and from Hilda Schuster in New York. She then taught Dalcroze eurhythmics, folk dancing, and German for 42 years at Duquesne University. Dorsch was part of the group of Dalcroze educators credited for founding the Dalcroze Society of America. In her memoirs she said, "Movement is basic to us. Rhythm is basic to us, and where there is rhythm, there is movement. I wanted my students to remember the joy of eurhythmics, as well as the [joy of] learning." Folk dance was often incorporated into Dorsch's eurhythmics classes as a tool for rhythmic reinforcement. Dorsch said, "Folk dance is a triple exploration of natural body movement: physical and emotional release, social interaction, and physical exercise." She also recognized the unity of the circle and the communal joy of cultural dance. The Greek *Misirlou*, danced throughout the world by amateur dancers, was created in Brunhilde Dorsch's studio.

Marta Sanchez was born in Chile and received her Dalcroze training at the Institute Jaques-Dalcroze in Geneva. After receiving her diploma from the Institute, Sanchez moved to the United States and taught eurhythmics at the Carnegie Institute of Technology for 40 years beginning in 1958. In the 1960s Sanchez established innovative music programs for preschool children in the Head Start Programs and in the Pittsburgh Public Schools, challenging the prevailing notion that three- and four-year-old children could not learn music. Sanchez believed that through good teaching students could and would learn music, and she is known internationally for her work as a Dalcroze educator. She has taught in every country in North and South America, as well as many parts of Europe, Asia, and Australia. Now retired from Carnegie Mellon University, Sanchez travels globally and continues to promote Dalcroze eurhythmics.

See also Kodály Method; Music Education; Orff Approach

For Further Reading

Becknell, Arthur Francis, Jr. "A History of the Development of Dalcroze Eurhythmics in the United States and Its Influence on the Public School Music Program." Ed.D. diss., University of Michigan, 1970.

Joseph, Annabelle S. "The Importance of Rhythmic Training in Music Education." In *The Eclectic Curriculum in American Music Education: Contributions of Dalcroze, Kodály, and Orff*, eds. Beth Landis and Polly Carder. Reston, VA: MENC [1972], 1990.

R. J. David Frego

Day, Doris (1924–)

Doris Day, singer and actress, is a beloved icon of American popular music. During the 1960s, Day was one of the 10 main box-office movie attractions; she was voted Star of the Year by the Theatre Owners of America, and Most Popular Actress in the World by the Hollywood Foreign Press Association. She made 40 movies over a 10-year period and enjoyed an eclectic persona that could equally display sensual innocent, tomboy heroine, and romantic protagonist. Her singing voice is characterized by a clear tone, and her performances convey a wide range of emotions with great ease.

Born Doris von Kapplehoff in Cincinnati, OH, on 3 April 1924 to parents who valued the arts (her father was a classically trained musician and voice teacher) and encouraged her artistic aspirations, Day took dance lessons, excelling both physically and artistically during her public school years. At age 12 she began touring with the Fancho and Marco Show and would have certainly continued in what promised to be a successful professional dance career had it not been for an accident at age 14 in which one of her legs was shattered. For nearly a year and a half, Day endured numerous hospitalizations and surgeries. It was during this difficult period that she began singing lessons with Cincinnati voice teacher Grace Raine. It soon became clear that although Day would probably never be able to dance professionally, she showed extraordinary promise as a singer. At age 17 she was encouraged by her teacher and mentor to audition for a local radio station. That fortuitous, although unpaid, performance earned her a paid job at a local nightclub owned by Cincinnati bandleader Barney Rapp. The song "Day after Day" became an audience favorite, and Rapp consequently renamed her "Doris Day."

Soon Day was performing regularly as a pickup singer with major bands—Bob Crosby's and Fred Waring's, among them—and later sang as the featured singer with the Bob Crosby Band. For three years she sang full-time in the Les Brown Band as the lead vocalist, and the Brown and Day single release on Columbia of "Sentimental Journey" became a best-selling record and helped to popularize Day's vocal stylizations.

During this period, film director Michael Curtiz saw her perform at New York's Little Club. Impressed with her singing, he was also awed by her wholesome good looks, poise, talent for comedy, and natural affinity with the audience. Curtiz invited Day to take a screen test, and Warner Brothers subsequently signed her. She appeared opposite Jack Carson in her first film, *Romance on the High Seas* (1948). Day left Warner Brothers in 1954, making movies for both Metro-Goldwyn-Mayer and Paramount.

Day continued, throughout her extensive film career, to release best-selling hit records, including "Que Sera Sera" and "Mister Banjo." Married and divorced four times, Day is now part owner of an animal-guest-friendly hotel and advocates for strict control of pet overpopulation on behalf of the Doris Day Animal League. She has remained largely reclusive since her Hollywood career ended in the late 1960s, but she appeared in 1993 for a charity screening of the romantic Western *Calamity Jane* and in 1995 for selective promotion of her previously recorded but unreleased recording *The Love Album* (Vision Music 2).

See also Musical Theater

For Further Reading

Kehoe, John. "Doris Day." *Biography* 2/11 (November 1998): 120.

Larkin, Colin (ed.). *The Guinness Encyclopedia of Popular Music*, vol. 2. London: Bath Press, 1995.

Stambler, Irwin. *Encyclopedia of Popular Music*. New York: St. Martin's Press, 1965.

Judith A. Coe

Dearie, Blossom (1926–   )

Blossom Dearie, called the last of the great supper club singers, is a singer, pianist, and songwriter, known for her little girl's voice and intimate style. Born of Scottish, Irish, and Norwegian descent, she was named for some peach blossoms that were brought to her house by a neighbor on the day she was born. Her girlish voice and flawless delivery characterize Dearie's performances.

Born on 28 April 1926, Dearie began piano studies at the age of five, and studied classical music throughout her teen years. Early influences included Duke Ellington, Art Tatum, and Count Basie. In the mid-1940s she joined the Blue Flames, a vocal group featured with the Woody Herman Orchestra, as well as the Alvino Rey band's Blue Reys. In 1952 she set off for Paris, where she founded the Blue Stars, a popular vocal octet. The group toured France and made six solo albums for Verve Records. Her early solo albums include *Blossom Dearie* (Polygram 837934), *Once upon a Summertime* (Verve 827757-4), and *Give Him the Ooh-La-La* (Polygram 517067). By the 1960s she had returned to New York and began singing regularly at various nightclubs. In 1966 she began annual performances at Ronnie Scott's Club in London. She started her own record company, Daffodil Records, in 1974. Johnny Mercer wrote one of his last songs for her before his death in 1976.

From 1983 on, Dearie has performed frequently at the Ballroom, a nightclub in Manhattan. In 1985 she was the first recipient of the Mabel Mercer Foundation Award, given annually to the year's most outstanding supper-club performer. During the late 1980s and early 1990s Dearie appeared frequently in both New York and London. Dearie's versions of Dave Frishberg's "Peel Me a Grape" and her original "Hey John" are some of her best-known songs.

See also Singer-Songwriter; Songwriter

For Further Reading

Erlewine, Michael (ed.), et al. *The All Music Guide to Jazz*, 2d ed. San Francisco: Miller Freeman Books, 1996.

Larkin, Colin (ed.). *The Guinness Encyclopedia of Popular Music*, 2d ed. Enfield, Middlesex, England: Guinness; New York: Stockton Press, 1995.

Brad Eden

Deason, Muriel

See Wells, Kitty

DeGaetani, Jan (1933–1989)

Internationally renowned mezzo-soprano Jan DeGaetani was an important singer and influential voice teacher who championed modern music. Many specialists believe that she is the most important song recitalist from the United States. With a range of two and one-half octaves, she interpreted the most difficult avant garde music with consummate artistry and technique. Her repertoire ranged from medieval and Renaissance song; to Joseph Haydn, Franz Schubert, and Johannes Brahms; to George Gershwin, Cole Porter, and other American masters. She made over 60 studio recordings for Nonesuch, New World, and other recording companies. In 1972 *Stereo Review* awarded the Record of the Year to the album *The Songs of Stephen Foster* (Nonesuch 79158), on which she was a featured artist.

She was born Janice Ruetz on 10 July 1939 in Massillon, OH. She married conductor Thomas DeGaetani, whose surname she retained even after their divorce in 1966. She married oboist Philip West in 1969. At an early age DeGaetani began singing in church choirs in her hometown, but according to her own account she learned to read music only after her admission to the Juilliard School in 1951. At Juilliard she studied singing with Sergius Kagen and met pianist Gilbert Kalish, with whom she formed a musical partnership that lasted over 30 years.

After graduation in 1955 she devoted one year to studying Arnold Schoenberg's *Pierrot Lunaire*, a 21-movement song cycle that was notated in *Sprechstimme*, a style of song that imitates gliding speech patterns rather than specific musical pitches. She continued to specialize in contemporary music in her work with the Gramercy and Contemporary Chamber Ensembles, supporting herself through secretarial work, waiting tables, babysitting, and occasional television commercials.

DeGaetani developed a vocal technique that allowed her to produce a variety of exotic and unusual sounds required by much contemporary music. She performed many world premieres, including that of George Crumb's *Ancient Voices of Children* (1970), one of several works that he composed for her. Elliott Carter, Peter Maxwell Davies, György Ligeti, William Schuman, and Richard Wernick also wrote vocal music with her voice in mind, often dedicating their scores to her.

In 1973 DeGaetani joined the faculty of the Eastman School of Music. She also taught regularly at the Aspen School of Music. With Norman and Ruth Lloyd, she co-authored the book *The Complete Sightsinger* (1980). In 1984 she made her first appearance in Carnegie Hall, 26 years after her formal New York debut in 1958. She developed leukemia around 1986 but continued to teach, present recitals, and give master classes. In January 1989 she gave her last full recital, and in that same year nine of her closest friends presented her with a portfolio of love songs that they composed for her. She died of leukemia on 15 September 1989 in Rochester, NY.

See also Experimental Music

For Further Reading

Slonimsky, Nicholas. "DeGaetani, Jan(ice)." In *Bakers Biographical Dictionary of Twentieth-Century Classical Musicians*, ed. Laura Kuhn. New York: Schirmer Books, 1997.

Staropoli, Barbara. "If You Encounter a Great Teacher: Remembrances of Jan DeGaetani." *National Association of Teachers of Singing Journal* 50/2 (1993): 27–33.

Victor Cardell

Deutsch, Diana (1938–)

The first woman to be internationally recognized as a leading scientist in the psychology of music, Diana Deutsch founded the scholarly journal *Music Per-*

ception and served as founding president of the Society for Music Perception and Cognition. Her edited volume *The Psychology of Music* (1982; 2d ed. 1999) is widely regarded as the authoritative guide in its field.

Deutsch was born in London, England, on 15 February 1938. She began piano lessons at age four and studied composition and music theory during her school years. She entered St. Anne's College, Oxford, in 1956 and obtained a First Class Honors Degree in psychology, philosophy, and physiology in 1959. She married J. Anthony Deutsch in 1957, and the couple immigrated to the United States following Diana's graduation. She entered the University of California, San Diego (UCSD), as a graduate student in 1966 and obtained her Ph.D. in psychology (1970). She joined the UCSD research faculty in that year and was appointed professor of psychology in 1989.

A wide-ranging and prolific scholar, Deutsch directed her initial work in music toward the field of music cognition. Out of these and other studies came the three striking musical illusions for which she is perhaps best known and for which she has garnered considerable attention from the popular scientific press. The "octave" and "scale" illusions aroused widespread interest because of their paradoxical nature and because the "octave" and "scale" are perceived quite differently from one listener to another. A similar instance of highly individualized perception can be found in the third illusion, the "tritone paradox." Whereas the individualized responses of people to the first two illusions seem to correlate with their left- or right-handedness, people's responses to the tritone paradox seem to correlate with their native speech dialect. These cases of individualized responses to musical stimuli have ramifications outside the laboratory, for they suggest that there may be times when no single mode of musical perception is shared by every listener. Music perception may be more idiosyncratic than was hitherto believed. One can no longer assume that music will necessarily be perceived as it appears in the printed score, or as a reader might imagine it from scanning the score. Neither will having a good "musical ear" necessarily lead to a "correct" perception. Rather, fine musicians may differ strikingly from each other in their perception of certain musical passages.

In recognition of her scholarly achievements, Deutsch has been elected fellow of the American Association for the Advancement of Science, the Acoustical Society of America, the American Psychological Association, the American Psychological Society, the Audio Engineering Society, and the Society of Experimental Psychologists. She was elected governor of the Audio Engineering Society, 1987–1989, and chair of the Section of Psychology of the American Association for the Advancement of Science, 1997–2000.

A commercial recording—*Musical Illusions and Paradoxes* (Philomel Records, La Jolla, CA, 1995)—makes available several of Deutsch's most famous stimuli and provides, in an enclosed booklet, a nontechnical introduction.

See also Music Psychology

For Further Reading

Deutsch, Diana (ed.). *The Psychology of Music*. New York: Academic Press, 1982.

Robert Gjerdingen

Diemer, Emma Lou (1927–)

Emma Lou Diemer is regarded highly as a teacher, composer, and performer in the last part of the twentieth century. Her compositions number several hundred works. Because of Diemer's background in organ and ongoing work as a church organist, she may be best known for her compositions for that instrument and her choral music. However, she has composed music in a wide variety of formats and media. Her catalog includes three symphonies, several overtures and piano concerti, and many chamber works for small ensembles, such as *Solotrio* (1981) for xylophone, vibraphone, and marimba, and *Toccata* for flute chorus (1968).

Diemer was born in Kansas City, MO, on 24 November 1927. As a child from a musical family, she was inspired and influenced by light classics and popular songs that she heard around the household. She often played the piano by improvising and from reading scores for family musical gatherings. Although she was involved in her high school women's glee club, it was not until later in her career that she began composing choral music.

Diemer's process of composition is closely tied to keyboard improvisation. Her music, even for large ensembles, contains pianistic qualities. Although many aspects of Diemer's music are conservative in style and rely on music of the past, she stretches and expands traditional elements of harmony, rhythm, and a sense of lyricism with newer styles and techniques such as serialism. Although she has not composed a large number of works of electronic or computer music, Diemer has experimented in these areas. Her music is available on *New Century Vol. 10* (MMC Recordings Ltd. 2067) and *Deferred Voices—Organ Music by Women* (Afka 527).

Diemer attended Yale University, where she studied with Richard Donovan and Paul Hindemith. She received a Fulbright scholarship in 1952, enabling her to study at the Royal Conservatory in Brussels. Following two years at the Berkshire Music Center studying with Ernst Toch and Roger Sessions, Diemer attended the Eastman School of Music. At Eastman she studied with Howard Hanson and received her Ph.D. (1960).

Between 1959 and 1961, Diemer was composer-in-residence for the secondary schools in Arlington, VA, under a Ford Foundation Young Composers Project grant. She has also served as composer-consultant under the Continuing Music Project of the Music Educators National Conference. As a result, many of Diemer's early works are conceived for school performance. She served on the faculty of the University of Maryland in composition and theory, and then at the University of California, Santa Barbara, from 1971 to the time she retired in 1991.

Diemer has been the recipient of many awards, dating back to her student days. She has received several research grants for electronic music, including a National Endowment for the Arts fellowship in electronic music. In 1981 Diemer received the Virginia Band Directors Association prize for wind band works, and in 1995 she was named the American Guild of Organists Composer of the Year.

See also Classical Music; Performer, Keyboard

For Further Reading

Brown, Cynthia Clark. "An Interview with Emma Lou Diemer: AGO 1995 Composer of the Year." *American Organist* (November 1995): 36–44.

Diemer, Emma Lou. "My Life as a Composer." *Piano Quarterly* 129 (Spring 1985): 58–59.

Cheryl Taranto

DiFranco, Ani (1970–)

Singer-songwriter Ani DiFranco is best known for her three-tier revolution against the corporate-music-industry norm: musical, with her alternative punk-folk music style; economic, with her independent label, Righteous Babe Records; and political, as an ardent feminist and an open bisexual. She has experimented over the years with her sound and style, where her music ranges from solo performer with guitar to full studio production and from spoken word to dance mixes. However, she has always remained true to herself with an empowering attitude, as described by her label's motto, "On Her Own."

Born in Buffalo, NY, on 23 September 1970, Ani DiFranco first began to learn how to play guitar at age nine from folk musicians in the Buffalo area. They helped her find her first gigs playing Beatles covers at bars and coffeehouses in the area. When she was 15 years old she moved out of her family's home and began writing her own songs. After graduating from the Visual and Performing Arts High School, where she also studied ballet and visual arts, DiFranco moved to New York City to continue playing the indie circuit, where her fan base had grown tremendously.

By age 19, DiFranco had written over 100 songs and had briefly studied art at the New School for Social Research. In 1990, besieged by requests from fans for recordings of her performances, she recorded her first album, *Ani DiFranco* (Righteous Babe 1), on her own label (which she ran out of the trunk of her Volkswagen) out of the necessity to distribute her music more effectively than commericial distributors would. With word-of-mouth and a frenetic concert schedule as her only advertising scheme, she continued to produce her own albums at a prolific rate, releasing at least one album a year for 10 years and seeing her popularity grow exponentially with each release. Though major labels soon became interested in her, she steadfastly held her own until Righteous Babe Records became a viable independent label. She has received three Grammy Award nominations, and Righteous Babe Records has been nominated for two Indie Awards from the Association for Independent Music.

DiFranco's lyrics, guitar playing, and voice are all very distinct. At one moment angry and biting and the next warm and sobering, she exudes a solid confidence that belongs to a positive, wise soul. Social consciousness is at the heart of her music, using poetic and sometimes piercing lyrics to express her thoughts. Her guitar playing is more rhythmic than melodic; her slapping-style gives her music a strong beat and an undaunted energy. She can scream and thrash as easily as she can "coo" and caress with her voice. In an open letter to her fans in 1997, Ani DiFranco described herself best as a "songwriter, musicmaker, storyteller, freak."

See also Rock and Popular Music Genres; Singer-Songwriter

For Further Reading

Misiroglu, Gina. *Girls Like Us: 40 Extraordinary Women Celebrating Girlhood in Story, Poetry, and Song.* Novato, CA: New World Library, 1999.

Post, Laura. *Backstage Pass: Interviews with Women in Music.* Norwich, VT: New Victoria Publishers, 1997.

Quirino, Raffaele. *Ani DiFranco: Righteous Babe.* Kingston: Quarry Music Books, 2000.

Woodworth, Marc. *Solo: Women Singer-Songwriters in Their Own Words.* New York: Delta, 1998.

Sarah Meyers

Disco

Disco as a musical style was primarily dance music, with a heavy, simplistic 4/4 beat. It was based on funk and soul styles and was often lyrically and musically repetitive with a penchant toward extended versions. These musical features served disco's function as dance floor fodder at flashy, glamorous nightclubs called discotheques, which flourished throughout the 1970s. Aside from this, disco was a cultural force that represented hedonism, fashion, youth, and sex. Disco hit the mainstream with the film *Saturday Night Fever* (1977), which brought the hitherto largely gay and black disco subculture to middle America and beyond. After dominating American pop music through the late 1970s, disco collapsed in the early 1980s, to resurface as various dance and electro-pop forms of the 1980s, and to influence hip hop and electronica in the 1980s and 1990s.

The most prominent role for women in disco was that of the so-called "disco diva," a glamorous, distant beauty, elegant and fashionable. The disco diva embodied many of the main aesthetic features of disco—glamour, slickness, fashion consciousness, and sexiness. Even drag queens like Sylvester (1944–1988) adopted the diva image in their public performances. As Nelson George has pointed out, the divas were "the great romantic icons of gay culture." Most important, the woman (usually black) disco singer provided human warmth and (often gospel-influenced) emotion against the often cold and impersonal instrumental backdrop of synthesizers and percussion.

Information is sketchy, to say the least, on roles for women in disco outside that of vocalist. Women have been significantly underrepresented in pop music historiography, just as disco has been all but erased from the pop historical canon. Thus women in disco are doubly ignored in the existing literature. Nonetheless, some brief biographical information does exist on several prominent women disco singing stars, including Donna Summer (b. 1948), Vicki Sue Robinson (1955–2000), Gloria Gaynor (b. 1949), and the group Sister Sledge.

Donna Summer met electro-pop producer Giorgio Moroder while living in Munich, Germany, as a member of a traveling troupe performing the musical *Hair*. In 1975 they recorded "Love to Love You Baby," a 16-minute reworking of Jane Birkin and Serge Gainsbourg's version of "Je t'aime . . . moi non plus." Summer's faux-orgasmic performance became an early disco staple and established the singer as one of disco's most visible stars. She was associated with the extended 12-inch remix single (a vinyl recording of a single song, in which elements of the original song are used as source material for a new setting, often longer than the original). This medium continued to be an important format in hip hop and in dance music of the 1990s. Summer continued her chart and club successes with "Hot Stuff" (1979) and "I Feel Love" (1980), then attempted to cross over to mainstream pop in the 1980s. Other than her hit single "She Works Hard for the Money" (1982), though, Summer's popularity declined in tandem with that of disco.

Vicki Sue Robinson, like Summer, was a product of the musical stage. Her "Turn the Beat Around" (1976) peaked at number 10 on the *Billboard* charts. Although Gloria Gaynor's 1975 hit "Never Can Say Goodbye" established her disco career, she is perhaps better remembered for her song "I Will Survive" (1979). Sister Sledge members Debra (b. 1955),

Joan (b. 1957), Kim (b. 1958), and Kathie (b. 1959) Sledge began recording as Sisters Sledge in 1971 but eventually dropped the "s" in "Sisters." After working various studio sessions through the early 1970s, they hit with "He's the Greatest Dancer" and "We Are Family" in 1979; but like many other disco-associated performers, they found their careers in decline at the dawn of the 1980s. The group disbanded in 1985.

See also Electronic Dance Music; Rock and Popular Music Genres

For Further Reading

Dyer, Richard. "In Defense of Disco." In *Record: Rock, Pop and the Written Word*, eds. Simon Frith and Andrew Goodwin. New York: Pantheon Books, 1990.

Negus, Keith. *Popular Music in Theory*. Hanover and London: Wesleyan University Press, 1996.

Mike Daley

Discrimination

Discrimination against women in music in the United States since 1900 has taken many forms. Music has historically been considered a feminine and feminizing and even effeminate art, and this may be the reason why efforts to preserve male control and masculinity have been particularly intense. Allegations of discriminatory treatment against women musicians are often considered newsworthy, perhaps because, at least to many outsiders, music appears to be one field in which women would not suffer devaluation and exclusion. Statistics concerning women's and men's employment and education are published by the federal Department of Labor and Department of Education and by many other public and private organizations. The College Music Society maintains records of academic employment in all fields and has published cumulative reports on women's status (College Music Society, 1988; Neuls-Bates, 1976; Payne, 1996; Renton, 1980). Member directories of musicians' unions provide records of other professional employment.

Women's unequal treatment in the early twentieth century derived from standards of behavior such as the doctrine of separate spheres and social Darwinism that rendered professionalism in music questionable and even impossible for middle- and upper-class women. Through World War I, with the exception of operatic, choral, and solo concert work, women were barred from the professional mainstream. Even symphony orchestras with women's committees providing the chief source of fundraising did not accept women players. With the war effort of the 1940s women musicians moved into jobs that men had left; at war's end, women had to give up their jobs.

In the second half of the century much anti-discrimination legislation resulted from the civil rights and women's rights movements. Although women have won legal equality with men in education and employment, and obvious discrimination is prohibited, women report sexual harassment, devaluation of their work, and other forms of discriminatory treatment as students, teachers, performers, and administrators. On college and university campuses women must either endure the chilly climate or actively oppose it; either way, their ability to accomplish their principal work is diminished. The catchphrase "glass ceiling" (a journalist's invention in 1985 and recognized as a legal problem in the Civil Rights Act of 1991), meaning the barrier between women and high-salaried, high-responsibility management positions, inspires similar phrases, often journalists' inventions—the "ivory ceiling" (faculty in the "ivory tower"), and the "brass ceiling" (brass players and band directors).

Devaluation. Behind most forms of discrimination against women in music—if not in all fields—is the devaluation of women and their work. Women are disproportionately perceived to be lacking in various respects and are denied hiring, promotion, and salary increases; it is still often said that a woman has to be "twice as good as a man" to be considered at all. The general tendency to devalue women and their work has been tested in several related studies in which two groups of people are asked to evaluate articles, résumés, and the like. The names attached to the items given to each group of evaluators are clearly either men's or women's, but they are reversed for each group; what one group believes is a woman's work, the other believes is a man's. Regardless of the items, when they are ascribed to a man they are rated higher than when they are ascribed to a woman. Further, because women internalize their devaluation and thus doubt their own competence, women evaluators are as likely as men to downgrade those items ascribed to women. In one study, women college students rated scholarly articles higher if they believed they were written by a man than if they believed they were written by a woman (Sandler and Hall, 6–7). In scholarship and in musical composition, women have sometimes tried to outwit the devaluation phenomenon by assuming a male pseudonym.

Another kind of devaluation exists in situations where response to the same behavior is different depending on the sex of the person exhibiting the behavior. A young woman who wants to be a conductor may be viewed as "unfeminine" or "too ambitious." If a woman student does exceptionally well, she may be praised for "thinking like a man"—a backhanded compliment that implies that there is something wrong with "thinking like a woman," which she is. An orchestral conductor (male) may urge a woman instrumentalist to "play like a man"; she notices that none of the men has been asked to play like a woman. A related tendency is to attribute men's success to skill or ability but women's success to luck or to the task's lack of difficulty. The implication is that only men have the ability to perform well or to improve, whereas women's success is owing to external factors over which they have little control and which they therefore cannot rely on for future achievement. Psychologists note a similar difference in the self-evaluation of talent and aptitude.

Feminization. Discrimination against women often increases with the feminization of an occupation, that is, when greater numbers of women succeed in finding employment in a formerly all-male occupation, resulting in a loss in pay and status. As many researchers have observed, women move into men's territory only to find that its occupants abandon it rather than share it with women, and they take their privileges with them. Women succeed only to find they have failed. When feminization has occurred in the past, notably in elementary school music teaching, men have moved to higher-status (unfeminized) positions such as high school teacher or music supervisor. In higher education, as more women obtain faculty positions, men have fewer places they can call their own, and thus women seeking promotion to senior faculty positions or administrative posts confront increasing difficulties. At elite institutions the backlash is especially intense; faculty women have the right to be there, but their authority and their ability to lead is challenged, if not actively undermined. Mistreatment is less accessible to legal remedy than is obvious discrimination.

Classical Music. A sampling of evidence of sex discrimination illustrates the general problem and possible remedies. In her survey "Women Band Directors in American Higher Education," Carol Ann Feather (1987) tabulates results of a questionnaire sent to women in the profession and draws conclusions about discriminatory behavior and attitudes on the part of administrators and students. In 1995 the *Wall Street Journal* ("Work Week: Brass Ceiling") reported new research by Linda Hartley, band director at the University of Dayton, showing that, at most, only 6 percent of college band directors in the United States are women. Most women band directors she surveyed find discrimination, discouragement, and discomfort in the predominantly man's milieu.

Barbara Jepson's study, "Women in the Classical Recording Industry" (1991), shows that with the influx of career-oriented women into the work force in the 1970s, women became involved in all facets of classical music recording. Yet the top decision-making authority, especially in larger conglomerates, remains in men's hands. Further, American women must deal with culturally ingrained prejudices within some of the major foreign labels. The relatively few successful women in the field through the 1980s include Wilma Cozart Fine, Judith Sherman, Alison Ames, and Teresa Sterne.

In 1997 the *Wall Street Journal* (Duff, 1997) reported a study by two economists at Harvard and Princeton Universities, funded by the National Bureau of Economic Research, that found that orchestras in the United States hired more women musicians after 1970 when, amid a general outcry of workplace discrimi-

nation against women, blind auditions were instituted. When women musicians auditioned behind a screen, such as a heavy cloth hung from the ceiling, so the judges could not know their gender, race, or age, their odds of making it past preliminary rounds were boosted by 50 percent. The researchers collected a sample of auditions for eight major orchestras in the United States; audition records listed the names of all candidates and whether they had advanced to subsequent rounds. Findings were adjusted for various factors and run through a traditional mathematical formula. The researchers concluded that the switch to blind auditions can explain from one-third to one-half of the women who were new hires between 1970 and 1995. In 1995 one-quarter of all players in the top 5 orchestras were women, compared to five percent in 1970. In response to the study as reported in the *Chicago Tribune*, one reader noted that her teacher told her to wear sneakers so that the judges could not hear her heels clicking; another reader attributed the greater number of hires to the fact that music schools were training more women; and another, noting the distressing underrepresentation of African American and other minority musicians in orchestras, suggested that blind auditions are no panacea (Kleiman, 1997).

In 1993 Jepson reported in the *Wall Street Journal* that the first International Women's Brass Conference counteracted the sense of differentness or isolation felt by many lone women players in the brass section. In 1998 the *Boston Globe* (Larson) described the "profile of gender bias" among working musicians as indicated by the Boston Musicians Union Member Handbook. Discrimination against women brass players seemed especially serious—the reporter noted that the "brass ceiling" in professional music is apparently impenetrable—owing to several factors: it is thought that women are too small; their arms are too weak; women are not aggressive enough to play brass instruments; or, if they are aggressive, this is considered unacceptable behavior for a girl. The Member Handbook listed no men harpists and no women tuba players. About 50 percent of the violinists were women, and eight out of 15 trumpet players (over 50 percent), but only one to two percent of the 50 timpani players, the 140 who play drum set, and the 150 trombonists. The reporter concluded that some young women were being steered away from what might be satisfying and productive careers. Other women formed all-women groups, often with whimsical, double-edged names like the Amazons Quartet (bassists playing string quartets) and the Jazzabels (Dixie-land).

Popular Music and Media. Reports of sex discrimination and related controversies are much more numerous in popular music, music videos, and music television (MTV) than in classical music, perhaps because the topics are more familiar to the general public and more people care about the outcome. In 1990 a guest columnist in the *Chicago Tribune* (Aaron) claimed that every type of popular music seen on MTV perpetuates sexist attitudes and offered opinions as to why those attitudes exist. In 1991 the *Atlanta Constitution* in an "Editorial: The Guy Awards" noted that the Grammy Awards, which televised all the "lesser" awards given to men while ignoring all the "lesser" awards given to women, might be renamed.

In October 1991 the *Washington Times* (Kowet) reported that the documentary film "Dreamworlds: Desire, Sex and Power in Rock Video," produced by Pro-fessor Sut Jhally of the University of Massachusetts, used clips from 165 music videos shown on the MTV cable channel to document MTV's tireless degradation of women; the headline suggested, perhaps ironically, that Jhally was "harassing" MTV. The *Boston Globe* (Davis, 1991) reported that MTV was challenging Jhally's contention that many music-video images of women are based largely on adolescent male fantasies and foster attitudes toward women that can lead to rape.

In 1993 Houston newspapers reported that 100 or more attendees at the National Association of Black Journalists convention walked out angrily after a Houston rapper told the group of several hundred journalists that all the women he knew were either "bitches or whores" and then cursed out a woman who asked if he would describe his mother that way (Asin, 1993; Weintraub and Perry, 1993). William Raspberry (1993), commenting on the incident in his *Washington Post* column a week later, touched on issues of race as well as gender under the headline "Foulmouthed Trash: If We Don't Respect Our Women, Why Should Anyone Else?"

A study published the next year in the *Journal of Broadcasting and Electronic Media* (Signorelli, McLeod, and Healy, 1994) examined gender portrayals and stereotyping in a sample of MTV commercials. Compared to men, women characters appeared less frequently, had more beautiful bodies, were more physically attractive, wore sexier and skimpier clothing, and were more often the object of another's gaze. As for executives, *Rolling Stone* reported that women in the music industry might be described as "Exiled in Guyville" (Ali, 1994).

See also Chilly Climate; Pseudonyms

For Further Reading

Duff, Christina. "Out of Sight Keeps Women in Mind for U.S. Orchestra Spots, Study Finds." *Wall Street Journal* (7 March 1997): 6B.

Feather, Carol Ann. "Women Band Directors in American Higher Education." In *The Musical Woman: An International Perspective II (1984–1985)*, ed. Judith Lang Zaimont et al. Westport, CT: Greenwood Press, 1987.

Kleiman, Carol. "Making Strides in Music Careers Merits Applause." *Chicago Tribune* (24 June 1997), Sect. 3, p. 2.

Larson, Susan. "Women Musicians Bend Brass Ceiling." *Boston Globe* (6 Sept 1998): N5.

Sandler, Bernice R., and Roberta M. Hall. *The Campus Climate Revisited: Chilly for Women Faculty, Administrators, and Graduate Students.* Washington, DC: Association of American Colleges, 1986.

"Work Week: Brass Ceiling." *Wall Street Journal* (15 Aug. 1995): 1.

Deborah Hayes

DJ, Club

A club DJ (or disc jockey) is the person who plays and mixes recorded music at a party, discotheque, or nightclub. In conducting the research on women DJs, specifically club DJs, one may quickly conclude that although the numbers of women DJs are rapidly increasing, women DJs continue to be marginalized in the club scene, journalistic discourse, and media representation. The main issues perpetuating this gender differentiation are threefold: accessibility, promotion, and professional connections within the community.

Accessibility is a major issue confronting not only women trying to break into the DJ scene but also those who are already established. To begin a DJ career, women must be able to access equipment (such as turntables and a mixer) and music either by purchasing their own, borrowing a friend's, or, perhaps like many women DJs, becoming involved in community radio. Once they have access to equipment and music they must gain the basic skills required to perform as a DJ. This often includes self-teaching or learning from others who are already experienced. The next step is locating the spaces to gain "spinning" experience with an audience. Opportunities for women DJs to play are often found in the queer and women-based communities because women DJs are favored to play for women-only spaces. There are also a number of DJs who suggest that the queer community, particularly queer-identified men, is less threatened than heterosexual-identified men are when the role of the DJ, often seen as a role of power in the music industry, is held by a woman. It is important to mention here that women DJs are often expected to prove their technical ability, more so than men, to gain equal respect and to be taken as seriously in the profession. Rosalind Gill and Keith Grint suggest, "the cultural association between masculinity and technology in Western societies . . . operates not only as a popular assumption—from which much sexist humour about women's 'technical incompetence' has been generated—but also as an academic truth" (Grint and Gill, 3). Stereotypes like this perpetuate the myth that women are unable to learn technical skills and maintain what is referred to as the "boy's club" in technical arenas.

Historically women have not been socialized to be self-promoters, yet promotion is a vital part of the DJ industry. Many women DJs talk about having to be aggressive, determined, and persistent in order to achieve success in the scene, as well as knowing someone who is already established on the inside, which can be problematic because the DJ circuit continues to be dominated by men.

There is a great need for women DJs

to come up with their own concepts and methods of promoting themselves, thus allowing women to be in control of their own DJ promotion. The focus may then shift from the associated novelty of their gender to their skills and reputation as a DJ. One important tool that many women DJs use to promote themselves and their fellow DJ "sisters" is the World Wide Web and related Internet services.

Establishing personal contacts through various DJ communities has historically been difficult for women DJs because of the lack of women on the circuit. In recent years this has changed drastically owing to the increased number of women DJs on the scene, as well as the women DJ collectives that have begun to surface. Sister, "a place for female DJ's to get gigs without bias," was co-founded in October 1997 by DJs XJS and Siren with MC Linzee, who were early to join. Sister evolved from a woman DJ cooperative that existed from 1993 to 1995 called Your Sister's House with the likes of DJs Polywog and Charlotte the Baroness. Primarily, Sister provides support for women DJs (new to, or established in the scene) and a space where women DJs are "viewed as a DJ first, and then as a woman, when you're behind the decks." Together this group of seven resident DJs and a long list of guest DJs throw monthly parties.

Another collective that acts as a "forum for information, networking and conversation about independent music from a [women's] perspective" is Indiegrrl, established by Holly Figuerao in May 1998. This group of DJs, performers, and managers is interested in women's roles in the independent music industry. SISTERDJS is World Wide Web community and an electronic mailing list founded by DJ Dazy, a guest DJ for Sister. The list includes more than 175 women who are well-established DJs as well as those who are trying to break into the DJ scene. DJ Dazy promotes the list as "a wonderful source of advice and resource-sharing for new and experienced selectors alike" (Palmer, 108).

At the turn of the millennium, the subject and status of women DJs is finally being addressed in other mediums. In 2001 Jane Walker and Jackie Pelle released a one-hour documentary entitled, *Spinsters*, which investigates the issues and concerns for women DJing in the Club scene. Walker and Pelle interview many women DJs from Canada, the United States, Britain, including DJ Heather, Misstress Barbara, Freya, Denise Benson, Jennifa Mayanja, Forest Green, XJS, etc. Throughout the documentary these DJs talk candidly about their experiences as women DJs and they also discuss the problematics of having to continually address their gender in relation to their DJ status. Although the documentary does, at times, rely on a male producer to validate some of the concerns raised by the women, Walker and Pelle have produced a valuable and educative tool for anyone who is interested in DJing and/or the club scene.

See also Electronic Dance Music; Music Technology; Underground

For Further Reading

Grint, Keith, and Rosalind Gill (eds.). *The Gender-Technology Relation: Contemporary Theory and Research*. London: Taylor and Francis, 1995.

Indiegrrl: For Women in the Independent Music Industry. Available: http://www.indiegrrl.com

The Official DJ Dazy Homepage. Available: http://www.djdazy.com

Palmer, Tamara, Len Sobeck, and Kieran Wyatt. "Review of *DJ Dazy*." *URB* 71 (January/February 2000): 108.

Sister: The Female DJ Collective in San Francisco. Available: http://www.sistersf.com

Charity Marsh

Dudziak, Urszula (1943–)

Polish jazz composer and vocalist Urszula Dudziak is known for her experimental vocal techniques. She concertizes around the world. Her music has won numerous awards and honors, including a National Endowment for the Arts award in 1985. Critics described her as "a walking space age machine" (*Billboard*) performing ad lib scat singing mixed with fascinating vocal effects, such as random, meaningless syllables, sweeping scales, guttural sounds, cries, and moaning, with results that are "exciting, haunting, inventive and beautiful" (*California Jazz*). Dudziak's style may be described as located between fusion and post-bop; she often uses electronics to highlight the broad range of her voice (through amplification, reverberation, echo) and focuses on unusual vocal techniques that she developed in the early 1970s.

Born on 22 October 1943 in Straconka, Poland, Dudziak began playing the piano at the age of five and started singing professionally at age 15. In the 1950s she performed with the legendary Polish jazz pianist Krzysztof Komeda, and in 1962 she met her future husband, jazz violinist Micha Urbaniak, with whom she has performed since 1964. After performing in Poland and Scandinavia (1965–1969), Dudziak emigrated to the United States in 1973, settling in New York.

In addition to recording voice, percussion, and electronics for many of Micha Urbaniak's albums, since 1972 Dudziak has released a number of solo albums, including *Newborn Light* (Cameo 101), *Urszula* (Arista AL 4065), *Midnight Train* (Arista 4132), *Future Talk* (Inner City 1066), and *Sorrow Is Not Forever . . . But Love Is* (Keytone 726). In 1979 Dudziak was called the Female Jazz Vocalist of the Year by the *Los Angeles Times*, and she ranked just behind Ella Fitzgerald (1917–1996) in the 57th annual Readers' Poll of *Down Beat Magazine* (1992).

Dudziak has worked with Adam Makowicz, Wojciech Karolak, Lester Bowie, Bobby McFerrin, Miles Davies, Laurie Anderson (b. 1947), Lionel Hampton, Chico Freeman, Nina Simone (b. 1933), and many others. Dudziak performed at major jazz festivals and such events as the Jazz Jamboree in Warsaw and the Gala Memorial Concert in tribute to Thelonius Monk at the Kennedy Center in Washington, DC (1986). She is a member of the vocal jazz group Vocal Summit but continues to perform as a soloist. Her concert tours in Europe and the United States have included performances in major jazz venues, and she also taught master classes and courses in Germany, Austria, Sweden, Poland, and the United States. Her project *Electronic Jazz Choir* was awarded a National Endowment for the Arts grant in 1985.

In addition to her activities as a performer and improviser, Dudziak composed music for Mieczyslaw Rogala's experimental video-opera *Nature Is Leaving Us* (1987–1989), for the film *Painted Boy* (1995) about Polish writer Jerzy Kosinski, and for the television series *Mondo Manhattan*.

See also Multicultural Musics

For Further Reading

Borkowski, Jan. "Urszula Dudziak: Newborn Light." *Jazz Forum* 24/4 (1973): 34–35.

Buchter-Romer, Ute. "New Vocal Jazz: Untersuchungen zur zeitgenossischen improvisierten Musik mit der Stimme anhand ausgewahlter Beispiele." Ph.D diss., University of Duisburg, 1989.

Maja Trochimczyk

Durbin, Deanna (1921–)

Deanne Durbin was one of the most popular box-office stars in the film musicals of the late 1930s and 1940s. She had a beautiful classically trained mature voice when her career began at age 13. She made the awkward age look graceful and gave many moviegoers their first experience with opera. Durbin was also commercially significant with a trade-marked line of clothing, dolls, and song-books.

She was born on 4 December 1921 in Winnipeg, Canada, and was christened Edna Mae. Because of her father's ill health, the family moved to Southern California a year later. None of the family was musical, but they recognized Edna Mae's outstanding voice. When older sister Edith began teaching school she insisted on using part of her earnings to help pay for voice lessons for her younger sister.

In 1935 Metro-Goldwyn-Mayer (MGM) was planning a movie based on the life of opera singer Madame Ernestine Schumann-Heink. An agent heard Edna Mae sing and took her to MGM, where she was hired to play the opera star as a child. Schumann-Heink became ill, and the movie was cancelled. MGM changed her name to "Deanna" and used her in a short musical film, *Every Sunday* (1936), with Judy Garland (1922–1969). MGM mogul Louis B. Mayer ultimately kept Garland under contract but dropped Durbin, who was immediately picked up by Universal Studios. At Universal her singing coach, Andres de Segurola, said her voice was as "rare and perfect as a blue-white diamond." Her first film, *Three Smart Girls* (1937), was a huge success and made Deanna Durbin a major star.

Throughout the 1930s Durbin made a series of highly successful films with director Joe Pasternak: *One Hundred Men and a Girl* (1937), *Mad about Music* (1938), *That Certain Age* (1938), *Three Smart Girls Grow Up* (1939), and *First Love* (1939). In 1938 she was awarded a special Oscar for her significant contribution in bringing the spirit and personification of youth to the screen. For most of the 1930s and 1940s Deanna Durbin was Hollywood's top woman attraction and was paired with leading men such as Robert Cummings, Walter Pidgeon, Franchot Tone, and Melvyn Douglas. However, when she wanted to change her image to a more sophisticated dramatic one, Universal was not interested. She had made 22 films for Universal but became convinced the studio would never allow her artistic freedom. In 1950, with two failed marriages behind her, she retired with her third husband, French film director Charles David, to Neauphle-le-Chateau, France, near Paris. Universal made repeated offers for her return, but Durbin refused. She was tired of being the girl-next-door who bursts into song over the poorest material, albeit the highest salary.

See also Musical Theater

For Further Reading

Ewen, David. *All the Years of American Popular Music*. Englewood Cliffs, NJ: Prentice-Hall, 1977.

Gammon, Peter. *The Oxford Companion to Popular Music*. Oxford and New York: Oxford University Press, 1991.

Wlaschin, Ken. *Opera on Screen*. Los Angeles: Beachwood Press, 1997.

Jeanne E. Shaffer

Early Childhood Music Educators

Early childhood music educators understand the importance of music for its aesthetic and utilitarian benefits—music has aesthetic (inherent) merit because it is an integral part of the human condition, which transcends history and culture. Music's utilitarian (attendant) elements have been shown to foster many aspects of personal and social proficiency (e.g., cognition, self-esteem).

The term "early childhood" is used to describe the span of life from birth to five years of age. Early childhood can be subdivided into five categories: neonate/infant (0–18 mo.), toddler (18–36 mo.), three-year-old, four-year-old, and kindergartner. Research has shown that children of these ages acquire information more rapidly than at any other stage of life. Consequently, early childhood is critical to the development of many aspects of a child's humanity. One aspect that can be actively developed at this stage is musicianship.

Researchers in early childhood music education suggest that high-quality and consistent experiences with music can enable children to more fully express, understand, and appreciate music. Musical experiences (or instruction) for children can be classified into two categories: informal music instruction and formal music instruction.

Informal music instruction typically occurs during the prekindergarten years and is often observed in the preschool or in the home. It consists of an adult exposing the child to musical culture and encouraging the child to absorb that culture. Parents and caregivers are encouraged to engage in musical babble and rhythmic movement with children and to provide an environment rich in musical stimuli. Examples of musical babble include encouraging a child to engage in vocal exploration and then imitating the child's vocal explorations. Rhythmic movement activities involve dancing, swaying, rocking, and patting to the beat of music. A parent or caregiver can provide an environment rich in musical stimuli by playing recordings of many different styles of music for the child. In addition, it is recommended that adults avoid having specific expectations regarding the musical responses of the child during this stage.

Formal instruction involves the parent or teacher planning specific musical material to teach the child and having expectations regarding the musical responses of the child. Formal instruction usually begins when the child reaches kindergarten and can be observed when an adult teaches a specific song to a child or instructs a child on how to play a musical instrument.

Informal music experiences for young children have traditionally been provided by parents, grandparents, other family members, or acquaintances. Musical play in the form of songs and games was an integral part of the adult-child interaction. Children were exposed to music in the home as many adults played instruments and sang. The advent of recording technology and radio brought a wider array of music into the home, giving young children a more diverse aural experience. However, a decline in adult music making seems to be the result of the availability of other musical sound sources. Consequently, the musical play once a standard component of adult-child interactions has waned.

Although some young children still benefit from a rich musical environment in their homes, specifically those from various cultures in which music is a fundamental part of everyday life, most children experience music outside the home or only through radio, television, and compact discs—usually a nonparticipatory experience. Church or community groups often encourage young children's engagement in some musical experiences. Preschool church choirs, women's groups, and informal music making at social events constitute some of these experiences. For those children enrolled in some sort of daycare or preschool setting, musical experiences may or may not be included in their daily activities. The comfort of the caregivers with their own musicianship often determines the level of musical engagement among the children and adults. Musical experiences in the form of recorded music are more likely to exist in these settings. When live music is included, the activities are usually songs that mark a specific time of day, task, or initiation of another activity. Examples include a hello song, a snacktime song, or a clean-up song.

Recognizing the inconsistency in quality and quantity of music experiences for young children, some people have established private music programs. These include: First Steps in Music, Kindermusik, Mini-Music, MUSICTIME, Music Together, Music for Young Children, Musical Awakenings, and programs offered through community music schools. Classes usually involve children and parents, and musical interaction among all participants is encouraged. Even though these programs have filled a void for some children, they are obviously available only to those children whose parents deem musical experiences necessary and are willing and able to pay the tuition. Consistent, enriching musical experiences are not available for all children.

Music experiences for young children are provided by nonspecialists, early childhood specialists, music specialists, and early childhood music specialists. Nonspecialists include persons such as parents, other siblings, Sunday school teachers, babysitters, and other family members and acquaintances. The quality and quantity of the music experiences included in their interactions with children are dependent upon their own musicianship and interest. Early childhood specialists are those persons who have training, often a college degree, in early childhood education or psychology. A music course or experience is sometimes included in their training. These specialists typically work in daycare and/or preschool settings and often include some music experience in the children's daily routine. Usually they understand the importance of music in the child's development, but their ability to offer appropriate nurturing musical experiences is mixed.

Music specialists are those persons who have had some training in music but not specifically in early childhood music education. They might be performers or private teachers, or they might just have more extensive musical background than most. Music specialists may provide music experiences to children by means of weekly visits to daycare or preschool settings, by working with a children's choir, by including music in a Sunday school class they are teaching, or by accepting young children as their students on the violin or piano. Although these persons provide an excellent musical model for young children, they frequently do not understand what sort of musical experiences are most appropriate for young children. Therefore some of their instruction may be developmentally inappropriate for the children with whom they work.

Early childhood music specialists are those persons who have training in music education for young children. Because most states do not offer teacher certification in this field, most colleges and universities do not offer degrees in the field either. Often these persons hold degrees in music education and then seek training on their own via workshops, classes, or private programs such as Music Together. The music experiences they provide for young children are probably the most appropriate. However, only a small percentage of children have opportunities to benefit from their expertise.

Although some men have contributed to knowledge and practice in early childhood music, women have provided most major contributions. Women have contributed to growth and interest in early childhood music education through their leadership as researchers and practitioners.

Many women have taken leadership positions in forwarding the cause of early childhood music education. Of particular note was the formation of the Early Childhood Special Research Interest Group (EC SRIG) in 1980. The EC SRIG is a subgroup in the Society for Research in Music Education, part of the Music Educators National Conference (MENC). The first national chair was Mary Tolbert, who presented the mission statement for the EC SRIG at the MENC national meeting in Miami in 1980. This group, open to any MENC member, has provided a vehicle for the dissemination of and support for research in early childhood music. Women who have served as chair of the EC SRIG include the following:

Mary R. Tolbert	(1980–1984)
Jonny Ramsey	(1984–1986)
Mary Palmer	(1986–1988)
Donna Brink Fox	(1988–1992)
Susan Tarnowski	(1992–1994)
Danette Littleton and Diane Persellin	(1994–1996)
Mary Lou VanRysselberghe	(1996–1998)
Lori Custodero and Rachel Nardo	(1998–2000)
Joanne Rutkowski	(2000–2002)
Joyce Eastland-Gromko	(2002–2004)

A body of literature in the form of doctoral dissertations and research articles currently exists to provide information regarding children's musical development and their responses to various types of instruction. Researchers in the field include Barbara Jo Alvarez, Beth Marie Bolton, Lori Almeida Custodero, Joyce Ann Decarbo, Patricia Flowers, Donna Brink Fox, Joyce Eastland Gromko, Lili Muhler Levinowitz, Danette Littleton, Dorothy McDonald, Rachel Lee Nardo, Mary Henderson Palmer, Diane Persellin, Jonny Hatmaker Ramsey, Maria Runfola, Joanne Rutkowski, Carol Scott-Kassner, Wendy Sims, Cynthia Crump Taggart, Wendy Hicks Valerio, and Marilyn Pflederer Zimmerman. Although leadership and research have been critical to the establishment of early childhood music as a vital and respected discipline, the many women who practice early childhood music contribute to the musical development of children daily. The following women are notable for their contributions in the practical arena, through publications and in-service presentations. Even though many of these women continue to be active in the field, the years indicated refer to the years in which their most notable works were published.

Andress, Barbara (ed.). *Promising Practices: Prekindergarten Music Education*. Reston, VA: MENC, 1989.

Campbell, Patricia Shehan, and Carol Scott Kassner. *Music in Childhood*. New York: Schirmer Books, 1995.

Levinowitz, Lili. "The Importance of Music in Early Childhood." *Music Educators Journal* 86/01 (1999): 17–18.

Palmer, Mary. "Lobbying for Music Education." *Music Educators Journal* 78/05 (1992): 41.

Sims, Wendy (comp. and ed.). *Strategies for Teaching Prekindergarten Music*. Reston, VA: MENC, 1995.

Tarnowski, Susan. "Musical Play and Young Children." *Music Educators Journal* 86/01 (1999): 26–29.

Zimmerman, Marilyn Pflederer. "Education in Music from Infancy through Maturity: A Continuing Process." *Canadian Music Educator* 19/02 (1978): 41–47.

Finally, some of the commercial early childhood music programs were founded, or co-founded, by women. Included among these are *Kindermusik* by Lorna Lutz Heyge, *Music for Young Children* by Frances Balodis, *Music Together* by Lili Levinowitz, and *MUSICTIME* by Donna Brink Fox.

See also Music Education; Music Learning Theory

For Further Reading

Gordon, Edwin E. E. *A Music Learning Theory for Newborn and Young Children*. Chicago: GIA Publications, 1990.

Rutkowski, Joanne, and Maria Runfola. *TIPS: The Child Voice*. Reston, VA: MENC; National Association for Music Education, 1997.

Joanne Rutkowski
Diana Dansereau

Eder, Linda (1961–)

Singer and actress Linda Eder, one of the most important woman vocalists on Broadway in the final decades of the twentieth century, made her Broadway debut as Lucy, the lady of the evening who encounters the two personalities of the title character in Frank Wildhorn's *Jekyll and Hyde*, a musical adaptation of Robert Louis Stevenson's literary classic. By the time *Jekyll and Hyde* opened on Broadway on 28 April 1997, the show had already amassed a loyal following through the release of a concept album followed by a 35-city tour. Eder, who was with the show from its inception, received the 1997 Theatre World Award and was nominated for the Outer Critics Award as well as the Best Actress Drama Desk Award.

Born on 3 February 1961 in Tucson,

AZ, and raised in Brainerd, MN, she was drawn to the music of previous decades at an early age. While other teenagers of the 1980s were listening to pop and rock, Eder was drawn to the styles of such singers as Judy Garland (1922–1969) and Barbra Streisand (b. 1942).

While still a teenager, Eder formed a duet act with pianist Paul Todd and played the hotel circuits for six years. Following those engagements she headed toward Los Angeles to try out her skills in front of a national television audience on the popular *Star Search Talent* competition. With an unprecedented 12-week winning streak and with the meeting of University of California Los Angeles student Frank Wildhorn, Eders's career and personal life took a dramatic turn.

At the time of their meeting, Wildhorn was working on a project that would become *Jekyll and Hyde*. From that moment the duel careers of Eder and Wildhorn have been on a steady climb. Although Broadway critics gave mixed reviews of the Wildhorn piece, audiences embraced the show. Although *Jekyll and Hyde* still plays to New York audiences, Eder has moved on to other projects, including several solo recordings. She and Wildhorn, whose romance has spanned the length of their professional relationship, were married on 3 May 1998. Eder recently fulfilled one of her childhood dreams when she made her debut at Carnegie Hall.

See also Musical Theater

For Further Reading

Block, Geoffrey, and Fred L. Block. *Enchanted Evenings: The Broadway Musical from Showboat to Sondheim*. New York: Oxford University Press, 1997.

Green, Stanley, and Kay Green. *Broadway Musicals Show by Show*. Milwaukee, WI: Hal Leonard Publishing, 1997.

Wildhorn, Frank. *Jekyll & Hyde: The Musical*. Port Chester, NY: Cherry Lane Books, 1997.

William G. Biddy

Electronic Dance Music

Electronic dance music (EDM), also known as electronica, is a genre of popular music that focuses on innovative electronic sounds and is intended for dance and listening. Women in electronic dance music are just beginning to gain recognition. Beginning in the early 1980s as an expression of a musical subculture, EDM has now reached the mainstream, where it maintains a stronghold in Europe and the United States; historically, electronica has had a stronger presence in Europe than in the United States, with London currently being the main center for emerging women artists in the genre. Because EDM is relatively new, commentary on the historical development of the subject is limited, although information from critics, artists, and aficionados may be found on the World Wide Web and in periodicals and ezines (electronic magazine) *DJ Times* and *Mixer Magazine*. Women in EDM are discovering their voices just as are their male counterparts; however, there are some salient differences worth noting.

Electronic dance music evolved from 1970s disco. Instrumentation in EDM differs notably from other musical genres by its predominant use of synthesizers and drum machines, those being the emerging technological instruments on the market at that time. EDM, a genre based on recorded songs as opposed to a "live band" scenario, was originally intended for clubs and parties and served as an outlet for an underground culture needing to break away from societal norms and the musical limitations of punk, rock and roll, and mainstream popular music. Since the mid-1980s, EDM has experienced continuing growth through clubs and "raves," usually large gatherings oriented toward drugs, dancing, and socializing. Within its short existence EDM has seen numerous subgenres emerge, each with a unique philosophical and musical bent, such as techno, house, trip-hop, jungle, gabba, ambient techno, trance, and drum'n'bass. Some of these subgenres, such as ambient techno, stray from the dance floor concept but still apply the same technology.

For the artist, there are many ways of approaching EDM: that of songwriter, producer, or DJ. The most prominent tools in the evolution of EDM have been the turntable, home computer, and home studio. Since the early 1990s, the affordability of the personal computer and accompanying musical software has closed the gap between professional and amateur. In this light, a look at the role of women in EDM can be viewed from several angles, in particular, through the continual progression of feminism in society and the more democratic distribution of technology via the World Wide Web and home computer. As more women break into the field of EDM and their exposure to technology increases, they are slowly infiltrating the formerly male-dominated areas of production and work as a DJ.

With various opportunities at hand, such as home studio production, the World Wide Web, and women's support groups and services, women are showing interest in using the computer as a tool of musical expression. Software and hardware development in the 1990s eliminated much of the technical detail work of electronic music composition, providing the individual the creative power of designing palettes of sound textures while at the same time offering a large range of ready-made drum tracks and sampled sounds. Many of the fundamental techniques of sound design developed by the research of composers and engineers from the 1950s to the 1980s have now become commonplace for amateurs and professionals.

There still exists an imbalance of male to female involvement in EDM. Technology is EDM; the genre requires mixing, spinning turntables, recording technology, and electronic instruments. In his book *Generation Ecstacy*, Simon Reynolds points out that "DJ culture is distinctly masculine. . . . This has to do with the homosocial nature of techno: tricks of the trade are passed down from mentors to males" (Reynolds, 274). The intrigue of gadgetry, equipment, and mysterious tricks and sleight of hand that come with this genre are indeed traits of the male stereotype, and one ponders if this is indeed why EDM has less involvement from women, particularly in production.

The growth in the number of women producers has been slow. Reynolds boldly states that there are distinct gender roles within EDM: "The DJ in his booth and his head-nodding acolytes are contrasted with the implicitly feminine abandon and hysteria of the dance floor proper . . . he is the maestro, seducing and arousing the 'feminine crowd,' guiding it through a multiorgasmic frenzy" (Reynolds, 274).

When women pioneers enter a male-dominated area, it takes a bit of mental reprogramming to move beyond the biased thinking such as a "woman doing man's work." Fortunately, as the DJ career opportunities grow, conferences, publications, and competitions have emerged, opening the way for more women to participate. In a personal interview (2000) Canadian DJ Misstress Barbara noted, "There are more [women] now, and there will be more. I just think that each new woman DJ or producer gets inspired by the other one, by actually realizing that it is indeed possible to become one, and since we're more and more, then there might be hope to get even more in the future."

No different than in popular music, a woman's role in EDM is still primarily as a vocalist. Hence the female vocalist, however significant her role may be in the interpretation of a song, is still only involved in one level of the creative process. Depending on the context, the woman vocalist is not necessarily in the spotlight because much of dance music is anti-narrative, sampled, and remixed, not to mention that there is no vocalist present during the playback.

On the other hand, the media are quick to grab the opportunity to make "stars" of women by playing on and exploiting their feminine appearance and on their portrayal as woman as vocalist rather than promoting or emphasizing a woman's direct involvement in studio production or service as a DJ. However, the electronica artist has emerged. A woman electronica artist can maintain a career as producer (of her works or others), songwriter, and DJ, although it seems that the majority of women interested in EDM still enter as vocalists. This may be seen in the early dance music pioneers such as Donna Summer (b. 1948), Annie Lennox, and Madonna (b. 1958). Many women artists are crossing over into popular music and gaining recognition through media exposure. Others try to explore the more experimental side of EDM.

Of all areas in EDM, women are gaining the most ground as DJs. The proliferation of DJs since the mid-1990s has been overwhelming. Once an exclusively male role, there are now many opportunities for women as DJs. As the career of DJ becomes more involved in marketing, DJs are exploring the areas of production, thus learning studio techniques and electronic music concepts. Perhaps it is in the act of becoming a DJ where women will make the greatest strides in bridging the gap between men and women in technology.

For an artist, the career of DJ offers an attractive blend of performance, creative input, and technology. For those women who do not care to sing or play a traditional instrument, being a DJ may fill that creative void. Mrs. Wood (Jane Rolink) of England is one of the first women DJs to gain popular recognition. Her album *Mrs. Wood Teaches Techno* is highly regarded in the repertoire of DJ "mixology." The late DJ Kemistry and DJ Storm, a British duo, were two other pioneering women DJs.

American DJ Susan Morabito has produced several albums of her mixes, such as *The Black Party* (1997), *Equinox* (1998), and *I Love to Dance* (1999). British DJ Rap (Charissa Saverio), known originally for her skill as a drum 'n' bass and jungle DJ, is probably the first woman DJ to take her knowledge of EDM and incorporate it into popular music—in her album *Learning Curve*. One True Parker (Karen Parker) maintains her career as DJ and has written and produced the album *Will I Dream?* Parker sticks closer to EDM than DJ Rap, who has shown more of an interest in hybridizing pop and EDM. With the exposure of studio production through creating mixes and remixes, women DJs may finally be making a home in the technology. Other emerging women EDM artists are the Austrian Susanne Brokesch, the Australian Lektrogirl (Emma Davidson), and the American Protocol (Nicole Caffarella).

See also DJ, Club

For Further Reading

DJ Times Magazine. Available: http://www. djtimes.com

Mixer Magazine. Available: http://www.mixermag. com/

Reynolds, Simon. *Generation Ecstasy: Into the World of Techno and Rave Culture*. Boston: Little Brown, 1999.

Santa Maria de los conejos

Electronic Music

See Music Technology

Ensembles, Jazz

All-women jazz ensembles have been an important outlet for women musicians since jazz became a popular American musical art form. Even before the turn of the twentieth century all-women brass bands, drum and bugle corps, and mandolin bands were popular in the larger communities. Most of the earliest all-women jazz bands, which played ragtime, cakewalks, and dance music in the early 1920s, were comprised entirely of black performers. Some of the most important bands were Estella Harris's Jass Band and Marian Pankey's Female Orchestra, both of which performed in the Chicago area. In New York City Olivia Porter Shipp's Jazz-Mines, the American Creolian Orchestra, and most important, Lil Armstrong's All-Girl Orchestra performed in hotels and clubs in the late 1920s and 1930s. Several of Armstrong's early recordings are available today on compact discs such as *Lil Hardin Armstrong* (Riverside OJCCD-1823-2), *Chicago: The*

Living Legends (Original Jazz Classics 1823), and *Lil Armstrong, A Documentary: Satchmo and Me* (Riverside 120).

In the 1930s all-women jazz groups proliferated. The Dixie Sweethearts, Harlem Playgirls, Harlem Rhythm Girls, and the Darlings of Rhythm all became touring bands with New York City as their home. However, many bands sprang up from other large cities and from the South. The Sepian Lassies of Harmony organized in St. Paul, MN, and the Sweethearts of Rhythm came from Piney Woods, MS. In the 1940s the Sweethearts toured throughout Europe as a United Service Organization group and became the International Sweethearts of Rhythm. The band featured both black and white performers. A recording of their early works is available on *International Sweethearts of Rhythm* (Rosetta 1312).

In the Los Angeles area Peggy Gilbert and her Metro-Goldwyn Orchestra, and later the Symphonics, and Babe Eagen and the Hollywood Redheads were popular and important bands, performing for radio shows, concerts, and films. Today, in her nineties, Peggy Gilbert and her Dixiebelles, made up of musicians drawn from the earlier all-women big bands, still perform in the Los Angeles area. Her music is recorded on *Dixieland Jazz* (Cambria CT-1024).

In 1934 Ina Ray Hutton, a dancer and singer from Chicago, known as "the blonde bombshell of rhythm," organized the Melodears, one of the most renowned all-women big bands. The band appeared in many Hollywood films and film shorts, including *Swing, Hutton, Swing* (1937), *Melodies and Models*, and *Feminine Rhythm* (ca. 1940). Even though the Melodears disbanded in 1949, Hutton put together another group, the Ina Ray Hutton Band, to perform a weekly television show in Los Angeles in the 1950s. Some of the best women musicians, however, including alto saxophonist Peggy Gilbert and trumpeter Norma Carson, had joined the Ada Leonard big band in the late 1940s. Leonard's band also performed on local television in Los Angeles. Both the Hutton and Leonard bands featured attractive, exquisitely dressed women playing difficult music and improvising remarkable solos.

In 1976 the group Alive! was formed by musicians from all over the country who had met at a jazz workshop in San Francisco and wanted to try working in a "leaderless" cooperative band. It was a successful union, and the band recorded several albums and toured. The group has several recordings, including *Alive!* (Urana 84) and *City Life* (Alive 543). Ann Patterson's Los Angeles–based big band, Maiden Voyage, for more than 25 years has gained critical acclaim for its performances at jazz festivals, in clubs, and on television. About them Leonard Feather wrote, "not just the best orchestra of its sex, but one of the most rewarding bands on the present scene." New York's Diva is another hard-driving band featuring exciting soloists and arrangements. In recent years many jazz festivals have featured all-women bands. In 1983 the Universal Jazz Coalition Big Apple Jazz Women festival brought many groups to the Tawes Theatre at the University of Maryland. In the 1990s the Mary Lou Williams Jazz Festival at the Kennedy Center focused on women groups and combos; and Nobuko Cobi Narita has produced the New York Women's Jazz Festival, which brings together the best contemporary women's jazz groups. All-women jazz ensembles are alive and swinging today.

See also Jazz

For Further Reading

Bindas, Kenneth J. *All of This Music Belongs to the Nation: The WPA's Federal Music Project and American Society.* Knoxville: University of Tennessee Press, 1995.

Dahl, Linda. *Stormy Weather: The Music and Lives of a Century of Jazzwomen.* New York: Pantheon Books, 1984.

Fry, Stephen M. *The Story of the All Women's Orchestras in California, 1893–1955: Bibliography.* With the assistance of Jeannie Pool. Northridge, CA: Dept. of Music, California State University, Northridge, 1985.

Stephen Fry

Equality

Issues of women's equality under U.S. law have affected women in music as in all fields. Since 1900, civil rights granted by the U.S. Constitution to white male property owners have been increasingly extended to women and minorities through Constitutional Amendments, new laws at the federal, state, and local levels, Executive Orders of U.S. Presidents, legal sanctions, case law, Supreme Court decisions, and voluntary compliance (Hartmann 1998). In the early decades the women's movement led to national women's suffrage. In the 1960s and 1970s, the so-called second wave of feminist activism or the Women's Liberation movement joined with efforts to extend civil rights to Negroes. Protection against arbitrary or discriminatory treatment by government or individuals is now guaranteed by law, regardless of sex, race, ethnicity, national origin, or disability. American society has undergone a transformation.

Early History. When the U.S. Constitution was being written in the 18th century, prominent women urged, unsuccessfully, the inclusion of women's emancipation. In 1848 leaders of a national women's convention at Seneca

Falls, NY, issued a declaration of independence for women, demanding full legal equality, full educational and commercial opportunity, equal compensation and the right to collect wages, and the right to vote. Early suffragists were usually also advocates of temperance and of the abolition of slavery. Though discouraged when the 15th Amendment (1870) gave the franchise to newly emancipated black men, but not to the women who had helped win it for them, women persevered. Little by little they gained rights such as access to higher education, entrance into all trades and professions, and property ownership. By 1913, 12 states and territories had granted suffrage to the women within their borders. In 1920 the 19th Amendment to the Constitution granted nation-wide suffrage to women. After that, women were divided on the question of equal standing with men (advocated by the National Woman's party) versus some kind of protective legislation as had been passed in the 19th century. While some historians believe the women's movement declined after 1920, others point to women's increased opportunities for employment during the New Deal of the 1930s (in the Work Projects Administration, for example) and in war time.

Later History. Beginning in the 1960s, the National Organization for Women, the National Women's Political Caucus, and other groups pressed for such changes as equal pay for women, the occupational upgrading of women, abortion rights, federally supported child care centers, and generally removing all legal and social barriers to education, political influence, and economic power for women. In 1963, President Kennedy signed the Equal Pay Act, which took effect in 1964. The act was amended in 1972 to extend to academic and profes-

sional employment. Under President Johnson, the Voting Rights Act of 1965 placed federal observers at polls to ensure equal voting rights, effectively extending suffrage to African-American women and men and other minorities. Title VII of the Civil Rights Act of 1964, as amended, prohibited discrimination in employment on the basis of sex, race, color, national origin, or religion. Its scope was enlarged by the Equal Employment Opportunity Act of 1972 to include academic employment. Title IX of the Education Amendments of 1972 prohibited discrimination based on sex. Although Congress passed the Equal Rights Amendment bill in 1972 to bar sex discrimination at the national level, the proposed amendment failed to be ratified by the required 38 states. Many states, however, passed their own equal rights amendments.

In 1980 the Equal Employment Opportunity Commission recognized sexual harassment as a form of sex discrimination and thus a violation of Title VII of the Civil Rights Act of 1964 as amended, under these guidelines: "Unwelcome sexual advances, requests for sexual favors, and other verbal or physical conduct of a sexual nature constitute sexual harassment when (1) submission to such conduct is made either explicitly or implicitly a term or condition of an individual's employment, (2) submission to or rejection of such conduct by an individual is used as the basis for employment decisions affecting such individual, or (3) such conduct has the purpose or effect of unreasonably interfering with an individual's work performance or creating an intimidating, hostile, or offensive working environment" (*Guidelines*). While such behavior has existed as long as women and men have worked together, only since the mid-1970s has there been official and public awareness that sexual harassment is a serious problem, that it is "less an expression of sexual interest than of power, and that it must be viewed not as an individual problem but as a societal one" (McCaghy, 3). Sexual harassment remains one of the most sensitive issues in women's attainment of equal rights.

Women in music have been concerned about equal access to education, equal pay, and equal employment opportunity, including legal remedies against sexual harassment. Efforts against sex discrimination in music are seen in such practices as blind auditions for orchestral musicians, blind judging of composition competitions, anonymous editorial review of submissions to scholarly journals, programs to encourage women to pursue careers in fields such as conducting in which they are underrepresented ("Equal Opportunity," 1987), and anti-discriminatory admissions policies for colleges and universities. Still, discrimination persists, as in the chilly climate often observed on campuses and in the workplace. It is the woman—the aggrieved party—who must document any alleged violation of her civil rights, file a grievance or take other legal action, gather evidence, seek remedies, and undergo a hearing or trial. Further, she risks being labeled a troublemaker or whistle-blower and suffering retaliation.

See also Chilly Climate; Discrimination

For Further Reading

"Equal Opportunity—Assessing Women's Presence in the Exxon/Arts Endowment Conductors Program: An Interview with Jesse Rosen." In *The Musical Woman: An International Perspective II (1984–1985)*. Ed. Judith Lang Zaimont et al. Westport, CT: Greenwood Press, 1987: 91–119.

"Equal Pay: A Thirty-Five Year Perspective." Washington, DC: U.S. Dept. of Labor, Women's Bureau, 1998. Also available via Internet from the DOL, Women's Bureau Web site.

Guidelines on Discrimination Because of Sex. 1980. Washington, DC: Equal Employment Opportunity Commission. In *Federal Register*, Vol. 45, No. 219, November 10, 1980: 74676–74677. Quoted in Bernice R. Sandler and Roberta M. Hall. *The Campus Climate Revisited: Chilly for Women Faculty, Administrators, and Graduate Students*. Washington, DC: Association of American Colleges, Project on the Status and Education of Women, 1986: 9.

Harris, William H., and Judith S. Levey (eds.). *The New Columbia Encyclopedia*. 5th ed. New York: Columbia University Press, 1993; q.v.: "Civil Rights," "Equal Employment Opportunity Commission," "Feminism," "Woman Suffrage."

Hartmann, Susan M. *The Other Feminists: Activists in the Liberal Establishment*. New Haven, CT: Yale University Press, 1998.

McCaghy, M. Dawn. *Sexual Harassment: A Guide to Resources*. G.K. Hall Women's Studies Publications. Boston: G.K. Hall, 1985.

Deborah Hayes

Essentialism

Essentialism is the belief that differences between men and women are biologically determined "essences" that are distinctly and outwardly manifest in the products of one's labor and the modes of one's expression, including music and other artistic endeavors. Essentialism assumes that there is a psychological or emotional temperament peculiar to women and that certain genres, forms, and types of discourse are grounded in the biological and reproductive characteristics of women. Further, the theory goes, by virtue of their unique sensibilities, women are bound by an almost self-defeating set of creative limitations. Essentialism is not generally accepted today, insofar as it involves examining creative efforts and in fact predicting their quality in advance, solely on the basis of their creator's biological sex, without consideration of the individual creator whose personality, including musicianship, is socially, experientially, culturally, and individually derived. The essentialist stereotypes that have resulted historically have been ascribed to women's artistic pursuits by critics who are predominantly men.

Patriarchal bias has usually defined women's "nature" or temperament as inferior or lesser in relation to what has been evaluated as male. History provides numerous examples of women's acceptance of their own supposed inferiority in music. American women, like the critics, have often been ignorant of women's historical contributions to musical life and have thus viewed achievement as a deviation from essential femaleness. Women musicians have often hesitated to assert their creativity in music composition, expressed shame over their efforts, and devalued their own success.

Writing in the late nineteenth century, the Chicago music critic George Upton (1880; quoted in Neuls-Bates, 1996) characterized woman as "emotional by temperament," which renders her "unable to give outward expression to other mysterious and deeply hidden traits of her nature." For Upton, woman "lives in emotion, and acts from emotion," whereas man, "who is sterner and more obdurate by nature, is able to see emotions quite clearly, is able to control them, and consequently reproduce them in musical notation as a painter imitates the landscape before him." Because of woman's nature, Upton forecast she would never be able to create music in its fullest and grandest harmonic forms.

The perception that certain genres, forms, and styles of music embody the characteristic "essences" of either men or women was prevalent in the writings of many of Upton's contemporaries. Hugo Riemann, whose aesthetics were deeply grounded in the Germanic tradition, described the sonata form as "having a strong, characteristic, first theme the rep-

resentative of the masculine principle, so to speak—and a contrasting, lyrical, gentle second theme, representing the feminine principle" (*Katechismus der Musik*, 1888). On the other side of the Atlantic, Charles Ives's memos (ca. 1900) supply similar commentary, wherein the composer touts some music for its "manliness" and disparages other works (opera and piano music, for example) as "effeminate" or "emasculated." The works by women composers who were Ives's contemporaries were evaluated according to similar perceptions. A review of Amy Marcy Cheney Beach's (1867–1944) *Gaelic Symphony in E Minor*, op. 32 (1896), the first symphony by an American woman, criticized it for being monotonous, spasmodic, and contrapuntally weak—not "Gaelic" or "masculine" at all. When Beach writes with "grace and delicacy" she is considered eminently feminine.

Women performers at the turn of the century were no less subjected to stereotyping than their composer counterparts. Of Teresa Carreño (1853–1917), a visiting Venezuelan pianist and composer, the *Chicago Evening Post* in 1909 stated, "her playing, no matter how full and rich in artistic insight, is womanly, with that charm, that tenderness, that sensibility which is her crown. There should be some word coined for those women who reach the heights of art where they are peers of men, but, praised by the fact, still with that untouched which marks them woman" (quoted in Neuls-Bates, 1996). Even when a woman transcended the perceived limitations of her gender, the result appears to have been her continued marginalization.

The psychologist Carl Seashore, writing in the 1940s, assumed a quasi-egalitarian view of women's musical capabilities and involvement. Acknowledging women's equal status to men in the areas of musical talent, intellectual endowment, musical temperament, education, and creative imagination, Seashore concluded that it is in their fundamental "urges" that men and women differ. Woman's fundamental urge, Seashore asserts, is "to be beautiful, loved, and adored as a person," whereas man's urge is "to provide and achieve in a career." Noting that there are exceptions to each of these characterizations, Seashore states that these theories govern the selections men and women make regarding the choice and pursuit of their life's goals. "Education, environment, motivation, obligations, and utilization of resources, often regarded as determinants in themselves, are but incidental modes," he writes, "for the outcropping of these two distinctive male and female urges" (quoted in Neuls-Bates, 1996).

As interest and research in the psyches of men and women continued, the psychologist Grace Rubin-Rabson, writing in *High Fidelity/Musical America* in 1973, when the women's rights movement was gaining momentum, continued to posit, as had others before her, that women are innately unsuited to a sustained effort at creative activity. In a companion essay in the same magazine, Judith Rosen countered Rubin-Rabson's essentialist ideas. Since then, with more feminists and musicologists entering into the debate, the tenor of the discourse has been refocused and essentialist ideologies challenged. Parallels between music and other arts have been examined for insights and applicability that could foster broader interpretation.

Gisela Ecker (1985) elucidates the transitory nature of that which is actually considered "feminine" in art. She suggests that where aspects of aesthetics are concerned, "feminist" is perhaps a more appropriate or suitable descriptor, for it considers what is relative to the moment in history and the specific necessities associated with it. Ecker cautions against letting the pendulum swing too far in the opposite direction from essentialism, to the point where an artist feels she has to suppress her gender. This, Ecker asserts, would be profoundly wrong.

In light of recent research and critical analysis, the possibility of identifying definitive style features in music based solely on the criterion of gender appear to be extremely remote. The feminist musicologist Marcia Citron in her study of women's marginal status (*Gender and the Musical Canon*, 1993) proposes that there are in fact no stylistic traits essential to all women or exclusive to women, but rather that certain tendencies that can be attributed to socialization more than to biological inheritance manifest themselves in many works by women. Citron acknowledges that gender is inscribed in music. Music is a human expression. She notes, however, that the same tendencies that are extant in the works of women through socialization are also available to men.

Ecker asserts that a truly genderized perspective would mean that the sex—female or male—of both artist and critic must be taken into account. Moreover, she asserts that it is impossible to deconstruct the myth of gender-neutrality in art if, at the same time, male artists and critics do not develop a consciousness of their own gender.

Because of essentialist stereotypes and the process of marginalization, it has been imperative for women to develop an acute and well-defined sense of gender. Now, in order to continue to engender the depth of analysis and the degree of critical inquiry currently being fostered, it appears that men will be challenged to do the same.

See also Female Inferiority, Theories of; Separate Spheres—Sexual Aesthetics

For Further Reading

Ecker, Gisela. *Feminine Aesthetics*. Translated from the German by Harriet Anderson. London: Women's Press, 1985.

McFadden, Margaret (ed.). *Women's Issues*. Pasadena: Salem Press, 1997.

Neuls-Bates, Carol (ed.). *Women in Music: An Anthology of Source Readings from the Middle Ages to the Present*. New York: Harper and Row, 1982. Rev. ed.: Boston: Northeastern University Press: q.v. sections 34 (Upton), 39 (Beach, Carreño), 47 (Seashore), 1996.

Maxine Fawcett-Yeske

Estefan, Gloria (1957–)

Cuban American Gloria Estefan is a very successful pop ballad songwriter and performer who achieved great popularity in the 1980s and 1990s with her productions in mainstream markets in both Spanish and English, in the United States and abroad. As a youngster in Cuba, Estefan joined a group called the Miami Latin Boys in 1975. This band, led by her husband-to-be, Emilio Estefan, soon changed its name to the Miami Sound Machine and became very active in the Cuban community in Miami.

Born on 1 September 1957 in Havana, Cuba, Estefan arrived in Miami from Cuba as a young child. During the early 1980s the Miami Sound Machine made a number of albums featuring Gloria Estefan, who sang sweet pop ballads in Spanish for the market in Latin America. By the mid-1980s Estefan began recording in English and achieved rapid success with the disco dance hit "Conga," which sold millions of copies and went to the top of the charts. Estefan and the Miami Sound Machine followed up with several highly successful albums that again sold

Gloria Estefan promoting her album *Mi Tierra* in 1993. *Photo couresty of Andrea Renault/ Globe Photos.*

in the millions and with a 20-month tour of Asia, Japan, Canada, and the United States. Her early albums with the Miami Sound Machine include *Primitive Love* (Epic EK-40131), *A Toda Maquina* (Song 10349), and *Anything for You* (Epic 4631252).

In 1988 the Miami Sound Machine received the American Music Award for Best Pop/Rock group. Estefan and the Miami Sound Machine toured the world in 1989, including three nights in London. Estefan continued to release successful albums in the early 1990s; these contained many of her own songs. In 1993 Estefan switched gears and released an album in Spanish, *Mi Tierra* (Epic 53807), supported by an impressive cast of the best Cuban musicians in the United States and emphasizing traditional Cuban music such as *son*, *bolero*, *danzón*, and Cuban American nostalgia for the homeland. *Mi Tierra* was a great commercial success in Latin America, Spain, and the United States, and it received a Grammy Award in 1994 as Best Tropical Latin album.

Following up on the success of *Mi Tierra*, Estefan produced a similar album in 1995, *Abriendo Puertas* (Epic 67284), this time focusing on the music of Colombia and other Latin American countries. Although not quite as successful as *Mi Tierra*, the effort afforded Estefan her second Grammy, again in the category of Best Tropical Latin. Her third Spanish-language solo album, *Alma Caribeña* (Sony 62163), mixes Afro-Cuban rhythms and styles.

See also Latin American Musicians

For Further Reading

DeStefano, Anthony M. *Gloria Estefan: The Pop Superstar from Tragedy to Triumph*. New York: Penguin Group, 1997.

Gonzalez, Fernando. *Gloria Estefan: Cuban-American Singing Star*. New York: Millbrook Press, 1993.

Raúl Fernández

Etheridge, Melissa (1961–   )

Melissa Etheridge is a singer-songwriter who came to prominence during the late 1980s with gutsy and impassioned performances of her songs of heartbreak and turmoil. Her raw vocals and bluesy guitar riffs have led to comparisons with blues legend Janis Joplin (1943–1970). The success of her 1988 self-titled debut album (Island 422-842303-2) proved her mass appeal, but it was with the album *Yes I Am* (Island 422-848 660-2) that she attained superstar status.

Born on 29 May 1961 in Leavenworth,

Melissa Etheridge. *Photo © (S.I.N.)/CORBIS.*

KS, Etheridge began her performing career while a teenager, playing piano and guitar in various cover bands around Kansas. She studied guitar at the Berklee College of Music in Boston while playing in coffeehouses and lounges at night. In the early 1980s she moved to Los Angeles, where she was hired to work on the film score for the movie *Weeds* (1987). In 1986 Island Records chief Chris Blackwell signed her after hearing her performing a club set. Etheridge's first album for Island spawned the single "Bring Me Some Water," for which she earned a Grammy Award nomination.

Etheridge's next three albums continued in her rock-confessional style. Her second album, *Brave and Crazy* (Island 422-842302-2), is slightly more reflective than her first release, in pieces such as "Testify," "You Used to Love to Dance," and "You Can Sleep While I Drive." Her third release, *Never Enough* (Island 314-512120-2), displays more range and diversity with the addition of thoughtful ballads and funk to her usual gutsy rock style. "Ain't It Heavy" earned Etheridge a Grammy Award for Best Female Rock Performance. The breakthrough album *Yes I Am* produced three hit singles: "Come to My Window," "I'm the Only One," and "If I Wanted To." Etheridge won her second Grammy Award for "Come to My Window" in the Best Female Rock Performance category.

In 1993 Melissa Etheridge came out publicly as a lesbian at the gay and lesbian Triangle Ball, part of the inaugural celebrations of President Bill Clinton. Since that time she has become an advocate for various gay and lesbian rights issues. The Hugh Padgham–produced *Your Little Secret* (Island 8042/524 154-2) addressed same sex–oriented emotional concerns in songs such as "I Could Have Been You" and "Nowhere to Go." In 1998 Etheridge and her partner, Julie Cypher, received an award for their efforts by the Human Rights Campaign, the nation's largest gay and lesbian political organization. Her 1999 album *Breakdown* (Polygram 546518) contains "Scarecrow," a tribute to hate-crime victim Matthew Shepard, and the autobiographical "Mama I'm Strange." *Breakdown*, departing from her hard-rocking style with intimate, emotionally revealing low-key moments, earned Etheridge Grammy Award nominations for Best Rock Album, Best Rock Song, and Best Female Rock Vocal Performance.

Etheridge has also worked as a composer and songwriter on other film projects, including *Teresa's Tattoo* (1994), *It Was a Wonderful Life* (1993), *Welcome Home, Roxy Carmichael* (1990), and *Scenes from the Goldmine* (1987).

See also Singer-Songwriter; Songwriter

For Further Reading

Gaar, Gillian G. *She's a Rebel. The History of Women in Rock and Roll*. Seattle: Seal Press, 1992.

O'Dair, Barbara (ed.). *Trouble Girls: The Rolling Stone Book of Women in Rock*. New York: Random House, 1997.

Rolling Stone.com. Available: http://rollingstone.com

Susanna P. Garcia

Ethnomusicology

Originally concerned with folk music of non-Western cultures, ethnomusicology has since grown to include folk music in urban contexts, urban popular music, and global music markets. The term "ethnomusicology" was coined by Jaap Kunst in 1950 to denominate a field that had gradually emerged since the late 1800s. Ethnomusicology has also come to address issues such as identity, ethnicity, nationalism, and multiculturalism.

American women scholars have made numerous contributions to the development of the field. During the early years of ethnomusicology, four women were recognized for their research activities in collecting and documenting music: Natalie Curtis Burlin (1875–1921), Alice C. Fletcher (1838–1923), Francis Densmore (1867–1957), and Helen H. Roberts (1888–1985). In 1955, 10 women ethnomusicologists helped found the Society for Ethnomusicology, and with their research, publishing, and teaching activities these women helped establish ethnomusicology programs nationwide. Today the number of women ethnomusicologists equals that of their male counterparts, and a significant portion of ethnomusicology's research comes from women ethnomusicologists.

Although it is unclear whether Burlin, Fletcher, Densmore, and Roberts communicated with each other, they shared an interest in American Indian music of North America. Their work provided an early model for conducting field research, that is, for documenting music in written and recorded formats and for communicating the results to and interacting with the research community.

In the 1880s Burlin documented the music of the Omaha, Dakota, and Pawnee Indians. At a time when the government's restrictions on American Indians living in reservations were such that they were prohibited by law from singing indigenous songs, Burlin obtained permission from President Theodore Roosevelt to record Indian songs at reservations. The president's endorsement of her work had a positive effect on governmental policy, which shortly thereafter began allowing freedom of expression for Native Americans living in reservations. Burlin's work among Native Americans culminated in the publication of *The Indians' Book* (1907, also published posthumously in 1923).

Also a pioneer in ethnomusicology, Alice C. Fletcher was a colleague of Burlin's. In the 1880s, with the assistance of her Indian collaborator, Francis La Flesche, Fletcher documented the music and folklore of the Omaha, Dakota, and Pawnee Indians. Francis Densmore became interested in American Indian music after reading reports of Alice C. Fletcher's research. Densmore contributed to ethnomusicology by documenting songs from the Sioux, the Chippewa, and the Seminoles. Her publications *Chippewa Music* (1910–1913) and *The American Indians and Their Music* (1926) earned her recognition among ethno-musicologists. In the 1950s, during the formative years of the Society for Ethnomusicology, Densmore was invited to join the association, and although she was unable to attend meetings, in 1957 she was nominated as the Society's second vice-president.

Helen H. Roberts was the most eclectic of the group, with research interests that included Jamaican, Hawaiian, Eskimo, and American Indian music. She was also one of the founders of the Society for Ethnomusicology, in addition to being both founder and secretary of the American Society for Comparative Musicology until its termination in 1937. Roberts published prolifically on Jamaican music, but her most prominent work was *Musical Areas in Aboriginal North America* (1936).

A second generation of women ethnomusicologists—Barbara Krader, Getrude Kurath, Nadia Chilkovsky, Rose Brandel, Roxane Connick McCollester, Johanna Spector, Rae Korson, and Barbara Smith—gained recognition for their leadership roles and their participation in the formation of the Society for Ethnomusicology (SEM). At the time of the Society's first annual meeting in 1956, these women were active in presenting papers and paving the way for women's scholarship in ethnomusicology. As the Society grew, Kurath, Chilkovsky, Brandel, and Spector used their leadership experience to found academic programs in both dance ethnology and ethnomusicology at several universities and colleges in the United States. From 1972 to 1973, Krader served as the first woman president of the SEM, paving the way for future women presidents such as Carol E. Robertson, Charlotte F. Frisbie, Charlotte Heth, Ruth Stone, and Kay Kaufman Shelemay.

Since the 1980s the number of women

in leadership positions within the SEM has increased dramatically. Notable contemporary scholars include Ruth Stone, Charlotte Heth, Charlotte Frisbie, Bonnie Wade, Helen Myers, Adelaide Reyes Schramm, Ann Briegleb Schuursma, Jane Sugarman, Ellen Koskoff (b. 1943), Kay Kaufman Shelemay, and Amy Catlin. Although still in its infancy, there has been impetus for feminist studies in ethnomusicology. Since the 1990s women researchers have been pursuing women's music making in various cultures, an area that until the latter part of the twentieth century was missing from ethnographies. Because past research has been done for the most part in patriarchal societies, women's music making in these societies has been largely overlooked. In addition to developing theoretical frameworks and widening the scope of ethnomusicology, women scholars such as Amy Catlin are demonstrating the importance of documentary film making as a useful educational resource. As in the past, women ethnomusicologists in the United States continue to shape the intellectual development of the discipline to accommodate the future.

See also Multicultural Musics; Musicologist

For Further Reading

Brandes, Edda. "The Role of the Female Ethnomusicologist in the Field: Experiences in Traditional Algerian Communities." *The World of Music: Journal of the International Institute for Traditional Music* 33/2 (1991): 35–49.

Kimberlin, Cynthia Tse. "What am I to be? Female, Male, Neuter, Invisible . . . Gender Roles and Ethnomusicological Field Work in Africa." *The World of Music: Journal of the International Institute for Traditional Music* 33/2 (1991): 14–34.

Koskoff, Ellen (ed.). *Women and Music in Cross-Cultural Perspective.* New York: Greenwood Press, 1987.

Vasana De Mel

Exceptional Woman

The concepts of the "exceptional woman" and the "women worthies" are the basic components of so-called compensatory history, a term that implies that research compensates or makes amends to women for past exclusion and neglect. Exceptional women are famous women of the past who, because their names have survived, are exceptions to the general rule that women and women's work are invisible in history. Identifying these few "token women" is intended to compensate for excluding all the rest; it also serves to isolate women from one another. In the history of women in music, especially classical music, the exceptional "women worthies" are women whose work seems to have met the standards of the accepted canon of great men composers and great works; these few women are thus deemed worthy of the kind of recognition usually bestowed only on men. They are the exceptions that prove the rule; if all the other women of the era had been as talented, they would not have remained invisible. The term "women worthies" is used somewhat sarcastically to emphasize the fact that this view of women's contributions to music, only perpetuates an inaccurate and destructive picture of women's actual work.

See also Canon; Compensatory History

For Further Reading

Kramarae, Cheris, and Paula A. Treichler. *A Feminist Dictionary.* Boston: Pandora Press, 1985.

Lerner, Gerder. "Placing Women in History: Definitions and Challenges." *Feminist Studies* 3/1–2 (Fall 1975): 5–14. Reprinted as "Placing Women in History: A 1975 Perspective" in *Liberating Women's History: Theoretical and Critical Essays,* ed. Berenice A. Carroll. Urbana: University of Illinois Press, 1976, 357–367.

Deborah Hayes

Experimental Music

Experimental music has widened the very definition of music to encompass sound as environment, healing practice, and tool for deepened or altered perception, in addition to the more mainstream view of music as an object of aesthetic appreciation. New and original approaches were most evident in the following aspects of contemporary musical practice of the last decades of the twentieth century: (1) an altered relationship among composer, performer, and audience; (2) alternative venues; (3) new media and technologies; (4) extended compositional and instrumental techniques; (5) the incorporation of non-Western musical and theatrical traditions; (6) redefinition of genres and invention of new ones, such as soundscape, installation, and "cinema of the ear"; (7) a focus on personal or political experience as a focus of the work; and (8) the creation of new institutions for the support and performance of new music. With regard to all these aspects, women have figured importantly in the exploration and creation of what is new about "new" music. And many of the composers discussed below integrate several of these approaches in their own highly personal and original work.

Four women have particularly distinguished themselves as pioneers of diverse contemporary musics through their originality, influence, and scope of work: Ruth Crawford Seeger (1901–1953), Pauline Oliveros (b. 1932), Meredith Monk (b. 1942), and Laurie Anderson (b. 1947). Ruth Crawford Seeger was the brilliant composer of such works as the String Quartet and Woodwind Quintet (Pulitzer Prize, 1953). She wrote a small number of influential pieces that display great care with regard to a dissonant and textural counterpoint. Her String Quar-tet in four movements is a landmark work of striking beauty and originality.

Pauline Oliveros has been one of the most influential and honored members of the American avant garde since the late 1950s. Her prolific output includes works for varied contexts, including traditional concert stage, theater, film, meditative gatherings, citywide happenings, and interactive World Wide Web environments. Among her innovations are "Sonic Meditations" compositions in the oral tradition utilizing a variety of meditation techniques, in which the distinction between audience and participant dissolves. Whether practiced in intimate settings of a few people or in the context of a ceremonial work like *Crow Two* (1974), particular listening strategies inform the group's interactive creation of sound. Trusting intuition, improvisation, and the educated ear, and with a penchant for the absurd, Oliveros's work has challenged traditional boundaries separating European and North American classical music from other styles and influences. Her extensive recordings range from older electronic such as *Bye Bye Butterfly* (CRI 728) to the recent *Ghost-dance* soundtrack of the music and dance collaboration between Oliveros and Paula Josa-Jones, commissioned by Lincoln Center Out-of-Doors.

Meredith Monk is an equally celebrated artist whose diverse roles include that of composer, singer, filmmaker, director, and choreographer. She is a pioneer in what is now called "extended vocal technique" and interdisciplinary performance. During a career that spans 30 years, she has been acclaimed by audiences and critics as a major creative force in the performing arts. The majority of her vocal music can be considered as songs without words. *Dolmen Music* (ECM New Series 78118-

21197-2) of 1979 was an early expression of her integration of gesture, textless singing, and music. *Our Lady of Late: The Vanguard Tapes* (Wergo Records SM 1058) were honored with the German Critics Prize for Best Records of 1981 and 1986. Her film *Ellis Island* won the CINE Golden Eagle Award, was honored at the Atlanta and San Francisco Film Festivals, and was shown nationally on PBS. The opera *Atlas* (ECM New Series 78118-21491-2), commissioned by the Houston Grand Opera in 1991, projects a heroine's search for spirituality as the dramatic fulcrum of action. All of Monk's works have been developed out of group improvisation, with herself as composer and performer.

Laurie Anderson is one of the most renowned multimedia artists of the last 25 years. Her first commercially successful song, "O Superman," launched a career that has included spoken word performance, sophisticated multimedia presentations, and music for theater, dance, and film. Integrating "high" and "low" art, personal reflections, humor, and sophisticated use of technology, she has produced a large body of consistently original work from the 1970s to the present.

The use of recording and electronic media has been central to the work of several influential women composers. Johanna Beyer (1888–1944) was one of the first composers fascinated with the potential of electronic instruments, and her hypnotic *Music of the Spheres* of 1938 (CRI 728) displays her interest in new media as well as in minimalist, cyclical counterrhythms. Although her music was not well known during her lifetime, it enjoyed a revival period at the end of the twentieth century.

Annea Lockwood (b. 1939), whose career has included teaching, publishing, and composing, has, among other interests, been interested in the sonic and spiritual connection with the environment, as well as with specifically feminine ritual. She has been known for her explorations into the rich and spontaneous world of natural acoustic sounds, in compositions such as *World Rhythms* of 1975 (CRI 728), a live 10-channel work utilizing multiple recorded sources that include such sounds as pulsars, earthquakes, volcanic activities, surf, and breathing, all of which are mixed live in extended performance. *A Sound Map of the Hudson River* (Lovely Music 2081) charts the path the river takes from its source to the sea.

Maryanne Amacher (b. 1946) has specialized in the performance of multimedia artworks, most especially the creation of large site-specific installations. Amacher combines a sensitivity to sculpture, architecture, and psychoacoustics of extremely loud sound, through which she contends the ear itself creates sounds. Priscilla McLean (b. 1942), in partnership with her husband, Barton, has been involved in the creation of several ambitious projects featuring multimedia presentation and source material recorded from such sites as the Amazon rainforest and the Malay peninsula. Their extended installations, one of the most celebrated being *Rainforest*, are typically featured in museums and college campuses; they include invented instruments, a "light board" in synchronization with musical events, and elaborate interactive schemas whereby the participant audience can assist in the creation of the work.

Other composers active in the years from the 1950s to the 1980s have been Ruth Anderson (b. 1928), Jean Eichelberger Ivey (b. 1923), Laurie Spiegel (b. 1945), and Vivian Adelberg Rudow (b. 1936). Judith Shatin (b. 1949) and Diane

Thome (b. 1942) were two of the first women to obtain doctorates in computer music and have been influential as both teachers and composers. Laurie Spiegel, a Renaissance woman who has been active in the creation of color video, has created a fascinating body of electronic music for stage, film, dance, and television, as well as the software program Music Mouse, a widely available program that permits real-time composition and performance. Carla Scaletti (b. 1956) developed the Kyma Sound Synthesis software, an environment that is widely used for the creation of computer music.

For several women, the "cinema of the ear" approach is one in which narrative and montage strategies are translated into audio imagery to create works of a strongly dramatic nature. Such composers as Judy Klein (b. 1943), Maggi Payne (b. 1945), Brenda Hutchinson (b. 1954), Cindy McTee (b. 1953), Alicyn Warren (b. 1955), Mara Helmuth, Lydia Ayers, and Anna Rubin (b. 1946) have created electro-acoustic works whose focus ranges from whimsy to environmental and highly personal material.

Women active in the new area of interactive Internet performances include Helen Thorington, whose World Wide Web site presents a variety of works by herself and other composers and sound artists. Sarah Peebles (b. 1964), an American composer living in Canada, has incorporated environmental concerns in a number of novel collaborative works including dance; calligraphy; the Japanese mouth organ, or *sho*; and World Wide Web interactivity. Pamela Z (b. 1956) works primarily with voice, live electronic processing, and sampling technology. In performance, she creates layered works combining operatic *bel canto* and experimental extended vocal techniques with a battery of digital delays, found

percussion objects, and sampled sounds triggered with a MIDI (Musical Instrument Digital Interface—a communications protocol for synthesizers and computers) controller called the Body-Synth. French-born performer Laetitia Sonami (b. 1957) is another pioneer in the area of interactivity, employing sophisticated digital technology that is worn on her body to gesturally activate rich sound landscapes.

Several composers have devoted serious study to non-Western traditions and incorporated that into their music. The Chinese American composer Chen Yi (b. 1953) has produced a wide variety of chamber and symphonic works that integrate classical and folk Chinese music with Western contemporary art music. Jin Hi Kim (b. 1957) is fully trained in the complexities of Korean traditional music as well as in Western avant garde composition. Her music retains the timbral and microtonal subtleties of her Korean heritage while incorporating the expressive concerns of experimental music. She often performs on the *komungo*, a Korean six-string zither, with a wide variety of performers from jazz and avant garde backgrounds. Bun Ching Lam (b. 1954) has been equally successful in integrating her Chinese musical background with Western compositional studies in music that spans chamber and orchestral genres as well as Chinese puppet theater.

Lois V. Vierk (b. 1951) has written a large body of work for stage and dance influenced by her study of *Gagaku*, or Japanese court music. Her dynamic works feature slowly unfolding structures of complex heterophony based on an exponential time structure that often creates a thrilling climax of complex textures. The world of gamelan has been nurtured by such women as Barbara Benary (b. 1946), composer, performer, instrument builder, and ethnomusicologist, who is a co-founder of Gamelan Son of Lion, a new music collective and repertory ensemble in New York City. Her colleague, Jody Diamond (b. 1953), has been extremely important in the nurture of gamelan music in the United States with her work in the Gamelan Institute. She has composed numerous works for gamelan groups throughout the world.

The voice has been the center of many women's compositional and performance careers. Women have been extremely influential in their exploration of advanced and extended vocal techniques. Singers such as Bethany Beardslee (b. 1927), Marni Nixon (b. 1930), Jan DeGaetani (1933–1989), Joan La Barbara (b. 1947), and Cathy Berberian (1925–1983) encouraged the composition of several seminal vocal works by such composers as Milton Babbitt, George Crumb, Phillip Glass, Steve Reich, Morton Subotnick, and Luciano Berio. La Barbara went on to develop her own compositional career based on the creation of works centered on the voice. Diamanda Galás (b. 1955), a singer with enormous range of expression, has created a number of striking multimedia performance works that dramatically testify to such modern-day horrors such as AIDS.

Women who have invented new instruments include Ellen Fullman (b. 1957), creator of the Long String Instrument, a box containing 85-foot-long wires that are stroked and plucked to magical effect. Brenda Hutchinson's Long Tube allows her to create microtonally fluctuating sounds of great variety.

Liz Phillips (b. 1951) has been making interactive multimedia installations for the past 30 years. These combine audio and visual art forms with new technologies to create a fascinating interactive experience. In a recent work presented at The Kitchen in New York, she builds a three-dimensional interactive human-scale sound and light structure that comes alive as members of the audience move through space to create an ever-changing environment of wonder. Interactive computerized circuitry and various sensor systems activate sounds made from processed samples of spinning objects—rings, Tibetan prayer bowls, rubbing metal, a rain-stick, or the rim of a wineglass. In addition, tubes of "Ecstatic neon" illuminate paths, furthering the experience of the tuning and weighted proportions of time and space.

As the twenty-first century begins, women may look ahead to a time of continuing technological change, increased multicultural interaction, and further corporatization of art making. Opportunities and challenges lie ahead as composers and performers await the next generation of inspired and empowered composers and creators to forge both the new expressive media and inspired music and sound that will enlighten the listener in the new millennium.

See also Music Technology; Performance Art; Performer, Live Electronics; Sound Installation Artist

For Further Reading

Chadabe, Joel. *Electric Sound: The Past and Promise of Electronic Music.* Upper Saddle River, NJ: Prentice Hall, 1997.

Gann, Kyle. *American Music in the Twentieth Century.* New York: Schirmer Books; London: Prentice-Hall International, 1997.

Anna Rubin

F

Falletta, JoAnn (1954–)

The first American-born woman to lead a regional orchestra, the Long Beach (CA) Symphony Orchestra (1989), JoAnn Falletta has had an increasingly successful career as one of few women in the conducting field. She has performed nearly 300 works by American composers, including over 60 premieres. She has received eight consecutive awards from the American Society of Composers, Authors and Publishers (ASCAP) and the American Symphony Orchestra League's John S. Edwards Award, all for her creative programming. A highly regarded conductor, Falletta is said to conduct "with clarity and precision, often producing raw power and rare sense of proportion" (*Washington Post*).

Born in Queens, NY, on 27 February 1954, she first learned to play the guitar. By the age of 12 she began to focus on the orchestra and being a conductor. Falletta entered the Mannes School of Music as a guitar student in 1972. In the following year she switched to conducting, an area where she first became aware of the difficulties she faced because of her gender. She received her B.M. from Mannes and her M.M. in a co-program from Mannes and Queens. In 1982 she entered the Juilliard School with the Bruno Walter Award, a full scholarship, and received her doctoral degree in conducting in 1989, the first woman to earn that degree. While at Juilliard she studied with Jorge Mester and Sixten Ehrling. In 1985 Falletta won both the Toscanini and Stokowski conducting awards.

Falletta's conducting career began in 1987 with the Queens (New York) Philharmonic. In addition to the Long Beach Symphony, she was music director of the Denver Chamber Orchestra (1983–1992), associate conductor of the Milwaukee Symphony (1985–1988), and music director of the Virginia Symphony Orchestra from 1991. For a period of nine years from 1986, she was music director of the Women's Philharmonic (formerly Bay Area Women's Philharmonic), based in San Francisco.

Through the National Women Composers Resource Center, a project of the Women's Philharmonic, Falletta was able to program neglected works and premiere new compositions. This center was important both as a clearinghouse for compositions and for commissioning new works by women. Falletta's programming often led to wider exposure and acceptance of the works. In 1990, Falletta and the Bay Area Women's Philharmonic recorded *Baroquen Treasures* (BTCS) for the Newport Classics label, a collection of eighteenth-century women's compositions. In 1992 a second compact disc was issued by Koch International featuring works of Clara Schumann, Lili Boulanger, Germaine Tailleferre, and Fanny Mendelssohn. Falletta has also recorded works by Shulamit Ran (b. 1949), Chen Yi (b. 1953), Jerome Moross, Elinor Armer, and others, primarily for Koch and New Albion Records.

In addition to the music directorships she has held, Falletta has guest conducted extensively, both in the United States and abroad, the latter where she has been the first woman to conduct many of the ensembles. Her conducting debut in Germany was with the Mannheim Orchestra, where she initially found great resistance but was engaged subsequently for a return appearance. Falletta is known for her innovative programming. In May 1998 JoAnn Falletta was appointed music director of the Buffalo Philharmonic Orchestra, making her one of only two women conductors to lead a major American orchestra.

See also Conductor, Instrumental and Operatic

For Further Reading

Brown, Royal S. "Call Her Maestra: An Interview with JoAnn Falletta." *Fanfare* 21/2 (1997): 108–122.

Edwards, J. Michele. "Congratulations to JoAnn Falletta!" *IAWM [International Alliance for Women in Music] Journal* 4/3 (1998): 16–17.

Lawson, Kay. "Women Conductors: Credibility in a Male-Dominated Profession." In *The Musical Woman: An International Perspective*, vol. 3. Westport, CT: Greenwood Press, 1991.

Annette Voth

Female Inferiority, Theories of

Theories of female inferiority are generally attempts to account for the absence of music composed by women from the mainstream concert repertoire, music histories, and academic curricula. Some writers, especially in the early 1900s, explain women's meager public record as the result of biologically determined or essential female qualities such as emotional subjectivity, lack of aptitude for the "higher" forms of music, and various female qualities of mind. Other writers, especially from about mid-century on, analyze women's inferiority as constructed by social and cultural factors, including inappropriate education, historians' neglect of women's contributions, and patriarchal religious doctrines in the Judeo-Christian tradition that suppress women and define women's work as less important than men's.

Besides explaining women musicians' apparent failure to excel in activities that might win them some renown, theories of female inferiority have served to exclude women or at least to discourage them. Women are as likely as men to accept patriarchal views of women's lesser worth. Because participation in the most public and highly valued areas of music has usually meant trespassing into traditionally male territory, as defined by the ideology of separate spheres, proclamations of women musicians' inferiority may be seen as efforts to counteract and deny any increased visibility and perceived strength.

Since 1900 a number of events have influenced assessments of women's supposed inferiority as creative musicians. By 1900 women were increasingly active as performers, music teachers, and patrons in the women's club movement; more women were seeking to enter the ranks of classical or "art music" composition as well. Some critics were alarmed at what they saw as the feminization of American music and an inevitable deterioration of the "masculine" European musical tradition. New American music was praised for its manliness and virility.

Beginning in the 1960s American women gained legal equality in many areas, including the right to equal pay and equal access to education, employment, and public funding for music. Women have come to be seen as participating more fully in musical life. Theories of women's inferiority have thus been supplanted somewhat by theories of gender difference. Yet issues of femininity, sexual politics, and women's contributions to American music remain controversial if not explosive. Feminists advocating gender equality continue to meet with strong antifeminist opinion, including accusations of upsetting the natural order.

Essential Inferiority. A classic statement of the essentialist point of view comes from the Chicago music critic George Upton, whose *Women in Music* (1880) was republished into the 1890s and whose theories were echoed by other writers, some of them women, well into the 1900s. According to Upton, women are not great composers owing to: the particular quality of feminine emotions; women's inability to endure the discouragements of the composer; and women's dependence on intuition rather than on the kind of musical training that binds the imagination "within the limits of form." Women's emotional feelings are personal and subjective, he writes; "she cannot project herself outwardly" as required to compose music. Women are essentially lacking in aptitude for serious musical study; they are rarely able to master music's "mercilessly logical and

unrelentingly mathematical" principles. Whereas women may excel at "ravishing melody" and "passionate outbursts," they have trouble with "the theoretical intricacies, the logical sequences, and the mathematical problems" of the larger forms of music. Upton goes so far as to say that as women age and their emotions become dulled or engulfed in sorrow, they drop their relationship with music altogether.

Essentialists have also used observations from biology and other sciences. One theory asserts that the female chromosomal makeup explains, biologically, why male geniuses greatly outnumber female geniuses. This theory has been widely discredited, as has the assertion that the female brain is smaller than the male brain.

Theories of women's inferiority have been refined by psychological data and psychoanalytical theories attributable to Sigmund Freud and others. In 1940 the psychologist Carl Seashore, a pioneer in measuring musical aptitude, in an essay entitled "Why No Great Women Composers?" for the *Music Educators Journal*, offered his "theories of urges" to explain why so few women's names were included on programs of "great and lasting music" or in two studies, David Ewen's *Twentieth Century Composers* (1937) and Claire Reis's *Composers in America* (1932). Seashore finds that "woman's fundamental urge is to be beautiful, loved, and adored as a person," whereas "man's urge is to provide and achieve in a career." For a woman musician, marriage is often a tragedy, he notes; "the promising Ph.D. settles down and gets fat."

Yet in the matter of innate musical attributes—native talent, intelligence, musical temperament, creative imagination, musical precocity, education, and endurance—women and men are equally endowed, according to Seashore. He finds "no clear support in genetics" for the theory that women's creative imagination is "less sustained" than men's, and he concludes that any difference is probably owing to "environmental influences." He wonders whether the "recent emancipation of women" (the 19th Amendment [1920] to the U.S. Constitution granting women the vote) will allow women to act like men and thus "pave the way for great composers"; in spite of these constructivist observations, however, he maintains that "the outcropping of genius is above social considerations." The *Music Educators Journal* reprinted Seashore's essay in 1979 to demonstrate, the editor explains, past ideas that have affected "how women have been treated in the music profession and how they have been taught music."

Culturally Constructed Inferiority. In the 1950s the behavioral psychologist Paul Farnsworth, rejecting theories of fundamental urges and innate genetic shortcomings, conducted research among American university students assessing feminine and masculine "roles" in music. In his essay "The Effect of Role-Taking on Artistic Achievement" (*Journal of Aesthetics and Art Criticism*, 1960) he attributes women's comparative lack of achievement to cultural conditioning, in particular a lack of self-confidence. Farnsworth notes the "preponderance of masculine values in the American culture" and "woman's acceptance of a role in society that is incompatible with great achievement." He reports that both women and men rate composing serious music, composing jazz, performing jazz, and listening to jazz as suitable to the "masculine" role. "Feminine" activities include listening to serious music and performing serious music, including singing in opera. Women, like men, he concludes, see creativity as "an enduring characteristic of the masculine role." Farnsworth predicts that owing to the "dismal picture" history has so far given of female creativity, few women "will be willing to put forth the effort essential to sustained creativity." Yet the future need not be so bleak: in one aspect of creativity, problem solving, he reports, increased self-esteem improves women's performance.

Essentialism versus Constructivism. In 1973, reflecting the intensity of the feminist revival and antifeminist reaction, *High Fidelity* magazine published a pair of essays with opposing answers to the question "Why Haven't Women Become Great Composers?" In one of the essays, Grace Rubin-Rabson, a psychologist and pianist, maintains the essentialist Freudian argument that women are biologically unsuited to sustained creativity. She notes Farnsworth's observations of women's lack of self-confidence and dismal history, but she sees these factors as resulting from what the psychologist Abraham Maslow calls "profound male-female differences": the "dedicated concentration" required for "superior musical creativity" is a "messianic male" trait that is "aberrant from the norm" of feminine personality. Rubin-Rabson characterizes women's musicianship as receptive rather than creative, echoing Upton and others, but uses explicitly sexual terms; she insists that with or without women's liberation, "men will remain actively penetrating, women receptive, accounting for their readiness to accept and interpret." This tendency, she concludes, is "innate and not culturally conditioned."

In the other essay, Judith Rosen, identified as a feminist, takes the constructivist approach, arguing that women composers have been excluded from opportunities in the public sphere. She notes that suppression and exclusion have been evident "until quite recently" at all levels of musical opportunity for women composers, including music education, symphony orchestras, and even the motion picture studio. To succeed, she observes, a composer needs cultural support that includes financial rewards, the incentive of a professional position, and audience recognition.

Since the 1980s and 1990s researchers have continued to investigate differences between men and women, in particular how ideas about composition, notions about appropriate instruments, and other stereotypes and prejudices have affected views of women's capabilities. The psychoanalyst Carol Gilligan's *In a Different Voice* (1982) offers analyses of contemporary gender relations and cognitive styles. She notes that education professionals have denigrated girls' ways of thinking as inferior and have effectively silenced them. Girls simply speak in a different voice, Gilligan asserts, one with as much validity as boys'. In 1990 the American Association of University Women (AAUW) directed a study, published in 1991 as *Shortchanging Girls, Shortchanging America*, that reports that boys and girls enter school roughly equal in ability and yet girls fall further behind boys, particularly in self-esteem, as the school years progress.

Patricia O'Toole's article "A Missing Chapter from Choral Methods Books: How Choirs Neglect Girls" (*Choral Journal*, 1998) applies Gilligan's theories to the choir. O'Toole finds that assumptions about aptitude and behavior are pervasive, giving boys several advantages over girls in choir. For example, because boys are expected to pose more discipline problems than girls, teachers may ignore girls in order to engage the boys. Further, because boys' voices encounter more vocal hurdles than girls' do, rehearsal time may be weighted toward working with the boys. At festivals, comments on the vocal quality of the ensemble focus on the boys, implying that girls' voices play an inferior role.

The musicologist Phillip Brett, in "Musicality, Essentialism and the Closet" (Chapter 2 in *Queering the Pitch*, 1994), explains women's suppression in European and American classical musical traditions as part of a patriarchal suppression of female sexuality—as well as male homosexuality, often equated with a man's being "musical." Brett suggests that music, like sexuality (other than male heterosexuality), arouses fears of instability and loss of control that threaten the social order. Theories of female sexuality, which are related to the Christian doctrine of Eve as evil and the Virgin Mary as good, also recall earlier fears of a "feminized" American music.

In both jazz and popular music, similar refrains of difference and inferiority run deep. The most common role for a woman in jazz is as singer. If she performs on an instrument, it is likely the piano. Lisa A. Lewis, in *Gender Politics and MTV: Voicing the Difference* (1990), finds the same traits in popular music, noting that women singers, unless they write their own songs, are regarded as lesser musicians. Whereas pop has women vocalists, the rock band represents, at least in its origins, an all-male team effort. Few women are hired to play. Drums are seen as too aggressive and synthesizers too mechanical for the woman musician.

According to Lewis, it was not until the 1970s when the punk movement celebrated "defiant amateurism" that the desegregation of professional-male and amateur-female helped redefine the performance space for women in rock. She traces women rockers' history in parallel with MTV's history; its videos visually highlight the singer, a role women are granted. Lewis sees this image as significantly responsible for the proliferation of all-women rock bands. In 1982 the Go-Go's scored the first Top 10 record for an all-woman band. This is one of many indications of change in assumptions and theories about female-male differences and feminine-masculine roles.

See also Aptitude; Constructivism; Separate Spheres—Sexual Aesthetics

For Further Reading:

Fuller, Sophie. "Dead White Men in Wigs." In *Girls! Girls! Girls! Essays on Women and Music*, ed. Sarah Cooper. New York: New York University Press, 1996, 22–36.

Gilligan, Carol. *In a Different Voice: Psychological Theory and Women's Development*. Cambridge, MA: Harvard University Press, (1982) reprinted 1993.

Green, Lucy. *Music, Gender, Education*. Cambridge: Cambridge University Press, 1997.

Carolyn Bremer
Deborah Hayes

Feminist Music Criticism

Feminist music criticism is a way of writing about music that makes use of critical theory to uncover ideologies and institutional power structures concerning women and gender that are contained in music and its effects. Feminist music criticism is closely related to feminist musical aesthetics, and many writers use the two designations interchangeably. If a distinction is to be made, feminist music criticism is something practiced by the listener and critic in attempting to explain music, whereas feminist musical aesthetics is about feminine and feminist qualities that women may express in their own music. The blurring of the distinction reflects the more general blurring of the boundary lines between critical the-

ory (of which feminist music criticism is an offshoot) and philosophy (including feminist aesthetics), as well as the growing conviction that the best and most interesting scholarship occurs at the borders of disciplines. (Feminist aesthetics is quite distinct from sexual aesthetics.)

In the first chapter of her book *Feminine Endings* (1991), Susan McClary outlines the beginnings of a feminist criticism of music by illustrating five general areas of concern: musical constructions of gender and sexuality; gendered aspects of music theory; gender and sexuality in musical narrative; music as a gendered discourse; and discursive strategies of women musicians. In ensuing chapters, written between 1987 and 1989, McClary analyzes constructions of gender and sexuality in some masterworks from the male canon and in the music of four American women: Diamanda Galás (b. 1955), Janika Vandervelde, Laurie Anderson (b. 1947), and Madonna (b. 1958). For McClary, the power of tonal music resides in its semiotic relationship with male sexuality and eroticism; a feminine or feminist aesthetic thus has much to do with female sexuality and eroticism, whether heterosexual or lesbian.

Renée Cox's essay "Recovering *Jouissance*: An Introduction to Feminist Musical Aesthetics" (1991) draws on writings by McClary and others in the late 1980s. Cox's term *jouissance* ("pleasure") comes from French feminist literary theory, where it describes a feminine mode of writing that disrupts conventional culture and meaning. (The term *jouissance* here refers to the pleasure of the rhythmic, presymbolic play of mother-infant communication in the infant's preoedipal stage of fusion with the mother.) Though found in the writing of either sex, the feminine mode of *jouissance* is most likely to occur in women's writing and in women's speech when men are not around. Because girls do not have to develop a gender identity different from that of the mother, they can maintain the *jouissance* of the preoedipal infant-mother connection longer; feminine writing results when traces of *jouissance* arise from the subconscious and are set against conventional modes of discourse (Cox, 334). Cox proposes that *jouissance* may be a useful analogy for the aesthetic pleasure of music—"music of all kinds by both sexes." Citing McClary's analysis of Anderson's construction of the feminine in "Langue d'amour (The Hothead)," which re-tells the biblical creation myth from the woman's perspective, Cox compares this construction to the "appropriated" femininity of "Be My Baby," a song written by a white man for the Ronettes, a black "girl group."

In music composed by women—Cox mentions Pauline Oliveros (b. 1932) and Ellen Taaffe Zwilich (b. 1939)—it is difficult to distinguish between the composer's expression of her own experience and her expression of male constructions of the feminine that she has internalized. Cox wonders whether women have "any authentically female experience unconditioned by patriarchal oppression and constraints." Because male composers' constructions of the feminine, even if they are found to be accurate, have often been intended to control and silence women, feminist music criticism could "expose these concepts or images and reformulate them." In "Langue d'amour" Anderson "takes a belief that has been most powerful in silencing women—the idea that woman was responsible for the Fall, and that this Fall had something to do with her sexuality—and turns it around, posits a female protagonist who combines thought, emotion, and desire and delights in them, refusing to accept shame or guilt" (Cox, 338)

Eva Rieger in " 'I Recycle Sounds': Do Women Compose Differently?" (1992) identifies seven elements of a feminine aesthetic in the work of Oliveros, Meredith Monk (b. 1942), Laurie Anderson, Ruth Anderson (b. 1928), Maryanne Amacher (b. 1946), Alison Knowles (b. 1933), Carole Weber, Annea Lockwood (b. 1939), Joan La Barbara (b. 1947), Ruth Crawford Seeger (1901–1953), Candace Natvig, Doris Hays, Kay Gardner, Barbara Benary, and several Europeans: an ability to create the maximum amount of music from minimal material; a preference for functional music; communication as a priority of composition; an interest in constituent substance over compulsive innovation; a striving to overcome binary oppositions; a desire to combine various fields of art with the human body and soul and with nature; and a close relation to their own bodies and to the human voice. Rieger discusses historical and stylistic reasons for these characteristics in various social constraints and opportunities that women have experienced.

The feminist qualities of Oliveros's music are the subject of several studies. Timothy Taylor (1993) shows how her works systematically undermine canonic aesthetics: they are not complex or virtuosic; they are less concerned with form, organic unity, and large-scale structural coherence; and they do not exclude and disempower the uninitiated. Taylor analyzes *Crow two* (1975) from a feminist viewpoint. Elisabeth LeGuin (1994) finds that feminist music such as Oliveros's creates a safe aesthetic place. For LeGuin, such music is "easy listening"; it avoids the problematic and reduces the reliance on focused attention to detail, without giving the listener license to refuse to think. Myrna Schloss (1993) finds a feminist aesthetic in certain characteristics of the music of Monk, Oliveros, and Joan Tower (b. 1938): cyclical structure; the cumulative growth of an idea; the disruption of conventional narratives; the equality of female and male musical performers and their music; a strong interest in myth, ritual, and physicality; the inclusion of autobiographical concerns and consciousness-raising issues; and the avoidance of definite closures. Schloss, like Cox and Rieger, concedes that men composers may employ feminine components; in the music of these three women, however, the feminine characteristics are consistent and predominant.

The relationship among feminist music criticism, feminist aesthetics, and feminist music theory is evident in Claire Detels's proposal (1994) of a feminist-based paradigm of "soft boundaries" as a way of understanding music. This kind of music theory examines important musical relationships neglected in traditional formalist musical theory and aesthetics—the relationship between physical motion and emotion, the relationship among musical constituencies, and the relationship between music and culture.

Feminist music criticism and feminist aesthetics are undergoing continuous change and refinement. Because women and their music constitute an "other" in relation to the male canon, McClary proposed early on that feminist music criticism could involve the analysis of related kinds of musical other-ness, including non-Western musics and popular genres, thus addressing the politics of several social constructs besides gender and sexuality, such as race, ethnicity, class, and nationality. Such political, social, and economic concerns have been vital to feminist musicology and most musicology in the United States since the 1990s—as to most academic disciplines.

As explained by McClary, Janaki Bakhle, Nicholas Cook, and others, critical theory, the basis of feminist music criticism, is a subdiscipline of Marxist sociology that developed in the 1930s from the writings of the musician and sociologist Theodor Adorno and the Frankfurt School; in the United States such work continued at the New School for Social Research in New York City. For Adorno, the transition from tonality to atonality to row theory was an expression of historical forces in German culture and society. Feminist criticism in music reflects more recent interdisciplinary methodologies as well: "deconstruction," which uncovers ideological premises; "postmodernism," which questions traditional boundaries such as those between classical and popular music; Marxism, which depicts women and laborers as victims of capitalism; "hegemony" theory, a branch of Marxism that holds that as members of a capitalist society we participate in our own oppression by consensus; "resistance theory," a main project of cultural studies that suggests that the consumer interprets popular culture (e.g., Madonna, Elvis, New Age music) against its ideological constraints, thus "resisting" the images or "exerting counter-hegemonic subjectivity"; and "critical aesthetics," which maintains the value of the canon of great music but investigates the politics behind the greatness. Feminist music criticism is at least as much about culture, gender, and the male canon as it is about women and their music.

See also Feminist Music Theory; Feminist Musicology; Gender in Music Analysis

For Further Reading

Cox, Renée. "Recovering *Jouissance*: An Introduction to Feminist Musical Aesthetics." In *Women and Music: A History*, ed. by Karin Pendle. Bloomington: Indiana University Press, 1991, 331–340.

McClary, Susan. *Feminine Endings: Music, Gender, and Sexuality*. Minneapolis: University of Minnesota Press, 1991.

Rieger, Eva. " 'I Recycle Sounds': Do Women Compose Differently?" *ILWC [International League of Women Composers] Journal* (March 1992): 22–25.

Deborah Hayes

Feminist Music History

Feminist history, or women's history, is a phase of historiography according to Gerda Lerner's 1975 classification that examines what most women were doing at a certain time and place. Rather than rewriting women into the conventional historical narrative, the historian provides a new historical narrative. Feminist history is differentiated from approaches labeled compensatory history (women judged by men's standards), bifocal history (women overcoming patriarchal oppression), and multifocal history (women and men being considered equally important), although it is closely related to the bifocal and multifocal approaches. In Betty Chmaj's 1990 review of the historiography of women in music in the United States, "Where Are the Women?" Chmaj describes how, using the methods of social history, American music historians have begun to focus not only on leaders and celebrities but also on anonymous women, poor women, nonwhite women, and collective music-making, and to consider audiences, especially women audiences, and women's patronage. It should be noted that the term "feminist music history" can have more general meanings. Some writers define it as any research about women in music that makes use of feminist theory or gender theory—that is, any approach except the compensatory (traditional). Other writers use the term to mean any historical research about women in music, no matter what the methodology.

In a pre-1970 and fairly radical example of feminist history in the United States, Sophie Drinker argues, in *Music and Women: The Story of Women in Their Relation to Music* (1948), that any kind of musical activity that truly represented women came to an end in ancient times with the beginning of patriarchal society and religion. She divides the history of the world's music into three phases. "Full Moon" describes women's music in full flower in ancient traditions, including goddess worship, until ca. 500 B.C.E. "The Dark of the Moon" describes the suppression of women and their music in early patriarchal societies, ca. 500 B.C.E. through the fourth century C.E. "New Moon," ca. 500 C.E. to the present, describes women's activities in more recent patriarchal societies. Chapters in this third section are arranged topically rather than chronologically: "The Nun"; "The Lady" (medieval noblewomen); "Priestess of Beauty" (court musicians); "The Prima Donna" (singers), "The Camillae" (women patrons and amateur performers); "St. Cecilia" (women inspiring male genius); and "Artemis Stirring" (intimations of new ideas, spirit, and flesh as one).

Concerning music in the United States, the cornerstone of recent feminist history or women's history (in Lerner's terms) is *Women in American Music: A Bibliography of Music and Literature*, compiled and edited by Carol Neuls-Bates and Adrienne Fried Block (1979). Drawing on a variety of sources both musical and extra-musical, the compilers document women's important contributions to music in the United States in the context of society's views, expectations, and proscriptions of women's activities. A nontraditional periodization delineates historical eras according to women's changing status and opportunities: colonial times to 1820, 1820–1870, 1870–1920, 1920–1950, and 1950–1978. In the "Historical Introduction" to the volume the compilers note the interrelationships between women and men, as well as the segregation of women in a world apart from men.

Similar woman-centered accounts may be found in several other studies from the 1980s and 1990s. Christine Ammer's *Unsung: A History of Women in American Music* (1980, revised 2001) is fairly inclusive as to genre and activity. The three volumes of *The Musical Woman: An International Perspective*, edited by Judith Lang Zaimont et al. (1984, 1987, 1991) contain essays on composers, critics, band directors, festivals, recording companies, and a wide range of activities, many of them in the United States. Neuls-Bates's *Women in Music: An Anthology of Source Readings from the Middle Ages to the Present* (1982; rev. ed., 1996), includes many readings from American history. Essays by Judith Tick, Neuls-Bates, and Matilda Gaume in *Women Making Music: The Western Art Tradition, 1150–1950*, edited by Jane Bowers and Tick (1986), discuss music in the United States in its economic and social context. Tick's "Women in Music" in the *New Grove Dictionary of American Music* (1986) reviews women's activities in their social, economic, and political context in a four-part chronology: colonial period to 1850; 1850–1900; 1900–1950; and after 1950. Karin Pendle's *Women and Music: A His-*

tory (1991) includes contributions concerning the United States by Block, Nancy Stewart, J. Michele Edwards, Leslie Lassetter, S. Kay Hoke, Michael J. Budds, and Linda Whitesett.

Among other recent historical studies, Helen Walker-Hill's "Chicago's Black Women Composers: Then and Now" (1992) highlights a number of women in classical music and explores the conditions that aided their artistic development: a strong and independent black community; the support of families, churches, social and music groups, schools, and teachers; and a highly charged metropolitan atmosphere. Bonny Miller's "Ladies' Companion, Ladies' Canon? Women Composers in American Magazines from *Gody's* to the *Ladies' Home Journal*" (1994) examines the representation of composers and performers in the women-oriented world of household magazines.

See also Bifocal History; Compensatory History; Historiography; Multifocal History

For Further Reading

Drinker, Sophie. *Music and Women: The Story of Women in Their Relation to Music.* New York: Coward, McCann, 1948. Rept., New York: Feminist Press of the City University of New York, 1995, with preface by E. Wood, afterword by R. Solie.

Neuls-Bates, Carol, and Adrienne Fried Block. "Historical Introduction." In *Women in American Music: A Bibliography of Music and Literature.* Westport, CT: Greenwood Press, 1979.

Tick, Judith. "Women in Music." In *The New Grove Dictionary of American Music*, eds. H. Wiley Hitchcock and Stanley Sadie. 4 vols. London: Macmillan, 1986.

Deborah Hayes

Feminist Music Theory

Feminist music theory is the study and practice of music theory from the perspective of its relationship to women. Its concepts developed during the 1980s, through the applications of feminist theory and gender studies to traditional music theory.

Traditional music theory is the systematic study of the structure of music, including the properties of musical sound and collections of sounds. Music theorists have searched for principles and consistent findings for analyzing and explaining musical phenomena and practice—plainsong and organum in the medieval period, modal counterpoint in the sixteenth century, harmony and tonality in the eighteenth century, tonal forms in the nineteenth century, and serial, atonal, and other post-tonal structures in the twentieth.

When feminist perspectives began appearing in music history and criticism in the 1970s, creating feminist musicology, it seemed that there was little applicability of a parallel movement in music theory. Analysis of systems and principles would seem to be independent of social concerns and immune to feminist approaches. Moreover, all the theories regarded as central were created by men, to explain music by men. To the new feminist critics, however, the all-male basis of music theory seemed highly significant. Perhaps in reflecting the interests of only one gender the discipline presented an incomplete and even distorted understanding of musical structures, processes, and aesthetic values. Like feminist musicologists, some music theorists began to recover women's work and women's influence and to analyze gendered relationships in traditional structures and concepts, thus expanding the field tremendously. By the 1980s writers such as Fred Maus and Marion Guck began describing the new feminist music theory.

The goal of feminist music theory is to understand how musical structures and systems—the material of traditional music theory—express and contribute to the social construction of gender roles. It explores how composers consciously and subconsciously use musical structures to express feminine images and sexuality. It also explores how and why compositions by women might differ from those by men. Feminist music theorists and those influenced by them now study a greater variety of scores (often deliberately choosing works by women composers), use a greater variety of approaches to analyze scores, and are more interested in relating musical structures to the contexts in which a work is created. They are more likely to include subjective interpretations and reception history in their work, and usually they have a more relativist position regarding aesthetic evaluation. Although the main focus is on women's perspectives, it is not only femaleness but also maleness that interests feminist theorists. Much of their work is feminist music criticism.

Sometimes feminist music theorists deliberately choose to focus on scores by women, such as Hildegard of Bingen from the medieval period, or Ruth Crawford Seeger (1901–1953) from the early twentieth century—composers ignored by the earlier canonic, male theorists. As the opportunity for women to become professional composers is greater today than in any other time, a great percentage of the available scores by women is from the last 20 years or so. Living composers such as Joan Tower (b. 1938), Ellen Taaffe Zwilich (b. 1939), Pauline Oliveros (b. 1932), and Libby Larsen (b. 1950) have received much attention. Feminist theorists are also much more likely than traditional theorists to write about popular and folk music from any period.

A more provocative aspect of feminist music theory is the viewpoint that analysis is not autonomous and objective. The theorist then either explores the underlying meanings of the analytical approach itself, or, finding traditional formal analysis inadequate, uses alternative and frequently cross-disciplinary approaches such as phenomenology, semiotics, or literary narratives. Evidence of strong interest in incorporating feminist critical theory with music theory may be found in the Feminist Theory and Music Conferences sponsored by the Society for Music Theory, the International Alliance for Women in Music, and leading universities, and held in alternate years since June 1991.

A number of writers have worked to "deconstruct" the nature of music theory's academic language itself. The term "deconstruction" is a concept from literary theory in which the text has no fixed meaning, thus allowing several equally viable "readings." When the "objectivity" of musical theoretical writing came under close scrutiny, a possible subtext was revealed: that analysts who are men have had a strong desire to avoid language that might seem unmanly. Emotional and personal responses were thus de-emphasized in preference for symbols, abstractions, pattern-identification, and rules. The small number of women theorists may be attributable to this restriction created by the language of music theorists.

In the essay "Masculine Discourse in Music Theory" (1993) Fred Maus recalls his experience as a music theory student at Princeton University in the 1980s and its reflection in the profession at large. The theoretical language, vocabulary, and approaches used by theory professors and students, all of them men, created mainstream and marginal groups. The mainstream approach, Schenkerian analysis and set theory used scientific, positivist, and therefore more masculine language. The work of James Randall and Benjamin Boretz, which relied more on cultural context and literary theory, used a more feminine discourse. Maus believes that the profession is still heavily weighted toward the traditional, male style of writing. In comparison to the feminine, emotional pursuit of music performance and listening, he notes, music theory is masculine and controlling.

An emphasis on the personal and the subjective characterizes much feminist music theory. Marion Guck is committed to using metaphors, personal language, and specific characterizations in her analyses rather than more objective technical jargon. In "A Woman's (Theoretical) Work" (*Perspectives of New Music [PNM]*, 1994), she analyzes Chopin's Prelude in B Minor using tapes of three groups of musicians in conversations. She argues that analyses benefit from the overt representation of the analyst and the analyst's gender. She comments on how the personal nature of her approach may be construed as being feminine (whether by her or someone else, man or woman) and is then marginalized within the field as a whole (even more so if by a woman).

Rosemary Killam, in "Women Working: An Alternative to Gans" (1993), analyzes Libby Larsen's *Songs from Letters* (1989), settings of Calamity Jane's letters to her daughter, describing her method as *feminist* analysis because of several features: a rich context derived from Killam's recent research, the specific inclusion of women's experiences, the analyst's attitude of non-oppression, and the inclusion of her personal experience and perceptions. Further, Killam uses concepts from disciplines other than music theory, namely, Eric Gans's theories of language, culture, feminism, and linguistics.

Marianne Kielian-Gilbert also deliberately and self-consciously explores women's identities linked to multiple connections within music. In her essay "Of Poetics and Poiesis, Pleasure and Politics—Music Theory and Modes of the Feminine" (*PNM*, 1994), she draws on Nattiez and the field of semiotics to discuss "subject position" and the feminine in music theory. She describes a range of notions and modes of the feminine and their corresponding social and theoretical implications. Her analysis of Miriam Gideon's Suite for Piano (1966) is unconventional in that she uses different descriptive "frames" without trying to unify them; each frame stands on its own as a different analytical voice. The frames, with labels such as "performing," "hearing the rhythms of pitches," "making intertextual connections," and "mediating identities," use a minimum of technical language. Again the personal is emphasized when Kielian-Gilbert briefly describes meeting Gideon and her world of Judaism.

Feminist musicologists and music theorists have explored musical forms not as objective isolated patterns but as expressions of sexuality. Sonata form has been interpreted specifically as an expression of male heterosexuality, a reading supported in part by historical descriptions of its thematic/tonal areas as masculine and feminine by the nineteenth-century theorist A. B. Marx and others. In *Gender and the Musical Canon* (1993), Marcia Citron presents a feminist analysis of the first movement of Cécile Chaminade's Piano Sonata, op. 21, and argues that Chaminade may have been challenging the gendered codes of nineteenth-

century sonata form by not using certain conventions of the form. Similarly, Susan McClary scoffs at the notion of "absolute" music in her numerous and provocative analyses that rely on narrative studies and semiotics. Her discussion in *Feminine Endings* (1991) of the gendered discourse of sonata form, and her subsequent analyses of Peter Ilich Tchaikovsky's Fourth Symphony and Georges Bizet's opera *Carmen*, have had widespread influence. She also connects gender to a fundamental Western "hero" plot, most notably in her analysis of Johannes Brahms's Third Symphony, in *Musicology and Difference* (1993).

Suzanne Cusick has discussed feminism and gender in a variety of contexts—seventeenth-century opera, a lesbian relationship with music, and as part of "embodied analysis." Most notable is her discussion of the potential of feminist music theory to solve what she identifies as "the mind/body problem" ("Feminist Theory, Music Theory, and the Mind/Body Problem," *PNM*, 1994). Using the basic feminist concept that gender descriptions are used as a metaphor for power relationships, Cusick proposes analyzing musical works as scripts for the performance of social relationships. She believes that musicologists and music theorists who focus on music as a fixed text (the score) and act upon it with their minds have neglected the bodily experience of performing; much of music's meaning, including its gender codes, is thus lost. She genders the mind as male, the body as female, and the composer as male, not because the majority of composers are men but because the composer is understood as a mind that creates music to which other minds assign meanings. She uses these metaphors to explain the tensions of Fanny Hensel's position as composer. Relying on writings by the feminist historian Joan Scott, the feminist philosopher Judith Butler, and the musicologist Edward Cone, Cusick discusses an approach for analyzing Hensel's Trio in D Minor, op. 11, in terms of gender encoding that would in part portray the piano as feminine and the strings as masculine.

Some feminist music theorists view changes in tonal language in earlier centuries as resulting from social changes, rather than representing inevitable changes of internal patterns. The replacement of modality with major/minor tonality in the seventeenth to eighteenth centuries has been explored in various writings by Ellen Rosand, McClary, and Cusick. Catherine Parsons Smith, in her essay " 'A Distinguishing Virility': Feminism and Modernism in American Art Music" (1994), using feminist literary criticism, suggests that American modernists ca. 1920–1943 used a highly dissonant style to distance themselves from the feminine and the European.

An example of the overlapping concerns of feminist work by music theorists and musicologists may be seen in studies of Ruth Crawford Seeger. The theorist Joseph Straus in *The Music of Ruth Crawford Seeger* (1995) shows how the composer, with her husband, Charles Seeger, devised a theoretical system for her compositions, a method many used to regard as exclusive to composers who are men. Then he devotes the final chapter to cultural contexts, including a section on the history of women in music. In her biography *Ruth Crawford Seeger: A Composer's Search for American Music* (1997) the musicologist Judith Tick analyzes several works to show how the composer's theoretical and compositional method reflect her spiritual and philosophical beliefs. In *Gendering Musical Modernism; The Music of Ruth Crawford, Marion Bauer, and Miriam Gideon* (2001), Ellis Hisama combines a new analytical approach with feminist theory and social criticism to examine the place of women in musical modernism.

Although there has been some resistance to feminist research in music theory, the work has irrevocably changed the nature of the field and influenced many of its practitioners. As a result of feminist theoretical studies, conditions for women (and men indirectly) may improve in a number of ways. Contemporary women composers are more likely to have their works performed, recorded, analyzed, appreciated, and documented. Women in general may find encouragement for their work by developing an awareness of historical women's successes in music. Many more types of music are available as models. More women may enjoy careers as theorists if the nature of the work includes women's perspectives. On a broader scale, as gender roles in music are studied, a better understanding of gender roles in the current time are developed, and decisions that enhance the quality of life are made.

See also Gender in Music Analysis; Music Theorist

For Further Reading

Maus, Fred. "Masculine Discourse in Music Theory." *Perspectives of New Music* 31/2 (1993): 264–293.

McClary, Susan. *Feminine Endings: Music, Gender, and Sexuality*. Minneapolis: University of Minnesota Press, 1991.

Perspectives of New Music. 32/1 (1994), *Towards a Feminist Music Theory* (special issue).

Sharon Mirchandani

Feminist Musicology

Feminist musicology is the study of some aspect of music from the perspective of its relationship to women. Feminist musicology began in the 1970s in connection with the feminist revival and the growth of women's studies as an academic discipline. Feminist scholars in music, as in other fields, wanted to recover the historical record of women, a group whom scholars had traditionally ignored. Because traditional musicology was concerned with men composers and their masterworks, feminist musicologists concentrated on famous women composers. This component of feminist musicology is often called "compensatory history," as it is intended to compensate for women's exclusion elsewhere. By the 1990s, however, feminist musicologists had widened their focus to include studies of women performers and patrons; audience response; social and political conditions as they affected women; the musical representation of gender differences and sexuality; ideologies of musical authorship, genius, and canon; and aesthetic values. The emphasis shifted somewhat from women to gender issues. Instead of feminist musicology, the term "new musicology" was often used, or simply, "musicology," as much of the new feminist methodology had been generally absorbed. Works from the male canon were examined for their political content in relation to gender as well as race, ethnicity, national origin, and socioeconomic class.

Musicological methods in compensatory history are fairly traditional, consisting primarily of the recovery and preservation of scores and other documentation needed for composer biographies and music analysis. By the 1980s many musicologists at American colleges and universities were offering classes in the history of women in music. New anthologies and histories appeared, such as James Briscoe's *Historical Anthology of Music by Women* (1987) and Diane Pea-cock Jezic's *Women Composers: The Lost Tradition Found* (1988). New enterprises such as ClarNan Editions, Hildegard Publishing Company, and Leonarda Productions issued historical editions and recordings. Joseph Straus's *Music by Women for Study and Analysis* (1993) helped bring new repertoire into the music theory classroom, illustrating the close relationship between feminist musicology and feminist music theory.

A broader approach to historiography not only finds the outstanding women composers but also examines cultural influences on women musicians and their status in relation to men. Carol Neuls-Bates's *Women in Music: An Anthology of Source Readings from the Middle Ages to the Present* (1982; rev. ed., 1996) contains invaluable reprints of writings, letters, interviews, and articles by and about women musicians, with editorial passages that frame the issues. Numerous writings address American topics, such as articles by the American pianist Amy Fay and the black American singer Marian Anderson (1897–1993), interviews with composers Nancy Van de Vate (b. 1930) and Joan Tower (b. 1938), and newspaper articles and reviews concerning women's symphony orchestras in the 1920s to 1940s as well as the Women's Philharmonic, established in 1981. The 15 essays in *Women Making Music: The Western Art Tradition, 1150–1950*, edited by Jane Bowers and Judith Tick (1986), place the musical achievements of women into a variety of historical contexts. Three authors address American topics: Judith Tick on women musicians' change from amateur to professional status from 1870 to 1900, Carol Neuls-Bates on women's orchestras from 1925 to 1945, and Matilda Gaume on Ruth Crawford Seeger (1901–1953).

In Karin Pendle's *Women in Music: A*

History (1991), chapters by Adrienne Fried Block and J. Michele Edwards on twentieth-century music in the United States examine many cultural factors—educational, economic, and political conditions for American women in general, and contemporary standards of taste and excellence—as the context for women's work in music. Besides composers, they discuss women who played other crucial roles in American music, including performers, patrons, and educators. Other chapters examine nonclassical genres: S. Kay Hoke discusses women in American popular music, and Michael J. Budds discusses African American women in blues and jazz.

Studies like these, of women's many kinds of participation in musical activities, attempt a more comprehensive view of music history. New research areas include: studies of the concept of separate spheres and the ideology of public (male) and private (female) music-making; studies of musical activities apart from concert performance; and the work of amateurs such as the historian Sophie Drinker. *Cultivating Music in America: Women Patrons and Activists since 1860,* edited by Ralph Locke and Cyrilla Barr (1997), examines women's patronage, including the work of Isabella Stewart Gardner, Elizabeth Sprague Coolidge, and Blanche Walton. New biographies of famous women, such as Tick's biography of Ruth Crawford Seeger (1997), Block's biography of Amy Marcy Cheney Beach (1998), and Heidi Von Gunden's biographies of Vivian Fine (1999) and Pauline Oliveros (1983), offer a more complete view of composers and historical women's issues. In the 1990s the International Alliance for Women in Music began providing a specific venue for feminist scholarship and reports on women composers with the *IAWM Journal* and

Women in Music: A Journal of Gender and Culture.

Among the methods of feminist musicology that have been almost universally adopted is a new kind of interpretation of musical works described as feminist music criticism. In a manner analogous to literary criticism, feminist music criticism explores the representation of women and the feminine in music, and it usually takes into consideration the identity of the composer and how it might affect that representation. Initially, only music with texts and explicit portrayals were considered. The field of opera provides a fascinating interplay of gender as it is represented on the stage, the gender of the performers, castrati, and the social milieu surrounding patronage and reception. American scholars investigating European lieder, troubadour songs, and chants have prompted studies of the relationship and possible effects of the genders of the composer, the singer, and the text's protagonist. In feminist music criticism musicologists often rely on interdisciplinary approaches, bringing in anthropology, sociology, and literary studies including mythology and symbolism. Questions that are asked include: Why have male composers and theorists often associated the feminine with the exotic Other, madness, and excess, as opposed to reason? Who is speaking through women characters? And, do these representations shed light on how women really are?

Feminist music criticism of music without text or explicit extramusical references has been explored most provocatively by the feminist musicologist Susan McClary in numerous publications, most notably *Feminine Endings: Music, Gender, and Sexuality* (1991). She argues that even absolute music may be regarded as a gendered discourse and that so-called pure musical forms are not without gendered cultural meaning. Her thesis that tonal forms and tonal theory are about desire, in particular male desire, has prompted the investigation of the nature of both male and female sexuality, the representation of that sexuality by men and women composers, and the role of homosexuality with regard to both. McClary's work has received great attention and influenced the entire musicological community.

A landmark publication in feminist musicology is *Cecelia Reclaimed: Feminist Perspectives on Gender and Music* (1994) edited by Susan C. Cook and Judy S. Tsou; five of its 10 essays concern American topics. An explanation of how forms and style changes may be value-laden is found in Catherine Parson Smith's " 'A Distinguishing Virility': Feminism and Modernism in American Art Music." Smith hypothesizes that American modernism developed from men striving to distance themselves from women professionally and from any feminine characterizations of their own work or natures. She comments on the possible negative consequences for several American women, including Ruth Crawford Seeger. Also included are essays by Block on the pianist/composer Amy Marcy Cheney Beach, by Bonny H. Miller on women composers in American magazines, by Venise T. Berry on images of women in rap music, and by Cook on narrative stereotypes of women and men in American balladry.

A number of authors have explored ways in which the feminine in music is linked to Westerners' images of foreign lands. Leo Trietler's "Gender and Other Dualities of Music History" in the anthology *Musicology and Difference* (Solie, 1993) explores binary opposites throughout music history that have been categorized as masculine/feminine, including Occidental/Oriental. Two essays in *The Exotic in Western Music*, edited by Jonathan Bellman (1998), are important to feminist studies: Mary Hunter's *The "alla Turca" Style* treats issues of gender and race in eighteenth-century musical representations of Turks that were laden with meaning at the time; and Linda Phyllis Austern's *Forreine Conceites and Wandring Devises* explores musical theoretical language in the Elizabethan period in which the feminine became associated with the foreign.

Feminist musicologists, like feminist scholars in other disciplines, have borrowed critical approaches from other disciplines. Musicologists use theoretical concepts from sociology, anthropology, literary criticism, and semiotics. They have called into question musicology's traditional emphasis on the role of composer and on specific genres and forms, revealed problems connected with the concept of genius, demonstrated the social conditions necessary to have one's works performed, and criticized the use of non-inclusive language such as the word "masterpiece" for art work. Marcia J. Citron's *Gender and the Musical Canon* (1993) is another landmark work, providing a critique of the Western canon and its implicit values.

Most feminist musicologists desire to expand the focus of musicology from Western art music to that of all ethnic groups, allying it frequently with the field of ethnomusicology. The 15 essays in *Women and Music in Cross-Cultural Perspective* (1987), edited by Ellen Koskoff, address the musical activities of women from a great variety of world cultures (Greek, Balkan, Moroccan, Tunisian, Afghan, Indian, Indonesian, Malaysian, Japanese, and Brazilian) and challenge the traditional view of anthropologists and ethnomusicologists that men alone influence musical culture. Topics on the United States include essays by Esther Rothenbusch on nineteenth-century hymnody, by Jane Hassinger on the New Orleans Boswell Sisters, by Karen E. Peterson on women-identified music, and by Koskoff on New York Hasidic Jewish women. Many of the essays do not address professional musicians but concentrate on women's musical roles and rituals that may concern religious matters, stages of life, or power relations between the sexes.

Although the term "feminist musicology" is still useful, increasingly much of the work is being absorbed into the broader and more recently identified category of "gender studies," a term that developed from the complexities that arise when trying to focus on women alone. Even though there are only two biological categories, there are numerous gender roles as a result of a particular society's cultural constructs, sexual orientation, life stages (age, marital status, parental status), and race/class/religious differences. Masculine, homosexual, transvestite, and transsexual perspectives have received greater attention. Many writers explicitly indicate their beliefs in the reason for gender differences as primarily constructivist or essentialist, and the implications of those beliefs. Jeffrey Kallberg's *Chopin at the Boundaries: Sex, History, and Musical Genre* (1996) explores gender definition, the notion of "feminine" genres, and Frederic Chopin's image as a "woman's composer." The collection of 14 essays in *Queering the Pitch: The New Gay and Lesbian Musicology*, edited by Philip Brett, Elizabeth Wood, and Gary C. Thomas (1994), address essentialism, friendship, the castrato, Georg Friederich Handel, Benjamin Britten, Franz Schubert, coun-

try music, compositional process, gay choruses, and growing up female. Nowhere is the diversity of gender roles and their effect on our understanding of music so apparent as in *Musicology and Difference: Gender and Sexuality in Music Scholarship*, edited by Ruth A. Solie (1993). Topics of the 15 essays include composers from Francesca Caccini to Charles Ives, "cross-dressing" in Robert Schumann's *Caranaval*, opera, ethnomusicology, and the importance of the "feminine" minor mode in Mozart.

Although there is much interaction between gender studies and feminist musicology, the latter places greater emphasis on women and their status in society. Though there is not universal agreement about what would constitute an appropriate balance, most feminist scholars believe that feminist musicology with its woman-centered orientation will help bring about a more accurate and even-handed approach to music history. In this new approach countless women of today may find encouragement in their various musical activities.

See also Feminist Music Criticism, Women's Sphere

For Further Reading

Citron, Marcia. *Gender and the Musical Canon.* Cambridge: Cambridge University Press, 1993.

McClary, Susan. *Feminine Endings: Music, Gender and Sexuality.* Minneapolis: University of Minnesota Press, 1991.

Neuls-Bates, Carol (ed.). *Women in Music: An Anthology of Source Readings from the Middle Ages to the Present,* rev. ed. Boston: Northeastern University Press, 1996.

Solie, Ruth A. (ed.). *Musicology and Difference: Gender and Sexuality in Music Scholarship.* Berkeley and Los Angeles: University of California Press, 1993.

Sharon Mirchandani

Festivals

See Conferences and Festivals

Film Composers

Women film composers were virtually unknown in this Hollywood-based business until the last few decades of the twentieth century. The American film industry, like so many other fields, offered few opportunities to women for most of its history, and the composition of music for films is no exception. One of the notable exceptions was Ann Ronell (b. 1908), who provided scores and songs for a few films in the 1940s and 1950s, including the Marx Brothers comedy *Love Happy* (1950), and received Academy Award nominations for the score of *The Story of G.I. Joe* (1945) and the song "Linda" from the same film. However, opportunities for women composers in Hollywood were severely limited until the 1980s.

Given their minimal presence in traditional film scoring, it is perhaps not surprising that some of the more remarkable contributions made by women film composers were in the realm of electronic music. Bebe Barron (b. 1927) collaborated with her husband, Louis Barron, on electronic scores for a number of films, most notably *Forbidden Planet* (1956). This score diverges wildly from the conventionally tonal, orchestral scores that are still the norm in Hollywood films. Rather, it combines sound effects and atonal music to create a seamless and otherworldly sonic environment for this science fiction epic.

Wendy Carlos (b. 1939), after achieving considerable fame for her electronic realizations of music by Johann Sebastian Bach, provided a score for Stanley Kubrick's *A Clockwork Orange* (1971) that blended her original music with synthesized versions of works by Beethoven, Rossini, and Purcell. She collaborated with Kubrick again in *The Shining* (1980),

a horror film that opens with Carlos's ominous electronic rendition of the "Dies Irae" plainchant. Carlos's score for the 1982 Disney-produced science fiction film *Tron* (1982) is an ambitious fusion of orchestral and electronic textures; this score, long unavailable on compact disc, is one of the scores most desired by film music collectors.

Throughout the 1980s women film composers seemed mostly limited to television; composers such as Nan Schwartz-Miskin (b. 1953) and Elizabeth Swados (b. 1951) have worked extensively in episodic dramas, made-for-television films, and miniseries. British composer Angela Morley (b. 1924) moved to the United States after composing several successful scores for British films, including *Watership Down* (1978); however, she has mostly worked in television since. New Age composer Suzanne Ciani (b. 1946) was one of the few women to compose for feature films in this decade, producing scores for *The Incredible Shrinking Woman* (1981) and *Mother Teresa* (1986).

Shirley Walker (b. 1945) was one of the first women to emerge as a major force in Hollywood film music in the last decade of the twentieth century. Walker first achieved prominence as orchestrator and conductor of Danny Elfman's score for *Batman* (1989); later, after other collaborations with composers such as Cliff Eidelman and Hans Zimmer, she began receiving solo scoring assignments, including *Memoirs of an Invisible Man* (1992), *Escape from L.A.* (1996), *Turbulence* (1997), and *Final Destination* (2000). Walker has shown great facility with large-scale orchestral scores and has excelled at the scoring of animated films, such as *Batman: Mask of the Phantasm* (1993) and the *Batman* and *Superman* animated television series. She is unique in that she is the only woman film composer to achieve consistent success in scoring violent action films and science fiction thrillers, genres traditionally aimed at men's tastes.

During the 1990s several British women composers achieved remarkable success in film scoring, with the inevitable effect of bringing them into the American film industry. Anne Dudley (b. 1956), a member of the rock band Art of Noise, won an Academy Award for her small-scale yet effective score for *The Full Monty* (1997) and later provided somber, chilling music for *American History X* (1998). She recently composed a complex and ambitious orchestral score for the huge television miniseries *The Tenth Kingdom* (2000). Rachel Portman (b. 1960), after scoring several notable British films, including *Antonia and Jane* (1991) and *Life Is Sweet* (1991), swiftly established herself as a major composer for Hollywood films as well. Portman excels in dramatic films, often featuring quirky characters; her extensive credits include *The Joy Luck Club* (1993), *The Road to Wellville* (1994), *To Wong Foo, Thanks for Everything, Julie Newmar* (1995), *Beloved* (1998), and *The Cider House Rules* (1999). She won an Academy Award for her score for *Emma* (1996).

Other women composers who are currently working in film include Laura Karpman, who has scored numerous made-for-television films; Debbie Wiseman, another British composer who has worked in American television; and Cynthia Millar, protégé of legendary film composer Elmer Bernstein.

See also Music Technology

For Further Reading

Jacquet-Francillon, Vincent. *Film Composers Guide*, 4th ed. Los Angeles: Lone Eagle, 1997.

Shropshire, Liz. "Where Are the Women Composers?" *Cue Sheet* 6/2 (1989): 53–62.

H. Stephen Wright

Fine, Vivian (1913–2000)

Composer, pianist, teacher, and performing artist Vivian Fine was a classical composer whose life spanned the twentieth century. Critics characterized Fine's early works as sternly dissonant and largely contrapuntal. With compositions like *The Race of Life*, a ballet inspired by James Thurber's contemporary drawings of the typical middle-class American family (1937), she displayed a lighter, more diatonic tone, however. *A Guide to the Life Expectancy of a Rose*, a stage work based on an article from the gardening section of the *New York Times* (1956), highlights yet a third period of artistic expression, one that returns to dissonance tempered by occasional tonality and a sense of humor.

Fine was born in Chicago on 28 September 1913. She began piano study at the age of five and soon became a scholarship student at the Chicago Musical College. Fine attended the American Conservatory from 1925 to 1931, studying piano with Djane Lavoie-Herz, counterpoint with Adolf Weidig, and composition with Ruth Crawford Seeger (1901–1953). Fine wrote her first composition for Crawford after beginning composition studies at the age of 12, and she quickly forged an important relationship with Crawford as mentor and role model. In 1931 Fine went to New York City, where she studied composition with Roger Sessions and orchestration with George Szell. While there, she participated in a circle of composers that met regularly with Aaron Copland as moderator. In addition, Fine served as piano accompanist and composer for modern

Vivian Fine. *Photo courtesy of Academy of Art and Letters.*

dance troupes led by Doris Humphrey, Hanya Holm, and Charles Weidman. In 1935 she married sculptor Benjamin Karp, with whom she had two daughters.

Fine's academic appointments as a composition teacher include New York University (1945–1948), the Juilliard School (1948), and Bennington College (1964–1988). One of the founders of the American Composers Alliance (ACA), she was also music director of the Rothschild Foundation (1953–1960). Honors include the Dollard Award (1966), a grant from the Ford Foundation (1970), election to membership in the American Academy and Institute of Arts and Letters (1980), and grants from the Rockefeller and Alice B. Ditson Foundations (1981). The ballet *Alcestis* (Composers Recordings Inc. 145), *Drama for Orches-*

tra, and the *Piano Trio* are among her most notable commissioned works. Recordings include *Canzonas y Dances* (Albany Records 86) and *Toccatas and Arias for Harpsichord* (Gasparo GSCD 266).

During the U.S. Bicentennial of 1976, Vivian Fine received a commission by the Cooper Union to compose a work celebrating the historic post–Civil War women's suffrage debates, many of which took place at Cooper Union Forum. Using excerpts from these debates, Fine produced *Meeting for Equal Rights 1866*, a cantata scored for orchestra, chorus, soloists, and narrator.

Vivian Fine died on 20 March 2000 as a result of injuries sustained in an automobile accident in Bennington, VT. She left an unparalleled legacy as a composer, mentor, and champion of composers' rights. Her career served to highlight, celebrate, and advance the contributions of women musicians within the field of twentieth-century composition.

See also Classical Music

For Further Reading

LePage, Jane Weiner. *Women Composers, Conductors, and Musicians of the Twentieth Century: Selected Biographies, Vol. 2.*, Metuchen, NJ: Scarecrow Press, 1983.

Von Gunden, Heidi. *The Music of Vivian Fine.* Lanham, MD: Scarecrow Press, 1999.

Judith Marley

Fitzgerald, Ella (1917–1996)

Ella Fitzgerald, often called the "First Lady of Song," overcame adversity to become one of the most popular singers of the twentieth century. With a buoyant, warm voice, she was famous for her interpretations of jazz as well as popular standards. She received numerous awards during her lifetime, including 13 Grammy Awards, the National Academy of Recording Arts and Sciences Lifetime Achievement Award, and an honorary doctorate in music from Yale University.

Known for her abilities to improvise, scat, mimic, and swing, Ella Fitzgerald influenced entire generations of performers and audiences. Though her light-hearted vocal style sometimes drew criticism for its lack of emotional depth, her enthusiasm and spirit make her music a joy to experience. As was once observed, "She shares with her audience her pleasures, not her troubles." (Pleasants, 178).

Fitzgerald was born in Newport News, VA, on 25 April 1917 (often incorrectly stated as 1918) and moved to Yonkers, NY, at a young age. When her mother died unexpectedly in 1932, Fitzgerald lived temporarily with an aunt in Harlem and later spent time at a state reforma-

tory for girls. A 1934 victory at an Apollo Theater talent show signified the beginning of her legendary career. After being noticed at the contest, she met bandleader Chick Webb; in 1935 she began singing with his orchestra. It was with this group that Fitzgerald made her first recording, *Love and Kisses* (Delta 17009) in 1935, and had her first hit, "A-Tisket, A-Tasket" in 1938. After Webb died in 1939, she stayed on as the honorary bandleader until beginning her solo career in 1942.

In the late 1940s, Fitzgerald joined forces with promoter and manager Norman Granz, performing with his touring series *Jazz at the Philharmonic* from 1946 to 1954. In 1955 she signed up with Granz's recording label, Verve. Here, Fitzgerald began her hugely successful "songbook" projects: over the years, she recorded individual collections of works by major American songwriters such as Cole Porter, George and Ira Gershwin, Duke Ellington, Rodgers and Hart, and Jerome Kern. These recordings include *Ella Fitzgerald Sings Cole Porter* (MGV 4049), *Ella Fitzgerald Sings Rodgers and Hart Song Book, Vol. 1–2* (Verve 821579-2), and *Ella Fitzgerald Sings the George and Ira Gershwin Song Book* (Verve V-4029). Fitzgerald's work with Granz proved to be one of the longest and most successful collaborations of her career; he remained her manager until her death. *Jazz at the Philharmonic* helped maintain her top status in the jazz world, and the huge success of the songbooks' popular standards attracted a large, non-jazz audience.

Fitzgerald continued to record and perform for decades, despite health problems caused by diabetes. She often appeared at major jazz festivals, performing alongside other jazz greats such as Duke Ellington, Count Basie, Oscar Peterson, and Louis Armstrong. A prolific recording artist, she won her 13th Grammy Award in 1990 for her album *All That Jazz* (Fantasy/Pablo PAB2310938).

After her death on 15 June 1996, Fitzgerald's estate donated an extensive collection of music, photos, and memorabilia to be divided between the Library of Congress and the Smithsonian Institution. Over 2,000 photographs and 1,000 musical arrangements, including those by Nelson Riddle for the songbooks, were included as part of this collection.

See also Grammy Award; Jazz

For Further Reading

Gourse, Leslie (ed.). *The Ella Fitzgerald Companion: Seven Decades of Commentary*. New York: Schirmer Books, 1998.

Nicholson, Stephen. *Ella Fitzgerald: A Biography of the First Lady of Jazz*. New York: Charles Scribner's Sons, 1994.

Pleasants, Henry. *The Great American Popular Singers*. New York: Simon & Schuster, 1974.

Kristina Lampe Shanton

Fluxus

The Fluxus movement began in the 1960s as an attempt to explore and break down the boundaries between art and life. Many women were involved in the development of Fluxus, including Mieko (Chieko) Shiomi, Charlotte Moorman (1933–1991), Alison Knowles (b. 1933), and Yoko Ono (b. 1933).

The Fluxus philosophy was committed to creating a democratic art form in which all things could be art and anyone could be an artist, and the founders of the movement wished to dismantle the institutions of "high art" and "serious" culture. They felt that art was a matter of perception rather than production, and this removed the artist from the center of the art-making process. Overall,

Fluxus urged a creative engagement with the world and life itself. The methods used by Fluxus reflected egalitarian concerns. Fluxus was meant to be inexpensive, reproducible, and accessible to all. These ideas run counter to the general structure of the art world with its emphasis on art objects as commodities with intrinsic value. Proponents of Fluxus sidestepped the gallery and museum system by organizing their own exhibitions and concerts in other venues and by operating a mail-order service to distribute their work.

Composer John Cage was a major influence on the Fluxus artists, particularly his work exploring the codes of musical composition and notation. Cage felt that all music scores were coded instructions for action of one sort or another. The bulk of Fluxus production consists of written scores for performances. These brief and cryptic texts were intended for interpretation by anyone, and even though many contained musical references, few would be mistaken for a traditional piece of music. George Brecht's *Solo for Flute* (1962), for example, instructed the performer to take the instrument apart and put it back together again. Nam June Paik's *Solo for Violin* (1962) called for the instrument's complete destruction.

Sound was often an incidental element to the compositions, but more often the combination of visual and aural information was meant to draw attention to the process of its own creation. In other words, the performer was supposed to concentrate on the action at hand and clear the mind of other information. La Monte Young's *Piano Piece for David Tudor* (1960) required such focus in that the performer was asked to open the piano's keyboard cover without making any sound at all. This action is repeated until successfully completed or until the performer gives up trying. Yoko Ono asked the performer to record the sound of a stone growing older in *Tape Piece I* (1963).

Fluxus works spanned every scale from the intimate to the global. Mieko (Chieko) Shiomi sent letters to people all over the world asking them to perform her *Spatial Poem* (1965–1972) and send her some record of what they did to complete the piece. The composition was a series of scores about wind and gravity. The results were assembled on a map of the world. Shiomi also created *Disappearing Music for Face* (1964), a work that exists as a performance and as a film (1966) of a mouth that slowly stops smiling. Her *Cello Sonata* (1977) was performed by Charlotte Moorman on top of a 500-year-old Italian clock tower; yet another Shiomi work is *Music for Two Players II* (1963), in which the performers remain in a closed room for two hours, doing anything except speaking.

Alison Knowles (b. 1933) also produced numerous performance scores, including *Identical Lunch* (1969), which calls for mindfulness in the daily act of eating. Knowles also wrote poetry using found texts from a myriad of sources ranging from seed catalogs to travelogues. Knowles was married to Fluxus artist Dick Higgins, who published a number of books by Fluxus artists through his Something Else Press. Higgins was an artist as well as a writer, and he described the notion of interdisciplinary art in his *Statement on Intermedia* (1966). Higgins also created a series of works called *Danger Music*, the second of which required Knowles to shave his head before an auditorium of uneasy spectators.

Cellist Charlotte Moorman and video pioneer Nam June Paik collaborated on numerous performances that added an erotic element to music. Moorman played her cello in various states of undress and in unusual locales such as atop an army tank in *Guadalcanal Requiem* (1976). Moorman was arrested for performing Paik's *Opera Sextronique* (1967) in the nude.

Yoko Ono also created pieces that questioned the role of woman's body in art. For *Cut Piece* (1964), Ono invited members of the audience to cut away pieces of her clothing with scissors. Her "instruction" works were scores that yielded paintings or sculptures. Ono interpreted many of the scores herself and showed the results, but like all Fluxus scores, everyone was welcome to perform them.

See also Experimental Music; Performance Art

For Further Reading

Armstrong, Elizabeth, and Joan Rothfuss. (eds.). *In the Spirit of Fluxus*. Minneapolis, MN: Walker Art Center, 1993.

Stiles, Kristine, and Peter Selz. *Theories and Documents of Contemporary Art*. Berkeley: University of California Press, 1996.

Jeffery Byrd

Folk Music

Folk music survives because people sing folk songs—for themselves, their families, and their communities—at work or play, to comfort or amuse, to tell a story or to make others dance. While speaking of courtship, complaint, rebellion, tragedy, virtue, salvation, and ancestral legend, the songs have a truthfulness about them, even "On Top of Old Smokey," a caution against false-hearted lovers and courting too slow. In twentieth-century America, women were essential in folk music, from seminal figures and folklorists to the modern stars of festivals, television, and the pop charts.

Whether doomed or saved, foolish or brave, some mortal women became immortal characters in song. We learn of darling Clementine, the lamented daughter of an 1849 miner, and Sweet Betsy from Pike (a county in Missouri), who with her husband, Ike, journeyed overland to the California goldfields enduring tremendous hardships. John Henry's wife, Polly Ann, picked up the hammer when her husband died of overexertion. Frankie killed her man, Johnny, because he done her wrong. Among the women murdered by their men are the stabbed Pretty Polly and the trusting, deceived Omie Wise, who was drowned. Barbara Allen, whose song originated in Britain, died for love; while refusing to admit she loved Sweet Willie, he expired pining for her. She so regretted her hardheartedness that she died the next day to be with him. And there are many more: the golden-haired Aura Lee, the neglected Wildwood Flower who refused to be sorrowful, the prostitute who warned her sisters to avoid the House of the Rising Sun in New Orleans, and all the daring ladies who dressed up in soldier's or sailor's clothes to be with their sweethearts.

Because they are supposedly made and played by ordinary folks, folk songs have a handformed quality in structure and sound. But who are these ordinary people? "The folk," a term that has come under much scrutiny, are portrayed as those who know and make folk music in their daily life as part of their rural upbringing. The "folkies" are characterized as people who learn and create it in their leisure time as part of a suburban awakening. The activities of the second group have led to several notable folk music revivals, such as the one that began in the late 1950s that brought fame to Bob Dylan and Joan Baez (b. 1941) in the 1960s.

At a 1956 concert in Chicago, bluesman Big Bill Broonzy got a big laugh when he said, "All the songs I ever heard in my life was folk songs, I never heard horses sing none of 'em yet!" Although all humans may be folks, not all of their songs are folk. The ideal folk song has a rustic pedigree. No one knows who wrote it, it has a social rather than commercial function, it was learned orally (person to person, not from recordings or books), it carries traces of antiquity, and different versions of it can be found in widespread regions. Even though recordings and print sources have now largely replaced oral tradition, songs with none of these characteristics—such as Joni Mitchell's (b. 1943) "Both Sides Now," made a hit by Judy Collins (b. 1939)—are still considered folk because of their acoustic instrumentation, poetic yet descriptive imagery, and commentary on worldly experience.

Folk songs express cultural character and heritage. In American folk music's earthiness, history, powerful language, and underlying morality, one hears the ethnic roots of the continent's founders. Alongside the ballads from the U.K. that persisted in the United States in remote mountain regions are songs and influences from European settlers, African slaves, Mexican cowboys, Native Americans, and other peoples.

Children in pioneer and rural households who were raised on songs usually heard them from their mothers. It was primarily the women, house-bound and devoted to their families, who passed the songs to their offspring, some perhaps performing them for diligent, inquisitive folklorists looking for vestiges of preindustrial life. When the Library of Congress Music Division started an Archive of American Folk-Song in 1928, the drive to preserve folk songs was already hundreds of years old.

The folklorists' passion was to document traditional music and culture by doing field research and recordings, to catalog and publish their findings, and sometimes to act as promoters of certain musicians they met. Men pursued this vocation, notably John A. Lomax, who served as the Archives director, and his son, Alan Lomax, and so did women, for folklore was seen as an honorable pursuit for middle-class ladies and social workers. Olive Dame Campbell, a schoolteacher from North Carolina, inspired, guided, and co-wrote with prominent British folklorist Cecil Sharp on his research in the Appalachian Mountains during World War I. Maud Karpeles worked with them also and edited the manuscript. Other prominent folklorists were Dorothy Scarborough and the Canadians Helen Creighton and Edith Fowke. The quest was to preserve oral traditions in the face of encroaching modernity, as improvements in transportation diminished isolation, and as radio, phonographs, and movies replaced home singing. Even though the very technology collectors used to record the songs altered oral tradition forever, their work has been invaluable. Their archival documents have served to revitalize and enchant diverse cultures and audiences.

With few exceptions, before women were known as individual performers they were part of ensembles. The most famous of the countless singing families was the Carter Family, a trio from Virginia, the first star group in country music, who drew heavily from folk sources. Sara Carter (1899–1979) sang and played autoharp; her husband, A. P. Carter, sang and organized the repertoire. Sara's cousin Maybelle Carter (1909–1978), married to A. P.'s brother, played guitar in such a distinctive way—with the thumb playing the melody on the bass strings—that the style is now known as Carter Picking. The Carter Family's first hit was "Single Girl, Married Girl" ("a single girl she goes to the store and buys, a married girl she rocks the cradle and cries"), from their historic recording debut in 1927. The emotional content of their songs and solemn delivery inspired folk, country, and pop acts to draw from their repertoire.

As a "voice of the people," folk music can be effective in protest, rallying for social change. From Kentucky, Aunt Molly Jackson (1880–1969) was a singing union organizer whose father, first husband, son, and two brothers were either blinded or killed in the mines. Jackson brought national attention to the abominable living and working conditions of the coal miners. Her half-sister Sarah Ogun Gunning also sang of the miners' struggles and was prominent in the 1960s and 1970s at folk festivals; in the 1940s both took part in the first "hootenannies" (folk song gatherings), held in New York City's Greenwich Village.

The link between leftist politics and folk music is strong. Woody Guthrie wrote about the plight of workers and inscribed "This machine kills fascists" on his guitar, and demonstrators today still sing "We Shall Overcome" on the front lines. One of the people who helped transform that song from its black spiritual origins to the anthem of the civil rights movement was banjo-playing activist Pete Seeger. He helped found the Weavers, a singing quartet that included Lee Hays, Fred Hellerman, and the robust contralto of Ronnie Gilbert (b. 1946). In the early 1950s they caused a sensation with their folk song repertoire set to pop arrangements, achieving a dozen Top 30 hits. Many of the songs they composed, arranged, or introduced became hits for other artists, from the Beach Boys to Creedence Clearwater Revival. The approach and harmony blend of the Weavers influenced later groups, including Jefferson Airplane, which began as a folk-rock unit, first with Signe Anderson (b. 1941) and then with Grace Slick (b. 1939) as the featured woman vocalist. The Weavers' career took a nosedive owing to their leftist leanings during a period when communist sympathies were officially condemned. After a couple of years they managed to regain their popularity as a live act until splitting up in 1964. An emotional reunion occurred in 1980.

When the Kingston Trio's "Tom Dooley" became a number one pop hit in 1958, it signaled a massive folk revival, nonpolitical at first, which soon swept the country. Young people gathered in coffeehouses in the shadows of many great universities, finding a social alternative to conservative values and a musical alternative to the increasing corporate forces bent on turning rock and roll into a formulaic product for preteens. At the Newport Folk Festival the next year, Joan Baez made a stunning debut, having only limited club experience previously. She became a queen-like presence in folk, and by 1962 she was on the cover of *Time* magazine. Bob Dylan soon became king, inspired by Woody Guthrie as well as Odetta (b. 1930), a classically trained vocalist who sang folk and blues songs from her black heritage. Though Joan Baez popularized many traditional ballads and recorded whole albums of Dylan songs, her own "Diamonds and Rust," a hit in 1975 that reflected on her personal relationship with him, is a fine example of her composing skills. Dylan's initial fame came when Peter, Paul, and Mary, a prominent folk act

featuring the voice of Mary Travers (b. 1937), made a major hit of his song "Blowin' in the Wind."

Two important folk duos of the 1960s were married couples: Richard and Mimi Fariña, and Ian and Sylvia. Though Richard Fariña's career as a folksinger and novelist was cut short by accidental death, Mimi ([1945–2001] Joan Baez's sister) continued singing, founding Bread and Roses in 1974, an organization that brings free live music to people living in institutions around San Francisco. Ian and Sylvia Tyson, a Canadian duo praised for their harmony singing, influenced folk and rock singers with their style and compositions: Ian's "Four Strong Winds" was revived by Neil Young, and Sylvia's "You Were on My Mind" became a folk rock hit when done by the We Five, featuring the voice of Beverly Bivens. In the 1990s, Sylvia Tyson formed Quartette, an all-female Canadian folk supergroup.

Buffy Sainte-Marie (b. 1941) was born on a Canadian Cree Indian reserve and raised in New England. Her songs encompass native issues and love ballads, and among her best known are the antiwar "Universal Soldier" and "Until It's Time for You to Go" (made famous by Elvis Presley). Beyond music, her career includes a five-year stint on the children's television show *Sesame Street* with her young son, as well as internationally acclaimed digital artwork. Also from Canada came Joni Mitchell, whose soaring voice, superb compositions, and willingness to follow her own muse has taken her from folk to jazz and beyond, earning the highest respect from her fans and peers. Kate and Anna McGarrigle emerged in the 1970s with inimitable sister-duet harmonies that derive from Quebec folk heritage; their poetic compositions have been covered by Linda

Ronstadt (b. 1946) and Emmylou Harris (b. 1947).

The 1986 debut album of Michelle Shocked (b. 1962) was recorded around a campfire at a Texas folk festival. On her 1992 *Arkansas Traveler* album (Polygram 512101) she highlighted the musical legacy of blackface traditions, creatively reworking minstrel songs and fiddle tunes. Ani DiFranco (b. 1970), of Buffalo, NY, showed that an independent artist could achieve massive acclaim and retain artistic and marketing control over her output.

The phenomenal success of Lilith Fair, a series of festivals instigated in 1996 by Canadian singer-songwriter Sarah McLachlan (b. 1968), has increased the profile of women performers of many styles. Its stages have featured numerous excellent folk acts, including Suzanne Vega (b. 1959), Shawn Colvin (b. 1956), Tracy Chapman (b. 1964), and the Indigo Girls. Despite the information revolution, folk music continues as strong as ever, and women's involvement in it seems assured.

See also Ethnomusicology

For Further Reading

Bufwack, Mary A., and Robert K. Oermann. *Finding Her Voice: The Saga of Women in Country Music*. New York: Crown Publishers, 1993.

Cantwell, Robert. *When We Were Good: The Folk Revival*. Cambridge, MA: Harvard University Press, 1996.

Graves, Anna Hunt. *Folk*. New York: Friedman/Fairfax Publishers (Life, Times and Music Series), 1994.

Craig Morrison

Foundation for Contemporary Performance Arts, Inc.

The Foundation for Contemporary Performance Arts, Inc., is a grant-giving organization whose annual awards are presented to individuals, groups, and organizations in five fields: dance, music, performance art or theater, poetry, and the visual arts. Founded in 1963 by John Cage and Jasper Johns, the foundation was initially funded by the sale of artworks donated to the foundation by visual artists and the 1969 book *Notations*, edited by John Cage and Alison Knowles (b. 1933), containing manuscripts donated from over 250 composers.

Candidates for the grants are nominated by a group of anonymous artists and art professionals and reviewed by the foundation directors. Selections are made based on the quality and imaginativeness of the work; awards range from $20,000 to $25,000. Women composers awarded in the past have included Maryanne Amacher (b. 1946), Zeena Parkins, Mary Jane Leach, Pauline Oliveros (b. 1932), Lois V. Vierk (b. 1951), Meredith Monk (b. 1942), and Susan Botti.

Organizations that provide professional services or opportunities for artists to present their work may apply directly to the foundation for awards of between $1,000 and $5,000, given annually. Grants for Immediate Needs are awarded each year in response to requests from artists and organizations and are designed to give support for urgent situations related to a current project. The John Cage Award in Music, established in honor of the late composer and founding director of the foundation, is awarded biennially in recognition of "outstanding achievement in the field of contemporary music." The $50,000 award is based on selections from invited nominations.

See also Organizations, Performer; Prizes, Composer and Performer

For Further Reading

CPCC [The Center for the Promotion of Contemporary Composers]—*Opportunities for Composers*. Available: http://www.under.org/cpcc/opps.htm

Edelson, Phyllis (ed.). *Foundation Grants to Individuals*, 11th ed. New York: Foundation Center, 1999.

Judge, Mary A. (ed.). "Foundation for Contemporary Performance Arts, Inc. 1998." New York: Foundation for Contemporary Performance Arts, 1999.

Erin Gee

Franklin, Aretha (1942–)

Called the "Queen of Soul," Aretha Franklin is foremost pioneer of the genre. Although she began her career as a gospel singer, she sought a broader audience and a different creative outlet, rising to stardom in the late 1960s. Her compelling, original style blurred established musical and social boundaries. She blended gospel sincerity with earthy and streetwise qualities, and she found an audience among black and white listeners alike.

Franklin was born on 25 March 1942 in Memphis, TN, and moved with her family to Detroit at the age of two. Growing up in Detroit, Franklin's earliest inspiration was her father, the Reverend C. L. Franklin, a charismatic preacher on the gospel circuit with whom she traveled and performed, even as a child. The Franklin home was visited by numerous well-known gospel and blues musicians who gave the young singer an abundance of musical experiences. She learned to play the piano from gospel musician James Cleveland, and she was guided and encouraged by renowned gospel singers Mahalia Jackson (1911–1972) and Clara Ward (1924–1973). By the age of 18 she possessed a rich and powerful, yet flexible voice that could belt low notes and float high ones, providing her with an uncommon range of expression.

Striking out on her own, Franklin signed with Columbia Records in 1961. However, Atlantic Records was the company that gave her the opportunity to release her gutsy, authentic talents, and she became an instant success with her first hit, "I Never Loved a Man" (available on *Aretha in Paris*, Rhino 71852). Her 1967 number one hit "Respect" (Rhino 71852) is regarded today as an American classic. In the two years that followed, she was a major force in popular music with numerous hit songs. At the height of her popularity she returned to gospel music, winning Grammy Award honors in 1972 for the album *Amazing Grace* (Atlantic SD2-906-2). In 1980 she appeared to acclaim in the movie *The Blues Brothers* (Atlantic 82787).

Franklin has remained a prominent figure in American music for her contributions to the development of a distinctive soul style, and she is an acknowledged inspiration for singers such as Whitney Houston (b. 1963). The subject and star of a 1986 retrospective television program, in the 1990s Franklin drew large audiences to live performances. She is the first woman singer to be inducted into the Rock and Roll Hall of Fame, and she has earned a Grammy Award for Lifetime Achievement.

See also Gospel Music; Rock and Roll Hall of Fame

For Further Reading

Franklin, Aretha, and David Ritz. *Aretha: From These Roots*. New York: Villard Books, 1999.

Jones, Hettie. *Big Star Fallin' Mama: Five Women in Black Music*, rev. ed. New York: Viking, 1995.

O'Brien, Lucy. *She Bop: The Definitive History of Women in Rock, Pop and Soul*. London: Penguin Books, 1995.

Paula Elliot

Fraternities and Sororities, Professional

Professional fraternities and sororities are organizations that have long been popular on college and university campuses as a means of bringing together students with common academic interests, hobbies, and professional aspirations. Some of the most important professional music fraternities and sororities devoted to women are Sigma Alpha Iota, Mu Phi Epsilon, and Delta Omicron.

Sigma Alpha Iota (SAI) International Music Fraternity was founded on 12 June 1903 by seven students in the University of Michigan School of Music. The founders were Mary Storrs (Andersen), Elizabeth A. Campbell, Frances Caspari, Minnie Davis (Sherrill), Nora Crane Hunt, Leila Farlin (Laughlin), and Georgina Potts. The objectives of SAI are to form chapters of music students and musicians who "uphold the highest ideals of a music education, and to raise the standard of productive musical work among the women students of colleges, conservatories and universities." Currently (2002), its membership includes 191 active college chapters and 114 alumnae chapters throughout the United States. Delegates at Triennial National Conventions elect province and national officers.

The Sigma Alpha Iota Philanthropies, Inc., is the philanthropic arm of the fraternity. Its projects support the American composer, undergraduate and graduate scholarships, the Inter-American Music Awards, the Sigma Alpha Iota Cottage at the MacDowell Colony, and a summer internship program at the Kennedy Center. The official publication of Sigma Alpha Iota is *Pan Pipes*, which began publication in November 1909. *Pan Pipes* is published quarterly, with the winter issue primarily devoted to information about the most recent compositions of living American composers.

Professor Winthrop S. Sterling, dean of the College, and Elizabeth Mathias, a member of the faculty, founded Mu Phi Epsilon on 13 November 1903 at the Metropolitan College of Music in Cincinnati, OH. They initially considered associate membership in Phi Mu Alpha, a men's professional music fraternity, but decided instead to establish an organization to advance the cause of music in America and at the same time encourage friendship among young women through music. At the first meetings of the Alpha chapter, the constitution and bylaws were adopted and the design of the badge and shield were selected, along with the sorority's colors, flower, aims, and ideals. Within a month the sorority expanded with the installation of Beta Chapter at the New England Conservatory in Boston and Gamma Chapter at the University of Michigan School of Music at Ann Arbor.

In 1936 the sorority changed status from a national music sorority, as it was originally chartered, to an honor society. It evolved into a professional music sorority in 1944, after definitions of general, honor, and professional sororities were formulated and accepted by the National Conference on College Fraternities and Societies. Mu Phi Epsilon became international with the installation of Alpha Tau Chapter at the Philippine Women's University in Manila, Philippine Islands. In compliance with Title IX of the Education Amendments Act of 1972, the fraternity became coeducational in 1977. Today, Mu Phi Epsilon has 134 chapters in three countries, 75 alumni chapters, and more than 60,000 members.

Delta Omicron International Music Fraternity is a professional music fraternity with collegiate chapters established throughout the United States and abroad. Hazel Wilson, Lorena Creamer, and Mable Dunn, undergraduate students at the Cincinnati Conservatory of Music, founded the fraternity in 1909.

From 1909 to the present, 26 Delta Omicron national presidents have worked to achieve the fraternity's objectives. These objectives include promoting American music and musicians, increasing a community's enjoyment of music, and improving and serving the "ultimate welfare of musicians." Legislative powers sit in the International Conference, which meets triennially and is composed of elected and appointed officers, music representatives, and delegates from each collegiate and alumni chapter. An executive office is maintained in Jefferson City, TN. Membership is on the "basis of talent, scholarship and character, and is open to music students enrolled in schools with Delta Omicron chapters, to music faculty members in those schools, and to professional musicians." The Delta Omicron International Music Fraternity and Delta Omicron Foundation, Inc., provide support for scholarships, grants, and awards to Delta Omicron chapters and members in good standing.

See also Tau Beta Sigma

For Further Reading

Anson, Jack L., and Robert F. Marchesani, Jr. (eds.). *Baird's Manual of American College Fraternities*. Indianapolis: Baird's Manual Foundation, 1991.

Delta Omicron. *Delta Omicron International Music Fraternity*. Available: http://deltaomicron.people.virginia.edu/home.html

Sigma Alpha Iota. "Sigma Alpha Iota History." Available: http://www.sai-national.org

Stevens, Albert Clark (ed.). *Cyclopædia of Fraternities*. Detroit: Gale Research, 1966.

Ellen Grolman Schlegel

Fulbright Fellowship Program

Named for Senator J. William Fulbright of Arkansas, the Fulbright Fellowship Program supports artists with monetary remuneration for travel, research, and creative activities. In 1947 the first Fulbright Program grants were awarded by Board of Foreign Scholarships. The Board established three divisions for the program: (1) student grants for study abroad, (2) primary and secondary teachers, and (3) university lecturers and researchers. Within the first year 65 grants had been issued to Americans to work in four countries. By 1952, the number had grown to 1,200 grants to 21 countries; and by 1960, 1,700 grants to 38 countries. Today grants are being awarded for research and lecturing to over 130 countries, and many of these awards are granted to women.

Women who played significant roles in the development and evolution of the Fulbright Program include Sarah Gibson Blanding, president of Vassar College, and Helen C. White, an English scholar from the University of Wisconsin, both of whom served on the First Board of Foreign Scholarships. Rose Bampton of the Metropolitan Opera and Dorothy Liebes of Dorothy Liebes Textiles, Inc., served on the first committees for selecting grantees. Several women were instrumental in establishing and administering foreign binational commissions, including: Cipriana Scelba, Italy; Olive Reddick, India; Dorothy DeFlandre, Belgium; Karin Fennow, Denmark; and Lillian Penson, vice-chancellor of the University of London. Anna Hawkes, then president of the American Association of University Women, served on the initial review committee and witness panel that took the Fulbright Program through the revisions of the Fulbright-Hays Act of 1960. Higher standards of selection, placement, and administration resulted from the changes of this Act.

Since 1989, 44 women have been

Women Fulbright Award Winners in Music

Fulbright Awards	Recipient	Country of Research
1989–1990	Amy Barber	Czechoslovakia
	Sandra Mangsen	Italy
	Teresa Perez	El Salvador
	Cynthia Schmidt	Sierra Leone
1991–1992	Beth Bullard	India
	Kimberly Marshall	Australia
1992–1993	Donna Coleman	Australia
	Constance DeFotis	Germany
	Abby Raboinovitz	India
	Amy Rubin	Ghana
	Kathleen Spillane	Venezuela
	Glennis Stout	Taiwan
1993–1994	Laura Harris	Guinea, Mali, and Sierra Leone
	Roberta Marvin	Italy
	Catharine Melhorn	Ghana
	Karolyn Stonefelt	Ghana
	Jan Walters	France
1994–1995	Margaret Donovan-Jeffry	China
	Jan Swafford	Austria
	Nancy Van Deusen	Hungary
1995–1996	Judith Becker	India and Sri Lanka
	Sharon Girard	Venezuela
	Glenda Goss	Finland
	Cynthia Kimberlin	Ethiopia
	Joyce Lindorff	China
	Jane Perera	Bolivia
	Susan Wheatley	Austria
	Katherine Wolfe	Bolivia
1996–1997	Isabelle L. Ganz	Israel
	Kay Kraeft	Bolivia
	Amy Lin	Brazil
1997–1998	Christine Getz	Italy
	Carol Hess	Spain
	Carol Marsh	Austria
1998–1999	Susan Berdahl	Honduras
	Susan Boynton	Italy
	Severine Neff	Russia
	Anne K. Rasmussen	Indonesia
	Nancy Walker	Germany
1999–2000	Ana Cervantes	Mexico
	Linda Maxey	Lithuania
	Cecelia H. Porter	Austria
	Kristin Olson Rao	India
	Sarah Ellen Smith	Botswana

awarded Fulbright Scholar Awards. A few examples of the types of research are as follows: Cecelia Porter, "Critical Assessments of Music by Women Composers in Vienna 1910–60"; Anne Rasmussen, "The Performance and the Experience of Holy Qur'an in Indonesia"; Judith Becker, "Relationship of Music and Trance in the Exorcist Rituals of the Sanni Demons of Sri Lanka and the Sofi Islamic Sama' of North India"; and Laura Harris, "Women, Marriage and Songs at Marriage among the Sankaran Maninka of West Afrika."

See also Prizes, Composer and Performer; Publication Awards

For Further Reading

CIES: Council for International Exchange of Scholars. Available: http://www.iie.org/cies/

Stephen J. Rushing

Fullman, Ellen (1957–)

Ellen Fullman—composer, sound artist, visual artist, teacher, and musical instrument inventor—has been one of the foremost experimental musicians of the last decade of the twentieth century. She has received fellowships from the New York Foundation for the Arts, a Visual Artists Fellowship in New Genres, an Interarts Artist's Project Grant, and a Meet the Composer Commission. The Los Angeles *Times* assesses Fullman quite well: "Paradoxically, her music is both intense and serene. The attractively eerie, acoustically unstable droning suggests urgency, while the slow formal development of the piece invites an intuitive, suspended-intellect sort of hearing."

Born in 1957 in Memphis, TN, she got an early start: her music career began "at the age of one, when Elvis Presley kissed her hand." Fullman received a B.F.A. in sculpture from the Kansas City Art Institute. Since then she has performed around the world on a musical instrument she invented, the Long String Instrument. Her work has been presented at the Kitchen, the Clocktower, and P.S. 122 in New York City; Mills College; the Walker Art Center in Minneapolis; L.A.C.E., Los Angeles; Wesleyan University; the ISCM Festival in Munich; Kunstlerhaus Bethenien, Berlin; Kunstverein, Stuttgart; and the Stedelijk Museum in Amsterdam. Between 1986 and 1989, Fullman, on a Meet the Composer Commission, worked with choreographer Deborah Hay in Austin, TX, on an extended collaboration entitled *The Man Who Grew Common in Wisdom*. Her recordings include *Suspended Music* (DLB-CD-8), *Body Music* (EF-CD-1), and *Change of Direction* (New Albion 102).

Fullman currently teaches classes in composition in her studio, "The Candy Factory." She also leads sound meditations there. She performs on her home-made instrument, the Long String Instrument, in which perfectly-in-tune wires up to 85 feet long are stroked as the performer walks along the length of the instrument. The wires are excited along their *longitudinal* modes—they vibrate along their lengths, rather than "up and down" as in a piano or violin, creating haunting melodies and textures in just intonation.

See also Experimental Music

For Further Reading

Hopkin, Bart, and Ellen Fullman. "The Long String Instrument Designed and Built by Ellen Fullman." *Experimental Musical Instruments* 1/2 (1985): 4–7.

Hovancsek, Mike. "Ellen Fullman's Long String Instrument." *Experimental Musical Instruments* 13/3 (1998): 28–30.

The Long String Instrument Home Page. Available: http://www.artcars.com/LSI/ellenhome

Colby Leider

G

Galás, Diamanda (1955–)

Diamanda Galás is a composer, performer, and activist. Her voice has been called "awesome," "frightening," and "angry." Her musical influences include Greek and Middle Eastern music, country, blues, gospel, jazz, classical, electronic, and rock music. Her music is often politically charged, and she possesses a powerful, primitive sound.

Born in 1955 in San Diego, CA, Galás began her musical training at the age of five, on the piano, and later accompanied her father's gospel choir. Galás made her classical debut with the San Diego Symphony performing Ludwig van Beethoven's Piano Concerto no. 1 when she was 14 years old. She began studying voice during college, and she earned bachelors and masters degrees from the University of California at San Diego (UCSD). While attending UCSD, Galás began experimenting with multiple microphones in quadraphonic space, creating such pieces as *Eyes without Blood* and *Wild Women with Steak Knives*. She used nontraditional and operatic vocal techniques, including simultaneously emitted multiphonic and *bel canto* vibrato production,

naturally produced octave transposition in speaking, inhaled screaming, and other extreme vocal techniques that she created through experimentation and improvisation. Her breakthrough performance came in 1979 when composer Vinko Globokar cast her as the lead in *Un Jour Comme Un Autre*, an opera based on Amnesty International reports about a Turkish woman torture victim who allegedly committed treason.

In the early 1980s Galás began performing her own compositions, including *Wild Women with Steak Knives* and *Tragouthia Apo to Aima Exoun Fonos* ("Song from the Blood of Those Murdered"). Her first album, *The Litanies of Satan* (Mute 71419-2), from the Charles Baudelaire text of the same name, was released in 1982 and re-released in 1989 by Mute Records.

Diamanda Galás was deeply affected by personal events when her brother, poet and playwright Philip Dimitri Galás, contracted HIV (he died in 1986 from complications of AIDS). On the fingers of her left hand are tattooed the words "We are all HIV+." Much of her creative output has centered on AIDS awareness. In 1983 she began working on

Diamanda Galás. *Photo by Austin Young © 2001.*

perhaps her best-known composition, *Plague Mass* (originally titled *Masque of the Red Death* after Edgar Allen Poe)—a trilogy with texts from the Bible, including Leviticus, Job, Revelation, and the Psalms. The three movements are entitled *The Divine Punishment, Saint of the Pit,* and *You Must Be Certain of the Devil.* The composition premiered on New Year's Day 1989 at the Queen Elizabeth Hall, London. In 1989 she and several

ACT UP (AIDS Coalition to Unleash Power) members were arrested at St. Patrick's Cathedral in New York City for participating in a "Die-In" to protest Cardinal John O'Connor's anti-homosexual statements. In October 1990 she performed the revised and expanded version of the *Plague Mass*, stripped to the waist and covered in "blood," featuring *There Are No More Tickets to the Funeral* at the Cathedral of Saint John the

Divine in New York. In 1990 Galás was denounced by a member of the Italian government for committing blasphemy against the Roman Catholic Church. *Vena Cava*, the companion composition to the *Plague Mass*, premiered in 1992 and examined the correlation of clinical depression and AIDS dementia.

Other important works include *Insekta*, *Schrei X Live/Schrei 27* (Mute 69037), and *Malediction and Prayer* (Asphodel 984). In 1996 Galás's first book, *The Shit of God*, was published. A leader in experimental composition and performance, Diamanda Galás was awarded Ford Foundation and Meet the Composer grants and has performed around the world, including festivals at Donaueschingen, Inventionen, Biennale de Paris, Musica Oggi, and Festivale de la Voce. Mute Records distributes her recordings.

See also Experimental Music; Music Technology

For Further Reading

Gaar, Gillian G. *She's a Rebel: The History of Women in Rock and Roll.* Seattle: Seal Press, 1992.

Galás, Diamanda. "Intravenal Song." *Perspectives of New Music* 20 (Fall/Winter 1981): 59–62.

Kristine H. Burns

Ganz, Isabelle

Mezzo-soprano Isabelle Ganz is an international performer and recording artist of Sephardic and contemporary music. Ganz is known as a champion of contemporary music and has premiered many works, including John Cage's *Ryoanji* for voice and percussion written for her and percussionist Michael Publiese.

Born in New York and a child prodigy on piano, she performed with the New York Philharmonic by age 10 and majored in flute at the High School of Music and Arts. Ganz began singing in college and specialized in both contemporary classical music and Sephardic music. She studied in Houston with Stephen Harbachick and Lois Alba, at the Juilliard School with Lotta Leonard, and with Jan DeGaetani (1933–1989) and Leonard Treash at the Eastman School of Music, where she earned a D.M.A. in voice and music literature (1980). Ganz received additional training at the School of Sacred Music of Hebrew Union-College and subsequently sang as a cantor in the United States, Canada, and Germany.

Ganz founded the Sephardic music ensemble Alhambra in 1981. Researching, collecting, and arranging the songs of native Sephardic singers (descendents of the Jews of Spain), she has as a goal the preservation of this Jewish heritage. She works closely with other ethnomusicologists who transcribe fieldwork of Sephardic music, providing arrangements for Alhambra based on her research. A renewed worldwide interest in Sephardic music generated tours in diverse countries, including the United States, Lithuania, Turkey, Columbia, Canada, Great Britain, and Spain. The ensemble's recordings include *The Joy of Judeo-Spanish Music* (Koch Schwann 1196), *Alhambra Performs Judeo-Spanish Songs* (Global Village 108), and *The Art of Judeo-Spanish Song* (Global Village 127). Ganz uses various instruments such as dumbek, recorders, lyre, piano, guitar, flute, krummhorns, and shepherd's shawm in her performances.

Isabelle Ganz divides her time touring as a singer, arranging music, making recordings, and teaching. She received a Fulbright Grant in 1997 to teach and to give master classes at the Rubin Academy of Music and Dance at Tel Aviv University and to research Sephardic music at the Jewish Music Research Centre at Hebrew University. She has also received a

National Endowment for the Arts Solo Recitalist Grant and toured throughout the United States in colleges, universities, and conservatories. Ganz won first prize of the Lind Solo Song Award sponsored by Cornell University in 1989 for her composition *Go Away Tango*. She toured with classical guitarist Sharon Isbin in duet recitals, appearing at the Frick Collection, the 92nd Street Y, the Vermont Mozart Festival, the Grand Teton Music Festival, and Aspen, as well as in Greece, Romania, and Korea.

She has performed with the Houston Ballet in *The Cruel Garden* and traveled extensively, giving recitals of contemporary music in Europe, Israel, and the United States. Isabelle Ganz's contemporary music recordings include *Dancer in a Garden*, *Three Songs of Pablo Neruda*, *Sundown Voyager*, *Sequenza*, and *Ryoanji*. She appeared with orchestras such as the Brooklyn Philharmonic, Seattle Symphony, and Slovak Radio Orchestra. Her compact disc *Composers of the Holocaust* (Leonarda LE342) features ghetto songs from Warsaw, Vilna, and Terezín. Ganz currently lives in Amsterdam and Houston, TX.

See also Jewish Musicians

For Further Reading

Ganz, Isabelle. *Isabelle Ganz: Mezzo Soprano*. Available: http://pws.prserv.net/usinet.lipschu/Isabelle.htm

Judith S. Pinnolis

Garage Rock and Heavy Metal Bands

All-women and women-dominated garage rock and heavy metal bands in the United States faced uphill battles for acceptance similar to those experienced by their pop-rock counterparts. The huge stateside success of glam-metal artist Joan Jett (b. 1960) in the 1980s proved the exception rather than the rule—though strong inroads, particularly among women-dominated mixed-gender garage-style indie-rock groups, would be blazed during the following decade. Accurately describing acts of this type is difficult (Babes in Toyland, L7, and Veruca Salt exhibit elements of both genres), but definite tendencies can be noted.

Bassist and vocalist Suzi Quatro's (b. 1950) career proved seminal to women's garage rock and heavy metal bands. Joined by sisters Patti and Arlene, she founded the Pleasure Seekers, one of few all-women garage acts during that movement's heyday in the 1960s. They released the single "Never Thought You'd Leave Me," which attained regional notoriety in their native Detroit. Despite constant touring, including a 1967 United Service Organization (USO) stint in Vietnam, the group never achieved national visibility. By 1971 the band had been renamed Cradle and another sister, Nancy, had replaced Arlene. At this time producer Mickie Most discovered Suzi and persuaded her to leave the ailing outfit and pursue a solo career in Britain. Initially backed by an all-men trio and assuming both a tough leatherette persona and glam-influenced metal style, she mellowed her approach and image in subsequent years. She enjoyed a profitable run in her adopted country that spanned 11 albums over a 17-year period and saw such hits in the United Kingdom as "Can the Can," "48 Crash," and "Devil Gate Drive." Success in her native land proved more elusive, but the single "Stumblin' In" (a duet with Chris Norman) did reach the U.S. Top 40 in 1978.

Quatro's work in the 1970s heavily influenced subsequent women metal rockers, particularly two alumnae of the Runaways, Joan Jett and Lita Ford (b.

1958). Jett, supported by the all-men Blackhearts, was one of the most commercially successful artists of the day. Her music, showing elements of punk, pop, and glam-rock, charted extremely well, reaching the U.S. Top 20 with "I Hate Myself for Loving You" and "Little Liar" as well as covers of "Crimson and Clover" and "Do You Wanna Touch Me." Her biggest hit, an anthemic version of the Arrows' song "I Love Rock and Roll," was one of the best-selling singles in 1982. Jett released nine albums, most notably *Bad Reputation* (Blackheart JJ 707-2), *I Love Rock and Roll* (Blackheart JJ 747-2), *Album* (Blackheart 371809), and *Glorious Results of a Misspent Youth* (Blackheart 371810). In the 1990s she expanded her considerable influence on women's bands by working closely as producer and performer with metal artists L7 and the Riot Grrrl group Bikini Kill.

Lita Ford's career was both slower to develop and less spectacular, but it saw two successful singles, "Kiss Me Deadly" and "Close My Eyes Forever" (the latter a duet with Ozzy Ozbourne). Of her six albums, the most successful were *Dancin' on the Edge* (Mercury 818864-2), *Lita* (Dreamland 6397-2-R11), and *Stiletto* (RCA 2090-2-R). Like Jett and Quatro, she fronted an all-men group and her heavy metal sound exhibited glam-rock touches.

The notoriety enjoyed by Quatro, Jett, and Ford unfortunately did not transfer to their all-women metal sisterhood; such bands generally received critical rather than popular notice and tended to have short careers. This was owing partly to a tendency for some of the genre's listeners—men and women—to embrace a sexist worldview: note such fans' suspicions of the rock-worthiness of women metal artists (witness the snide nickname

"Bimbo Monkees" appended to the all-women band Vixen) while vociferously cheering their all-men counterparts decked out in makeup, spandex, and elaborate hairdos.

The Los Angeles club scene was home to some of these distaff metal outfits, such as the glam-influenced quintet Precious Metal. Consisting of Leslie Wasser (vocals), Mara Fox (guitar), Janet Robin (guitar), Alex Rylance (bass), and Carol Control (drums), they released three albums—*Right Here, Right Now* (Mercury 826146-1), *That Kind of Girl* (Chameleon D2-74753), and *Precious Metal* (Chameleon D2-74834)—before splitting up. The aforementioned Vixen, a sleek pop-metal migrant from St. Paul, MN, recorded two albums—*Vixen* (EMI America E2-46991) and *Rev It Up* (EMI America E2-92923) with a lineup including vocalist Janet Gardner, guitarist Jan Kuehnemund, bassist Share Pederson, and drummer Roxy Petrucci—and folded soon afterwards. A revived version of the group, joining Gardner and Petrucci with Gina Stile, put out the compact disc *Tangerine* (CMC International 86246). The Clams, a Minneapolis band influenced by the Rolling Stones and New York Dolls, lasted for one album, *Exile on Lake Street* (CD Imaginary). Its members were Cindy Lawson (voice), Roxie Terry (guitar), Patty Janson (bass), and Karen Cusak (drums). More successful was L7, an overtly feminist punk-metal act with ties to the grunge and Riot Grrrl scenes. Also hailing from Los Angeles, its members were guitarists Suzy Gardner and Donita Sparks, bassist Jennifer Finch, and drummer Dee Plakas. Unlike other such groups, they charted with "Pretend We're Dead" and their albums *L7* (Epitaph 86401-2), *Smell the Magic* (Sub Pop SP79B), *Bricks Are Heavy* (Slash 2-26784), *Hungry for Stink* (Slash/

Reprise 45624), and *Beauty Process: Triple Platinum* (Warner Brothers 46327) sold well. They also founded Rock for Choice, a concert-presenting organization that raised funds to support women's reproductive rights.

The classic garage-rock genre of the 1960s including such groups as ? and the Mysterians, the Standells, and Shadows of Knight, was (despite the Quatro sisters' efforts) almost exclusively a male enclave. Garage rock did exercise strong posthumous influence through its rerelease on the Nuggets and Pebbles record series, providing a blueprint for American indie-rock and spawning a modest revival of the style in the 1980s. The most important all-women exponent of this revival was the band the Pandoras, a Los Angeles–based act. The one constant in this star-crossed band's variable lineup was singer/guitarist Paula Pierce. After releasing a debut EP and two albums, *It's about Time* (VOXX 2021) and *Stop Pretending* (Rhino RNLP-70857), their big break collapsed, resulting in the shelving of a third completed album. They continued for a few more years, recording *Live Nymphomania* (Restless 72318-2) and another EP before folding after Pierce's death in 1991.

Garage-inflected all-women indie-rock groups enjoyed slightly more visibility, achieving cult or critical successes and influencing the Riot Grrrls movement of the 1990s. One of the earliest groups was Ut, founded amid New York's no-wave scene in 1978. Consisting of Nina Canal, Jacquie Ham, and Sally Young, its members' penchant for trading instruments between songs was partly responsible for the band's primitive, noisy sound. They finally released their first of four proper albums, *Conviction*, eight years after forming, followed by *Early Live Life* and *In Gut's House* (Blast First BFFP 17); they

disbanded shortly after the release of their last disc, *Griller* (Blast First 36).

Founded in 1985, the unpretentious, outspokenly feminist Scrawl experienced notoriety more quickly, recording the albums *Plus, Also, Too* (Rough Trade ROUGH-US 64), *He's Drunk* (Rough Trade ROUGH-US 51C), and *Smallmouth* (Rough Trade 76). Founded in Columbus, OH, the all-women trio consisted of guitarist Marcy Mays, bassist Sue Harshe, and drummer Carolyn O'Leary. After O'Leary's departure the outfit added a male drummer and released two more compact discs, *Velvet Hammer* (Simple Machines 20) and *Travel on Rider* (Elektra 61934).

Also known for their no-nonsense women's empowerment lyrics, San Francisco's short-lived Frightwig provided a clear blueprint for grunge rock with their abrasive, bass-dominated sound. Initially a trio consisting of Mia (guitar), Deanna (bass), and Cecilia (drums), they released the album *Cat Farm Faboo* (Subterranean) and then expanded to a quartet for *Faster, Frightwig, Kill! Kill!* (Caroline 1334).

Lunachicks, a neo-Ramones-style New York act tinged with performance art elements, featured Theo Kogan (lead singer) frequently decked out in blood-splashed gowns or similar regalia backed initially by the tumultuous foursome of Squid (bass), Gina (guitar), Sindi (guitar), and Becky (drums). The titles of five of their albums, *Babysitters on Acid* (Blast First 52), *Binge Purge* (Plan9/Caroline 2107), *Jerk of All Trades* (Go Kart 13), *Pretty Ugly* (Go Kart 34), and *Luxury Problem* (Go Kart 51), mirrored the group's gleefully squalling approach.

Massachusetts-based Salem 66 opted for a more sedate jangle-pop and folk-based sound. This changeable-member group began as an all-women trio (Judy Grunwald, Beth Kaplan, and Susan Merriam) but, like Scrawl, later added male players. This prolific band released a self-titled EP in 1984 with its original threesome, followed by five non-compilation albums, *A Ripping Spin* (1985), *Frequency and Urgency* (1987), *Natural Disasters, Natural Treasures* (1988), *Something's Rockin' in Denmark* (1988), and *Down the Primrose Path* (1990) before disbanding.

Babes in Toyland, from Minneapolis, with founding members guitarist Kat Bjelland, bassist Michelle Leon, and drummer Lori Barbero, received critical acclaim as a result of touring with the bands Sonic Youth and Faith No More. They released an EP and four albums, *Spanking Machine* (Twin/Tone 89 183), *Fontanelle* (Reprise 2-26998), *Painkiller* (Warner Brothers 45339), and *Nemesisters* (Reprise 45868)—the last exhibiting a heavy metal approach.

Women-dominated mixed-gender groups fared better. The most celebrated of these groups was Hole, a Los Angeles–founded, Seattle-based act flamboyantly fronted by singer/guitarist Courtney Love that was closely allied with the Seattle grunge scene. This group was formed in 1989, and its small but visible catalog contained two best-selling albums, *Pretty on the Inside* (Caroline CAROL-1710-2) and *Live through This* (DGC 24631); their single "Doll Parts" attained modest chart success.

Boston was home to two such bands, Throwing Muses and the Blake Babies. The Blake Babies released three full albums, *Nicely Nicely* (Mammoth 86), *Earwig* (Mammoth MR-0016-2), and *Sunburn* (Mammoth MR-0022-2), featuring vocalist/bassist Juliana Hatfield's breathy, confessional singing backed by a ringing pop guitar sound. Their brief existence ended when Hatfield went solo in 1991. Conversely, Throwing Muses had an especially lengthy career spanning the period 1983 to 1997; its most visible members were stepsisters Kristin Hersh (b. 1966) and Tanya Donelly. Although this band's work was often harsh and intense-sounding, it could also be more melodically oriented, even pop-like. Noteworthy albums from their sizable catalog included a self-titled debut (4AD 292), *House Tornado* (4AD/Sire 2-25710), *The Real Ramona* (4AD/Sire 2-26489), and *University* (Sire/Reprise 945796).

Pixies bassist Kim Deal joined Donelly in founding the Dayton, OH, group the Breeders in 1990 (Deal's twin sister, Kelley, signed on in 1992). Showing kinship to the lo-fi movement, their music was a unique and raw pop version of indie-rock. Their two proper albums, *Pod* (4AD/Elektra 61331-2) and *Last Splash* (4AD/Elektra 61508), attracted significant attention and spawned a charting single, "Cannonball." By 1992 Donelly had severed ties with both groups to form Belly, a successful Providence, RI, alternative pop act. During the band's short run, they released two brisk-selling albums, *Star* (Sire/Reprise 45187) and *King* (Sire/Reprise 45833), and three EPs; they also reached the charts with "Feed the Tree."

Chicago's Veruca Salt played music veering from harmony-laden, bubblegum-oriented power pop (though setting disturbing lyrics) to metal-oriented rock. Their work, including two full compact discs, *American Thighs* (Minty Fresh 7) and *Eight Arms to Hold You* (Outpost 30001), found significant chart success (particularly via the single "Seether") but generated little critical appeal. Singer/guitarists Louise Post and Nina Gordon headed up this band, which ended in 1998. Concrete Blonde, formed in 1982, was the oldest of these groups. Originally named Dream 6, their roots were grounded in the Los Angeles punk scene that produced X and the Go-Go's, though Concrete Blonde's independent attitude scared off record labels until 1986, when their eponymous debut was released. Four further albums, *Free* (IRS X2-13001), *Bloodletting* (IRS X2-13037), *Walking in London* (IRS X2-13137), and *Mexican Moon* (IRS 81129), followed, as did a Top-20 single, "Joey." Fronted by vocalist/bassist Johnette Napolitano, their style ranged from post-punk to polished garage rock to Hispanic influences. Mention should also be made of indie-rock stars Sonic Youth; although not the dominant force in this band, singing-songwriting bassist Kim Gordon was a highly visible presence and proved a direct inspiration for many of these acts.

Other U.S. groups, either all-women or mixed-gender, in these styles included Dickless, Gut Bank, Stone Zoo, STP, and Vomit Launch.

See also Indie-Rock; Rock and Popular Music Genres; Underground

For Further Reading

Dunn, Jancee. "True Confessions: Alternative Sounds." In *Trouble Girls: The Rolling Stone Book of Women in Rock*, ed. Barbara O'Dair. New York: Random House, 1997.

Gaar, Gillian G. "Step into the Future." In *She's a Rebel: The History of Women in Rock and Roll*. Seattle: Seal Press, 1992 363–435.

McDonnell, Evelyn. "Rebel Grrrls." In *Trouble Girls: The Rolling Stone Book of Women in Rock*, ed. Barbara O'Dair. New York: Random House, 1997.

David Cleary

García, Adelina

During the 1940s singer Adelina García was one of the leading performers of the *bolero*, a song form popular throughout Latin America, and she made several highly successful recordings including *Desesperadamente*, *Vereda tropical*, *Mi tormento*, *Perfidia*, and *Frenesí*. At different points in her career García performed at Los Angeles venues such as the Mason, Maya, and Million Dollar theaters. Interestingly, after achieving international acclaim for her Columbia recording in Los Angeles, García toured Brazil before touring Mexico. On the Brazilian tour she was featured with the highly popular Mexican composer Gonzalo Curiel, who also performed on piano and directed an accompanying orchestra.

Adelina García was born in Phoenix, AZ, but she lived in Juárez, in the state of Chihuahua, Mexico, from the age of three to 13, after which she returned to Phoenix in 1937. In 1939 she moved to Los Angeles, where she began to perform on live radio and to record on the Columbia label. In 1944 García arrived in Mexico City, where she was warmly received by the public. She worked with numerous composers and various artists including Curiel, Mario Ruiz Armengol, Juan Garcia Esquivel, and José Alfredo Jiménez. In Mexico City she sang extensively on live radio, notably radio station XEW, and also began to record for RCA Victor. In Brazil she recorded on the Odeón label, a subsidiary of Capitol Records. García also toured extensively in Cuba, Argentina, and many other Latin American countries, in addition to California and the southwestern United States. In Mexico she also appeared in singing roles in three motion pictures. In 1955 García returned to Los Angeles and two years later married José Heredia, a professional musician active in Los Angeles. Performing only for a few special events in the ensuing years, she dedicated herself to her family, which included three sons, one of whom (Joey Heredia) became a highly recognized drummer in the 1980s.

See also Latin American Musicians; Multicultural Musics

For Further Reading

Loza, Steven. *Barrio Rhythm: Mexican American Music in Los Angeles*. Urbana and Chicago: University of Illinois Press, 1993.

Steve Loza

Garland, Judy (1922–1969)

Judy Garland was one of the most important singers on stage and in movie musical history during the first half of the twentieth century. Her long career began in vaudeville and continued through both stage and film. Her two daughters—Liza Minnelli (b. 1946) and Lorna Luft (b. 1952)—have both followed in their mother's famous footsteps. Because of her vivacious attitude, wholesome persona, and song stylings, Garland's legacy as an entertainer is one that will never be equaled.

Judy Garland was born on 10 June 1922 in Grand Rapids, MN, as Frances Ethel Gumm to aspiring vaudeville performers. The three Gumm daughters (Mary Jane, Virginia, and Frances) began performing regularly at the family's theater and in outlying areas, but the youngest, Frances "Baby" Gumm, was the exceptional performer of the trio. The family moved to Los Angeles, CA, in 1926 hoping to further their careers in vaudeville and expand into movies.

While performing at the 1934 Chicago World's Fair, the Gumm Sisters replaced another act performing at the Oriental Theater. George Jessel introduced them as the "Garland" sisters, a change that was quickly adopted by the group. The girls changed their first names as well. Mary Jane became "Suzy," Virginia became "Jimmy," and Frances chose the name "Judy," after the Hoagy Carmichael song of the same name.

Garland auditioned for Metro-Goldwyn-Mayer (MGM) in 1935 and

Judy Garland during an appearance on the *Jack Paar Show* in the early 1960s. *Photo courtesy of NBC/Globe Photos.*

was signed for a seven-year contract starting at $100 per week. The trio broke up, and Judy's solo career began. In 1936 MGM teamed her up with Deanna Durbin (b. 1921) in the movie short *Every Sunday*. Judy's breakthrough performance came in 1937 with *Broadway Melody of 1938* (available on Sound of the Movies 3106) when she sang "You Made Me Love You" to a picture of actor Clark Gable. She also performed with Mickey Rooney in several MGM movies, including *Thoroughbreds Don't Cry* ([1937] available on Sound of the Movies 3108), *Love Finds Andy Hardy* (1938), and *Babes in Arms* ([1939] Sandy Hook 2077). Garland won the coveted role of Dorothy Gale in *The Wizard of Oz* ([1939] MGM

E-3464), for which she received an honorary Oscar as Outstanding Juvenile Performer, and the song, "Over the Rainbow," became her lifelong signature tune.

Beginning in the late 1940s, Garland had a series of breakdowns and attempted suicide several times over the following decades. She was replaced in several MGM films, and her contract was dropped in 1950. Garland accepted an invitation to perform at the London Palladium in 1951; this was followed by a resurgence in her career with performances in New York at the Palace and years later at Carnegie Hall, for which she won two Grammy Awards.

Following a four-year absence from acting, she returned in 1954 to play the lead role in *A Star Is Born* (1954), for which she received her first Oscar nomination as Best Actress. In the years that followed she continued acting with small parts in movies including *Judgement at Nuremberg* (1961), for which she was nominated for another Oscar for Best Supporting Actress. From 1963 to 1964 she starred in her own television variety series, *The Judy Garland Show* (CBS).

Even though her professional life was filled with successes, feelings of inadequacy plagued her. Dependency on alcohol and diet and sleeping pills took their toll. Her last concert appearance was in Copenhagen, Denmark. She died at the age of 47 of a drug overdose on 22 June 1969 in London.

See also Musical Theater

For Further Reading

Clarke, Gerald. *Get Happy: The Life of Judy Garland*. New York: Random House, 2000.

Frank, Gerold. *Judy*. New York: Harper and Row, 1975.

Shipman, David. *Judy Garland: The Secret Life of an American Legend*. New York: Hyperion, 1992.

Torme, Mel. *The Other Side of the Rainbow*. New York: William Morrow, 1970.

Kristine H. Burns

Geisman, Eleanor

See Allyson, June

Gender and Curricula

Music is one of the last disciplines to attempt a culturally pluralistic transformation in gender and curricula. This is true for pre- through postsecondary education in the United States. Until Roberta Lamb (b. 1952) designed the *Women Composers Curriculum Project* for American middle school students, she could find no nonsexist curriculum guides in music, though several such guides exist for other subjects, at both elementary and high school levels. At the university level, culturally pluralistic, gender-inclusive curricular work was finally being developed at the end of the twentieth century.

Ethnomusicology. Ethnomusicologists have shown a serious commitment to studying works and traditions that the dominant musical canon has excluded. Ethnomusicologist Ellen Koskoff (b. 1943) helped to break ground for beginning explorations of gender issues in her field by editing a collection of essays entitled *Women and Music in Cross-Cultural Perspective*. Koskoff examined the cross-cultural experiences of women through exploring two central questions: "First, to what degree does a society's gender ideology and resulting gender-related behaviors affect its musical thought and practice? And second, how does music function in society to reflect or affect inter-gender relations?" (Koskoff, 1).

Musicology. Musicologists, on the other hand, have made more progress in addressing gender issues. In response to the famous question often asked in music history classes—"Where were all of the women?"—feminist musicologists, in particular, have created new ways of studying and highlighting both the musical contributions of women and the musical limitations placed on women by society. Some of these limitations were, and continue to be, lack of access to education and employment, lack of childcare combined with household responsibilities, lack of recognition, lack of access to public performance opportunities, and blatant discrimination. These exclusions, especially from education and contact with colleagues, discouraged women from developing as composers. Therefore, few women have appeared in the standard music history textbooks.

Feminist Musicology. Through the study of these contributions of (or limitations placed on) women musicians and composers, feminist musicologists have created new ways of thinking about topics in music history. Instead of focusing on a series of "great" musical works through a European male–defined history, aspects of power and control over women musicians and compositions by women are being investigated. Specifically, the concepts of "greatness" and "genius" in music are being interrogated as to their appropriateness when considering compositions by women. Instead of "greatness" or "genius," feminist scholars are seeking a cultural interpretation of music and music making. Wishing to view music based more on its social function, they look directly at music in its context, rather than seeking innate meaning in the music itself. These new approaches to music history have been considered a threat to the entire foundation of the discipline of music, but the

changes can also be considered complementary to earlier modes of thought and methods of inquiry.

Queer Theory. Queer theory is developing more rapidly, led by the first collection of lesbian and gay musicological essays, *Queering the Pitch* (Brett, Wood, and Thomas, 1994). The preface points out much common ground with feminist musicology: "The concern in this book, then, is less with identities than with representations, performances, and roles. Its emphasis is on throwing into question old labels and their meanings so as to reassociate music with lived experience and the broader patterns of discourse and culture that music both mirrors and actively produces" (viii–ix). This book, and many others like it, are being integrated into the music curriculum on many campuses across the United States.

In higher education, women increasingly outnumber men in the student population, though this fact is seldom reflected in the music curriculum. The College Music Society has encouraged its members to reflect on this discrepancy, through its National Committee on Music, Women, and Gender. Several workshops on Teaching Women and Gender have been offered in recent years, including themes of World Music and Popular Music, with future offerings in Women and Music Technology. The World Wide Web page for the International Alliance for Women in Music includes space for sharing course syllabi for courses on women and music. The addition of these courses with a special emphasis on women's contributions to music, past and present, notated and improvised, is a vital step toward achieving a culturally pluralistic, gender-balanced curriculum in music. However, if adding such courses is the only attempt at curricular revision, the European male–based curricular canon is likely to remain fixed in American higher education. A new curricular model must be created that will simultaneously challenge, yet complement, the existing curricular canon, if the contributions of women musicians and composers are to be fully included rather than excluded.

See also Gender and Repertoire; Gender in Music Analysis; Gendered Aspects of Music Theory

For Further Reading

Brett, Philip, Elizabeth Wood, and Gary C. Thomas (eds.). *Queering the Pitch: The New Gay and Lesbian Musicology*. New York: Routledge, 1994.

Koskoff, Ellen (ed.). *Women and Music in Cross-Cultural Perspective*. Contributions in Women's Studies, no. 79. New York: Greenwood Press, 1987.

Lamb, Roberta. "Women Composers in School Music Curricula, Grades 5–8: A Feminist Perspective." In *The Musical Woman: An International Perspective*, vol. 3, eds. Judith Lang Zaimont et al. New York, Westport, London: Greenwood Press, 1991.

Anita Hanawalt

Gender and Feminist Research in Music Education

Gender and feminist research in music education is a broad field of inquiry that explores the cultural politics of power as it relates to the experience of gender in music teaching and learning. Political in orientation, it seeks to redress and eliminate inequalities brought about through ideologies of domination by creating an openness to musical experience that promotes access to all. Given the absence of women's voices in the history of music education, this agenda has often led the research to be characterized as work by and for women. Gender, however, has increasingly been approached not as male or female, but as a continuum of possibilities sustained by socially and historically constructed notions of masculinity and femininity that interact in complex, often competing and contradictory, ways. Although believed a fundamental facet of self-identity, gender is also understood to be intertwined with other forms of socially constructed inequality such as class, race, ethnicity, religion, and so forth.

Early gender and feminist research in music education was limited by a narrow scientific research paradigm that, in its emphasis on observation and quantification, could do little more than establish gender as a category for analysis. The possibilities of the field, however, were transformed in the 1980s by a new interdisciplinary orientation that, drawing on developments in other disciplines such as anthropology and sociology, radically expanded how the cultural work of music education has been conceived. The interdisciplinary orientation also infused a variety of new methodological approaches that have lead to three distinct, albeit related, branches of inquiry: philosophical rationales for music education; pedagogical practices; and music education as critical pedagogy.

Philosophical Rationales. Philosophical rationales for music education became an issue when developments in musicology, lead by Citron (1993), cast music education as caretaker for a privileged class of musical works by composers who were men. Initial debate, as such, sought to identify not only the presence of gender inequalities but also the ideologies and political processes through which the canon has come to assume its power. For some, this power has been a matter of a philosophical rhetoric that favors rationality, objectivity, and the mind over subjectivity, emotions, and the body. For Lydia Goehr (1992) and Claire Detels (1999), among others, it is more deeply embedded in a museum culture that has isolated music from its social context by transforming it into something to be collected and cherished independent of time and place. It is a concept of "music as work" that has functioned in tandem in the curriculum with conceptions of knowledge, correctness, and genius to place the learner in the shadows and, in so doing, mask the play of meanings through which musical experience unfolds.

Whereas early debate centered primarily on accounts of music education as aesthetic education, new philosophical directions have challenged gender and feminist research to maintain a vigilant watch over its own practices as the profession's social conscience. Wayne Bowman (1998), for example, reveals the limitations of essentialist arguments that treat women's musical experiences or modes of knowing as singular. Others, like Elizabeth Gould (1994) and Charlene Morton (1994), identify a pattern of argumentation that, unfolding through binary dualisms, potentially maintains music education's already marginal status in the curriculum as inferior to other intellectual pursuits. The rhetoric celebrating multiplicity and difference has also been found problematic, particularly in multicultural accounts of music education where fixed and rigidly bound conceptions of authenticity and tradition continue to cast music education in a caretaking role by treating cultural and individual identities as static and unchanging.

Pedagogical Practices. This branch of inquiry turns from the philosophical ideologies and processes shaping the definition of music education's raison d'etre to the hidden subtexts of its pedagogical practices. Developments reflect a methodological shift that has progressively re-defined research as an evolving dialogue in which the perspectives of researchers, teachers, and learners are considered integral components. Although much of the research has been fragmented and disconnected, the most significant developments cluster around four topics: instrument selection, published teaching resources, composing, and performance as instructional context.

Instrument selection has been an issue since it was first linked to social stereotypes on the basis of biological sex. It has remained an issue as one of a variety of factors affecting career options later in life, particularly for roles and occupations historically perceived as gender-specific. Recent research, consequently, has turned from the instrument selected to the processes and mechanisms through which such choices are framed. Cross-cultural studies have proven a particularly fertile ground for exploring the power of instructional model, musical genre, and popular artists as cultural icons. Instrument, however, has also been implicated in ethnomusicological studies of performance, both in terms of the power relationships within an ensemble and the body-instrument connection more generally. The metaphors of love and desire, combat, struggle, and adaptation used by jazz musicians to describe the body-instrument relationship when "in the groove" seem particularly rich avenues for further exploration. Published teaching materials have played an important role in gender and feminist research for both the symbolic meanings of the images they present and the ways in which they define instructional content. Julia Koza (1990, 1992, 1993, 1994) was the first to push the boundaries of this work by using nineteenth-century illustrations of music as feminine pasttime to account for the presence and absence of boys and girls in different instructional contexts. Recent analyses of song texts by Barongan (1995), Took (1994), Goodman (1998), and other have pushed the boundaries even further to encompass race and ethnicity, as well as themes of violence and aggression common to representations of gender in popular music traditions such as rap. To date, however, attention has focused primarily on the teaching materials themselves. The language of power and control found in computer software promotional materials also suggests a need to address what Stephen Feld has described as the "politics of curation," particularly with respect to the benefits certain representations of gender have for publishers.

Until recently, studies of composing as gendered practice have focused primarily on professional women composers and their absence in positions of higher education. Much of this research seems to have been motivated by a need to understand (and dispel) eighteenth- and nineteenth-century characterizations of women as lacking both the intelligence and personality traits necessary to be successful as a composer. Historical studies identifying education as an enabling factor, however, have broadened the focus of exploration to include classroom interactions. Work by Lucy Green (1997) has been particularly fruitful in that it links patriarchic conceptions of knowledge and a model of musical meaning as socially constructed to explain how students' and teachers' perceptions of competence interact in the classroom to affect both confidence and participation. Other studies add to the mix conceptions of technology as a largely masculine domain.

Interpretation of these findings must be cautious, however, as technology has also been found to be an enabling factor for women composers, particularly when the compositional strategy or orientation emphasizes play and exploration over product and musical work.

Performance has to date received less attention as instructional context than composing. This has been owing in large part to a general pedagogical orientation that, focusing on the development of technical skills, has limited gender/feminist research to studies exploring differences in aptitude and achievement seemingly attributable to biological sex. Performance, though, also involves a variety of power relationships that have been shown to sustain both cultural and individual gendered meanings. Referencing her own instrumental experiences, for example, Marianne Kielian-Gilbert (1994) identifies a conflict between the authority of the conductor and performance as a mode of self-expression. In the choral ensemble setting, Patricia O'Toole (1994, 1997, 1998) also finds problematic institutional constructions of the women's (or all-girl's) ensemble as inferior (to the mixed); functional relationships between voice parts within an ensemble; and the loss of power and control experienced as the voice changes. In the studio, Roberta Lamb (1999) implicates the dynamics of the master-teacher/apprentice relationship, focusing in particular on the contradictory feelings of empowerment and oppression that this relationship can have for both men and women. Interestingly, competition was a factor in all three instructional contexts, having both institutional and individual dimensions warranting further study.

Critical Pedagogy. This branch of inquiry explores how music teaching and learning can be used to change the status quo. Much of the work, to date, has centered on what Sandra Harding (1989) describes as "add and stir" projects intended to fill holes in the curriculum. Although these projects validate the achievements of women (and other marginal groups), they do little to change the ideologies and practices that created the holes in the first place. Change, as such, is no longer a matter of simply enriching the curriculum, but of actually transforming it. As to the specific nature of the transformation, some have sought inspiration by studying music teaching and learning in other cultural traditions. This work has done much to expand the metaphors through which we understand musical experience and its potential educational values. It stands to suffer the same fate as many of the "add and stir" projects, however, unless its infusion into the curriculum is accompanied by significant softening of the boundaries that have come to separate academic subjects as distinct disciplines. To this end, attention is focusing more and more on the transformative power of music as a site for both self- and cultural regeneration. This work changes the focus of music teaching and learning from "music as work" to the experience of the performing self as "a moving subjectivity" (Lather, 1991) or "identity in the making" (Stubley, 1998). It also collapses the boundaries among research, education, and art by showing how the play of meanings involved in the act of making music can open the self to possibilities of gender and identity not yet theorized or even imagined.

Dissemination. Gender and feminist research has been promoted through a wide variety of mainstream music education journals and through support networks established by GRIME, an organization sponsored by the Music Educators National Conference and devoted specifically to gender and feminist

issues in music education. Impact, however, has been felt most dramatically in general educational forums where music has become increasingly seen not simply as another subject matter discipline, but as a site for enriching and transforming conceptions of learning, power, and self-possibility more generally.

See also Gender Issues; Music Education

For Further Reading

Detels, Claire. *Soft Boundaries: Re-visioning the Arts and Aesthetics in American Education.* Westport, CT: Greenwood Publishing, 1999.

Gaskell, Jane, and Willinsky, John (eds.). *Gender In/forms Curriculum: From Enrichment to Transformation.* New York: Teachers College Press, Columbia University, 1995.

Green, Lucy. *Music, Gender, Education.* Cambridge: Cambridge University Press, 1997.

Eleanor Stubley

Gender and Repertoire

In spite of the increased visibility and influence of women in American musical life in the twentieth century, most major U.S. orchestras, choruses, and opera companies remain committed to the mainstream, European-American, male repertoire when choosing music from the past, thus helping perpetuate the historical bias in gender and repertoire against music composed by women. The growing recognition of women's work, especially since the 1970s, and the increase in performance opportunities are indicated in successive volumes of Judith Lang Zaimont's *The Musical Woman* (1984, 1987, 1991). Two projects are particularly significant for the performance of repertoire by women: the Women's Philharmonic, and Leonarda Productions.

The Women's Philharmonic, founded in San Francisco in 1981, is unusual among professional orchestras in that it is dedicated to the performance of orchestral works by earlier women and the promotion of contemporary women composers. Unlike the women's orchestras from the 1920s to the 1940s that were primarily vehicles for the advancement of players and conductors, the Women's Philharmonic was created for the advancement of composers. The orchestra's repertoire is quite large, owing to the greater number of women writing for orchestra and also to the rediscovery and publication, beginning in the 1970s, of a great wealth of historically important music. In accordance with prevailing U.S. laws and attitudes concerning equality, membership in the orchestra, as in regular "mixed" orchestras, is open to all, but few men have chosen to audition for the Women's Philharmonic.

Leonarda Productions, which issued its first two recordings in 1979, was founded by Marnie Hall to record music by earlier women composers and by twentieth-century women and men. Although wanting to call attention to women's work, Hall decided not to record music by women exclusively. She recognized the general belief that if it is by a woman, it must not be very good. She feared that if she recorded only music by women, potential buyers would assume the music was second-rate because she was not free to choose from all music. She noted also the outright hostility on the part of some people, women and men, toward music composed by women.

For these and similar reasons, many women composers prefer that their music be performed on the same programs as music by men, not on women-only programs. Like other marginalized groups, women composers fear separation from the larger musical world. Many object to the label "woman composer" itself, as it implies that the music should be judged according to different standards or that the composer requires special treatment in light of past oppression. Yet special effort may in fact be required if women are not to be lost in that larger, male-dominated concert world. When composers and performers intentionally choose women's work, audiences can learn new repertoire and develop new preferences. If preference is shown, demand will follow, as is demonstrated in many successful organizations such as the Women's Philharmonic, Ars Femina, and Anonymous 4.

Many local and regional performing groups and soloists continue to rediscover, commission, and perform music written by women. Music educators at all levels, from elementary school through university, are attempting to develop more inclusive repertoires for their orchestras, bands, and choirs by choosing music by women and other musics outside the canon. Women who compose frequently express a commitment to ensuring that girls and young women considering a future career in composition will hear more music by women. All these efforts are helping to create a new reality in the music marketplace.

See also Canon; Publishers, Women's Music

For Further Reading

Boone, Clara Lyle et al. "All-Male Programming: An Antitrust Violation?" *IAWM [International Alliance for Women in Music] Journal* (October 1995): 2–4.

Hall, Marnie. "Chronicling Women Composers on Disc." In *The Musical Woman: An International Perspective*, Vol. eds. Judith Lang Zaimont et al. Westport, CT: Greenwood Press, 1984.

"The Women's Philharmonic." Section 51 in *Women in Music: An Anthology of Source Readings from the Middle Ages to the Present*, ed. Carol Neuls-Bates. New York: Harper and Row, 1982. Rev. ed., Boston: Northeastern University Press, 1996.

Anita Hanawalt

Gender Coding

Gender coding in music involves using musical effects to demarcate gender differences. Identifying gender codes and conventions a composer uses to signify contrasting feminine and masculine stereotypes is part of musical semiotics, the theory of signs and symbols in music and their function in conveying meaning. Common examples of gender coding include *masculine* force and energy contrasted with *feminine* grace and elegance, or *masculine* diatonicism with *feminine* chromaticism. The study of gender coding is a technique of feminist music criticism that, like critical theory in general, seeks to uncover political meaning and ideology. The ideological meaning of gender coding in Western music, including music in the United States, is typically the subjugation of the female or the feminine. Chromaticism can also be said to destabilize the "normal" diatonic structure of tonal music just as women destabilize the patriarchal social order; the female is the "other" that must be controlled. Gender coding can also involve associating musical constructions with heterosexuality and homosexuality.

Gender coding has been analyzed in masterworks of the European classical tradition and in several forms of American music. In musical modernism after World War I dissonance and experimentalism were coded male, consonance and romanticism female. The lyrics of North American folk balladry are said to be coded masculine, as the stories are almost always men's stories about men's occupations. Gender coding has also been discussed in rock and rap music and videos. Gender codes may be used by women as well as men composers; women may parody and subvert accepted codes, either in an attempt to remedy the assumption of women's subjugation or for other reasons.

See also Feminist Music Criticism; Gender in Music Analysis

For Further Reading

Cook, Susan C., and Judy S. Tsou (eds.). *Cecilia Reclaimed: Feminist Perspectives on Gender and Music*. Urbana and Chicago: University of Illinois Press, 1994.

McClary, Susan. *Feminine Endings: Music, Gender, and Sexuality*. Minnesota and Oxford: University of Minnesota Press, 1991.

Deborah Hayes

Gender in Music Analysis

Consideration of feminine and masculine gender in music analysis generally follows one of two models: either the projection of attributes of gender onto musical materials, or the mapping of specific musical techniques onto a particular gender. These associations may be explicit in narrative musical contexts such as dramatic music (opera and ballet) and program music, where specific musical techniques are often aligned with the gender of a character or set of characters. In absolute, or non-programmatic, music, these associations are often less well defined and thus more subjective; writings contemporary with the music, however, contain information regarding correlations between music and gender that may be taken to represent general societal norms and expectations.

Throughout history, writers on music have made such correlations. Comparisons between musical materials and attributes of gender are often intended to demonstrate the relative strength or weakness of a particular musical element or set of elements. As a complement to the male gender, which represents relative strength, action, and independence, the female gender represents relative weakness, passivity, and dependence. For example, a cadence that concludes on a metrically accented beat is considered strong and is thus a "masculine cadence," whereas a cadence in a metrically unaccented position is considered weak and referred to as a "feminine cadence."

Similarly, analyses of tonality and tonal forms have included gendered descriptions of specific harmonic functions. The "sisterly" subdominant chord is subordinate to the "brotherly" dominant triad. The major triad and the major mode are often associated with the male gender and the minor triad and minor mode with the female gender. Some writers describe the declamatory first theme of a sonata form movement as masculine and the more lyric second theme as feminine.

A further aspect of gender in music analysis has been the association of the male gender with normalcy and naturalness and the female gender with abnormality and unnaturalness. The major triad (masculine) derives from simple frequency ratios, whereas the minor triad (feminine) does not occur among low members of the harmonic series. Again, these correspondences have often mirrored values and attitudes of society.

The role of gender in music analysis expanded in the course of the twentieth century. Reference to aspects of gender in musical analysis from the early and middle parts of the century, as in writings from before 1900, consisted typically of the types of associations cited above. No serious effort was made, however, to consider these correlations as anything more than analogies. Since the late 1980s aspects of gender have taken on a significant and more formalized role in the analysis of music. This new scholarship draws largely from theories of gender in such fields as sociology, psychology, women's studies, and political feminism, as well as from literary criticism and studies in the visual and other art forms. Recent directions in music analysis that incorporate readings of gender usually fall into one of three interrelated categories: (1) analyses that seek to reveal binarisms based on gender; (2) the application of these dichotomies in light of larger societal forces and patterns; and (3) the examination of the functioning of one particular gender in a single piece of music, throughout a composer's oeuvre, or transcending a genre or style.

One of the central questions of gender studies, and one that is fundamental to any system of musical analysis based on it, is whether gender is essential (an inherent quality that is inevitably characteristic of a person who is born either male or female) or a construct (a sum of collective behaviors and behavioral patterns suggesting either a male or female gender). In either case one may associate the female gender with the social conception of woman or womanhood, and the male gender with the corresponding concepts of man or manhood. Beyond the question of whether gender is an innate or a societal force is the question of the relationship between the genders. Specifically, the analyst must decide whether female and male are diametric to one another in a binary opposition, whether they are dualist, or whether there is some continuum between genders. If there is a continuum, it becomes necessary to define wherein the boundaries remain intact, what is unquestionably male or female, and where they overlap or blur.

Particularly when adopting the constructivist view, the analyst must further delineate the relationship of gender to sex (as a biological category, female or male) and to sexuality. A person of either sex may choose to live according to the societal norms and behavioral patterns of the opposite sex. In this case, an individual who is female would have "man" as her gender. Similarly, it is possible for a male to live in society as a "woman." This phenomenon, referred to as transgendering, is not necessarily dependent on sexuality or sexual orientation. People who take on the opposite gender are not always or inevitably homosexual. Like gender, sexuality may exist on a continuum, whereas the concept of sex remains a binarism.

Once the analyst has decided what constitutes masculinity or femininity, establishing a definition of gender, he or she may use this definition as the basis for relating music to culture. This process normally entails creating a musical semiotics of gender and then drawing on hierarchical binarisms relating to the various gendered signs; it also involves examining aspects that stand between genders or are to some extent contradictory with regard to gender. It is important for the analyst to study carefully the musical and societal conventions and attitudes of the historical period in question, and to assess the extent to which a musical composition, or a composer, appears to have been influenced by the prevalent attitudes of the time. Another avenue for considering gender in musical analysis is to examine how these conventions may change over time or remain unchanged.

See also Feminist Music Theory; Gendered Aspects of Music Theory

For Further Reading

Citron, Marcia J. "Gender and the Field of Musicology." *Current Musicology* 53 (1993): 66–75.

Cook, Susan C., and Judy S. Tsou (eds.). *Cecilia Reclaimed: Feminist Perspectives on Gender and Music*. Urbana: University of Illinois Press, 1994.

McClary, Susan. *Feminine Endings*. Minneapolis: University of Minnesota Press, 1991.

Robert Peck

Gender Issues

Gender issues surrounding women's activities in music in the United States since 1900 have reflected not only changes in musical life and in ways of thinking about music but also changing interpretations of female and male sexuality, social roles, sexual politics, and the cultural conditioning of women and men. Since the 1980s the word "gender," originally a classification of words according to grammar rules, has been accepted as a general term for classifying feminine and masculine behavior, expectations, and characteristics. Musical genres and effects and musicians' activities are said to be "gendered" feminine or masculine according to whether they are associated with women or men. Some writers maintain a distinction between the words "gender" and "sex," using gender to refer to elements of femininity and masculinity that are culturally constructed and socially conditioned, beyond the biological and genetic fact of female and male sex. Others use the words interchangeably; for instance, the phrase "gender-based discrimination" seemed to be preferred in the 1990s over the equivalent phrase "sex discrimination" from the 1960s and 1970s. In music as in most activities, it is often impossible to differentiate gender-based (cultural, social) factors from sex-based (biological) factors. Women have usually faced discrimination because of their sex, that is, because they are female; the various forms of sex discrimination and their remedies may be said to be gender issues, that is, part of women's experience.

Around 1900 the term "feminism,"

used in Europe in the late nineteenth century, entered American English usage; feminist was an appropriate designation for the activities of the suffragists who were actually pressing for women's rights and equality in many areas besides votes for women. As chronicled in music histories, discussions of historiography, music criticism, and journals, the early 1900s saw the continuation of a wave of feminism in music in the form of increased professionalism and visibility of women musicians, especially among the upper middle class in urban cultural centers. Throughout history, feminist efforts such as these, resulting in greater recognition of women and equitable treatment of their work, have typically inspired antifeminist reactions—the "backlash"—in an effort to restore the status quo. In the early 1900s antifeminist sentiments included the ideologies of social Darwinism, the women's sphere, separate spheres, and sexual aesthetics in music criticism, holdovers from the domestic feminism of previous decades; according to the prescriptive literature, a woman's activities in music were properly in the home in keeping with her role as guardian of the moral and religious life of the family, and public performance and publishing would be immodest.

Yet women persisted. According to the 1910 federal census, women constituted 60.6 percent of those reporting occupations in "Music and Music Teaching." Women were more visible as composers of symphonies and choruses and other large classical forms. Women singers were well-established, well-paid professionals, and women piano teachers were increasingly professional. Beginning in the 1920s, new conservatories (Eastman, Curtis, Juilliard) produced more qualified women players who, when denied places in regular, mixed orchestras, could find

work in women's orchestras that flourished until about 1945; such groups, organized by women, provided opportunities for women conductors and entrepreneurs as well as instrumentalists. Women's patronage, both individually and collectively through music clubs, helped build musically educated and receptive audiences for orchestral concerts, opera, and other classical performances. In reaction, some critics decried the feminization of American music and held women responsible for what they heard as sentimentality, in contrast to the profound feelings in the best of the European tradition. The supposed inferiority of women in the higher forms of music, then, was linked to the supposed inferiority of American music. Further, the feminization of music was said to have created the American "manliness complex" that would make it difficult for a man to choose to be a musician. The exclusion of women was thus important to the success of the American modernist movement in the 1920s.

An expanded range of gender issues in American music emerged in the so-called second wave of feminism in the 1960s and 1970s, which advocated women's liberation from historic restrictions and brought unprecedented legal guarantees of women's rights. Women's studies departments developed rapidly in U.S. colleges and universities in direct response to the aims of the contemporary women's movement for improving the status of women in society. Women formed associations and organized festivals and conferences for the performance and study of music by women and the discussion of gender issues in music. Women's influence gradually transformed the traditional disciplines of music theory and musicology. American researchers sought once again to reclaim women's history, not only in the European-American classical tradition but also in other American musical traditions, including African, Asian, Pacific, and Latin American. A basic premise of feminist music theory and feminist musicology is that issues of gender and sexuality in music are inseparable from issues of race, ethnicity, and economic and social class. Women, however, unlike other marginalized groups, are not a minority and thus seem to pose a greater political threat. Recent research about music and gender addresses men's work more often than women's and can thus be seen as an antifeminist reaction in the direction of the academic status quo.

Assessing women's place in American musical life has usually involved the question of whether women are men's musical equals, albeit suppressed and marginalized, or may instead constitute a separate group with special abilities and interests. Two important historical surveys, one by Adrienne Fried Block and Carol Neuls-Bates (1979) and the other by Judith Tick (1986), review women's progress since 1900 in achieving recognition, status, and commercial success as singers in classical and popular genres and also in traditionally male-dominated musical activities such as orchestral playing, conducting, composing, and college teaching. Tick provides statistics concerning women in musical occupations based on federal census data and *Billboard* magazine's charts of women's commercial success in popular music, rhythm and blues, jazz, country music, and easy-listening categories. Women's strategies in male-dominated fields have included the use of male pseudonyms and their support of performers of music by women, thus linking gender and repertoire.

Among the studies that investigate women's special abilities, some explore a separate feminist history that takes into account not only women's public work but also work conducted from privatized spheres to support public culture. Women-identified music in the 1970s and the history of a more general category of lesbian music represent women's efforts to be heard in public performance but as separate from the male, heterosexual mainstream. Feminist music criticism focuses on gender issues in music by women and men, including the possibility of a feminist musical aesthetics and a woman's voice, or women's sound, distinct from the perceptions of the male gaze. Essentialism and constructivism provide alternative explanations of women's roles in music. Scholars in music, as in all disciplines, examine power and gender in the American patriarchal system. Studies of gender in music analysis, gender coding, and other gendered aspects of music theory examine musical effects considered feminine and masculine, and how such effects may serve to devalue women. For some critics, men composers' adoption of supposedly feminine qualities is a kind of cultural appropriation.

Women and men in music in the United States share certain advantages and disadvantages. Music is part of an industrial capitalist system in which vastly greater public funding goes to preserve the nation's military might than to sustain the arts. American musicians work in a predominantly commercial world in which women and men compete for rather limited resources. To many critics and academics, American music in the classical tradition is almost as marginal as music by women, perhaps because of the nation's colonial past, in popular genres, however, American music is predominant throughout the world. In the American music industry gender issues are carefully considered in the marketing of performers in classical and popular fields to potential audiences; sexual attractiveness is often as important as musical excellence. Debates about gender and music are ongoing. They reflect music's innumerable and often ambiguous ways of expressing emotion and personal, sexual, and social identity. They also reflect the eternal ambivalence of relationships between women and men.

See also Discrimination; Gender Coding

For Further Reading

Block, Adrienne Fried, and Carol Neuls-Bates. "Historical Introduction." In *Women in American Music: A Bibliography of Music and Literature*. Westport, CT: Greenwood Press, 1979.

Cook, Nicholas. "Music and Gender." In *Music: A Very Short Introduction*. London: Oxford University Press, 1998, Chapter 7.

Tick, Judith. "Women in Music." *The New Grove Dictionary of American Music*, 4 vols. Eds. H. Wiley Hitchcock and Stanley Sadie. London: Macmillan, 1986.

Deborah Hayes

Gendered Aspects of Music Theory

Only in the past 20 years or so have music theorists and musicologists paid serious attention to the gendered aspects of music theory, in particular the ways in which thinking about music theory has influenced women's work in music. Three areas have been of particular interest: (1) the absence of women from the historical record of influential theorists, (2) gendered terminology in classic theoretical concepts as taught in American colleges and universities, and (3) the application to music theory of feminist theories of the body, performance, and cultural context.

European and American music theorists trace the origins of the scientific study of music to Aristotle and other ancient Greek writers. In medieval Europe, music was one of the four essential scientific disciplines of the quadrivium—music, geometry, arithmetic, astronomy. Another categorization distinguished three aspects of music: *musica theoretica*, or the speculative, mathematical approach; *musica practica*, or composition, plainsong, mode, interval, rhythm, and notation; and *musica poetica*, or affect and rhetoric. Music theorists generally analyze music according to two approaches, adopting either a traditional, scientific, positivist method or a multidisciplinary approach that includes consideration of the effect of culture and context on the construction, performance, and reception of the musical work. The multidisciplinary approach has expanded greatly since the 1980s with the development of feminist music theory and feminist musicology.

According to contemporary critiques of the patriarchy, cultural context as it relates to scientific knowledge is largely responsible for women's relative invisibility in the history of music theory. The concept of separate spheres in the early 1900s encouraged women to maintain a house and rear their children rather than pursue advanced study. A few American women musicians published pedagogical methods in music theory, and several devised systematic methods in writing their own music. Yet industrialization, technology, and science continue to play a role in music theory and composition in the development of sound recording, World Wide Web–based information, music synthesis, and computer applications in music, and many contemporary music theorists and musicologists continue to associate music analysis, theory, and technology with masculinity.

In recent years scholars have analyzed the patriarchal ideologies embedded in the gendered terminology of traditional music theory. Susan McClary's highly influential *Feminine Endings* (1991) alerted musicians to the cultural and political meanings in nineteenth- and twentieth-century writings on music that associate masculine/feminine with weak/strong, major/minor (harmony or key), principal theme/subordinate theme, tonic/dominant, diatonic/chromatic, normal/abnormal, natural/unnatural, and the like. For example, a "masculine" cadence ends on a strong beat and a "feminine" cadence ends on a weak beat. Such concepts seem to reinforce the lesser status of the feminine, not only in music but also in society at large. (Interestingly, in the revised edition of Walter Piston's well-known textbook, *Harmony* [1987], Mark DeVoto refers to downbeat and upbeat cadences rather than masculine and feminine, terms that he describes as archaic.) Examination of gender in music analysis continues to occupy musicologists and theorists. Marcia J. Citron's study, *Gender and the Musical Canon* (1993), shows how the language of music theory and criticism in the European-American art-music tradition has been constructed to exclude women from the canon.

McClary analyzes the sexual implications of tonal forms; thwarting and delaying tonal resolution until a climactic moment—postponing fulfillment of tonal expectations—is not simply a musical technique but also a way of constructing a musical narrative of desire. McClary also notes the age-old associations of musical performance with feminine elements—the body, dance, sensuousness—that go beyond the written score. She maintains that musicians who are men have tried to destroy these associations by rejecting women's participation and stressing such masculine traits as objectivity, transcendence, and omnipresence. Restoring the mind-body connection is a major concern in feminist music theory. Whereas positivist music theorists may regard human physical expression and social context as unworthy of study, contextualists view social mediation as inseparable from musical detail.

See also Feminist Music Theory; Gender in Music Analysis

For Further Reading

Burnham, Scott. "A.B. Marx and the Gendering of Sonata Form." In *Music Theory in the Age of Romanticism*, ed. Ian Bent. Cambridge: Cambridge University Press, 1996.

Cusick, Suzanne G. "Feminist Theory, Music Theory, and the Mind/Body Problem." *Perspectives of New Music* 32/1 (1994): 8–27.

Kielian-Gilbert, Marianne. "Of Poetics, Poiesis, Pleasure and Politics: Music Theory and Modes of the Feminine." *Perspectives of New Music* 32/1 (1994): 44–67.

Susan Epstein

General Music

General music refers to music education provided in school classrooms, kindergarten through 12th grade. It enjoys the longest history of any type of public school music instruction in the United States and is distinguished from large ensemble performance courses such as concert, marching and jazz bands, orchestras, and choirs. Contemporary general music usually includes a concept-based academic curriculum about which students are evaluated and graded so that they may advance to the next level. This curriculum may vary widely depending on grade level and teacher interest. General music instruction, however, is ubiquitous throughout the country as virtually every state provides certification for music specialists, and most states have developed some type of curriculum statement in which general music is included.

The earliest general music instruction in the public schools is considered to have been provided in 1838 when Lowell Mason was hired by the Boston School Board as music specialist for the Hawes Elementary School. Mason and others argued that music instruction would not only benefit every student but also could be learned by every student, given appropriate instruction. Influenced by the ongoing singing school tradition, music used for this instruction was intended to uplift students morally, physically, and socially.

Most public school general music teachers during the nineteenth century were former singing school masters who often were acquainted and recommended each other for positions. Many of these men created tune books, which formed the basis of the materials from which they taught. Initially purported to be based on the pedagogical principles of Johann Pestalozzi, the content of general music instruction consisted of singing and note reading. Many different teaching techniques were used, however, and a protracted debate ensued over the merits of teaching by "note" (reading and writing European music notation) as opposed to teaching by "rote" (singing before reading and writing). Regardless of method, the results of nineteenth-century general music instruction were regularly put on display in extravaganzas that often included hundreds of students.

Music textbook publishing is an integral component of general music, that began in the nineteenth century. Luther Whiting Mason's National Music Course books (1870–1875, revised in 1885) are considered to be the first music texts to gain national acceptance. Note reading was taught through a rote method using movable "do" solfege (a mnemonic syllable system for hearing melodic intervals) and hand signs first developed by Sarah Glover (1786–1867). Later, the C major scale was introduced on a five-line staff. Although most teachers did not use the solfege system, the method of teaching songs by rote became increasingly widespread. *The Normal Music Course* by Hosea Holt and John W. Tufts, first published in 1883, also became enormously popular. Holt was an outspoken critic of rote teaching, and his text's graded approach emphasized note reading, the evaluation of which was done by monitoring students' ability to sing music at sight. By the last 15 years of the nineteenth century, rote teaching had virtually disappeared as concerns were raised about the educational content of singing rote songs, and music specialists' primary responsibilities were to supervise classroom teachers who provided music instruction to their students.

Several changes in educational philosophy occurred around the turn of the twentieth century. Among these were the kindergarten practices of Friedrich Froebel, the child-study movement of G. Stanley Hall, and the progressive, child-centered curriculum of John Dewey. Having worked with Dewey, Eleanor Smith (1858–1942) co-authored with Robert Foresman in 1898 the *Modern Music Series*, a graded music series that reflected new educational ideas of using movement and rhythm in general music. Similarly, Satis Coleman (1878–1961) advocated in the 1920s that general music instruction should develop students' creativity, giving them opportunities to experience music as their own. Teaching rhythm and movement represented a shift from exclusively teaching singing and note reading, which had recently moved to the song method in which exercises for note reading were taught as they appeared in the music the students sang. This broadening of the general music curriculum early in the twentieth century coincided with the return of music specialists to providing general music instruction directly to students.

Rhythmic education was comprehensively introduced in general music education in the United States through the principles of Emile Jaques-Dalcroze. Developed in Switzerland, these techniques were not widely available or understood in the United States until the 1920s. Mabelle Glenn (1881–1969) incorporated in her *Music Appreciation for Every Child* (1926) her experiences with Dalcroze's eurhythmics. Her textbook series *World of Music* (1936) also emphasized movement responses to music. Similarly, psychologist James Mursell advocated rhythmic training in general music. Thaddeus P. Giddings, however, was opposed to this shift in emphasis in general music, and in 1925 he co-authored with Will Earhart and Ralph Baldwin a set of Music Education Series textbooks that emphasized singing.

Amid debate over rhythmic teaching, Frances Elliott Clark (1860–1958) began using the Victrola to play records for her students. Initially she used recordings of songs the students were singing as exemplary models. Clark left her teaching position in 1911 to work for the Victor Company, for which she developed an extensive classroom music appreciation program. Another alternative to the emphasis on music reading in general music education, recordings, player pianos, and later radio broadcasts were used regularly to teach music appreciation at the elementary and secondary levels well into the 1930s. This contributed to the popular music memory contests, the first of which was presented by Mabel Bray in

1916, and which became widespread in the 1920s. These contests were very competitive but ended within a decade as emphasis was placed on performance. Music appreciation and listening experiences, however, became part of an expanded general music curriculum during the rest of the twentieth century.

Between the world wars, instrumental music became extremely popular, contributing to teaching specializations of instrumental music, choral music, and general music. A significant impetus of general music specialization occurred after World War II when several approaches to teaching general music were introduced. The two most influential of these are attributed to Zoltan Kodály and Carl Orff. Kodály's approach evolved from the Hungarian schools and is based on using folk songs of the students' cultural heritage to involve them in singing, dancing, reading and writing music, and playing instruments. Orff's approach is based on developing student creativity; it emphasizes improvisation, composition, and movement using percussion and tuned barred instruments Orff developed. Contemporary general music educators teach in separate classrooms and select from a variety of approaches. Most, however, use Kodály, Orff, or Dalcroze approaches separately or in various combinations, although debate continues about the merits of adhering strictly to one approach or combining them in an eclectic approach.

During the late 1950s and 1960s, the Ford Foundation and federal government took an interest in music education that impacted general music, funding several national projects. These projects, and others, evaluated music education in terms of materials, repertoire, and pedagogy, which again broadened the scope of general music, making it more relevant to students' lives. Implementation of this began in the 1970s. General music gained more status as a profession with the establishment of the Society for General Music in 1981, which has contributed to extensive research in the field. Current issues salient to general music educators include nontraditional learners of all kinds, curriculum integration, multicultural music, testing, education-related standards, and the relationship between music and cognition.

Although it was once part of most high school offerings, general music is now typically found at the elementary level and as an elective at the middle school or junior high level. This association with young students has ensured the predominance of women among general music teachers and among those preparing general music teachers. Indeed, general music is the only area in music education in which the proportion of women exceeds that of men. Women leaders in general music include, for instance, Julia Crane (1855–1923), who in 1884 founded the Crane Normal Institute at Potsdam, NY, the first college-level institution to prepare music specialists. Frances Elliott Clark chaired the 1907 meeting at which the Music Educators National Conference (MENC) was founded. Lilla Belle Pitts (1884–1970), president of MENC from 1942 to 1944, was senior editor of the series book *Our Singing World*. Vanett Lawler (1902–1972) worked nationally and internationally and helped to found the International Society for Music Education in 1953. Many contemporary leaders in general music are associated with a particular general music education methodology or specialty. Eunice Boardman (b. 1926), however, is well known in general music teacher preparation, and Patricia Shehan Campbell (b. 1950) received national recogni-

tion for her book *Songs in Their Heads* (1998), an ethnographic study of children's ideas and feelings about music and its place in their lives.

General music instruction is more vital, dynamic, and diverse now than ever before. This is owing to the efforts of general music teachers who provide relevant and comprehensive music instruction to meet the needs of every student they teach. The profession suffers, however, from (1) an image problem in regard to its separation from performance classes that have more visibility, and (2) its tenuous relationship to general education, particularly at the secondary level. Factors contributing to this situation range from the educational values of the music education profession in general to the feminization of general music teaching in particular. Responding to these issues and defining the role and mission of general music will provide significant challenges for the profession in the century just beginning.

See also Music Education

For Further Reading

Alig, Kelley Joseph. "Factors in the Development of Leading General Music Educators." Ed.D. diss, Arizona State University, 1993.

Britton, Allen. "Music Education: An American Specialty." In *One Hundred Years of Music in America*, ed. Paul Henry Lang. New York: Da Capo Press. Reprint of G. Schirmer, 1961, rev. 1985.

Coffman, Don D. "Vocal Music Instruction and the Classroom Teacher, 1885–1905." *Journal of Research in Music Education* 35 (1987): 92–102.

Gould, Elizabeth S. "Music Education in Historical Perspective: Status, Non-Musicians, and the Role of Women." *College Music Symposium* 32 (1992): 10–18.

Growman, Florence. "The Emergence of the Concept of General Music as Reflected in Basal Textbooks: 1900–1980." D.M.A. diss., Catholic University of America, 1985.

Humphreys, Jere T. "Sex and Geographic Representation in Two Music Education History

Books." *Bulletin of the Council for Research in Music Education* 131 (1997): 67–86.

Lamb, Roberta. "Including Women Composers in Music Curricula: Development of Creative Strategies for the General Music Class, Grades 5–8." Ed.D. diss., Columbia University Teachers College, 1988.

Elizabeth Gould

Gideon, Miriam (1906–1996)

Composer Miriam Gideon wrote over 50 works covering the gamut from orchestral to piano to vocal to choral works that were never limited to passing styles, but reflected her own deeply personal musical idioms. Her music used only that which was needed to get a point across; there are very few uses of thick textures. Her music reflected a spartan taste that expressed thoughts in as succinct a manner as possible, giving every note and chord specific purpose. In the application of poetic text, Gideon's fascination was life-long and achievement high.

Born a second-generation German Jew on 23 October 1906 in Greeley, CO, to Abram and Henrietta Gideon, Miriam became interested in composition as a young child. She started studying piano after the family moved to Chicago in 1912. She viewed her early musical accomplishments modestly, but recognized her own drive, and was committed to her compositional work by her late teens. Summers in Dedham, MA, turned to full-time musical studies. In 1920, Gideon's parents sent her to study with an uncle, who was an organist and choir director at Temple Israel in Boston.

Miriam studied piano with Felix Fox and Hans Barth and attended Boston University, graduating in 1926. In 1931 she left for New York and studied composition with Lazare Saminsky and Roger Sessions. Gideon felt fortunate to study with Saminsky, one of the foremost Jewish composers in America at that time. Saminsky helped coordinate her training and lent her valuable experience in the area of orchestration. Sessions, with whom she studied for eight years, helped to develop her sense of musical form and proportions and taught her a great deal about modal counterpoint.

After an aborted European study in Switzerland and France owing to impending war, Gideon returned to New York. She studied with Eric Hertzmann and Paul Henry Lang, and in 1946 she earned a master's degree from Columbia University. She then taught at City College, Brooklyn College, the Manhattan School of Music, and the Jewish Theological Seminary. She received a doctorate of sacred music in composition from the Jewish Theological Seminary at age 64. She then returned to City College, became a full professor, and retired in 1976.

Gideon's early experience setting text are *a cappella* choral settings such as *Slow, Slow Fresh Fount* (1941) and *Sweet Western Wind* (1943). She wrote the *Lyric Piece for String Orchestra* (1944) and was commissioned to write the vocal chamber work *The Hound of Heaven* (1945). In 1948 she was awarded the Bloch Prize for choral work for *How Goodly are Thy Tents—Psalm 84* (1947), a work that reflects Ernst Bloch's music in a modal idiom expressing a Jewish melodic contour.

In 1953 she completed a full orchestral work, *Symphonia Brevis*, and in 1954 *Adon Olom* was commissioned by Hugo Weisgall. She completed her opera, *Fortunato* in 1956. In 1958 she wrote *Three Biblical Masks* and that same year was awarded the American Society of Composers, Authors, and Producers (ASCAP) award for symphonic music contribution. She wrote the cantata *The Habitable Earth*

(1965), based on the Book of Proverbs and dedicated it to the memory of her uncle, Henry Gideon. Other vocal chamber works include *The Condemned Playground* (1963), *Questions on Nature* (1964), *Rhymes from the Hill* (1968) and *Nocturnes* (1976).

While Gideon found designations such as "woman composer" or "Jewish composer" somewhat limiting, she is known as the first woman ever commissioned to compose a complete *Sacred Service for Sabbath Morning* (1971) for the Jewish (Reform) liturgy. The composition was commissioned by and performed at The Temple in Cleveland, OH. Her *Shirat Miriam L'Shabbat*, commissioned by the Park Avenue Synagogue, was completed in May 1974 and published in 1976. Other sacred text settings include *Eishet Chayil (A Woman of Valor)* (1982). Her sacred compositions reflect the influences of her early exposure to synagogue music, yet are introspective, personal, and in a style she termed "free atonality."

In 1975, along with Louise Talma (1906–1996), she became one of the first women admitted to the American Academy and Institute of Arts and Letters. She received a National Endowment for the Arts Award in 1974. Gideon died after a long illness at her home in New York on 18 June 1996.

See also Jewish Musicians

For Further Reading

Ardito, Linda. "Miriam Gideon: A Memorial Tribute." *Perspectives of New Music* 34/2 (1996): 202–214.

Gray, Anne. "In Memoriam: Miriam Gideon (1906–1996): A Jewish Pioneer." *IAWM [International Alliance for Women in Music] Journal* 3/1 (1997): 20.

Petersen, Barbara A. "The Vocal Chamber Music of Miriam Gideon," In *The Musical Woman: An International Perspective*, vol. 2, eds. Judith L.

Zaimont et al. New York: Greenwood Press, 1991.

Judith S. Pinnolis

Glanville-Hicks, Peggy (1912–1990)

The Australian composer Peggy Glanville-Hicks was a major figure in American musical life as a New York City critic, composer, and concert organizer from the late 1940s into the 1960s. Glanville-Hicks received several major awards, including a grant from the American Academy of Arts and Letters (1953–1954), two Guggenheim fellowships (1956–1958), a Fulbright Fellowship (1960), and a Rockefeller Grant (1961–1963).

She was born on 29 December 1912 in Melbourne and studied at the Melbourne Conservatorium and the Royal College of Music in London. In 1938 she married English pianist and composer Stanley Bate, whom she divorced in 1949. In 1940–1941, she accompanied Bate on his concert tours to Melbourne and Sydney, then Boston and New York, where they decided to settle. In 1948 she took U.S. citizenship. In 1951 she married Austrian-Israeli critic Rafael da Costa, whom she divorced in 1953.

From 1947 to 1955 the *New York Herald Tribune* published over 500 of Glanville-Hicks' concert reviews, mostly of new music. She also published reviews and essays in the *New York Times, Musical America, Music and Letters, Musical Quarterly*, and other journals. She updated the material on American composers in *Grove's Dictionary of Music and Musicians*, 5th edition (1954). Glanville-Hicks was active in the League of Composers and the American Composers Alliance; she also served as director of the New York Composers' Forum. She organized concerts and commercial recordings of new music, usually including a work of her own.

Between concert seasons Glanville-Hicks traveled widely. As a composer she was inspired by the melodies and rhythms of Spain (in the *Sonata for Harp*, 1951; available on Tall Poppies CD 71), India (*The Transposed Heads*, 1954; available on ABC Classics CD43139-2), North Africa (*Letters from Morocco*, 1952; available on Tall Poppies CD112), Black Africa (*Sonata for Piano and Percussion*, 1951; available on CSM CD24), the Italian peninsula (*Etruscan Concerto*, 1954; available on MusicMaster Classics CD0162-067089-2), England (*Concerto Romantico*, 1956), and ancient Greece (in the operas *Nausicaa*, 1960, and *Sappho*, 1963). The plots of her operas and ballets involve subjects close to her heart. *The Transposed Heads* explores the dilemma of a woman who, having married a high-born man and enhancing her social position, falls in love with his less ascetic–type best friend and is unable to live without both of them. In both *Nausicaa* (Composers Recordings Inc. 695) and *Sappho* she portrays women of ancient Greece who work through a tangle of political intrigues among the powerful men in their lives. The plot of *Nausicaa* explores female authorship, specifically the female tradition in Greek mythology. Glanville-Hicks saw herself, however, as part of a male tradition. She rarely acknowledged, let alone praised, the work of any of the women among her contemporaries.

From about 1960 she lived mainly in Greece. In 1967 she underwent surgery in New York to remove a brain tumor; she recovered but composed almost nothing more. In 1975 she returned to Australia, where in 1987 the University of Sydney awarded her the honorary D.Mus. degree. She died in Sydney on 25 June 1990.

See also Music Critic

For Further Reading

Hayes, Deborah. *Peggy Glanville-Hicks: A Bio-Bibliography*. Westport, CT: Greenwood Press, 1990.

———. "Peggy Glanville Hicks." *New Grove Dictionary of Music and Musicians*. 2d ed. Ed. Stanley Sadie; executive director, John Tyrell. 29 vols. New York: Grove, 2001. Also available to online subscribers, London: MacMillan Reference; New York: Grove's Dictionaries, 2000– .

Wood, Elizabeth, and Thérèse Radic. "Peggy Glanville-Hicks." *New Grove Dictionary of Women Composers*. London: Macmillan. *Norton/Grove Dictionary of Women Composers*. New York: W.W. Norton, 1994/1995.

Deborah Hayes

Glenn, Mabelle (1881–1969)

Mabelle Glenn cut an impressive swathe in American music education circles for 42 years from 1908 to 1950. She championed music in schools, held leadership positions, initiated influential programs, and generated innovative teaching materials. Community outreach featured significantly in Glenn's vision; she believed music supervisors should reach beyond the school curriculum to catalyze music in every aspect of every child's life. Mabelle Glenn wrote eloquently on reasons and ways to teach music: "The ability to read the score . . . to sing, the abilities represented by the various instrumental techniques, the auditory abilities developed by ear-training—all of these are to be created . . . for the sake of a deeper and wider appreciation, a wiser and more potent love of music" (Holgate, 101).

Born in 1881 in Oneida, IL, Glenn attended Galesburg Kindergarten Normal School, where she was later certified to teach (1902), and studied music at Monmouth College Conservatory in Illinois (B.M. 1908) and in Europe. In later life she attended Northwestern and Columbia Universities and received an honorary music doctorate from Chicago Musical College (1930). Glenn became supervisor of music at Monmouth, IL (1908–1912), then supervisor of music in Bloomington, IL (1912–1921). Her exceptional abilities to inspire music supervisors became apparent at this time.

From 1921 to 1950, Glenn was music director of the Kansas City Public Schools. Under her guidance these music programs became models for the country. By 1925, all children in elementary school in Kansas City were receiving classroom music. She implemented piano classes, with 3,000 students enrolled by the second year. School music festivals, music memory contests, music appreciation, and instrumental music, as well as enrollment in private lessons, flourished. Glenn promoted active participation in orchestra youth concerts attended by 10,000 children. She ceaselessly sought to improve instructional quality and teacher effectiveness.

Mabelle Glenn led with enthusiasm and skill: she was president of the Music Supervisors National Conference (MENC) (1929–1930); president of the Southwest division of MENC (1927–1928); president of the National School Vocal Association (1936), among other roles. During her MENC presidency she championed a constitutional revision that allowed any music teacher to become part of the organization.

Glenn wrote and co-authored a dozen books and textbooks, including *The Psychology of School Music Teaching* (1931). She collaborated on two basic music series, *The World of Music* (1936) and *Our Singing World* (1950). *The World of Music* featured innovative developments such as a teacher's handbook to sequence learning throughout the student's schooling, a system of melodic patterns derived from songs to facilitate sight singing and improvisation; and movement ideas inspired by Dalcroze eurhythmics.

Upon her retirement in 1950, Mabelle Glenn moved to La Jolla, CA, where she died in 1969.

See also Dalcroze Eurhythmics; Music Education; Music Educators National Conference

For Further Reading

Goodman, A. Harold. *Music Education: Perspectives and Perceptions*. Dubuque, IA: Kendall Hunt, 1982.

Holgate, G. *The Life of Mabelle Glenn, Music Educator*. West Yarmouth, MA: Rainbow Press, 1965.

Kari K. Veblen

The Go-Go's

The Go-Go's were an all-woman band in the 1970s and 1980s. In September 1981 *Beauty and the Beat* (IRS 44797-5021-2), the Go-Go's double-platinum debut album, climbed onto the *Billboard* chart where it was to stay for 38 weeks, six of which were at the number one position. The album was an unexpected hit and propelled the all-girl group from underground punk phenomenon to new wave sensation. The historical significance of the Go-Go's might be as pop music feminists, artists who wrote and performed their own music—still a rarity among women rockers at the time—and influenced countless subsequent women's groups such as Hole, Veruca Salt, and the Bangles, to name a few. But in 1981 their appeal resided in the dual image they projected as innocent, sweet girls (lead singer Belinda Carlisle was a high school cheerleader) and gritty, rough-

The Go-Go's in a publicity photo from October 1984. From left to right, the band members are Charlotte Caffey, Kathy Valentine, Jane Wiedlin, Gina Schock, and Belinda Carlisle. *Photo courtesy of Frank Driggs Collection.*

edged punks who produced short, danceable songs with simple tunes, memorable lyrics, and catchy hooks. The Go-Go's were daringly confident and eminently likeable.

The Go-Go's recording career actually began in 1980 during a tour of England where they recorded an early version of "We Got the Beat" for Stiff Records. As the single found its way among American underground audiences, the band's small but dedicated fan base grew, and I.R.S. Records signed them and released *Beauty and the Beat*. A new version of "We Got the Beat" appeared on the album and scored a hit on the U.S. charts, as did "Our Lips Are Sealed." Two subsequent albums followed; *Vacation* (IRS 44797-5031-2), with its eponymous hit single, and *Talk Show* (IRS 44797-5041-2). Although *Vacation* went gold and *Talk Show* sold fairly well, each was of diminishing popularity and the group disbanded in May 1985.

In 1978 a band called the Misfits was formed in Los Angeles, including vocalist Belinda Carlisle (b. 1958), guitarist/vocalist Jane Wiedlin (b. 1958), bassist Margot Olaverra, and drummer Elissa Bello. The band changed its name to the Go-Go's, and guitarist/keyboardist Charlotte Caffey (b. 1953), who had completed classical piano studies in college, was recruited. A final lineup was complete by 1980 when Kathy Valentine (b. 1959) and Gina Schock (b. 1967) replaced Olaverra and Bello. The Go-Go's played clubs and parties in California, progressing from a novelty act to a serious band. Caffey and Wiedlin produced the most notable contributions as songwriters, separately but also as frequent collaborators. As their amateurism receded so too did their edgier musical side, suggesting an untamed punk band that became new wave.

However, their reputation as poorly behaved rockers did not imply a calmer lifestyle. Legends of sex, drugs, and trashed hotel rooms maintained their image as bad girls. The pressures of constant touring and promotion took their toll on the band. Caffey, who was rumored to have been thrown out of Ozzy Osbourne's dressing room in 1985 for excessive rowdiness, eventually checked in to a clinic to shake her chemical dependencies, and soon thereafter Carlisle cleaned up as well. With sober outlooks, and prompted by Wiedlin's departure in 1984, the band decided to call it quits.

Since 1985 the five new wave cheerleaders continue a prolific schedule of music making, both in their frequent reunion tours and in their solo careers and offshoot bands. A 1990 reunion tour was produced to promote the release of a greatest hits album and to focus attention on the California Environmental Initiative. In 1994 the group reunited again for a tour to promote *Return to the Valley of the Go-Go's* (IRS 29694), a two-disc retrospective containing three new songs. Caffey, who was pregnant at the time, missed the tour and was replaced by former Bangles guitarist Vicki Peterson. Legal bickering over royalties between Schock and Caffey was eventually set aside in 1999 for a massive reunion tour. Two additional albums came out in 2000 and 2001, *VH-1 Behind the Music: Go-Go's Collection* (Interscope 490617) and *God Bless the Go-Go's* (Beyond 78182).

As a solo artist Carlisle has been the most successful, with seven albums plus a greatest hits compilation. Her 1987 song "Heaven Is a Place on Earth" was a number one hit in the United States; since then her popularity has been strongest in Europe and in Asia. Wiedlin produced the hit single "Rush Hour" in 1988 from her album *Fur* (EMI America E2-48683), acted in a few Hollywood films, and later formed the band FroSTed. In the 1990s she teamed up with Caffey to form the acoustic duo Twisted and Jaded. Caffey also worked with her band, Astrid's Mother (named after her daughter with whom she was pregnant in 1994), wrote songs for Courtney Love, and made arrangements for Jewel. Meanwhile, Schock formed the band House of Schock and with Valentine started the Delphines. In 1999 4 Alarm Records released *Unsealed* (Four Alarm 447), a 12-song tribute album of Go-Go's classics performed by various indie bands. When asked if the Go-Go's would perform at the all-women Lilith Fair festival, Carlisle expressed reluctance, citing her support of women but a reticence to be involved in a gender-exclusive event.

See also Bands, Pop Rock

For Further Reading

Beatnik: The Go-Go's Ezine! Available: http://www. beatnikbeat.com

Mark S. Applebaum

Goetze, Mary (1943–)

Mary Goetze—music educator, composer, and conductor—became an ardent advocate for multicultural music education in the 1990s. She is the author of *Share the Music*, a music series for grades kindergarten through six, published in 1995 by Macmillan McGraw-Hill, that exposes children to a wide variety of native languages, scripts, songs, and holidays as they study music. *Share the Music* includes texts for pupils and teachers, accompanied by a set of compact disc recordings for each grade level. Passionate about including non-Western music and musical styles in classrooms and choral ensembles in all settings, Goetze has been a pioneer in the use of new technologies for music education. In 2000 Mary Goetze created the CD-ROM *Global Voices in Song*, a resource that allows teachers and students to experience world musics performed by natives of the culture and incorporate these varied styles into their own performances. At Indiana University, where she is professor of music in music education, she has directed the 55-voice International Vocal Ensemble, a group dedicated to diverse musics, since 1995.

A native of rural Missouri, Mary Goetze was born on 20 January 1943. She grew up singing at home and in choirs, studying piano, playing flute in band and orchestra, and arranging for vocal trio. With degrees from Oberlin Conservatory of Music (B.M. 1965), Indiana University (M.M.E. 1971), and the University of Colorado (Ph.D. 1985), her diverse musical career has included teaching as an elementary vocal music specialist and college professor, directing children's and adult choirs, arranging music for the classroom, and composing. Goetze's numerous compositions and arrangements for treble voices are staples in the repertoires of children's choirs throughout the world. The *Mary Goetze Choral Series*, published by Boosey and Hawkes, is known for well-crafted, interesting, and artistic music for young singers, including folk songs, original melodies, and editions of works by Johannes Brahms, Hugo Wolf, and Melchior Franck.

In demand throughout the nation as a workshop leader and festival clinician, Goetze has received numerous awards, including the President's Award for Distinguished Teaching from Indiana University and the Outstanding Educator of the Year award from the University of Colorado College of Music.

See also Music Education

For Further Reading

Goetze, Mary. "The Challenges of Performing Music from Diverse Cultural Traditions." *Music Educators Journal* (July 2000).
———. *Share the Music*. New York: Macmillan McGraw-Hill School Publishing, 1995.
———. "Wanted: Children to Sing and to Learn." *Music Educators Journal* 75/4 (1988): 28–32

Pamela Schneller

González, Celina (1928–)

Singer Celina González combines the Hispanic-based country *guajiro* music of Cuba with the songs and chants of the Yoruba-based Santería religion to produce a unique musical mixture. The new style became part of Cuban popular traditions and made her successful in the United States and other Latin American countries, especially Colombia.

González was born into a peasant family on 16 March 1928, near Jovellanos, in the province of Matanzas, Cuba, a region well known for its deep African cultural roots. When she was very young Celina's family moved to the eastern city of Santiago de Cuba, in the former province of Oriente. Their house in Santiago was a meeting place where singers and troubadours met at fiestas to improvise and play in the old country traditions of versification. She was only 15 years old when she met Reutilio Domínguez at one of those parties.

Celina and Reutilio would soon form a duo, and later marry. Reutilio was an excellent guitar player with a formidable right-hand technique, which enabled him to produce what appeared to be the sound of two guitars. With Reutilio's accompaniment Celina González began to perform on local radio stations and, in 1947, on the Cadena Oriental de Radio, a Santiago de Cuba radio station powerful enough to reach most of eastern Cuba. The duo Celina y Reutilio provided musical variety in a radio drama that addressed the poor social conditions affecting Cuban peasants. It was through this early connection with social issues that the duo caught the public's attention.

Musically, Celina and Reutilio broke with established patterns that separated the guitar-based Spanish melodies of country music from the more percussive chants and songs of African-derived religions. In 1948 they wrote the song "A Santa Bárbara" (available on International Music 110017), which became an immediate hit in Cuba and neighboring Spanish-speaking countries.

Celina and her husband decided to stay in Havana, where they became a fixture on radio and television programs featuring country music. In the early 1950s they traveled twice to New York City, where they performed for the local Latin American community. This exposure to the New York Pan-Latino audience resulted in the spread of their music in the United States and in other Latin American countries. After the death of her husband in 1971, Celina continued to perform with her son Lázaro and has recorded tunes of the new generation of *nueva trova* artists.

Among her recordings are *La Rica Cosecha* (Tumi 056), *Salsa* (International MSC7025), and *Que Viva Chango!* (Pure Sounds 1002). Celina's influence on current U.S. pop music can be detected especially in the style and repertoire of Cuban American singer and Miami celebrity Albita Rodríguez (b. 1962), whose musical career followed the path opened up by Celina González.

See also Latin American Musicians; Multicultural Musics

For Further Reading

Broughton, Simon et al. *World Music: The Rough Guide*. London: Rough Guides Ltd., 1994.
Martínez, Mayra. *Cubanos en la Música*. La Habana, Cuba: Editorial Letras Cubanas, 1993.

Raúl Fernández

Gore, Lesley (1946–)

The "All-American girl-next-door," Lesley Gore was one of the most successful singers of teenage-oriented songs in the United States during the 1960s. Just 16 years old when she burst onto the music scene in 1963 with "It's My Party," she appealed to teenage girls who perceived that Lesley was suffering the same traumas they were. With follow-up hits like "Judy's Turn to Cry" and "You Don't Own Me," she has been called the first of the "tell it like it is" female pop singers. In fact, in "You Don't Own Me," a feisty statement of independence, Gore refused to be seen as the possession of a boy out of desire for establishing her own autonomy. Though it personified a defiant attitude for the time, it became Gore's second-biggest single.

Gore was born on 2 May 1946 in New York City and raised in Tenafly, NJ. In her mid-teens, while attending the exclusive Dwight Preparatory School for Girls in Englewood, NJ, she decided she had the potential to become a vocalist. While performing with a seven-piece jazz ensemble at New York's Prince George Hotel, she was discovered by Mercury Records producer Quincy Jones. In February 1963 Jones and Gore picked out a tune for her first single—"It's My Party"—from over 250 demos. It was a million seller in less than four weeks, and in 1964 received a Grammy Award nomination as Best Rock and Roll Record of the Year.

Gore continued having Top-40 hits through 1967, among them "Sunshine, Lollipops and Rainbows," "That's the Way Boys Are," "Hey Now," "Maybe I Know," and "Look of Love" (all songs are available on *The Golden Hits of Lesley Gore*, Mercury 810370). She was featured on *The Ed Sullivan Show* a number of times as well as on most other major network TV variety shows. Gore made several appearances in teen-oriented films and television shows, including *Batman*. By the end of 1964, *Record World*, *Music Business*, and *Cashbox* magazines all named Gore the "Year's Best Female Vocalist."

Despite her phenomenally successful recording debut in the early 1960s, Gore held her career in music partly in abeyance until she received her bachelor's degree in English and American literature from Sarah Lawrence College in Bronxville, NY, in the late 1960s. In the 1970s Gore worked to re-establish herself as a singer in New York and West Coast clubs and also honed her skills as a composer. She recorded two albums, and other singers began recognizing her composing skills. Dusty Springfield recorded a cover of the title song from her second album from the 1970s, *Love Me by Name* (A&M 4564). During the 1980s Gore recorded less frequently but made greater impact as a composer. Her song "Out Here on My Own," co-written with her brother Michael and sung by Irene Cara (b. 1959) in the movie *Fame* (PolyGram 800034), was nominated for an Oscar. In the 1990s Lesley continued to compose and sing, and in 1999 she appeared on Broadway as a guest star in the musical review *Smokey Joe's Cafe*. She maintains an active performing schedule on the oldies circuit.

See also Rock and Popular Music Genres

For Further Reading

Gaar, Gillian G. *She's a Rebel: The History of Women in Rock and Roll*. Seattle: Seal Press, 1992.

Stambler, Irwin. *The Encyclopedia of Pop, Rock and Soul*. New York: St. Martin's Press, 1989.

Warner, Jay. *Billboard's American Rock 'n' Roll in Review*. New York: Schirmer Books, 1997.

Lisa Dolinger

Gospel Music

Reacting against the rigid and stifling Puritan church regulations and long, dry sermons in the newly forming America, the new preachers of personal salvation of the mid-eighteenth century brought fervor and emotional enthusiasm to the religious experience. This fundamentalist "Great Awakening" brought with it a new exuberance in church music. The standard hymns were sung with a new intensity, and newly composed hymns frequently reflected a kind of religious folk music. The tunes were often drawn from familiar secular songs of the day, including art songs, spirituals, and even drinking songs. Many were newly composed by musicians who were often itinerant singing teachers. From around the beginning of the nineteenth century these hymns were sometimes sung in parts. Indeed new song books, like William Billings's *Continental Harmony* (1794), Jeremiah Ingalls's *The Christian Harmony: or, Songster's Companion*, Andrew Law's *The Art of Singing in Three Parts* (1800), and Richard Allen's *A Collection of Spiritual Songs and Hymns* (1801) brought musical sophistication to the traditionally monophonically sung hymns. The texts were based loosely on the stories, teachings, and experiences of Christ as set forth in the four gospels of the King James Bible, but also from other books of the Bible, mostly in the Old Testament.

The gospel music of the white Protestant churches and the black congregations developed separately but along parallel paths, with women participating in both venues. The spirituals of the black slaves were important precedents to the black gospel musical style. The camp meeting was influential in the development of the white gospel tradition. Following the Civil War, modern traditions of gospel hymnody emerged, and with its proliferation in many and diverse denominational churches certain characteristics developed. Gospel music is characterized by themes of spiritual salvation and living by Jesus's illustration,

by the participation of all, and by a straightforward informality. Lois Blackwell writes, "The earmarks of a gospel song are simplicity, optimism, and pragmatic hope" (Blackwell, 18).

From about 1900 black and white traditions were being defined, and performance style more than the tunes and text seem the more important distinctions. The white style derives from the music of country, hillbilly, bluegrass, and other popular music genres. The black style draws on elements of blues, jazz, and call and response. The gospel quartet, or small group, seems more important to the white commercial gospel milieu, whereas the excited and animated chorus interacting with soloists—often the minister—is an important focus of the black church gospel environment.

Although both gospel traditions were dominated by men as leaders, directors, composers and singers, many women were important exponents. Among the important white women gospel singers were members of the Carter Family, who brought their hillbilly-style gospel music from the hills of Virginia to the nation. A. P. (Alvin Pleasant) Carter and his wife, Sara (1898–1979), and her sister-in-law Maybelle (1909–1978) sang together as the Carter Family from 1926 to 1943. In 1943 Maybelle's children June (b. 1929), Helen (b. 1927), and Anita (b. 1933) joined her as the Carter Sisters and Mother Maybelle at the Grand Ole Opry and on *The Johnny Cash Show* on television. June married Johnny Cash.

Mahalia Jackson (1911–1972), the "Queen of Gospel Music," grew up in New Orleans but began her long career in Chicago. Aretha Franklin (b. 1942) refers to her roots for her rich career in popular and soul music from singing gospel music in Detroit. The remarkable popular and soul music singer Gladys

Knight (b. 1944) toured with the Morris Brown Gospel Choir through Georgia and Alabama as a young woman. Among the famed Staple Singers, led by Roebuck "Pops" Staples, were his daughters Mavis (b. 1940), Cleotha (b. 1934), and Yvonne (b. 1939). Sister Rosetta Tharpe (1915–1973) was a pioneer in the gospel music tradition. Shirley Caesar (b. 1938) sang with James Cleavland and toured with the all-women group the Caravans. Cissy Houston (b. 1932) is a gospel music icon and Whitney Houston's (b. 1963) mother. Sweet Honey on the Rock is an internationally renowned *a cappella* gospel quintet. Two recent gospel music stars are Vanessa Bell Armstrong (b. 1953) from Detroit and Tramaine Hawkins (b. 1951) from San Francisco. Among the newer generation of white gospel singers are Sandy Patti (b. 1957) and Twila Paris (b. 1958).

See also Church Music; Grand Ole Opry; Hymnody

For Further Reading

Allen, Ray. *Singing in the Spirit: African-American Sacred Quartets in New York City.* Publications of the American Folklore Society, New Series. Philadelphia: University of Pennsylvania Press, 1991.

Blackwell, Lois S. *Wings of the Dove: The Story of Gospel Music in America.* Norfolk, VA: Donning, 1978.

Reagon, Bernice Johnson (ed.). *We'll Understand It Better By and By: Pioneering African American Gospel Composers.* Washington, DC: Smithsonian Institution Press, 1992.

Stephen Fry

Gottlieb, Susan

See Phranc

Grammy Award

The Grammy Award is granted yearly by the Excellence in Recording Academy to honor outstanding work in the recording industry. The Recording Academy, also known as the National Academy of Recording Arts and Sciences (NARAS), was established to improve "the quality of life and the cultural condition for music and its makers." In 1957 the Hollywood Beautification Society requested five of the most important recording company executives to recommend performers who were worthy of honor stars on Hollywood Boulevard in Los Angeles. In addition to those recommendations, Sonny Burke of Decca, Lloyd Dunn of Capitol, Jesse Kaye of Metro-Goldwyn-Mayer, Henri René of RCA Victor, and Paul Weston of Columbia ultimately began to explore other means for honoring outstanding recording industry professionals; thus was born the Grammy Award.

The Recording Academy honors many different styles and genres of music, including classical, country, gospel, Latin, new age, rap, rock, rhythm and blues, and jazz, in combinations of solo, duo, and group performances. Awards for technical merit including recording, producing, and editing are also presented. For every category the members of the Academy cast preliminary votes, which are tabulated to choose five finalists. Encompassing a variety of creative and technical professions, the Academy's voting members determine the finalists and the ultimate winners of each category.

First awarded in 1959 (for work completed in 1958), the Best New Artist Award has been presented to 14 American women musicians and duos or groups with prominent women: Lauryn Hill (1998), Paula Cole (1997), Leann Rimes (1996), Sheryl Crow (1994), Toni Braxton (1993), Mariah Carey (1990), Jody Watley (1987), Sade (1985), Cyndi Lauper (1984), Ricky Lee Jones (1979), Debby Boone (1977), Bette Midler

Grammy Award Winning Women

Album of the Year	Artist	Album
1998	Lauryn Hill	*The Miseducation of Lauryn Hill*
1995	Alanis Morissette	*Jagged Little Pill*
1993	Whitney Houston	*The Bodyguard* (soundtrack)
1991	Natalie Cole	*Unforgettable*
1989	Bonnie Raitt	*Nick of Time*
1981	John Lennon, Yoko Ono	*Double Fantasy*
1971	Carole King	*Tapestry*
1963	Barbra Streisand	*The Barbra Streisand Album*
1961	Judy Garland	*Judy at Carnegie Hall*

Recording of the Year	Artist	Recording
1994	Sheryl Crow	"All I Wanna Do"
1993	Whitney Houston	"I Will Always Love You"
1991	Natalie Cole	"Unforgettable"
1989	Bette Midler	"Wind beneath My Wings"
1984	Tina Turner	"What's Love Got to Do with It?"
1981	Kim Carnes	"Bette Davis Eyes"
1975	Captain and Tennille	"Love Will Keep Us Together"
1973	Roberta Flack	"Killing Me Softly with His Song"
1972	Roberta Flack	"The First Time Ever I Saw Your Face"
1971	Carole King	"It's Too Late"

Song of the Year	Songwriter(s)	Song
1990	Julie Gold	"From a Distance"
1987	Barry Mann, Cynthia Weil, and James Horner	"Somewhere Out There"
1986	Carole Bayer Sager and Burt Bacharach	"That's What Friends Are For"
1981	Jackie De Shannon and Donna Weiss	"Bette Davis Eyes"
1977	Paul Williams and Barbra Streisand	"Love Theme from A Star Is Born (Evergreen)"
1974	Alan Bergman, Marilyn Bergman, and Marvin Hamlisch	"The Way We Were"
1971	Carole King	"You've Got a Friend"

Hall of Fame Induction	Artist(s)	Recording
2000	Lena Horne	"Stormy Weather"
2000	Andrews Sisters	"Boogie Woogie Bugle Boy"
2000	Dionne Warwick	"Don't Make Me Over"
2000	Ella Fitzgerald	*Ella Fitzgerald Sings the Cole Porter Song Book*
2000	Nina Simone	"I Love You, Porgy"
2000	Billie Holiday	"Lady in Satin"
1999	Marian Anderson	Schubert: "Ave Maria"

Grammy Award Winning Women (*continued*)

Hall of Fame Induction	Artist(s)	Recording
1999	Fanny Brice	"My Man" (from *Ziegfeld Follies* of 1921)
1999	Wendy Carlos	*Switched-On Bach* (album)
1999	Rosemary Clooney	"Hey There"
1999	Doris Day	"Secret Love"
1999	Ella Fitzgerald	*Ella in Berlin* (album)
1999	Ella Fitzgerald	*Ella Fitzgerald Sings the Rodgers and Hart Song Book* (album)
1999	Roberta Flack	"Killing Me Softly with His Song"
1999	Aretha Franklin with James Cleveland and the Southern California Community Choir	"Amazing Grace"
1999	Aretha Franklin	"A Natural Woman (You Make Me Feel Like)"
1999	Marvin Gaye and Tammi Terrell	"Ain't No Mountain High Enough"
1999	Etta James	"At Last"
1999	Gladys Knight and the Pips	"Midnight Train to Georgia"
1999	Brenda Lee	"I'm Sorry"
1999	Peggy Lee	"Is That All There Is?"
1999	Martha and the Vandellas	"Dancing in the Street"
1999	Big Maybelle	"Candy"
1999	Joni Mitchell	"Blue"
1999	Laura Nyro	*Laura Nyro* (album)
1999	The Ronettes	"Be My Baby"
1999	Shirelles	"Will You Love Me Tomorrow"
1999	The Staple Singers	"I'll Take You There"
1999	The Staple Singers	"Uncloudy Day"
1999	The Supremes	"You Keep Me Hangin' On"
1999	The Supremes	"Where Did Our Love Go?"
1999	Ike and Tina Turner	"River Deep, Mountain High"
1999	Sarah Vaughan	*Sarah Vaughan* (album)
1999	Dinah Washington	"Teach Me Tonight"
1999	Mary Wells	"My Guy"
1999	Tammy Wynette	"Stand by Your Man"
1998	Carpenters	"We've Only Just Begun"
1998	The Carter Family	"Can the Circle Be Unbroken (Bye and Bye)"
1998	Aretha Franklin	"Respect"
1998	Judy Garland	"(Dear Mr. Gable) You Made Me Love You"
1998	Judy Garland	*Judy at Carnegie Hall* (album)
1998	Mahalia Jackson	"Move On Up a Little Higher"
1998	Carole King	*Tapestry* (album)
1998	Peggy Lee	"Fever"
1998	Loretta Lynn	"Coal Miner's Daughter"
1998	Helen Morgan	"Bill"
1998	Patti Page	"The Tennessee Waltz"
1998	Kay Starr	"Wheel of Fortune"
1998	Barbra Streisand	"People"
1998	Sarah Vaughan	"If You Could See Me Now"

Grammy Award Winning Women (*continued*)

Hall of Fame Induction	Artist(s)	Recording
1998	Dionne Warwick	"Walk On By"
1998	Dinah Washington	"What a Difference a Day Makes"
1998	Ethel Waters	"Dinah"
1998	Kitty Wells	"It Wasn't God Who Made Honky Tonk Angels"
1998	Lauryn Hill	*The Miseducation of Lauryn Hill*
1996	Andrews Sisters	"Bei Mir Bist Du Schon"
1995	Sophie Tucker	"Some of These Days"
1994	Mamie Smith and Her Jazz Hounds	"Crazy Blues"
1993	Bessie Smith with Louis Armstrong	"St. Louis Blues"
1992	Patsy Cline	"Crazy"
1989	Billie Holiday	"Lover Man (Oh, Where Can You Be?)"
1986	Chick Webb and His Orchestra with Ella Fitzgerald	"A-Tisket, A-Tasket"
1986	Wanda Landowska	"Bach: Goldberg Variations for Harpsichord"
1983	Bessie Smith	"Empty Bed Blues"
1982	Kate Smith	"God Bless America"
1981	Judy Garland	"Over the Rainbow"
1979	Les Paul and Mary Ford	"How High the Moon"
1978	Billie Holiday	"Strange Fruit"
1977	Wanda Landowska	"Bach: The Well-Tempered Clavier"
1976	Billie Holiday	"God Bless the Child"

(1973), Carly Simon (1971), and the Carpenters (1970).

Special awards such as the Lifetime Achievement Award, the Trustees Award, the Grammy Hall of Fame Award, the Technical Grammy Award, and the Grammy Legends Award honor those significant performers and technicians of the past and present. Marian Anderson (1897–1993), Patsy Cline (1932–1963), Ella Fitzgerald (1917–1996), Aretha Franklin (b. 1942), Judy Garland (1922–1969), Billie Holiday (1915–1959), Lena Horne (b. 1917), Mahalia Jackson (1911–1972), Peggy Lee (1920–2002), Leontyne Price (b. 1927), Bessie Smith (1894?–1937), Barbra Streisand (b. 1942), Sarah Vaughan (1924–1990), and Kitty Wells (b. 1918) have all been honored with the Grammy Lifetime Achievement Award.

Numerous women have won Grammy Awards since its establishment in 1957. The preceding is a chart of women winners for Album of the Year, Recording of the Year, Song of the Year, and Hall of Fame awards.

See also Audio Production; Organizations, Professional Audio

For Further Reading

The Recording Academy. Available: http://www. grammy.com

Kristine H. Burns

Grand Ole Opry

The Grand Ole Opry is a performance venue for country musicians—performers, singer-songwriters, and entertainers alike. The Grand Ole Opry began on 28 November 1925 with a premier performance featuring 80-year-old fiddler Uncle Jimmy Thompson. Pioneer radio showman George D. Hay, also known as the "Solemn Old Judge," broadcast that performance over a new radio station whose call letters were WSM, an abbreviation for "We Shield Millions," sponsored by the National Life and Accident Insurance Company in Nashville, TN. Hay's program, the WSM Barn-Dance, taken from his National Barn Dance program in Chicago, changed its name in 1928 to the Grand Ole Opry.

Men performers wore cowboy hats and overalls, and women performers wore the full skirts like those worn at barn dances. Since 1925, WSM Radio's Grand Ole Opry has featured country music for live Saturday night broadcasts, introducing to the nation most of country music's greatest artists. So many fans flocked to the studio to see the show performed live that the Opry has changed location five times, each venue seating more and more people. It even charged an admission in its early years to discourage the large numbers of fans that turned out for the show, but to no avail. The first Grand Ole Opry location was the Hillsboro Theatre; then, it moved to the Dixie Tabernacle and also to the War Memorial Auditorium. In 1943 it moved to the Ryman Auditorium, which had perfect acoustics, and finally in 1974 to its current location, the Grand Ole Opry House, which seats 4,400 people, located in Opryland, USA, an entertainment theme park outside Nashville.

In 1939 NBC Radio began broadcasting the Opry and featured artists such as Roy Acuff, Uncle Dave Mason, the Weaver Brothers, the Solemn Old Judge, Elviry, and Little Rachel. Artists such as Roy Acuff, up to and including the 1970s and 1980s, have helped to establish the

Opry and keep it flourishing through the many stylistic changes of country music. Performers have included Jimmie Rodgers, the Carter Family, Roy Rogers, Gene Autry, the Sons of the Pioneers, Hank Williams, Bob Wills, Jim Reeves, Eddy Arnold, Flatt and Scruggs, Charley Pride, Conway Twitty, the Charlie Daniels Band, Willie Nelson, Johnny Cash, Waylon Jennings, Merle Haggard, John Conlee, and Alabama, to name a few.

Leading women artists who established their careers by way of the Grand Ole Opry include the Opry's first woman singing star, also known as the "Queen of Country Music," Kitty Wells (b. 1918), who in the 1950s became an overnight success with her hit single "Honky Tonk Angels," and Patsy Cline (1932–1963), whose 1961 hit "I Fall to Pieces" enabled her to become the top woman country singer and a regular featured performer on the Opry. Patsy Cline has been a major influence and inspiration to other women country singers, including Loretta Lynn (b. 1935), Reba McEntire (b. 1954), and Sylvia.

Other women artists for whom the Opry paved the way include Texas Ruby (1908–1963), Hazel Dickens (b. 1935), Jean Shepard (b. 1933), Dolly Parton (b. 1946), Molly O'Day (1923–1987), Minnie Pearl (1912–1996), Skeeter Davis (b. 1931), Connie Smith (b. 1941), Tammy Wynette (1942–1998), Barbara Mandrell (b. 1948), Patty Loveless (b. 1957), Goldie Hill (b. 1933), and many others.

Today's country artists featured at the Opry include Randy Travis, Alan Jackson, Garth Brooks, George Straight, Alison Krauss (b. 1971), the Judds, Lorrie Morgan (b. 1959), Shania Twain (b. 1965), Kathy Mattea (b. 1959), Jeanne Pruett (b. 1937), Joni Harms (b. 1959), Jan Howard (b. 1932), Wilma Lee Cooper (b. 1921), Holly Dunn (b. 1957), Lee

Ann Womack, Porter Wagoner, Diamond Rio, and Ricky Skaggs. The Opry, now televised, is 75 years old and has vaulted the careers of nearly every country artist—man and woman alike. George D. Hay, announcer for the National Barn Dance, who gave the Grand Ole Opry its name, depicted the music of the Grand Ole Opry as American working-class music.

See also Country Music; Country Music Association; Country Music Hall of Fame

For Further Reading

Grand Ole Opry. Available: http://www.opry.com
Wolfe, Charles K. *A Good Natured Riot: The Birth of the Grand Ole Opry.* Nashville: Vanderbilt University Press, 1999.

Susan Epstein

Grant, Amy (1960–)

Known primarily for her work in gospel and contemporary Christian music (CCM), singer-songwriter Amy Grant has also experienced success as a mainstream popular music artist. Her crossover success has paved the way for other CCM musicians desiring exposure and recognition in various musical markets.

Born on 25 November 1960 in Augusta, GA, Grant learned to play the guitar at a young age and performed frequently at school, often singing original compositions that expressed her Christian faith. While working part-time at a recording studio, she made a tape of her music for family and friends that, without her knowledge, was played for executives at Word recording studios. At age 15 she was approached by Word's Myrrh label to sign a record contract; in 1976 she released her first album, *Amy Grant* (RCA 66260).

Grant's popularity grew steadily with later releases, and with her 1983 *Age to Age* (Reunion 701-6697-274) album she became the first CCM artist to achieve Platinum sales. *Heart in Motion* (A&M 5321), issued in 1991, was considered her first cross-over album into pop music and spent 52 consecutive weeks on the U.S. album chart. This album, with its high-charting singles "Baby, Baby" and "Every Heartbeat," evoked conflicting feelings among the CCM community, as many felt that Grant's flirty videos and ambiguous lyrics did not represent the values her music once had ("too much talk about falling in love and too little talk about the need for a personal relationship with Jesus Christ," Howard and Streck, 102). Her continued success with CCM audiences and her new-found pop marketability opened the door for other Christian musical artists (representing genres such as rap, soul, and country) to attract mainstream audiences, as the pressure to extol Christ in song lyrics gradually lessened. The success of Grant's 1997 *Behind the Eyes* (A&M 540760) confirmed her position as a popular recording artist in both gospel and pop music circles.

Grant has been the recipient of numerous awards, for both her music and her humanitarian efforts. She has received five Grammy Awards for Gospel Performances and over 25 Gospel Music Association Dove Awards. In 1994 she received the Pax Christi award from Saint John's Abbey and the University of Minnesota for her work with terminally ill and poor children.

See also Church Music

For Further Reading

Howard, Jay R., and John M. Streck. *Apostles of Rock: The Splintered World of Contemporary Christian Music.* Lexington: University Press of Kentucky, 1999.

Millard, Bob. *Amy Grant: A Biography*. New York: Doubleday, 1986.

Romanowski, William D. "Move over Madonna: The Crossover Career of Gospel Artist Amy Grant." *Popular Music and Society* 17/2 (Summer 1993): 47–68.

Kristina Lampe Shanton

Grawemeyer Award for Music Composition

The Grawemeyer Award for Music Composition is an international prize awarded in recognition of outstanding achievement by a living composer for a large-scale genre, including orchestral, chamber, choral, electronic, dance, music theatre, opera, song-cycle, or lengthy solo work. The cash award is currently $200,000 and is the largest international cash prize to be awarded for composition. The award's benefactor was Louisville, KY, native H. Charles Grawemeyer, a graduate of the University of Louisville Speed Scientific School and the founder of Plastic Parts, Inc., a Louisville-based industrial company. Grawemeyer, a lover of music, created the prize to recognize current music mastery and encourage the development of new composers. Awards have been made in music composition since 1985; recipients include such notable composers as György Ligeti, Krysztof Penderecki, John Corigliano, Karel Husa, Ivan Tcherepnin, Toru Takemitsu, Chinary Ung, Tan Dun, and Thomas Ades. There is no requirement that an award be made every year.

Joan Tower (b. 1938) is the only woman composer to receive the Grawemeyer Award to date. Tower's orchestral work *Silver Ladders* (Nonesuch 79245), a 22-minute commission by the St. Louis Symphony Orchestra and Meet the Composer, Inc., that premiered on 9 January 1987, received the Grawemeyer Award in 1990.

The composition competition is overseen by the University of Louisville's Grawemeyer Award Committee, which consults three internationally known music professionals. Entries must be sponsored by an individual or a professional music organization. Such sponsors may include conductors, music critics, performers, publishers, and chairpersons of music schools. A composer may not submit his or her own work, and only one work by any given composer may be entered. Submissions should include the full score, a cassette or compact disc recording of the work, documentation of the work's premier (e.g., a printed program), a letter of support in English by the sponsor, the composer's photo and biography, an official application form, and an entry fee. Official entry forms may be obtained by writing to the Grawemeyer Music Award Committee, School of Music, University of Louisville, Louisville, KY 40292.

See also Prizes, Composer and Performer

For Further Reading

Grawemeyer for Music Composition. Available: http://www.louisville.edu/library/music/speccoll/grawemeyer.html

Susan Epstein

Grigsby, Beverly Pinsky (1928–)

Influential teacher, composer, and lecturer, Beverly Pinsky Grigsby is noted for her work in computer music. Professor of music theory–composition and musicology at California State University, Northridge (1963–1993), and California Institute for the Arts (1997), she established and directed the California

State University, Northridge (CSUN), Computer Music Studio from 1976 until 1993, when she retired as professor emerita. Her output spans chamber music through stage works, and her commercial and documentary film music includes scores for Francis Ford Coppola (1962) and Ray Bradbury (1987, 1990).

Born on 11 January 1928 in Chicago, IL, Grigsby studied violin, piano, ballet, and elocution as a child. In 1942 she moved to Los Angeles, CA; and following three years of medical school at the University of Southern California (1944–1947), she studied conducting at Southern California School of Music and the Arts (1947–1949) as well as music theory, counterpoint, composition, and musicology with Ernest Krenek and Arnold Schoenberg at the University of California, Los Angeles (UCLA). She worked in electronic music from the late 1950s and earned degrees from CSUN (B.A. 1961, M.A. 1963) and the University of Southern California (D.M.A. with honors, 1986). She pursued further studies in computer music at Stanford University (1975) and the Massachusetts Institute of Technology (1976), in medieval instruments at the Royal College of Music in London (1981), and Gregorian chant at Solesmes, France (1981, 1997).

Grigsby has received awards from National Endowment for the Arts; the Rockefeller Foundation; the American Society of Composers, Authors and Publishers; International Educators; International Alliance for Women in Music (IAWM); and universities in California, Kentucky, Mexico, and Brazil. She has served as master composer at Ball State University (1993) and the Ernest Bloch Music Festival (1994), and as master composer and professor in the California State University Summer Arts Program (1996). She chaired the IAWM International Congress on Women in Music,

London (1999), and the International Composition Competition, Rome (1999–2000), and is coordinator of the International Institute for the Study of Women in Music Library at CSUN. Grigsby was named a Carnegie-Mellon fellow in 1987 and has been a research scholar at the New Getty Museum in Bel Air, CA, since 1997.

Much of Grigsby's computer music has been realized by direct synthesis on the Fairlight Computer Music Instrument (CMI) and involves sounds and textures that are often symphonic in nature, creating accompaniments for live performers and occasionally incorporating acoustic sampling to provide orchestral and choral timbres.

Significant works by Grigsby include large-scale compositions: *Fragments from Augustine the Saint* (dramatic cantata, tenor, chamber ensemble, 1975), *Moses* (opera, 1978), *The Mask of Eleanor* (opera, soprano, computer music instrument, 1984), *The Vision of St. Joan* (dramatic cantata, soprano, CMI, 1987). Solo and chamber music includes: *Songs on Shakespeare Texts* (soprano, 1949), *Two Faces of Janus* (string quartet, 1963), *Five Studies on Two Untransposed Hexachords* (piano, 1971), *Love Songs* (tenor, guitar, 1974), *Dithyrambos* (violin, violoncello, 1975), *Three Movements* (guitar, 1982), the Shakti cycle: *Shakti I* (flute, CMI, 1983), *Shakti II* (soprano, CMI, 1985), *Shakti III* (clarinet, tabla, CMI, 1987), *Shakti IV* (oboe, CMI, 1988), *Trio* (violin, clarinet and piano, 1994), *Saxsong* (saxophone, 1998), *A Little Background Music* (computer, 1976), and *Spheres* (computer soundscape, 1998).

See also Music Technology

For Further Reading

Burns, Kristine H. *WOW/EM (Women on the Web/ ElectronMedia)*. Available: http://music.dartmouth. edu/~wowem/

Sadie, Julie Anne, and Rhian Samuel. *The Norton/ Grove Dictionary of Women Composers*. New York and London: W.W. Norton, 1994.

Stewart, John L. *Ernest Krenek: The Man and His Music*. Berkeley: University of California Press, 1991.

Deborah Kavásch

Guggenheim Award

The John Simon Guggenheim Memorial Foundation was established by former U.S. senator Simon Guggenheim and his wife, Olga, as a memorial to the death of their son to provide fellowships for research and artistic creation. In the winter of 1923–1924, Senator Guggenheim consulted with Carrol A. Wilson, general counsel for Guggenheim Brothers. Wilson later contacted Frank Aydelotte, president of Swathmore College, to solicit advice on establishing the program. With the assistance of these two professionals, the Guggenheims arrived at the basic concept of the foundation by April 1924. On 23 February 1925 the foundation was established with an initial endowment of $3 million. Monetary awards were given for a period of time from six months to one year. In 1973 the average amount for a fellowship was $11,252; in 2001 the average was $35,931.

In a letter dated 26 March 1925, Senator Guggenheim outlined the purpose of the award: to "promote the advancement and diffusion of knowledge and understanding, and the appreciation of beauty, by aiding without distinction on account of race, color or creed, scholars, scientists and artists of either sex in the prosecution of their labors." In June 1929 he also wrote: "Such aid should be afforded under the freest possible conditions." Consequently, no special conditions are attached to the fellowship awards. The grants are made freely, and the recipients may spend the grant funds in any manner they deem relevant to

Guggenheim Awards

Composer	Year of Award
Ruth Porter Crawford (Seeger)	1930
Louise Juliette Talma	1946, 1947
Julia Amanda Perry	1954, 1956
Peggy Glanville-Hicks	1955, 1957
Leni Alexander	1969
Barbara Kolb	1971, 1976
Mary Lou Williams	1972, 1977
Meredith Monk	1972, 1982
Ann E. McMillan	1972
Carla Bley	1972
Pauline Oliveros	1973
Thea Musgrave	1974, 1982
Pril Smiley	1975
Lucia Dlugoszewski	1977
Joan Tower	1977
Vivian Fine	1980
Ellen Taaffe Zwilich	1980
Sheree Clement	1983
Judith Lang Zaimont	1983
Laura Clayton	1984
Jean Eichelberger Ivey	1986
Michelle Ekizian	1986
Susan Morton Blaustein	1987
Melinda Jane Wagner	1988
Augusta Read Thomas	1989
Juliana Hall	1989
Anne LeBaron	1991
Jessica Williams	1994
Ursula Mamlok	1995
Chen Yi	1995
Jennifer Elaine Higdon	1997
Melissa Hui	1997
Tamar Diesendruck	1999
Mariana Villanueva	1999
Shih-Hui	2000

Researcher	Year of Award
Margaret Helen Hewitt	1947
Isabel Pope Conant	1950
Eta Harich-Schneider	1953, 1954, 1955
Angela Diller	1953
Carleen Maley Hutchins	1959, 1962
Carol Cook MacClintock	1962
Sylvia W. Kenney	1963
María Ester Grebe Vicuña	1964, 1977
Janet E. Knapp	1966
Mary Helen Rasmussen	1967
Vera Brodsky Lawrence	1976
Rose R. Subotnik	1977
Marian McPartland	1980

their work. The fellowships are offered to those professional writers, scholars, and scientists who have made significant contributions in their respective professions. In regard to the field of music, the foundation limits its music awards to those in composition or music research. Professionals who interpret works created by others are not considered for Guggenheim Fellowships.

Many significant women have won this award, beginning with Ruth Crawford Seeger (1901–1953) in 1930. Other composers such as Louise Talma (1906–1996), Barbara Kolb (b. 1939), Joan Tower (b. 1938), Vivian Fine (1913–2000), and Chen Yi (b. 1953) have won the Guggenheim since its inception. Women researchers of music have also won several of these very prestigious awards. In 1947, Margaret Helen Hewitt was the first music researcher awarded the Guggenheim. More recent recipients include Vivian Perlis, Carolyn Abbate, and Cristina Magaldi.

See also Prizes, Composer and Performer; Publication Awards

For Further Reading

John Simon Guggenheim Memorial Foundation Page. Available: http://www.gf.org/

Stephen J. Rushing

Guillot, Olga (1925–)

Olga Guillot became renowned in Latin America during the 1950s for her characteristic singing of the Cuban *bolero*. She has appeared three times at Carnegie Hall, and 30 of her recordings have reached Gold status, selling over 1,000,000 copies. For nearly 40 years Olga Guillot has lived and worked in southern Florida, where she is highly revered by the mostly Cuban American community in the area. She is both a regional icon in the United States and a figure of continental dimensions when it comes to the singing of the classic Latin American *bolero*.

She was born on 9 October 1925 in Santiago de Cuba into a family with a significant arts background. When Guillot was five years old her family moved to Havana, where she spent the next 30 years and reached success as an interpreter of popular song, particularly the *bolero*.

When she was nine years old, Olga began singing duets with her sister Ana Luisa. The Dúo de las Hermanas Guillot performed at family gatherings and other social celebrations. By 1938 they were entering amateur singing contests on Havana radio stations, where they interpreted tangos and other current popular styles. Around this time Olga received voice training at the Havana Conservatory and began to appear on radio programs on a regular basis.

In 1944 she joined a group, the Cuarteto Siboney, with which she recorded her first song in 1945, a Spanish version of the popular American tune "Stormy Weather." This recording led to an increase in her performing activities. In 1946 she was voted the most popular singer on Cuba's radio stations. The next year she traveled abroad for the first time. She spent several months in Mexico and then went on to New York and South America in a tour that lasted one and a half years.

In 1954 she made a recording of the Mexican *bolero* "Miénteme" that became an overnight hit throughout Latin America. This number, which remains to this day her signature song, is one of the best examples of her dramatic, speaking-voice approach to the interpretation of the *bolero*. In the years following, Guillot traveled throughout Latin America influencing other vocalists of romantic songs throughout the areas. Guillot remained at the top of her popularity in Cuba until 1961, when she left for Mexico and then settled permanently in the United States.

Her recordings include *Epoca de Oro* (Antilla 29), *Reina Del Bolero* (AF 8009), and *Eterna Voz Del Bolero* (AF8026).

See also Latin American Musicians; Multicultural Musics

For Further Reading

Ayala, Cristóbal Díaz. *Cuando Salí de La Habana, 1898–1997, Cien años de música cubana por el mundo*. San Juan, PR: Editorial Cubanacán, 1998.

Duque, Hernán Restrepo. *Lo que cuentan los boleros*. Bogota, Colombia: Centro Editorial de Estudios Musicales, 1992.

Raúl Fernández

Gumm, Frances Ethel

See Garland, Judy

H

Haasemann, Frauke Petersen (1922–1991)

A specialist in group vocal techniques, a soloist, and a music educator, Frauke Petersen Haasemann developed an approach to choral vocal techniques that has influenced the choral profession worldwide. Her accomplishments range from performing as a contralto soloist in over 90 recordings to preparing choirs for performances and recordings with leading orchestras including the New York Philharmonic, the Philadelphia Orchestra, and the Vienna Philharmonic.

Born on 25 November 1922 in Rendsburg, Germany, Haasemann received early musical training from her mother, who was an accomplished singer. After being widowed during World War II, Haasemann studied church music at Westfälische Landeskirchenmusikschule, Herford, West Germany. In 1948 Dr. Wilhelm Ehmann and Haasemann co-founded the Westfälische Kantorei. This professional chorus became the cultural crown jewel of postwar Germany. The Kantorei was sponsored by the Goethe Institute, the German Embassy, and the Lutheran Church and was the first mu-sical organization after World War II to represent the German people outside their borders. The Kantorei toured throughout the world and made numerous recordings of the music of Johann Sebastian Bach and Heinrich Schütz in particular.

Through her work with the Kantorei, Haasemann was recognized as an innovator in building a choral sound based on healthy vocal production informed by her own voice training. Subsequently she worked extensively with the Rias-Kammerchor, Berlin, and the Broadcast-Choir of Belgium and presented seminars in Germany and Switzerland. In collaboration with Ehmann she published the book *Voice Building for Choirs* (rev. ed. 1981), which has become the definitive work on the subject.

In 1971 Haasemann and Ehmann presented an interest session for the American Choral Directors Association national convention in Kansas City. They discussed their group vocal techniques as it related to the performance of Bach. On the basis of this successful venture Haasemann and Ehmann were invited to numerous workshops and festivals throughout the United States as well as to repeated summer sessions at Westminster Choir College (WCC) in Princeton, NJ.

In 1977 Haasemann moved to the United States and became the assistant conductor for the Westminster Choir and professor of conducting at WCC. For the next 14 years Haasemann shared her vision of group vocal techniques with countless singers and conductors, through classroom instruction, rehearsals, and hundreds of workshops. Her collaborations with Joseph Flummerfelt, director of the Westminster Choir, and James Jordan, professor of conducting at WCC, have resulted in numerous concerts, recordings, and publications relating to her choral vocal methods. Most notable of the publications is Haasemann's *Group Vocal Techniques* (1992), which delineates her approach to choral singing through prose, an extensive sequenced collection of vocalise cards (vocal melodies without texts), and an instructional video (1989).

Honors and awards received in recognition of her life's accomplishments include the title of church music director, Evangelical Lutheran Church of Westphalia, 1974; an honorary Doctor of Music degree from Westminster Choir College, 1991; and a Certificate of Appreciation, Eastern Division American Choral Directors Association, 1991. Haasemann died of cancer on 12 April 1991. In testimonies by her peers and students she was celebrated not only for her outstanding musicianship but also for her love of life, friendship, and undying desire to help all whom she met.

See also Choral Education; Music Education

For Further Reading

"Frauke Peterson Haasemann, Famed Westminster Professor." Obituary. *Trenton Times*, 16 April 1991.

Haasemann, Frauke. "Thoughts on Choral Music in America: Report of a Sabbatical Trip to Six American Institutions." Trans. Brenda Smith. *Choral Journal* (August 1986): 23–27.

Schisler, Charles. "A Woman for All Choirs." *Westminster Choir College Newsletter* (November 1978) Princeton, NJ.

Eric Johnson

Hackley, Emma Azalia Smith (1867–1922)

Throughout her career as concert artist, teacher, and writer, Emma Azalia Smith Hackley strove to improve music education in black communities. She performed, taught, and championed works by black composers along with traditional spirituals. In addition to almost ceaseless touring and teaching, she organized the Hackley Foreign Scholarship Fund in 1908 to assist black musicians in their pursuit of European study. In 1915 she founded the Hackley Normal Vocal Institute in Chicago, and in 1916 she opened a publishing firm, the Azalia Hackley Music Publishing House, to help black composers and music educators distribute their works. Her tireless commitment to music education inspired the Detroit Public Library to name their extensive collection of African American arts holdings in her honor: the E. Azalia Hackley Memorial Collection of Negro Music, Dance, and Drama.

Hackley was born on 29 June 1867 in Murfreesboro, TN. Racial hostilities forced the family to flee Murfreesboro in 1870 and move to Detroit to be closer to family members and friends. Hackley's musical training began in her formative years with lessons in piano, voice, and violin. In 1883 she was the first black student to graduate from Detroit Central High School, and in the fall of that year she became the first black student to be admitted to the teacher training program at Detroit's Washington Normal School. After completing her training she taught in the Detroit elementary schools for several years. In 1894 she married Denver attorney and newspaper editor Edwin Henry Hackley and moved to Colorado. She entered the University of Denver and in 1901 earned a bachelor's degree in voice performance and pedagogy. In 1905–1906 and again in 1907 she toured Europe, concertizing and studying voice, conducting, and pedagogy with two renowned teachers: Jean de Reszke in Paris and William Shakespeare Hays in London.

Between 1890 and 1910 Hackley was best known throughout the United States, Canada, and Europe for her solo recitals and occasional opera appearances. In 1910 she announced her impending retirement from the stage and commenced a three-year farewell concert tour. She devoted a portion of her recitals to "vocal demonstrations" that featured talks about singing techniques, note reading, and music appreciation. Throughout her retirement tour she visited dozens of schools and taught thousands of students, earning the sobriquet "the vocal teacher of ten thousand." She gradually relied far less on European choral classics to achieve her pedagogical goals and instead turned to spirituals, along with new pieces by black composers, for teaching materials. Her innovative programming and teaching philosophy inspired the initiation of folk song festivals—a format she used almost exclusively after 1913. Her festivals not only served her goals of music education but also became potent vehicles for building community solidarity and individual social and political empowerment, or what she referred to as "musical social uplift" (Marshall, 235).

In 1919 Hackley's health began to de-

teriorate. She was hospitalized with a cerebral hemorrhage in 1921 after a whirlwind tour of Japan and never completely recovered. She died in Detroit at the home of her sister on 13 December 1922.

See also Music Education

For Further Reading

Brevard, Lisa Pertillar. *A Biography of E. Azalia Smith Hackley, 1867–1922, African-American Singer and Social Activist*. Lewiston, NY: Edwin Mellen Press, 2001.

Hackley, E. Azalia. *The Colored Girl Beautiful*. Kansas City, MO: Burton, 1916.

———. "Hints to Young Colored Artists." *New York Age* [series of 12 articles], 1914–1915.

Karpf, Juanita. "E. Azalia Hackley (1867–1922): Artist, Educator, Philanthropist." *Notable Black American Women*. Ed. Jessie Carney Smith. Detroit: Garland, 1992, 429–434.

———. "Hackley, Emma Azalia." In *African American Women*. Ed. Dorothy C. Salem. New York: Garland, 1993, 219–220.

———. "The Vocal Teacher of Ten Thousand: E. Azalia Hackley as Community Music Educator, 1910–22." *Journal of Research in Music Education* 47, no. 4 (Winter 1999): 319–330.

Marshall, M.M. "Emma A. Hackley." In *Homespun Heroines and Other Women of Distinction*. Ed. Hallie Q. Brown. Xenia, OH: Aldine, 1926; reprint, New York: Oxford University Press, 1988.

Juanita Karpf

Hair, Harriet Inez (1935–)

A nationally recognized leader in music education, Harriet Inez Hair is well known for her service to professional organizations and for her research on children's musical responses. Hair's research focuses on technology in teaching and on musical development, especially children's verbal, visual, and auditory responses to music. She continues to publish in leading journals, including the *Journal of Research in Music Education*, *Psychology of Music*, *Psychomusicology*, and the *Bulletin of the Council for Research in*

Music Education. In addition, she has presented her research at conferences and symposia throughout the United States and in Europe, Asia, and South Africa. She was selected as one of seven musicians to present her research at six seminars of the International Society in Music Education during the years 1986–2000.

Born in Spartanburg, SC, on 28 June 1935, she received her initial music instruction in piano at age eight. During junior high school she wanted to play trumpet in the band but was informed that girls were not allowed to participate in the band program. Only after considerable persuasion from her mother did the band director relent, enabling Hair to become one of the first girls in her school's band. After graduating from high school Hair entered Mount Holyoke College and earned a B.A. in music with a minor in French. During her junior year she was selected to participate in the prestigious Sweet Briar Program, which sponsored studies overseas. She spent the academic year 1955–1956 at the University of Paris, France, and had lessons in music theory with Nadia Boulanger. She recalls her experiences in Paris as being among the most influential of her entire career. After the completion of her undergraduate degree Hair earned an M.A. from Harvard University Graduate School of Education, an M.M. from Converse College, and an Ed.D. from Teachers College, Columbia University.

Hair has held teaching positions in the public schools of Waltham, MA, where she taught music and French, and at Converse College as assistant professor of music. She joined the faculty of the University of Georgia in 1971 and was promoted to the rank of professor in 1984. During the years 1988–1991 she was a General Sandy Beaver Teaching Professor at the University of Georgia, an honor bestowed on only 10 faculty members. In fall 1992 she held an endowed chair of music education at the University of Alabama, Tuscaloosa, and in fall 1999 she was an invited lecturer for the Joint Seminar in Music Education at Arizona State and the University of Arizona.

Throughout her career Hair has been a mentor for new and aspiring teachers, especially through service to professional music education organizations. She has held a variety of state, regional, and national offices in the Music Educators National Conference (MENC) and the Association for Technology in Music Education. In addition, she has served on the editorial board of the *Journal of Research in Music Education*, as chair of the Society for Research in Music Education, and as national chair of collegiate chapters of MENC.

See also Music Education

For Further Reading

Hair, Harriet I. "Divergent Research in Children's Musical Development." *Psychomusicology* 16 (1999): 26–39.

———. "Microcomputer Tests of Aural and Visual Directional Patterns." *Psychology of Music* 10/2 (1983): 26–31.

———. "Verbal Identification of Music Concepts." *Journal of Research in Music Education* 29 (1981): 11–21.

Juanita Karpf

Handy, D[orothy] Antoinette (1930–)

D[orothy] Antoinette Handy has made an important contribution to the American music scene through her works as a musician, writer, and director of the music program at the National Endowment of the Arts (retired in 1993). Her outstanding efforts in so many phases of music have been recognized by two honorary doctorates, from the Cleveland Institute of Music (1993) and Whittier College (1997), along with awards from the governor of Louisiana, the National Association of Negro Musicians, the National Black Music Caucus, the New England Conservatory of Music, and the Northwestern University School of Music. Though slowed by physical problems in recent years, Handy maintains a busy schedule of professional activities: conducting site visits and evaluations for the National Endowment of the Arts, lecturing, music consulting, and choir directing, in addition to her work as a music author.

Handy was born on 29 October 1930 in New Orleans, LA. She studied piano, violin, and trumpet before settling on the flute at age 14. After finishing high school she earned a B.M. in flute performance at the New England Conservatory (1952), an M.M. at Northwestern University School of Music (1953), and a Diploma at the Paris National Conservatory (1955). While at Northwestern she played a season on scholarship with the Chicago Civic Orchestra. Following her work in Paris at the conservatory she pursued a very successful career as a flutist both in Europe and the United States.

In the years that followed she was a member of the International Orchestra of Paris (1954–1955); Musica Viva Orchestra of Geneva (1955); the Symphony of the Air under Leonard Bernstein (1956); the Bach Festival Orchestra in Carmel, CA (1957); the Orchestra of America under Richard Korn (1960–1962); the Symphony of the New World (1968–1971); and the Richmond (VA) Symphony (1966–1976). From 1954 to 1976 she toured widely in the United States and Europe as a concert flutist performing concerti, solo recitals, and other concerts with her own ensemble, the Trio Pro Vivo. This trio featured the music of black composers.

During the latter part of these years she served as radio commentator on a weekly program she created called "Black Virginia," wrote articles for the Richmond *African American*, and held music faculty positions at Florida A&M University, Tuskegee Institute, Jackson State College, and Virginia State College. Since that time she has continued her work as a music writer on black music as well as a very distinguished career as an arts manager at the National Endowment for the Arts (1985–1993). She first went to the endowment as the assistant director of the music program; she later became the director and made a significant contribution in making changes to the panel procedures and in defining jazz as a chamber music medium. She also conceptualized three very successful programs for the Smithsonian Institution on "Black Concert Music."

As a truly outstanding musician, writer, and arts administrator, Handy has created a special role for her many colleagues and for those to follow in daring to pursue her dreams and goals as an African American woman in the United States. She is a pioneer for all who labor diligently on behalf of the arts.

See also African American Musicians

For Further Reading

Handy, D. Antoinette. *Black Conductors*. Lanham, MD: Scarecrow Press, 1995.
———. *Black Women in American Bands and Orchestras*, 2d ed. Lanham, MD: Scarecrow Press, 1998.

———. *The International Sweethearts of Rhythm.* Metuchen, NJ: Scarecrow Press, 1983.

Greg Steinke

Harry, Deborah (Debbie) (1945–   )

Deborah (Debbie) Harry is a pop rock singer and actress who is best known as the lead vocalist for the new wave band Blondie. She also enjoyed a notable solo career and appeared in a number of films. Sporting platinum blond hair, an attractive singing voice, and a model's good looks and sexual allure, Harry was one of the most charismatic pop performers of the late 1970s and early 1980s. Her image can perhaps be most succinctly characterized as a punk updating of Marilyn Monroe.

Born in Miami, FL, on 1 July 1945, Harry was adopted. Despite singing appearances in a sixth-grade school play and with her local church choir, she was not considered musically precocious. After obtaining an associate degree from Centenary College (NJ) in 1965, she moved to New York City, where she began her career with various obscure local bands. The most notable of these were Wind in the Willows, a 1960s folk-rock act, and the Stilettos, an early 1970s neo girl-group outfit. During this time she held various odd jobs, among other things working as a waitress at Max's Kansas City and as a Playboy bunny.

Harry and boyfriend Chris Stein founded Blondie (initially calling themselves Angel and the Snake) in 1974 from the remains of the Stilettos. Along with Television, Talking Heads, and the Ramones, Blondie was one of the vanguard New York new wave acts associated with the club CBGB, although the group's approach was somewhat more pop-oriented than that of their peers. After a slow start,

Debbie Harry, lead singer of Blondie, in performance c. 1980. *Photo courtesy of Hulton/Archive Photos.*

by the end of the decade Blondie had become the most commercially successful of these bands, enjoying major hits with "Denis" (a remake of the 1963 Randy and the Rainbows' hit "Denise"), "Hanging on the Telephone," "Heart of Glass," "One Way or Another," "Call Me," "The Tide Is High," and "Rapture." Blondie's best albums, including *Blondie* (Chrysalis 21165), *Plastic Letters* (Chrysalis 21166), *Parallel Lines* (Chrysalis 21192), *Eat to the Beat* (Chrysalis 21225), and *Autoamerican* (Chrysalis 21290), received both popular and critical acclaim. Harry's singing proved very amenable to the band's eclectic approach, which ranged from punk to pop, reggae to rap.

By 1981, Blondie was beset with interpersonal difficulties; at this juncture, Harry released her first solo album, *KooKoo* (Chrysalis 6082), which reached Gold status. One year later Stein developed a serious genetic-based illness, precipitating the demise of Blondie and forcing Harry into temporary retirement. Harry resumed her singing career in 1986, recording solo albums such as *Rockbird* (Geffen 2-24123), *Def, Dumb, and Blonde* (Sire 25938), and *Debravation* (Sire/Reprise 45303). Although no American hits resulted, she charted in the United Kingdom with "French Kissing" and "I Want That Man." In 1997 Harry and a now-recovered Stein reformed Blondie and recommended recording and touring.

See also Rock and Popular Music Genres; Rock Music

For Further Reading

Bangs, Lester. *Blondie*. New York: Simon & Schuster, 1980.

Che, Cathay. *Deborah Harry: Platinum Blonde. A Biography*. London: Andre Deutsch, 1999.

Harry, Debbie, Chris Stein, and Victor Bockris. *Making Tracks: The Rise of Blondie*. New York: Da Capo Press, 1998 (originally published 1982, London: Elm Tree Books).

David Cleary

Hayes, Pamela Tellejohn (1946–)

Pamela Tellejohn Hayes is a nationally recognized string educator, orchestra clinician, consultant, conductor, teacher, and author. Particularly recognized for her outstanding work in the public schools, Hayes is an active and important resource person in the initiation, development, and management of exemplary public school orchestra programs.

Hayes was born in Little River, KS, in 1946. She earned a bachelor's degree in music education at Wichita State University (1968), and a master of education degree in educational administration from the University of South Carolina (1979), followed by an education specialist certificate from the University of South Carolina (1995). Hayes taught orchestra in numerous public school districts in Kansas and in South Carolina from 1968 to 1999. She has also served on the faculty at Columbia College (SC), the University of South Carolina, and Presbyterian College (Clinton, SC).

One of the outstanding leaders in music education, Hayes has published numerous articles in the *Music Educators Journal*, the *Instrumentalist*, *Orchestra News*, *The Glasel World of Strings*, and the *South Carolina Musician*. She has co-authored the best-selling string class method series *Essential Elements for Strings* and is a contributing author for several Music Educators National Conference (MENC) publications, including the *State Leadership Guide*, the *Complete String Guide*, and the *Orchestra Curriculum Guide*.

Hayes has served as president of numerous professional organizations, including the National School Orchestra Association, the South Carolina Music Educators Association, and the South Carolina chapter of the American String Teachers Association. Hayes is a well-recognized leader, having received many honors including the Elizabeth A. H. Green School Educator Award from the American String Teachers Association (1998) and the Merle J. Isaac Lifetime Achievement Award from the National School Orchestra Association (1996).

See also Music Education; String Education

For Further Reading

Allen, Michael, Robert Gillespie, and Pamela Tellejohn Hayes. *Essential Elements for Strings*. Milwaukee: Hal Leonard Publishing, 1994.

Andrea Olijnek

Heavy Metal

See Garage Band and Heavy Metal Music

Hensley, Virginia Patterson

See Cline, Patsy

Hill, Emily (1911–1988)

Emily Hill was a composer and performer whose lifelong performance and love of Wind River Shoshone songs sprang from her strong commitment to her culture. A Native American, she spent her entire life on the Wind River Reservation in Wyoming. The Wind River Shoshones originated in the Great Basin and moved onto the Plains in the sixteenth century. There they adapted to Plains culture as nomadic hunters and warriors. Great Basin and Plains singing styles are very distinct: Great Basin singers sing with a "relaxed" throat, whereas Plains singers sing with greater tension, producing a more intense, "pinched" sound. In addition, Plains singers employ "pulsation" on long notes—steady, rhythmic surges, or pulses of sound. Hill sings all her songs using Plains singing style, with the exception of Ghost Dance songs, in which her singing is a modified Plains/Basin style.

At the time of her birth, families lived in tents or small log cabins and depended on government rations of meat and other staples to supplement garden produce, wild foods, and hunting. Emily attended a boarding school on the reservation, counterbalancing warm memories of work experiences with the painful punishments students suffered for speaking Shoshone.

Researcher Judith Vander has recorded Hill's performance of 213 songs, a repertoire that reflects both Great Basin and Plains cultures. It includes 147 Ghost Dance or *Naraya* songs, the largest number ever recorded from an individual singer. *Naraya* songs were a vital part of the Ghost Dance, a nineteenth-century religious performance by Shoshones and others. Song and dance were used to help achieve the prophecy for the return of dead relatives and the creation of a new, pristine world. Shoshones layered these Ghost Dance beliefs on top of an older Round Dance tradition of the Great Basin. Like the Round Dance, the *Naraya* was supposed to ensure an abundance of plant and animal life, as well as water, a central concern to Great Basin peoples. The *Naraya* also prevented disease and maintained health. Transcriptions of music and texts (in both Shoshone and English) of Hill's performances appear in three publications by Vander.

Another important religious performance among the Shoshones, the Sun Dance, is reflected in 48 of Hill's songs. Sixteen Round Dance songs and two Wolf Dance songs round out her repertoire, reflecting the importance of old social dances and their accompanying songs in community occasions of the past.

See also Multicultural Musics; Native American Musicians

For Further Reading

Vander, Judith. *Ghost Dance Songs and Religion of a Wind River Shoshone Woman*. Monograph Series in Ethnomusicology, no. 4. Los Angeles: University of California, 1986.

———. *Shoshone Ghost Dance Religion: Poetry Songs and Great Basin Context*. Urbana and Chicago: University of Illinois Press, 1997.

———. *Songprints: The Musical Experience of Five Shoshone Women*. Urbana and Chicago: University of Illinois Press, 1988.

Judith Vander

Hill, Lauryn (1975–)

As a founding member of the hip hop group the Fugees, Lauryn Hill first found prominence in 1996 with the release of the trio's second record, *The Score* (Sony 67147). Following that release Hill spent time as a songwriter for Aretha Franklin's *A Rose Is Still a Rose* and gave birth to her first child, Zion, with husband Rohan Marley, son of Bob Marley (the couple had a second child, Selah Louise, in 1998). Hill has received praise for her compassionate lyrics and moral approach to hip hop. A critic writing for *The Source* states that *The Miseducation of Lauryn Hill* (her 1998 release) is "Thoughtful, passionate, purposeful and unmistakably female . . . the overall emotional and musical effect is potent."

Lauryn Hill was born on 26 May 1975. As with the song "To Zion," her children emerge as a focus in her music. Her 1998 release, *The Miseducation of Lauryn Hill* (Sony 69035), claimed the number one position on the *Billboard* chart the week of its release. With this achievement, *The Miseducation of Lauryn Hill* became the first record by a woman solo artist to sell over 400,000 copies in its first week of release. She was accompanied by guest appearances by performers such as Mary J. Blige, D'Angelo, and Carlos Santana. Santana's performance in "To Zion" helped to focus musically on the extremely personal and profound nature of the text—an exploration of Hill's decision to carry a baby to term rather than explore alternatives.

See also Rap

For Further Reading

"Hip-Hop Pages." *Rolling Stone* (3 September 1998): 98.
The Source (September 1998): 230.

Kristen Stauffer Todd

Lauryn Hill performs at the MTV Video Music Awards in New York City in September 1999. *Photo © Jeff Christensen/ Reuters NewMedia, Inc./CORBIS.*

Hillis, Margaret (1921–1998)

The founder of the Chicago Symphony Chorus and the first woman to conduct the Chicago Symphony, Margaret Hillis was a pioneer among women conductors. At the time of the Chicago Symphony Chorus's founding in 1957, there were few professional vocal ensembles. Hillis was determined to create an outstanding professional chorus and at the same time make a name for herself as a conductor. Her efforts established the standard of excellence for symphonic choruses and led to her widespread recognition as a gifted conductor.

Margaret Hillis was born on 1 October

A 1979 photo of Margaret Hillis, founder and longtime director of the Chicago Symphony Chorus. *Courtesy of Rosenthal Archives, Chicago Symphony Orchestra.*

1921 in Kokomo, IN. She was educated at Kokomo High School and the Tudor Hall School in Indianapolis. She received a bachelor's degree in composition from Indiana University and a master's degree in choral conducting from the Juilliard School, where her primary teacher was Robert Shaw. Hillis made her conducting debut when she led the Kokomo High School orchestra in the Overture to Carl Maria von Weber's *Der Freischütz.* Although she led various ensembles during her graduate work, including serving as Shaw's assistant conductor for the Collegiate Chorale in New York City, her true professional debut came in 1952 when she conducted the Tanglewood

Alumni Chorus (later the American Concert Choir and Orchestra) in two Carnegie Hall concerts.

In 1957, Hillis was invited by Fritz Reiner, then music director of the Chicago Symphony Orchestra, to start the Chicago Symphony Chorus. For five years Hillis commuted between Chicago and New York before leaving New York permanently in 1962. Although she held many other positions concurrently, it was with the Chicago Symphony Chorus that she became best known. She served the Chorus as director until her retirement in 1994.

Originally Hillis wanted to be an instrumental conductor, but at that time there were no women instrumental conductors. She was advised to pursue vocal conducting as a means of establishing herself, thereby opening the door to instrumental conducting engagements. The strategy was most successful. By the end of her career she had conducted many of the major orchestras in the United States, including the Chicago Symphony Orchestra. Her most notable appearance there came in 1977 when she stepped in for an ailing Sir George Solti, conducting the orchestra in a performance of Gustav Mahler's Eighth Symphony at Carnegie Hall. Still remembered and respected in New York City for her earlier work there, Hillis became known across the country as a result of the national headlines occasioned by the concert.

Although she was best known for her conducting, teaching was also important to Hillis. She taught at the Union Theological Seminary (1950–1960), the Juilliard School (1951–1953), and Northwestern University (1970–1977). She founded not only the Chicago Symphony Chorus but also the American Concert Choir and Orchestra, the American Choral Foundation, and the Elgin (Illinois) Symphony Orchestra. She received many awards and recognitions, including nine Grammy Awards.

Following Hillis's death from lung cancer on 4 February 1998, the Margaret Hillis collection containing her scores, papers, and awards was established at the Samuel and Marie-Louise Rosenthal Archives of the Chicago Symphony Orchestra at Symphony Center.

See also Conductor, Choral

For Further Reading

LePage, Jane Weiner. *Women Composers, Conductors, and Musicians of the Twentieth Century: Selected Biographies.* Metuchen, NJ: Scarecrow Press, 1980.

Wager, Jeannine. *Conductors in Conversation: Fifteen Contemporary Conductors Discuss Their Lives and Profession.* Boston: G. K. Hall, 1991.

Michele Wolff

Historiography

The historiography of American women in music—how women's past is to be interpreted—has undergone many changes since 1900. Through the 1960s the relatively few researchers investigating women's work were concerned with documenting women's increasing recognition as men's intellectual and musical equals. At the same time, an all-male art-music repertoire, or canon, became entrenched in American academic curricula, concert life, and musicology. Textbooks for classes in music history, theory, and appreciation reinforced the notion that important music consisted in the masterworks of a succession of men composers, most of them European and few of them still alive. In the 1970s and 1980s, feminist music historians were thus less optimistic than in earlier decades about improvements in women's opportunity and status; the task of recovering women's history and documenting the present seemed more urgent. Like civil rights leaders advocating racial equality, feminist music historians advocated women's right to equal recognition, but not necessarily on existing terms. Critical theory and feminist theories of cultural context inspired new paradigms of women's history. Feminist musicology and feminist music theory introduced gender as a factor in history, analysis, and criticism. In the 1990s, as many music historians adopted the inclusiveness and political awareness of feminist scholarship, the emphasis shifted from women's history to gender issues.

Early Optimism. Rupert Hughes, in his chapter "The Women Composers" in *Contemporary American Composers* (1900), asserts that "it is impossible for a rational mind to deny that the best work done in the arts by women is of better quality than the average work done by men." He calls Amy Marcy Cheney Beach's (1867–1944) works "markedly virile" and Margaret Rutheven Lang's "supremely womanly." In *Woman's Work in Music* (1903) Arthur Elson notes the many women composers in the United States "who do earnest work, and who lead lives of activity and production that afford them equal rank with the men in this respect." His survey of women in music begins with antiquity and includes mythical figures, composers' wives, and a chapter on American women.

Similarly, Otto Ebel in *Women Composers: A Biographical Handbook of Woman's Work in Music* (1902), dedicated to the Women's Musical Clubs of America, predicts the end of "prejudice and the rules of fashion and custom" that earlier barred women from serious study of harmony and counterpoint, and from studying the violin, cello, and other stringed and wind instruments. He observes, optimistically, that the time has passed when "to be told that a composition was the work of a woman, was equivalent to its condemnation beforehand." Ebel provides biographical sketches of composers, biographers, and other writers in Europe and the United States beginning in the sixteenth century, including over 100 recent Americans. These and similar surveys by Hughes, Elson, and Ebel went through several revised editions, some of which were reprinted in the 1970s.

Edwin Barnes's *American Women in Creative Music* (1936), a 44-page chronology, highlights 200 composers active since 1900. William Treat Upton, in *Art-Song in America* (1930; *Supplement*, 1938), discusses works of Amy Marcy Cheney Beach, Clara Rogers, and Ruth Crawford Seeger (1901–1953) in some detail; John Tasker Howard in *Our American Music* (1931) mentions Beach, Crawford Seeger, and Ethel G. Hier. Toward mid-century, Claire Reis in *Composers in America* (1947) presents information about the lives and works of 17 prominent women. Sophie Drinker's *Music and Women* (1948), on the other hand, develops the thesis that women in the United States, as in other modern patriarchal societies in which women are suppressed, cannot be truly creative as musicians.

The 1970s and 1980s. The revival, or "second wave," of feminism brought renewed interest in women's history, including music history; women rediscovered the effectiveness of collective political action, and women's studies became an academic discipline. During this era the historian Gerda Lerner ("Placing Women in History," 1975) described methods of historiography that may be discerned in music history as well. She introduced the term "compensatory history" for feminist research that identifies the "women worthies"—women who, when judged by traditional, male standards, may be deemed worthy of the kind of attention usually afforded only to men. Although compensatory history is an improvement over all-male history, it should be superseded by more productive and informative feminist methodologies. In the bifocal history of women, or Lerner's "contribution history," which examines women's contributions to male-dominated society, human experience is conceptualized primarily in dualist categories—female/male, private/public, nature/transcendence—and women's status and oppression are taken into account. In feminist history, historians investigate what most women were doing at a certain time and place, in the private, women's sphere as well as the public, men's sphere. Finally, in multifocal history, the ideal phase that Lerner calls "universal history," historians discuss gender roles along with race, ethnicity, class, marital status, and sexual preference, in considering women's work; a balanced perspective serves to fuse women's and men's work into a holistic view.

By the 1970s, influenced by women's studies and feminist scholarship in other disciplines, feminist researchers in music were producing biographies of women musicians, worklists, new editions of music, bibliographies, and indexes. Many feminist historians advocate the mainstreaming, or "integration," of women into the academic music curriculum. For Americanists, one of the most significant historical studies is *Women in American Music: A Bibliography of Music and Literature*, compiled and edited by Adrienne Fried Block and Carol Neuls-Bates (1979), which contains abstracts of books, journal articles, and other literature by and about women in art music and vernacular music from colonial times to 1978. The introduction provides a chronological survey of women in music and an analysis of the historical and historiographical issues.

In the 1970s the move to interpretive, interdisciplinary studies was also reflected in the work of Judith Tick (b. 1943), Jane Bernstein, Jane Bowers, Elizabeth Wood, and Jeannie Pool, among others. Wood, in her "Review Essay: Women and Music" (*Signs*, 1980), asserts that current discussions of women's work "in terms of the dominant musical culture or methodology alone" are lacking in "scholarly substance." She urges researchers to address "the conditions women have had to create, exploit, defy, deny, or succumb to, in order to have their music heard at all"; she recommends "probing research of an interdisciplinary and comparative nature," without which "musical scholarship on women will remain conceptually irrelevant to work in other fields." Pool, in "A Critical Approach to the History of Women in Music" (*Heresies*, 1980), likewise argues for feminist analysis of women's history; it is not enough to produce biographies of notable women, she writes, which merely constitute a defensive response to questions of greatness.

In 1989 and 1990 in the *College Music Symposium*, Jane Bowers reviews "Feminist Scholarship and the Field of Musicology" over the previous two decades. Bowers lists and documents five general facts that American research has revealed concerning the history of women and music throughout the world: (1) women have been active in musical life in totally unanticipated numbers; (2) women's (as well as men's) music making has reflected the social/sexual roles assigned them by the societies in which they lived; (3) women's activities have been limited by

exclusionary techniques and social control; (4) women have complied with imposed limitations and often worked behind the scenes to nurture their communities' musical environment; and (5) a historical process has been at work to render women's activities invisible. If "feminist methods and perspectives" are to make "a substantial impact on the mainstream of American musicology," she continues, then the fact-finding must be informed by "imaginative new research methodologies" and "broad new organizing ideas" drawn from anthropology, ethnomusicology, sociology, history, folklore, language studies, and other disciplines. She describes in detail several possible interdisciplinary modes of inquiry, most of them applicable to the history of music in the United States.

Five Stages. In 1990 in the *Sonneck Society for American Music Bulletin*, Betty Chmaj, chair of the society's newly formed interest group on gender issues, describes the shift over the previous 25 years, from research about women and music in the United States to multifocal, multidisciplinary research on gender issues. Chmaj describes "how women's perspectives are not only restoring unsung women to music history but are changing the way the culture thinks and knows, the way it judges music and chooses canons, the way it looks at its own past and transforms the future." To this end, she reviews five stages in women's studies research as applied to American music history. Stage one, "Women Worthies and Image Studies," combines the compensatory and bifocal approaches. Besides identifying Lerner's "women worthies," Chmaj notes, historians begin looking at images of women in lyrics of parlor songs, mother songs, and hymns to help illuminate the doctrine of separate spheres and the "cult of true womanhood." Images in the lyrics of rock music, country music, popular music, and women-identified music, Broadway musicals, blues, and various ethnic musics also attract scholarly attention.

Chmaj labels stage two, which begins in the mid-1970s, "Where Are the Women?" Researchers use the methods of the new social history and focus not only on leaders and celebrities but also on anonymous women, poor women, nonwhite women, and collective music making. Historians also begin to consider audiences, especially women audiences, not simply music critics, as a measure of response, and they consider women's participation in musical patronage. This stage is similar to Lerner's feminist history.

Stages three and four are refinements of Lerner's multifocal history. In Chmaj's stage three, "Critique of Patriarchy," the focus on women gradually gives way to a focus on gender as a concept, including ideas of feminine and masculine, female and male, and how they have structured Americans' beliefs and actions. Men join women in the discourse over feminist theory and gender issues. They ask how patriarchal values and procedures have been built into the society as a whole. Why must the girl Frank Butler marries be as soft and pink as a nursery? Why *can't* Annie get a man with a gun? ("The real Annie did," Chmaj writes, "and the real Frank adored her for her talent.") What does it mean to describe Lester Young's saxophone style as "feminine" and Charlie Parker's as "masculine"?

Stage four, evident in the late 1970s and early 1980s, is "Equality or Difference?" A conceptual shift develops into a split. Although some historians believe that women speak and write "in a different voice" (Carol Gilligan, author of the book by that name, was named *Ms. Magazine*'s Woman of the Year in 1983), others maintain that women and men share ideas, concepts, and attitudes. Stage five, "Hearing Women and Hearing Anew," constitutes investigation into what Chmaj calls "re-hearing"—a way of listening from a woman's point of view that will cause us to "hear anew." Chmaj also envisions a further stage, "Complicity Research," that involves investigation of how women, while living within patriarchal restraints, have used cultural gestures that are ironic or quixotic in order to subvert such restraints and escape censure.

The 1990s. In the 1990s various interdisciplinary approaches were widely used, except that men's work—men composers' representation of women and gender issues—was usually the focus, not women's work as in Bowers's description, and not women's and men's work in a holistic approach such as Lerner and Chmaj envisioned. Many studies of gender in music did not mention women composers or performers at all. Calls for the integration, or "mainstreaming," of women in the curriculum were less frequent than in the 1970s and 1980s. Male history prevailed, even if its status had been called into question and its methods and results transformed. Among historians of women, the usual approach was now the inclusive feminist history, although compensatory and bifocal approaches were also evident in the ongoing critique of patriarchy and debates over equality versus difference. Many researchers tended to denigrate archival research, including the production of editions and chronologies of women's work, which they may have associated with old-fashioned compensatory history. It seems too early to abandon such research methods, however, which inform and enrich studies that are interpretive, contextual, and interdisciplinary.

See also Feminist Music Theory, Feminist Musicology

For Further Reading

Barnes, Edwin N.C. *American Women in Creative Music*. Tuning in an American Music series. Washington, DC: Music Education Publications, 1936. Ebel, Otto. *Women Composers: A Biographical Handbook of Women's work in Music*. Brooklyn, NY: F.H. Chandler, 1902, Bvd. ed.; New York: Chandler Ebel, 1913.

Chmaj, Betty E. M. " 'Reality Is on Our Side': Research on Gender in American Music." *Sonneck Society for American Music Bulletin* 16/2 (Summer 1990): 53–58.

Hisama, Ellie M. "Musicology: Feminist." *Reader's Guide to Music: History Theory, Criticism*, ed. Murray Steib. Chicago and London: Fitzroy Dearborn, 1999.

Lerner, Gerder. "Placing Women in History: Definitions and Challenges." *Feminist Studies* 3/1–2 (Fall 1975): 5–14. Reprinted as "Placing Women in History: A 1975 Perspective" in *Liberating Women's History: Theoretical and Critical Essays*, ed. Berenice A. Carroll. Urbana: University of Illinois Press, 1976, 357–367.

Deborah Hayes

Hoffman, Mary E. (1926–1997)

Mary E. Hoffman was a leader and innovator in music education in several areas. Beyond her 25-year tenure at the University of Illinois Urbana-Champaign, her distinguished career ranged from elementary classroom teaching and school district leadership to serving as president of the Music Educators National Conference (MENC). She co-authored widely used music education textbooks and toured internationally as a guest choral conductor and clinician. Hoffman stands out for her emphasis on life-long learning and for her outspoken advocacy to secure the place of music education in schools through public policy.

Hoffman received her bachelor's degree from Lebanon Valley College, earned her master's from the Teachers College at Columbia University, and pursued advanced studies at Northwestern University. In the 1950s she taught elementary music in Delaware, Connecticut, and Pennsylvania. She became known as a pied piper of sorts, reaching 17,500 pupils in 29 Philadelphia schools as the "roving music teacher." She was revolutionary in her day, going beyond the standard note reading and songbooks; her inventive use of rhythm sticks, marching, classroom instruments, and props fostered children's participation in music making and has been widely imitated. She became elementary district music supervisor in Philadelphia and then supervisor of elementary and junior high school music in Milwaukee, where she served on the board of the Wisconsin Music Educators Conference from 1963 to 1967.

Moving into higher education at the University of Illinois, she rose to the rank of professor of music education. Her primary focus was to improve music curricula for the general music student as a way to encourage life-long learning and participation in music. Respected for both her teaching and her musicianship, Hoffman was guest conductor of over 90 district and all-state choruses, and as a guest clinician and speaker she traveled throughout the United States, Austria, and Canada. In 1978 she served on the curriculum committee for the educational television project "MUSIC . . ."

As president of MENC in 1981–1982, Hoffman led the movement to strengthen the music education profession through improved teaching, assessment, and advocacy. She appealed to teachers to strive for full understanding of music's benefits to children, to further investigate how students of all ages learn music, to improve assessment of music learning, and to bring a clear message to policy makers and communities in order to secure the future of music programs in school district budgets. She called for increased grass-roots involvement and urged MENC to continually reevaluate its Goals and Objectives Project in the service of improving and sustaining music education nationwide.

Hoffman also influenced the music education profession as a writer. In addition to numerous journal articles, she was co-author of two college music education texts: *Teaching Music: What, How and Why* and *Teaching Music*. She contributed to sixth- through eighth-grade editions of three classroom texts: *World of Music*, *Silver Burdett Music*, and *The Music Connection*. Her numerous choral arrangements are published by the Lawson-Gould Choral Catalogue. Hoffman received alumna citations from Lebanon Valley College and Teachers College, Columbia University, and was honored with the Distinguished Service Award from MENC.

See also Music Education

For Further Reading

Hoffman, Mary E. "For President-Elect." *Music Educators Journal* 65/5 (1978): 101.

———. "Goals and Objectives for the Eighties." *Music Educators Journal* 67/4 (1980): 48–49.

———. "The Heart of the School Music Program." *Music Educators Journal* 68/1 (1978): 42–43.

Kilissa M. Cissoko

Holiday, Billie (1915–1959)

Musical legend Billie Holiday was perhaps the most outstanding jazz singer of her time. She did not scat, but instead phrased her vocal lines as a jazz instrumentalist might do. She took the melody

Billie Holiday before a New York City performance c. 1950. *Photo © Bradley Smith/ CORBIS.*

from the beat and stretched or minimized it—singing behind the beat. In doing so, she was following the style of Louis Armstrong. The other inspiration for her singing was blues singer Bessie Smith (1894–1937). Although she did not have Bessie Smith's vocal power or wide repertoire, Holiday still used blues style in most of her work. There are numerous recordings of Holiday's performances, including *Lady Sings the Blues* (Polygram 521429), *Body and Soul* (Mobile Fidelity 658), and *Lady in Satin* (Sony 53814).

Details of Holiday's early years, at least until approximately age 15, are speculative. Born Eleanora Fagin on 7 April 1915 in Philadelphia, PA (some earlier accounts stated Baltimore), she spent part of her earlier years with her mother, Sadie Fagan. Her father, Clarence Holiday, a big band musician, was disinterested in and absent from her life. While her mother found work as a maid, primarily in New York, Holiday stayed with relatives or friends. In 1929, when she finally moved north to be with her mother, Holiday was not interested in working as a maid and subsequently moved to Harlem, where she began singing in nightclubs. Music was a panacea for her, and singing was a way to earn a living.

By the early 1930s Billie Holiday's impressive vocal talents were gaining her recognition. She sang with Benny Goodman's band in 1933, and in 1935 she began a fruitful and rewarding recording career. The musicians with whom she worked were the giants of jazz. Saxophonist Lester Young nicknamed her "Lady Day." She worked with Count Basie's band in 1937, and in 1938 she became the first African American singer to tour with a white band (Artie Shaw). Unhappy as a band singer, Holiday left Artie Shaw's band in 1939 to begin a solo act in nightclubs.

During the early 1940s while she was performing in nightclubs, Holiday was also drinking excessively and using hard drugs. By the mid-1940s her excesses began to affect her performances. She was arrested and served 10 months in jail for drug possession. She made several comebacks, continued recording, and even toured Europe. However, Billie Holiday died of a drug overdose on 17 July 1959 in a New York hospital.

See also Jazz

For Further Reading

Gourse, Leslie (ed.). *The Billie Holiday Companion: Seven Decades of Commentary*. New York: Schirmer Books, 1997.

Holiday, Billie, and William Dufty. *Lady Sings the Blues*. Garden City, NY: Doubleday, 1956.

Nicholson, Stuart. *Billie Holiday*. Boston: Northeastern University Press, 1995.

Monica J. Burdex

Holt, Patricia

See LaBelle, Patti

Hood, Marguerite Vivian (1903–1992)

Marguerite Vivian Hood, a prominent music educator, made major contributions in education and publishing. She was the first woman chairperson of the editorial board of the *Music Educators Journal* and an important force in the founding of the *Journal of Research in Music Education*. She published numerous articles on elementary music education, rural education, and teacher training. Additionally, she authored books on singing and classroom music, and she edited music textbook series that were published by Summy-Birchard and Ginn.

Hood was born in Drayton, ND, on 14 March 1903. She received a B.A. degree in music, French, and Spanish from Jamestown College, ND (1923). She taught music in Montana public schools in Havre and Bozeman in the 1920s and then was appointed Montana's first state supervisor of music (1930–1936). Hood continued her education by taking courses at Northwestern University and the Chicago Musical College, and she taught piano at the University of Montana. After studying radio techniques at New York University in 1936, Hood worked in Missoula, MT, and Spokane, WA, at stations operated by the Columbia Broadcasting System. She was a radio announcer and wrote news and advertising. In 1939 she accepted a teaching position in the School of Music of the University of Southern California, Los

Angeles, where she completed an M.M. degree (1941). In 1942 Hood continued her career in Michigan. She accepted a joint position as supervisor of music of the Ann Arbor public schools (1942–1958) and professor of music education at the University of Michigan. At the University of Michigan she directed the program that prepared students to teach choral and general music education, and she taught doctoral seminars.

Hood was an important leader of the Music Educators National Conference (MENC). She was president of the North Central Division of MENC (1945–1947), second vice-president of MENC (1948–1950), and president (1950–1952). She also served on the MENC Research Council (1944–1950). As president, Hood worked with the National Association of Schools of Music to develop policies for national accrediting of collegiate music education programs and continued this work as chairman of the MENC commission on accreditation (1952–1968). Articles and speeches by Hood during her presidency urged music educators to take more responsibility, be more assertive, and set high standards.

Active in the International Society for Music Education (ISME), Hood attended all the conferences from ISME's founding in Brussels (1953) to Warsaw (1980). Before the 1966 conference in Interlochen, MI, she was the administrative director for a successful International Seminar on Teacher Education in Music, held in Ann Arbor. Hood became an honorary member of ISME in 1947, received an honorary doctorate from Jamestown College in 1947, and was elected to the MENC Hall of Fame in 1986.

Marguerite Vivian Hood died on 22 February 1992 in her retirement home in Pomona, CA.

See also Music Education

For Further Reading

Britton, Allen P., George N. Heller, and Bruce D. Wilson. "Obituary, Marguerite Vivian Hood (1903–1992)." *International Journal of Music Education* 19 (1992): 47–48.

Sondra Wieland Howe

Hoover, Katherine (1937–)

Composer and performer Katherine Hoover is a widely recognized and performed composer, as well as an accomplished flutist who appears frequently in concerts and recordings. She has taught theory, composition, and flute at the university level. She was the driving force behind a pathbreaking series of women's music festivals. In recent years she has also begun producing recordings and conducting.

Hoover was born in Elkins, WV, on 2 December 1937. Her family was not musical and did not encourage her professional musical ambitions. As a result, she chose to enroll at the University of Rochester initially instead of its Eastman School of Music. She eventually transferred to Eastman, studied flute under Joseph Mariano, and graduated with a Performer's Certificate in flute and a B.M. in music theory (1959). After further study with flutist William Kincaid, she began teaching at the Juilliard School and later the Manhattan School of Music, where she received an M.M. degree in music theory (1973).

It was not until 1966, however, that a composition of Hoover's was performed in public. Diane Peacock Jezic (1988) traces this delay to prejudicial attitudes. In music school, Hoover encountered negative attitudes toward women composers that resulted in her pursuit of degrees in music theory instead of composition. Since the early 1970s she has been composing steadily, and many of her works have appeared under the imprints of major publishers like Carl Fischer, Theodore Presser, Boelke-Bomart, and Papagena Press. Recognition has come in the form of awards from the American Society of Composers, Authors and Publishers (ASCAP) and the American Academy of Arts and Letters; grants from the National Endowment for the Arts, Meet the Composer, and the Alice M. Ditson Fund; and an impressive array of commissions and recordings.

Between 1978 and 1981, Hoover organized annual festivals of women's music, by far the most ambitious effort that had been undertaken up until then to bring the history of women's music to the attention of the concert-going public. In all, nearly 200 works by 69 women composers from the Middle Ages to the present were performed. Broadcasts and recordings reached an international audience.

Hoover has written many excellent flute compositions with works such as *Kokopeli* (available on *Gaubert, Casella, et al: Works for Flute*, Summit 226) and the *Medieval Suite* (available on *A Distant Mirror*, Bayer 100246) becoming new standards in the flute literature. She has written idiomatically and with great success for other media, including chamber music and large ensembles. Hoover composes with the effects peculiar to each individual instrument in mind, incorporating such effects into the thematic and emotive content of the work at hand. Whereas such works as the piano quintet *Da pacem* (Koch International Classics 3-7147-2H1) demonstrate a great gift for expressive lyricism, characteristic works such as *Homage to Bartók* (1975), the *Sinfonia* for bassoon quartet (1976), and the Oboe Sonata (1991) are notable for rhythmically dynamic passages laced with incisive dissonance but often mingled with elements of jazz and well-timed humor.

See also Classical Music

For Further Reading

Hoover, Katherine. "The Festivals of Women's Music I–IV." In *The Musical Woman: An International Perspective*, vol. 1, ed. Judith Lang Zaimont. New York: Greenwood Press: 347–377.
Jezic, Diane Peacock. "Katherine Hoover (b. 1937): Virtuoso Flutist and Composer." In *Women Composers: The Lost Tradition Found*. New York: Feminist Press, 1988, 165–172.

Steve Luttmann

Horne, Lena (1917–)

Lena Horne, a legendary singer, talented actress, and stunningly beautiful woman, has received many accolades for her performances and career, including Tony and Grammy Awards for her 1981 one-woman Broadway show *Lena: The Lady and Her Music*, a lifetime achievement award from the Songwriters Hall of Fame (1994), the Ella Award for Lifetime Achievement by the Society of Singers (1997), and Kennedy Center honoree (1984). Numerous recordings of Horne are available from all periods of her life, including *Lena on the Blue Side* (RCA 2465), *An Evening with Lena Horne* (Blue Note 31877), and *Being Myself* (Blue Note 34286).

Born Lena Calhoun Horne on 30 June 1917 in Brooklyn, NY, the young Lena wanted a career in the performing arts rather than the teaching profession preferred for her by her grandmother, with whom she sometimes lived. She agreed to her grandmother's wishes until her mid-teenage years, when she became a member of the chorus at the famed Cotton Club in Harlem.

Her grandmother died in 1933, and Lena's mother "persuaded the 16-year-old to quit school and join the chorus at

Lena Horne performing in *Two Girls and a Sailor* in 1944. Accompanying Ms. Horne are Olivette Miller (harp), Phil Moore (piano), and "T-Bone" Walker (guitar). *Photo courtesy of Frank Driggs Collection.*

Harlem's famous Cotton Club" (Matsumoto and Gliatto, 120). In 1935, while performing at the Cotton Club, she accepted an offer to tour with Noble Sissle's band. Although Horne was not initially as successful as other vocalists were, her superb acting ability and beauty enabled her to become an exceptionally strong performer.

In 1936 Horne married Louis Jones and moved to his family's home in Pittsburgh. They had two children, Gail and Teddy, but the marriage ended in 1940. Lena returned with her daughter to New York City and began performing again in nightclubs and in theatrical productions. She also worked with Charlie Barnet's band (1940–1941) and recorded with Artie Shaw. In the early 1940s Louis B. Mayer, head of Metro-Goldwyn-Mayer (MGM), enticed her to come to Hollywood. She starred in two all-black musicals, *Stormy Weather* (1943) and *Cabin in the Sky* (1943). The title song "Stormy Weather" became her signature tune. In 1947 Lennie Hayton, an MGM arranger and conductor, became Lena's second husband. They married in Paris because of the miscegenation laws of California at that time. He also became her accompanist and musical director for her highly successful shows and recordings throughout the 1950s and until his death in 1971.

See also Jazz; Musical Theater

For Further Reading

Haskins, James, and Kathleen Benson. *Lena: A Personal and Professional Biography of Lena Horne.* New York: Stein and Day, 1984.

Horne, Lena, and Richard Schickel. *Lena.* Garden City, NY: Doubleday, 1965.

Matsumoto, Nancy, and Tom Gliatto. "Horne of Plenty." *People Weekly* 49, no. 26 (July 6, 1998): 120–121.

Monica J. Burdex

Horne, Marilyn (1934–)

Marilyn Horne, mezzo-soprano, is widely acclaimed as one of the foremost interpreters of both Baroque and *bel canto* repertoire, particularly in the operas of Georg Friedrich Händel, Gioacchino Rossini, and Vincenzo Bellini. She has received equal acclaim as a recitalist, with over 1,300 performances to her credit. Her numerous recordings include *Rossini: Barber of Seville* (Sony Classics 37862), *Recital—Donizetti, Gounod, Offenbach* (Wea/Atlantic/Erato 98501), and *An Evening with Marilyn Horne, Volume 1* (Opera D'Oro 2017).

Marilyn Berneice Horne was born in Bradford, PA, on 16 January 1934 to Bentz J. Horne, a semi-professional singer, and Berneice P. Hokanson Horne. Marilyn and her older sister Gloria began performing in public as the Horne Sisters. The family relocated to Long Beach, CA, in order to take advantage of the superior educational opportunities for the children, and both sisters began singing with the Roger Wagner Chorale. Horne graduated from the Polytechnic High School (1951) and matriculated at the University of Southern California (USC), where she studied voice with William Vennard. During this time she also studied with singer Lotte Lehmann (1888–1976) in a series of master classes. In 1954 she auditioned for a chorus part in Otto Preminger's *Carmen Jones* (RCA 1881, soundtrack recording) but was hired instead to dub Dorothy Dandridge's singing in the title role.

In 1956 Horne was offered a contract at the opera house in Gelsenkirchen, Germany. She made her debut as Guilietta in *The Tales of Hoffmann*. Over the next three years she performed a wide range of repertoire, from Händel to Alban Berg. Upon returning to the United States in 1959, she made her San Francisco Opera debut as Marie in Berg's *Wozzeck*, which she also performed at Covent Garden in 1964.

In 1960 Horne married African American conductor Henry Lewis, a former classmate from USC. During Lewis's tenure as conductor of the New Jersey Symphony, the two made a number of performances and recordings together. The couple had one daughter, Angela Turnham, born in 1965. Horne and Lewis formally announced their separation and subsequent divorce in 1974.

Horne made her Metropolitan Opera debut in 1970 as Adalgisa in *Norma*, appearing with Joan Sutherland. Over the next two decades she enjoyed extraordinary success in a variety of roles in the United States and Europe.

Horne has received numerous awards, including the Handel Medallion (1980), Premio d'Oro from the Italian government (1982), Commendatore al merito della Republica Italiana (1983), Gold Merit Medal from the National Society of Arts and Letters (1987), Fidelio Gold Medal from the International Association of Opera Directors (1988), and George Peabody Award (1989). She has received medals for outstanding service from the Covent Garden Royal Opera House (1989) and the San Francisco Opera

(1990), the National Medal of Arts (1992), Kennedy Center Honors for lifetime achievement (1995), five honorary doctorates, and four Grammy Awards. In 1994 she created the Marilyn Horne Foundation, a nonprofit organization devoted to the art of the vocal recital. In 1995 she was named director of the vocal program at the Music Academy of the West.

See also Performer, Vocal

For Further Reading

Horne, Marilyn, and Jane Scovell. *Marilyn Horne: My Life*. New York: Atheneum, 1983.

Sargeant, Winthrop. "Marilyn Horne." In *Divas*. New York: Coward, McCann and Geoghegan, 1973.

David L. Bruner

Hutchinson, Brenda (1954–)

Sound artist Brenda Hutchinson is one of the most significant avant garde musicians of the late twentieth century. She explores the concept of sound in many different ways. At times she operates as a physicist delving into the very structure and shape of tone and timbre. At other times she takes the role of sociologist or ethnographer documenting the role that sound and music play in the lives of others.

Hutchinson was born on 15 June 1954 in Trenton, NJ. She studied piano and violin from a very early age and eventually earned degrees from Carnegie Mellon University and the University of California at San Diego. Hutchinson's compositions include live performances, radio pieces, and mixed-media installations. She began recording sounds at age five when she was given a pink and white plastic tape recorder for Christmas. She combined this early impetus to collect ambient sounds with an open attitude toward composition inspired by John Cage.

Hutchinson explores the world with a tape recorder much like a documentary photographer uses a camera. She records an aural "picture" of a situation, including "portraits" of people by collecting their personal narratives. In some compositions, this exploration is guided by a theme.

In *How Do You Get to Carnegie Hall?* (1998) Hutchinson explored the piano as a cultural icon. To complete the piece, she traveled cross-country in a van with a piano in the back, asking people along the way to play and tell her stories about their relationship with the piano and with music. Hundreds of people shared their skills at the keyboard, their memories of music lessons, conflicts with parents, and other poignantly touching stories. Hutchinson then edited the interviews into a sound collage that provided the basis for a live performance work scored for piano. The composition posits the piano as a unifying element in the American landscape and "Heart and Soul" as a tune that anyone can play.

Hutchinson continues her interest in music as a part of a larger human experience in *Voices of Reason* (available though the Pauline Oliveros Foundation, Inc., item BH-C-1). For two years Hutchinson recorded the voices of patients in a psychiatric hospital. Again, music was found to be a unifying force. The patients sang songs as Hutchinson played the organ. The resulting performance included personal stories told by the patients and Hutchinson playing the Giant Music Box, an instrument that she built that is now housed as an interactive exhibit at San Francisco's Exploratorium museum.

Hutchinson has also produced work in a more abstract style, including *Long Tube Solo* (1990), a work performed on a copper tube that is over nine feet long.

Hutchinson buzzes and sings through one end of the tube, creating an eerie soundscape of overlapping harmonics. *EEEYAH!* (AER 1991/4) is another impressionistic work that is based on a Thai pig call. Inspired by recent deaths in her family, Hutchinson created a work of dense layers that is structured in two parts. The first section is the shrieking call repeated again and again, overdubbed to produce a jarring dissonance. A hushed yet urgent chanting of Hutchinson's genealogy follows.

See also Experimental Music; Music Technology; Sound Design

For Further Reading

Boone, Charles. "Vanguard Composers in San Francisco." *P-Form Magazine* 33 (1994): 20–22.
Gann, Kyle. *American Music in the Twentieth Century.* New York: Schirmer Books; London: Prentice-Hall International, 1997.

Jeffery Byrd

Hymnody

Hymnody, the writing and performance of hymns, dominated American Protestantism in the nineteenth century. Major changes in worship and doctrine, as well as the rise of feminism, permitted women to play a more active role in the growing importance of hymns in the American religious landscape. The Second Great Awakening of 1790–1835 produced an insatiable desire for music and lyrics that reflected religious experience and ideals. It also produced a doctrinal shift from Calvinist conservatism toward an emphasis on God's love and redemption. Women were especially drawn to and converted by this message, becoming a major force as writers and composers of hymns and hymnals.

Even though the nineteenth century was the most productive and inspirational period for women's influence on American hymn writing, much carried over into the twentieth century. A representative sample of 70 hymnals for formal worship published between 1849 and 1917 reveals that only 8.7 percent of the texts are by women, and 1.7 percent by American women. A similar sample of 70 social hymnbooks reveals that 26.7 percent are by women, 13.7 percent by American women (De Jong, 144). The social hymnbooks not only permitted women the opportunity to contribute their unique emotional and transforming perspectives on religion to the public, but also allowed American Protestantism to integrate women and their talents into the religious experience, which led to the societal and political inroads in women's rights of the twentieth century.

Leading the field in both the production and emotional content of hymns in the late nineteenth and early twentieth centuries was Frances J. "Fanny" Crosby (1820–1915). Blind since infancy, Crosby was one of the first graduates from the New York School for the Blind in 1835. She studied music with George Frederic Root, collaborated with the most famous men hymnists of her day, and composed over 9,000 hymns, 3,000 of which were published. She began writing hymns during the 1858 revival, and her lasting success and contemporary appeal can be attributed to her social and evangelistic ministry. Her most familiar hymn is probably "Blessed Assurance."

Clara H. Scott (1841–1897) was an anthem and hymn composer who published her work in music collections and journals. Her *Royal Anthem Book* (1882) was the first such book published by a woman. Her best-known hymn is "Open My Eyes, That I May See." Her musical style is closer to English Victorian hymnody, with its slower harmonic movement and strong European orientation.

One of the most prolific early composers of Sunday school hymns was Phoebe Palmer Knapp (1839–1908). A child of Methodist evangelists, Knapp became a leading figure in New York social circles, and her home was a meeting place for women reformers such as Harriet Beecher Stowe and hymnists such as Fanny Crosby, with whom she wrote many successful hymns. She composed more than 500 gospel hymns and published two children's hymnals. Knapp's position in American hymnody is unique, owing primarily to her family's role and involvement in both music publishing and revivalism. Her 14 songs in *Woman in Sacred Song* (1885) made her the best represented composer in this first-of-its-kind collection of 2,500 works of texts and songs by women. Knapp's first book, *Notes of Joy for the Sabbath School*, contains her own hymns introduced by her husband, president of Metropolitan Life Insurance Company.

Few women hymnodists were blessed with Knapp's connections or social standing. Most were from upper- to middle-class northern families, attended girls' schools, had musical instruction and education, taught Sunday school, and volunteered in reform movements and social work in the inner cities. The demands for hymn tunes and texts, as well as inexpensive songbooks suited to large crowds, helped to spur the new urban revivalism and religious efforts toward the destitute. Young educated women, already involved in missionary efforts in this area, brought their education and experience into the production of these songs.

Susan Parkhurst (1836–1918) was better known for her popular songs than for her hymns. She was a well-known composer during the 1860s in the northeastern United States after she became a war widow. Her daughter Effie's singing of her mother's songs helped to popularize the temperance song.

Eliza Edmunds Hewitt (1851–1920) helped to make Philadelphia a center for gospel hymnody during the Civil War by compiling over 60 collections of gospel hymns and other sacred music in collaboration with William Kirkpatrick and John Sweney, both Civil War bandleaders and church choir directors. Most of these collections featured texts and melodies by women. Hewitt, typical of many nineteenth-century women hymnodists, suffered a physical ailment that shaped and colored her texts and musical production. Soft theology and an optimistic flavor apparent in postwar American thought characterize her "heaven songs."

Anna B. Warner (1822–1915) and her sister Susan wrote the most popular and durable children's hymn, "Jesus Loves Me." They were lifelong Sunday school teachers at West Point Academy. In their best-selling book *Say and Seal* (1860), this text is sung by the child hero on his deathbed and was given music by William B. Bradbury.

Post–Civil War opportunities for women in religious writing and music composition was enhanced by four growing institutions: the Sunday school; professional revivalism characterized by Dwight L. Moody and Ira D. Sankey; weekly services with anthems featuring music for quartet choirs; and the reform movements in temperance, suffrage, and pacifism. Moving into the twentieth century, Victorianism and its sentimentality were strongly integrated into hymnody by women, but the conflict between Protestant evangelicals and social gospel proponents reached its peak between 1910 and 1915 with the publication of *The Fundamentalists*, 12 paperback volumes that supported fundamentalist doctrines by a variety of American and British conservative writers. Promoting premillennialism, evangelism, and a strong exclusionary Scripture interpretation, many fundamentalists directly challenged empowered women in religion and their role in religious song and music.

A leader of the temperance movement was Anna Gordon (1853–1931). She gave up professional studies in organ to push for temperance. She edited *Marching Songs for Young Crusaders* in the 1890s, and her marches emphasized borrowed melodies, hand clapping, and the "heaven song."

Ida L. Reed (1865–1951) believed that God called her to be a hymnist. Raised in rural West Virginia, she mailed her hymns to urban publishers and struggled to earn a living. Her "heart-cries to God," as she called her hymns, have not made many inroads in the male-dominated publishing industry, however.

Finally, May Whittle Moody (1870–1963) was the daughter of a famous evangelist, Major D.W. Whittle, and the daughter-in-law of another, D. L. Moody. She was one of the first women singers and hymn writers in professional revivalism. She published the *Northfield Hymnal #3* (1918) with the gospel composer Charles Alexander. She attended Oberlin College and the Royal Academy of London. Her most popular hymn is "Moment by Moment."

Women played a major role throughout the nineteenth and early twentieth centuries in writing and composing hymns and producing hymnals in American Protestantism. Their current participation in this activity has been strongly curtailed by the resurgence of religious conservatism and fundamentalism, especially in the South. Despite these restrictions, women still express their unique interpretation and perspectives regarding God and religion through the contemporary Christian music market, and in their local and regional church life.

See also Church Music

For Further Reading

De Jong, Mary. " 'Theirs the Sweetest Song': Women Hymn Writers in the Nineteenth-Century United States." In *A Mighty Baptism: Race, Gender, and the Creation of American Protestantism*, eds. Susan Juster and Lisa Mac-Farlane. Ithaca, NY: Cornell University Press, 1996, 141–167.

Hobbs, June Hadden. *"I Sing for I Cannot Be Silent": The Feminization of American Hymnody, 1870–1920*. Pittsburgh: University of Pittsburgh Press, 1997.

Rogal, Samuel J. *Sisters of Sacred Song: A Selected Listing of Women Hymnodists in Great Britain and America*. New York: Garland Publishing, 1981.

Brad Eden

Improvisation

Musical improvisation may be defined as music created as it is performed. Traditionally in Western music this may involve: (1) the complete extemporization of music with few or no preconceived guidelines, (2) the realization of music from a score that provides an outline or instructions for performance (e.g., basso continuo realization; interpreting a graphic score; or performing a jazz tune from a lead sheet), or (3) ornamenting a notated musical line according to contemporary traditions. Thus, by its nature, a completed improvisation cannot be recreated exactly and is durable only through a recording.

Although documentation of early music improvised by women is scanty, music was important in the life of ancient Greece, and its manifestations are represented in the myths of the muses, all of whom performed music. It is not known how the music actually sounded—less than two dozen notated fragments of early Greek music have survived. However, epic poems, hymns, and other texts were sung extemporaneously in appropriate modes, reflecting the natural rhythm of the language, and these often developed into traditional melodies. The nine muses—Calliope, Clio, Erato, Euterpe, Melpomene, Polyhymnia, Terpsichore, Thalia, and Urania—represented a variety of arts and sciences, but they all performed music on the lyre, kithara, aulos, and other instruments, and they sang. Mythology further suggests the muses competed in improvised music contests at the "Mouseai" festivals in the sixth century B.C. in the famous Valley of the Muses, Thespies, on the eastern slopes of Mt. Helikon. Sappho, Pythia, and Polygnota are other women musicians who may have improvised in these traditions. Little is known about improvisation by medieval women composers, among whom the most important include Kassia (ninth c.) and Hildegard von Bingen (twelfth c.).

The Western European women troubadours, or trobairitz, of the twelfth and thirteenth centuries, including the Comtessa de Dia, of whom one manuscript survives, carried on the tradition of improvisation in performed poetry and stories. Although melodies were created for specific works, they were often used for subsequent works.

Skill in improvisation was often expected of musicians trained in Western traditions, and from the sixteenth century there is evidence of its use by well-trained performers and composers. Church and concert organists, accompanists of singers and instrumentalists, dance musicians, and even in church services, musicians were trained in improvising on a *cantus firmus*. Donna Cardamone writes: "By 1550 the cultural scene in Venice was completely open to women, and in entering the coterie world of the urban salon, they joined men in literary and musical improvisation" (Cardamone, 112). It is not known the extent to which women participated in these musical activities, except that many women were prominent as composers and keyboard performers and would have surely freely improvised preludes, intonations, and sets of variations as was the custom of the Baroque period. Formulaic elements allowed improvisation within such traditional forms. In composed music, elaborately improvised embellishments and ornamentation were also expected of singers and instrumentalists, as well as cadenzas within the concerto forms.

Many early women performers, however, were acclaimed for their improvisational skills at the harpsichord or organ, and as singers for their ornamentation. Elizabeth-Claude Jacquet de la Guerre (1665–1729), daughter of composer and harpsichord-maker Claude Jacquet, was distinguished as a composer and harpsichord recitalist throughout her life, and she performed for King Louis XIV as well as for the greatest musicians of France. Her skill at improvising on the harpsichord is extensively documented.

Francesca Caccini (1587–1630), eldest daughter of composer Giulio Caccini, was a renowned singer for both Henry IV of France and the courts of Rome and Florence. She composed and performed in several remarkable operas, focusing on beautiful improvised and written-out embellishment of the monadic lines. Maria Teresa Agnesi (1720–1795), associated with the court of Milan as a composer and performer, improvised harpsichord sonatas from composed musical outlines. Anne-Marie Krumpholtz (1755–1813), a renowned harpist, was well known for improvising variations on themes familiar to her audiences. Josepha Barbara von Auernhammer (1758–1820), a protégé of Wolfgang Amadeus Mozart, also excelled at improvising on familiar tunes for her audiences. Elisabetta de Gambarini (1731–1765); Juliane Reichardt (1752–1783), daughter of Franz Benda; Sophia Corri Dussek (1775–1830), who married Jan Ladislav Dussek; her daughter Olivia Dussek Bulkley (1799–1847); and Maria Wolowska Szymanowska (1789–1831) were harpsichord performers with noted improvisational skills.

Cadenzas became an even more important venue for improvisation in the nineteenth century, as did the ubiquitous "fantasy" that often appeared on the programs of acclaimed performers. Clara Wieck Schumann (1819–1896), a prolific composer and interpreter of the works by her husband, Robert Schumann, was renowned as a virtuostic pianist skilled at improvising fantasy works. In her letters she wrote that she used improvisation in creating "authentic" interpretations of her husband's music. Her preludes "constitute unusually direct evidence of the practice of improvising introductions to piano pieces, a practice carried over to the piano from lute and harpsichord music in the 18th century and continued into the twentieth" (Goertzen, 238).

In music of the twentieth century, improvisation takes on a new face with many graphic scores by women composers deliberately calling for improvisation to create aleatoric or chance music. In a large body of works, including *Deep Listening*, Pauline Oliveros (b. 1932) calls for improvisations on a diverse range of instruments, including the accordion and voice. Cathy Berberian's (1925–1983) *Stripsody* for solo voice (1966), with graphics by Roberto Zamarin, called for improvised interpretation of comic strip characters with onomatopoetic words and sounds. These women, and many more, experimented with improvisation techniques.

Jazz is an improvisatory art, and as women joined their male colleagues to perform jazz, improvisation became a universal expression for Western women musicians. Early jazz women players noted for their improvisational abilities include Mary Lou Williams (1910–1981), one of the great early jazz pianists and improvisers recorded into the 1960s. Lil Hardin Armstrong (1898–1971) played piano in the King Oliver and Louis Armstrong bands in the 1920s and performed with groups ranging from Johnnie Dodds to Sidney Bechet. Lovie Austin (1887–1972) improvised accompaniment for many of the great women blues singers, including Ida Cox (1896–1967), Ethel Waters (1896–1977), and Gertrude "Ma" Rainey (1886–1939). Other noted improvisers include trombonist Melba Liston (1926–1999), pianist Carla Bley (b. 1938), the Dizzy Gillespie protégé Clora Bryant (b. 1927), and pianist Barbara Carroll (b. 1925).

Larger all-women bands have also been an important outlet for women improvisers. The International Sweethearts of Rhythm in the 1940s featured breakout solos by both black and white performers. Alive! was an exciting San Francisco group. Ina Ray Hutton's Los Angeles big band, which gained fame from their weekly television show and several film appearances, featured attractive, exquisitely dressed women improvising solos.

For 25 years Ann Patterson's Los Angeles–based big band, Maiden Voyage, provided an environment where hard-driving jazz improvisers thrived, including such instrumentalists as Carol Chaikin (alto sax), Sue Terry (saxes, flute), Virginia Mayhew (saxes), Rebecca Coupe Franks (trumpet), and Ingrid Jensen (trumpet). Susie Hansen fronts her own Los Angeles salsa band, providing grand solos on her custom electric violin. New York's Diva is another hard-driving band featuring exciting soloists. In recent years Nobuko Cobi Narita has produced the New York Women's Jazz Festival, which brings together the best women jazz musicians on the East Coast.

Two of today's most accomplished jazz improvisers on piano remain Marian McPartland (b. 1918) and Toshiko Akiyoshi (b. 1929). Both are proponents of free jazz, which incorporates remote harmonic structures in their improvised solos.

Scat singing, for example, vocalizing rhythmic syllables and sounds in an improvised solo, is a form of improvising in which singers use their voice as if it were a horn. Ella Fitzgerald (1917–1996), heralded as the "Queen of Scat," always scatted solos in her shows and sometimes substituted improvised lyrics for those she "forgot" in performance. Most jazz vocalists working today scat solos, and their scatting technique helps define their vocal style.

See also Jazz

For Further Reading

Cardamone, Donna G. "Lifting the Protective Veil of Anonymity: Women as Composer-

Performers, ca. 1300–1566." In *Women Composers: Music Through the Ages*, Vol. 1, eds. Martha Furman Schleifer and Sylvia Glickman. New York: G. K. Hall, 1996, 110–115.

Goertzen, V.W. "Setting the Stage: Clara Schumann's Preludes." In *The Course of Performance: Studies in the World of Musical Improvisation*, ed. Bruno Nettl with Melinda Russell. Chicago: University of Chicago Press; 1988, 237–260.

Unterbrink, Mary. *Jazz Women at the Keyboard*. Jefferson, NC: McFarland, 1983.

Stephen Fry

Indiana Home Economics Club Choruses

The first Indiana Home Economics Club Choruses were brought to regional attention when, in 1934, the women of the Tippecanoe County Home Economics Chorus club wanted to publicize club activities on the radio. The chorus of 20 women from across the county attracted considerable attention, and in 1936 it traveled to Washington, DC, to sing for the Conference of Rural Women. Shortly thereafter the U.S. Department of Agriculture's Extension Service supported a statewide expansion of the idea within Indiana under the direction of Al Stewart, music director at Purdue University. Stewart supervised a plan whereby each local home economics club selected two women singers by audition to participate in a county chorus. The county units performed locally and combined into the Indiana State Home Economics Club Chorus for a yearly conference at Purdue. The conference featured critiqued performances by each county chorus and a mass chorus of all participants.

Stewart selected the state repertoire and traveled from county to county to ensure similar interpretation. Additionally a late summer clinic was held for county directors and accompanists so that they could learn the year's new music in advance. Recordings from some of these events arc cxtant. Stewart's focus was on what he called popular and semi-classical repertoire, and he developed the motto "No fun without music, No music without fun." A review of the yearly repertoire (compiled into songbooks that each participant bought) reveals an emphasis on sacred anthems, Christmas and holiday selections, folk and patriotic arrangements, and a few pop hits. Often one *a cappella* piece is included, but most call for piano accompaniment; only occasionally are non-English works present. There is some evidence that some compositions were commissioned by the state chorus, but no specific repertoire has yet been located. Stewart's rehearsals also included time devoted to vocal pedagogy and a modicum of music theory and history.

By 1948, 49 counties sent 1,382 singers to the annual conference; and in 1950, 2,500 women representing 84 Indiana counties traveled again to Washington, DC, to sing for the Capital Sesquicentennial celebration. In subsequent years the ensemble sang in Toronto, Los Angeles, Oregon, and Hawaii, raising money for the trips through local fundraising ventures, many of which reflected the rural backgrounds of the women.

Stewart retired in 1974, and the choir program declined as women's societal roles and time commitments expanded in the 1980s and 1990s. The organization plan also was revised, eliminating the need for a choir participant to be a member of a Homemaker Club, and rehearsals were scheduled (with babysitting provided) to be more convenient for working mothers. Some Indiana counties continued to sponsor choirs to the end of the twentieth century, and the yearly summer concert at Purdue University continued. As would be expected, the choirs played both a musical and a social role in the lives of the participants.

See also Performer, Choral and Vocal Ensemble

Linda Pohly

Indie-Rock

The groundswell of women indie-rock artists in the 1990s was one of the most important developments of the decade in U.S. rock music. When the Seattle-based, all-men band Nirvana achieved enormous commercial success for its top-selling album, *Nevermind* (DGC 24425), in 1991, the noisy sound and rebellious ethic of independent rock artists suddenly found themselves in the mainstream. Women musicians played a large role in filling the void left in the underground music scene then known as "alternative." As alternative artists flirted with corporate label success, "indie-rock" emerged as the resistant voice in rock music. Women found themselves in a unique position among indie-rock artists and left an indelible mark on this traditionally all-boys culture.

Women artists have always played some part in every rock counterculture, since Janis Joplin (1943–1970) of the Velvet Underground and Grace Slick (b. 1939) of Jefferson Airplane in the 1960s. The era of alternative music prior to Nirvana's ground-shifting success was no exception. The work of these artists would be a huge influence on, and precursor to, the women involved in indie-rock and its spin-off feminist movement, Riot Grrrl.

Perhaps the most important of these is Kim Gordon (b. 1953), the bassist who, along with husband Thurston Moore and Lee Ranaldo, form the band Sonic Youth. Formed in the early 1980s, Sonic Youth is known for its harsh, dissonant, and noisy percussive guitar sounds. Combined with Gordon's self-taught bass style and restrained, raspy vocals, the avant garde techniques of Moore and Ranaldo make Sonic Youth a central figure in the genealogy of underground rock music in the United States. Similarly, in the late 1980s, Kim Deal, as bassist and sometimes-singer for the Boston-based band the Pixies, provided a uniquely women's voice to a noisy, high-decibel underground band. In both cases, Kim Gordon and Kim Deal have been essential parts in highly influential alternative bands, Sonic Youth and the Pixies. Their strong, tough-girl presence lent considerable credibility, inspiration, and influence toward the opportunities for women rock artists in the indie-rock movements shortly to come.

Not coincidentally, the women's indie-rock movement of the 1990s began where alternative music merged with the mainstream: in the state of Washington, home to Nirvana. In 1991 the International Pop Underground (IPU) Convention was held in Olympia, also the site of Evergreen College, well known for its Women's Studies Program. It may well have been "Girl Day" at that IPU festival that catapulted the growing network of women's bands, which had already been rudely and purposely defying the norms of bouncy cuteness expected from girl-centered rock, into a full-fledged musical, artistic and political feminist rebellion.

The movement, which became known as Riot Grrrl, was not as much a musical style as it was an artistic consortium of women rock musicians. Held together by their confrontational, punk-infused intensity and their passionate appeals to feminist activism, Riot Grrrl was a network of women in Olympia as well as

Washington, DC. Through their distinctly low-tech recordings, impromptu live shows, lyric sheets and fan-zines, this branch of indie-rock served to distribute manifestos and slogans and provide support groups for women to express uniquely female experiences in the language of rock music.

As a post-punk feminist movement, Riot Grrrl was personified in the Olympia band Bikini Kill. Founded by Evergreen College students Kathleen Hanna, Tobi Vail, and Kathi Wilcox in the late 1980s, Bikini Kill, also the name of a feminist magazine published by the students, became renowned for their radical live shows in which they called to task not only the sexism that existed generally in American culture, but specifically that which they found in the underground music culture itself. They typically asked audience members who were men to move their aggressive dancing to the back of the crowd so women audience members could remain, unthreatened, in the front. Their songs bluntly addressed issues of sexual abuse, incest, rape, and women's empowerment, often allowing audience members turns at a microphone to tell their own stories during a show. Many early song titles, including "Resist Psychic Death," became slogans for the Riot Grrrl movement, both chanted and often drawn onto the performers' bodies in a ritual reminiscent of performance art of the early 1990s.

Bikini Kill's first recording, a cassette distributed independently in 1991, was tellingly called *Revolution Girl Style Now* (Kill Rock Stars 204). Subsequent recordings were released by Olympia-based Kill Rock Stars (KRS), an independent label synonymous with the indie-rock movement and the determination to turn away from major-label rock music. KRS helped Bikini Kill tour the United King-dom with British Riot Grrrl leaders Huggy Bear, which increased the visibility of women's indie-rock tremendously.

KRS also signed and recorded the other major Riot Grrrl band in the United States, the trio Sleater-Kinney. Formed from the remnants of two other early Riot Grrrl groups (Heavens to Betsy, and Excuse 17), Sleater-Kinney consisted of singer/guitarist Corin Tucker, Carrie Brownstein, a classically trained pianist, and drummer Lora MacFarlane. The most popular and critically acclaimed of Riot Grrrl bands, Sleater-Kinney released its first album in 1995 and continued the Riot Grrrl tradition of turning feminist critiques in on the indie-rock music world itself in addition to the anti–pop culture rantings of their male counterparts.

Ultimately, the Riot Grrrl movement died a relatively quick death under the weight of its own heavy expectations and, at times, self-righteous elitism. Independent artists who embraced notoriety more easily, such as Courtney Love, lead singer of the band Hole, railed against Riot Grrrl's exclusionary ethic and aesthetic. Faced with the impossible task of trying to move people politically and socially while, understandably, refusing to speak in a language accessible to many, and rejecting what media attention they did receive, Riot Grrrl's indie-rock influence would pass to other women artists.

Liz Phair (b. 1967) was born in New Haven, CT, and, like indie-rock godmother Kim Gordon, studied art in college, where she became infatuated with indie-rock's sound and culture. With her debut album, *Exile in Guyville* (Matador 51), Liz Phair combined the low-tech production and recording techniques of indie-rock, along with its sense of alienation from the male-dominated indie-rock world, with a singer-songwriter stylistic approach, as opposed to the garage-band style of Riot Grrrl artists. *Exile in Guyville* received significant critical acclaim, including many best-album-of-the-year honors.

Phair's work and popularity helped gradually move the female indie-rock influence away from the noise-rock roots of Sonic Youth and the Pixies and toward the more folk-based songwriting of emerging young artists such as New York City's Ani DiFranco (b. 1970), who started her own independent label, Righteous Babe Records, and began releasing her own successful albums as a teenager. Difranco's honest expressions of openly feminist ideals and concerns—songs about sexism, rape, and abortion—while maintaining control of the production of her music, is a perfect demonstration of the artistic possibilities inspired by the pioneering indie-rock women of the late 1980s and early 1990s. Despite still being severely outnumbered in the world of non-mainstream rock music, women have forged ways to make their voices heard in the realm of underground music generally and the brutal directness of indie-rock in particular.

See also Garage Rock and Heavy Metal Bands; Rock and Popular Music Genres

For Further Reading

O'Brien, Lucy. *She-Bop: The Definitive History of Women in Rock, Pop and Soul.* New York: Penguin Books, 1996.

O'Dair, Barbara (ed.). *The Rolling Stone Book of Women in Rock: Trouble Girls.* New York: Random House, 1997.

Don Byrd

Indigo Girls

One of the most popular folk-rock groups of the late 1980s and 1990s, the Indigo Girls are best known for their inspiring recordings and performances, their contemplative lyrics, and their instantly recognizable sweet blend of two women's voices with their guitars. Hailing from Atlanta, GA, the duo of Amy Ray and Emily Saliers were catalysts for the folk singer–songwriter revival and its mainstream success. The Indigo Girls' 1989 debut album, *Indigo Girls* (Epic EK-45044), and its most popular song, "Closer to Fine," with its acoustic roots, won them critical acclaim and their first Grammy Award for Best Contemporary Folk Recording. They have since produced several albums, including their most recent *Come on Social Now* (Sony 63773), each of which is increasingly complex and adventurous in both its music and lyrics. All the while, they have been outspoken social activists for a number of issues, including environmentalism, feminism, human rights, gay/lesbian sexuality, and inner-city resource development.

Ray and Saliers met in the sixth grade in their hometown of Decatur, GA, and began to play music together at Shamrock High School under the name the B-Band. They continued developing their music while in college at Emory University, where Saliers earned her degree in English and Ray earned her degree in religion and English. They began to play on the indie circuit regularly in 1985 and released their first album, *Strange Fire* (Epic EK-45427), in 1987. However, it was only after Suzanne Vega (b. 1959) and Tracy Chapman (b. 1964) found their radio success that the Indigo Girls had the perfect opportunity to break the airwaves with their album *Indigo Girls*. The accolades poured in rapidly. Ten years and eight albums later, the Indigo Girls have sold seven million albums, including one double platinum disc, three platinum, and four gold, and

Amy Ray (left) and Emily Saliers are the Indigo Girls. *Photo courtesy of Frank Driggs Collection.*

have earned another five Grammy Award nominations.

The Indigo Girls have benefited greatly from collaborating with other musicians over the years. They have shared the stage with other artists at the Newport Folk Festival, the New Orleans Jazz Festival, the Lilith Fair, and hundreds of other benefit concerts. Ray set up Daemon Records, a nonprofit independent label focusing on Atlanta-area bands, having benefited greatly from performing with other Georgian bands (including R.E.M.). The Indigo Girls tour very frequently and often speak to audiences in a personal way in order to connect with them. They are known for their down-to-earth attitudes and for the intimate nature of their concerts, even in large stadiums.

Even though both women compose music, each has a very distinctive style. Saliers's sound is gentle and abstract, with more traditional influences by Joni Mitchell (b. 1943) and Joan Baez (b. 1941), whereas Ray's sound is heavy and direct, drawing inspiration from aspects of punk rock. However, their voices and guitar playing blend seamlessly, and the women are well known for their impassioned performances both in the studio and on stage.

See also Lilith Fair; Rock and Popular Music Genres

For Further Reading

Childerhose, Buffy. *From Lilith to Lilith Fair: The Authorized Story*. New York: Griffin, 1998.
Indigo Girls—The Official Site. Available: http://www.indigogirls.com

Sarah Meyers

Industry, Rock Music

Women made impressive gains behind the scenes in the rock music industry. Even as recently as the 1980s, women predominantly occupied office management or secretarial positions and the industry was still very much a man's world. But beginning in the late 1980s and early 1990s, more women began to move into senior-level executive positions. Women's rise behind the scenes arguably paralleled women's notable popular rise as performers, musicians, singers, and songwriters through out the 1990s. Women's increased presence in all forms of the music industry is in no small part owing to the women's rights movement, passing of civil rights legislation, and enforcement of nondiscrimination policies.

Marketing, publicity, and press relations are areas in which women have historically maintained their greatest presence. Many argue that women were commonly placed in these types of positions because they were, and still are, often perceived as the "softer," more "feminine" side of the recording industry. It is common industry knowledge that publicists do not become top-level record company executives. More recently, women have branched into many other occupations within the recording industry, including high-level positions at music publishing companies, licensing organizations, and record labels.

Some of the most influential publishers have women at top levels of management; these include Donna Hilley at Sony Tree Publishing and Celia Froehlig at Nashville/Screen Gems-EMI Records. Division heads of music licensing organizations include Connie Bradley (Nashville office) and Frances Richard (vice-president for concert music) of the American Society of Composers, Authors and Publishers (ASCAP) and C. Diane Petty at the Society of European Stage Authors and Composers (SESAC). Frances Preston has held the presidency at Broadcast Music Inc. (BMI).

Record label heads include Michele Anthony as executive vice-president at Sony Music Entertainment and Nancy Berry as vice-chair at Virgin. Nancy Jeffries has served as vice-president at Elektra and Sheila Shipley-Biddy as senior vice-president and general manager at Decca. Motown senior vice-president Cassandra Mills has headed two Motown labels; one focused on soundtracks and the other on adult rhythm and blues. Polly Anthony has headed Sony's Epic Records, and Denise Brown has headed Warner's Black Music division. Monica Lynch has served as president of Tommy Boy Music.

Some of the most notable women in the music industry include Sylvia Rhone (b. 1952), Judy McGrath, and Hilary Rosen. Sylvia Rhone was the first African American woman to head a major record label, serving as chair and chief executive officer of Elektra Entertainment Group. Having grown up with an appreciation of music instilled by her parents and earning a degree in marketing and economics, Rhone first made an impression at Atlantic Records by reestablishing its suffering Black Music division in just four years' time in the 1990s. Rhone is viewed not only as an executive but as a woman with a real interest in music and breaking new artists. She has launched such artists as Third Eye Blind, Busta Rhymes, and Better Than Ezra. She has also been a guiding force in reinvigorating Tracy Chapman's (b. 1964) career with her comeback album *New Beginning* (Elektra 61850) and guiding Natalie Merchant (b. 1963) into solo artist territory after leaving the group 10,000 Maniacs. Rhone continues to stay involved at the music and artist level, searching out new talent and involving herself in the production of music videos.

Music Television (MTV) president Judy McGrath is another woman who rose through the ranks from the ground floor level, beginning in 1981 as an MTV on-air promotional spot writer. McGrath has played a substantial role in MTV success stories, including *MTV Unplugged* and MTV's *Choose or Lose* election coverage. Hilary Rosen, another impressive figure in the male-dominated field of the music industry, serves as president and chief executive officer of the Recording Industry Association of America, Inc. (RIAA). She has played a leading role in various copyright and licensing disputes throughout the years. Herself a lesbian and cognizant of her high-profile position, Rosen has also been vocal about gay rights and gay adoption.

Publicity, an area that has been traditionally considered one of the lower rungs of the recording industry corporate ladder, has remained a unique area where women can thrive. Many women have headed up their own successful firms. Susan Blond is one such example, having started her own publicity firm in 1987 and representing artists such as Janet Jackson (b. 1966) and Pet Shop Boys. Anita Mandell has had success with publicity at Decca Records, and Erin Yasgar is senior director of marketing at Universal/Motown Records.

The most difficult arena for women to break into is producing, and particularly engineering. Engineering has largely remained a male bastion allowing women little access. Some suggest that lingering myths that men fare better technologically than women is a leading cause for this. As recently as the mid-1990s the number of women engineers could be counted on one hand. One of the first women to break the ranks was Tena Clark, who produced for Patti LaBelle (b. 1944), Rita Coolidge, and Mary Wilson (b. 1944). Angela Winbush is another early notable, having garnered production credit on Janet Jackson's *Control* (A&M 75021-3905-2). Women serving as sole producer is remarkably rare; it is more common to see women serving as producer alongside a male counterpart. For example, Wilma Cozart Fine produced alongside her husband on projects that included Mercury Records' *Living Presence* release.

The most common road for women to take that can lead to the role of producer is for women musical artists themselves to act as producer on the production of their own record. Grammy Award nominations for production have been extremely rare. Exceptions include Janet Jackson (with Jimmy Jam and Terry Lewis) as the first woman to be nominated for Producer of the Year; Paula Cole was the first woman to receive a nomination for production for Record of the Year in 1996. No women made the list of nominations for the 1999 Grammy Awards. Low numbers persist in terms of women's wide and mainstream acceptance as engineers.

The second most difficult area for women to break into is arts and repertoire (A&R). A&R representatives are highly valued at record labels and are in charge of signing new artist, monitoring the progress of already signed artists, and overseeing what songs are recorded and by whom. However, strides have been made. The few women who have broken this barrier include Renne Bell at RCA Records/Nashville, Kim Buie and Susan Levy at Capitol, Susan Collins at Virgin, Margie Hunt at Sony, and Paige Levy at Warner.

Similar to women striking out on their own to develop publicity firms, many women have launched their own record labels. One of the most successful music industry insiders, particularly of the 1960s and 1970s, is Estelle Axton, co-founder of Stax Record. Marian Leighton is another pioneer. She founded Rounder Records in 1970 with Ken Irwin and Bill Nowlin. Rounder Records remains a strong and successful label today. The now-defunct Olivia Records was another early startup label in the support of music by women, for women, and about women. Having begun in 1982, Ladyslipper is another small independent label seeking to further new musical and artistic directions for women musicians. Often musical artists themselves launched independent labels, sometimes in an effort to support unsigned artists, at other times in resistance to major label control. In the 1990s, startup women fronted labels include Missy "Misdemeanor" Elliott's Gold Mine Label, Lil' Kim (b. 1975) and Queen Bee Records, and Indigo Girl Amy Ray's Daemon Records. Madonna's (b. 1958) Maverick Records broke new artists such as Prodigy and Alanis Morissette (b. 1974). Another standout independent is Ani DiFranco (b. 1970); most concerned about maintaining creative control and artistic integrity, she launched her fiercely independent Righteous Babe Records.

Women have also made inroads at radio stations, with increasing numbers of women holding positions as DJs and station programmers. Historically, men were the dominant record buyers; however, recent statistics suggest that there has been a shift, with women now buying more music than men. In response to women listeners' increased interest in music, radio stations have developed formats to target women specifically—namely, modern adult contemporary,

which combines modern rock with adult contemporary. The trend of increasing numbers of women rising to top-level decision-making positions at record labels and radio stations is likely to continue. Women have clearly established a presence, both as consumers and behind the scenes. However, despite this optimism, the truth remains that in comparison to men the number of women, and in particular women of color, remains alarmingly low.

See also Rock Music

For Further Reading

Andrews, Suzanna. "Taking Care of Business." *Rolling Stone* 773 (November 13, 1997): 169.

Dickerson, James. *Women on Top: The Quiet Revolution That's Rocking the American Music Industry*. New York: Billboard Books, 1998.

Ann Savage

Inskeep, Alice C. (1875–1942)

Alice C. Inskeep played an important role in the history of American music education during the first half of the twentieth century. A founding member of the Music Educators National Conference (MENC), she was also one of the original members of the Music Education Research Council, on which she served for 10 years. For more than three decades, until 1941, she was supervisor of music in the Cedar Rapids Public Schools. During much of this period she taught at the American Institute of Normal Methods and was director and professor of public school music at Coe College (Cedar Rapids, IA).

Inskeep was born on 1 April 1875 in Ottumwa, IA. As a high school student she was active in a variety of dramatic and musical activities. After graduation she became a grade school teacher. Inskeep credited Frances E. Clark as being one of her primary mentors. In 1927 Inskeep wrote: "Mrs. Clark knew of my ambition to 'elevate the stage,' and knew that I had arrangements all made to enter the dramatic class at Northwestern University, but she argued 'you have done so much in directing the choir and you get such lovely music from your grade children, why not train yourself for supervision?'" Clark was successful in convincing Inskeep to change her career path. "'Now,' Clark said, 'the first step in your development is to attend a meeting of music supervisors which is to be held in Keokuk, Iowa'" (Inskeep, 1956). Inskeep did attend the 1907 Keokuk conference, at which the MENC was proposed. This event proved to be a pivotal experience in her career. It was the inspiration of the Keokuk gathering that brought Inskeep to Chicago for further studies in public school music at the American Book Company School. She went on to become assistant supervisor of music in the public schools of Cedar Rapids, and then supervisor of music in Sioux Falls, SD. She finally returned to Cedar Rapids as supervisor of music, where she spent the rest of her career.

Inskeep had a particular affinity for choral music, and under her supervision the public school vocal program flourished. An instrumental program was also launched under her watch and grew impressively. More than 1,600 students were playing instruments in the Cedar Rapids schools by 1941. In addition to her work in Cedar Rapids, Inskeep taught in the summer school program at Northwestern University for 33 summers. She retired from a long and fruitful career in 1941 and died shortly thereafter on 23 February 1942 at age 66. Inskeep will be remembered as a passionate and extremely effective leader and advocate of American public school music. Her tireless work to demonstrate that public school music contributes productively to the life of the community has become a model that is relevant to the advocacy challenges for public school music in the twenty-first century.

See also Music Education; Music Educators National Conference

For Further Reading

Alice Inskeep, "Some Recollections and Experiences of Pioneer Days: Written by Alice Inskeep in 1927." *Music Educators Journal* (April–May 1956): 73–75.

McConathy, Osbourne. "We Salute You, Alice Inskeep." *Music Educators Journal* (January–February 1941): 11.

Nancy Uscher

Instrumental Education

Instrumental education in U.S. public schools can be traced to the large interest in town bands after the Civil War. This interest led to the formation of school bands somewhere between 1872 and 1883. Students in these school bands learned to play their instruments at home or from a private teacher. Extracurricular bands were formed and led by the music supervisor (who taught singing during the school day) or another teacher with musical interest. The growth of school bands was encouraged by the highly visible professional touring and military bands of early bandmasters Patrick Sarsfield Gilmore (1829–1892) and John Phillip Sousa (1854–1932). Although there were a few school bands in the late nineteenth century, it was at the height of Sousa's popularity in the early twentieth century that school bands became more common. In fact, the Sousa band served as the model for most school bands. The band members were men, as was the bandmaster, who was considered the expert on all matters concerning the band. The role of the band members was to produce the music in the way the bandmaster dictated. The goal for these groups was entertainment of the audience through upbeat marches, show tunes, and elements of the spectacular. Although the professional American concert bands disappeared by 1930, school bands of this model have continued to be re-created and emulated in schools.

Currently, instrumental education in most public schools throughout the country begins sometime between fourth and sixth grade. If begun in elementary school (fourth or fifth grade), students often leave the regular classroom instruction for weekly group lessons on woodwind (flute, oboe, clarinet, bassoon, saxophone), brass (trumpet, trombone, French horn, tuba), and percussion instruments. In addition, these elementary students often meet in a large group for beginning band. Instruction at this level focuses on the development of musicianship, music reading, and the basic skills of performing on the instrument. Several public performances are usually presented as a part of the beginning band experience.

At the middle school level (grades 6–8) students often meet in a large ensemble (50 or more) for daily rehearsals. As students become more skilled on their instruments, they may begin to study privately outside of school with a professional musician. In addition, they may begin to perform solo literature. Most states hold annual solo and ensemble festivals at which intermediate and advanced players perform for comments from adjudicators. Many intermediate bands also participate in band festivals and competitions at which the entire ensemble performs for an adjudicator for comments and suggestions for improvement. Middle school band also includes regular public performances.

Most public high schools offer a variety of programs in instrumental education. The core of the band program is the concert band. In some schools students may be required to audition for placement in a specific ensemble based on musical achievement. Although there are a variety of names for these ensembles, including concert band, wind ensemble, symphonic band, and others, all these terms refer to a large ensemble of wind, brass, and percussion instruments. Although the number of players in the ensemble may vary from 40 to 200, most concert bands include some combination of the following instruments: flute, piccolo, oboe, English horn, clarinet, bass clarinet, bassoon, alto saxophone, tenor saxophone, baritone saxophone, French horn, trumpet, cornet, trombone, euphonium, tuba, snare drum, bass drum, xylophone, and auxiliary percussion. As players become more advanced, they often continue to take private lessons and participate in solo and ensemble festivals. Many high school bands attend multiple competitions and festivals each year in addition to local concerts, tours, and trips where performances are given.

The literature performed by the high school band is quite varied and may include marches, transcriptions of orchestral works, concert pieces composed just for the band medium, and popular music of various kinds. Well-known composers who have contributed to the band repertoire include Percy Grainger, Paul Hindemith, David Holsinger, Gustav Holst, Karel Husa, Darius Milhaud, Vincent Persichetti, Sergei Prokofiev, Arnold Schoenberg, William Schuman, and Ralph Vaughan Williams. There are few women composers of band music and no women composers who would be considered "mainstream contributors" to the current band repertoire.

In addition to the concert band, most high school programs have a marching band that performs for high school football games and local parades. Some schools become very involved in marching band competitions as well. Many school programs also offer jazz band as part of the high school band curriculum. Although some programs allow any student to participate in jazz band, most programs restrict participation to traditional jazz instruments including saxophone, trumpet, trombone, keyboard, guitar, bass, and drums. Many band players continue to play in concert and marching bands after their school experiences. Most colleges have a concert band, and many have marching bands as well.

There are many gender issues associated with instrumental education, and considerable research has been conducted on the relationship between gender and the choice of which musical instrument to play. This work has suggested that stereotypes regarding which instruments are most "masculine" and which instruments are most "feminine" have historically had an impact on what instruments girls and boys choose to play. Although recent research has suggested that girls are beginning to play instruments that were stereotypically considered "masculine" (tuba, euphonium, percussion), the large majority of girls still choose to play instruments considered "feminine" (flute, oboe, clarinet). These choices often result in fewer women in jazz and marching bands, because "feminine" instruments are not always used in these ensembles.

Due to the history of the band deriving from the male-dominated military band tradition, only in the last 30 years or so have girls been allowed to participate in marching bands at the college level. The perception that marching band in particular but band directing in general is a "male" activity is still quite common in secondary and college band programs and among community members today. Although there are certainly more women in high school band director positions today than 30 years ago, the largest percentage of women in the band profession are women working with elementary and intermediate bands. Several studies have documented the lack of representation of women in the college band directing profession.

Those women who do work with secondary school band students and college bands continue to discuss the prejudice they feel in their communities regarding being a woman band director. As suggested earlier, there are few women composers of band music. Thus young women conductors and composers have few role models. However, there are important women who have contributed to the success of instrumental education in America. Gladys Wright was the first woman elected into the American Bandmasters Association in 1984. She founded the Women Band Directors National Association (now changed to Woman Band Directors International) and in 1999 was the first woman inducted into the National Band Association Hall of Fame. Paula Crider (b. 1944), retired director of bands at the University of Texas at Austin, was the first woman president of the National Band Association.

Kathryn Scott, director of marching band at the University of Alabama, was the first woman director of a marching band in a major university. Patricia Hoy, director of bands at Northern Arizona University, was the first woman director of bands in a large university. Mallory Thompson, currently the director of bands at Northwestern University, was the first woman director of bands in a Big 10 university. Maxine Lefever, a percussionist, worked with the National Band Association and the Sousa Foundation as well as serving as a percussion instructor at Purdue University. She is also known for her compositions for percussion ensembles.

Elizabeth Green, now deceased, was a conducting faculty member at the University of Michigan and is currently being inducted into the Hall of Fame for Distinguished Women Conductors. Barbara Buehlman, now deceased, was a middle school director in Round Lake, IL, who served as secretary for the Midwest Clinic (a national conference held annually in Chicago attended by over 12,000 band and orchestra directors) for many years. She did a lot of arranging for bands.

See also Music Education; Women Band Directors International

For Further Reading

Conway, Colleen M. "Gender and Musical Instrument Choice: A Phenomenological Investigation." *Bulletin of the Council for Research in Music Education*, 146 (2000): 1–17.

Grant, Denise Elizabeth. "The Impact of Mentoring and Gender-Specific Role Models on Women College Band Directors at Four Different Career Stages." Ph.D. diss., University of Minnesota, 2000.

Keene, James A. *A History of Music Education in the United States*. London: University Press of New England, 1982.

Mark, Michael L., and Charles L. Gary. *A History of American Music Education*. New York: Schirmer Books, 1992.

Miles, Richard. *Teaching Music through Performance in Band*. Chicago: G.I.A. Publications, 1997.

Wright, Gladys. *Women in the Band World (1850–2000)*. West Lafayette, IN: John Phillip Sousa Foundation, in progress.

Zervoudakes, J., and J. M. Tanur. "Gender and Musical Instruments: Winds of Change." *Journal of Research in Music Education*, 42/1 (1994): 58–67.

Colleen Conway

International Alliance for Women in Music

With a membership of over 1,000, the International Alliance for Women in Music (IAWM) is the largest organization devoted to issues regarding women in music. Two events during musicALASKAwomen, an International Congress on Women in Music (ICWM) held in Fairbanks, AK, in 1993, served as catalysts for the establishment of the IAWM in January 1995: Jeannie Pool's keynote speech entitled "The Passionate Pursuits of Musical Women: Feminism, Unity and Advocacy," and a panel discussion entitled "The Future of Women in Music," led by Tera de Marez Oyens of the Netherlands.

The Interim Executive Committee of the International League of Women Composers (ILWC), acting on a member mandate to explore opportunities for cooperation with American Women Composers (ILWC general membership meeting, Alaska, August 1993), began informal discussions with AWC past-president Judith Shatin (b. 1949) during the musicALASKAwomen festival in August 1993. Ensuing conversations among Stefania de Kenessey, American Women Composers (AWC) president, and various ILWC board members resulted in an invitation from AWC to the ILWC to attend an AWC Board of Directors meeting in Washington, DC, on 12–13 November 1993. The AWC Board (with the approval of the ILWC) appointed a six-member merger committee to further explore the merger concept.

The merger committee included two members of the ILWC Interim Executive Board (Sally Reid and Hilary Tann), two members of the former ICWM (Lucille Field Goodman and Jeannie Pool), and two members of the AWC Board

(Stefania de Kenessey and Judith Shatin); de Kenessey and Reid served as co-chairs. AWC president Stefania de Kenessey wrote to the AWC membership, "The immediate benefits of such a union are clear—a broader membership, a shared pool of resources, a wider range of activities, and the avoidance of duplication and competition . . . and an opportunity to form a single, vigorous organization (which) holds enormous promise for the future."

Beginning with their "Points of Agreement," committee members prepared a merger proposal document, a general plan for achieving orderly unification, for the boards of both the AWC and the ILWC. "Convinced that the time is right to eliminate duplication of effort and to combine our energies to achieve common purposes, we propose the formation of an International Alliance for Women in Music that unites the International Congress on Women in Music (ICWM), American Women Composers (AWC) and the International League of Women Composers (ILWC). This new entity will not abandon its heritage or the obligations of its former identities, but rather will embrace anew the original visions and purposes of all three parent organizations. . . . We believe a merger can be accomplished without disrupting ongoing projects or services to the combined memberships. We have prepared this proposal in good faith with high hopes for our shared future." (AWC/ILWC Merger Committee, June 1994). This document, with amendments, was approved on 12 June 1994. A nominating committee for the new IAWM Executive Committee and IAWM Board of Directors included Lucille Field Goodman, Catherine Pickar, Clare Shore, and Hilary Tann.

In January 1995, the International Al-liance for Women in Music was born, calling itself a "coalition of professional composers, conductors, performers, musicologists, educators, librarians, and lovers of music, men as well as women, the IAWM encourages the activities of women in music; by encouraging the publication and distribution of music by women composers; by supporting performances and recordings of women composers; by fostering scholarly research on women-in-music topics; by facilitating communication among members and with other organizations; implementing various broadcast series, competitions and educational programs; by encouraging member participation in other composer groups; by continuing the International Congresses on Women in Music as International Alliance for Women in Music Congresses; by initiating advocacy work on behalf of women in music; by actively seeking diversity in participation on the board and in IAWM projects, activities and events." Short-range goals focused on creating unity; medium-range goals focused on becoming the principal information resource for the international music community; and long-range commitments included increasing the inclusiveness of all women and the encouragement of, cooperation with, and support for other women in music organizations. Stefania de Kenessey served as IAWM president from 1995 to 1996; Deon Nielsen Price, from 1996 to 1999; and Sally Reid, from 1999 to 2001.

Publications of the Alliance include the *IAWM Journal* (three issues per year); *Women and Music: A Journal of Gender and Culture*, a refereed academic journal published annually since 1997 and by the University of Nebraska Press beginning in 1999; and an annual membership directory. The IAWM maintains the

IAWM electronic distribution list, an electronic mail service with over 500 subscribers hosted by Abilene Christian University.

The IAWM has initiated several new cooperative ventures, including support for concerts at the Fourth and Fifth International Festivals of Women Composers at Indiana University of Pennsylvania in 1996 and 1998, organized by Susan Wheatley and Sarah Mantle.

The IAWM sponsored a panel discussion on women composers in Asian countries during the Asian Composers League Conference in Manila, the Philippines (1997), at the initiation of board member Jin Hi Kim (b. 1957). In collaboration with the Asia Society, the IAWM also presented concerts and panel discussions at the World Music Institute and Thomas Buckner's Interpretations in New York City on 22–23 October 1999 entitled "Asian Women in Music Today." The IAWM has also sponsored concerts in New York City and Chicago in collaboration with American Composers Midwest (AWC). Each concert featured IAWM member works chosen through a blind score selection process.

The IAWM continues to present annual concerts in collaboration with the National Museum of Women in the Arts (in the museum's recital hall in Washington, DC). The concerts feature compositions by IAWM members chosen through an anonymous score selection process. The program was expanded to include performer members and commissions of works by American women of color in 2000. The IAWM co-sponsored a concert to celebrate the placing of the American Women Composers' score collection in the Gelman Library of George Washington University (GWU) in September 1997. Scores for the performance were selected by GWU faculty perform-

ers from the collection. The score archive of the International Congress on Women in Music is housed at the International Institute for the Study of Women in Music at California State University, Northridge.

The IAWM produces biennial Congresses alternating between international venues and the United States, most recently in London, England (July 1999), and Valencia, CA (May 1997). The annual IAWM Search for New Music (SNM) makes five annual awards: Zwilich Prize (composers age 21 and under); Aaron Cohen Prize (for composers age 22 to 49); Miriam Gideon Prize (for composers over age 50) and the 1st and 2nd IAWM SNM awards (for student composers of any age). The 1997 Pauline Alderman Awards were made in conjunction with the Tenth International Congress on Women in Music in Valencia, CA. Coordinators for these awards included Susan Cook, Ev Grimes, Nancy Bloomer Deussen, and Marilyn Shrude (SNM); and Stephen Fry, Jeannie G. Pool, Beverly Simmons, and Lance Bowling (Alderman).

The IAWM was one of the first music societies in the United States with an Internet presence. Beginning in December 1994, the IAWM site provided an initial Web presence for several small publishers of music and recordings by women, including Arsis Press, ClarNan Press, Hildegard Publishing, Vienna Modern Masters, and Leonarda Recordings. Each used this experience as a first step in establishing a successful commercial World Wide Web site. The IAWM Internet community archive is developed and maintained by members and contains nearly 4,000 pages of materials on women composers and women in music. Online projects include: the award-winning Early Women Composers mod-

Winners of the ILWC/IAWM Search for New Music

Search for New Music	Composer
ILWC	
First Search for New Music	
First Prize	Sarah Aderholdt
Honorable Mentions	Debborah S. Van Ohlen
	Linda Catlin Smith
Second Search for New Music	
First Prize	Katherine Hafemeister
Third Search for New Music	
First Prize	Catherine Schieve
Second Prize	J. Katherine Harvey
Third Prize	Karen Thomas
Honorable Mentions	Laura Goldfader
	Elizabeth Bevan
	Janet Ivcich
	Merilin Michele Perry-Paris
	Catherine Schieve
	Karen Thomas
Fourth Search for New Music	
First Prize	Alice Ho
Second Prize	Ie Don Ho
Honorable Mentions	Julia Anderson
	Susan Calkins
	Janice Macaulay
	Elizabeth Sheidel
Fifth Search for New Music	
First Prize (tie)	Janice Misurell Mitchell
	Violeta Dinescu
Honorable Mentions	Janice Macaulay
	Jae Eun Park No
	Elena Ruehr
Sixth Search for New Music	
First Prize	Christina Kuzmych
Second Prize	Dorothea Ferrari-Stone
Honorable Mentions	Linda Bouchard
	Violeta Dinescu
Seventh Search for New Music	
First Prize	Ruth Meyer
Second Prize	Renée Silas Waters
Honorable Mentions	Brigitte Condoret
	Christina Kuzmych
Eighth Search for New Music	
First Prize	Nack-Kum Paik
Second Prize (tie)	Mary Wright
	Elizabeth Alexander

Winners of the ILWC/IAWM Search for New Music (*continued*)

Search for New Music	Composer
Honorable Mention	Patricia Morehead
	Elena Ruehr

Ninth Search for New Music

First Prize	Hillary Kruh
Second Prize (tie)	Karin Swanson
	Lori Dobbbins
Honorable Mentions	Elizabeth Alexander
	Jennifer Higdon

Tenth Search for New Music

First Prize	Lori Dobbins
Second Prize (tie)	Simona Simonini
	Carolyn Yarnell
Ellen Taaffe Zwilich Prize	Penka Kuneva
Honorable Mentions	Renée Silas Waters

Eleventh Search for New Music

First Prize	Serra Hwang
Second Prize	Simona Simonini
Zwilich Prize	Hollie Thomas
Honorable Mentions	Renée Silas Waters

Twelfth Search for New Music

First Prize	Joanne Metcalf
Second Prize	Jennifer Higdon
Zwilich Prize	Luna Woolf
Honorable Mentions	Ellen Ruth Harrison
	A. E. Sierra
	Stacy Garrop
	Sheila Forrester
	Stacey J. Willer
	Renée Favand
	Mei-Chun Chen

Thirteenth Search for New Music

First Prize	Stacy Garrop
Second Prize	Deborah J. Monroe
Zwilich Prize	Betsey Rosenblatt

Fourteenth Search for New Music

First Prize	Alissa L. Roosa
Second Prize	Lisa Rainsong
Zwilich Prize	Heather Schmidt
Honorable Mentions	Renée Favand
	Ellen Harrison
	Sally Lamb
	SoYeon Lee
	Belinda L.
	Terry Vosbein
	Anna Weesner

Winners of the ILWC/IAWM Search for New Music (*continued*)

Search for New Music	Composer
Fifteenth Search for New Music	
First Prize	Gabriela Lena Frank
Second Prize	HyeKyung Lee
Zwilich Prize	Heather Schmidt
Nancy Van de Vate Prize	Andrea Clearfield
Sixteenth Search for New Music	
First Prize	Laurie San Martin
Second Prize (tie)	Stacy Garrop
	Rona Siddiqui
Zwilich Prize	Mary Jane King
Van de Vate Prize	HyeKyung Lee
Seventeenth Search for New Music	
Student Composer Prize (tie)	Erika Foin
	Jennifer Furr
Zwilich Prize	Nancy Koe
Miriam Gideon Prize	
First Prize	Elizabeth R. Austin
Second Prize	Janice Misurell-Mitchell
Eighteenth Search for New Music	
First Prize	Stacy Garrop
Second Prize	Sarana Tzu-Ling Chou
Zwilich Prize	Erin Hollins
Gideon Prize (tie)	Janice Hamer
	Ruth Lomon

ule, developed by Sarah Whitworth; WOW/EM, Women On the Web/ElectronMedia, a site for young women interested in music and art, hosted by Kristine H. Burns; Women'sMusic.com, a site that includes a composer chat room and archives of radio broadcasts of Eine Kleine Frauenmusik provided by Jeanne Shaffer; "Webliography": an introduction to music research online compiled by Judith A. Coe; and the IAWM Publisher Contact Service, which connects performers with publishers.

Additionally, the IAWM used its electronic communication network to protest the Vienna Philharmonic Orchestra's (VPO) historic exclusion of women musicians during the orchestra's 1997 U.S. tour (in New York and California). This helped pressure the VPO to grant full membership to their harpist of 26 years, Anna Lelkes. The Alliance maintains the "VPO Watch" to evaluate the progress/failure of the VPO in the auditioning and accepting of qualified women instrumentalists into the orchestra.

Individual members of the IAWM produce a number of radio shows featuring music by women, including "Eine Kleine Frauenmusik," hosted by Jeanne Shaffer on the Southeastern Public Radio Network; "Listening to Women and Men," hosted by Jeanne Brossart in Provincetown, MA; "The Latest Score," hosted by Canary Burton in Provincetown, MA; broadcasts featuring women composers by Casper Sunn and Tracy Dietzel in Madison, WI; and "Into the Light," hosted by Kathryn Mishell in Austin, TX.

The IAWM participates in the National Music Council, the American Alliance of Composer Organizations, and maintains affiliate relationships with the National Federation of Music Clubs, Sigma Alpha Iota, the Association of Canadian Women Composers, American Women Composers, Midwest, and the Honor Committee of Donne in Musica Foundation. A member of the IAWM Board of Directors has presented a world report on the status of women in music in the United States during the Donne in Musica Festival held each fall in Fiuggi, Italy, since 1996.

See also American Women Composers, Inc.; International Congress on Women in Music; International League of Women Composers

For Further Reading

Marez Oyens, Tera de. "Future of Women in Music," Introduction to Panel, Future of Women in Music, presented at musicALASKAwomen, 14 August 1993. *ILWC [International League of Women Composers] Journal* (October 1993): 21.

———. "Reports from the Interim Executive Committee." *IAWM [International Alliance for Women in Music] Journal* (February 1994): 35.

Pool, Jeannie. "The Passionate Pursuits of Musical Women: Feminism, Unity and Advocacy." *ILWC [International League of Women Composers] Journal* (October 1993): 1–5

Reid, Sally. "Toward the International Alliance for Women in Music." *IAWM [International Alliance for Women in Music] Journal* (October 1994): 33.

———. "Toward the International Alliance for Women in Music: A Progress Report from the AWC/ILWC Merger Committee." *IAWM [International Alliance for Women in Music] Journal* (June 1994): 43.

Sally Reid

International Congress on Women in Music

In 1978, Jeannie Pool founded the National Congress on Women in Music (later named International Congress on Women in Music [ICWM]), a series of meetings, concerts, and workshops devoted to women musicians. The first project was a conference and workshop of twentieth-century string quartets by women, a collaboration with the International League of Women Composers. Broadcast Music, Inc. (BMI), the American Society of Composers, Authors and Publishers (ASCAP), and other organizations provided the $12,000 needed to host the event and its 200 attendees on International Women's Day, 8 March 1980. National Public Radio won an award for its presentation of eight string quartets in concert and interviews with the composers in a series called *A Woman's Work Is . . . Music.*

Because of this success, Jeannie Pool organized the first National Congress on Women on 26–29 March 1981. It was sponsored by New York University's (NYU) Music Department and met at a number of sites in New York, including NYU. Pool then moved to Los Angeles and organized an international Congress on the West Coast. On 1–4 April 1982, 150 people from 29 countries heard music by women composers and performers, as well as lectures and scholarly papers. Highlights included a rare performance of Mary Carr Moore's opera *David Rizzio*, gospel music, and a session on Mexican women's music. It was here that the ICWM was formalized as an organization. Its goals were to facilitate the international exchange of information on music by women; to plan future ICWM Congresses and other meetings for women musicians; to initiate advocacy work with governments; and to recognize outstanding women in music. The quarterly ICWM newsletter began in January 1983 and included a member directory.

Successive Congresses were held in Mexico City (1984), Paris (1985), Atlanta (1986), Germany (1988), and New York City (1990). What is impressive about the Congresses was the level of inclusion: professional and amateurs, well-known and student composers, old and new music, and a variety of racial and ethnic cultures. This attitude fostered connections with other organizations, such as Frau und Musik in Germany; Kinder I Muscek in Denmark; Donne in Music in Italy; Movement d'Action Musical in France; and the Association of Japanese Women Composers. After the merger with the International League of Women Composers in 1990, Congresses continued to be held under the auspices of the ILWC in Utrecht, the Netherlands (1991), Madrid, Spain (1992), and Fairbanks, AK (musicALASKAwomen, August 1993).

In 1985 the ICWM became affiliated with the International Institute for the Study of Women in Music at California State University, Northridge, chartered by the California State University, Northridge, in 1985. The institute houses research materials donated by Aaron Cohen, which he assembled for the landmark books *The International Encyclopedia of Women* (published in 1981 by Bowker), including information on more than 4,800 women composers and thousands of books, scores, manuscripts, records, scrapbooks, and other materials about women and music. Jeannie Pool and Beverly Grigsby (b. 1928) served as the institute's directors. Its purpose was to encourage use of the Cohen Collection by scholars; to expand the holdings of the collection to include new works by

women composers, particularly of Latin America, Eastern Europe, the Soviet Union, and Asia; to organize, promote, and produce various events to increase awareness of the accomplishments of women in music, particularly as composers; to bring scholars to present and discuss research methodology and results; to encourage performance of music by women composers; and to build a network among scholars involved in the study of women in music. In 1985 Pool produced *Working Papers on Women in Music*, a collection of articles jointly published by the ICWM and the International Institute.

Beginning in 1986 the Pauline Alderman Awards were presented by the Congress for new research on women in music, bestowing honor and distinction on the winning scholars. Pauline Alderman (1893–1983), for whom the award is named, was one of the pioneering woman musicologists interested in women and music. She was a member of the faculty at the University of Southern California for 45 years, where she chaired the music history department from 1952 to 1960. As a composer, performer, and music historian, and as a teacher and mentor to hundreds of students and colleagues, she exemplified the highest standards in musical pedagogy and research. The prizewinning research projects included books, articles, papers, essays, dissertations, and other published and unpublished materials. The 1993 awards were made in conjunction with musicALASKAwomen (Fairbanks, 1993).

With the merger of the International Congress on Women in Music with the International League of Women Composers and the American Women Composers into the IAWM in 1995, the scope of the Pauline Alderman Awards continued to expand. Awards were presented for (1) the most important book-length

Pauline Alderman Recipients, 1986–1997

Year	Prize	Author	Title
1997	First Prize	Marcia Citron	*Gender and the Musical Canon*. Cambridge and New York: Cambridge University Press, 1993.
1997	Second Prize	Bonnie Jo Dopp	"Numerology and Cryptography in the Music of Lili Boulanger: The Hidden Program in Clairières dans le ciel." *Musical Quarterly* 78/3 (Fall 1994): 557–583.
1997	Third Prize	Julie Anne Sadie and Rhian Samuel	*The Norton/Grove Dictionary of Women Composers*, 1st American ed. New York and London: W. W. Norton, 1995.
1993	First Prize	Judith Lang Zaimont, editor-in-chief, and Jane Gottlieb, Joanne Polk, and Michael J. Rogan, associate editors	*The Musical Woman: An International Perspective, Vol. III: 1986–1990*. Westport, CT: Greenwood Press, 1991.
1993	Second Prize	Susan McClary	*Feminine Endings: Music, Gender and Sexuality*. Minneapolis: University of Minnesota Press, 1991.
1993	Third Prize	Karin Pendle	*Women and Music: A History*. Bloomington: Indiana University Press, 1991.
1989	First Prize	Diane Jezic	*Women Composers: The Lost Tradition Found*. New York: Feminist Press of the City University of New York, 1988.
1989	Second Prize	Judith Vander	*Songprints: The Musical Experience of Five Shoshone Women*. Urbana: University of Illinois Press, 1988.
1988	First Prize	Virginia Bortin	*Elinor Remick Warren: Her Life and Her Music*. Metuchen, NJ: Scarecrow Press, 1987.
1988	Second Prize	Edith Borroff	"The Apprentice System and the Music of Women." Typescript, 1987. Unpublished paper given at the Fourth International Congress on Women in Music, Atlanta, GA, 1986.
1988	Third Prize	Susan Finger	"The Los Angeles Heritage: Four Women Composers, 1918–1939." Typescript, 1987. Ph.D. diss., University of California, Los Angeles, 1986.
1987	First Prize	Jane Bower and Judith Tick	*Women Making Music: The Western Art Tradition, 1150–1950*. Urbana: University of Illinois Press, 1987.

Pauline Alderman Recipients, 1986–1997 (*continued*)

Year	Prize	Author	Title
1986	First Prize	Catherine Parsons Smith and Cynthia S. Richardson	*An American Woman: The Life and Music of Mary Carr Moore*. Typescript, 1985. Subsequently published by the University of Michigan Press, 1987.
1986	Second Prize	Nancy B. Reich	*Clara Schumann: The Artist and the Woman*. Ithaca, NY: Cornell University Press, 1985.
1986	Third Prize (shared)	Judith Rosen	*Grazyna Bacewicz: Her Life and Works*. Los Angeles: Friends of Polish Music, 1985.
1986	Third Prize (shared)	Joanne Riley	"Tarquinia Molza (1547–1617): A Case Study of Women, Music, and Society in the Renaissance." Typescript, 1985. Subsequently published by Greenwood Press in *The Musical Woman II*, 1987.

monographic study about women in music (including a biography, history, or study of some specific aspect of women in music; a book, dissertation, master's thesis, or other substantial academic paper); (2) the most important journal article dealing with an aspect of women in music; and (3) the most important bibliographic study, research tool, or reference work in any medium, including electronic, about women in music. The Pauline Alderman Committee was to consider (1) evidence of thorough research and the presentation of factual, useful information with proper documentation; (2) clear and concise presentation of the material; (3) appropriate, timely, and focused topics; (4) the integration of the methodology for women's studies with that for musicology; and (5) analysis of the material presented, demonstrating a thorough understanding and synthesis of the subject.

See also International Alliance for Women in Music; International League of Women Composers

For Further Reading

Fry, Stephen M. "The History of the ICWM." *IAWM Journal* (June 1995): 4–8.

Pool, Jeannie. "Silent No More: Women in Music," which includes reminiscences of her experiences with the ICWM [International Congress on Women in Music], in *Festival Essays for Pauline Alderman: A Musicological Tribute*, ed. Burton L. Karson. Provo: Brigham Young University Press, 1976.

Alicia RaMusa

International League of Women Composers

The League of Women Composers, founded in 1975 by Nancy Van de Vate (b. 1930), creates change and provides women musicians the opportunity to enter the professional mainstream. Van de Vate also founded the first National Organization of Women chapter in Tennessee in 1970, as well as the Vienna Modern Masters Recording Company, to ensure equality to women composers and conductors. Van de Vate provided strong leadership as League chairperson from 1975 to 1981.

In 1978 "International" was added to the organization's name. Composer members were admitted by score review. Performers and others held affiliate member status. Original board members included Radie Britain, Claire Polin, Marga Richter, and Pauline Oliveros (b. 1932). Assistant chairpersons, Doris Hays and Elizabeth Pizer, were added for the East and West Coasts in 1981. Pizer succeeded Van de Vate as chairperson, continuing until 1993. Others who served on the ILWC board during the early years were Susan Cook, Tina Davidson, Jane Frasier, Katherine Hoover (b. 1937), Susan Cohn Lackman, Linda Mankin, Kimberly McCarthy, Valerie O'Brien, Ann Silsbee, Elizabeth Vercoe, and Judith Lang Zaimont (b. 1945). International leaders have included Jane O'Leary (Ireland), Betty Beath (Australia), Violeta Dinescu (Germany/Europe), Ruth Gipps (Great Britain), Mary Mageau (American living in Australia), and Teresa Procaccini (Italy).

Some of the projects given life by the League include the publication of *Contemporary Concert Music by Women: A Dictionary of Composers and Their Works*, edited by Judith Lang Zaimont et al. (Greenwood Press, 1982); the Australian Broadcast Series begun by Mary Mageau on 2MBS-FM Radio, and later coordinated by composer member Betty Beath and airing on two additional Australian radio stations, 4MBS-FM Brisbane and 3MBS-FM Melbourne; and *Expressions*, a radio series produced by Doris Hays. The annual Search for New Music (SNM), coordinated by Susan Cook and later Ev Grimes, recognized and encouraged student composers. Meetings of ILWC membership were held in conjunction with various festivals, including the 4th International Congress on Women in Music, Atlanta, GA, March 1986; and the Opus 3 Conference, University of Kansas, March 1985.

The League developed an association with Arsis Press to promote music by women composers and presented many concerts. America in Concert programs were organized by Clara Lyle Boone. Meet the Woman Composer, later known as the League Lecture Project, featured an 11-concert series in New York, organized by Doris Hays and Beth Anderson. A Library of Congress Concert included works performed by the Contemporary Music Forum (CMF) on 17 May 1982, a collaborative effort organized by Frances McKay of CMF and supported by Arsis Press, the ILWC, and the Music Division of the Library of Congress.

By 1980 the International League of Women Composers (ILWC) budget had grown to $7,000. Advocacy projects included efforts to have women placed on various boards and panels within the music community. Press releases and letters were sent to hundreds of music magazines and newspapers, and sample newsletters were mailed to libraries in the United States supported by a National Endowment for the Arts grant (1981). A representative was sent to the American Symphony Orchestra League Conference. Clara Lyle Boone appeared before the Music Advisory Panel of the National Endowment for the Arts (1981) citing statistical evidence to show that women do not receive their fair share of Endowment funds. The group lobbied for blind judging in composition competitions and to have works by women included on various performance competition lists. Van de Vate, as editor of the *ILWC Newsletter*, published a review by J. Carol Dixon of the Music Educators National

Conference's (MENC) Selective Music Lists. Dixon observed there were no works by women in either the orchestral or the choral works lists. Van de Vate sent copies of Dixon's report to the *Journal of Research in Music*.

Vital to the growth of the organization was the *ILWC Newsletter*, documenting the activities of its members and providing a sense of connection among them. Early issues included information about the increasing number of festivals of music by women, book reviews, and opportunities for members. Member news began to be included in 1982. Extensive information about radio programs that would receive tapes and records of music by women provided many composers with their first opportunities for airplay. Valerie O'Brien succeeded Van de Vate as editor, followed by Hilary Tann (1982–1987), Mary Chaves (1987–1990) and Sally Reid (1991–1995). The newsletter was renamed the *ILWC Journal* in 1989, and it grew to 60-plus pages, including photographs and scholarly articles. Assistant editors during these years included Deborah Hayes, Laura Hoffman, Fern L. McArthur, Valerie Hubbard, Laurine Elkins-Marlow, Julie Scrivener, and Elizabeth Vercoe. Lively newsletter discussions addressed whether or not "all-women's" or "all-contemporary" composer concerts were "ghettoizing" the music and the composers; equity in competition judging; and how some women preferred not to be called "women composers."

In 1990 the ILWC merged with International Congress of Women in Music (ICWM). Congress founder Jeannie Pool wrote, "this joining together sends a signal to the music community of our strong commitment to best serve the women-in-music community and the unity of purpose in creating new oppor-

tunities for women in music." ICWM members Lucille Field-Goodman, Jeannie Pool, and Deon Nielsen Price were added to the ILWC Board of Directors. Following the merger, additional congresses were held in Utrecht, the Netherlands (1991), Madrid, Spain (1992) and Fairbanks, AK (musicALASKAwomen, August 1993).

It was in Alaska that conversations leading to the subsequent merger with American Women Composers began. An Interim Executive Committee guided the day-to-day activities of the League from the summer of 1993 until the merger with American Women Composers in January 1995. It was governed by Lucille Field Goodman, Tera de Marez Oyens, Jeannie Pool, Deon Nelson Price, Sally Reid, and Hilary Tann, who served as coordinator. The League's communication network moved online in 1993 with the participation of three dozen members on the ILWC electronic mail list, hosted by Abilene Christian University. The ILWC (which later became the International Alliance for Women in Music) Web site was unveiled in December 1994 in preparation for the merger with American Women Composers. By the close of 1994 the ILWC had 450 members in 36 countries and on five continents. The increased membership included performers, musicologists, educators, and librarians.

See also American Women Composers, Inc.; International Alliance for Women in Music; International Congress on Women in Music

For Further Reading

Beath, Betty. "The International League of Women Composers." *ILWC [International League of Women Composers] Journal* (July 1991): 1–2. [This article first appeared in *Sounds Australian*, and was reprinted in the *ILWC Journal* by permission.]

Peterson, Barbara A. "Women Composers Yesterday, Today, and Tomorrow, or Yes, Nancy, There is Life after Fifteen!" *ILWC [International League of Women Composers] Journal* (July 1991): 8–9.

Pool, Jeannie. "The Consolidation of the ILWC and the ICWM." *ILWC [International League of Women Composers] Journal* (September 1991): 10–11.

———. "The Women-in-Music Movement, Then and Now." *ILWC [International League of Women Composers] Newsletter* (Spring 1985): 6–10.

Straughn, Greg. "The International League of Women Composers." *ILWC [International League of Women Composers] Journal* (June 1995): 8–10.

Alicia RaMusa
Sally Reid

International Women's Brass Conference

The International Women's Brass Conference (IWBC), founded by Susan Slaughter in 1990, provides opportunities for the education, support, development, and inspiration of women brass players. Slaughter, principal trumpet of the St. Louis Symphony Orchestra and currently the only women brass player with a principal chair in a major U.S. orchestra, served as IWBC president from 1990 to 1998. Marie Speziale, associate principal trumpet, Cincinnati Symphony (retired), succeeded her.

The IWBC sponsors conferences every three to five years featuring guest artists, master classes, a solo competition, premieres of commissioned works for brass by the IWBC, workshops, and other related presentations. The first two conferences (May 1993 and June 1997) were held at Washington University in St. Louis; the third conference was held in June 2000 at the University of Cincinnati. Attendance at IWBC conferences ranges between 300 and 400, with men accounting for 15 percent of the registrants.

The "Pioneers Awards" of the IWBC honor outstanding women brass players and commemorate and document their accomplishments. In 1993 this award was granted to trombonists Betty Glover and Melba Liston (1926–1999) and trumpeter Leona May Smith. In 1997 this award was granted to trumpeters Jane Sager and Clora Bryant and tubist Constance Weldon. In 2000 the award was granted to Nadine Jansen, Ethel Merker (horn), and Betty O'Hara (euphorium).

The IWBC strives to increase the visibility of women brass players through international tours of Monarch Brass, a large brass ensemble with an all-women membership. The solo competition, open to women and men, awards $18,000 in prize money to winning candidates, with $2,000 in first prizes and $1,000 in second prizes given in each of six categories (trumpet, horn, trombone, bass trombone, euphonium, and tuba). The IWBC commissions new works for brass, which are premiered at each conference.

In July 1999 the IWBC's membership was 1,533, with the distribution of the members' primary instruments as follows: trumpet (418), horn (665), trombone (193), euphonium (21), and tuba (112). IWBC publications include *Women Brass Musicians, Past and Present*, compiled by the Pioneers Committee to document the history of women brass players and stimulate further research; the *Directory of Women Brass Performers and Teachers*; and a biannual *Newsletter* to members.

The IWBC also serves as the central clearinghouse for an international Behavior Study, where women brass players can report incidences of sexual discrimination or harassment occurring on the job. Because of the isolation of women brass players from each other, the IWBC believes that gathering this information is essential and that the survey results are necessary to document and identify the extent of the difficulties women brass players encounter. With that knowledge the IWBC and individual women can consider joint efforts to address the problems.

See also Organizations, Performer; Performer, Brass

For Further Reading

International Women's Brass Conference. Available: http://iwbc-online.org.
International Women's Brass Conference *Newsletter.*
Jepson, Barbara. "Sexism in the Brass Section." *Wall Street Journal*, 7 July 1993, p. 10.
Maloof, Lisa. "Focus Story: Women in Brass." *Women's Philharmonic Newsletter* (Spring 1998).
Monique Buzzarté

Internet Resources

At the end of the twentieth century, Internet resources provided not only sources of reference and research but also means of personal support for many women. Because the Internet offers an environment in which gender is hidden, women are capable of thriving both economically and socially as well as men. Traits such as age, sex, race, and gender may remain anonymous when using the Internet, so discussion can focus on content, ideas, and meaning. And the Internet is no stranger to women: as a group, they make up some 40 to 50 percent of those using commercial online services.

Although numerous national and regional women's organizations exist, and many have extensive World Wide Web sites, many organizations exist primarily, if not entirely, on the World Wide Web. These Internet organizations still may require dues but are able to offer free services such as electronic mail, disk space for World Wide Web publishing, electronic mailing lists, and ezines (electronic magazines). iVillage.com: The Women's Network is the leading source of World Wide Web resources devoted to women's issues. Along with World Wide Web sites such as Cybergrrl.com and its sister site, Webgrrls.com, these sites are similar to the women's magazines available on newsstands, covering careers, fashion, and general news. YIN: The Women's Guide to the Best of the Web, as well as the Women's Internet Information Network, offer information on arts, business, health, and food.

Many electronic mailing lists offer advice and information by and for subscribers. The more significant women's mailing lists for general information include the National Organization for Women (NOW) Action List; the GLB-NEWS, gay, lesbian, and bisexual news; and WMST-L, the women's studies list. A variety of electronic newsgroups also allow users to read and reply to messages, but without the day-to-day contact that many electronic mailing lists offer.

Search engines are used to locate specific information on various World Wide Web sites. The three major women's search engines are Women's Search, FeMiNa, and WWWomen. Women's Search offers a searchable directory of women-owned World Wide Web sites and issues of special interest to women, and FeMiNa provides women with a searchable database of "women-friendly" World Wide Web sites. The WW-Women search engine finds sites relevant to women's issues, including information about child rearing and pregnancy, civil liberties, careers, and religion.

Numerous music World Wide Web sites, including those of many professional music societies, exist on the Internet. The College Music Society (CMS), National Association for Teachers of Singing (NATS), International Double Reed Society (IDRS), International Clarinet Association (ICS), National Flute Association (NFA), and Percussive Arts Society (PAS) all have World Wide Web sites for their members. Music research organizations such as the American Musicological Society (AMS), the Society for Music Theory (SMT), the Society for American Music (formerly the Sonneck Society), and the Music Educators National Conference (MENC) also have World Wide Web sites. The composer's organizations such as the American Music Center (AMC), the Society of Composers, Inc. (SCI), and the Society for Electro-Acoustic Music in the United States (SEAMUS) have sites. These professional music organizations usually provide information such as membership fees, conference and festival information, and brief histories of the organizations, and they sometimes even offer Web space for members to post their own World Wide Web sites. Many of the groups also have electronic mailing lists. Performing rights organizations such as Broadcast Music, Inc. (BMI), and the American Society of Composers, Authors and Publishers (ASCAP) have Web sites that provide information on royalties, membership fees, and member news. Many of these societies have subcommittees for studying women and gender issues. The AMS Committee on the Status of Women, the SMT Committee on the Status of Women, and the Sonneck Interest Group, Research on Gender in American Music, all provide information of specific interest to women and gender studies.

The number of Internet resources for women in the United States involved with various genres including pop, rock, jazz, indie, and classical is growing rapidly. The Female Musician, GoGirls, Womanrock, and Harmony Ridge are World Wide Web sites devoted to indie music, rock, folk, bluegrass, and country music. Popular music fans have nearly unlimited resources now available on the Internet. Most performers now have their own World Wide Web sites, electronic mailing lists, and sometimes even ezines. Browsers can log on to locate concert dates and venues, biographical information, discographies, and much more. Additionally, organizations such as the Country Music Hall of Fame and the Rock and Roll Hall of Fame provide browsers with historical information, entrance fees, and pictures of the key figures within each genre.

Music professionals and enthusiasts alike can easily locate Internet resources specifically on women in music. Even though the International Alliance for Women in Music (IAWM) is a women's music organization, and not just a Web site, the IAWM site is one of the most comprehensive World Wide Web sites for women in music, covering historical women musicians, women and music competitions and festivals, and even course syllabi for women and music classes. The Women in Music National Network provides a networking base for women in the music industry. Member services, donations, and sponsorships are used to support the organization's goals, including seminars, mentor programs, a newsletter, and a variety of other activities. Additionally, the Cyberspace Music Resources Web site offers a *webliography* (a Web-based bibliographic listing). This tool provides links to hundreds of World Wide Web sites that include popular music, music technology, women's studies, and women in music World Wide Web sites.

Many online services have special subjects for young women. One such site is WOW/EM (Women On the Web/ElectronMedia), a World Wide Web site devoted to young women with interests in digital media arts including multimedia. This site serves as a resource for girls with interests in music and visual art, including band, choir, photography, or pottery, as well as mathematics, science, and computers.

The World Wide Web provides a wide range of resources relating women in music, and new Internet sites are being developed daily. Never before have technology and education been open to such a large audience of women.

See also Music Technology

For Further Reading

Cosola, Mary. "Resources for Women in Music." *Electronic Musician* 13/1 (January 1997): 96–102, 159.

Sinclair, Carla. *Netchick: A Smart-Girl Guide to the Wired World*. New York: Henry Holt, 1996.

Kristine H. Burns

J

Jackson, Janet (1966–)

Award-winning singer, dancer, and actress, Janet Jackson was one of the most important pop music singers of the 1980s and 1990s. In addition to recognition for creativity and versatile expression, her career as a performer is distinguished by a notable humanitarian element as she contributes generously to causes for education and the advancement of African Americans.

The younger sister of superstar Michael Jackson and members of the earlier group the Jackson Five, she was born on 16 May 1966 in Gary, IN, but soon moved to California, where her brothers pursued their career in entertainment. First known as a child and teenage actress, she appeared in the late 1970s and early 1980s in the television series *Good Times*, *Diff'rent Strokes*, and *Fame*. She promoted her debut recording, *Janet Jackson* (A&M 75021-4907-2), by visiting schools and encouraging students to graduate. A second recording, *Dream Street* (A&M 75021-4962-2), followed in 1984. Although the material on these early recordings was considered unremarkable by critics, she achieved considerable visibility as an attractive entertainer.

The young singer achieved stardom with her 1986 album *Control* (A&M 75021-3905-2). With the popularity of the singles "What Have You Done for Me Lately?," "Nasty," and others, the album moved to Platinum status. *Control* gave rise to numerous original videos, of which "Nasty" won an MTV Video Music Award. The material on the popular 1989 album *Rhythm Nation 1814* (A&M 75021-3920-2) expresses the singer's personal observations of social problems and contemporary situations confronting youth in the United States. Well-received recordings followed, including *Janet* (Capitol 87825), *Design of a Decade 1986/1996* (A&M 540400), and *The Velvet Rope* (Virgin 44762), a probing, mature expression of the singer's personal experiences.

In 1993 Jackson made her film debut in John Singleton's *Poetic Justice*, going against the advice of her managers and showing her daring independence. The world tour following the release of *The Velvet Rope* (Virgin 44762) was an extravagant production of dance and music with sophisticated high-tech effects.

Janet Jackson performing in London in April 1995. *Photo courtesy of Press Association/Neil Munns/Archive Photos.*

During the tour Jackson often met with civic leaders and groups of young people, demonstrating her conviction that as a popular entertainer she has a responsibility to the community. Her ambitious business sense, appearance, and versatility in dance and song combine to make Jackson a formidable presence in turn-of-the-century popular music.

See also Rock and Popular Music Genres; Rock Music

For Further Reading

Nathan, David. *The Soulful Divas: Personal Portraits of over a Dozen Divine Divas from Nina Simone, Aretha Franklin, and Diana Ross, to Patti LaBelle, Whitney Houston, and Janet Jackson.* New York: Watson-Guptill, 1999.

Ritz, David. "Sex, Sadness, and the Triumph of Janet Jackson." *Rolling Stone* 796 (1998): 38–45.
Paula Elliot

Jackson, Mahalia (1911–1972)

Singer Mahalia Jackson was known as the "Queen of Gospel Music." Her rich contralto voice became a national institution in the annals of gospel music history, and throughout her life she used her voice as an inspirational tool to interpret the music that touched audiences around the world. Early in her childhood Jackson realized that her role was to evangelize the world through the power of song.

She was born in New Orleans on 26 October 1911 to a poor family. Jackson

Mahalia Jackson in performance in the 1960s. *Photo courtesy of Frank Driggs Collection.*

was only five years old when her mother died, and as one of the oldest children she helped take care of her younger siblings. As her voice changed from soprano to alto, Jackson listened for hours to the recordings of legendary blues singers such as Mamie Smith (1883–1946), Bessie Smith (1894–1937), and Gertrude "Ma" Rainey (1886–1939). In much of her music she attempted to imitate these blues sounds. In addition, she blended the blues with the gospel sound of the Holiness Churches of the South. Thus by the age of 15 her vocal style was formed. At the age of 16 Jackson moved to Chicago, where she joined the church choir at the Greater Salem Baptist Church. Her vocal skills were superior to those of the other singers, and by 1934

she had not only begun singing at special events but also issued her first recording, "God's Gonna Separate the Wheat from the Tares."

From 1939 to 1944 Jackson toured throughout the country with Thomas Dorsey, "the father of gospel music," singing at tent revivals and churches. During this time Jackson's reputation as a singer and interpreter of spirituals grew. Although she had achieved great success with her singing career after touring with Dorsey, to earn extra income she open a beauty salon and flower shop in Chicago. Then, in 1946, while she was practicing in a record studio, a representative from Decca Records heard her sing one of her childhood favorites, "Move On Up a Little Higher." Jackson was encouraged to record the song, and recording sold over two million copies. Later it became her signature piece. On 4 October 1950, Jackson performed at Carnegie Hall to a sold-out audience. She also became equally popular overseas and performed throughout France, England, Denmark, and Germany. In the late 1950s and early 1960s Jackson turned her attention to the civil rights movement in the United States. On 28 August 1963 she sang for the March on Washington at the Lincoln Memorial in Washington, DC, before Dr. Martin Luther King Jr. delivered his famous "I Have a Dream" speech. She also sang at his funeral ceremony in 1968.

There are numerous recordings of Mahalia Jackson. These include *Bless This House* (CBS 08761), *Live at Newport 1958* (Columbia 53629), *The Power and the Glory* (Sony 65201), and *In the Upper Room* (Vogue 601 3117).

On 27 January 1972 Jackson died in Chicago of complications from a heart condition. Her funeral at the Greater Salem Baptist Church was attended by thousands of mourners who gathered to pay tribute to her as one of the world's greatest gospel music innovators.

See also Gospel Music

For Further Reading

Boyer, Clarence Horace. *How Sweet the Sound: The Golden Age of Gospel*. Washington, DC: Elliott and Clark, 1995.
Young, Alan. *Woke Me Up This Morning: Black Gospel Singers and the Gospel Life*. Jackson: University Press of Mississippi, 1997.

Clarence Bernard Henry

Jarjisian, Catherine (1946–)

Catherine Jarjisian's outstanding career encompasses the full range of public school music educator, college professor, clinician, author, and administrator.

While focusing her research on music in early childhood, Jarjisian has remained active as a professional performer. Observing her former music education students while developing a database of exemplars-in-music-teaching videotapes led her to reflect that "Not only are they astounding music educators, they are completely different from each other. I recognize in each something of myself, but I delight in what each has added to create uniqueness as a teacher. The students of my students are very fortunate, so I feel fortunate as well."

Jarjisian was born on 29 September 1946 in Fort Lauderdale, FL, and lived in and around Philadelphia, PA, from infancy until 1980. As a child she played clarinet and piano. At Susquehanna University, Jarjisian majored in piano while continuing to study voice and clarinet. She focused on vocal performance since the 1970s and was a member of the Robert Page Cleveland Singers.

Jarjisian taught high school choir and elementary music while earning a M.M.E. degree at Temple University; she returned to Temple as a teaching assistant and earned a D.M.A. degree in music education. After teaching at the University of Wisconsin—Whitewater and Iowa State University, she joined the faculty of the Oberlin College Conservatory of Music in 1983 and later served as director of the Music Education Division. Seeking a new direction, Jarjisian became director of the Conservatory at Baldwin-Wallace College in 1998, the first woman to hold the position in the 100-year history of the Conservatory.

Jarjisian has published articles in the *Bulletin* of the Council for Research in Music Education and *Psychology of Music*; she has also served on the editorial boards of *Update: The Applications of Research in Music Education* and the *Kodály*

Envoy. She was a contributor to the Music Educators National Conference (MENC) series *Strategies for Teaching* and *TIPS.* While on the faculty at Oberlin, Jarjisian received grants to support her research in multicultural materials for preschool instruction, Kodály and Orff pedagogy, and additional work in early childhood music education. She has given presentations for the National Association of Schools of Music, MENC, the International Society for Music Education, and at state and regional music education conferences. In the summer of 1999, Jarjisian's new administrative responsibilities took her to "Leading Transformation and Change" at the Institute for Higher Education at the Harvard Graduate School of Education. As a scholar, educator, and performer, Catherine Jarjisian is as an exemplar of the ideals of the teaching musician.

See also Music Education

For Further Reading

Jarjisian, Catherine S. "The Effects of Pentatonic and/or Diatonic Pitch Pattern Instruction on the Rote-Singing Achievement of Young Children." D.M.A. diss., Temple University, 1981.

Carolyn Bryan

Jazz

Traced to many cultures and many genres, the jazz genre rose in popularity during the early part of the twentieth century in the United States. Although women were primarily singers [Gertrude "Ma" Rainey (1886–1939), Bessie Smith (1894–1937), and Ethel Waters (1896–1977)] during the early part of the twentieth century, there were some notable exceptions who performed as instrumentalists, including Lil Hardin Armstrong (1898–1971), Clora Bryant (b. 1927), and Peggy Field. African tribal music, "call and response," spirituals, and gospel all contributed to the jazz-related idioms of blues, swing, bebop, and other more experimental forms.

Ragtime. Early ragtime composers and performers were predominantly men who often had training in the European classical music tradition. It was difficult for women to play ragtime music because it required a level of proficiency that was available to few women and because ragtime was associated with the debauchery for which New Orleans was infamous.

Nevertheless, there were women ragtime composers and performers scattered throughout the country. Ida Emerson co-wrote the popular ragtime song "Hello, Ma Baby!" with her husband, Joseph E. Howard, in 1899. Mary Frances Aufderhiede composed many popular rags, including "Dusty Rag" (1908), "Richmond Rag" (1909), and "A Totally Different Rag" (1910). Her friend Julia Lee Niebergall was also a successful ragtime composer. Aufderhiede's father published some of her music, including "Horseshoe Rag" (1911) and "Red Rambler Rag" (1912). Adelaide Shepherd published several popular ragtime compositions, including "Pickles and Peppers" (1906) and "Wireless Rag" (1909). Many of these early rags by women composers are available on *Fluffy Ruffle Girls: Women in Ragtime* (NR 9003 Koch International Classics #7457).

Early Blues Vocalists. Although portrayals of female roles in vaudeville were often caricatures and stereotypes played by male actors, many early women blues singers got their starts on the vaudeville stage. The gender and racial stereotypes that existed in American popular culture at the turn of the twentieth century had deep roots. Black women were often depicted as the "Mammy" character, a kind and soft-spoken female servant who was unattractive and asexual. When Gertrude "Ma" Rainey thrilled vaudeville audiences with her powerful voice and show-stopping stage antics, she curbed some entrenched race and gender barriers. Rainey, known as "Mother of the Blues," introduced a new character to the vaudeville stage: the strong, self-respecting black woman blues singer. Rainey's contributions to jazz did not end with her own groundbreaking accomplishments. She also helped Bessie Smith, who became a blues superstar, achieve her title as the "Empress of the Blues." Although significantly more subtle in style than her mentor, Smith put on stunning shows that drew a significant following.

The earliest blues recordings were issued by Mamie Smith (1883–1946), a remarkable singer who also began her career in vaudeville. Her landmark recording of "Crazy Blues" (available on Document 551) on the Okeh label signaled the rise of jazz in popular culture. Okeh Records took a great risk in having a black woman sing on one of its first jazz recordings, and the company met with much opposition and hostility from political organizations all over the country. However, the record was so successful that Okeh eventually called her back for follow-up recordings. Smith became one of the highest paid black entertainers of the 1920s, and she earned the respect of other great musicians of the day, including Fletcher Henderson, Coleman Hawkins, and Bubber Miley.

Several other important women blues singers came from the vaudeville stage from 1900 to 1920, each adding something to the vocal aesthetic. Ida Fox (1896–1967) defined the term "blues queen" with her extravagant performances alongside such jazz and blues greats as pianist James P. Johnson, trumpeter Henry "Red" Allen, and saxophonist Coleman Hawkins. Clara Smith (1894–1935) brought a crass sense of humor to her blues singing and gathered a significant following. Memphis Minnie (1897–1973) raised social awareness through her music, calling attention to the problems of poor black communities. Monette Moore (1902–1962) helped spread blues through her successful recording career with Charlie Johnson's Paradise Orchestra.

Vocalists. The vaudeville scene faded as blues singers left the stage and entered the jazz clubs. Despite the economic devastation that plagued the United States in the 1930s, this time proved to be a "Golden Era" for jazz vocalists. Women singers were revolutionizing the face of popular music, inventing new styles, and creating the classic image that we still associate with jazz today. Among these talented singers was Ethel Waters, who helped facilitate the transition from blues to jazz. In her singing Waters put an emphasis on lyrical content, and every musical technique she implemented was to further the listener's understanding of the text. Waters brought the jazz singing style to a new level of sophistication. In the early 1920s, singer and entertainer Josephine Baker (1906–1975) destroyed popular perceptions of black women. Through her "Jungle Music" shows she portrayed her culture as something beautiful and exotic, and most important, she added an element of sensuality to the image of the black woman.

Aside from breaking down social barriers, women singers also became more prominent as regular band members over the next few decades. Male bandleaders were employing women for their musical value. Ivey Anderson, for example, was known for her work with Duke Ellington, who wrote arrangements specifically tailored to the performance styles of Anderson, and his band members. Lena Horne (b. 1917) was the highly energetic singer for Charlie Barnet and His Orchestra. Helen Humes (1913–1981) was the lead vocalist for Count Basie's band, as well as the only woman. Anita O'Day (b. 1919) was also a spirited singer, and she created controversy in Stan Kenton's orchestra by wearing a band uniform instead of the usual gown. This forced audiences to see her as a musician, not as a decoration to the orchestra.

Ella Fitzgerald (1917–1996), Sarah Vaughan (1924–1990), and Billie Holiday (1915–1959) were among the leading jazz singers of the swing era of the 1930s. These women helped to define the female voice as a solo instrument. Billie Holiday had a unique vocal tone and style of phrasing that was impossible to duplicate. Sarah Vaughan emphasized lyrical content and simplicity in her singing. Ella Fitzgerald pioneered "scatting," a type of vocal improvisation that gives the singer the freedom to express herself like any horn player. Whereas Holiday separated the voice from other instruments in the orchestra, Fitzgerald and Vaughn proved that the voice was a necessary instrument in any orchestra.

Popular women jazz singers were quite common by the 1950s. Blossom Dearie (b. 1926) made a name for herself as a solo singer and pianist. Her 1952 rendition of "Peel Me a Grape" (available on *Needlepoint Magic, Vol. 5*, Daffodil 105) is still widely used today in film and television. Peggy Lee's (1920–2002) 1958 recording of "Fever" (available on EMI-Capitol Special 57358) is classic. In the 1960s, Betty Carter (1929–1998) reinterpreted "My Favorite Things" and "Tea for Two." Nina Simone (b. 1933) was another talented singer, whose version of "I Loves You Porgy" is remembered as a classic.

Instrumentalists. Although the 1930s seemed to be alive with the high-energy dance music of swing orchestras, America was suffering an economic depression that reflected a social tension that percolated into the music world. Women in jazz who were not singers felt the most pressure during this time to prove themselves worthy musicians. At a time when jobs were scarce, minorities were often blamed for the nation's state of economic distress. Thus women who were employed were seen as "stealing jobs from men." Racial tensions were also on the rise, and black entertainers such as Josephine Baker, Duke Ellington, and Louis Armstrong found themselves leaving the country to play in Europe.

Oddly, all-women orchestras gained popularity during the 1930s. General opinion held that women were not bold or aggressive enough to play jazz, and reviews of these groups often compared women musicians to men musicians. To say that any one of these women "played like a man" was considered a high compliment. Although first seen as a novelty act, all-women orchestras and women bandleaders managed to declare themselves as valid musical talents. Lil Hardin Armstrong's All-Girl Orchestra was quite successful during this time, led by the highly talented pianist and composer. The Sweethearts of Rhythm boasted several gifted musicians, including trumpeters Clora Bryant and Flo Dreyer. Ada Leonard's Big Band featured saxophonist Peggy Gilbert and trumpeter Norma Thompson. The Melodears, under the direction of Ina Ray Hutton (1916–1984), were popular not only on stage but also in Hollywood films and on television.

The onset of war in the 1940s created

a need for women entertainers, as many of the nation's men were called to duty. Trombonist, composer, and arranger Melba Liston (1926–1999), saxophonist Vi Redd, and pianist Mary Lou Williams (1910–1981) were among many women accepted into predominantly male orchestras to substitute for drafted men. Williams, along with British pianist and jazz innovator Marian McPartland (b. 1918), did more than just substitute for men. These two women were known for always being on the cutting edge of the jazz scene, taking music that was usually reserved for the background of conversation at dinner clubs, and making it the center of attention.

Innovators. Up until the 1960s, women in jazz had been challenged with overcoming stereotypes. Once the world was able to appreciate the talent and genius of trail-blazing women musicians, women in jazz ceased to be a special minority. They no longer had to fight so hard to get noticed. After a certain point the focus on women as an underprivileged group changed to a focus on the music they created. After the female jazz vocal aesthetic had been firmly established, there was a wave of women who helped to develop it further by mixing in elements of gospel music. Mahalia Jackson (1911–1972) was a leader in this area, being one of the first women to incorporate gospel music into jazz. "Move On Up a Little Higher" was a very successful record for Jackson in 1945. Dinah Washington (1924–1963) was also very popular with her gospel-infused records *What a Diff'rence a Day Makes!* (Mercury 543300) and *Unforgettable* (Mercury 314-510602-2). Abbey Lincoln (b. 1930) was a product of this genre, with influences like Billie Holiday evident on her star-studded 1961 record "Straight Ahead."

Jazz itself was also rapidly changing.

The 1960s brought on an experimental era in jazz, which incorporated sounds from other genres as well as other areas of the world. Rock and roll influenced almost all of popular music, and jazz was no exception. Classic jazz singers from earlier decades such as Sarah Vaughan and Betty Carter were suddenly faced with Aretha Franklin (b. 1942), demanding "R-E-S-P-E-C-T!," while Janis Joplin (1943–1970) created her own synthesis of blues and rock that shook the pop music world. Joni Mitchell (b. 1943) created a unique blend of folk, blues, and jazz with poetry and defined the sound of a generation.

As lines began to blur, more and more musicians rejected Western classical theory and instead were interested in exploring other cultures. The 1960s brought on a wave of international influences on jazz, America's own folk music. A wave of *bossa nova* came from South America, bringing with it many sensuous Brazilian singers such as Flora Purim (b. 1942) and Astrud Gilberto (b. 1940). From Japan came the gifted pianist, arranger, composer, and conductor Toshiko Akiyoshi (b. 1929). She was the first successful Asian woman in jazz, and she paved the way for many others to come.

Contemporary Jazz. Today's influential jazz leaders have brought on a kind of jazz revival, calling on the works of old masters such as Ellington and Count Basie. Of course, many of the older jazz musicians are still alive and performing, reliving the jazz that once was. But it seems that fewer musicians are concentrating on furthering jazz and taking it to the next level. Among these musicians is pianist and composer Geri Allen (b. 1957), who incorporates African rhythms as well as funk into music. Canadian vocalist Diana Krall shows great skill in experimenting and re-arranging old tunes. Dee Dee Bridgewater (b. 1950) is a jazz vocalist who was very active in Broadway musicals. One of her Broadway successes was a musical called "Lady Day," which was a tribute to Billie Holiday. Nancy Wilson (b. 1937) is a highly acclaimed vocalist who has also won several Emmy Awards for her television projects.

There are a myriad of academic institutions that train musicians to compose and perform jazz, and women are prominent among these apprentices. To earn admission into today's jazz institutions, one requires only talent and not a specific gender. These women pioneers in jazz have laid the groundwork for years to come.

See also Blues; Ensembles, Jazz; Jazz Education

For Further Reading

Dahl, Linda. *Stormy Weather: The Music and Lives of a Century of Jazzwomen*. New York: Pantheon Books, 1984.

DjeDje, Jacqueline, and Eddie S. Meadows. *California Soul: Music of African Americans in the West*. Berkley: University of California Press, 1998.

Placksin, Sally. *American Women in Jazz*. New York: Seaview Books, 1982.

Southern, Eileen. *The Music of Black Americans: A History*. New York: W. W. Norton, 1997.

Rossanna Skupinsky

Jazz Education

Jazz began around the turn of the century but did not appear in the public schools and colleges until the 1930s with the institution of jazz education programs. During this early period, jazz groups formed for the purpose of entertainment at school dances and were referred to as "dance bands." There is no record of any school offering academic credit for participation in dance bands until the 1940s.

In 1947 North Texas State Teachers College (later North Texas State University, and currently the University of North Texas) was the first college to have a jazz program and offer a bachelor's degree with an emphasis in dance band. Prior to the establishment of that degree, Gene Hall taught an arranging class that used a "lab band" to play jazz arrangements. Administration and faculty were skeptical about including jazz in the official music curriculum but recognized it would establish the college as having unique course offerings. The University of North Texas offered the first degree to include jazz courses in fall 1947, and it has remained a leader in jazz education since.

After World War II, the General Issue (GI) Bill created opportunities for soldiers to return to school. Many of these men had played in service big bands and were looking for educational opportunities in jazz and popular music. These men helped to bolster the University of North Texas's jazz program and to encourage other universities to begin additional jazz programs.

The September 1948 issue of *Metronome* magazine listed requirements for the North Texas degree, which included the following performing ensembles: Dixieland, Bop, "Mickey Bands," jump bands, a radio orchestra, and a lab jazz band. The radio orchestra and lab jazz band were equivalent to orchestra, band, or chorus, requiring five clock hours per week. Dance Band Arranging was also a degree requirement.

The Berklee College of Music in Boston began in 1945 as the Schillinger House, an institution designed to teach the Joseph Schillinger music theory method. The school attracted a large number of jazz musicians, and the program grew, eventually changing its name in 1954 to the Berklee School of Music and later to the Berklee College of Music. The Berklee College of Music now offers one of the most comprehensive programs in jazz education at the tertiary level.

Other universities to begin offering jazz programs in the 1940s and 1950s were Indiana University, the University of Illinois, the Eastman School of Music, and the University of Miami. Higher education was slow to include jazz in the curriculum, and departments of jazz studies were not common until the 1980s.

Jazz festivals are often associated with college music programs, and the first one, the Tall Corn Festival, at the University of Northern Iowa, occurred in 1939. It was not until 1949 that Gene Hall of North Texas State University added a second collegiate festival—the Brownwood Festival at North Texas. *Down Beat Magazine* sponsored the third festival in 1959—the Notre Dame Festival. By 1960, 11 collegiate jazz festivals were offered across the country; by 1974, there were 160 festivals.

Beginning in 1959, Stan Kenton (leader of the popular Stan Kenton Orchestra) and Gene Hall began the first summer jazz band clinics to be offered on college campuses. These camps were open to all ages of students and evolved into the National Stage Band Clinics. The popularity of the summer clinics inspired secondary school jazz clinics that took place during the school year. Popular clinicians in the 1960s included Stan Kenton, Clark Terry, and Rich Matteson. Other musicians who occasionally participated were Dizzy Gillespie, Doc Severinson, Ubie Green, Buddy Baker, Cannonball Adderley, Billy Taylor, Louis Bellson, and Ed Shaugnessey. In addition to guest clinicians, there were

clinics and concerts performed by big bands that were in residence in the schools. Big bands that were popular among educators were the bands of Don Ellis, Maynard Ferguson, Woody Herman, Thad Jones/Mel Lewis, and Stan Kenton.

Until the mid-1960s, programs in jazz education focused primarily on developing instrumental jazz groups. College and high school band directors were in need of jazz training and therefore created a new market for jazz pedagogy. The clinics and summer camps served as the primary means through which the college and high school band directors learned how to teach improvisation and how to improve their rehearsal techniques.

In 1964 a group of music educators that included Gene Hall, Clem DeRosa, Jack Wheaton, John Roberts, William Lee, and Matt Betton met at a Music Educators National Conference (MENC) in St. Louis to discuss the need for greater visibility of jazz education and jazz music in MENC. Meetings were organized with MENC leaders, and at the 1968 MENC conference a handful of high school and college jazz groups performed. Following the MENC performances, this group of jazz educators along with Stan Kenton created a formal organization for jazz educators named the National Association of Jazz Educators (NAJE). Kenton was an important supporter of jazz education, which gave the movement credibility among jazz musicians and educators. John Roberts, supervisor of music for the Denver Public Schools, was active in lobbying MENC to add jazz education as a constituency group.

Both Kenton and Roberts attended the Tanglewood Symposium during the summer of 1967. Their presentation persuaded MENC to support jazz education by offering NAJE an associate status. The constitution and bylaws for NAJE were presented and accepted by MENC in 1968. Soon thereafter NAJE decided to split from MENC over philosophical differences and became an independent organization.

NAJE began as a grass-roots organization with a small membership and a single-page newsletter but gradually grew and offered its first conference in 1973. The newsletter eventually became the *Jazz Educators Journal*, now published bimonthly. Over 8,000 people attended the organization's year 2000 conference, and strong links have been made with MENC once again.

One looks back on the development of jazz education and notices the absence of women. Indeed, women jazz educators are as rare as women performers and composers in jazz. In 1983 NAJE members Anita Clark and Kimberly McCord (b. 1955) attended the NAJE conference in Kansas City and noted the absence of women. Although women wore badges indicating they were attending the conference, many were there as wives of jazz educators who were men. Clark and McCord decided there was a need to form an organization for women jazz educators and performers to meet and establish professional connections. The NAJE Women's Caucus held its first meeting at the 1984 conference in Columbus, OH.

With the announcement of the meeting, women NAJE members requested that it be closed to male NAJE members, because many women wanted to discuss issues of sexism within the organization and did not feel comfortable doing so with men present. The meeting indeed was closed to men, and over 40 women attended. Within two years this ambi-

tious and well-organized group managed to have a woman, Julie Hudson, elected to the Executive Board, have sexist language removed from the journal and literature, and was instrumental in NAJE's decision to title the 1986 conference "Women in Jazz."

During the early 1990s the Women's Caucus leader, Sunny Wilkinson, established the Sisters in Jazz Mentoring Program as an offshoot of the Women's Caucus. State chapters have instituted Sisters in Jazz mentoring programs and connect aspiring female high school and college students with professional women jazz mentors. In 1998 IAJE established the first Sisters in Jazz Collegiate Competition, directed by J. B. Dyas. Each year college jazz musicians compete for a coveted spot in the Sisters in Jazz group, which performs at IAJE conferences and international jazz festivals.

In addition to a lack of women in NAJE leadership roles, there has been an absence of women teaching jazz in higher education. In a 1976 survey of women in college teaching positions, only 23 women were found to have taught jazz in the 615 positions identified. By 1977 there was an increase to a total of 829 positions, but women still taught only 30 of those courses.

The most prominent woman to hold a position of significance in higher education was Mary Lou Williams (1910–1981), who became an artist-in-residence at Duke University in 1977. She is most remembered for her History of Jazz classes, but she also composed and conducted for many of the Duke ensembles, including the Duke Wind Symphony, choral groups, and jazz orchestra.

In 1984 the University of Connecticut was the first major university to name a woman, Ellen Rowe (b. 1958), as director of jazz studies. Since that time more women have held leadership roles in university jazz programs, including: Rowe, who is now coordinator of the undergraduate jazz studies program at the University of Michigan; Dianthe (Dee) Spencer, director of jazz studies at the San Francisco State University; and Karyn Quinn (b. 1962), jazz studies program director at the University of Wisconsin—LaCrosse. Further, there are a few women who teach in university jazz programs: Sunny Wilkinson teaches vocal jazz at Michigan State University; Patrice Rushen (b. 1954) teaches at the University of Southern California at the Thelonious Monk Institute. Another important figure in jazz education is Laura Johnson (b. 1958), who directs the education division at Jazz at Lincoln Center. The division coordinates jazz concerts for children, publications and materials for teachers, and the high school jazz band competition, Essentially Ellington.

During the 1990s women enjoyed increased acceptance in jazz education and as performers and composers. Women are now more visible as high school and college ensemble directors and performers, as festival adjudicators, and in leadership positions as administrators in jazz organizations. However, the jazz education profession is far from being gender-balanced.

See also Jazz; Music Education

For Further Reading

Brown, Charles T. "The Relative Position of Jazz in Higher Education." *NAJE Educator* (1977): 4–5.

Cochran, Al. "Jazz Education: Its Utilization into Existing College/University Programs." *Jazz Research Papers* (1982): 74–77.

McCord, Kimberly A. "The Conceptualization of Women in Jazz." *Jazz Research Papers* (1986): 93–97.

Kimberly McCord

Jewish Musicians

The role of Jewish women musicians has grown with each generation in the twentieth century. Although feminist studies point to some women in ancient leadership roles, in more recent centuries Jewish women were essentially excluded from positions of music leadership in synagogues. At the turn of the twentieth century there were no women serving as *hazzan* (cantor, singer of synagogue song) or *meshorim* (singing helpers). Women were not present in synagogue choirs except in Reform synagogues, and women's participation was also rare in Jewish instrumental playing. Even though some women regularly participated as folk singers or on the stage, many were relegated to separate performances in *shul* (synagogue). Orthodox adult Jewish women are not allowed to sing in front of men owing to a religious proscription. The voice of a woman, *kol ishah*, is considered a distraction to the higher duties of spiritual contemplation.

In the late nineteenth and early twentieth centuries, attitudes began to change in the liberal movements in America. Reform and Conservative congregations allowed women to sing and to participate fully in worship services, but leading was a different matter and was not permitted until mid-twentieth century. Jean Gornish (1916–1981), born in Philadelphia and known as *Shaindele de Chazante* (cantor's wife), sang religious music in concerts and over the radio but never served as cantor in a synagogue. It was not until September 1955 that Betty Robbins officiated at a worship service as the first woman cantor in the United States, at Temple Avodah in Oceanside, NY. The first woman formally invested as a cantor was Barbara Ostfeld Horowitz, who graduated from Hebrew Union College in 1975. The Reform movement began increasing the number of women trained as cantors, and in 1987 Cantor Benjie Ellen Schiller became the first full-time faculty member of the School of Sacred Music in New York.

Orthodox Jewish women have always sung religious music, but separately from men. Ellen Koskoff, in her groundbreaking investigations of musical participation in the Lubavitcher Hasidic community, discovered an inverse relationship between a woman's status in the community and her participation in music making. Young girls are encouraged to sing at the Sabbath table and other festivities until they reach sexual maturity. Women can participate musically in a *forshpil*, an all-women gathering on the Sabbath before a woman's marriage, but married older women often give up active music performances and regard such singing as youthful activities. Nevertheless many adult women reported singing and composing religious melodies, or *nigunim*. Others adapted tunes appropriated from the outside culture into spiritual compositions. One Hasidic group established an all-women choir that performs for certain social occasions within the community in New York.

The contributions of Jewish women as liturgical composers were not generally recognized as recently as 1975. The *Concise Encyclopedia of Jewish Music* does not mention a single Jewish woman composer. Composer Miriam Gideon (1906–1996) became the first woman commissioned to write a sacred service in 1969–1970, and she completed *Shirat Miriam L'Shabbat* for Park Avenue Synagogue in 1974. Since then, other women have composed Jewish religious settings, such as Judith Lang Zaimont's (b. 1945) *Sacred Service* and Maxine Warshauer's (b. 1949)

Shacharit, An Interpretation of the Sabbath Morning Service.

Among the greatest body of twentieth-century popular Jewish religious music are the songs set for voice and guitar by Debbie Friedman. Influenced by both the American and Israeli folk song traditions, her musical compositions are widely used in congregational, community center, and camp settings as expressions of authentic Jewish devotionals with simple and memorable melodies. Despite hostility from many cantors, Friedman's popularity runs deep within segments of the American community, and she performs widely in Reform and some Conservative settings.

Ruth Rubin published her collections of Yiddish folk songs in 1973, *Voices of a People: The Story of Yiddish Folksong*; and Nahma Sandrow wrote *Vagabond Stars: A World History of Yiddish Theater* in 1977, opening the worlds of Yiddish folk song and theater to a new generation of Americans. Among protagonists of Yiddish preservation and revival is Eleanor Mlotek, whose compilations of Yiddish songs, such as *Mir Trogn a Gesang! Favorite Yiddish Songs of Our Generation* (1982) and *Pearls of Yiddish Song: Favorite Folk, Art and Theatre Songs* (1988), have provided Yiddish texts, music, transliterations, and historical background. Women in each generation since 1900 have specialized in various styles of Yiddish stage and song interpretations; representative among them are Isa Kremer, the Barry Sisters, Martha Shlamme, Adrienne Cooper (b. 1946), and Ilana Kochinski. Modern Yiddish productions include such musical stage works as *The Memoirs of Gluckel of Hameln*.

Although A. Z. Idelsohn (1967) documents that Jewish women were in organized instrumental bands as early as the fifteenth century, few women participated as instrumentalists in performance bands in the first half of the twentieth century. In America, despite the famous depiction of Molly Picon as a klezmer violinist in the 1936 *Yidl Mitn Fidl*, women were used primarily as singers, not instrumentalists, in Jewish settings before the revival of klezmer music in America in the 1970s. Elaine Hoffman Watts, a third-generation klezmer drummer from Philadelphia, relates that as a young girl she was asked to play drums, but only as a fill-in member of her father's band. Women in klezmer music have experienced a meteoric rise during the last 30 years, with such featured performers as cutting-edge violinists Alicia Svigals (b. 1963) and Deborah Strauss, vocalists Judy Bressler and Lori Lippitz, clarinetists Margot Leverett and Ilene Stahl, and drummer Eve Sicular.

In the classical music world, Jewish women are tackling compositions based on Jewish themes; examples are Deborah Drattell's operas *Festival of Regrets* and *Lilith* (Delos 3159) and an *a cappella* piece, *Eishes Chayil*, and Elizabeth Swados's composition *Bible Women*. In the popular arena such superstars as Barbra Streisand (b. 1942) sang in *Funny Girl* (1968), based on the life of Fanny Brice, and *Yentl* (1983).

Many Jewish women have devoted themselves to the preservation and dissemination of Sephardic music in America. Among them, Flory Jagoda not only performs music from her native Sarajevo but also composes new songs in Ladino, such as *Ocho kandelikas*. Judith Wachs researches extensively and arranges material for Voice of the Turtle, a Sephardic music ensemble based in Boston. Others performing Sephardic music include Judy Frankel, Lauren Pomerantz, and Isabelle Ganz. Musicologists and ethnomusicologists such as Johanna Spector, Judith

Cohen (a Canadian), and Kay Kaufman Shelemay use fieldwork to investigate Sephardic/Asian music. Shelemay recently focused on *pizmonim* (adorations) of the New York Syrian Jewish community in her 1998 book *Let Jasmine Rain Down*.

Many Jewish women, such as Leah Abrams, Julie Silver, Cindy Paley, Linda Hirschhorn, and Deborah Katchko-Zimmerman, are educators, writing and singing songs for children. Among feminists, Linda Hirschhorn's 1997 collaboration with Marcia Falk in setting music to *The Book of Blessings* is a landmark source for Jewish-feminist prayer and inspiration.

See also Ethnomusicology; Multicultural Musics

For Further Reading

Heskes, Irene. "Miriam's Sisters: Jewish Women and Liturgical Music." *Notes* 48/4 (1992): 1193–1202.

Koskoff, Ellen. "The Sound of a Woman's Voice: Gender and Music in a New York Hasidic Community." In *Women and Music in Cross-Cultural Perspective*. New York: Greenwood Press, 1987.

Musleah, Rahel. "An Explosion of Jewish Women's Popular Music." *Lilith* 20/4 (1995): 18–29.

Rubin, Ruth. *Voices of a People: The Story of Yiddish Folksong*. Philadelphia: Jewish Publication Society of America, 1979.

Judith S. Pinnolis

Jones, Shirley (1934–)

Named after Shirley Temple, singer and actress Shirley Mae Jones was one of the most popular American musical theater performers of the mid-twentieth century. Known for the role of Laurey in Rodgers and Hammerstein's screen production of *Oklahoma!*, Jones instantly became America's new sweetheart in 1955 when the film was released. Following this were leading roles in several other successful film musicals, including *Carousel* (1956), *April Love* (1957), and *The Music Man* (1962). Her sweet voice, clear tone, and cheery personality were characteristic of Jones' performances during her career on stage and screen.

Born on 31 March 1934, Jones grew up in Smithton, PA, near Pittsburgh. She exhibited talent early in life and was taking voice lessons from a well-known Pittsburgh vocal coach by the time she was 12 years old. In 1952 during her senior year in high school, Shirley Jones won the Miss Pittsburgh contest, which came with a scholarship to the Pittsburgh Playhouse drama school. After her apprenticeship at Pittsburgh Playhouse, she intended to go to a junior college in New Jersey to study drama, but first she took a brief vacation trip to New York in August 1953. While there, a friend arranged for her to sing at an open audition for chorus parts in several currently running Richard Rodgers and Oscar Hammerstein musicals. Her clear soprano voice and wholesome looks immediately caught the attention of the casting director, and subsequently the celebrated song-writing duo themselves.

Promptly signing on the 19-year-old Jones in a multi-year personal contract, Rodgers and Hammerstein first cast her in minor roles in the Broadway productions of *South Pacific* and *Me and Juliet* to give her professional experience. When *Me and Juliet* went on tour, they advanced her to a leading role.

Wishing to prove her acting ability in dramatic roles as well, Jones auditioned for and was reluctantly given (at Burt Lancaster's insistence) the part of prostitute LuLu Bains in the 1960 film *Elmer Gantry*. Her performance won her the Academy Award for Best Supporting Actress. Subsequently Jones was awarded dramatic roles in films such as *Two Rode*

Together (1961), *The Courtship of Eddie's Father* (1962), *The Happy Ending* (1969), *Beyond the Poseidon Adventure* (1979), *Tank* (1983), and *Gideon* (1998).

By the late 1960s, Shirley Jones began to turn her attention to television roles, playing in such movies and specials as *The Lives of Jenny Dolan* (NBC, 1975), *Yesterday's Child* (NBC, 1977), *Last Cry for Help* (ABC, 1979), and *Inmates: A Love Story* (ABC, 1981). Her performances in *Silent Night, Lonely Night* (NBC, 1969) and *There Were Times, Dear* (PBS, 1987) won her Emmy Award nominations. Jones is perhaps best remembered for her role as Shirley Partridge, mother of the musical *Partridge Family*, a popular series that ran on ABC from 1970 to 1974, which also starred her stepson, David Cassidy. She briefly had her own series, *Shirley*, on NBC in 1979. Jones has made guest appearances in other television series and has also hosted numerous television documentaries. Intertwined between acting assignments have been live musical theater, nightclub, and concert appearances.

Shirley Jones was married to singer and actor Jack Cassidy from 1956 to 1975. They had three sons—Shaun, Patrick, and Ryan, who have also had show business careers. Jones married actor, producer, and agent Marty Engels in 1977.

See also Musical Theater

For Further Reading

Contemporary Theatre, Film, and Television, vol. 6, s. v. "Jones, Shirley, 1934– ." Detroit: Gale Research, 1989, 215–216.

Jones, Shirley, Marty Ingels, and Mickey Herskowitz. *Shirley and Marty: An Unlikely Love Story*. New York: William Morrow, 1990.

Laurie Eagleson

Johnston, Karen Michelle

See Shocked, Michelle

Jones, Ruth Lee

See Washington, Dinah

Joplin, Janis Lyn (1943–1970)

Janis Lyn Joplin, renowned blues and folk-rock singer of the 1960s, was one of the most influential performers of the mid-twentieth century. Her raspy, high-energy performances left an unforgettable mark on many future women performers. Her many recordings have had tremendous success and include Gold, Platinum, and Triple-Platinum sales.

Joplin was born on 19 January 1943 in Port Arthur, TX. Her adolescence was somewhat difficult because of her preference for African American music styles, including Bessie Smith's (1894–1937) blues and Odetta's (b. 1930) folk music, instead of the rock music preferred by her classmates, who were mostly white children. While in high school she began singing in some of the nightclubs and bars in the Austin and Houston areas. Restless, she moved to Los Angeles in 1961 and thrived in the artistic atmosphere of Venice Beach. The beatnik folk scene in San Francisco became a life-expanding magnet for Joplin, but she only remained there a year.

She returned to Texas in 1962 and became a member of the Waller Creek Boys, a local country folk music group. There she began to assert her independent views on culture, politics, and lifestyles. Unfortunately she also began drinking and using drugs. After some unfortunate incidents, she hitchhiked to New York City and performed folk music in a few Greenwich Village nightclubs. In 1963–1964 she returned to San Francisco and intensified her alcohol and drug use, but by the spring of 1965 she

Janis Joplin c. 1969. *Photo courtesy of Hulton/Archive Photos.*

again returned to Texas in hopes of recovering her health.

In the Austin, TX, nightclubs of 1966 Joplin's strong brassy voice and uninhibited bluesy style made her an instant success. She joined Big Brother and the Holding Company, a San Francisco blues-influenced rock band, in 1966. She performed with the band for two years, recording such songs as "Easy Rider," "Piece of My Heart" (both available on *Box of Pearls: The Janis Joplin Collection*, Sony 65937), and "Ball and Chain" (Columbia CGK-31160), which have become rock classics. In 1969 she formed a new group, the Kozmic Blues Band, to back her performances.

While Joplin's fame and performing acumen grew, her personal problems with alcohol and narcotics usage and, to some extent, her uninhibited style began to affect her ability to obtain bookings. Briefly, however, in late 1969 she stopped using drugs. Spring 1970 saw her perform again with Big Brother and the Holding Company in San Francisco. But shortly thereafter she reorganized the Kozmic Blues Band into the Full Tilt Boogie Band. With this band she recorded two more hits, "Me and Bobby McGee," and "Mercedes Benz" (both now available on *Janis Joplin's Greatest Hits*, Sony 65869), and in July 1970 she toured Canada. At the end of the tour she began recording another album, but on 4 October 1970 she died in Hollywood, CA, at the Landmark Hotel from an accidental overdose of heroin.

See also Blues; Rock and Popular Music Genres; Rock Music

For Further Reading

Dalton, David. *Janis*. New York: Simon & Schuster, 1971.

———. *Piece of My Heart: The Life, Times and Legend of Janis Joplin*. New York: St. Martin's Press, 1985.

Echols, Alice. *Scars of Sweet Paradise: The Life and Times of Janis Joplin*. New York: Metropolitan Books, 1999.

Friedman, Myra. *Buried Alive: The Biography of Janis Joplin*. New York: William Morrow, 1973.

Monica J. Burdex

Jorgensen, Estelle Ruth (1945–)

Music educator and researcher Estelle Ruth Jorgensen advocated for and broadened philosophical discourse in music education during the last part of the twentieth century. In 1988 Jorgensen founded and acted as the national chair of the Philosophy of Music Education Special Research Interest Group of the Music Educators National Conference. Jorgensen edited the *Philosophy of Music Education Newsletter* from 1988 until 1991. Owing to the popularity of the newsletter Jorgensen established an independent journal in 1992, the *Philosophy of Music Education Review*, now in its eighth edition. As editor of this journal Jorgensen has worked to create an open forum for scholarly philosophical debate and diverse perspectives on music education.

Jorgensen was born on 28 May 1945 in Melbourne, Victoria, Australia; she received her Honor's Degree in economics and geography from the University of Newcastle, New South Wales, Australia (1967, 1968). Throughout her university years Jorgensen received an Associate of Music degree in piano performance through the Australian Music Examinations Board, sang in the Avondale chorale under the direction of Allen Thrift, and directed a women's vocal ensemble. Jorgensen's career in education began in 1968 teaching geography and economics at Epping Boys High School in Sydney, Australia. Wanting to find a way to combine her love of music with her love of education, Jorgensen left Australia at the opportunity to teach music and social studies in Canada. From Canada she came to the United States to obtain her M.M. degree from Andrews University in Michigan (1970). During her doctoral work at the University of Calgary, Jorgensen committed to pursuing her interests in philosophy and developing theories of music education. The main thrust of her work is philosophical, but she also explores theoretical, sociological, and historical perspectives. After 10 years on the music faculty of McGill University (1977–1987) in Montreal, Quebec, Jorgensen began teaching at Indiana University in Bloomington. She has held a position as professor of music in the School of Music there since 1987.

Jorgensen states that philosophy "enables us to clarify and refine our ideas critically and carefully to make informed judgments about all aspects of music education that touch us as musicians, teachers, and students" (Jorgensen, 1990). Beyond philosophy as a means for clarification of ideas about music education, Jorgensen's current work addresses notions of transforming music education through philosophical questioning, and the creation of new, inclusive visions and models of music education.

See also Music Education

For Further Reading

Jorgensen, Estelle. "The Artist and the Pedagogy of Hope." *International Journal of Music Education* 27 (1996): 36–50.

———. "Philosophy and the Music Teacher: Challenging the Way We Think." *Music Educators Journal* 76/5 (1990): 17–23.

Julie Bannerman

Journals

Music journals, magazines, and other periodicals have long been a feature of musical life in America. In the nineteenth century many journals published interviews with women musicians and reviews of their work. In the twentieth century discussions of issues relevant to American women in music increased dramatically, both in the number of articles and in their scope. Contributing to this growth were the rising tide of the suffragist movement in the early decades and the increasing professionalization of women musicians. Journals such as *Hot Wire* and *Ear Magazine* that target women readers came into existence in the last decades of the twentieth century.

Music journals have covered almost every aspect of the music scene for women. The following overview highlights five topics that have been discussed in a substantial number of journal articles from the twentieth century: performance, including conducting; composition; music business and administration; music education; and surveys and studies of women in music.

Performance. Women performers, including vocalists, instrumentalists (orchestral and solo), and conductors, have contended with a wide range of issues, including the practical difficulties of living alone in large cities while pursuing advanced music training, ways of combining a career with motherhood, gender-based discrimination in employment, and proper stage attire and appearance. From 1901 to 1919 *Musical America* and *Etude* published articles on the everyday dangers facing women music students in New York City and Europe ("Alma Gluck Warns against Evils of Study-Life Abroad," *Musical America* 19/8 [27 December 1913]). Interviews with prominent women musicians reported their opinions on balancing the demands of motherhood and career ("Motherhood and Careers: or, the Mother Artist," Musician 21/12 [December 1916]; "Don't Give Up Music at the Altar," *Etude* 37/7 [July 1919]).

Individuals whose careers had been affected by gender-based criteria publicized their experiences in journals. Women instrumentalists, both orchestral and solo, and orchestral conductors were most heavily represented in this group. Luminaries such as Maud Powell (1867–1920), Ethel Leginska (1886–1970), and Teresa Carreño spoke about developing their careers in the climate described by titles such as "Critical Attitude towards Women Violinists" (*Musical America* 15/14 [10 February 1912]), "Are Women Men's Equals as Pianists?" (*Musical America* 25/7 [16 December 1916]), and "Are Women Musicians People?" (*Mu-*

sical Courier 115/8 [20 February 1937]). After the 1960s when sex discrimination became illegal, titles of the articles became even more explicit (Susan Starr, "The Prejudice against Women," *Music Journal* 32/3 [March 1974]).

Women instrumentalists who wanted to join regular orchestras repeatedly asked for auditions behind screens. Many women played in smaller ensembles such as hotel or beer-garden ensembles, until the war broke out and regular orchestras had to fill spots left by drafted men. Women's strength and endurance for certain instruments, rehearsals, and the standard concert repertory were debated (Raymond Panzer, "Stepdaughters of Orpheus," *Independent Woman* 15/2 [February 1936]; Jerzy Bojanowsky, "Championing the Woman Orchestral Player," *Musical Courier* 131/2 [15 January 1945]). The even harsher environment for women conductors led in part to an increase of all-women symphony orchestras in major American cities in the 1920s and 1930s ("Make Way for the Ladies," *Musical America* 55/19 [10 December 1935]; Florence Frame, "Women Also Conduct Orchestras," *Music Journal* 15/2 [February 1957]).

The fate of women as choristers and choral conductors received considerable attention up to the 1970s. Writers commented on: the formation of women's choruses; how husband-and-wife teams might divide the job of church choir director and organist; and the necessity for new, innovative music for women's choruses. Several journals addressed problems of dress and appearance for women performers ("Should a Woman Singer Wear a Corset?" *Musician* 19/5–6 [May–June 1914]; "How Fashion's Dictates Handicap Woman Climbing Artistic Heights," *Musical America* 21/20 [20 March 1915]).

Composition. Music composition as a professional pursuit for women generated strong debates in the printed media, especially in the first two decades of the century and then again in the 1970s, reflecting strong phases in the women's liberation movement. Women's ability for creative work came under the scrutiny of male writers, who elaborated at length about what they thought women lacked (Dr. H. Moeller, "Can Women Compose?" *Musical Observer* 15/5–6 [May–June 1917]; and George T. Ladd, "Why Women Cannot Compose Music," *Yale Review* 6/4 [July 1917]). Women writers on the same topic, on the other hand, advocated improving the climate of acceptance of women composers, urged traditional institutions such as symphony orchestras to perform women's works, and discussed the impact of gender roles on composing (Clara A. Korn, "Women Composers and the Federation," *Musical Courier* 55/6, [7 August 1907]; Judith Rosen, "Why Haven't Women Become Great Composers?" *High Fidelity/Musical America* 23/2 [February 1973]).

One writer revealed that American women composers received more support than did their European counterparts (Marie Wurm, "Women's Struggle for Recognition in Music," *Etude* 54/11 [November 1936]). Advocates recommended that American women improve the situation by joining groups such as the League of Women Composers (founded in 1975) and by subscribing to publications such as the *Journal of Women and Music*. Interviews with established women composers like Undine Smith Moore (1904–1989) (*The Black Perspective in Music* 13/1 [1985]) provided encouragement and practical guidance for women students in composition.

Music Business. The roles of women in music business and administration in the twentieth century are probably documented more clearly in music journals than in any other printed media. Reports from around 1900 reveal that a considerable number of women were working as piano tuners, music engravers, designers, and publishers (*Etude* 18/1 [January 1900] and 18/4 [April 1900]). Women urged each other to gain business skills by working in music clubs and organizations and by managing artists and symphony orchestras. Music criticism, instrument-making, and library work were also recommended as professional options. Women continued to produce journals, such as *Women in Music* (1935–1940, founded by the conductor Frederique Petrides), *Bitch* (1985–, see Cheryl Cline, "Bitch: The Women's Rock Mag with Bite," *Hot Wire* 3/3 [July 1987]), the *Association of Women's Music and Culture Newsletter* (1988–), and the *IAWM [International Alliance for Women in Music] Journal* (1995–). Women were also the force behind the formation of organizations such as the Musical Union of Women Artists, music sororities (Mu Phi Epsilon, Sigma Alpha Iota, Phi Beta, etc.), professional and amateur associations (Women Band Directors' National Association, National Federation of Music Clubs, Women's Philharmonic Society of New York, Organized Women Musicians of Chicago) and major events like the International Congress for Women in Music.

Music Education. Many music journals covered the topics of women in music education and music in women's education. Much of the discussion in the first half of the twentieth century was based on the traditional belief that music improved a middle-class woman's marriage prospects, domestic life, and children's education. Women were strongly urged to take music lessons and become music educators in the home, community, and elementary schools (Richard Hageman, "Shall the Young Woman Choose Music as a Profession?" *Musician* 30/3 [March 1925]; William Revelli, "Women Can Teach Instrumental Music," *Etude* 61/5 [May 1943]; Guy Maier, "Shall I Major in Music?" *Etude* 72/8 [August 1948]). Famous women music educators such as Carre L. Dunning were featured in articles of considerable length. The development of musical taste among young lady pianists was debated (James Gibbons, "The Girl Who Plays Chopin," *Harper's Bazaar* 33/25 [23 June 1900]; William Henderson, "Why Woman Loves Chopin," *Etude* 28/3, [March 1910].

Several articles countered traditional paradigms about women in music education (Ann Hebson, "Women Can Become Successful University Music Professors," *School Musician* XL/5 [January 1969]; "You Won't Have 'Lady Musicians' to Kick Around Much Longer," *Music Educators Journal* 59/1 [September 1972]; Susan Parenti, "Composing the Music School: Proposals for a Feminist Composition Curriculum," *Perspectives of New Music* 34/1 [1996]).

Surveys and Studies. Surveys and studies of women in music—historical, statistical, and analytical—and reports of meetings, conferences, and colloquia appeared in journals in great numbers, reaching a peak in the 1970s. Many writers concluded that women musicians were not attaining positions for which they were qualified (Nancy Barnes and Carol Neuls-Bates, "Women in Music: A Preliminary Report," *College Music Symposium* 14 [Fall 1974]; Sarah Fuller, "Report of the Committee on the Status of Women," *American Musicological Society*

Newsletter 8/1 [January 1978]). Women active as teachers, composers, performers, and administrators were featured in articles and publicly acknowledged for their contributions to music ("I Am Woman: A Tribute to Women in Music," *BMI: The Many Worlds of Music* 4 [1977]; Ruth Julius, "Showcasing Women Composers," *Feminist Art Journal* 6/2 [Summer 1977]).

Journals continued to publish compelling statistical evidence that women were still underrepresented in some areas ("Statistics in Music," *School Musician* 45/10 [June–July 1974]; Gladys Wright, "Career Opportunities for the Young Woman Graduate," *School Musician* 46/10 [June–July 1975]). The rising profile of women performers in the last two decades of the twentieth century, especially in popular music, received considerable coverage and support in journals such as *The Music Scene* (J. Murphy, "Climb to Fame Easing for Women in Country Music," Nr. 305 [January–February 1979]), *Jazztimes* (L. Gourse, "Beating the Odds: Emerging Women Drummers," Nr. 21 [1991]), and *Billboard* (E. Oumano, "The Billboard Report: Women Increase Number, Scope of Roles in Reggae," Nr. 108 [27 January 1996]).

Many journals published special issues featuring women in music. Early in the century, *Etude* published a series of four issues on "Woman's Work in Music" (1901–1929). Special issues later in the century included: *Music Journal* 31/1 (January 1972); *Symphony News* 24/6 (December 1973–January 1974); *Pan Pipes* 68/2 (January 1975); *High Fidelity/Musical America* 25/1 (June 1975); *ASCAP in Action* (Winter 1987); *Journal of American Folklore* 100 (October–December 1987); *Flutist Quarterly* 15/2 (Spring 1990); *Journal of Country Music* 15/1 (1992); *Music Educators Journal* 78/7 (March 1992); and *Opera News* 57 (July 1992). More recent journals focusing on women and gender issues included: *Hot Wire: The Journal of Women's Music and Culture* (1985–1994); *Women and Performance: A Journal of Feminist Theory* (1983–); *Women of Note Quarterly* (1993–); and *Women and Music: A Journal of Gender and Culture* (1997–).

See also International Congress on Women in Music; International League of Women Composers

For Further Reading

Block, Adrienne Fried, and Carol Neuls-Bates. *Women in American Music: A Bibliography of Music and Literature*. Westport, CT, and London: Greenwood Press, 1979.

Ericson, Margaret D. *Women and Music: A Selective Annotated Bibliography on Women and Gender Issues in Music, 1987–1992*. New York: G. K. Hall, 1996.

Fellinger, Imogen, and John Shepard. "Periodicals." In *The New Grove Dictionary of American Music*, Vol. 3, eds. H. Wiley Hitchcock and Stanley Sadie. London: Macmillan, 1986.

Roe-Min Kok

The Judds

The Judds, mother Naomi and daughter Wynonna, were by far the most popular and successful all-woman country recording group of the 1980s and early 1990s. Their unprecedented success as a duo, leading to Wynonna's subsequent domination of the country charts as a solo artist, was owing in no small part to Naomi's vision and tenacity. Their stage productions were notable for blending a winning combination of Wynonna's expansive vocal abilities and breadth of expression with Naomi's harmonies, fashion flair, and outgoing personality. Their music videos also broke new ground, mixing technical innovations with family photos.

Naomi was born Diana Judd on 11 January 1946 in Ashland, KY. Although a number of her relatives were mountaineer folk, Diana was raised in middle-class circumstances. Fragile and shy, she was a straight-A student who enjoyed a happy childhood until her brother's death from cancer drove her father to alcoholism, resulting in her parents' divorce. She became pregnant, married high school sweetheart Mike Ciminella, and gave birth to her first daughter, Christina Claire, on 30 May 1964 shortly before her high school graduation.

In what would be the first of many relocations, the Ciminellas moved to Los Angeles, where their second child, Ashley, was born in 1968. When they divorced in 1972, Diana was left with few resources to care for her children and had to struggle through numerous odd jobs during the following years in Los Angeles. To escape the hippie culture prevalent on the West Coast, Diana moved the family to a small Kentucky town where she and the children lived without many modern conveniences. Diana studied toward a nursing degree while Christina learned to play the guitar. Soon mother and daughter began singing together while Diana taught her daughter old folk tunes and hymns.

As mother and daughter learned the traditions of, and acquired an appreciation for, Southern country culture, they underwent a metamorphosis, finally changing their names to "Naomi" and "Wynonna" Judd. Naomi, Wynonna, and Ashley moved to Northern California late in the 1970s but stayed only a year. Convinced that Wynonna possessed extraordinary talent, in 1979 Naomi moved the family again, this time to Nashville, TN, so that Wynonna might pursue a singing career. While Wynonna finished high school, Naomi worked as a nurse. During the next two years they wrote songs, sang for anyone who would listen, and performed periodically on Ralph Emery's morning television show. They came to the attention of record producers and major label executives in 1981 and, supported by a collaborative effort of both Curb and RCA Records, began a career that has made history in the recording industry.

In 1983 their first release reached the Top 20, and in the following eight years the Judds garnered eight consecutive number one records. The second of these, *Why Not Me* (RCA PCD1-5319), won the Country Music Association's Song of the Year award in 1984. In 1985, 1987, 1988, and 1990, respectively, they saw their albums *Rockin' with the Rhythm* (RCA PCD1-7042), *Heartland* (RCA 5916-2-R), *Greatest Hits* (RCA 8318-2-R), and *Love Can Build a Bridge* (RCA 2070-2-R) all reached Platinum status. The songs, sung by women, clearly spoke to women. They were sassy, tough, fun-loving, inspirational, and sentimental; the lyrics emphasized strength and determination and idealized old-fashioned rural values contrasted with a fun-loving, free-spirited attitude. Becoming the most-awarded all-woman group in country music, the Judds collected more than 50 awards and sold in excess of 10 million records.

Naomi retired from performing in December 1991 after being diagnosed with chronic hepatitis, a serious liver disease. Wynonna continued to perform as a solo artist beginning with the 1992 million-selling album *Wynonna* (MCA/Curb MCAD-10529). As the Judds had led the field of harmonizing "girl groups" in the country music industry of the 1980s, the

1990s saw Wynonna's solo career lead the way for the success of an unprecedented number of women country singers, many of whom effectively crossed over into pop music record sales. To celebrate Naomi's remission, as well as the new millennium, the duo reunited in December 1999 for the "Power to Change Tour."

See also Country Music

For Further Reading

Bufwack, Mary A., and Robert K. Oermann. *Finding Her Voice: The Saga of Women in Country Music*. New York: Crown, 1993.

Dew, Joan. *Singers and Sweethearts: The Women of Country Music*. Garden City, NY: Doubleday, 977.

Haslam, Gerald W. *Workin' Man Blues: Country Music in California*. Berkeley: University of California Press, 1999.

Amy Corin

K

Kaye, Carol (1935–)

Electric bassist and pedagogue Carol Kaye has been active in the fields of jazz and jazz education since the 1960s. She won the Lifetime Achievement Award from Dusquesne University for "Outstanding Dedication to Bass Performance and Pedagogy," in addition to performing on numerous television series and films such as *Cannon, Room 222, Wonder Woman, Guess Who's Coming to Dinner*, and *Airport*. Her musical influences include Duke Ellington, Artie Shaw, Sonny Stitt, Miles Davis, Horace Silver, and Ray Charles.

Born on 24 March 1935 in Everett, WA, to musical parents, Kaye began playing guitar in jazz clubs in Los Angeles and started giving guitar lessons around 1949. She got involved in recording studio work in 1957 when she played guitar on several recordings with Sam Cooke. Her big break came in 1963 when a bassist missed a recording scheduled at Capitol Records. In that performer's place, Kaye picked up a Fender bass and began playing. Following that session she quickly became one of the most important electric bassists in Hol-

lywood, working in television, film, commercials, and industrial films.

In 1969 she wrote the first of her many electric bass books, *How to Play the Electric Bass*. Her other pedagogical books include *Jazz Improv for Bass, Rock Funk Bass*, and *Electric Bass Lines No. 1–6*.

Carol Kaye has performed with numerous groups both live and in the studio, including the Beach Boys, Ray Charles, Herb Alpert, Elvis Presley, Lou Rawls, Simon and Garfunkel, Frank Sinatra, Sonny and Cher (b. 1946), and Barbra Streisand (b. 1942). Kaye currently teaches electric bass at the Henry Mancini Institute at the University of California, Los Angeles.

See also Bands, Pop Rock

For Further Reading

Kaye, Carol. "The Official Carol Kaye Website." Available: http://www.carolkaye.com/
National Public Radio interview, *Morning Edition*, Thursday, June 15, 2000. Available: http://www.npr.org

Kristine H. Burns

Kemp, Helen Hubbert (1918–)

Inspired by a love for children and the sound of young voices in song, Helen

Hubbert Kemp achieved international recognition in the field of music education as a composer, innovator, and advocate for children's choirs. In 1949 her husband, John Kemp, accepted a position as music director at First Presbyterian Church in Oklahoma City, OK. Kemp served with her husband for 18 years as a nonpaid associate director. Together the Kemps developed a church choral program that included eight choirs with up to 500 voices. Helen Kemp was primarily responsible for the choirs designed for singers age 12 and under. During these years she honed her philosophy and techniques in children's voice development and achieved a national reputation as a specialist in this field. Through her essays published in the *Chorister's Guild Letters* and her many workshops, Helen Kemp became a profound influence in the resurgence of the children's choir in the United States.

Kemp was born on 31 March 1918 in Perkasie, PA. She cites her family as a significant influence in the development of her musical interests. The Hubbert parents made their home one that was filled with music, and the Kemp family frequently performed throughout the community. Edward Moyer, Kemp's high school music teacher, encouraged young Helen to audition for the school operetta, in which she received the leading role. Her musical interests were further developed during her college studies at Westminster Choir College, where she met her husband, studied voice with Lorean Hodapp Powell, and was significantly influenced by John Finley Williamson. Kemp was recognized as an outstanding vocal soloist and performed frequently throughout her career.

John and Helen Kemp had five children who also became involved in lifelong musical activities. The Kemps toured in Europe and the United States as a singing family. The experience of raising children played a significant role in the development of Kemp's philosophy for working with children. One of the primary approaches she used with choirs and taught in her workshops was the use of visual and mental imagery in musical instruction. She developed specific images for use with various musical or vocal challenges. The use of images allows children to develop understandings of the concepts based on their own life experiences. Kemp also believed that instruction for children should focus on the positive rather than emphasize the negative.

In 1968 Helen and John Kemp left the Presbyterian Church in Oklahoma to accept positions with the Choristers Guild—John as executive director and Helen as associate editor and director of workshops and festivals. Helen Kemp returned to teaching at the Westminster Choir College between 1972 and 1983. After a 15 year absence, the Kemps resumed their work at the First Presbyterian Church in Oklahoma City in 1983, where they stayed until their retirement in 1986. Helen received two honorary doctorates for her contributions to the field of music education and her work with children's choirs, one from Westminster Choir College in 1989 and the other from Shenandoah University in 1998.

See also Church Music; Music Education

For Further Reading

Kemp, Helen. *Of Primary Importance.* Garland, TX: Choristers Guild, 1989.

———. *Of Primary Importance, Vol. II.* Garland, TX: Choristers Guild, 1991.

Tagg, Barbara, and Dennis Shrock. "An Interview

with Helen Kemp." *Choral Journal* 30 (November 1989): 5–13.

Alan Rieck

King, Carole (1942–   )

Singer-songwriter Carole King, both in collaboration with Gerry Goffin and as a soloist, penned some of the most popular songs of the 1960s and 1970s. Hired as a songwriter at the Brill Building, a popular songwriting establishment in New York, King and Goffin co-wrote numerous songs, including their first hit, "Will You Still Love Me Tomorrow?" and later hits such as "One Fine Day," "Pleasant Valley Sunday," and "(You Make Me Feel) Like a Natural Woman."

Born Carole Klein on 9 February 1942 in Brooklyn, NY, she began playing piano as a young child. She formed her first band, the Co-Sines, a vocal quartet, during high school and went on to attend Queens College. During her years at college she met singer-songwriters Paul Simon and Neil Sedaka, as well as Goffin. Sedaka penned the 1959 hit "Oh! Carol" for King. Carole King and Gerry Goffin had a highly successful partnership, both professionally and personally. They married in 1958 but later divorced.

After years of writing songs under the aegis of the Brill Building, King pursued a solo career beginning in the 1960s. However, not until the 1971 release of her very popular solo album *Tapestry* (Sony 66226) did King find solo success. The album featured several hit songs, including "So Far Away," "It's Too Late," and "I Feel the Earth Move." Other albums include *Thoroughbred* (Epic/Legacy EK-34963), *Touch the Sky* (Capitol 11953), *Speeding Time* (Wea International 80118), and *City Streets* (Capitol C2–90885).

Carole King was inducted into the Rock and Roll Hall of Fame in 1990.

See also Rock and Roll Hall of Fame; Singer-Songwriter

For Further Reading

Erlewine, Michael, et al. (eds.) *All Music Guide to Rock*, 2d ed. San Francisco: Miller Freeman Books, 1997.

King, Carole. Available: http://www.caroleking.com/

Perone, James E. *Carole King: A Bio-Bibliography*. Westport, CT: Greenwood Publishing, 1999.

Kristine H. Burns

Kitt, Eartha (1927–   )

Eartha Kitt is a chanteuse, dancer, actress, and linguist. Her career both on stage and in film and theater has outlasted even the heartiest performers. Her refined and sophisticated attitudes, as well as her overt sexiness, are further revealed in her steamy vocals that incorporate cat "purrs," growls, and other gutteral sounds.

She was born Eartha Mae Kitt on 17 January 1927 in Columbia, SC. Her mother abandoned her, she never knew her father, and she worked in the cotton fields when she was a young child. The family who raised her mistreated her. As a child she moved to New York to live with her aunt, and according to Kitt she was encouraged by a teacher to study literature, music, and other performing arts. She successfully auditioned to study at the New York High School for the Performing Arts, and there the impetus for her performing career was launched.

Kitt joined the famed Katherine Dunham dance troupe in 1945. She toured Europe with the troupe in 1947, and the European audiences and critics were enchanted and impressed by her. She left the dance troupe in 1950 in Paris to begin a singing career, and soon her sono-

Eartha Kitt performs at the Plaza Hotel in New York City in April 1961. *Photo © Bettmann/CORBIS.*

rous voice and exotic beauty captivated her audiences. Orson Welles billed her as "the most exciting woman in the world" when she toured as Helen of Troy in his stage production of *Dr. Faust.*

In 1951 she returned to New York to continue performing in cabarets and nightclubs. She began a recording career in several languages. Among her hits are "An Old Fashioned Girl," "C'est Si Bon," "I Want to Be Evil," "Santa Baby," and "Uska Dara." Her many recordings include *That Bad Eartha* (BMG International 89439), *In Person at the Plaza* (GNP 2008), and *Eartha Kitt Songs* (BMG International 89477).

She debuted in the Broadway revue *New Faces of 1952,* which was also filmed in 1954, and where she had a hit performance singing "Monotonous." Her other Broadway musical roles include those in *Shinbone Alley* (1957) and *Timbuktu* (1978). The latter role occurred after her infamous luncheon at the White House, where she stated her opposition to the Vietnam War to First Lady "Lady Bird" Johnson. In exercising her right to freedom of speech, she was ostracized and unable to work in the United States for a few years. However, she did continue her successful European career.

Throughout the late 1980s and 1990s Kitt appeared in many roles on television shows. She also played Catwoman in the *Batman* television series and had roles in such movies as *Ernest Scared Stupid* (1991) and *Boomerang* (1992). She was also featured in the Miramax film production of Isaac Mizrahi's documentary *Unzipped* (1995). Even in her seventies, she continues to perform and record her special brand of music.

See also Musical Theater

For Further Reading

Kitt, Eartha. *Alone with Me.* Chicago: H. Regnery, 1975.
————. *I'm Still Here: Confessions of a Sex Kitten.* New York: Barricade Books, 1989.
————. *Thursday's Child.* New York: Duell, Sloan, and Pearce, 1956.

Monica J. Burdex

Klein, Judith (Judy) Ann (1943–)

Electronic music composer Judith (Judy) Ann Klein has been active as both an electro-acoustic composer and an advocate for the furtherance of all kinds of electronic music. She was instrumental in the creation and implementation of the electro-acoustic music archive of the New York Public Library for the Performing Arts at Lincoln Center. In recent years she has served as both an instructor and the director of New York University's Computer Music Studio, as well as on the advisory board and music selection committee of the Society for Electro-Acoustic Music in the United States (SEAMUS). At present she is also the curator for the Exhibit of the History of Electro-Acoustic Music in the United States at New York City's Lincoln Center.

Klein was born on 14 April 1943 in Chicago and was educated in California, New York, France, and Switzerland. In 1998 she completed *The Wolves of Bays Mountain*, a 21-minute tape composition. The piece used both processed and unedited recordings of wolf howls, cries, and barks, as well as the sounds of insects, frogs, and other forest dwellers captured on tape by the composer over a two-year period as she became familiar with a pack of wolves and their habitat in Bays Mountain Park (Kingsport, TN). The work's opening of processed howls results, rather than in the depiction of wolves in their habitat, in sounds like an Eastern plucked string instrument, or perhaps a peculiarly tuned and particularly resonant zither. Unprocessed howls emerge from this, and the listener is soon confronted with a very physical representation of forest life. Here the concreteness of crows flying past, and of cicadas and frogs nearby, gives way to growled "commands" as well as the quick movement of wolf feet passing, as it seems, mere inches from the listener. Throughout the work the physical backdrop of the forest's many sounds intermingles with the otherworldly sounds that wolves produce in their communications with each other and with those same wolf sounds made even more alien by the use of digital signal processing. The moving final result is shaped as a traditional ABA

form. The composer even dedicates the work to the wolf Navarro, a male of the pack who died during the months of her field recordings.

Klein received Phi Beta Kappa honors at the University of California, Berkeley, in 1967, continuing her music studies next at the Sorbonne in Paris. She received the Sorbonne's Diploma d'Études Française (1969), a diploma from the Konservatorium der Musik Academie der Stadt Basel (1972), and an M.A. from New York University (1987). As a composer of both acoustic and electro-acoustic works and as an experimental musician, Klein has studied with such notables as Charles Dodge, Ruth Anderson (b. 1928), Lilli Friedemann, Reynold Weidenaar, and Thomas Kessler. Her computer music has been performed in Lucerne and Basel, Switzerland, and in New York City; it has also been installed in the Koizumi Gallery in Tokyo, Japan, and in Princeton, NJ. Her tape composition *From the Journals of Felix Bosonnet* received Special Honors from the 16th Bourges International Competition, and *The Wolves of Bays Mountain* was written for a commission from the Forum Neue Music and premiered in Lucerne in 1998. Her composition *Elements 1.1: sulphur, phosphorus; diamond* is available on the SEAMUS CD Series, Vol. 4.

See also Music Technology

For Further Reading

Dodge, Charles, and Thomas Jerse. *Computer Music Synthesis, Composition, and Performance.* New York: Schirmer Books, 1997.

Alan Shockley

Knight, Gladys (1944–)

The remarkable African American singer Gladys Knight, is associated with the rhythm and blues, soul, gospel, and popular music genres. Her vocals, backed by the close harmonies of the Pips, influenced the popular music sound of the 1960s and 1970s with such hits as "I Heard It through the Grapevine" (available on *All the Greatest Hits*, Motown 37463-5303-2) and "Midnight Train to Georgia" (available on *Imagination*, Kama Sutra 5141).

Gladys Maria Knight was born on 28 May 1944 in Atlanta, GA. She started singing as a child in the Mount Moriah Baptist Church Choir in Birmingham, AL, and toured with the Morris Brown Gospel Choir through Georgia and Alabama in 1950–1953. In 1952 Knight appeared on *Ted Mack and the Original Amateur Hour* and won $2,000.

The Pips were formed in 1952 with sister Brenda, brother Merald, and cousins William and Elenor Guest. Brenda and Elenor left around 1957, and Edward Patten and Langston George joined the Pips. George left in 1961, but the remaining singers stayed with the Pips throughout their existence. Gladys Knight and the Pips recorded primarily for Motown, Buddha, and Columbia. They discontinued recording as a group in 1977 owing to a contract dispute, but in 1980 they resumed recording for Columbia.

Knight and the Pips won Grammy awards for "Neither One of Us (Wants to Be the First to Say Goodbye)," "Midnight Train to Georgia," and "Love Overboard." Gladys Knight, Elton John, Dionne Warwick (b. 1940), and Stevie Wonder won the Grammy for Best Pop Vocal Performance by a Duo, Group or Chorus in 1986 for "That's What Friends Are For."

Gladys Knight and the Pips were inducted into the Rock and Roll Hall of Fame in 1996. Their legendary recording "Midnight Train to Georgia" received a Grammy Hall of Fame Award in 1999. Knight continues to perform today.

See also Gospel Music; Grammy Award; Rock and Popular Music Genres

For Further Reading

Knight, Gladys. *Between Each Line of Pain and Glory*. New York: Hyperion, 1997.

Nathan, David. *The Soulful Divas: Personal Portraits of over a Dozen Divine Divas from Nina Simone, Aretha Franklin, and Diana Ross, to Patti LaBelle, Whitney Houston, and Janet Jackson*. New York: Watson-Guptill, 1999.

Soufas, Leigh D. "Gladys Knight and the Pips." In *Dictionary of Twentieth Century Culture: American Culture after World War II*, ed. Karen L. Rood. Detroit, MI: Gale Research, 1994.

Laura Gayle Green

Knowles, Alison (1933–)

Experimental composer Alison Knowles focuses her art on detail; her music can perhaps best be described as meditations on the miniscule. She explores the mundane through her art. Knowles was born in New York City and graduated from the Pratt Institute in Brooklyn. She has worked in a variety of forms, including poetry, radio, installations, and performance scores that can be performed or interpreted by anyone. She taught at the California Institute of the Arts and won a Guggenheim Fellowship for the computer instigated dwelling *A House of Dust*.

Born on 29 April 1933 in New York City, Knowles was a founding member of Fluxus in the early 1960s. The group was composed of artists from all over the globe who were dedicated to the idea that anything could be perceived as art and that anyone could be an artist. Knowles was married to Dick Higgins, another member of the group, who coined the term "intermedia" to describe work that broke boundaries between traditional art forms.

Identical Lunch (1961), her most widely

known composition, was generated by a daily ritual whereby Knowles ate exactly the same lunch every day (a tuna fish sandwich on wheat toast with lettuce and butter, no mayonnaise, and a large glass of buttermilk or a cup of soup). Once written as a score, this menu turns a commonplace event into a ritual that others may execute. Knowles produced a journal in 1971 describing various interpretations of the score. The outcomes proved that it was quite difficult for two people to have exactly the same experience while eating the same lunch. There were many varying factors, such as personal taste (different soups were eaten) and economics (participants paid different amounts for the meal owing to mistakes in addition). In each case, the performer was not merely eating but also paying attention to minor details associated with the experience of eating. It is this induced attentiveness that is at the heart of Knowles's work. Knowles believes that through mindfulness, any experience can be art.

In other pieces, activities that generate barely audible sounds prompt acute awareness. In *Nivea Cream Piece* (1962), performers apply hand cream in front of a microphone. The minute sounds crescendo as more people enter and join in the process. When performed *en mass*, the sound suggests a flock of birds. In most cases Knowles's compositions do not operate metaphorically. Rather, she seems interested in investigating the ways in which common things (words, objects, and events) reflect human experience at its most specific and universal. *California Sandals* (1991) is a lengthy and thorough description of a pair of shoes. As the piece progresses, the identical nature of the shoes is revealed to be untrue (one has more finishing nails than the other does), and the history of the wearing is

recorded in scuffs related to accidents and broken bones.

Although most of Knowles's compositions are performed live and are not intended for recordings, her music is available on the compact disc *Frijoles Canyon* (NONF-CD-11), a compilation of text and recordings made in New Mexico.

See also Experimental Music; Fluxus; Performance Art

For Further Reading

Knowles, Alison. *Event Scores*. Barrytown, NY: Left Hand Books, 1992.
———. *Spoken Text*. Barrytown, NY: Left Hand Books, 1993.

Jeffery Byrd

Kodály Method

The Kodály method, a system for teaching solfege, was developed by Zoltan Kodály, a prominent music educator, composer, and ethnomusicologist. Born on 16 December 1882, Kodály revitalized music education in the Hungarian school system beginning in the 1920s. His singing-based approach to music development focused on the ability to read, hear, and think in music through the use of folk music. Kodály suggested that through singing, students learn to know the pulsation, rhythm, and shape of melodies. He advocated the use of folk music for the instruction of singing, because it is the music of the people of each culture and, consequently, is beloved by those who know and share it. Further, folk music contains all the characteristics needed to teach the basics of music. He suggested that folk music is the musical "mother tongue" of a language and that the skills and concepts necessary to develop musical literacy are best taught through this musical foundation. In addition to using folk music in music education, solfege (a system of using syllables to indicate the sound of the interval between the pitches and the ways in which they function harmonically) was to be taught to assist in learning to sing on pitch and in building basic musical skills. Finally, students learn to read and write music at an early age and eventually learn to sing in parts, improvise, and develop excellent intonation and musical memory.

The approach emphasizes the Prepare-Present-Practice teaching format. Preparation exposes students to a variety of musical experiences to develop readiness and involves problem solving to discover the elements of music before they are presented and practiced. Preparing students through physical, aural, and visual experiences helps them gain familiarity and security while they develop musicianship skills. The presentation stage occurs when the teacher provides a name, symbol, and sound for new musical concepts. Practice and evaluation occur next as students are given opportunities that reinforce concepts. During this process, students are prepared for new musical concepts so that all phases of learning overlap in each lesson, and evaluation is ongoing. The Kodály curriculum is carefully sequenced according to experience; and includes hand signs, rhythm solmization, flash cards, echoing, picture symbols, musical ladders, and stick notation.

Early leaders of the Kodály approach in the United States had strong ties to Hungary. Katinka Daniel (b. 1913), graduate of the Franz Liszt Academy of Music in Budapest, and pupil of Kodály, introduced the Kodály approach to North American teachers in 1959. She presented the Kodály method in 1974 at the first International Kodály Conference held at Holy Names College (CA).

Although she felt her greatest gift to music education in the states was to make American music teachers aware of their own folk songs, she also influenced music educators directly. Sister Lorna Zemke (b. 1933) wrote her master's thesis and doctoral dissertation on the Kodály method with the assistance of Daniel. Zemke later developed one of the foremost Kodály teacher preparation programs in the United States at Silver Lake College (WI).

Lois Choksy (b. 1928) visited Hungary at Daniel's encouragement and attended the Danube Bend Summer University at Estergon. She returned to study music education at the Franz Liszt Academy in 1970–1971. Choksy adapted the Hungarian method using North American traditional music and pedagogical strategies appropriate to North American children. As a researcher, speaker, teacher, and author, Choksy has expressed her indebtedness to Sarolta Kodály, wife of Zoltan Kodály, who gave freely of her time to help with the history of the approach. Choksy also gives credit to Erzsebet Szonyi (b. 1924), dean of the School of Music Education at the Franz Liszt Academy of Music in Budapest, who was her teacher and mentor during the writing of her book *The Kodály Method: Comprehensive Music Education from Infant to Adult* (1974).

Jean Sinor (1946–1999) studied in Hungary in 1968. Her leadership in the Kodály approach was evident at all levels from local to international through her courses, workshops, and addresses. Similarly, Mary Helen Richards (1921–1998) also studied in Hungary. She, however, developed her own approach based on the educational philosophy of Kodály. Richards's book *Threshold to Music* (1964) used an extensive system of experience charts, songs, and movement activities, emphasizing reading and singing because she viewed them as being inseparable, whereas it placed less emphasis on music writing. Mary Alice Hein (b. 1927) studied in Hungary in 1970–71 and returned to the United States to develop the first graduate degree program in Kodály studies at Holy Names College.

Denise Bacon (b. 1920) studied both the Kodály method in Hungary and the Orff approach in Germany. She delineates to music educators the differences in the two methods. The Kodály approach, she feels, balances Orff's emphasis on rhythm and playing instruments by stressing the importance of music literacy, which is developed through experience before it is learned conceptually.

Although he died on 6 March 1967, Kodály influenced music education throughout the world for many years to come. Since it was first introduced in the United States, the Kodály method has been used by music educators at all levels. Its influence is evident in the classroom as well as in the preparation of music educators throughout North America.

See also Dalcroze Eurhythmics; Music Education; Orff Approach

For Further Reading

Daniel, Katinka S. *Kodály Approach*. Champaign, IL: Mark Foster Music, 1978.

Jaccard, Jerry. "What Is the 'Real' Kodály Method?" *Kodály Envoy* 21/1 (1994): 4–9.

Sandor, Frigyes (ed.). *Music Education in Hungary*. New York: Boosey and Hawkes, 1975.

Delta Cavner

Kolb, Barbara (1939–)

Since the 1970s, Barbara Kolb has been recognized as an American composer on the contemporary international scene who makes use of new idioms to create her distinct style. In her music she establishes a twentieth-century brand of Impressionism while also incorporating serial, aleatoric, and electronic techniques. Many of her compositions contain impressionistic characteristics and, although freely atonal, still evoke a sense of traditional harmonic language. Kolb's compositional style has been described as "eclectic," drawing on many different sources and idioms. Her works draw heavily on sources from literature and the visual arts.

Kolb was born in Hartford, CT, on 10 February 1939. She attended Hartt College of Music, where she studied with Arnold Franchetti. Kolb received a B.A. (1961) and an M.M. in composition (1964). In 1964 and 1968 she spent the summer at the Berkshire Music Center at Tanglewood, where she studied with Lukas Foss and Gunther Schuller. Kolb recognizes both these composers as major influences in the development of her style. She has been the recipient of numerous awards, including a Fulbright fellowship, several MacDowell Colony fellowships, Guggenheim fellowships, and National Endowment for the Arts grants. Kolb became the first woman to receive the American Prix de Rome in music composition in 1969; as a result she spent one year studying at the American Academy in Rome.

Kolb has been active as artistic director of contemporary music at the Third Street Music School Settlement, Marlboro Music Festival composer-in-residence (1973), and American Academy in Rome composer-in-residence (1975). During 1983–1984, Kolb spent nine months in residence at the Institut de Recherche et Coordination Acoustique/ Musique (IRCAM), where she received a commission for *Millefoglie* (New World Records 80422) for chamber ensemble and computer tape. She has held teaching positions at Brooklyn College, CUNY (1973–1975), and Temple University (1978). She was a visiting professor of composition at the Eastman School of Music in 1984–1985. Under the auspices of the Library of Congress in 1986, Kolb created a music theory instruction program for the blind and physically impaired.

Kolb has explored and used new electronic technology in some of her works, albeit sparingly. For example, *Solitaire* (1971) for piano and tape was her first work utilizing tape. *Solitaire* is a largely atonal work with some diatonic effects, including a direct quotation from Chopin. *Appello* (CRI 576), a serial work for solo piano from 1976 that makes use of tone clusters, borrows a tone row from Pierre Boulez's *Structures Ia*.

More recently Kolb has been active with commissions. Her most performed work in recent years, *Voyants* for solo piano and chamber orchestra, premiered in Paris in February 1991. *All in Good Time*, commissioned by the New York Philharmonic for the Orchestra's 150th anniversary season, premiered in February 1994. Her more recent compositions include a mixed sextet on a commission by Elisa Monte Dance, *New York Moonglow*; *Sidebars*, a duet for bassoon and piano; and *Virgin Mother Creatrix*, a choral work inspired by Hildegard of Bingen. *Virgin Mother Creatrix* premiered in March 1998 at the International Festival of Women Composers at Indiana University of Pennsylvania, where Kolb was the featured composer. Kolb's publishers are Boosey and Hawkes, Peters, and Carl Fischer.

See also Classical Music

For Further Reading

Gage, Cole, and Tracy Caras. *Soundpieces: Interviews with American Composers*. Metuchen, NJ: Scarecrow Press, 1982.

Perconti, Ellen S. "Three Keyboard Pieces by Barbara Kolb." *Women of Note Quarterly* 4 (2) (May 1996): 20–26.

Cheryl Taranto

Krauss, Alison (1971–)

Through honing her talent as a vocalist and fiddler, Alison Krauss became a prominent figure in bluegrass while still a teenager, and in the 1990s she was the style's most famous ambassador. By the time she entered the University of Illinois in her home state as a 16-year-old voice major, Krauss had already played in bands for years, won several state fiddle championships, been signed as a recording act, and performed at the Newport Folk Festival. Amid the rising expectations, she was able to keep her characteristic professionalism and sense of perspective. Her fine fiddle playing, along with her high, clear vocals, made Alison Krauss one of the most outstanding young bluegrass musicians in the latter half of the twentieth century.

Born on 23 July 1971 in Champaign, IL, by age 19 she had won not only the International Bluegrass Association's Entertainer of the Year Award but also a Grammy Award for Best Bluegrass Recording. That album's title track, "I've Got That Old Feeling," was made into an acclaimed video, a bluegrass first. The resulting publicity in mainstream and music magazines gave her a higher public profile than any bluegrass musician had achieved. In 1993 she was the youngest person to ever join the ranks of Nashville's Grand Ole Opry. Producer Ken Irwin, an executive of the Boston-based independent Rounder label, has long boosted her career. A 1994 anthology of her work for the company—*Now That I've Found You—A Collection* (Rounder 0325)—was the first bluegrass album to sell one million copies in a year.

First picking up the fiddle in elementary school, Krauss developed an uncanny musical memory and the motivation to master the instrument. Early stints in bluegrass bands taught her how to improvise within a song's structure and the details of ensemble playing. Being inspired from seeing top performers in action and working alongside other excellent musicians in her band, Union Station, have kept her standards high. The beauty and precision of her music, as well as its dynamic presentation, show that the publicity is well-founded. Alison Krauss's influence is felt throughout the field of bluegrass.

See also Bluegrass

For Further Reading

Bufwack, Mary A., and Robert K. Oermann. *Finding Her Voice: The Saga of Women in Country Music*. New York: Crown Publishers, 1993.
Willis, Barry R. *America's Music—Bluegrass: A History of Bluegrass Music in the Words of Its Pioneers*. Franktown, CO: Pine Valley Music, 1998.

Craig Morrison

Krumhansl, Carol L. (1947–)

Carol L. Krumhansl is professor of psychology at Cornell University, where she has conducted an active program of research into the psychology of music since 1980. Using the experimental techniques of cognitive psychology, her research addresses the following questions: How do we perceive and remember music? What are the structural properties of music that affect these processes? What can music tell us about human abilities to encode, organize, and reproduce complex auditory patterns? To what degrees do experience, musical training, acculturation, and development influence how we understand music?

Born on 17 September 1947 in Providence, RI, Krumhansl grew up in Ithaca, NY, where she began to study the violin. That training continued at the Interlochen National Music Camp and at Wellesley College. While she was in college, her academic interests turned to mathematics. She earned a master's degree in abstract mathematics (algebraic topology) at Brown University and then moved to Stanford to study mathematical psychology. Roger Shepard's theoretical and methodological contributions had a great influence on her, and he encouraged her to apply some of the new techniques of mathematical psychology to questions of music.

With Shepard, Krumhansl developed a method that has become standard in the field of music psychology. The listener hears a recording of a small musical context, perhaps a scale, chord, or chord progression, which is immediately followed by a "probe" tone or chord. The listener rates, on a numerical scale of perhaps one to seven, how well the probe tone or chord fits with the previously played musical context. Mathematically analyzing such ratings from many different contexts can reveal a great deal about how the listener evaluates musical relationships. The results of the first study using the "probe-tone technique" were extended with similarity and memory accuracy measures in Krumhansl's Stanford dissertation. This led to a wide-ranging series of experiments, the results of which are summarized in her book *Cognitive Foundations of Musical Pitch* (1990).

Working with a number of collaborators, including several musicians, Krumhansl has explored a full range of musical phenomena. Building on her early studies on the cognitive bases of tonal and harmonic organization, she has done research into the experience of rhythm and time; melodic expectancy; crosscultural studies including Indian, Chinese, Finnish, and Javanese musics; infants' sensitivity to phrase structure in music; and the perception of musical timbre.

Krumhansl's work has been recognized both nationally and internationally. She has been a member of the editorial board of *Music Perception* since its founding, and currently she serves on the editorial board of the *Journal of Experimental Psychology: Human Perception and Performance*. The American Psychological Association awarded her its Distinguished Scientific Award for an Early Career Contribution to Psychology in 1983, and in 1993 she was elected both a member of the Society of Experimental Psychologists and a fellow of the American Psychological Society. Twice a fellow at the Center for Advanced Study in the Behavioral Sciences, Stanford, she organized in 1993–1994 a Special Project on Music Cognition, a collaboration of psychologists and music theorists. Her Fulbright Fellowship year at the University of Jyväskylä, Finland, was capped by that institution awarding her an honorary doctorate in musicology (1998). She served as president of the Society of Music Perception and Cognition in 1998–2000 and is on the International Advisory Board for the European Society for the Cognitive Sciences of Music.

See also Music Psychology

For Further Reading

Krumhansl, Carol L. *Cognitive Foundations of Musical Pitch*. New York: Oxford University Press, 1990.

Perlman, Marc, and Carol L. Krumhansl. "An Experimental Study of Internal Interval Standards in Javanese and Western Musicians." *Music Perception: An Interdisciplinary Journal* 14/2 (Winter 1996): 95–116.

Robert Gjerdingen